LAND
BETWEEN
THE RIVERS

LAND BETWEEN THE RIVERS

A 5,000-YEAR HISTORY OF IRAQ

BARTLE BULL

Atlantic Monthly Press
New York

FIRST EDITION

Published simultaneously in Canada
Printed in the United States of America

This book is set in 11.75-pt. Dante by Alpha Design & Composition of Pittsfield, NH.

First Grove Atlantic hardcover edition: September 2024

Library of Congress Cataloging-in-Publication data is available for this title.

ISBN 978-0-8021-6250-2
eISBN 978-0-8021-6251-9

Atlantic Monthly Press
an imprint of Grove Atlantic
154 West 14th Street
New York, NY 10011

Distributed by Publishers Group West

groveatlantic.com

24 25 26 27   10 9 8 7 6 5 4 3 2 1

To Claudia

Contents

List of Maps

Preface

*L*and *Between the Rivers* is the result of over a decade's research and writing. The topic is large: five millennia, beginning somewhat before Gilgamesh, king of the Sumerian city-state of Uruk in about 2700 BC, at the edge of historical time. More than anywhere else, Mesopotamia, the famous land between the rivers, where civilization was born, where East and West have mixed, clashed, and fed each other since long before Alexander the Great died at Babylon in 323 BC, has led an existence that could be called, from a Eurasian perspective at any rate, one version of a history of the world.

A theme emerges. It is the theme of all politics, and perhaps ultimately of all culture: humanity's innate freedom, the expression of this in humanism, and the struggle of this with tyranny. By humanism we mean not secularism but rather those qualities that inhere definitively in mankind: reason, natural law, autonomy. There are no grounds, depending on the faith, to find these at odds with religion.

Iraq has uniquely formed and manifested the phenomenon. The thesis revealed itself gradually over the years of working on this history, an insight picked up, piece by piece, from the soil like the discoveries of an archaeologist. Looking back, maybe the idea should be no surprise. What else would we expect from the axial land?

The earliest antecedent posited for Iraq's name is the ancient Sumerian city of Uruk, birthplace of writing, the place where Gilgamesh was

king, and greatest of the early cities in the small region in southern Iraq
where civilization was born. The term "Iraq" has been used by Arabs to
describe much of the present-day country of that name since at least the
sixth century AD. Other terms have included "Mesopotamia," "Turkish
Arabia," and more. Generally these expressions reflect their users, with
their own times and contexts. While the latter inevitably change, there is
no question that the place referred to has for millennia been a distinct, if
internally variegated, part of the world. Through much of ancient history
the components were "Babylonia" in the south and center and "Assyria"
in the north. Under the five centuries of the Ottoman Turks, it was the
three provinces, north to south, of Mosul, Baghdad, and Basra.

"Mesopotamia" is a Greek name that has meant differing things over
the centuries. Literally meaning "between rivers," it has always referred
to land associated with the Tigris and Euphrates. Its widest definition
includes country as far north as parts of southeast Turkey and as far
south as Kuwait. Parts of western Syria can also be included. In Hellenistic times, "Mesopotamia" referred to the northern third of this area.
In this book, as many have done before, we use the term to describe
the area more or less embordered by the modern frontiers of Iraq. It
can broadly be said that while "Mesopotamia" is the ancient Greek and
European name, the name "Iraq," in its various forms, has been more
local. Similarly, with the usual caveats about the dangers of generaliza-
tion, "Persia" is the ancient Greek and hence European name for the
land more locally known as "Iran." In the latter case, as with "Iraq" and
"Mesopotamia," we use the terms for the most part interchangeably.

———

The last word on the question of whether Iraq really is a distinct place,
historically, can be given to the following fact. If one divides the five
thousand years of human civilization into ten periods of five centuries
each, during the first nine of these the world's leading city was in one of
the three regions of current-day Iraq, while none was in a neighboring
land, much less—with the relatively brief (by Iraq's standards) exception
of ancient Rome—anywhere else.

First came the great cities of the Sumerian civilization of southern Iraq, including Uruk and Ur. Then Babylon rose, north of Sumer.

Nineveh—at Mosul which long gave its name to the northernmost of Iraq's three traditional regions—rose in the seventh century BC, to be followed by Babylon again through the time of Alexander. Babylon was followed by Seleucia-on-Tigris, city of Alexander's Hellenistic successors, in the center of the country. After the interlude of Rome in the centuries around the time of Christ, Seleucia rose again as Ctesiphon, principal city of the Sasanian Persian Empire in the first half millennium after Christ. The last of the major Mesopotamian cities was Baghdad during the Abbasid dynasty, with its heyday in the ninth and tenth centuries AD.

Other cities in other lands rose and fell: Thebes and Alexandria in Egypt, for example, or Patna in India and Tang Dynasty Xi'an in China. But none of these defined historical epochs for a broader world like the urban centers of the land that invented civilization and that continued through all these periods to be the essential crossroads.

I first came to know Iraq during the four years I spent reporting and writing for newspapers and magazines during the 2004–2008 war there that erupted after a year or so of lesser violence following the 2003 US-led invasion. I was a freelancer, with no resources for security but also none of the restrictions that come with working for corporate media in a war zone. I worked and survived by the generosity and courage of the Iraqi people amongst whom I lived and moved. I placed myself at their mercy, as a guest in their houses and in their land. It paid off. I came to owe the place a great debt. Wanting to understand Iraq better, and to share what I learned about its longer and more fundamental story, as I had previously shared some of its more recent stories during my years in journalism, I embarked on this book.

Apart from the main theme of humanism versus the various outlooks of power, other principal threads emerge. One is that Iraq—the Mesopotamian floodplain with its southern wetlands and northern foothills—is very much a place, and one whose modern borders reflect this well. Another is Iraq's extraordinary centrality to broader cultural and political history over the millennia. A third is how this, thanks partly to Iraq's location and its mostly flat and open landscape, also means that the story, from the beginning, is so often driven by outsiders.

Another is the extraordinary length of what might be called an East-West conflict in Iraq. The Roman-Persian wars lasted from 54 BC until 628 AD.* Nine centuries later a version of the conflict resumed, when the Ottoman Turks made Constantinople again the capital of a strong empire, taking on much of the organization of the Second Rome; and when Iran's Safavid Empire saw Persia at last whole and imperial once more for the first time since the Muslim invasions of the seventh century AD. The Ottoman-Persian wars, adding an additional layer of Sunni versus Shia, lasted from 1507 until 1823. More than anywhere else, these conflicts took place in Iraq. An expansive view would have them beginning on Iraq's soil with Alexander the Great in 331 BC and continuing well into the twenty-first century.

Iraq's historical status as the locus for these many conflicts is indisputable, and it has been interesting to discover how long that has been the case. That said, a parallel and probably more important narrative also emerges. This is the extraordinarily fruitful cross-pollination of cultures in the region, without which our existence today would be incalculably poorer. There is also the profound depth of liberal humanism—to put it in Western terms—in the region, embodied in the teachings of Zoroaster and in the many strands of Sufism, in Persian mystical poetry and in the dazzling cosmopolitanism of Ottoman government and society, and in other ways that readers will encounter here. All of this stands as an essential antidote to the influential narratives that have predominated since the "War on Terror" period when I first worked in the region.

If we limit ourselves to truisms and received wisdom, there is as little point in reading history as in writing it. Thus, at a more specific level than the broad themes outlined above, we are led to some surprising

---

* These conflicts saw the Parthian and then Sasanian Empires of Persia fight republican and subsequently imperial Rome, based from 330 AD at Constantinople.

historical conclusions when we take an unusually long perspective that brings its own look at the facts.

To take an example from the realm of religion, naturally a central topic in *Land Between the Rivers*, from this longer perspective Shiism emerges as, in essence, a faith of its own, rather than as a sect or heresy within some greater "Islam." (Alternatively, one could use a definition of Islam as a constellation of traditions that, while dramatically distinct in their roots and usually opposed to each other in message, happen to share a broad regional origin while making reference back to the Prophet. The view here is that this definition is so broad as to be of doubtful value.) The Sunni-Shia split is often described as a family feud over a disputed succession; in fact, it represents something far deeper, which Iraq itself reflects, namely a profound fault line between the Semitic and Perso-Hellenistic traditions. To take another example of an interesting, unexpected conclusion that was revealed by the unusual perspective taken here: the ideas that killed the project of Iraqi rebirth, freedom, and moderation in the twentieth century were indeed foreign, but the culprit ideologies were those of Berlin circa 1880–1945, not those of London— ethnic nationalism and collectivism, not constitutional liberalism. A third example: the Versailles conference of 1919 was indeed the "peace to end all peace" for Iraq as for almost everywhere else of importance that it addressed—but not in the way that is most commonly repeated. The early Iraqi state's British partnership would have emerged, and with strong Iraqi support, regardless of Versailles. The sin of Versailles, in this context, was to impose an offensive and coercive "mandate" status that said Iraq was not a sovereign, if weak, state capable of undertaking such a relationship bilaterally; the League's third-party Mandate is what poisoned modern Iraq's crucial fragile founding years.

Land Between the Rivers is a sweeping story. The structure, as we cover the five thousand years, is chronological and mostly episodic, concentrating on key people and events but also focusing on bit players who illuminate the wider picture.

Human stories, human dramas—it was these that largely drew me to the work I did in wartime Iraq. *Land Between the Rivers* tells much of its tale through individual narratives: Abraham, the Man from Ur, setting off over the horizon in roughly 1850 BC, leaving behind the circular fatalism of earlier outlooks and establishing a future for free will; Alexander, pupil of Aristotle, bringing Classical humanism into the East as he attempted a fusion of the Greek and the Persian, in his new capital at Babylon, only to die there at the age of thirty-three; Imam Hussein, grandson of the Prophet, his martyrdom at Kerbala in 680 AD setting forever the bloody fault line of Sunni and Shia; Caliph Mamoun in the heady, violent, lascivious atmosphere of Baghdad's early medieval High Noon, representing a culture that preserved and passed along the Classical Greek heritage for a Europe that still slumbered in its Dark Ages; Sultan Suleiman the Magnificent, conquering Baghdad and wresting it from the Persians at the beginning of five centuries of Ottoman rule; Austen Henry Layard and the nineteenth-century archaeologists, bringing yet another layer of imperial rivalries to Iraq's soil as the painful encounter with the modern West began; and the brave, wise, elegant, cunning, and ultimately tragic King Faisal I, who almost turned the birthplace of cities and kingship into the first successful constitutional nation-state of the postimperial, postcolonial twentieth century.

Most of the chapters that follow tell their story through these individuals, some humble and some great. A smaller number of chapters cover the interstices between these dramas.

Research for a work like this takes many forms. Shelves, and in some cases entire rooms, of books have been written about subjects that here might be treated in a page, a paragraph, or even a sentence. Much of *Land Between the Rivers* is primary history, from original sources, in translation or otherwise depending on the material. Many of the sources are secondary. The discovery of chains of reference, attributed or not, has been an interesting part of writing this book. I hope any of my own failures to cite references properly, perhaps unavoidable in a book of this length, written over so many years, are not too egregious; they are, at any rate, unintentional.

Iraq's story is necessarily also that of its neighbors: Iran, Turkey, Syria, Arabia. Libraries in Tehran and Damascus were sources of my early research, as much as booksellers in London, Istanbul, New York, and Baghdad, where the famous bibliopoly of Mutanabbi Street is still going strong.

Some of the primary sources have been delightful surprises: fine, extended pieces of writing by principals participating first-hand in events. Ogier de Busbecq's account of Sultan Suleiman the Magnificent's empire in the 1550s provides an extraordinary keyhole view into the apogee of Ottoman power at a time when Europe trembled before Suleiman, the Shadow of God on the Earth. Like de Busbecq, Amr ibn Bahr al Jahiz, the ninth-century Baghdad polemicist, has left behind an unsung gem— *The Epistle on Singing Girls*—that amply rewards an excursion into the story he tells. Austen Henry Layard is a witty, modest, engaging travel companion of the 1850s.

Underlying everything, there is *Gilgamesh*, the first epic of all. Like Jahiz's tale and Busbecq's, but more profoundly, Gilgamesh's story is well worth retelling here. It, and the Abraham saga that follows it, reach a deeper place than early Iraq's countless material contributions to our world. From the wheel to writing itself, the latter are remarkable; but Iraq's contributions to the life of spirit and intellect are even greater.

None of this bookish research would mean much without a sense of the place. *Land Between the Rivers* is a straightforward piece of third-person history, with nothing of the memoir about it. But without the years of travel that inform it—across Iraq, from north to south and east to west, and in its neighbors of Syria, Iran, Turkey, Jordan, and Arabia— this would be a different work.

At Persepolis, in its megalomaniacally vast spaces, the traveler senses the difference in imperial tone that came to ancient Iran when Cyrus, the imperial founder, was followed by Darius and Xerxes; recalling that Alexander then sent the whole place up in flames, the modern visitor imagines the wild longing, the *pothos*, that ultimately led to an early death for the conqueror at Babylon. In Baghdad, embedded in 2005 with the Mahdi Army in the immense Shia slum of Sadr City, watching old women don their white funeral shrouds as they prepared to brave the suicide bombers and vote, I learned more about the Shia sense of martyrdom—the preoccupation with victimhood and justice that came down from Ali's death at Kerbala fourteen centuries earlier—than I could learn from any book.

In frontline Mosul at the height of the siege of the ISIS-held city in
2015, deep in catacombs freshly dug in a modern-day mining for antiquities, I thought of the first archaeologists, who had begun digging into
those same mounds in the 1850s; then too, as order frayed in the long
Ottoman twilight, there had been drama and gunplay. Now, as the low,
damp, tight earth walls around me quaked with the battle going on,
I found the discarded orange jumpsuits of the Islamic State prisoners
who had been forced to dig there for relics of Nebuchadnezzar and
Ashurbanipal. The Mosul Museum, where I found many of Layard's
nineteenth-century finds half destroyed, changed hands three times in
the fighting while I was there. Spending a night alone in 2006 atop the
Ziggurat of Ur, the Iraqi insurgency hot in the plains all around in what
was already the deadliest war in the history of journalism, I could not
ignore that these stars above me, and eventually the dawn glow in the
east, had been Hammurabi's too. At Babylon, and in the Marshes, and
at Palmyra and Isfahan, it has been the same.

I did not know that Alexander, with his dream of fusing East and
West, had died at Babylon. I did not know that the famous glory of early
medieval Baghdad had been part of an intellectual conflict within Islam
that might have made the faith of the Caliphs a humanist enterprise, long
after the Prophet; or that the eastern *limes*, or limit, of the Roman world
had run through Iraq for centuries, or that the Sunni Ottomans and Shia
Persians had also had their shifting border there. I was unaware that the
builders of Iraq's twentieth-century monarchy—fascinating characters
like Faisal I, Gertrude Bell, and T. E. Lawrence—had created something
of such decency and potential. I had never understood that the generals
of the Prophet Mohammed may well have been the greatest of all time,
or that if Hitler had gone east through Mesopotamia, the world, as it
briefly had been for Alexander, may well have been his. I had forgotten
that Abraham's father was a maker of idols, that these idols were living
gods, that Saladin was a Kurd, and that Sinbad the Sailor hailed from
Basra.

———

The story of *Land Between the Rivers* begins with ancient Sumer, and
Gilgamesh building the walls of Uruk to make a great name for himself

around the turn of the third millennium BC. It ends in 1958, as Iraq's last royal family is slaughtered on the steps of a small royal palace in Baghdad, a city that up to that point had been effervescent and strikingly free, the most promising capital in the Middle East.

Ending in 1958, with a brief epilogue taking us to the US-led invasion early in 2003, *Land Between the Rivers* does not address the Iraq of more recent decades. From the perspective of a story spanning five millennia, the events of 1958 more or less speak for the period they initiated.

The world of Iraq that followed the bloody 1958 revolution—the emergence of Saddam Hussein as the crowning and inevitable expression of the "Arab Socialism" of the Baath Party, his wars against his own people and their neighbors, the American-led invasion of 2003 and its aftermath—is better suited to a sequel. We already know that story's essential contours: thuggery, tragedy, some promise. From the long perspective, the one taken here, these particular names and chronologies do not matter much. The job of *Land Between the Rivers* is not to tell the stories of our time but to provide their background.

Writing from Baghdad eleven days after the 1958 coup, the great James (later Jan) Morris filed a report for the *Guardian*. Morris was always after the essence of a place, and uncannily good at finding it. Visiting Iraq to report on what the bloody change of regime meant, Morris soon realized that even if it meant much, right then, it also meant very little: that in Iraq more than anywhere these things are merely a matter of the length of your outlook. The insight Morris achieved for his readers was not about which party or individual would prevail in that week or year; rather, it was about the essentially ephemeral quality of any politics, wars, factions, foreigners, and rulers in Iraq.

"We have only to look out across the grand old Tigris down to Babylon," wrote Morris, "and realise what a contemptible flicker of history we are witnessing by the Titanesque standards of Mesopotamia."

Gilgamesh, young king of Uruk—perhaps the fifth historical king of the tiny Sumerian state that may have given Iraq its name—was compelled above all else by a desire to escape his own mortality. He would achieve immortality by building up his city and "becoming a famous name," as the poet wrote. Gilgamesh did build up the great city. Then his story, by name, was the one most frequently told over the first two thousand years or so of civilization in ancient Mesopotamia. And when English explorers dug into the mysterious mounds by Mosul in the 1850s, and found clay tablets with his story on them, Gilgamesh became a famous name again. He has been ever since.

The city, where Gilgamesh wanted the bricks to bear his name, meant civilization, and writing meant that instead of mere legend, now there would be history. *Gilgamesh* was a living part of Iraq's culture into the time of the patriarch Abraham, four thousand years ago, and then onward for a thousand years after that. To a unique degree Gilgamesh's epic informs and reflects the worldview of the people who, more than any others, during that period created the foundations of our own world. Ambition, fulfillment, immortality, control of one's destiny: man, born free, seeks the life of the gods.

Prologue

> In Uruk he built walls, a great rampart, and the temple of blessed
> Eanna for the god of the firmament Anu, and for Ishtar the goddess
> of love. Look at it still today: the outer wall where the cornice runs,
> it shines with the brilliance of copper; and the inner wall, it has no
> equal. Touch the threshold, it is ancient.
>
> —*The Epic of Gilgamesh*, ca. 1750 BC

In the middle of the fourth millennium before Christ, men and women could feed themselves and their families, much of the time, but almost nobody else. They did not yet have the wheel. They could fight, but they did not have the capacity to make war. They could not read or write, for there was no writing. Without writing, there was no history. There were stories but no literature. Art was something that people might produce on their pottery, but never for a living. There were customs but no laws. There were chiefs but no kings, tribes but no nations. The city was unknown.

And then, around that time, civilization was born: urban life, based on nutritional surplus and social organization, characterized by complexity and material culture, much of it made possible by writing.[1] This happened in a very particular part of the world: the flood-prone, drought-wracked, frequently pestilential plain of southern Iraq, where the rivers Tigris and Euphrates meet the Persian Gulf. The plain could be fertile, very fertile, but only when people worked together to irrigate it and control the floods with channels and earthworks; this necessity, most likely, accounts for much of the early surge in social complexity that distinguished the area. Later civilizations would arise independently in two great river valleys not so far away, the Indus and the Nile, but the original organized, literate, urban culture was produced by a far crueler and more challenging environment than either of those.

This first civilization came to be known as Sumer. By about the year 3000 BC, a city called Uruk near the mouth of the Euphrates River, just inland of the head of the Persian Gulf, had eighty thousand residents.[2] A thousand years later Iraq, the land along the Euphrates and its sister stream, the Tigris, would be named for this early metropolis of Uruk. Sharing the land of Sumer, about the size of Belgium, with a dozen other city-states, Uruk was not always the foremost among its rivals in the land. But for most of its existence, spanning the two millennia of the Sumerian world, Uruk was the greatest city on earth.

The Sumerians invented kingship, priesthood, diplomacy, law, and war. They gave the West its founding stories: the opposition of darkness and light at the Beginning; the Flood, with its ark and dove and surviving patriarch; the tower of Babel; the distant ancestors of Odysseus and Hercules. The Sumerians established the outlines of our political, legal, and temporal structures too, with the first kings and assemblies, the first written laws, the first legal contracts, and the sexagesimal system of counting that regulates the hours and seconds of our days.

The Sumerians wrote the first epics and constructed the first monumental buildings. They invented the wheel, the sailing boat, the dome, and the arch. They were the first people to cast, rivet, and solder metals. They were the first to develop mathematics, calculating the hypotenuse of a right triangle two thousand years before Pythagoras and enabling extraordinary achievements in civil engineering. Compiling methodical lists of plants and animals, the Sumerians were the first people to apply rational order to our knowledge of the natural world.

The Sumerians wrote down almost everything they knew, much of it on disposable clay tablets that have survived the millennia. Some thirty-nine centuries after the last of the Sumerians died, another inventive and curious people, the Victorians of the nineteenth century AD, initiated a remarkable period of foreign exploration in Iraq. Thanks to this colorful and dramatic intellectual adventure, which began in the 1840s, today we can follow the course of Sumerian lawsuits, track Sumerian inventories, and study the terms of Sumerian marriages, wills, and loans. We read the overtures of Sumer's diplomats. We follow in detail the provisioning of Sumer's armies and the triumphs or disasters of their expeditions. We know intimately the pleadings of Sumerian students for more money from their fathers, and the pleadings of their fathers for more diligence from their sons. We track the transactions of Sumerian merchants in copper or onions. We admire the complex and perfect calculations of Sumerian engineers.

Human life on the alluvial plain of the two rivers at the birth of civilization five thousand years ago was precarious. Again and again, through the ancient stories and archaeological records that illuminate the dawn of history, plagues and pestilence swept the hot, low country. Terrifying floods killed and destroyed everything within reach of the raging waters that came every spring when the snow melted in the mountains five hundred miles and more to the north, in what is now Armenia and southeast Turkey. At Ur in Sumer's far south, the great archaeologist Sir Leonard Woolley, digging in 1929, discovered a layer of "perfectly clean clay" more than eight feet thick separating the remains—pottery and much more—of two distinct cultures from some time before 3000 BC.[3] A single flood, in other words, had created a temporary lake that deposited this eight-foot-thick layer. The catastrophic scale of such a deluge is almost beyond the powers of imagination. Woolley naturally surmised that it was the great flood of Genesis. Other floods have left similar records in southern Iraq. Most were smaller than Woolley's Ur deluge. One left eleven feet of new flood soil.

Meanwhile neighbors from the higher, rougher country to the east, north, and west were greedy for the wealth of the settled plain, then as now. The invasions of barbarians from the Persian hill country, the Kurdish and Turkish mountains, and the Arabian steppe sometimes paused, but never ended. Within Sumer, Uruk and its neighboring city-states fought against each other almost constantly during the twenty-odd centuries of Sumerian civilization.

The soil of southern Iraq is a dusty, flinty accumulation of silt from the two shifting rivers that originate far to the north. In the areas where Iraq's alluvial soil is not dry, it is marshy, especially in the south; it was more so in ancient times, when the Tigris and Euphrates were bigger. The ground is home to no minerals or ores, although bitumen seeps from the earth in places. The land contains no stones for building. Almost no tree, aside from the date palm, grows on it successfully.* Trade with the far-off source-lands of raw materials—for tin and copper to alloy into bronze for weapons, for gold and silver to please the rich and the divine, for hardwood timbers for the roof beams of palaces and temples—required the pooling of resources.[4] Organization and leadership were required to conduct commerce at scale with places as far afield as Anatolia for tin, Lebanon for cedar timbers, "Oman for copper, south-west Iran for carved stone bowls, eastern Iran for lapis lazuli, the Indus for carnelian."[5]

———

The water of the two great rivers irrigated the rainless plain. It also raged as a violent killer, to be restrained with dykes and channels. This required cooperation on a much larger scale than the individual village or town could offer. Better irrigation led to increasing harvests. As the land of Sumer became crowded with more and more people, food was another reason for increasingly sophisticated social arrangements. Each of these catalysts—trade, water, sustenance—also led to humanity's first organized conflicts. War was born. Every Sumerian city had its own principal deity, and the many gods also sent men into their earliest battles there on the hot plain.

———

Late in the fourth millennium BC, a couple of thousand years after the advent of agriculture with the Neolithic revolution, Sumer was one of several distinct cultures around the world. In none of these cultures had true urban life and, with it, civilization yet developed. Then the Sumerian genius produced its greatest innovation: writing.

The eighty thousand people living in Uruk by 3000 BC sheltered behind walls that were forty feet high and six miles long. Archaeologists estimate these to have cost over five million man-hours to build. The fourth-millennium city occupied about 1.7 square miles, a little bit

———

* Pace Stephen H. Longrigg, writing in 1925 of Iraq ca. 1500 AD: "Willow and poplar, rare today, then lined the banks of the southerly river courses." *Four Centuries of Modern Iraq* (Oxford: Oxford University Press, 1925), p. 3.

less than imperial Rome at its peak (2.1 square miles) and larger than classical Athens.

At the archaeological site of Uruk, the residential buildings, workshops, and barracks have not yet been excavated. Thus it is still the case that "very little about the actual conditions of life in the city is known."[6] Yet this is certain: Uruk was the world's only major city of the fourth millennium BC, marked by public buildings that were "unprecedented and unrivaled at the time."[7] Most of the labor for such civic projects in Sumer came from free laborers requiring recompense for their work. Trade in livestock and agricultural produce fed them and the residents of nearby towns. The Sumerians needed a way to keep track of it all. This was the setting in which writing was born.

The earliest writing and the earliest direct precursors of writing, all from the second half of the fourth millennium, have been found at Uruk. Initially, clay tokens the size of a thimble would be formed to represent the sorts of things that a person might own and trade, such as sheep. For convenience, these tokens would then be put into a larger, hollow clay ball a little smaller than a grapefruit. These clay spheres, called "bullae," served as something like sealed wallets or envelopes for the information within. On its exterior, the bulla would then be impressed with authenticating marks from cylindrical seals rolled upon the clay surface.

At Uruk some of these bullae have been found with additional marks impressed onto their surfaces. These marks indicated the number of tokens contained inside. It was an obvious step. The next step then suggested itself. With the contents marked on the exterior, there was no need for the little tokens rattling around inside. By 3300 BC, the information was instead simply scratched onto the surface of the spheres. The Sumerians had invented writing.*

It is the only invention that has ever rivaled that of agriculture for its transformational effect upon human existence. Eventually flat clay tablets replaced the bullae.

---

* Egypt, which developed its first writing system a little after 3000, not long after the Sumerians invented theirs, did so without Uruk's clear chain of precursors, suggesting that the notion of writing, if not the script itself, may have been borrowed from Sumer. Elsewhere, writing developed in the Indus civilization in about 2500, and in China five hundred or a thousand years later. Jean Bottéro, *Mesopotamia: Writing, Reasoning, and the Gods* (Chicago: University of Chicago Press, 1992), p. 67.

At this stage writing was almost purely pictographic. Characters signified their objects through more or less recognizable images. Any given
pictograph might mean several different things. "Mountain"—a right-
side-up pyramid formed by three convex half circles—also meant "foreign
lands," for Sumer was completely flat. Consequently the same character
also signified "conquest." Shown together with the symbol for "woman,"
a downward-pointing triangle with a notch at the bottom tip, the two
symbols meant a woman captured from far away: "slave-woman."*

Pictographs were originally drawn on wet clay with a sharp-pointed
object. Clay was an ideal medium for the Sumerians. It was cheap and
abundant on the floodplain. Clay tablets were easy to make and prepare,
although it is still not known how the larger ones were kept wet and
impressionable. Sumerian scribes eventually wrote for the most part as
we do, from left to right, top to bottom. A typical tablet might be two
to three inches high and half again as wide, with writing often going all
the way to the margins. Incisions toward the bottom of archaic Iraq's
writing tablets tend to be visibly less deep and clear than those at the
top of tablets, as the drying clay became harder to work. Once the
inscribed clay had dried in southern Mesopotamia's hot sun, it would
endure for scores of centuries, and possibly forever, if left somewhere
still and dry. Tablets made from such cheap and ubiquitous material were
easily discarded once no longer needed. To the delight of archaeologists
dozens of centuries later, they were thrown into heaps or used to fill
the spaces beneath floors.

The original pictographs were for the most part recognizably indica-
tive of something physical: a plow or a mountain, a head or a hand. But
clay as a two-dimensional medium is ill-suited to both detail and curves.
Around the year 2900, scribes discovered that impressing a sequence
of lines with a straight-edged implement such as a cut reed was easier
than tracing with a pointed implement. Reeds are flat, with a spine
along one edge. Thus the mark made by each impression of the cut-off
reed comprised a straight line with a wedge at its tip. By 2100, Sumerian

---

* Some symbols used by the pioneers at Uruk had no representational value. The sign
for a sheep, for example, was a circle divided into four quarters by a horizontal and a
vertical line. This was an artifact from the days of the bullae, when a single sheep had
been represented by a small spherical ball with a cross marked onto its surface. Bottéro,
Mesopotamia, p. 7.

scribes possessed a fast, well-developed script. Almost four thousand years later, in 1700 AD, cuneiform was named after the Latin word for wedge, *cuneus*, by the court interpreter of Eastern languages at the court of William III of England.*

The rigid straight lines of the new technique pushed the characters away from the representational and toward the symbolic and the stylized. As centuries passed, the pictographs lost their illustrational quality. They were now "ideographs." "Mountain," for example, became three semicircles. By 2500 BC the recognizably representational had disappeared.

A representational writing system has significant limitations. It is not practical to have a symbol for everything. The symbols must mean the same to all who use the writing. Users must memorize thousands of these symbols and must also be familiar with that which is being expressed.[8] Tenses, cases, and voices are mostly impossible to depict.[9] In the first centuries of writing, an image illustrating a foot meant "walk," "stand up," "ground," "foundation," and more besides simply "foot." This made things difficult enough, but how would one say, "She will walk"? Or, worse, "Will she walk?" or "How will she have walked?" The ideographic method also had great limitations, as it connected writing not to words themselves, but rather to whatever it was that the words expressed. Ideographic writing bypassed spoken language, in other words. Restricted to known events and objects, unconnected to the spoken word, such a system can never cover all that language covers.

The next great innovation in the development of writing derived from puns. Early in the third millennium before Christ, Sumerian scribes perceived that homophones allowed them greatly to expand the verbal territory covered by the symbols they had mastered. For example, the Sumerians originally lacked a pictograph for their word *sum*, "to give." To signify "give" in writing they used the pictograph for another word ("garlic") that also was pronounced "sum." In English such a visual pun is called a rebus. We might remember these from school. The picture of an eye next to that of a reed is one such, challenging us to remember,

---

* Thomas Hyde (1636–1703) believed that cuneiform was decoration employed by artisans of the Persian Achaemenid Dynasty (550–330 BC). Hyde left Eton for Cambridge at fifteen, was librarian of the Bodleian Library at Oxford at twenty-nine, and became court interpreter of Eastern languages, including Chinese, Hebrew, Turkish, Persian, Arabic, Syriac, and Malay, to Charles II, James II, and William III.

dimly, the Sumerians with the sentence "I read." With this development, writing was now attached to sounds, to the "signifier" and not the "signified." By the time of what is known as the Old Babylonian period, about 1500 BC, the Sumerian discovery of the power of paronomasia had helped the Uruk period's written lexicon of two thousand characters halve in number, even as it covered more meaning. Writing was more accessible. During the Old Babylonian period even a king might be able to read, where hitherto that skill had been largely the province of scribes.

Shortly after the earliest development of writing, an ominous cloud appeared on Sumer's northern horizon: a people called the Akkadians. In contrast to the native Sumerians, the Akkadians were Semitic pastoralists living in what came to be known as the Arabian Desert, the huge, dry steppe to the south and west of the Mesopotamian floodplain. By about 3000 BC, the Akkadians had moved eastward out of the desert. They settled north of Sumer in the part of Iraq that later came to be known as Babylonia.

The Sumerians and Akkadians lived next to each other for a thousand years. The two peoples mixed and fought constantly. There was a great degree of bilingualism, and all manner of sharing between the two languages over time. But the Sumerian and Akkadian tongues are entirely different.* How, in such a setting, might a Sumerian scribe record the name of an Akkadian merchant? The need for a single script to serve a geography using two such dissimilar languages almost interchangeably was a great spur to the development of early Mesopotamian writing. Eventually the increasingly cosmopolitan quality of life on the Mesopotamian floodplain would force the script to make itself usable by people of different tongues.

The demands of the emerging southern Mesopotamian sprachbund required that the script deliver more and more of the nuances of speech. With writing no longer able to ignore spoken language, a crucial change happened. Most of writing's symbols came to represent not meaning—an

---

* The great French cultural historian of Sumer Jean Bottéro compares the difference to that between his own language and Tibetan.

Ancient Sumer

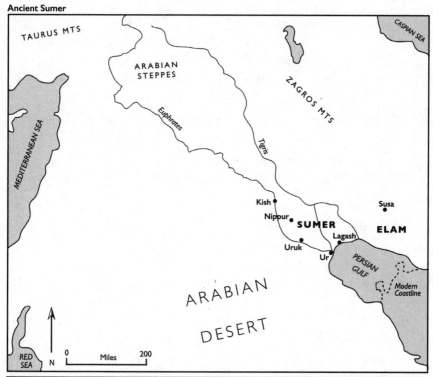

Persian Gulf
Over the 5,000 years covered by the maps in this book the northern coast of the Persian Gulf moved south as both the Tigris and Euphrates Rivers deposited silt. Thus, this and following maps depict the coast as gradually changing at regular intervals until reaching its present line in 1500. The maps of the earliest eras have a modern coast guide to show the extent of this silting.

object, activity, or idea, for example—but rather sound. Here was the evolution from the ideographic to the phonetic.[10] The impact was revolutionary. The boundaries of writing were now as infinite as those of speech. Once the Sumerian script became phonetic, the civilization that cuneiform defined would spread until it reached from Iran to the Mediterranean and from the Persian Gulf to Anatolia.*

---

* The Phoenicians of the Syrian coast developed the first alphabet, in about 1500 BC, with about twenty consonants and, initially, no vowels. When the Greeks filled this out by adding vowels, in around 750 BC, the development of phonetic writing had reached its natural conclusion: a concise and efficient alphabet, with every sound in a language covered by a symbol or short combination of symbols. Bottéro, *Mesopotamia*, p. 86.

Chapter 1

"In Search of the Wind"

Gilgamesh, 2700 BC

> I will proclaim to the world the deeds of Gilgamesh. This was the
> man to whom all things were known; this was the king who knew
> the countries of the world. He was wise, he saw mysteries and knew
> secret things, he brought us a tale of the days before the flood. He
> went on a long journey, was weary, worn-out with labor, returning
> he rested, he engraved on a stone the whole story.
>
> —*The Epic of Gilgamesh*, ca. 1750 BC[1]

Forty-six or -seven centuries ago, a king of Uruk, one Gilgamesh, left
home on a vital mission. His growing city required timber for its temples
and palaces. The journey became the basis of a story that is at the heart
of the pioneering literary work known as *The Epic of Gilgamesh*.

The most complete single version of the epic found to date, providing
about three quarters of the text as we know it, was also the very first
version of the epic to be discovered. Dating from the seventh century
BC, it was found among much other material at Nineveh, in northern
Iraq, by a British Museum expedition in 1853. The clay tablet on which
it was inscribed lay untranslated and wholly unremarked in the alluvial
depths of the museum until 1872. The tablet's discovery then caused
a sensation throughout the Western world, for the story included an
account of a great flood very much like that in Genesis. The rest of the
Gilgamesh epic has since been filled in from a variety of other versions
discovered elsewhere. These include the oldest Sumerian Gilgamesh
material, dating from perhaps 2100 BC and uncovered over the period
1889–1900 amid a trove of thirty thousand clay tablets excavated by

a University of Pennsylvania dig at the buried city of Nippur, once Sumer's religious capital. Scholars and translators also use a Gilgamesh fragment from Megiddo in Palestine, raising the exciting notion that Biblical authors may have known directly of Gilgamesh and his gods and exploits. The narrative is also partly filled in by fragments bearing versions of the Gilgamesh epic in the Hittite and Hurrian languages from archaeological finds in what is now southern Turkey, dating from perhaps the fourteenth century BC.[2]

We are confident today, through a sort of historical triangulation, that Gilgamesh the king did indeed exist.[3] He was likely a real, flesh-and-blood historical figure, living at the exact (if we may use that word) dawn of historical time, twenty-seven or -eight centuries before Christ. Copies exist of an ancient Sumerian text known as the King List; the oldest of these is from about 2100 BC, during what is known as the Third Dynasty of Ur. The kings with whom the list begins are fantastical characters who enjoyed reigns of hundreds or thousands of years in the darkness of prehistory. Then, according to the list, there is a catastrophic flood. The postdiluvian kings on the list are real historical people. The list gives them reigns of realistic length, and their names begin to appear on the bricks, pottery, and tablets since found in the ruins of Sumerian cities.

The flood clearly marks the boundary between the historical past and the antediluvian world of myth beyond. On the King List, the fifth of the post-flood rulers of the great city of Uruk was one Gilgamesh.

"When the gods created Gilgamesh," says the poet, "they gave him a perfect body." The sun god gave the hero beauty; the storm god gave him courage.

Two-thirds god and one-third man, this son of a goddess and a priest wins the kingship of his city with his all-vanquishing force of arms. He builds famous walls and great temples. But these walls of civilization constrain him. Within them he thrashes furiously, "terrifying like a wild bull," appalling his neighbors. He sounds the war drum as if for fun. "No son is left with his father," the men of the city complain to their gods, "for Gilgamesh takes them all." And this is the king, the shepherd of his people? His lust leaves no virgin to her lover, neither the warrior's daughter nor the wife of the noble.

The gods hear the lament. They decide that Gilgamesh, this rampaging king whose appetites are too much for civilization, even within the very large walls that he himself has built for it, needs a companion, "stormy heart for stormy heart." He needs a friend to channel his arrogance and desires. And so, from a piece of clay dropped into the wilderness, the gods make Enkidu. Enkidu is wild, with wavy hair like the golden hair of the corn goddess. His skin is covered with matted hair like the hair that mats the skin of the cattle god. He eats grass in the hills with the gazelle, watering with the wild beasts, "innocent of mankind."

One day in the wilderness a humble trapper from Uruk spies Enkidu. The man sees that the fur-covered savage is releasing wild animals from the traps and pits of humanity. The trapper returns to Uruk to seek the help of his king. Gilgamesh, who has already learned in his dreams of the wild man, sends the trapper back to the wilderness with a prostitute from the city, "a wanton from the temple of love." She is to seduce the savage. Their congress will sever forever Enkidu's bond with the wild beasts. What Gilgamesh wants, in other words, is to inoculate Enkidu with the spirit of civilization and the city. To do so will require the wiles of the courtesan.

On their third day of waiting by a waterhole, the prostitute and the trapper see the herds come, and Enkidu with them. The trapper says to her,

> Now, woman, make your breasts bare, have no shame, do not delay but welcome his love. Let him see you naked, let him possess your body. When he comes near uncover yourself and lie with him; teach him, the savage man, your woman's art, for when he murmurs love to you the wild beasts that shared his life in the hills will reject him.

When the wild man finally sees her, he is helpless before his desires. For six days and seven nights, Enkidu and the prostitute lie with each other, having sex. Enkidu then tries to return to the wild beasts, but they flee from him. He tries to run after them but the strength in his legs is gone. He has wisdom within him now, and the thoughts of a man, and so the woman persuades him to come with her to the city. There, she says, "every day a festival is held, the lyre and drum are played, the temple prostitutes stand around, lovely, radiating sexual prowess, filled with sex-joy."

"You are wise, Enkidu," she says in convincing him to come to the city, "and now you have become like a god." It is the first time we know of in our entire experience that humanity is equated with godliness. In many ways the grand narrative of Iraq ever since would be the story of a conflict between this notion and the submission that mortals owe to the divine.

First Enkidu and the woman go to live among shepherds. He learns to eat bread, "the staff of life," and to drink wine, "the custom of the land." One day Enkidu learns from a passing man that King Gilgamesh is planning a debauch in Uruk. In one version of the epic, the king is going to have an orgy in a civic building. In another, a wedding is to take place in the city and Gilgamesh plans to assert his prima-noctial right. In either case, Enkidu comes to Uruk and blocks Gilgamesh's path. The two giants fight. Gilgamesh wins and they embrace as friends.

The Sumerian King List tells us that just before the time of Gilgamesh, a monarch called Enmebaragesi ruled over Kish, a nearby city that was a perennial rival of Uruk. According to the list, Enmebaragesi's son, Agga, followed his father on the throne of Kish while Gilgamesh reigned at Uruk. Both Enmebaragesi and Agga are now known, from references discovered elsewhere in the documentary record, to have been living, historical individuals. The list's reference to Gilgamesh living alongside them is part of the confirmation of his own likely historical veracity.

Supporting the King List, there is a Sumerian poem known as "Gilgamesh and Agga of Kish." This tells the story of Agga demanding the submission of Gilgamesh and his city, Uruk. Gilgamesh, according to the poet, takes the matter to "the convened assembly of the elders of his city." Gilgamesh hopes for war but the elders counsel peace. King Gilgamesh then consults a younger assembly, "the fighting men of the city." This body, saying, "Do not submit to the house of Kish," advises war.

It is a notable moment in world events. At the very sunrise of history, in an episode that probably actually happened in some form, the greatest king of the world's first civilization is consulting on the most important of matters with the fundamental institution of democracy, an assembly (bicameral, no less) of citizens.* The poem tells us that Gilgamesh rejects the ultimatum. Agga then besieges Uruk. But when Agga's forces see Gilgamesh glowering down at them from Uruk's famous city walls, the invaders are stricken with terror. It is they who "bite the dirt," surrendering and submitting. Thus Agga becomes Gilgamesh's vassal.⁴ The King List appears to confirm this, reporting independently that Kish becomes a vassal state to Uruk at about this time. Another text details repairs made by a succession of historical rulers to a temple built by Gilgamesh at Nippur, Sumer's religious capital.

The upshot is that while hard proof has not yet been found to establish Gilgamesh's existence irrefutably, as has been done for many of the contemporary rulers who inhabit the Sumerian record alongside him, there are easily enough credible indirect references to persuade scholars of his historicity.⁵

One of the exciting things about Gilgamesh is precisely this: his inhabiting the shadow lands at the very edge of history itself.⁶ Occasionally he comes into view, when the sunlight of written records peeks through the thick fog of deep historical time. More frequently, he lurks in the misty gloaming of illiterate prehistory. Enmebaragesi of Kish, the father of Gilgamesh's real-life rival Agga, illuminates the hero's liminal quality, for Enmebaragesi is himself the first person ever whose identity is attested verifiably in writing.† In 1959, fragments of two alabaster vessels were identified by a German scholar in the Baghdad Museum as having Enmebaragesi's name on them.⁷ Since then, contemporaneous objects have been translated mentioning Enmebaragesi by name as a ruler of Kish.

---

* The American professor who discovered and translated this particular Gilgamesh poem in 1956 noted how remarkable it was to see this happen in a part of the world that was viewed as being "traditionally the home of tyrants and despots, a part of the world where political assemblies were thought to be practically unknown." Samuel Noah Kramer, *The Sumerians: Their History, Culture, and Character* (Chicago: University of Chicago Press, 1971), p. 2. In most versions, Gilgamesh's more rapacious and brutish behavior comes before he achieves kingship, learns the ways of civilization, and matures.

† Gilgamesh "himself" died about 2660 BC. Georges Roux, *Ancient Iraq*, 3rd ed. (London: Penguin, 1992), pp. 123, 140. Roux dates the writing of the Gilgamesh epic (p. 196) to the era of the reign of Hammurabi (d. ca. 1750 BC), "when the Akkadian language reached perfection" and the Akkadian scribes "continued to copy the major Sumerian texts, but . . . also wrote original works."

Enmebaragesi has been called the "starting point" of Iraqi history.[8] He is in fact, as the first nonfictional king attested in writing anywhere, the starting point of all political history. It began with a conflict that continues to this day, one that flares up again and again, if indeed it ever truly stops, throughout the long story of the world's central land. The King List tells us that Enmebaragesi "carried away as spoil the weapons of Elam."[9] Elam was Sumer's eastern neighbor, the first great civilization in what is today Iran. The city-states of ancient Iraq were at war with Elam—a regional power with its main capital at Susa—almost ceaselessly for about three thousand years, until shortly before the Persian king Cyrus conquered Iraq in 539 BC.[10]

The historical Gilgamesh was almost certainly a great builder. Uruk, which lies a hundred miles southeast of Baghdad, was renowned in its day for its city walls. In the ancient accounts it is always Gilgamesh the king who receives the credit for them. Forty-six or -seven centuries after the walls of Gilgamesh's city were built, two Englishmen of the 1850s, William Loftus and Henry Rawlinson, became the first people to pay serious attention to the place since the sack of the city during the Muslim invasion of Iraq in 654 AD. Loftus and Rawlinson were impressed with Warka, as it continues to be known locally, swiftly realizing that, notwithstanding the many other sites in the Near East beginning to attract study, they had found the "mother-city."

The walls of Uruk around the time of Gilgamesh were undoubtedly impressive. The measurement of six miles around and forty to fifty feet high was made by German archaeologists who dug there in the 1920s and 1930s, when the earliest examples of writing were found. Inside Uruk's huge walls, the Germans observed, the city of the historical Gilgamesh was divided along lines that reflect the city that the legendary king shows to the ferryman in the Gilgamesh epic.* The archaeologists discovered that the historical city was divided into thirds, one for the formal buildings of government and the rich, one for the poor, and one for open

---

* The Germans had a reputation in the world of nineteenth- and twentieth-century Mesopotamian archaeology as the leading experts in the very fine work of identifying structures of unfired bricks buried deep in the same Iraqi earth from which the bricks were made. The Iraqis who did the physical digging for them made a sort of inherited guild of their skill, confining the secrets to the "closed shop" of their home village of Tel Al Rabiy.

spaces such as gardens and cemeteries. Many cities of the region are not very different today.[11]

The archaeological sites of Mesopotamia look, in their untouched form, like simple mounds in the flat landscape. Known as *tels*, they are the remnants of ancient cities, towns, or even individual buildings such as temples, eroded down and covered with thousands of years of dust and dirt until they are mere rounded humps on the level countryside, anywhere in area from a square mile or two to fifty or a hundred yards square. Some are dozens of feet high and more, others no higher than a contemporary house. Driving around modern Iraq, the number of modestly sized *tels*, as well as of larger ones, untouched as yet by the archaeologist, is astounding.

The *tel*, or hill, at Warka was one of these: just a bump, if one of the bigger ones, in the even, brown floodplain. But Loftus and Rawlinson were correct in their intuition. For the twenty-five centuries following Gilgamesh, the land between the rivers continued to produce cities, such as Ur, Nineveh, Babylon, Ctesiphon, and Baghdad. Today, after 150 years of archaeological discovery, with extensive digs by many nations at scores of important sites in Iraq, Uruk-Warka still possesses "the earliest, grandest, and most numerous monumental buildings in Mesopotamia."[12] Gilgamesh's capital was indeed the ur-city of all humanity.* Within about three hundred years of the time of Gilgamesh and the walls he built at Uruk, the "urban revolution"—civilization itself, underwritten by writing—had spread beyond the Mesopotamian floodplain. Only in southern Iraq, however, did the urban population outnumber the rural population.[13]

After roughly a thousand years of encroachment by the Semites, the barbarians from neighboring Arabia who settled in Akkad, north of Sumer, the Sumerian civilization died its final death around the turn of the third into the second millennium BC. For another thousand years, the memory of Sumer lived on in Mesopotamia, much as the memory of Rome was to live on in the Europe of the Middle Ages, providing a language of scholarship and liturgy, and a reference for aspirations. During this time the walls of Uruk reappear repeatedly in the poems,

---

* The English prefix "ur-," meaning original or primordial, comes not from the Iraqi city of Ur but from an Old High German word, *ur*, meaning "thoroughly."

stories, and myths of the cultures that succeeded Sumer. Gilgamesh, the
builder of the walls, nearly ubiquitous, like a Mesopotamian Hercules,
was the greatest hero of Iraqi mythology through these long centuries.
Of the nine Sumerian epics known to us, Gilgamesh is the leading figure
in five: "Gilgamesh and the Land of the Living," "Gilgamesh and the
Bull of Heaven," and so on.

Gilgamesh's stature in the extensive literature of two millennia of
Sumerian culture makes it likely that he was a conqueror as well as a
civic builder. This is partly confirmed by the King List's mention of the
subjugation of Kish by Uruk. Like any archaic conqueror and builder
on the stoneless Sumerian floodplain—a place with neither ores below
ground nor trees above it—Gilgamesh would have had to go far from
home to acquire the raw materials to achieve his ambitions.

The Gilgamesh of the epic heads off from Uruk to the distant forests and
returns with precious wood for his growing city. Gilgamesh the historical
king would have gone either east toward Elam; north to the forested hill
country of Amanus, now northern Syria; or west to the cedar-rich mountains of Lebanon. But the epic hero is really questing for something far
greater than building supplies. "I will set up my name," he says before
setting off on his journey to the far-off forests, "in the place where the
names of famous men are written."

What he really wants, then, is immortality. That is what he achieves.
The Gilgamesh saga is the great original story of civilization, the earliest
epic sequence ever written. For the first twenty centuries of historical, literate, and urban life, the most popular stories in the land where
civilization and history began are about one person: him. In the epic,
Gilgamesh refers again and again to immortality as a function of the
written word, that world-changing invention of his very own Uruk.

The threads of the Gilgamesh story, the characters, their concerns and
biographies, are woven through the narrative of Western culture. Many
of the epic's themes—friendship, civilization, mortality—exist beyond
any specific time and culture. They would be recognizable in almost
any place or epoch. And yet, as universal as some elements of the tale
certainly are, there is also much about it that is distant and weird. When

we read the epic, only sixty pages long in its leading English version, we feel an odd excitement. The sensation results from the surprising mixture of familiarity and strangeness. It is the sort of thing that we might sense during an encounter with a cousin from far away who shares so many of our physical features that we are rattled when she speaks in a strange tongue. It is the sensation of the extraordinary distance of our own journey since the day five thousand years ago when Gilgamesh, king of Uruk, set off to find eternal life far away over the sea of death.

———

Living in Uruk, Gilgamesh and his friend Enkidu become restless. Enkidu finds himself grown weak. Idleness oppresses him like a heavy weight. For Gilgamesh the pain is different: "I have not established my name stamped on bricks," he laments.

The two friends resolve upon a great adventure. They will journey to the land of cedars, there to slay the giant Humbaba, who has grown overweening in his god-appointed guardianship of the trees. Enkidu is frightened, but Gilgamesh reminds him that "only the gods live forever," and that to die in such an endeavor would at least mean leaving behind "a name that endures forever."

Shamash, the sun god, appoints the many winds to protect the two friends. The armorers and craftsmen of Uruk make weapons for them; the axes weigh nine score pounds and the swords four times more. On their way out of the city, Gilgamesh and Enkidu stop to visit Ninsun, the queen, Gilgamesh's mother. To receive them she puts on a dress that shows off her figure, "jewels to make her breast beautiful," and a tiara. Her skirts sweep the ground at the altar of the sun upon the roof of her palace. She burns incense and says a prayer for the heroes. Gilgamesh and Enkidu depart after receiving final advice from the city elders.

In three days the heroes walk the equivalent of a month and a half's journey, crossing seven mountains. At the gate of the cedar forest, things are different from the plain of Uruk. The way is broad and clear, the trees enormous, and their shade cool. But now Enkidu's hand has lost its strength. Gilgamesh persuades his friend to press ahead. "When two go together," says Gilgamesh, "each will protect himself and shield his companion, and if they fall they leave an enduring name."

After campfires in the forest and dreadful dreams and more long journeys, Gilgamesh finally takes his axe in hand and fells a mighty cedar. The tree happens to be sacred to Humbaba. The giant, somewhere far off in the forest, cries out in rage. When Humbaba appears, Gilgamesh loses his nerve. He begins to cry, calling out to Shamash for help. The god summons the winds. They come,

> the great wind, the north wind, the whirlwind, the storm and the icy wind, the tempest and the scorching wind; they came like dragons, like a scorching fire, like a serpent that freezes the heart, a destroying flood and the lightning's fork.

As the winds paralyze Humbaba, Gilgamesh cuts down more cedars. Humbaba blazes out in impotent fury until the seventh tree has been felled. Then he begs Gilgamesh for freedom, but Enkidu reminds the king of Uruk that fate is pitiless to men of weak judgment, and Gilgamesh takes his sword to the neck of the giant. Enlil, the lord of the gods, is furious. But Gilgamesh and Enkidu return safely to Uruk, with their cedars, victorious in civilization's first war for natural resources. Man has stood up to the gods.

The next scene provides one of the far-off epic's many moments of recognizable humanity. With their textures of immediacy, these seem to leap across the millennia and bridge the broad waters of fantasy, making this story fresh even today. Gilgamesh is now returned home from the journey. It has been arduous, frightening, and successful. The king of Uruk washes his hair. He cleans off his weapons and exchanges his filthy travel-worn clothes for sweet-scented royal robes. He flings his clean hair back over his shoulders and puts on his crown.

But there is no rest for his anxious spirit. "Glorious Ishtar," the goddess of love and war, spies Gilgamesh's beauty. "Come to me, Gilgamesh," she says, "and be my bridegroom; grant me seed of your body, let me be your bride." Gilgamesh replies temperately enough. He would gladly give Ishtar her due as a goddess. He will even provide her with food and wine befitting a queen. But his wife? That she will never be. "How would it go with me?" he asks her of a marriage between them:

Your lovers have found you like a brazier that smoulders in the cold, a backdoor that keeps out neither squall of wind nor storm, a castle that crushes the garrison, pitch that blackens the bearer, a water-skin that chafes the carrier, a stone that falls from the parapet, a battering ram turned back from the enemy, a sandal that trips the wearer.

Gilgamesh goes on to name some of those most hurt by the rapacious goddess. "Listen to me," he says, "while I tell you the tale of your lovers." There was Tammuz, the lover of Ishtar's youth, condemned to a life of tears; the bird, the many-colored roller, whose wing she broke and who laments this forever on a branch; the stallion, magnificent in battle, for whom Ishtar decreed the whip and the spur and that he must muddy his own water before he drinks; and even her own father's gardener, now a blind mole digging in the earth, his desire always beyond his reach.

Ishtar, enraged, goes to her father in heaven among the gods. She persuades him to send down a mighty beast, the Bull of Heaven, to punish Gilgamesh. The bull comes down to Uruk and with his first snort rends the earth, killing a hundred men. With his second he kills a hundred more. Enkidu grabs the bull's tail and Gilgamesh kills the animal with a sword through its nape. As Ishtar rails at them from the walls of Uruk, Enkidu hurls the right thigh of the bull at her. Victorious, Gilgamesh and Enkidu wash their hands in the Euphrates and drive through the rejoicing streets of the city before celebrating in the palace.

Soon after, Enkidu tells Gilgamesh of a trip to the underworld in his dreams. This report is still our main account of how the people of ancient Sumer saw the afterlife. It was a miserable place.

Holding me fast, he took me down to the house of shadows, the dwell-
 ing of hell, To the house whence none who enters comes forth,
On the road from which there is no way back,
To the house whose dwellers are deprived of light,
Where dust is their fare and their food is clay.
They are dressed like birds in feather garments,
Yea, they shall see no daylight for they abide in darkness . . .
When I entered that house of dust I saw crowns in a heap,
There dwelt the kings, the crowned heads who once ruled the land.[14]

All people went there, whether they had been good or bad in life. Even princes and kings sat there in the dark, wearing feathers for clothes. All ate dust for ordinary food. Clay was their meat. There was no hope for anything better. The message was that any chance of paradise happens in this world, in this life. Gilgamesh understands this. "The dream was marvelous," he says, "but the terror was great; we must treasure the dream whatever the terror; for the dream has shown that misery comes at last to the healthy man, the end of life is sorrow." For Gilgamesh, the peerless Sumerian king, he who was constantly seeking immortality, the lesson of Enkidu's gloomy vision is *carpe diem*: life must be lived in the here and now.

When Enkidu then dies of illness, Gilgamesh lays a veil, "like the veil of a bride," over his friend. He orders a statue of Enkidu to be made. Its body will be of gold. He sets out in offering to the sun a carnelian bowl full of honey and a lapis lazuli bowl full of butter.

Fearing his own death—"what my brother is now, that shall I be when I am dead"—Gilgamesh sets himself another quest. He will seek Utnapishtim, the man who has survived the great flood on a wooden ark, the one man to whom the gods have given eternal life. Gilgamesh and Enkidu have adventured around the world in search of endless fame, but now Enkidu's death has persuaded the child of the gods that even an immortal name is not enough. He himself must live forever.

Eventually Gilgamesh's quest brings him to the sea. It was probably at the Phoenician coast beyond the mountains of Lebanon. There he comes to Siduri, "the divine barmaid."[15] We meet her, "the woman of the vine," sitting in the sun where the blue waters lap on that once-enchanted coastline. She sits "in the garden at the edge of the sea, with the golden bowl and the golden vats that the gods gave her." There is a strong sense here, in this beautiful scene, of the long, strange Mesopotamian epic, like a trader's ship from far away, nosing its prow up the beach of the more familiar Homeric world.

The idea of a classical connection is not far-fetched. Gilgamesh lived perhaps twenty centuries before Homer (ca. 700 BC), but a major surviving version of the Sumerian epic dates from no earlier than 650 BC. The lands of the Greek bard and the Assyrian scribe of the seventh century BC were separated only by the well-traveled trade routes of Syria and Anatolia, and we know from several sources that the Greeks and Assyrians had been in contact since at least the thirteenth century BC.[16]

It is in tablet XI of one of the epic's versions that Gilgamesh asks Utnapishtim, "You then, how did you join the ranks of the gods and find eternal life?" Later in this penultimate tablet of the epic, Gilgamesh invites Urshanabi, the ferryman of Utnapishtim, to visit him at home, and there "pace out the walls of Uruk. Study the foundation terrace and examine the brickwork."[17]

Siduri herself seems a direct ancestor of Circe, the Mediterranean enchantress who entertained Odysseus in her own slow-paced waterside idyll. The sea, that particular sea, and the vine and the wine and the golden bowl, and the weary hero resting on his quest, give the episode a distinctly classical atmosphere. Siduri, in her mellow Mediterranean arcadia, is alarmed at the sight of this disheveled man approaching. She bars her gate and bolts her door. The visitor explains that he is Gilgamesh, not some common thief. Why, she asks, does he wander about like this, looking dreadful, "in search of the wind"? Gilgamesh describes his pain at the death of Enkidu. "Because of my brother," says Gilgamesh, "I am afraid of death." Fear of mortality and the journey toward self-knowledge that this fear causes: for the divine barmaid, Gilgamesh expresses in a handful of words the very theme of the epic.

Siduri is the most human and realistic figure in the story. She is not a Scorpion Man with a stare that kills. Her hair is not golden waves of grain. She is not like a noble wild bull chained to the mountainside. She is simply a veiled woman who makes wine by the glinting sea. Her answer to Gilgamesh is important:

"You will never find that life for which you are looking," she tells the restless Sumerian. She continues,

When the gods created man they allotted to him death, but life they retained in their own keeping. As for you, Gilgamesh, fill your belly with good things; day and night, night and day, dance and be merry, feast and rejoice. Let your clothes be fresh, bathe yourself in water, cherish the little child that holds your hand, and make your wife happy in your embrace; this too is the lot of man.

Siduri's advice accords perfectly with the central Sumerian outlook of wonder and excitement at the quotidian. These were the people who invented it all, and then wrote it all down. But Siduri's guest is still the slave of his restive desires. He insists on pressing ahead, and the woman of the vine shows him the way. He must go with Urshanabi the ferryman. But, she warns, the journey over the waters of death will be extremely difficult. Only the sun and the god Shamash have ever crossed the ocean.

Gilgamesh and Urshanabi set out, poling carefully over the waters of death—in an early reference to crude oil, their poles are covered in pitch—and then they sail into Utnapishtim's harbor with the arms of Gilgamesh himself as a mast and his clothing as a sail.

"Oh father," says Gilgamesh to the flood survivor when they meet, "how shall I find the life for which I am searching?" Utnapishtim replies that we are all of us, master and servant alike, the same once death comes; the judges and the "mother of destinies" decree our fates and the moments of our deaths. His words are gloomier than Siduri's, but fundamentally the two points are the same. We must accept our lot. It follows that we must do what we can with the present. Gilgamesh does notice that Utnapishtim is not the vigorous, heroic physical specimen that he expected. Is immortality, then, truly so desirable? Again the message is to make the most of one's potential in the life that one has. It is an understandable message from the Sumerians, an early foreshadowing of the struggle between fatalism and humanism that will be their land's key theme through the millennia to come.

The ferryman now provides Gilgamesh with an account of the great flood. The Sumerian Noah, Utnapishtim, built a pitch-covered ark and loaded pairs of animals aboard it to escape the deluge. Afloat upon the floodwaters in his ark, he welcomed back a far-flying bird returning with the good news of dry land. Then they drifted to a mountaintop mooring. When the clay tablet bearing this part of the epic was first translated, in the reading room of the British Museum in 1872, it caused an extraordinary commotion. This flood story, so clearly a close ancestor of the Old Testament's version, inspired the Victorians to send explorers back to Iraq to seek the rest of the epic. Almost miraculously, they found it, buried deep in the northern Mesopotamian dust. This discovery gave Gilgamesh the immortality he sought, more than forty centuries after his death.

When the story of the flood is finished, Gilgamesh turns once more to his physical immortality. "There is a plant," Utnapishtim tells him, "that grows under the water, it has a prickle like a thorn . . . but if you succeed in taking it, then your hands will hold that which restores his lost youth to a man."

Gilgamesh dives to the bottom of the sea with the help of heavy stones tied to his feet. He finds the thorny flower on the seabed, returns to the surface, and promises to give it to the old men of Uruk to restore them. And then on the long journey home he swims in a cool well of water. "But deep in the pool there was lying a serpent, and the serpent sensed the sweetness of the flower." The snake emerges from the deep, takes the flower of youth from Gilgamesh, and swims away with it forever, sloughing its old skin as it goes.

When the serpent swims off with the spiky flower of immortality, Gilgamesh is disconsolate. The hero understands at last the futility of trying to change his final destiny. At last he grasps the great concept of his civilization: if heaven is anywhere, it is here, on earth, today. So he travels home to Uruk. There he has the ferryman do something that is remarkable given the transcendent preoccupations of the rest of the story. "Urshanabi," Gilgamesh commands,

> climb up on to the wall of Uruk, inspect its foundation terrace, and examine well the brickwork; see if it is not of burnt bricks; and did not the seven wise men lay these foundations? One third of the whole is city, one third is garden, and one third is field, with the precinct of the goddess Ishtar. These parts and the precinct are all Uruk.

Here, at the end of the Gilgamesh epic, we are right where something so quintessentially Sumerian would have us be. We are inspecting the brickwork of the mother city, proud of our practical accomplishments, anchored with curiosity and dirty fingernails in the here and now. After boasting of this busy, thrusting achievement, showing it off to the boatman of the only survivor of that antediluvian world when all was myth, Gilgamesh engraves the story on a stone.*

---

* When the latter-day Iraqi despot Saddam Hussein rebuilt part of Babylon in the 1980s, he, like Hammurabi and Nebuchadnezzar before him, had bricks stamped with his name. In 2010, when the Iraqi prime minister of the day laid a cornerstone for a new port on the Persian Gulf, he immortalized himself in stone with the inscribed words "The same hand that signed Saddam's execution warrant will be the hand that rebuilds Iraq."

So in the end there is no flower of eternal life for our hero. We all die, we do not progress, and there is neither lasting reward nor punishment. We all end up equally pale and dusty in our dreary, monotonous, uniform afterlife, feathered wretches eating clay in the gloom.

Make the most of today, Gilgamesh tells us, because nothing we do here in this life will get us anywhere special tomorrow. The ancient Mesopotamians had a curious, questing fascination with the immediate, a concern visible in their meticulous recordkeeping and correspondence and in their avid tabulations of all that they knew about zoology, mineralogy, botany, geography, mathematics, grammar, and more. It is the spirit of the awakening infant full of wonder in its crib. In Gilgamesh's time this spirit is far from developing into the full thrust of conscious human freedom. But in his turbulent, frustrated quest, we can begin to see the origins of an outlook of free will.

Two thousand years later, to the northeast in Iran, a religion would emerge that gave humanity a day of judgment, leading to an afterlife of either heaven or hell. This faith was Zoroastrianism. There can be no judgment without free will, and thus the Iranian religion would also introduce the concepts of human agency and ethical choice into the moral resources of the region. By the brown Euphrates waters of another Mesopotamian city, Babylon, seventy miles north of Uruk, an exiled people called the Judaeans would then encounter this theology. They adopted elements of it into their own faith during a series of mass captivities there that lasted through much of the sixth century BC. They then returned to Israel with a new religion, Judaism, that had Zoroastrian end times, judgment, and moral freedom at its heart, marrying these with the omnipotent god of the Jews' Israelite forebears.

The Jews' Zoroastrian legacies of ethics and free choice, leading to an eschatology of the judgment day, were natural complements to the humanism of the ancient Greeks. When the two outlooks met in the time of the Roman Caesars, a third great monotheistic faith resulted: Christianity. Islam, the fourth of the Fertile Crescent's major one-god religions, would eschew these developments and return to the pure will of the older Semitic Almighty who demanded complete submission.

Chapter 2

The Father of Many

Abraham, 1800 BC

In about 1900 or 1800 BC, seven or eight centuries after Gilgamesh, another Sumerian set off on an epochal quest. This traveler did not know his destination as he left his father's house at the behest of his god.

Life was different now in southern Iraq. Sumer, the civilization of the man's birth, was in its last throes. Centuries of pressure from invaders to the east, west, north, and south—from lands we now call Iran, Syria, Kurdistan, and Arabia—had beaten it down. A new city, Babylon, established by the desert dwellers known as the Semites, had risen as Sumer's northern neighbor, taking control of political and economic life in south and central Mesopotamia. When the Semites had begun to encroach upon the Sumerians four hundred years earlier, the people of Ur had derided the newcomers as "tent-dwellers."* Now the Semites of Babylon were copying Sumerian culture in sterile ways, as the vibrant language and refined literature of Abraham's fathers atrophied and died.

"Get thee out of thy country," the man's god tells him, "and from thy father's house, unto a land that I will show thee."[1] The man from Ur obeyed the divine call without question. His trek would lead him to a land called Canaan and a posterity in which his various descendants—Jews, Christians, and Muslims—would be as countless as the dust on the ground of the Middle East.

---

* In much the same way, as shall be seen in due course, the Muslim invaders of Iraq in the days of the Prophet Mohammed's successors thirty centuries later, also Semitic nomads from the deserts south and west of Iraq, were sneered at as uncouth, "lizard-eating" camel riders by the Persians and Babylonians of the day.

The Book of Genesis calls the man Abram. God would later rename him Abraham, meaning "father of many." The Abraham of the Book of Genesis, the prophet, patriarch, and father of nations, the founder of Middle Eastern monotheism with its luminous clarity and dangerous intensity, took the culture of Sumer with him. Sumer informs Abraham's legacy to a remarkable extent. As we reconsider the father of Judaism, Christianity, and Islam in the light of this powerful Mesopotamian heritage, Abraham's story takes on new substance. In turn, restoring the legend of Abraham to its Sumerian context underscores how great an influence ancient Mesopotamia has had on our world.

Around the year 2000 BC, almost seven hundred years after Gilgamesh and a century or so before Abraham, 90 percent of the people in Sumer were living in cities.[2] Ur, where Abraham would be born two hundred years later, was now foremost among these. The merchants of Sumer traded with lands as far away as India. The scale of Sumerian life in the centuries before Abraham's birth is astounding. At Ur in 2000 BC there were five hundred yards of walled docks lining the harbor at what was then an estuary at the head of the Persian Gulf.* Fifteen centuries before classical Athens walled the road to its port at Piraeus, a Sumerian merchant ship departing from these docks would have carried ninety tons of cargo for the Indian spice trade, or to barter for copper in Oman.

Sumer at this time was home to as many as ten cities of at least thirty or forty thousand inhabitants. Feeding a Sumerian city of that size, and some that were much larger, required more than three tons of barley every day. Grapes were also part of the Iraqi menu then, as were dates, apricots, and chickpeas. A large merchant in a Sumerian city might order 150,000 bunches of onions at a time. Beer, the national drink, was invented in Sumer and brewed in the temples. The training to become a qualified cook in a Sumerian city such as Abraham's Ur took sixteen months of apprenticeship. Certification as an expert builder required eight years of formal training.

The ashes of this Sumerian milieu of Abraham's ancestors were still warm when he was born around the nineteenth century BC. Eventually Babylon, in the course of its own extraordinary longevity, would preserve and radiate much of Sumer's legacy in intellectual and material

---

* Today, thanks to the gradual southward extension of the head of the gulf due to river-borne siltation, the site of Ur is a hundred miles inland.

culture. Abraham's contribution passed along something different: parts of Sumer's spiritual inheritance.

———————

While Gilgamesh comes to us from the dawn of historical time, Abraham came from a different world. Writing, and history with it, had spread far beyond Sumer. Yet, as with Gilgamesh, no final and indisputable item of proof—no contemporaneous brick or votive bowl or clay tablet with Abraham's name on it—has reached us.

We do know that people from southern Mesopotamia were emigrating to Canaan during this period. At the end of the third millennium BC, on the early side of the range of likely dates for Abraham, the settled, civilized lands of Palestine saw an intense disruption caused by immigrant bands from Mesopotamia, one of which was known as the Habiru or Hapiru. These Mesopotamian migrants "spoke West Semitic languages, of which Hebrew is one."[3] Perhaps Abraham led one of these Hebrew bands. We are told in the Old Testament that he was a substantial chief, with "318 trained men, born in his house."[4] *

Besides the reference to Ur in the chapter of Genesis that introduces him, perhaps the most salient clue to Abraham's historicity—or at least his strong historical plausibility—is the journey that is then described. After telling us that Abraham's family had come out of Ur, Genesis refers to their sojourning in Harran (latterly Urfa in southeast Turkey, 720 miles by road northwest from the Iraqi city of Nassiriya, by the site of Ur), a city culturally and geographically at the far northern tip of Mesopotamia. From here, Abraham makes his way south to Canaan, then travels into Egypt and back to Canaan.

The arc of these travels describes perfectly the historical Fertile Crescent, the band of green lands forming an upside-down U from southern Iraq up to an apex in southern Turkey and down again through the green west of Syria into Palestine, Israel, and Egypt. The two tips of the crescent are rooted in great river deltas: the eastern in the Sumerian wetlands of southern Iraq, the western in the Nile delta that fed the slightly younger civilization of ancient Egypt. Busy trade and migration

———————

* This is from Genesis 14, when Abraham mounts an expedition to rescue his nephew Lot. The "trained men" would have meant a retinue of fighting men.

The Ancient Fertile Crescent

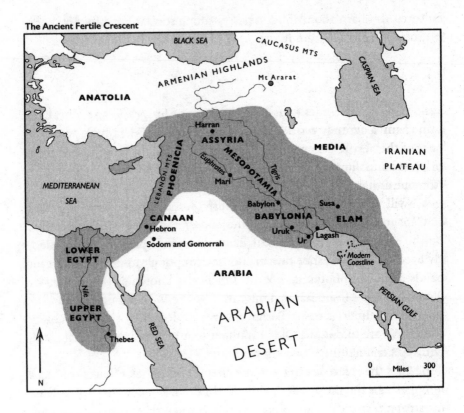

along the Fertile Crescent at the time make the course of Abraham's physical journey to his promised land a familiar one for the period.

When Abram is seventy-five and has sojourned at Harran long enough to have gathered "substance" there as well as various new "souls" for his wider household or band, his father, Terah, dies.* As God had earlier told Abram to "get thee out of thy country, and from thy kindred, and from thy father's house,"[5] he now sets off for the land that God has promised to show him. There, Abram is told, he will become the father of a great people. God's promises of paternity will henceforth pound like a drumbeat throughout the Abraham story, underscoring a deep preoccupation with posterity and immortality while also marking the

---

* Terah died at the age of 205, a descendant of Shem and thus (like everyone, according to the Genesis story) of Noah and ultimately Adam and Eve.

progress of his journey. Where Gilgamesh's immortality came through the establishment of a name made eternal by writing, Abraham's would come from the establishment of a tribe of descendants and from the beliefs they spread.

The man from Ur sets off from Harran accompanied by his wife, Sarai, with whom he has been unable to conceive children. They bring with them a nephew named Lot, among others. Tracing the western horn of the Fertile Crescent southward from Harran, Abram's group of relatives and followers eventually arrives at the land of Canaan, modern Palestine and Israel. There God makes him another promise: "Unto thy seed I will give this land."

In Canaan, however, Abram's party finds famine, so they move on to Egypt. There, Pharaoh is struck by Sarai's beauty. Abram, fearing that Pharaoh will murder the husband of such a woman, passes Sarai off as his sister. As the brother of a favorite concubine of the king, Abram goes on to prosper at court.

Eventually returning to Canaan "very rich in cattle, in silver, and in gold," Abram allows his band to split. He encourages Lot and his followers to take the green plain with its rich cities, including Sodom and Gomorrah. God directs Abram himself to look toward the four points of the compass and pledges to him all the land that he can see, for him and his descendants forever. Enjoying this legacy, God promises, will be a progeny as numberless as the dust of the earth.

When Abram laments that he is still childless, God makes him a fourth promise of a great lineage, this time as numerous as the stars in heaven. God follows this with yet another, but much larger, promise of land. "Unto thy seed," he says, "I have given this land, from the river of Egypt unto the great river, the Euphrates." The reference to the Euphrates, the river of Babylon, follows a forewarning from God that there will come a time when Abraham's "seed shall be a stranger in a land that is not theirs."

Ten years after first arriving in Canaan, Abram and Sarai still have no children. God's promises become ever harder for them to believe. Abram is now eighty-six, and Sarai ten years younger. So Sarai, as was the Sumerian custom when a woman was infertile, gives Abram her Egyptian serving girl, Hagar, to bear him a child. Eventually pregnant by Abram, Hagar sets herself up above her mistress, and Abram allows his insulted wife to force the pregnant serving girl out into the desert. There the angel of God finds Hagar by a spring and tells her to return to Sarai, reassuring Hagar that the baby will be a boy and have offspring beyond counting. The boy, says the angel, will be called Ishmael: *ish* for "man," and *mael* meaning "from God." But he will be a "wild ass of a man, his hand against everyone and everyone's hand against him," and between him and his kin relations will be violent.

When Abram turns ninety-nine, and Sarai's monthly periods have stopped, God comes to him again, but this time the message is different. "I am God Almighty," he says. "Live always in my presence and be perfect, so that I may set my covenant between myself and you and multiply your descendants."

This statement was different from the divine promises that had come before it. "God Almighty" is a new formula. The injunction to live perfectly is also new. More important, what had heretofore been one-way promises by God to Abram have now been replaced by a "covenant." There will be a contract that goes both ways, binding both parties. Abram now does something he has never done before. He abases himself, face down to the ground. From the Almighty, who now renames his follower Abraham, the words roll out in a new tone that is huge and stern:

> I make this covenant, and I make it with you: you shall be the father of a host of nations. Your name shall no longer be Abram, it shall be Abraham, for I make you father of a host of nations. I will make you exceedingly fruitful. I will make nations out of you, and kings shall spring from you. I will fulfill my covenant between myself and you and your descendants after you, generation after generation, an everlasting covenant, to be your God.

For a sign of commitment, God requests that Abraham and his entire male household circumcise themselves. It is part of the covenant, a symbol of submission and devotion.

God now changes Sarai's name too. She will be called Sarah, meaning "princess," in recognition of her future as the mother of a nation. Abraham finds this so funny that he falls to the ground laughing.* He

---

* It is said to be the earliest laughter ever attested. Paul Johnson, *A History of the Jews* (New York: Harper Perennial, 2008), p. 15.

was nearly a hundred years old and Sarah ninety. This laughter echoes in the next episode of Abraham's story, after circumcision has bound him to God and prepared him ritually to father a host. Abraham is sitting at the opening of his tent in the heat of the day when God arrives with two angels, disguised as travelers. Abraham recognizes them and welcomes them with a feast. Sarah, listening just inside the tent, hears yet more promises of children and a great progeny. Now she laughs. God hears her and asks,

"Wherefore did Sarah laugh?"

"I laughed not," she answers.

"Nay," says God, "but thou didst laugh."

The episode ends there. It is a scene of remarkable intimacy between Abraham, Sarah, and God. It is one of many such scenes in which Abraham's relationship with God takes the form of near equals sharing the most personal of confidences.

The intimacy continues as Abraham learns of God's purpose in the region. God is on His way to Sodom and Gomorrah to punish the people there for their sinful ways. Abraham argues that God should save Sodom if there are fifty righteous men in it. Abraham asks, "Shall not the Judge of all the earth do right?" Bowing to this rather impertinent moralizing, the Almighty accedes. It does not end there. Abraham now bargains God down, step by step, from fifty righteous men to forty-five, and thence to forty, and thirty, and twenty, and finally ten. So much for the terrifying Jehovah who shortly before the Abraham story had flooded the earth.

When Abraham is one hundred years old, he and Sarah finally have a child together, a boy whom they call Isaac, meaning "laughter." With a legitimate son at last, and one who is by blood fully Sumerian, Abraham disinherits Ishmael and banishes him and his servant-girl mother.

Before sending the half-wild Ishmael off, however, Abraham receives a promise from God that Ishmael, too, will found a "great nation." According to Muslim tradition, Ishmael—son of Ibrahim, as Abraham is known in Arabic—then fathers the Arab peoples.

In the crowning episode of Abraham's story, God calls on him to deliver the ultimate proof of his devotion. The patriarch-elect must sacrifice his own son, Isaac. Once again, the man from Ur is prepared to obey without question. But at the last moment, as Abraham raises his knife to slaughter his precious son like a sheep, God stops him. Abraham has passed the ultimate test. God acknowledges the extent of Abraham's devotion with a final promise of a progeny as numerous "as the sand on the seashore and the stars in the heavens."

For Jews, Christians, and Muslims, Abraham's story is one of parentage and posterity. His great adventure, which takes him physically farther than Gilgamesh's journey to the forest of cedars, derives its drama from the tension between, on one side, the protagonist's quest to be the father of an heir and, on the other, God's long series of tests. The man from Ur must prove his devotion. In return he receives frequent promises that entire nations will be his bequest.

We have seen the Sumerian concern for posterity before. In the Abraham story, the urge manifests in many ways through the themes of paternity, progeny, and patrimony. It is no accident that Abraham's covenant with God is followed quickly by the birth of Isaac. Both Isaac's birth and the covenant are preceded by the episode at Sodom and Gomorrah, where the Genesis account tells us that the people have sex for mere pleasure and in unnatural ways that cannot produce children. God's punishment of the Sodomites occurs because they insult the gift that the entire Abraham story is about, the one blessing that truly honors God and His gift of human potential: human offspring. Abraham's discovery of the one true God, meanwhile, would mean nothing without descendants to worship Him. Thus is the narrative concerned with propagation. But the emphasis on posterity, on the great name that a millennium earlier was Gilgamesh's main concern, is eminently Sumerian.

The thematic link to Gilgamesh should not come as a surprise. Even geographically, the Old Testament is framed by Mesopotamia. When humanity first appears in Genesis, we are told that the garden of Eden is situated at the junction of four rivers, which the book names. Two of these are mythical—the Pishon and the Gihon—and the other two are real—the Tigris and the Euphrates.* Thousands of years and dozens of

---

* In the original Hebrew, the third river is called the Hiddekel. The Sumerian name was Idigna, which via the Elamite and then Old Persian "Tigra" became the Greek "Tigris." In the Semitic languages, the Sumerian Idigna entered the Akkadian language as "Idiqlat," which became the Hebrew Hiddekel. "Euphrates" is the Greek for the Hebrew "Phrat."

books later, the historical narrative of the Old Testament concludes with the exile in Babylon and the return from it.* Then, at the conclusion of the Bible, closing the New Testament, the Book of Revelation ends with lurid descriptions of that "mother of harlots and abominations of the earth," the Whore of Babylon, "which did corrupt the earth with her fornication."[6]

Mesopotamia's myths inform the Old Testament as broadly as do its places. The Babylonian creation story, the *Enuma elish,* is a clear forebear of its successor in the Torah. It tells of a chaotic darkness at the beginning, and of the first land emerging as an island of reeds from a world of water. Eventually the gods form man from a piece of clay and a minor god. This new being is the gods' servant, not their equal. The creation of a world of order from a primordial chaos, the seminal birth of light from a comprehensive darkness, the first emergence of dry land from the watery murk, and the idea of mankind fashioned by God in God's own image, and from clay at that—all of these Biblical foundations come straight from Sumer.

The great flood, in both its Sumerian and its Biblical versions, is sent by the divine being to chastise sinful humanity. Utnapishtim, threaded into Sumerian civilization through the Gilgamesh compilation and beyond, specifically anticipates Noah with his ark, from the divine command to make a ship to "save the seed of all living creatures," as the Babylonian version puts it, to the pitch that makes the vessels watertight, from the animals on board and the harbinger bird that at last discovers dry land to the mountaintop resting place at the end.[7] †

After the flood, Genesis tells us, humanity settles on "the plain of Shinar." The place name itself is a rendition of Sumer. In subsequent books of the Old Testament, this name for Sumer appears repeatedly as a Biblical name for southern Iraq.

The King James Version of the Bible refers to them thus: "And the name of the third river is Hiddekel: that is it which goeth toward the east of Assyria. And the fourth river is Euphrates."

* The books addressing the Babylonian Exile are Ezekiel, Daniel, and Esther. Ezra, Nehemiah, and various minor prophets deal with the Return. In between the Garden of Eden and these are many other references to people, places, and events in Iraq.

† There are other flood stories in ancient cultures as far afield as China and Peru, and as close to Mesopotamia as Egypt.

Absent a divine command, why might someone like Abraham uproot himself and his family to leave Ur for the uncouth backwater of Canaan? Why would he do this at a time when, as Babylon rose and Sumer fell, southern Mesopotamia remained the center of civilization, the richest and most sophisticated place in the world? The answer is suggested by Sumerian history from the first centuries of the second millennium BC.[8]

Throughout the Sumerian civilization, its rich cities had attracted the interest of tough peoples from the wild periphery: Kassites from the Iranian mountains, Gutians from the Kurdish ranges, and various Semites from the Syrian and Arabian steppes. This conflict between the rich Mesopotamian plain and the desert and highlands on all sides— between "the desert and the sown," as Gertrude Bell put it in the title of a 1907 book—would be a defining feature for Iraq throughout its history.

The era when Gilgamesh stalked the floodplain is known as Sumer's Early Dynastic Period (ca. 2900–2334 BC). It was the time when the city-states of fertile and crowded southern Mesopotamia developed in intense rivalry with each other, as in the rivalry between Uruk and Kish that featured in Gilgamesh's career as king. The competition for power and resources sparked immense cultural creativity. Something similar would happen in the city-state systems of classical Greece and Renaissance Italy. Eventually, attracted by the wealth of the settled plain, barbarians from the dry wastes to the south and west began to move in. These were the Semites. In the twenty-fourth century BC, one Sargon of Akkad (r. 2334–2279 BC) arose among these newcomers and conquered his neighbors on every side. Thus came the end of Sumer, except for a brief renaissance two hundred years later. Sargon's was the world's first empire. He ruled it with what was, after Egypt's Old Kingdom (ca. 2575–2130 BC), the first centralized state, providing a forceful model that foreshadowed the subsequent Mesopotamian history.

The Akkadian Empire founded by Sargon collapsed in 2193 BC, precipitating nearly a century of chaotic rule by a detested foreign hill tribe, the Gutians, from the northerly mountains of what is now Kurdistan. In about 2119 BC, a coalition of Sumerian cities managed to expel the

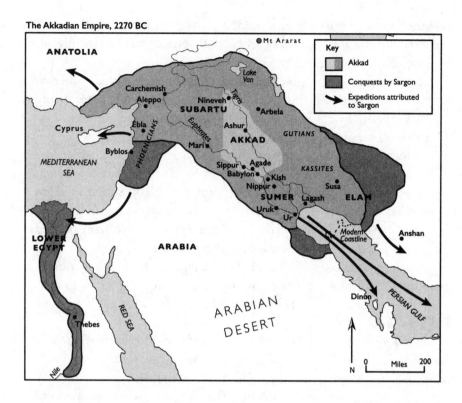

The Akkadian Empire, 2270 BC

barbarians. Seven years later the leader of Ur, one Ur-Nammu, brought all of Sumer and Akkad under his rule, initiating a brief, final flowering of Sumerian civilization that culminated shortly before Abraham's time.

This so-called Third Dynasty of Ur provided a golden moment of order and high culture. Ur-Nammu inscribed the earliest body of law that has been discovered, making capital crimes of murder, robbery, and the deflowering of another man's virgin wife.[9] * Trade with India and the Mediterranean revived. Poetry and the plastic arts flourished, and the Sumerian King List was compiled. The kings of this dynasty emphasized their connections to the original kings of Uruk, Gilgamesh foremost among them, from six or seven hundred years earlier. Subsequent Mesopotamian

---

* The penalty for knocking out a man's tooth was two shekels of silver, but for cutting his foot off it was ten shekels; sleeping with a widow was exempted from punishment; and somebody returning an escaped slave was owed two shekels by the owner. The more famous legal code of Hammurabi, king of Babylon, came about three hundred years later.

cultures, many centuries later, would look to this moment—to Ur of the Sumerian Renaissance—much as people of that time and place themselves looked back to Uruk in the time of Gilgamesh.

A full thousand years later, cuneiform texts from this Neo-Sumerian period, not only poems but even administrative records, were being copied verbatim by students in successor Mesopotamian cultures, long after the Sumerian language had died.[10]

The Sumerian Renaissance was Sumer's swan song. In the final decades of the twenty-first century BC, Ur's short-lived revival was collapsing. The Semites seized back province after province. Elam, Sumer's old foe to the east, in southwest Iran, revived its ancient pressure. In 2004 BC an Elamite army sacked Ur itself. The Elamites were eventually pushed out of Iraq, but the Semites stayed at Babylon. Under their great king Hammurabi (r. 1792–1750), famous for his legal code, the Babylonians cemented the establishment of Mesopotamia's new center of gravity 150 miles north, away from Sumer and the marshy lands at the head of the great gulf.

Meanwhile the Semites in Mesopotamia, like the barbarians who flooded over Rome's borders during Late Antiquity, were assiduous in adopting the trappings of Sumerian high culture. Babylon, originally the upstart neighbor and rival aping Sumer's sophisticated ways, and then the heir to Sumer's cultural wealth, would dominate the Middle East for most of the next fifteen centuries. Through this millennium and a half, the Babylonians would preserve and radiate Sumer's legacy as Sumerian survived as the written language of scribes and scholars. In Babylon, the Sumerian cuneiform script, the definitive achievement of Abraham's Sumerian forefathers, lasted longer than their civilization itself had done. It was used in Mesopotamia for a further twenty centuries, not disappearing until the second century after Christ.

"Sumer in those days was like the declining Roman Empire where everything was Latin, save the emperors," writes one historian of the century before Abraham.[11] After their brief renaissance under the Third Dynasty of Ur, the Sumerians disappeared as a people. Personal names found in the clay tablets of the documentary record suggest that the use of the Sumerian language began to decline around the middle of the third millennium, and that by 1800 BC it had died as a spoken language. By the time Abraham would have been born, the collapse of Sumer was nearly complete.

In the Bible's telling, the event immediately preceding Abraham's departure from Ur is the Lord's scattering of the people of Babel. It is the story of the abandonment of a great civic project, heralding a time of confusion. Undoubtedly, Abraham was born into a period of great disruption. He was probably a member of Ur's educated class; Jewish oral traditions assign his family a degree of prominence in the life of the city. The elite would have been the leading victims of the collapse of Sumerian society. Perhaps this, from a secular perspective, is why Abram's father took the family north to Harran.

For the authors of Genesis, writing much later when Babylon was in its long apogee, the city represented peerless prestige as well as overweening power. But for a man from Ur in 1850 BC, the burgeoning city on his homeland's northern border probably represented the barbaric new order that he was escaping. For both, Babylon's ambitious ziggurat, or stepped pyramid, meant nothing good. In the aspirations of the Biblical people of the Tower of Babel, there are strong echoes of Gilgamesh and the Sumerian link between buildings, fame, and immortality: "Go to," the builders of the tower say to each other in Genesis, "let us build us a city, and a tower, whose top may reach unto heaven, and let us make us a name."[12] God worries about the threat of these people and thwarts their profane dreams by throwing them into a confusion of languages, a babble.

An important poem from the Sumerian canon, "The Nam-Shub of Enki," presages this divine punishment for humanity's noisy and arrogant self-absorption at Babel:

> The lord of wisdom, who scans the land, the leader of the gods,
> Changed the speech in their mouths, put contention into it,
> Into the speech of man that had been one.[13]

The world that Abraham leaves behind is this same new, thrusting Babylonian society that failed to respect man's duty of humble, direct

communion with the divine. Abraham's instruction from God to leave
his "country" and his "father's house" comes a mere six lines after the
Tower of Babel episode. And the reward for Abraham should he heed
the call?

> I will make of thee a great nation, and I will bless thee, and make thy
> name great; and thou shalt be a blessing.[14]

Seeking fame and a form of immortality is all very well, in other
words, but only so long as it is done in humility and devotion to God.
The Abraham story projects the old Mesopotamian concerns in its
emphasis on posterity, that form of immortality. But it also signals a
change. Mere physical achievement, like Gilgamesh's walls or the tower
at Babel, is no longer the concern. It is spiritual posterity, based on
spiritual achievement, that is now paramount. When Abraham swaps
the tower of the vulgar Babylonians for the tent of their lowly Semitic
forebears, it is his own version of the spiritual riches of Sumer that
he brings with him.

As Abraham began the journey to leave the wreckage of his old civilization and pursue the promise of founding a new nation, he would
have carefully packed his personal god among the chattels in his caravan.
Traveling north from Ur, after 150 miles or so Abraham would then
have passed Babylon. There he would probably have seen its ziggurat.
The transition between the two stories—from the Tower of Babel to
Abraham—is a key moment in the Old Testament. The Tower story is
remarkably short, just nine brief verses, and its tone throughout is one
of fantastical deep time. Then, with Abraham following immediately
afterward, the Old Testament moves from this foggy allegorical past to
a detailed family history involving individuals who, living in real places,
following real migration routes, dealing with challenges and achievements that are human in scale, for the first time seem real and human
across the centuries.

When Abraham obeyed God's call in Harran to "go forth," he led
his little band to a far edge of their known world. Leaving home for
he knew not where, for the place that God would show him, Abraham
became the first figure in the broad cultural background of the West

to set off over the horizon for what seems to have been the purpose of staying over the horizon. There would have been traders in Abraham's day who went back and forth, and some probably stayed in the far-off lands that they reached. But before Abraham, the great heroes of myth and faith had remained in their small worlds—or those who left home had returned—to end their stories where they had begun. Even Gilgamesh finished his days back in Uruk.

Abraham was different. Just as his story marks the start of a historical tone in the Bible, it also shatters the circular notion of life that prevails in the accounts of those who came before him. Where man in polytheistic Sumer and its neighbors was on a mythological treadmill, a slave of fate living life in a cycle like the seasons, Abraham becomes the first to break this cycle and bring his life to an end point. Taking hitherto circular human existence and making it linear was revolutionary. Abraham makes his own destiny. God's call may well be a command, but after Abraham receives it there is a real sense that he, the mortal, is exercising his own agency at every stage of his long relationship with the divine. Consistent with the Sumerian outlook that placed humanity in a strong position vis-à-vis the divine, this process emphasizes free will in the Bible story just as a true sense of human history is beginning.

The first five books of the Old Testament are known by Christians as the Pentateuch and by Jews as the Torah. Prevailing scholarship about the textual origins of the Bible holds that the Abraham story in Genesis has two main sources, which were written down in about 950 BC and 850 BC, respectively. According to the theory, known as the Documentary Hypothesis, this material and other sources were eventually redacted into the Torah's final form in the first half of the fifth century BC, by Israelites in Babylon in the wake of the Babylonian Exile.[15]

The internal complexions of Canaan and southern Iraq changed greatly during the roughly fourteen centuries that elapsed between Abraham's time and that of the final editors of his story in the Old Testament. But the relative situations of these two lands stayed more or less the same. While Canaan remained a backwater, southern and central Mesopotamia continued to be without peer as the indispensable cultural, economic, and political force of the Fertile Crescent.

The Iraqi floodplain was probably still home to almost a million people when the Torah was produced there around 450 BC.[16] Mesopotamia's temples and urban archives by then contained a thousand years of written history, detailed and unbroken. Its scribes descended from the men who had invented writing. Its dozen and more large cities boasted ziggurats the size of ten-story buildings; the one at Babylon was three times that size.[17] In the shadows of these man-made mountains worked priests and mathematicians with fifteen centuries of a broadly consistent culture behind them. Nowhere else on earth came close to this level of cultural achievement.

The Genesis text anachronistically refers to Abraham's Sumerian hometown as Ur "of the Chaldeans." There were no Chaldeans in Abraham's day. At the time when the main Genesis texts were composed, so long after Abraham, the Chaldeans were a famous group—a sect, in ways—of Babylonians associated with high learning, especially mathematics. The Genesis writers were connecting themselves, through their ancient patriarch, to the land that was dominating the arts, sciences, and politics of their own day.*

There is a distinct mood of loss and decline in the literature of the period leading up to Abraham's departure from Ur. The "Lament for the Destruction of Ur," a poem written perhaps a century before Abraham, just after the Semites and Elamites had crushed Ur's final renaissance, reflects the elegiac tone:

Though I would tremble for that night,
that night of cruel weeping destined for me, I could not flee before
that night's fatality.

---

* At roughly the same time, the Greek historian and traveler Herodotus (ca. 450) still considered Babylon to be "surpassing in splendor any city of the known world." He too called the people who lived there Chaldeans. Roman authors used the same appellation for centuries more. Babylon was especially famous by Classical times for the sophistication of its astrologers and mathematicians. Later, through the Medieval times in Europe, "Chaldean" was a term for sorcerer or magician.

Dread of the storm's floodlike destruction weighed on me, and of a
   sudden on my couch at night
upon my couch at night no dreams were granted me.
And of a sudden on my couch oblivion, upon my couch oblivion was
   not granted.[18] *

The pressures on Sumerian society near the turn of the third into
the second millennium led to an evolution in the hierarchy of Sumer's
gods. Each city in Sumer originally belonged to its own city god. In early
Sumerian cities, the temple of this god, positioned atop its ziggurat, was
by far the dominant building. Today, Ur's ziggurat, even in its current,
decapitated condition, stands over a hundred feet above the flat southern Iraqi landscape, ten miles from the city of Nassiriya. It remains one
of the great structures of the ancient world. Even in the twenty-first
century AD, even during wartime, to sleep on its uppermost platform
and awaken as an orange dawn begins to warm the cool floodplain is
to feel a step closer to the gods of long-forgotten days.

As Sumerian culture evolved, the city gods dominating Sumerian life
receded in importance. We see in the ancient remains that during this
period the temples in Sumerian cities were becoming ever smaller and
poorer. Royal palaces and municipal establishments were growing larger
and richer. Perhaps this was a function of the constant need to organize
for war, especially as Sumer declined.

Excavations from southern Iraq show that as the official temples
declined in power and wealth, worship shifted to the home. Individual
household gods gradually take the place of the shared city gods. By
Abraham's time, every Sumerian household has a principal, fatherly
god: a "god of gods," a "god of our fathers." He would be a humanoid
figure of stone or clay, perhaps a foot tall, with wide almond eyes and
hands clasped before a bare chest above a calf-length skirt.

The god of gods lived in a niche in a wall of his Sumerian house. He
was fed and watered daily. Sometimes he was shaven-headed. Sometimes
he sported shoulder-length ringlets and a long beard. The Sumerian's

---

* This and other examples of Sumerian "city laments" are distinctly echoed in the Old
Testament's Book of Lamentations, which bewails the destruction of Jerusalem at the
hands of the Babylonians in 586 BC.

god of gods would enjoy a dominant, patriarchal role among other, lesser gods in the household and among the human family around him. Perhaps the most difficult part of this to grasp today is that these clay family idols were not mere representations of the Sumerians' gods. They were real, living gods. Connected to the greater prominence assumed by Sumer's household gods, in particular the fatherly god, was another key development. Personal gods emerged, with whom the worshipper had an individual relationship of devoted service. This direct relationship between worshipper and deity was something new.

According to Jewish oral tradition, written down in the Talmud at Babylon around 500 AD, Abraham's family in Ur were by profession makers of these clay gods. Such was the way of Sumer, seedbed of civilization's ingenuity, where even King Gilgamesh could find neither stone nor wood: god and man alike made each other from clay. Whatever the accuracy of the ancient Talmudic tradition about Abraham's idol-making family, a historical young man from Ur such as Abraham would almost certainly have taken his own private god of gods—the "god of his fathers"—with him on any long journey such as the trek north to Harran and thence to Canaan.[19] When Abraham sets off over the horizon on the advice of his personal deity, it is to found a new nation devoted to the God of gods.

The single Almighty that Abraham bequeaths to his numberless seed would seem to have a great debt to the personal gods of ancient Sumer, those clay deities that had provided the livelihood of Abraham's fathers. Most telling is God's warm intimacy with the laughing Sarah and the wheedling Abraham in the scene just before the punishment of Sodom and Gomorrah. Here the same God who would rain brimstone upon the stiff-necked showed that He could also be something like a household intimate. The amiable conversation outside Abraham's tent—"I did not laugh . . . Nay, but thou didst"—holds strong echoes of the Sumerian idol in his cozy domestic nook. The thundering Semitic God before whom believers tremble in awe is difficult to imagine in such a context.

The covenant is a bargain. God's power is manifestly not absolute: it is circumscribed by an obligation, and the obligation is to a mortal. After the aborted sacrifice of Isaac, God reaffirms His commitment with an extraordinary statement that begins, "By myself I have sworn . . ." The Almighty, who believes He must explain Himself, is subject to rules.

This God is so human that He will visit you at your tent. He will allow your wife to laugh at Him. He will then, as with the negotiation over the punishment of the Sodomites, let you shame Him over the course of a lengthy bargaining session into tempering His wrathful plans. He can be held to account. This is what Abraham buys with the completeness of his faith.

The notion of a contract as the basis for faith may well find its roots in the legal and economic conventions of Sumerian society. Certainly, like no other ancient people, the Sumerians cared about contracts. Thousands of agreements, and references to agreements, have survived, dealing with marriages and divorces and commitments between buyers and sellers of anything from barley to land to slaves, between lenders and borrowers, landlords and tenants, tradesmen and clients, shepherds and flock owners. This particular agreement, Abraham's covenant, places man and God on equal footing with respect to the mutual obligation at the core of the patriarch's new faith. It implies an essential human sovereignty. This may have sources in another part of Abraham's heritage, Sumer's religious mythology.

Sumerian society in the time of Gilgamesh had crystallized around the temples at the top of stepped pyramids, the ziggurats that were like stairways to heaven at the center of every city. Inhabiting a remarkably inhospitable natural environment, the Sumerians found themselves dramatically at the mercy of the gods. Nature in the Mesopotamian floodplain was so violently unpredictable—vastly more so than in Egypt, where the great river's flood gift of new soil every year was generally as gentle and reliable as a tide—that the Sumerians, and the Semitic Akkadians, Babylonians, and Assyrians who followed them, marshaled much of private and public life to the service and propitiation of the divine.

Even the Sumerian kings were in theory servants of the Sumerian gods. The Atrahasis, a Babylonian epic of which the oldest known version was written in the Semitic tongue of the Akkadians in about 1700 BC, explains this. The Atrahasis tells the story of Utnapishtim, the Noah figure discussed in Chapter 1. Long before the emergence of humans, when only the gods existed, the lesser gods served the material wants of the greater gods, preparing their food, maintaining their dwellings, and harvesting their crops. Exhausted, the lesser gods eventually laid down their tools and burned them. In response, the gods convened their assembly. Ea, the high intellect and the solver of problems among the gods, suggested that they create a new kind of servant: a being sufficiently intelligent and capable to do the work, but mortal and therefore aware of his inferiority. The gods adopted Ea's suggestion.

Clay and the blood of a minor god were used to make the first progenitor of man, this new and acquiescent servant.

The enthusiastic newcomers were so successful, and eventually so numerous, that the noise they made soon kept Enlil, leader of the Sumerian gods, from his sleep. To silence the mortals, Enlil sent first disease, then drought, then famine. But the plan was foolish. The new servants were indispensable to the gods. Each time Enlil tried to thin the ranks of humanity, Ea foiled his divine colleague. Finally Enlil decided to destroy mankind completely. The god decided to send a massive flood, the most feared of all calamities in the flat, disaster-wracked land between the rivers. Sworn not to tell the mortals about this plan, Ea instead sent a dream of warning to his favorite among them, Utnapishtim. When the flood came, Utnapishtim and his family survived in a wooden boat and repopulated the earth. Thus, long before Noah, humanity had already endured disaster to fulfill forever its original and only purpose on earth: to serve the gods.

This first written story of our origins has elements of the humanism that Mesopotamia would help to contribute to the foundations of Western culture. The story satirizes the overweening, mercurial behavior of flawed leaders, criticizing the gods for acting as bad kings do upon the earth. The episode of the lesser gods refusing to work establishes the notion of a fundamental relationship of consent between rulers and the ruled. It goes farther, acknowledging man's resulting right of argument and refusal. And it offers the concurrent idea that the gods are themselves subject to consequences.

Any such notion is anti-absolutist by nature. It drastically circumscribes whatever innate prerogative gods or kings might claim. Only one can be sovereign: ruler or justice. The implications of this—for religion, philosophy, government—would dominate much of Iraq's subsequent history.

As an account of human origins, the story of Enlil and the noisy servants assigns to humanity an indispensability in the workings of the universe. This status further limits any ideas of the divine's omnipotence or of man's total submission. The creation story helps explain the fact that in Sumerian and later Mesopotamian medical treatises, there is never mention of spells, goblins, spirits, or other superstition.[20] Similarly, in the Sumerian legal texts there is no hint of divine interference, or even interest, in earthly justice or law. In the worldview of Abraham's ancestors, much was given over to the gods. But the Sumerians were a practical people. However great the sphere of the divine, more was held back for humanity. This would be a large part of Sumer's legacy to the world, with Abraham a key agent of the bequest.

When his son Isaac—the improbable child whose name meant laughter —is mature enough for marriage, Abraham sends a servant back to Mesopotamia to find the young man a wife from among their own people. Isaac, in turn, would eventually send his own son Jacob to do the same. Even into the third generation of life in Canaan, Abraham's family kept the Sumerian bloodline pure and renewed the cultural connection to the land of Ur.

Later, Abraham visits his other son, Ishmael, in a tiny town called Mecca in far-off Arabia, according to the Muslim version of the story. There Abraham helps Ishmael, the wandering black sheep and illegitimate son of the family, to build a shrine where people would worship forever. Ishmael's offspring are to be a great nation too, numerous beyond counting, their hand against everyone, according to the Old Testament, and everyone's hand against them.

The old man dies at 175. He is buried, after his wishes, next to Sarah in a cave that he has bought for her tomb near Hebron, in the promised land. The life of the last Sumerian had been long. His covenant, and the incipient humanism at its heart, would last much longer.

Chapter 3

Babylon and Assyria

1800–539 BC

The rise and fall of the Akkadian empire offers a perfect preview of the rise and fall of all subsequent Mesopotamian empires: rapid expansion followed by ceaseless rebellions, palace revolutions, constant wars on the frontiers, and in the end, the coup de grace delivered by the high-landers: Guti now, Elamites, Kassites, Medes or Persians tomorrow.
—Georges Roux (1914–1999), Assyriologist

Of the hundred thousand or more paintings in the collection of Paris's Louvre Museum, *The Death of Sardanapalus*, painted in 1827 by Eugène Delacroix, may well be the most striking. The canvas is vast, sixteen feet wide by twelve feet high. But it is the imagery that truly stuns. A swarthy, bearded, heavy-lidded king reclines on a vast bed. Gasping, fleshy beauties of his harem writhe around him in anticipation of the agony to come, for his magnificent city burns in the background. Soon, and on the king's orders—we infer this from Sardanapalus's comfortable, imperious posture—the flames will consume them all.

Burly, near-naked slaves follow the king's command. As the flames approach, the retainers slaughter whom they can: a frantic steed here, a supple, buxom slave girl there. Treasures of gold and velvet and stones fill the interstices. With King Sardanapalus languishing while all around him the grotesque indulgences of a voluptuous life face the fire, it is clear that the bed, indeed the entire scene, is the king's own funeral pile. The painter's message is unmistakable. The great couch is a pyre for vanity, luxury, and corruption: an altar for final sacrifices to the gods of some vast and tragic hubris.

The scene represents a day in 612 BC. Roughly twelve centuries after Abraham, the Assyrian Empire, the mightiest on earth, is falling to a vengeful coalition of former subject peoples and bullied neighbors, the Babylonians foremost among them. Assyria had been the world's first great empire; where Sargon's Akkad had conquered Mesopotamian neighbors, Assyria was the first state to conquer and rule truly foreign, alien lands far beyond the homeland. During its heyday, Assyria was probably the most violent long-lived state—not only in the uniquely long and peerlessly violent history of Iraq but in the history of the world. The city burning in the background of the painting is Nineveh, Assyria's last capital. It and Babylon were likely the largest metropolises in the world at the time.[1]

Based in northern Mesopotamia, the Assyrians had dominated Iraq and its environs, militarily overshadowing even their great, older rival Babylon, for the previous three centuries. Assyria's first subjugation of its southern neighbor had occurred in 1234 BC. Culturally, throughout the Assyrian period, as for the eight centuries before and the two centuries after, Babylon remained nonpareil in the region. The year 612 BC, with the sacking that Delacroix depicts, is when the Babylonians, with their allies, had their revenge for over six centuries of Assyrian depredations.

The "Sardanapalus" of the painting is something of a Greek concoction, combining the classical ideas of the effeminate luxury of the East with the name of the last truly great Assyrian despot, Ashurbanipal (d. 627).[2] The last Assyrian king in Nineveh was called Sin-Shar-ishkun and likely died in street fighting at the end of the siege.[3]

The Assyrians dominated their world, which stretched from the deep Nile valley and the west coast of the Red Sea to the Mediterranean coast from Libya through the Levant. In the east, the Assyrian Empire ran from the western littoral of the Persian Gulf to the southern coasts of the Black and Caspian Seas. From the Ethiopian highlands to the Scythian and Cimmerian steppes, neighbors paid them tribute. The scene in Delacroix's painting, the blazing destruction of the imperial capital at the hands of its own subjects, was an end well suited to Assyria's long epoch of vicious, grandiose glory.

Just as the Sumerians, long before and far to the south, had invented writing, kingship, the wheel, and the city, the Assyrians invented the standing army. The first to fight with weapons of iron, they invented the

The Assyrian Empire, 650 BC

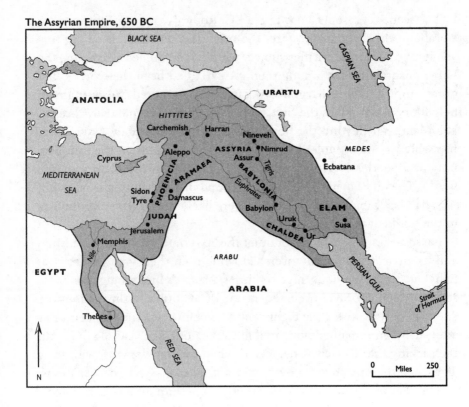

society organized for war. They invented siege-craft and organized cavalry. They had the first military schools, where students learned to mine and destroy city walls. Other Assyrian innovations include mass enslavement and the wholesale deportation of populations. When the Assyrian king Shalmaneser I defeated the Mitanni state to his north in about 1250 BC, he boasted of blinding 14,400 of their soldiers in one eye. The grim stone reliefs and statuary of the vast Assyrian palaces are among the most terrifying and monumental artworks in history. The friezes of their palaces show scene after horrifying scene from hunt, battle, and war: lions bristling with arrows, their claws in the haunches of chariot horses; cities, soon to be pillaged, with their slaughtered defenders tumbling through the air from the besieged walls; enemy soldiers decapitated in various settings; populations marched off in serried ranks into a life of slavery.

The Assyrian king Tiglath-Pileser I (1115–1077 BC), from his capital at Assur on the northern Tigris, waged war from Armenia to the Syrian desert, from the Levantine coast to southern Iraq. He sacked the royal palaces at Babylon. In the hunting field, Tiglath-Pileser was equally fierce. According to his own records, he killed wild bulls—"mighty and monstrous in size"—in central Anatolia, elephants at Harran and in eastern Syria, and a narwhal on the shores of the Mediterranean. He claimed to have killed 120 lions on foot and 800 from his chariot.[4]

Tiglath-Pileser's conquests failed, however, to establish any lasting dominion beyond the Assyrian heartland. It was not until the turn of the ninth to the eighth century BC that the true Assyrian Empire arose. Ashurnasirpal II (r. 883–859), the third monarch of this period, would provide the exemplar of an Assyrian prince. Among conquests elsewhere, Ashurnasirpal, like his predecessor Tiglath-Pileser, reached the Mediterranean. "I washed my weapons in the deep sea," he claimed of one campaign. "The tribute of the seacoast—from the inhabitants of Tyre, Sidon, Byblos . . . [included] gold, silver, tin, copper, copper containers, linen garments with multi-colored trimmings, large and small monkeys, ebony, boxwood, ivory from walrus tusk."[5]

The following is a list boasting of Ashurnasirpal's spoils from a minor town near Diyarbakir in what is now southeast Turkey:

40 chariots 'equipped with the trappings of men and horses'
460 horses 'broken to the yoke'
2 talents of silver, 2 talents of gold*
100 talents of lead, 100 talents of copper
300 talents of iron
1,000 vessels of copper, 200 pans of copper bowls and cauldrons of copper
1,000 brightly colored garments of wool and linen 'couches made of ivory and overlaid with gold' from the ruler's palace
2,000 heads of cattle
5,000 sheep[6]

---

* A talent was a measure of weight equivalent to approximately seventy pounds.

Ashurnasirpal also killed the local king and helped himself to the man's sister as well as the "daughters of his nobles with their rich dowries." Fifteen thousand ordinary members of the local population were herded off to the Assyrian heartland. During the same campaigning season, Ashurnasirpal harvested spoil and tribute from "no less than five countries and nine major cities," all of them likely to have been richer than this small provincial town.

Ashurnasirpal, who left countless inscriptions in his palaces and elsewhere, immortalized his treatment of several cities that imagined they could deny him, including this unfortunate case:

> With battle and slaughter I stormed the city and captured it. 3,000 of their warriors I put to the sword; their spoil and their possessions, their cattle and their sheep I carried off. Many captives from among them I burned with fire, and many I took as living captives. From some I cut off their hands and their fingers, and from others I cut off their noses, their ears, and their fingers, of many I put out the eyes. I made one pillar of the living, and another of heads, and I bound their heads to posts round about the city. Their young men and maidens I burned in the fire, the city I destroyed, I devastated, I burned it with fire and consumed it.[7]

Ashurnasirpal also boasted of immuring large numbers of foes in the palaces of their leaders; others, he claimed, "I consumed with thirst in the desert of the Euphrates."[8]

The great palace that Ashurnasirpal built at Nimrud, twenty miles south of the present-day city of Mosul, would be discovered by an English explorer, Austen Henry Layard, in 1845. Over the following six years, the finds from Nimrud electrified the European world, giving birth to the field of professional archaeology generally and initiating a near-frenzy of interest in Mesopotamian archaeology in particular. Nimrud's palace was burned down in the same invasion of Assyria that led to the destruction of Nineveh in 612 BC, probably in the same year. Fueling the fire at Nimrud was the precious lumber that had been used to build the palace: "cedar, cypress, juniper, boxwood, mulberry, pistachio-wood and tamarisk for my royal dwelling," boasted Ashurnasirpal. The building zeal of the great king, and the foreign construction materials that required far-flung adventures, recall Gilgamesh, whose name, like those of Tiglath-Pileser and Ashurnasirpal, would wait so long in the dust—in that very dust, in that very place—to claim its immortality. Ashurnasirpal celebrated the completion of the palace at Nimrud in about 684 BC with a ten-day feast for 69,754 guests. The stele that memorializes this event for posterity briefly makes us forget "the other, unsavoury aspects of this great monarch."⁹

It was all based on endless war. For the Assyrians, what was originally opportunistic brigandage eventually became an engine of self-sustaining necessity. Facing a ceaseless succession of tough neighbors on all sides, lacking both access to the sea and natural defensive frontiers of their own, constantly provoking those around it with never-ending rapine, the Assyrian state would die if it stopped fighting. Ashurnasirpal's son and successor, Shalmaneser III (r. 858–824 BC), devoted thirty-one years of his thirty-five-year reign to war. Soon enough, the machine of looting and tribute extraction became an administrative empire.

Year after year, under king after king for three centuries, "these masters of war, these strange people of Assyria" sallied to war almost every spring.¹⁰ "In Assur war was not only a means," wrote the French archaeologist L. J. Delaporte in 1925, "it seems often to have been an end—battle for the exercise of violence, victory for the pleasure of torturing." Soon enough, the constant warfare became a matter of faith. It was "at the command of Ashur," their city god, that the Assyrians set out to war each spring, and they appear to have compelled observance of his cult wherever they ruled.¹¹

The Assyrians expanded the empire inexorably in every reign, from 911 BC until 625 BC. Then finally, suddenly, the most comprehensive, sustained war machine that history has ever witnessed stopped. The death of Ashurbanipal in 627 BC was followed by a contested succession and rebellion in Babylon. The economy and army, meanwhile, seem to have suffered from war fatigue at last. Assyria found itself surrounded by bitter ancient enemies, surging nomads from the northeastern steppes and rising new local powers. Fifteen years after the death of the greatest king in its fifteen-century history, Assyria fell forever. It was at this point that Sardanapalus, according to the Greeks, immolated himself and his harem in the palace at Nineveh as the vengeful Babylonians and ambitious Medes closed in.

Twelve years before Delacroix completed his painting, Byron celebrated the Assyrians, this time in rare defeat, in lines that became some
of the most famous he was ever to write. "The Destruction of Sennacherib" (1815), about an unsuccessful Assyrian siege of Jerusalem in about
701 BC, opens in the galloping cadences for which the poem is known:

The Assyrian came down like the wolf on the fold,
And his cohorts were gleaming in purple and gold;
And the sheen of their spears was like stars on the sea,
When the blue wave rolls nightly on deep Galilee.

The Assyrian in this case was the emperor Sennacherib (r. 704–681 BC),
who later, in 689 BC, razed a rebellious Babylon to the ground for the
first time in its history and spitefully sent its dust "to the most distant
peoples." (The city soon recovered.) Before Sennacherib, the many preceding Assyrian monarchs who had repeatedly subdued Babylon always
treated the ancient and holy city with "infinite patience and respect."[12]
Sennacherib moved the Assyrian capital to Nineveh, there building a great
palace using imported "beams of cedar" and "door leaves of cypress." He
would die there in a temple he had built, "stabbed to death by one of his
sons or . . . crushed by the winged bulls that protected the sanctuary."[13]
    In about 701 Sennacherib invaded Palestine, where his predecessor
Shalmaneser had already conquered the Hebrews' northern kingdom of
Israel and its capital Samaria. Shalmaneser had "carried Israel away into
Assyria,"[14] according to the Old Testament's Second Book of Kings, and
this part of the Israelite people then disappeared from history forever.
Invading the southern Hebrew kingdom of Judah twenty years later,
Sennacherib claims to have taken forty-six of the Israelites' towns and
"carried off 200,156 persons, old and young, male and female." From
Jerusalem he boasted of extracting a tribute of thirty talents of gold
and three hundred of silver.
    Sennacherib had these details recorded on several fifteen-inch-high
hexagonal clay prisms. The first of these to come to light was discovered by an English colonel at Nineveh in 1830. Supporting Sennacherib's
claims, the Second Book of Kings says that the same amount of tribute
was extracted from the cities of Judah during this campaign. As for the
capital, Jerusalem, this part of the Old Testament tells a different story,

the tale that inspired Byron. One night during the Assyrian siege of Jerusalem, says Kings, "the angel of the Lord went out, and smote in the camp of the Assyrians a hundred fourscore and five thousand: and when they arose early in the morning, behold, they were all dead corpses. So Sennacherib king of Assyria departed, and went and returned, and dwelt at Nineveh."[15]

The Assyrian era began nine or so centuries after Abraham. For much of the intervening period, the most important city in Mesopotamia and the world had been Babylon. Great cities came and went elsewhere, particularly in Egypt (Memphis and Thebes in this period) and China (Yinxu, Haojing, Chengzhou). But Babylon's eminence among the metropolises of earth, as a cultural touchstone, a living city, and a strategic prize, would last until a couple of centuries before Christ. For most of these sixteen centuries, Babylon's status was rarely contested by any long-term rival other than Assyria. Sometimes, as just before the end, Assyria would have the upper hand. Occasionally, invaders from Iraq's rugged frontiers would succeed in their wars against the successive Babylonian powers. In 1595 BC Hittites from the Anatolian highlands carted off Babylon's god Marduk. Twenty-five years later, the horse-riding Kassites of Luristan in eastern Iran conquered the Hittites and restored Marduk to Babylon. The Kassites then ruled there for four hundred years.

Throughout the period of Assyria's military dominance, Babylon retained its cultural supremacy. When Nineveh finally came crashing down in flaming ruins in 612, it was at the hands of a broad uprising of subject peoples led by a Babylonian alliance with an assertive new nation called the Medes. Babylon then enjoyed a seventy-year revival known as the Neo-Babylonian period. This was the Babylon, cruel and imperial, that, even more than Assyria's Nineveh, looms so large in the Old Testament: the Babylon that repeatedly acts as God's rod to chastise the wayward Israelites, sending their elites into exile by the banks of the river Tigris.*

---

* Strictly speaking, the Hebrews of sixth-century Jerusalem were not Israelites but Judaeans. Jerusalem was not in the northern kingdom of Israel but rather in the southern breakaway kingdom of Judah.

The Old Testament's book of Kings tells of the siege of Jerusalem in 587 BC by Nebuchadnezzar II, greatest of the kings of the Neo-Babylonian Empire.* Successful in taking the city after an eighteen-month siege, he carries off to Babylon the city's elite, "all the princes, and all the mighty men of valor," right down to the "craftsmen and smiths." After these events, in Jerusalem "none remained, save the poorest."[16] In the Book of Isaiah, we learn that the fate of "Babylon, the glory of kingdoms . . . shall be as when God overthrew Sodom and Gomorrah."[17] The Book of Daniel is about a child of the Captivity who has been "made master of the magicians, astrologers, Chaldeans, and soothsayers" at the Babylonian court; when the doomed Babylonian regent Belshazzar (d. ca. 539 BC) notices during a feast that a hand is writing on the wall, it is Daniel who interprets the message: "Thou art weighed in the balance and found wanting," it says. "Thy kingdom is divided, and given to the Medes and the Persians."[18]

The Medes soon became masters of their own regional empire based in what are now the Kurdish mountains of northwest Iran. Out of this Median power came Cyrus the Great of Persia. Cyrus would manage one of the more remarkable double feats in history. He built the first "world empire," the first genuinely intercontinental polity, vastly larger than that of the Assyrians at their peak. And he became the archetype of a good ruler, the beau ideal of kingly clemency, wisdom, and virtue, in two of the most influential cultural traditions in history, neither of them his own: the Jewish tradition of the Old Testament and the classical tradition of Greece. If Christianity can be said, from a secular perspective, to flow in equal measures from the Jewish and Greek traditions, this Persian king is second only to Jesus as its exemplar. The epoch that Cyrus initiated would lead directly to the birth—political, philosophical, and spiritual—of the Western world.

The story of Iraq during the period of Cyrus and his successors would be a story of Iranian domination. It is perhaps only natural that the end of Iraq's long greatness in the ancient world should come at

---

* Nebuchadnezzar is credited with building Babylon's famous Hanging Gardens.

the hands of this eastern neighbor. Throughout Iraq's earliest historical periods, first Sumerian and then Akkadian, Babylonian, and Assyrian, Elam had been a recurring foe. Sometimes subjected, sometimes silent in the record, sometimes conquering Sumerian cities or carrying off by force the gods of Babylon and other cities of southern Mesopotamia, Iran-based Elam was fundamentally—again and again, on and on, for almost three thousand years—the mortal rival of the leading Iraq-based states of the day.[19]

When at last the Assyrians, under their great king Ashurbanipal, flattened the Elamite capital at Susa in 645 BC, their destruction of the city expressed the hatred of thirty centuries. This went far beyond the usual looting, burning, and rape. It went beyond the customary stealing of local gods and repatriation of captive gods. "The tombs of the ancient heroes were broken open," wrote an impressed Sir Percy Sykes, one of the two or three foremost English-language historians of Iran, in 1915, "and their bones despatched to Nineveh, where, in a supposed exquisite refinement of cruelty, libations were offered, by means of which the souls chained to the crumbling bones were kept alive to taste to the full the cup of bitterness of fallen Elam!"[20]

The prophet Ezekiel summed up Elam's fate: "There is Elam and all her multitude round about her grave, all of them slain, fallen by the sword."[21] Elam would never rise again. Her millennia of rivalry with the cities of Iraq were over. However, new Iranian powers would rise to the north soon enough to continue the ancient struggle.

Thirty-three years after the destruction of Elam, Nineveh itself would be destroyed, with Sardanapalus and his household immolated in the burning city, as the Greek legend has it. Two years later, in 610 BC, the Elamite heartland in the southwest of Iran was divided between the same victors who had conquered Assyria: the Babylonians and the Medes. The Median king who accomplished all of this was Cyrus the Great's great-grandfather. With the annihilation of Elam, power in the lands directly east of Iraq had now shifted north for the first time, to the highlands of two "Iranic" or "Aryan" groups. These Medes and Persians were related peoples who had come to Iran from somewhere along the broad belt of southern Russia around the turn of the second to the first millennium BC. Some research suggests that the early Aryans came from near the Black Sea; other research suggests various points east of there.

Both peoples settled in the west of Iran. The Medes alit farther north and west, higher in the mountains than their cousins, while the Persians established themselves farther south, down the slopes of the mountains and into the plateau at the northern edge of Elam. Cyrus, son of a Persian father and a Median mother, united the two peoples under Persian rule in 550. Doing so, he formed what would become the heart of the Iranian nation.

The Medes and Persians were both members of what is known as the Indo-European linguistic family. The Indo-Europeans, with their likely origins in the southwestern steppes of Russia, settled a wide swath of Eurasia in the late third millennium BC. An indication of the range settled by these peoples, and of their notable cultural potency, is found in the distribution of their word for the great sky god. The original has been reconstructed by scholars as *Deiwo*. It provides the common root for the Latin *Deus*, the Greek *Zeus*, and the Old English *Tiw*, whence Tuesday. In Sanskrit, the original Indo-European language of Hindu India, it is *Dyaus*. In Persian it is *Dyaos*.[22] *

The speakers of Avestan, the original Iranian tongue, were close Indo-European linguistic relatives of the speakers of Old Sanskrit in ancient India. Both of these branches of the Indo-European lineage used the term *arya* to mean something like "noble." The ancestors of these peoples seem to have used the word as their name for themselves. Nineteenth-century European ethnologists and linguists concluded that those common ancestors, the Aryans, formed a distinct group descended from a very ancient people called the Proto-Indo-Europeans. The ancient name "Iran" refers to this land of "Arya."

———

Herodotus was an Ionian Greek of the fifth century BC. He came from Halicarnassus, now Bodrum, on the southern Aegean coast of present-day Turkey. With his only known work, *The Histories*, it can be said that Herodotus personally created the practice of research-driven nonfiction narrative writing. For this, Cicero rightly dubs him the Father of History. By the mid-fifth century BC, the boasts of kings, the songs of

———

* A similar relationship is posited in "the correspondence of Latin *rex*, Sanskrit *rajan* and Irish *ri*." Richard N. Frye, *The Heritage of Persia* (Cleveland, OH: World, 1963), p. 20.

priests and poets, the exercises of students, and the records of merchants, scribes, and scholars had existed in writing for two thousand years. But Herodotus was the first to harvest facts in the service of a rational inquiry into historical events. He was also the first private individual to record historical facts in a single prose account for the future.

Where Herodotus was able to see firsthand the cities and battlefields of his histories, he did so—traveling to Sicily, the Greek mainland, the Levant, Egypt, and elsewhere. He wrote about Babylon at length and in some detail and may well have gone there. Where Herodotus's pioneering inquiries uncover conflicting accounts or explanations, he provides as many of these as he can. Where he has not been able to confirm something picked up in his travels, he lets us know that his account comes from the locals and reminds us that he himself has not verified it. "As legend would have it," is a typical guidepost in his writing. As for the gods, they play a role in the minor sketches from time to time, but it is man who drives events in these chronicles.

Herodotus's main focus is the repeated ill-starred campaigns of Cyrus's successors, the Great Kings of Persia, to conquer Greece in the early fifth century BC. The bulk of the *Histories*, five of its eight books, is an investigation into the origins of the conflict. The story of Cyrus takes up a full fifty pages near the start of the account, comprising the Greek's longest narrative until he arrives at the main event, the Greco-Persian Wars themselves. In Herodotus's story of Cyrus and the rise of Persia, Iraq, as usual, plays a central role. Babylon was the administrative capital of the mighty Persian Empire that Cyrus founded, and Mesopotamia provided by far the empire's richest provinces.

Herodotus's account of Cyrus begins with Cyrus's grandfather, Astyages, the third ruler of the Median Empire that emerged after the fall of Nineveh and the defeat of Assyria. Astyages was the son of Cyaxares, the Mede who had sacked Nineveh with his Babylonian and nomadic allies in 612 BC. When eventually, in 539 BC, Cyrus and his Persians took Babylon, it marked one of the handful of truly key dates in Iraq's prodigious history: the end of indigenous sovereignty in Mesopotamia until the twentieth century AD.

Chapter 4

Persians, Greeks, and Jews

Cyrus the Great and the Universal Vision, 550 BC

O man, whoever thou art, from wheresoever thou comest, for I know you shall come, I am Cyrus, who founded the empire of the Persians. Grudge me not, therefore, this little earth that covers my body.

—Original inscription, now lost, on the tomb of Cyrus the Great, 530 BC

Herodotus of Halicarnassus here displays his inquiry, so that human achievements may not be forgotten in time, and great and marvelous deeds—some displayed by Greeks, some by barbarians—may not be without their glory; and especially to show why the two peoples fought with each other.

—Opening of *The Histories*, by Herodotus, b. ca. 490 BC

Astyages, king of the Medes, had a daughter and, according to Herodotus, "he dreamed one night that she urinated in such enormous quantities that it filled his city and swamped the whole of Asia."[1] Alarmed, Astyages consulted with his priests, the magi. They knew immediately what the dream meant. The girl's progeny would usurp her father's kingdom. To avoid this, Astyages married her off to a vassal, the ruler of a poor and backward people, related to his own, from the benighted neighboring province of Persis. Astyages chose his son-in-law with care. Considered by the king to be "well below a Mede even of middle rank," the Persian was also a man "of good family"—by local standards, at any rate—"and quiet habits."

After a year of this marriage the king's daughter was pregnant. He had another dream. "A vine grew out of her private parts, and spread over all Asia."

Astyages immediately ordered his pregnant daughter brought home, and eventually she gave birth to a son. The king instructed his chief steward to lay hold of the baby, "take it home, and kill it." The man accepted the charge. But then, bringing the child "dressed in grave clothes" home to his wife, the courtier could not bear to "take a hand in such a brutal murder." Instead he gave the baby to a cowherd from the mountains, with orders to leave the boy to the wild animals. But the cowherd's wife had just given birth to a stillborn child. So the couple swapped the living royal baby for the corpse of their own son.

Ten years later a Persian nobleman brought a complaint to the Median ruler. In a village back in Persia, the nobleman's son and some other local boys had been playing the "game of kings," in which one boy rules over the others. The boys had selected a humble herdsman's son to play the king, and the nobleman's son had refused to take orders from this upstart. The make-believe monarch had then arrested the make-believe rebel and "beat him savagely with a whip." So the nobleman came to see Astyages, seeking redress. Astyages, to placate his vassal, sent for the boy. When the little despot arrived at court, Astyages was struck by his lordly mien. This was no slave, said the king to himself. "Moreover," writes Herodotus, "the cast of the boy's features seemed to resemble his own." The youngster was called Cyrus. Astyages investigated the matter and learned that Harpagus, his trusted counselor, had in fact failed to kill the augured infant all those years ago.

The king arranged a feast to celebrate the news that his grandson had survived. Harpagus, meanwhile, was delighted "to have come off so lightly" for his deception and was thrilled when the king asked him to send his son to the palace to visit the royal newcomer. "When Harpagus's son arrived at the palace, Astyages had him butchered, cut up into joints, and cooked." At the banquet, while others ate savory mutton, Harpagus was served the flesh of his son. The courtier ate heartily. Only when his son's head arrived on the platter bearing his second portion did he discover the truth.

After the feast, Astyages again consulted with his magi. They were not concerned. The royal destiny of this youth, Cyrus, had already been

The Median and Neo-Babylonian Empires, 550 BC

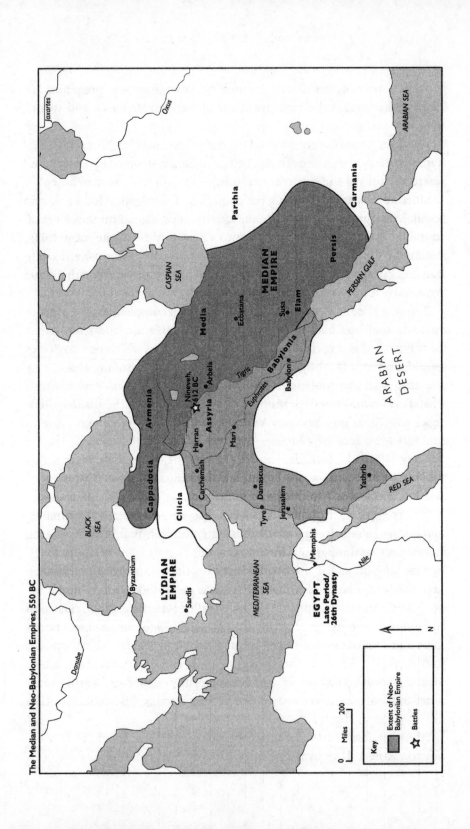

fulfilled, they said, "by the mere fact that the boy has been called king" by other children in their game. Emperor and magi were in agreement: Astyages's dream had safely reached "this trifling conclusion." The boy would pose no threat to his grandfather's throne. So the emperor sent Cyrus home to Persia with good-luck wishes and an escort, to be reunited for the first time with his true parents.

More years passed, and "Cyrus grew up to be the bravest and most popular young man in Persia." Harpagus, meanwhile, still at the imperial capital in Media, had never really come to terms with Astyages's evil trick. Eventually the courtier began to approach the young prince secretly from afar, finally sending him a message sewn inside a hare. "Persuade the Persians to revolt," implored Harpagus, "and march against the Medes."

Cyrus heeded. He prepared a false document assigning himself command of the Persians. Then he gathered his tribesmen and put them through a brutal day of physical labor, clearing thorns from a patch of rough land in their hill-country homeland. These were men whose land was so rough and poor that all they wore was leather. They ate only what they had, as Herodotus puts it, and never what they wanted. The next day, Cyrus gave them a lavish banquet, with the finest wine he could procure. Then he addressed them.

"Men of Persia," said their prince, "listen to me. Obey my orders, and you will be able to enjoy a thousand pleasures as good as this without ever turning your hands to servile labor."*

Shortly afterward, Cyrus marched against his grandfather. Median soldiers began deserting to the side of the charismatic young rebel. Soon the empire was his. The year was 549 BC. "The Persians under Cyrus," Herodotus tells us, "from then onwards were masters of Asia." Where once the Medes had been rulers and the Persians slaves, now the Medes were slaves and their Persian cousins ruled. As for Astyages, Cyrus kept him comfortably by his side for the rest of the defeated man's days.

Cyrus's conquests had only begun. In 546 he attacked a neighbor, the legendarily rich Croesus, whose local empire of Lydia comprised by and large the western half of what today we call Turkey. Once again Cyrus benefited from the good advice of Harpagus, who suggested deploying

---

* Persia (*Persis*) was the Greek name for Iran. It was derived from *Pars* or *Fars*, the local name for the Iranian province from which Cyrus and his forebears came. Mesopotamia ("between the rivers") was the Greek name for Iraq.

camels against the horses of the famous Lydian cavalry. The smell of the exotic beasts frightened the Lydian horses, and Cyrus carried the day.

Within five years, turning east toward the rising sun, Cyrus had extended his domain into the mountains of the Hindu Kush in what is now Afghanistan. Of the great provinces of the known world, all that remained outside Cyrus's possession were Babylon and, beyond it, Egypt and Ethiopia. By 539, Babylon was his. Conquering the green steppes to the north and east as far as the distant reaches of current-day Kazakhstan and Kyrgyzstan, Cyrus eventually died in battle in August 530. From the Aegean Sea to the Khyber Pass, he was the first to rule on a genuinely intercontinental scale. Where the Assyrians before him had originated the very notion of empire and held the region in a gruesome grip, Cyrus introduced the idea of empire as something tolerant and potentially desirable for its far-flung members. During the twenty-odd years of his imperial career, the Persians, the obscure and backward hillsmen of his youth, had become the greatest people on earth.

Cyrus further demonstrated his desire to reassure the conquered Medians when he included many of them in his administration. He retained their capital, Ecbatana, as his own. Croesus too, Herodotus is careful to tell us, was brought into Cyrus's circle after succumbing in battle.* In Babylon, Cyrus spared the king, Nabonidus, and his heirs. A year after conquering Babylon, Cyrus proclaimed a state of mourning when the former ruler died.

Alongside the picture of the perfect prince, with so much war and empire-building there is also, unavoidably, a Cyrus story of ego and bloodshed. Herodotus's tales, like the one he tells of Croesus, are often about nemesis of one kind or another—about what the Greeks call "retribution, and . . . the instability of human things." The Father of History recognized the Cyrus dilemma that would later bedevil the emerging

---

* Croesus survived to become an advisor to Cyrus's son Cambyses II (r. 530–522 BC). In that capacity, Croesus provided one of the better courtier's lines on record. Shortly after Cambyses's acquisition of Egypt, the new emperor asked how he compared to his great father. "Son of Cyrus," replied Croesus, "I at least do not think you are equal to your father; for you have not yet a son like the son he left behind him in yourself."

Western culture: the strong relationship between vision and coercion. At the end, the bloody fate that came for Cyrus was directly related to the rest of his destiny.

The imperial dynasty that Cyrus founded is remembered as the Achaemenids, after an ancestor called Achaemenes. It lasted for 219 years, from 549 BC, when Cyrus seized his grandfather's Median Empire, until Darius III, Cyrus's twelfth and last successor, was murdered in 330 BC by a confidant after losing three battles to Alexander the Great. In Cyrus's day the Persians' military strength lay in their mounted bowmen, unarmored and mobile. Later, the vast armies of Cyrus's successors would encompass an exotic variety of subject men-at-arms from across the wide empire, but the spine would consist of Greek mercenary heavy infantry. From the three Persian invasions of Greece in the years 492–480 until Alexander the Great finally settled the issue by conquering the same Persian Empire a century and a half later, in any given battle, the Persians, thanks to these mercenaries, frequently had more Greeks fighting for them than the Greeks had troops of any description on their own side.

The Achaemenid emperors governed in consultation with a loose council of the great men of their realm. Among these, the Medes tended to be foremost. Long after Cyrus, his successors generally continued his effective diplomatic style: treating vanquished princes with respect, declining to plunder or enslave the conquered nations, and inviting their subjects into the imperial government and army. It was the policy of the mailed fist gripped lightly, for those who submitted. For those who did not, it was war.

As for religion, Cyrus never mentioned his own faith. Cyrus's true religion, it might be said, was statecraft. In the records he left behind, Cyrus spoke only of the gods of his various subject peoples.

Ten years after Cyrus defeated his grandfather, in 539 BC, the people of Babylon opened the city's gates to Cyrus. A few days before, he had defeated the Babylonian army at Opis, sixty miles to the north, but now the welcome was warm. It seems mostly to have been that way with Cyrus.

The city, of course, was a historic prize. With a population of perhaps two hundred thousand, it was still the largest in Iraq and the world. Babylon brought its conquerors huge wealth. More, it brought prestige, the ineffable aura of the Mesopotamian cities that had formed the core of the civilized world since the beginning of history. In Cyrus's time, Babylon brought with it Syria, including Judah, Palestine, and the Levantine coast. For Cyrus, the conquest crowned an empire that now extended from the mountains and high plains of Afghanistan to the shores of the eastern Mediterranean.

From the usual varied sources—the ancient Greeks, the Jewish Bible, and the physical record, in this case the walls and buildings uncovered by German archaeologists at Babylon in the early twentieth century AD—we can attempt a picture of the day that Cyrus entered Babylon.

There appears, in the words of the *Cyropaedia*, a semi-fictional biography of Cyrus from the fifth century BC by the Athenian Xenophon, "Cyrus himself upon a chariot." Crowds surround him on either side. He has restored their god Marduk, shelved by the last Babylonian ruler. The people would have cheered wildly: without Marduk they had been unable to celebrate their louche feasts. Cyrus, in Xenophon's description of the great procession, is "wearing his tiara upright, a purple tunic shot with white (none but the king may wear one), trousers of scarlet dye about his legs, and a mantle all of purple."[2]

The Persian was likely bedecked in gold and stones. The Roman biographer Plutarch wrote five hundred years later that one of Cyrus's successors wore "three million pounds of gold on his body."[3] Xenophon, using Cyrus to teach princely leadership to future generations, could not resist a final didactic detail about the entry into the city that was the Persian's greatest trophy. "With him," according to the *Cyropaedia*, "rode a charioteer, who was tall, though neither in reality nor in appearance so tall as he."

Under Cyrus, Iraq's first period of Persian rule began well. On occupying Babylon, he launched a campaign to win over the local population, "taking the hands" of Marduk in a public procession.[4] As he had done with local divinities throughout his empire, Cyrus called on the Babylonian god for support. Where the last Babylonian king had confiscated numerous local statue gods from around the Babylonian realm, laagering them in the capital, Cyrus restored them to their temples in their own towns and cities. He was also careful to perform the key acts of kingship that all great Mesopotamian kings were expected to perform, acts of near ritual with distinct echoes of Gilgamesh: rebuilding temples, city walls, and palaces. He had stellae and tablets inscribed with the record of these deeds, adopting for his inscriptions the style of his local predecessors.

Herodotus writes that on the golden altar outside the temple of Marduk (or Bel, as sources sometimes call him), the Babylonians burned twenty-eight and a half tons of frankincense every year during the god's festival. Now here was Cyrus, taking the god's hand among the sweet, billowing clouds, the foreign conqueror strolling down the festive boulevard hand in hand with the local deity.

In Babylon as elsewhere, Cyrus left administrations in place but established above them a layer reporting directly to himself: satraps, treasurers, and military commanders. His basic administrative system was to endure until the arrival of Alexander two centuries later. The Macedonian then retained so much of the administration of the Persian Empire that he has frequently been called the last of the Achaemenids.

Babylon had a special place in the Persian imperial system bequeathed by Cyrus. Home to much of the great king's treasury and royal archives, the city was also the empire's bureaucratic capital. The court remained at Ecbatana, the old capital of Astyages and the Medes. Later in the Achaemenid dynasty, Susa, the ancient Elamite capital farther south, became the court's winter capital. Mesopotamia was by far the largest and richest region in the empire. Its two great provinces, Assyria in the north and Babylonia in the south, were places of transcendent antiquity and distinction. Iraq provided a full third of the tax revenues of the Persian Empire stretching from Egypt to India, and the satrap of Babylonia and Assyria was ex officio the second man of the empire.

Herodotus tells us that for expenses such a personage received five bushels of silver coin daily and possessed, "as his personal property, in addition to war horses, eight hundred stallions and sixteen thousand mares, twenty for each stallion, and so many Indian dogs that four large villages" were devoted to their feeding.*

---

* These dogs were likely mastiffs used as guard dogs. The modern Indian mastiff, or Bully Kutta, can weigh up to two hundred pounds.

After Cyrus's entry into Babylon, he followed Mesopotamian tradition by emplacing an inscribed clay cylinder within the walls of the city's main temple.* Other Mesopotamian conquerors before Cyrus had taken care to make claims not far short of the Persian's, but the Cyrus Cylinder is widely called the world's first declaration of human rights. Much of the text follows a somewhat standard litany used for legitimizing new kings in Babylon and its neighbors.[5]

Presenting himself as "Kurash [Cyrus], King of the World, Great King, Legitimate King, King of Babilani, King of Kiengir and Akkade, King of the four rims of the earth, Son of Kanbujiya, Great King, King of Hakhamanish, Grandson of Kurash, Great King, King of Hakhamanish, descendant of Chishpish," Cyrus presents a litany of the tolerant acts that made him such a model to the Greeks and Hebrews:

> When I entered Babylon as a friend and when I established the seat of the government in the palace of the ruler under jubilation and rejoicing, Marduk, the great lord, induced the magnanimous inhabitants of Babylon to love me, and I was daily endeavoring to worship him . . . I returned to the sacred cities on the other side of the Tigris, the sanctuaries of which have been ruins for a long time, the images which used to live therein and established for them permanent sanctuaries. I also gathered all their former inhabitants and returned them to their habitations. Furthermore, I resettled all the gods in their former temples, the places which make them happy.[6]

At Babylon, Cyrus found perhaps fifty thousand Israelites living in exile.[7] Nebuchadnezzar, the Neo-Babylonian emperor, had brought them there in three waves during his forty-three-year reign (605–562 BC), including the 587 BC deportation described in the Second Book of Kings. Other Hebrews had been in Mesopotamia since 722 BC, when the Assyrian Empire began the mass expatriations of Abraham's "stiff-necked"

---

* In 1879 the cylinder was discovered by a British Museum archaeological expedition led by an Assyrian Christian from Mosul, Hormuzd Rassam. A copy is on permanent display at the United Nations in New York. The original resides in the British Museum.

descendants. Jewish and Christian Scripture described Nebuchadnezzar's destruction of Jerusalem's great temple, built by King Solomon, and the subsequent Babylonian exile, as both punishment (Isaiah) and trial (Ezekiel) for the erring Israelites.[8] These events would mark the first steps in an eventual transformation of the Israelites' faith itself, as the spiritual legacies of Abraham and Zoroaster merged among the exiles in Babylon.

When Cyrus helped thousands of the Babylonian Israelites return home to Jerusalem, many others, perhaps most, chose to remain in the cosmopolitan capital, where they were to thrive under the tolerant rule of Cyrus and his successors.* Although the Return was naturally a major event for the Biblical authors, the event did not earn remark by either Herodotus or Xenophon. Cyrus returned numerous other peoples from exiles by previous conquerors, and from the imperial perspective there was nothing notable about the Israelites. But for the people of Abraham it was an event of the highest importance. In the Old Testament, the prophet Ezra tells us that Cyrus ordered, "both by word of mouth and in writing," the rebuilding of the Hebrew temple in Jerusalem.

Cyrus, says Ezra, decreed:

> Let the house be builded, the place where they offered sacrifices, and let the foundations thereof be strongly laid . . . and also let the golden and silver vessels of the house of God, which Nebuchadnezzar took forth out of the temple which is at Jerusalem, and brought unto Babylon, be restored, and brought again unto the temple which is at Jerusalem.[9]

For Cyrus, it was not enough to end the exile of the Israelites. It was not enough to order their temple in Jerusalem rebuilt, and to restore its riches. Ezra writes that Cyrus also commanded that the peoples of the empire en route assist the returning Israelites "with silver, and with gold, and with goods, and with beasts, besides the freewill offering for the house of God that is in Jerusalem."[10]

---

* One hundred and fifty thousand of their descendants, the oldest community of Jews in the world, would remain in Iraq until a mass expulsion and exodus in the aftermath of the creation of Israel in 1948, and a further expulsion with the ascendancy of the Baath Party in 1968.

From the perspective of the Israelites, Cyrus, working these extraordinary deeds on their behalf, was an instrument not of his own wishes, but of God's. This much had been foreseen by the prophet Isaiah. While certain that the terrible destruction caused by the Assyrians in Israel and Judah in the late eighth century was God's "rod of mine anger" to punish the wayward Hebrews for their idolatry, Isaiah knows that eventually God will see to it that His city of Jerusalem is restored. Isaiah reports God saying,

> I am the Lord . . . who says of Cyrus, "He is My shepherd, and he shall perform all My pleasure, even saying to Jerusalem, 'You shall be built,' and to the temple, 'Your foundation shall be laid.'"[11]

"Messiah" is originally a Hebrew word meaning "daubed in oil." It eventually came to mean a person who has been chosen—anointed—to effect God's will. Later it would mean the eschatological savior figure himself. Cyrus's appointment as the instrument of God's will, his selection for the special task of rebuilding the temple at Jerusalem, makes him a messiah for the Jews. As a messiah—"God's anointed," in Isaiah's words—Cyrus is an Old Testament forerunner of the Christian messiah, Jesus.[12] * Chosen by God to save the Israelites, the founder of the Persian Empire becomes the only foreign ruler mentioned positively in the entire Hebrew Bible.[13] The Jewish God, according to Isaiah, has "held the pagan Cyrus by the right hand and subdued nations before him." God promises to "loosen the armor of his adversaries, smooth the high places for him, and break any gates that bar him."

———

Perhaps a dozen centuries before Cyrus, the founder of the ancient religion of Persia—the prophet Zoroaster—lived among the nomadic pastoralists of northeast Iran and the green steppes beyond. Zoroaster's story and that of Abraham would eventually converge in Cyrus's time in

---

* For this reason, Vernon Wayne Howell, leader of the Branch Davidian sect at Waco, Texas, in 1993, called himself David Koresh, "Koresh" being Cyrus's name in many English Bible translations.

Babylon, where the Israelites in exile had absorbed key ideas of Zoroaster and—thanks to Cyrus—brought these back to Israel.

Little is known about the historical Zoroaster. Even Gilgamesh and Abraham are easier to descry, triangulate, and flesh out. Nothing of Zoroaster's biography was recorded, or even passed on orally, by his followers or anyone else. Historians cannot agree where the prophet came from or even where he received his revelations and preached. The leading theories run from southern Russia, or just west of the Black Sea, to Turkmenistan and Afghanistan. We can locate Zoroaster's lifetime within no narrower range than a century or two either side of about 1700 BC. If these estimates are correct, he may well have been a contemporary of Abraham's. Not one word of Zoroaster's teachings was written down until well over a thousand years after he lived.

Yet today we possess much of Zoroaster's prophetic work. This is thanks to events that are possibly as close to us in time as they are to him. In 226 AD, six centuries after the fall of the Achaemenids, Iran's second great dynasty arose: the Sasanians. Seeking to shore up their rule, the Sasanians used Zoroaster's preaching, still preserved in oral form—probably nineteen centuries or so after the prophet's lifetime— as the basis for a new state religion linking the new rulers to ancient Iranian culture.

Like Cyrus, the Sasanians came from the ancient Persian home province of Fars. They took pains to claim descent from his dynasty. As part of their new faith, the Sasanians produced a new holy book, the *Avesta*. This included seventeen hymns, called the Gathas, that the Sasanian writers attributed to Zoroaster himself. It is these hymns that today provide our clearest link back to the prophet. Oral transmission can be remarkably accurate, keeping its integrity for many centuries in cultures or faiths where the spoken word is the only form of record. Despite the distance in time between Zoroaster's likely dates and the articulation of Sasanian Zoroastrianism, most modern scholars are confident that the six thousand words of the Gathas are indeed likely to be very nearly the words of the prophet himself.[14]

The Iranian priests who first committed the Gathas to writing, in the third century AD, did not know what the texts meant. The language, now called Ancient Avestan, was by then long dead in Iran. A further sixteen hundred years would pass before Zoroaster's hymns were translated. Then, in the early nineteenth century AD, French and English philologists discovered that the language of the Gathas was close to the early Sanskrit language of the Rig Veda. The latter is the key text of Hinduism, dating from sometime around 1700 BC.[15] The link allowed the Gathas to be translated, or as nearly translated as is possible, into a living language for the first time. The linguistic connection to the Rig Veda also would seem to be a clue about Zoroaster's dating, placing him at perhaps 1700 BC, alongside the Hindu writings. The Rig Veda connection is further evidence of the strong Indo-Iranian connection that makes Iran the central piece of what might be termed the Indo-European metaculture.[16]

The written records of the Achaemenids do not mention Zoroaster. About ten years after Cyrus's death, however, Achaemenid royal inscriptions begin to mention Zoroaster's god, Ahura Mazda. Numerous classical authors, from Plato in the fifth century BC to Plutarch in the first century AD, refer to Zoroaster as if he were a historical figure.

Long before Zoroaster, Ahura Mazda had been one of several ancestral deities in greater Iran. Zoroaster made Ahura Mazda the sole God. To this move from polytheism to monotheism, the prophet added an extraordinary innovation: morality in religion. "Good thoughts, good words, good deeds" was the prescription at the heart of Zoroaster's revelation. The world, he explained, is dominated by two main forces, the Truth and the Lie. People, responsible for their actions, must make the choice between them. It is the choice between good and evil.*

The religions of the region had not hitherto placed ethics at the core of belief. No deity had required, or promised, goodness. Few if any had bothered themselves with moral conduct at all. The gods of the ancient Near East had required devotion in various strict and literal forms, and perhaps propitiation when a flood or plague expressed divine anger. Then the God of Abraham had demanded strict spiritual monogamy. Abraham's bargain had been a practical one: it never mentioned right or wrong, and on Abraham's side what was owed had nothing to do with good or honest behavior and everything to do with loyalty.

---

* It was from the moral constraints of Western civilization, created by Zoroaster's choice and its consequences, that Nietzsche sought to free mankind in *Thus Spake Zarathustra* (i.e., Zoroaster) and *Beyond Good and Evil*.

Abraham's covenant and Zoroaster's introduction of ethics nonetheless represented moves in the same direction. In a theology of pure power, there is no room for either natural law or a bargain between man and God. The very notion of justice or virtue suggests, as does the Abrahamic covenant, that there is some other set of rules to compete with the unfettered will characteristic of the Semitic Almighty.

Zoroaster's injection of morality into religion worked in tandem with another spiritual novelty: end times. Eventually, taught the father of Persian religious thought, the world would come to an end, and on that last day we will all be judged. Some will have lived well, embracing the life of "good thoughts, good words, and good deeds," choosing Truth over the Lie. These would enjoy an afterlife in paradise forever afterward. For the rest, those who had chosen the lie, eternal damnation awaited. A savior figure would then redeem the world at this End of Days.

Zoroaster's twin revolutions—ethics and eschatology—could not have worked without a third great innovation: free will. With Zoroaster, this is far more central and explicit than it is with Abraham. Without the power to make their own decisions, people cannot choose between Truth and Lie, cannot elect the life of "good thoughts, good words, good deeds." Without full agency, individuals cannot be judged after they die. Long before Cyrus, Zoroaster's formulations began to take root in Iran and Mesopotamia.

Xenophon (b. ca. 427 BC) was an Athenian soldier of fortune and gentleman philosopher whose works on Socrates, leadership, the art of war, and the training of horses (and wives) made him a fundamental part of the canon of the educated classes of Western civilization from Roman times through the first half of the twentieth century AD. Alexander exhorted his men with Xenophon's example. Scipio Africanus carried the author's works with him everywhere. Queen Elizabeth I's tutor Roger Ascham ranked Xenophon alongside Plato and Aristotle.[17]

Xenophon's *Cyropaedia* is one of his two greatest works.* It is a treatise on kingship, presented as a biography of Cyrus—a historical novel

---

* The other was his *Anabasis, or March of the Ten Thousand*, an account of his leadership in 401 BC of a Greek mercenary army that had fought for an Achaemenid pretender calling

of sorts, based on his life. Influential for well over two thousand years, its purpose is instructive, prefiguring medieval European "mirrors of princes" and, later, Machiavelli's *Prince*. For the Greeks, the Persian Wars against the successors of Cyrus were to provide the events that eventually crystallized their self-definition as free, individualistic, and rational. The Greek idealization of Cyrus may be seen as part of the same process, setting the Greek epitome that Cyrus embodied for them against his tyrannical, hubristic, and ultimately defeated heirs who would repeatedly invade Greece, lose there in battle to its free citizen soldiers, and ultimately succumb to Alexander, pupil of Aristotle.

In the *Cyropaedia*, Xenophon provides a corroboration for the impression of Zoroaster's ideas that we receive from the Gathas and other Zoroastrian traditions. At the end of the book, Xenophon gives Cyrus a peaceful end after a three-day illness. (The near-contemporary Herodotus, preoccupied with downfall, gave Cyrus a very different death.) In a spirit of reflection alternating calm with a sense of restrained emotion, Xenophon's Cyrus delivers an oration from his deathbed. This remarkable speech, for the first time ever in writing, posits the momentous ideas of the one Almighty God, the cosmic struggle of right against wrong, the individual's ethical imperative, and the freedom of human will upon which the latter is based. Xenophon's audience was the literate Hellene of the fourth century BC. His narrator was an idealized Persian of two centuries earlier. The ideas were distinctly Zoroaster's:

> The everlasting God above, who beholds all things, with whom is all power, who upholds the order of this universe, unmarred, un-ageing, unerring, unfathomable in beauty and in splendour, fear Him my sons, and never yield to sin or wickedness, in thought, in word or in deed.

> And after the Almighty, I would have you revere the whole race of man, as it renews itself forever; for God has not hidden you in the darkness, and your deeds will be manifest in the eyes of all mankind. If they be righteous and free from iniquity, they will blazen forth your

---

himself Cyrus the Younger. After Cyrus was killed in a battle that the Greeks won fifty miles north of Babylon, they were left in enemy territory with no local support. Xenophon led them on a long retreat to safety on the Greek-dominated southern shore of the Black Sea and thence home to Greece.

power; but if you meditate evil against each other you will forfeit the confidence of every man.[18]

During his mercenary days, Xenophon had spent the better part of a year in Persian lands, mostly Mesopotamia, and among Achaemenid courtiers. The deathbed oration that he gives to Cyrus is at least quasi-fictional, and it is undoubtedly imbued with a Greek perspective. But it also shows a notable understanding of the Zoroastrian fundaments. One God, ethics at the heart of faith, and individuals determining their fate through their own decisions: this Greek appreciation of the Iranian prophet clearly contains key ideas in the eventual Judaeo-Greek synthesis that became Christianity. Before Xenophon, the Athenian, these Eastern concepts had not been immortalized in writing. With Xenophon, the Greeks and their heirs acknowledge with enthusiasm the origins of these ideas in "barbarian" lands.

From the perspective of the early Achaemenid Persians in their great cities of Susa, Ecbatana, and Babylon, the political status of the Greeks was a minor matter. Herodotus tells a story of the Spartans, honoring treaty obligations to the Ionian Greeks, sending an envoy to Cyrus to warn him not to harm a single Greek city. The emperor, bemused by the impertinence, turned to "some Greeks who happened to be with him" and asked who the Spartans were.[19] This response was shocking to the Greeks, among whom the Spartans towered at the time.*

For the Persians, the Greeks were a small and distant people. By contrast, Cyrus's imperial creation would become a realm so universal, so apparently permanent, so much at the heart of the natural order of things, that even to the self-reliant Greeks, the Persian emperor was often known simply as *basileus*, "the king." When, after some insolence

---

* Herodotus has Cyrus follow his question with a little-noticed response to the Spartans. "I have never yet been afraid of men who have a special meeting place in the center of their city, where they swear this and that and cheat each other," says the emperor. The comment is, says Herodotus, "intended as a criticism of the Greeks generally, because they have markets for buying and selling." It is a precursor of Napoleon's equally hubristic comment on the English, that "nation of shopkeepers."

or another, the time came for Cyrus to chastise the Ionian Greeks for their independent ways, the task was unworthy of his presence. He would send a deputy instead.

Herodotus provides us with a neat ordering of how the world looked to Cyrus, the first ruler of Persian Iraq: "He did not think the Ionians important enough to constitute a primary objective, for his mind was on Babylon and the Bactrians and the Sacae and the Egyptians."[20] The Bactrians inhabited the then-rich lands of what is now much of Afghanistan; the Sacae were the Scythians of the great steppe north of Iran.

After Mesopotamia's two principal contributions to the world— civilization itself, and the ideas of free will and humanity's dignity in relation to God that are embedded in Abraham's story—the essentially Iranian idea of individual responsibility for one's eternal fate, based on right and wrong, would be among the most momentous gifts from East to West. That would come seven or eight centuries after Cyrus. After taking Babylon in 539 BC, the father of the Persians returned his attention eastward. Herodotus tells us,

> There were many things which roused his ambition and gave him courage to undertake this new war, the two most important being his belief in his superhuman origin and the success of all his previous campaigns; for it was a fact that until then it had been impossible for any nation to escape, once he had marched against it.

To any mind imbued with the Greek tradition of Herodotus's readers, the undertones of hubris are impossible to miss. From here to Nemesis could not be far. For Cyrus it would be quite unlike the peaceful death that Xenophon gave him.

Toward the end of Cyrus's life, in 530 BC, the largest unconquered power in the easterly reaches of his orbit was the Massagetae, steppe nomads living to the northwest of his earlier conquests in the Hindu Kush. The Massagetae, who seem to have been mostly based in what is now Uzbekistan, were led by a queen, Tomyris. Cyrus's opening gambit was a request for marriage. Tomyris saw through the overture—"The

The Empire of Cyrus the Great, 530 BC

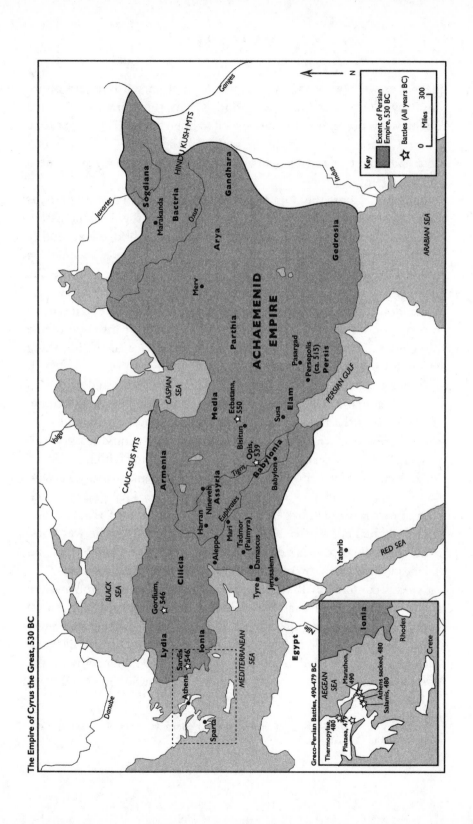

Key

Extent of Persian Empire, 530 BC

☆ Battles (All years BC)

0   300
Miles

N

Ganges

HINDU KUSH MTS

Sogdiana

Marakanda

Bactria

Gandhara

Arya

Oxus

Jaxartes

Indus

ARABIAN SEA

Gedrosia

Merv

ACHAEMENID
EMPIRE

Parthia

Pasargad
Persepolis
(ca. 515)

Persis

CASPIAN
SEA

Media

Ebatana,
550

Bisitun ☆ 550

Susa

Elam

PERSIAN GULF

CAUCASUS MTS

Volga

Armenia

Assyria

Nineveh

Harran

Euphrates

Mari

Tigris

Opis,
539

Babylon ☆

Babylonia

Aleppo

Tadmor
(Palmyra)

Damascus

Jerusalem

Yathrib

RED SEA

BLACK
SEA

Cilicia

Gordium,
☆ 546

Tyre

Lydia

Sardis
☆ 546

Ionia

Athens

MEDITERRANEAN
SEA

Sparta

Greco-Persian Battles, 490–479 BC

AEGEAN
SEA

Thermopylae,
480

Plataea,
479

Marathon,
490

Athens sacked, 480

Salamis, 480

Ionia

Rhodes

Egypt

Nile

Crete

queen was well aware that he was wooing not herself but her dominions," says Herodotus—and rejected it. "Cyrus, therefore, having failed
to achieve his object by cunning, turned to open force." The story's tone
toward Cyrus has changed. In the ascent of the king's remarkable arc,
there had been tact and a laudable inclination to diplomacy. Now there
was mere cunning.

Marching against the nomad queen, Cyrus reached a river, perhaps
the Oxus, today's Amu Darya forming much of the Turkmenistan-
Uzbekistan border.* There Cyrus began to build a bridge and modify
the local ferries so that his army could enter the lands beyond. He
received a message from Tomyris. "King of the Medes," wrote the
queen who had recently scorned his marriage proposal, "I advise you
to abandon this enterprise, for you cannot know if in the end it will do
you any good. Rule your own people, and try to bear the sight of me
ruling mine. But of course you will refuse my advice, as the last thing
you wish for is to live in peace."

Tomyris went on to suggest that if Cyrus really wanted to try his
strength against her people, he could give up the laborious bridge-
building, cross the river in peace, march three days inland, and fight
where there was space to do so. Or, she proposed, she could cross over to
his side of the Araxes and give battle there. Consulting with his officers,
Cyrus decided to let Tomyris cross to the Persian bank of the river. Wise
old Croesus was still alive, and still at Cyrus's side. "I have learnt much
from my own misfortunes," Croesus said. Only sixteen years before,
he himself had enjoyed famous wealth and power. Now he was but a
living specimen of Cyrus's diplomatic touch and bloody ambition, and
of Herodotus's grand theme of the mutability of human affairs.

Croesus continued: "If you recognize the fact that both you and the
troops under your command are merely human, then the first thing I
would tell you is that human life is like a revolving wheel and never
allows the same people to continue long in prosperity." In the event of
a defeat, Croesus argued, it would be better to have the enemy on the
far side of the river. And should Cyrus win the battle, he would want

---

* Herodotus calls it the Araxes, but that river, the modern-day Aras, is in the Caucasus,
well west of the Caspian Sea.

to be able to press his victory into the undefended heartland of his foes. Tactically, Croesus's advice seems sound enough. What is more notable is the wafting scent of the dish that Herodotus serves best: comeuppance.

Croesus had a final suggestion for Cyrus. The Massagetae were, as had been the Persians until quite recently, a rough lot. They were unaccustomed to life's pleasures. Cyrus must prepare a great banquet, leave it badly defended, and then fall upon the savages of the steppe once they had slaughtered the small Persian guard and abandoned themselves to the feast.

Croesus's banquet trap succeeded. Cyrus took Tomyris's son prisoner as the drunken Massagetae were cut to pieces in the Persian camp. The queen's response to Cyrus was withering.

"Glutton as you are for blood," said the queen of the steppes in a message to the greatest empire-builder their world had seen, "you have no cause to be proud of this day's work, which has no smack of soldierly courage. Your weapon was the fruit of the vine . . . Give me back my son and get out of my country with your forces intact . . . If you refuse I swear by the sun our master to give you more blood than you can drink, for all your gluttony."

These were harsh words for history's model of diplomacy and tolerance. Cyrus paid no heed. Tomyris's son, freed from his fetters, promptly killed himself.

Herodotus, who wrote of scores of conflicts, goes on to say that the ensuing battle was the bloodiest ever fought between two peoples. Cyrus died in the fighting. Twenty-nine years had passed since he made war upon his grandfather Astyages. Tomyris, meanwhile, kept her promise. When the messiah's body was found, she put its severed head into a wineskin that she had filled with human blood. Her words are history's only eulogy for its paragon of princely virtue. Cyrus was at last enjoying, she said, his "fill of blood."

———

Through most of the two centuries of Persian rule that began with Cyrus's conquest in 539, daily life for Babylonians continued with few changes apart from those wrought by an increasingly arduous imperial tax harvest.* Babylon's population of locals, Jews, other Semitic peoples, Egyptians, Persians, and more inhabited a sophisticated urban world of commerce, religion, and learning. Babylonia was at the time also known (mostly to the Greeks) as Chaldea. The Old Testament uses the term not only anachronistically in the Abraham story, but also more accurately in later stories such as that of Daniel, soothsaying child of the Captivity. It was now, during this renaissance known as the Neo-Babylonian period, that the region's astronomers and astrologers became so renowned for their skillful and arcane calculations that "Chaldean" became a byword for practitioners of magic and the occult.

The cuneiform script continued to be favored for religious and scientific writing in Iraq. Meanwhile the far more practical Aramaic script, with its simple and versatile alphabet of only twenty-odd letters, all of them consonants, was gaining dominance in government and commerce. With it came Aramaic, a Northwest Semitic language that would replace Akkadian, Babylon's native East Semitic tongue, as the main spoken language of daily life. Eventually, a generation or two after Cyrus, Aramaic would be the lingua franca and bureaucratic language of the whole empire, continuing to dominate until the Arab conquests of the seventh century AD.[21] In Cyrus's day, Babylonians were already beginning to abandon their Semitic names for Persian ones.

Herodotus provides colorful details about life in many of the places that he writes about. He reports that a Babylonian gentleman of the period perfumed himself all over and wore his hair long under a high turban-like hat. Like his woman, he scented himself with a smoky potpourri after sex. The Babylonian boulevardier of the day carried his own cylinder seal and a bespoke walking stick capped with an "apple or rose or lily or eagle or something of the sort." In death he would be embalmed in honey.

---

* Herodotus claims that Darius the Great, Cyrus's third successor, was the first of the Achaemenid Persian emperors to impose a regular tax on the imperial provinces. The Greek lists the twenty provinces of the empire and their tax burdens in the time of Darius. Herodotus's unit of measurement for all of the provinces is the Babylonian talent, a unit of weight by then relatively standard for the previous twenty-five centuries, equivalent to about sixty-six pounds. Herodotus puts the contribution of "Mesopotamia" (Babylonia and Assyria) at one thousand Babylonian talents (over thirty tons) and five hundred "eunuch boys." No other province is listed as having to provide the latter. *The Histories*, trans. Aubrey de Selincourt (London: Penguin, 2003), Book 3, pp. 212–213.

Herodotus has rightly been called "the first great travel writer as well as historian."[22] The Greek suggests, but does not state, that he visited Babylon in person, writing, "I was told by the Chaldeans that..." and "I have this on the authority of the Chaldeans, though I never saw it myself" and so on. Perhaps Herodotus visited Babylon, perhaps not. Regardless, we can imagine what some of his "Chaldean" friends would have looked like. At Persepolis today, the life-sized carved images of Babylonian emissaries stand like old friends of the traveler, tassel-hatted companions whom the Greek, with his noted taste for the ribald, might have known from a visit to that notoriously sinful city.[23]

Babylon was by then unfathomably old, fourteen centuries at least. It was peerless in wealth, size, and sophistication. It was nourished by a uniquely cosmopolitan blending of peoples. Ripening these qualities, undoubtedly, would have been the unmistakable sense of cruel indecency that, for many a traveler from afar, hangs in the hot, still air of the Mesopotamian floodplain. As Herodotus implied, Babylon was already thought of as a center of lasciviousness long before it became the emblem of evil and sin in the Jewish and Christian traditions.

———

In the 530s BC Cyrus sent the Hebrew exiles back to Jerusalem. They had been in Babylon for fifty-odd years. The Hebrews of the Captivity had been the elite of the Israelites, for Nebuchadnezzar had abducted the rich and the educated, leaving the lumpen masses behind. In Babylon they had prospered. Many of them would choose to stay in cosmopolitan Iraq, where their community continued to thrive for a further twenty centuries.[24]

Under Cyrus's son Cambyses II (the first Cambyses had been Cyrus's father, the lowly Persian prince of "good family and quiet habits" chosen by Astyages the Mede for his daughter), the Persian Empire conquered Egypt in 525 BC. "The third great power of the old world"—along with Media and Babylonia—Egypt was the only one that had escaped Cyrus.[25]

Darius made himself King of Kings in 522 BC after killing the reigning king (Bardiya, another son of Cyrus, who had succeeded Cambyses II earlier that year upon the latter's death) and reigned until 485 BC. The train of events that would ultimately topple the empire now began.

Darius fixed the imperial coinage, standardized weights and measures, and imposed across the wide realm—except in Egypt where the size and age of the place made such changes harder—a single legal system. Like Cyrus, Darius built temples to local gods in various parts of the empire. He turned ancient overland routes into efficient royal roads. He dug a canal from the Nile to the Red Sea. It was all very efficient, but the vision had changed.

In a grandiose new palace at Susa, the winter capital, Darius left an inscription boasting of how almost every nation of his empire contributed to its building. "The cedar timber," recorded the King of Kings, "was brought from a mountain named Lebanon."[26] Twentieth-century explorer and writer Freya Stark paraphrased the next part of the inscription in 1966: the cedars were "brought by Assyrians to Babylon and thence by Carians and Ionians; the timber from north-west India and Kerman; gold from Sardis and Bactria; lapis lazuli and cornelians from Sogdiana; turquoises from Chorazmia; silver and copper from Egypt; and ivory from Kush and Sindh. Ionian masons had built their limestone walls and carved the pillars, and the goldsmiths were Medes and Egyptians."[27]

At Bisitun, in western Iran, 120 miles from the border with Iraq, there is a spectacular inscription on a cliff, two hundred feet above the plain below, that illuminates what it took to make possible all this shipping and building.

The purpose of the Bisitun inscription is to commemorate and legitimize the political triumph of Darius, the fourth Achaemenid emperor, over his rivals for the throne. The inscription includes an image of Darius, a usurper only distantly related to the family of Cyrus, facing representatives of nine defeated peoples. In an echo of the Assyrian reliefs at Nineveh, Darius's left foot rests on the chest of a vanquished rival.* Lengthy inscriptions in three languages detail the Persian's victories, repeatedly presenting them as the victory of "Truth" over the "Lie." There is not one specific truth or lie referred to here, but rather a generalized self-benediction according to the terms set by Zoroaster.

"By the favor of Ahura Mazda I became king," Darius proclaims. The message of favor from the One God is echoed again and again through the Bisitun inscription as if it is a mantra. The peculiar power

---

* The craftsmen who created the carvings at Bisitun were themselves most likely Assyrians.

of monotheism is so thoroughly shackled to brutal kingcraft in Darius's inscription that the effect is almost sinister.

Subsequent successors to Cyrus's throne would also make aggressive use of the political potential so latent in their monotheistic faith. The great Swiss historian Jacob Burckhardt, who in the late nineteenth century "discovered" the Italian Renaissance and invented the study of what became known as cultural history, wrote in reference to Darius's inscription at Bisitun, "Ahura Mazda had been thoroughly exploited by the Persian King to ensure submission of all nations to the ruler under the god's protection. No other religion of antiquity was so perfectly adapted to foster the arrogance of perpetual self-righteousness and omnipotence as this version of Zoroastrianism."[28]

A thousand years later, under a subsequent dynasty—the Sasanians, who formalized Zoroastrian texts and rituals in service of a political project—Iranian monotheism had much the same character as the ancient faith that Burckhardt describes. In Iran in the late twentieth century AD, Khomeinism drew on these deep roots. Iraq, without this tradition, would never welcome state religion as Iran did.

When Darius succeeded to the throne in 522 BC, the Persian Empire had grown to include Cyprus and the south coast of the Mediterranean as far west as Libya. In the east, the realm of the Great Kings extended to the Indus Valley. The empire's western territories included the prosperous Greek trading cities of western Asia Minor, known as Ionia, as well as several Greek islands. The Ionian cities were, like other Greek cities of the time, lively, independent-minded places. Herodotus's hometown of Halicarnassus was one of them. There was an ambitious, aspirational quality to life in these former colonies of mainland Greek city-states. An existence as subjects—slaves, formally—of the Persian Great King was not among these aspirations.

The Greeks had translated their great cultural idea, the freedom of the citizen living in his city-state, into a hard military fact of extraordinary power. The Greek hoplite, a rigorously drilled heavy infantryman, trained and fought shoulder to shoulder with his peers of the city. The hoplite provided his own equipment. He elected his officers. Fighting as a mercenary across the broader world of the ancient Hellenes, from Egypt to Afghanistan, he was the dominant soldier of his day. Money itself, in the form of stamped coins from a ruler's central mint, was invented to pay him—in about 600 BC, by a predecessor of Croesus. An Egyptian pharaoh retained thirty thousand Greek hoplites.[29]

Given the expansionist nature of the Achaemenid Empire, it may have been no more than a matter of time before the Persians invaded Greece proper. Toward the end of his reign, stung by Athenian support for revolts in the thriving Greek cities of the Asia Minor coast, Darius sent an army against Greece. There the local oracles, grateful for the enlightened imperial policy of supporting local cults—bought off by Persian gold, in other words—advised against resistance to the huge armies of the Great King. But the Greeks did resist.

In 490 Darius's Persians landed ashore twenty-five miles north of Athens, at the plain of Marathon. There the Athenians, outnumbered perhaps four to one, attacked and defeated the Persian army. They then made the twenty-five-mile forced march back to Athens to fend off a threat from the Persian fleet. Humiliatingly repulsed, Darius's generals abandoned the expedition. In Babylon, where inhabitants were taxed heavily to fund the Persian imperial adventure against the free Greek city-states, there were revolts and economic unrest.

Darius trained his eldest son, Xerxes, for the throne by installing him as satrap in Babylon. Xerxes, "Ahasueras" from the Book of Esther, ascended the throne upon Darius's death in 486 BC, reigning for twenty years. "Famous for his radiant beauty and splendid physique," he was also "indolent, weak, and easily swayed."[30] First Egypt rose against him, in the year after his accession. In Babylon the tax screw tightened again, revolt followed, and in 483 Xerxes was forced to besiege his own principal city.* Prevailing after three months, he dismantled the famous walls, burned Marduk's temple to the ground, and confiscated the god for what would prove to be the final time in the peripatetic deity's millennium of prominence.

---

* The notion of an imperial Achaemenid "capital" is complex. For most of the period, the summer residence of the ruler, and his treasury, was at Ecbatana, the former Median capital; in winter the ruler and his treasury moved south to Susa. Babylon, political capital of the Mesopotamian satrapies, served as the empire's administrative capital. Persepolis was the ritual or ceremonial capital and the capital of the province of Persis itself.

Herodotus writes that the golden god-statue, including Marduk's gold throne and the gold plinth on which it sat, weighed over twenty-two tons.* Xerxes broke Babylonia into pieces administratively, with one part given to the successor province of the old enemy, Assyria. The estates of Babylon's grandees were distributed to Persians. The empire wrung taxes yet more viciously from the ancient province, and this time the Babylonians were carried off into captivity. Sixty years had passed since Cyrus's very different entry into the city. Babylon would never recover, although Alexander the Great tried to bring back the glory a century and a half later.

———

In 480 BC, five years after Marathon, the Persian Empire is estimated to have encompassed 44 percent of the world's population, making it the largest empire in world history by that standard.[31] † Athens, including foreigners and slaves, may have been home to four hundred thousand at the time. There is a school of thought that the Greek victory at Marathon, without doubt an epic achievement for the comparatively tiny Athenian state, had been for the mighty Persians barely noticeable: a mere "pinprick" on the margins of the empire.[32] We cannot know whether the Persians saw it this way, for they recorded little about it. But ten years later, when they invaded Greece again under their new emperor, Xerxes, they did so with the largest army and most extensive preparations that the Persian Empire ever devoted to an imperial adventure; it was "the greatest of recorded expeditions in ancient times."[33]

The planning for this second invasion of Greece had begun under Darius, over four years before Xerxes launched it. When the attack finally came, the expeditionary force comprised two hundred thousand men and six hundred ships.[34] In 480, Xerxes's army crossed into Europe over a bridge of triremes, narrow ships built for ramming and powered by

———

* Herodotus quotes this figure for the Bel-Marduk statue. He erroneously states that it was another gold statue, of a standing man, that Xerxes stole.

† The Persian Empire "accounted for approximately 49.4 million of the world's 112.4 million people in around 480 BC—an astonishing 44%." *Guinness Book of World Records*, https://www.guinnessworldrecords.com/world-records/largest-empire-by-percentage-of-world-population/.

triple banks of slave-manned oars, that spanned the Hellespont (the strait known today as the Dardanelles).

After a minor delay at Thermopylae, Xerxes's Persians arrived at Athens and sacked it. Within a few weeks, the Athenians gained revenge by leading the Greeks to a major naval victory off the nearby island of Salamis. The next year, 479, Greek land forces led by the Spartans delivered the Persian invasion its deathblow at the battles of Plataea and Mycale.

The great majority of Greek cities united against the invaders, although several city-states among the ever-fractious Greeks fought on the Persian side.* The Hellenes of the early fifth century BC, despite their various differences, shared definitive commonalties. These included a basic language, even if its various dialects could be mutually incomprehensible; the pantheon of Olympian gods; a tendency toward political organization into city-states of free male franchise-holders living atop a substantial slave class; an intellectual atmosphere encouraged by such clearinghouses of ideas as the agora, the gymnasium, and the symposium; and a set of cultural institutions including the Olympic Games, the Delphic Oracle, and the poems of Homer. The key to all of this was a powerful innovation: a basic belief in "the freedom of citizens to share in their own government and make their own decisions about their future."[35]

Herodotus's work captures the critical role of the Persian invasions in forging all of these similarities into a sense of shared nationhood and unique values. He imbues his *Histories* with a strong feeling of a generalized Hellenic identity. "Such, then, is the story of the Greeks' struggle at Thermopylae," he writes, for example, even though the battle in question was very specifically a Spartan-dominated affair.

The importance of the idea of freedom to the Greeks during this struggle, and in the intense reflections that came in its aftermath, is equally evident in what the Greeks wrote about the Persians.[36] "Better a small city perched on a rock, so long as it is well governed, than all the splendours of idiotic Nineveh," wrote the Greek poet Phocylides at the time of Cyrus's great expansion. Nineveh was long dead by then, so the poet was using the city metaphorically, to invoke a notion of eastern

---

* The independent Greek city-states that fought on the Persian side tended to be either long-time opponents of the principals in the anti-Persian alliance, as Thebes was with Athens or Argos with Sparta, or more geographically exposed to the Persian threat, as Byzantium was.

excess. Locating this as he does in Mesopotamia, not in the culturally shallower Iranian home provinces of Persia and Media, is what gives the comparison power. The Greek perception of Achaemenid culture and might revolved around Babylon and its neighbors during this period of Hellenic development, placing Iraq at the center of the story as the idea of the West is born.

Through a Greek lens, "Oriental" characteristics were by implication of a piece with the tyrannies of the barbarians, by which term the Greeks originally meant non–Greek speakers. According to Herodotus and other Greek writers who followed him, luxury, effeminacy, and dissipation were all a natural part of the life of despots and slaves that characterized the East. This is the East of Sardanapalus in Delacroix's 1827 painting. On the Greek side, by contrast, "hand in hand with freedom went the adulation of supposed virtues, among them moderation and self-restraint."[37]

With plays, histories, debates (both historical and rhetorical), works of political philosophy, and even plastic arts of revolutionary human perceptiveness, the Greeks left behind them an entirely new kind of historical record. As a result of these developments, exhibited first by Herodotus, from this time onward the history of Iraq and the surrounding lands becomes known and understandable through sources that are not material, ritual, political, or administrative. This record makes it clear that the successive Greek defeats of enormous Persian armies during these wars meant far more than simply the territorial independence of the Greek world and the survival of its gods.

Absolute despotism, the dominant feature of political life in Mesopotamia and its neighbors since the time of Sargon at least, eighteen centuries previously, was prominent in the Greek characterization of the Persian power. When the Greeks, with tiny numbers of citizen soldiers led by elected citizen generals, defeated vast Persian armies at Marathon or Plataea, the victory was one of the city-state. On the Greek side, citizens and slaves fought for "Hellenic liberties." On the Persian side, even the generals were slave-subjects of the Great King.

What is important in this Greek self-definition, exemplified in Herodotus but with a strong legacy elsewhere from Thucydides to Aeschylus and others, is not whether it was objective or wholly accurate but rather which values the Greeks chose, in the aftermath of the clash, to express as their ideal. These Greek ideas eventually found common ground with Zoroaster's free will and Abraham's humanlike Sumerian God.

In 490, shortly before Marathon, Darius had sacked Eretria, an Athenian ally in supporting the rebellious Greeks of Asia Minor. Darius had then sent Eretria's entire population to Mesopotamia.[38] The mass removal of peoples was by then not uncommon. The practice had been invented long ago by the Assyrians and used by them and the Babylonians in the land of the Hebrews and elsewhere. A defeated Athens would most likely have suffered Eretria's fate, which in 483 Xerxes had inflicted on the rebellious Babylonians themselves. Socrates would have been born alongside the children of the Israelites on the banks of the Tigris at Babylon.

A severe curtailment of Greek religious freedoms might have been another consequence of Persian victory. Greece's varied pantheon made for an easygoing religious culture. There was little that was numinous about a spirit world in which the mortal princeling Paris is invited to choose a lover among the greatest goddesses of Olympus—Athena, Aphrodite, and Hera—as if they were apples on a cart. In worshipping such gods, who fought, schemed, and made love with the mortals, the Greeks essentially worshipped themselves. An Athenian might favor her city goddess Athena, but she would never deny the power of Poseidon, patron of rival Corinth. At certain times of the year she might happily choose to join the rites of Dionysus, Poseidon, or Apollo. The heterodoxy and humanness of the Greek pantheon reflected the independence of mind at the heart of the classical outlook.

The Persian invasions of Greece started not long after the Iranian religion that had been so relaxed in the reign of Cyrus—relaxed enough for Cyrus to walk hand in hand with Marduk through the streets of Babylon—had mutated in the absolutist direction expressed in Darius's inscription on the cliff at Bisitun. "Perhaps victory over the Hellenes would have allowed this . . . to erupt into complete madness," Burckhardt writes of a tendency to which he finds the nearest comparison to be "the vanity of Louis XIV." Legend had it that ever since the Ionian revolt, Darius had commanded a servant to say to him "Remember Athens" three times every night, as the imperial dinner was served.

About a generation after the Persian Wars, a group of Israelites returning from Achaemenid Babylon had an astonishing announcement for those whom they found back home. Only they, the returnees, possessed the true religion, and they would teach this to the benighted Hebrews of Israel. The new preaching called in part for a return to strict observance of the old Israelite faith. This had been maintained carefully by the elite in their exile by the Tigris, even as it had slid into laxity among the *hoi polloi* left behind in Judah. But the religion preached by those come home from Babylon was also in large measure something new, developed at the Persian court of Babylon amid the followers of Zoroaster.[39]

In the Jewish and Christian Scriptures, the story of the return is told in the books of Ezra and Nehemiah. Ezra was a scribe and priest of the Captivity who enjoyed favor at the Persian court. In about 457, the Great King—Artaxerxes, son of Xerxes—commanded Ezra to return to Israel as a religious magistrate to "judge all the people that are beyond the river."

Supported by Persian "silver and gold," Ezra arrived in Jerusalem with an ardent mission and ample resources. In Babylon, the exiles had compiled their holy book, the Torah. Corresponding to the Pentateuch, the first five books of the Christian Old Testament, this collected and edited the history and laws of the Israelites, all of it said to have been written down under divine inspiration by the patriarch Moses. The priest-scribe Ezra is thought to have been the last editor and custodian of these books as they took their final form toward the end of the exile. As the Torah's author in Babylon and its propagator in Jerusalem, Ezra is credited as the founder of Judaism: the new, post-Captivity faith of the Babylonian returnees.

Arriving back in Jerusalem to judge the locals and require them to accept his holy book, Ezra had "prepared his heart to seek the law of the Lord . . . and to teach in Israel statutes and judgments." While the Judaean elite were living through their Babylonian exile, the humbler people back home had taken "strange wives" from among neighboring peoples and bred with them. Upon his return, Ezra insisted that the community cleanse itself of this stain. It was a sacrifice reminiscent of that which Abraham was called upon to make with his son Isaac. Perhaps Ezra knew the example of the tribes of the northern kingdom, who, in similar circumstances, after being forcibly deported by the Assyrians two and a half centuries before, had apparently slackened in their faith and were now well on the way to disappearing forever.

The erring poor of a still-wrecked Jerusalem had little chance of resisting Ezra, this reforming zealot who appeared suddenly among them with the strong backing of the distant Persian overlord. Arriving at Jerusalem, Ezra commanded "all Israel" to swear to follow his rules and the teachings of his holy book—"and they sware." For this moment perhaps more than any other, Ezra is remembered as the "father" of the new religion. A measure of the change marked by Ezra can be found in the use of the word "Jews" in the Old Testament. The term appears just once before him, when the people of Judaea suffer their exile in the Second Book of Kings; here the term is geographical, a shorthand for "Judaeans." After Ezra, the word "Jews" appears repeatedly. In the Scripture's postexilic books, the term refers to the people of a religion, not a place.

How different from the ancient faith was this new creed of Judaism? The Israelites who had gone off to Mesopotamian exile had been believers in the God of Abraham. They had been followers of the laws of Moses. They had been loved by God when they submitted to His jealous ways. They had been scourged and chastised when they prostituted themselves to other deities. For this sin their God judged and punished them collectively, not individually.[40] They were Hebrews, but they were not yet Jews.

The returnees from the Babylonian Exile were different. After this point, marked by the introduction and acceptance of the Torah, the Jewish Bible—corresponding to the Old Testament—has no more collective crime and punishment among the Israelites. There is no further mention of idolatry, of the whorish worshipping of other gods, of mass chastisement for these headstrong tendencies. Thirteen or fourteen centuries after Abraham, and perhaps a similar amount of time after Zoroaster, the Jewish religion was now born as the legacies of these two prophets mixed by the waters of Babylon. In life, the Jews would be guided by angels. In death, an afterlife and resurrection would await, with different fates for the righteous and the sinful. The Jews would trust in the arrival of a savior. At the end, when he arrived, there would be a day of judgment.

Every one of these ideas in Judaism—individual responsibility for one's fate, life and resurrection after death, a messiah heralding a final judgment and the End of Days, including the angels and their halos—had been introduced in the Babylonian exile. Each of these concepts had been central to the faith of Ahura Mazda for many centuries. Before the return from the Captivity the Hebrew Bible did not concern itself with Zoroaster's individual "moral choices and the good life." There was instead the Semitic God, whose desire and power were all, for whom the human free will hinted at by Abraham had not yet developed much beyond the choice to be faithful or faithless, and for whom submission was ultimately the requirement.[41]

After Ezra, other books of the Hebrew Bible contain additional ancient Iranian concepts that are not present in the preexilic books. The apocalyptic visions in the Book of Daniel and the Satan figure in Job are Zoroastrian infusions with no precedent before the successors of Cyrus sent Ezra, Nehemiah, and the others home from their time in Babylon. In the pre-Captivity portions of the Old Testament, the books of Genesis through Kings, the dead—good and bad alike—join their forebears underground for a dreary eternity in the grave. It is an afterlife much like the Sumerian one that Gilgamesh dreaded. The resurrection of the dead is unheard of until Daniel speaks of the "end of the days."[42] Heaven too (although not Hell) begins to be elaborated in the religion of Abraham's descendants only after the return from exile. "Paradise"— paradeisos—is a Greek word coined by Xenophon from pairidaeza, the Median–Old Persian word for a protected garden.[43] Later Greeks, translating the books of the Hebrew Bible, used the Persian term to describe the Garden of Eden.[44]

Some of the postexilic reforms and additions to the Hebrew Bible are not so much Zoroastrian and Iranian as they are Babylonian. Only after the exile did the descendants of Abraham begin to observe the Sabbath. Putting to use the work of the famous Chaldean astronomers and mathematicians, they began to mark out the religious year with regular celebrations: Passover and Pentecost, the New Year and the Day of Atonement.

Judaism's Zoroastrian borrowings would prove immensely important for the wider world. Like Abraham's revolutionary journey out of Sumer and ultimately over the western horizon into a future of individual agency, the End of Days does away with two of the heavier existential shackles. The first of these is the treadmill of a human condition that is cyclical in nature. The second is slavery to a preordained individual fate. Both of these brakes on human development were demolished by the day of judgment at the end of time. The classical Iranian eschatology, well predating the rise of the Persians, meant that individuals were going somewhere, and that the choice of where they went lay with the individuals themselves, not with some distant master or prewritten script.

———————

Zoroaster's notions, as Xenophon's funeral oration for Cyrus illustrates so well, were markedly more serious and sophisticated than the offerings of ancient paganism. The prophet's concepts, fundamentally binary and so powerfully concentrated, also had the potential for a darker manifestation, as exemplified by the massive cliff carving of the usurper Darius at Bisitun.

The tombs of Cyrus and Darius show the contrast between the two men. At Pasargadae, in the old tribal heartland of Fars, in the southeast of central Iran today, Cyrus built himself a remarkable tomb: a tiny rectangular mausoleum that sits on a simple plinth in the center of what is today a broad and empty green valley. At Persepolis, just twenty miles distant, and only fifteen or twenty years later, Darius would build something entirely different: a vast, megalomaniacally scaled ritual complex on a platform fourteen hundred feet long and a thousand feet wide, rising fifty feet above the green-brown countryside below.

The roof of Darius's audience hall at Persepolis was held up by seventy-two columns that were over sixty-five feet high. Donald Wilber, a colorful American spy in Iran during the 1950s who wrote four books on Persian architecture, writes, "In 1621 Pietro della Valle recorded that twenty-five of the columns were still standing, while in 1828 an observer saw only thirteen, the number standing today."[45] All of these still stand.

Darius decorated the massive stairways leading to his audience hall with images depicting twenty-three subject nations rendering their fealty. The reliefs have survived relatively well. Ethiopians lead an okapi and carry an elephant's tusk. Bactrians bring a two-humped camel. Indians carry vases in baskets. Libyans offer a kudu. Bulls are led in by Egyptians, by Gandarians in long capes, and by Babylonians in tasseled conical hats.[46] The entrance to the complex is formed by a pair of fifteen-foot-tall bull-men installed by Darius's son Xerxes in the bellicose style found at Nineveh and other Assyrian cities. The craftsmen and artists at Persepolis appear to have been mostly Assyrians and Asian Greeks.

For a visitor to Pasargadae and Persepolis, these two valleys at the historic core of the ancient Persian home province of Fars, the contrast between Cyrus's modest tomb and the vast, histrionic spaces of Darius presents a poignant testament to the stunning evolution that took place over a single generation following Cyrus's death. It was the change from empire as a vision of universal enlightenment to a more familiar view of empire as a machine for tribute and control. It is impossible not to think of Gilgamesh here. Cyrus would live on, especially in the Western tradition, in princely manuals, quasi-mythic romances, great religious texts, and ideas. Darius and the others would live on in the ghostly stonework of Persepolis and Bisitun, and in memories of a string of Greek victories. Gilgamesh had set out to build walls and a city for his immortal name, but it was his story that lasted.

Chapter 5

Aristotle in Babylon

Alexander the Great, 356–323 BC

See God not as an autocratic despot, but as the common father of all and thus your conduct will be like the lives of brothers within the same family. I, on my part, see you all as equal, whether you are white or dark-skinned. And I should like you not simply to be subjects of my commonwealth, but members of it, partners of it.

—The Oath at Opis, attributed to
Alexander the Great, 324 BC

On a hot late-summer day in 331 BC, a twenty-five-year-old Macedonian stood with his army before Babylon's vast walls, rebuilt since Xerxes had pulled them down a century and a half earlier. For hundreds of years thereafter, Alexander would be worshipped as a god on three continents. That day he was a young king a thousand miles from his throne.

The Macedonian was "fair-skinned, with a ruddy tinge" to his complexion, according to the biographer Plutarch; his hair was parted in the middle and hung in blond ringlets. His height was average. There was a permanent leftward tilt to his neck, a mild condition present since birth, but he was exceptionally fit and visibly athletic.[1] His native language was likely Greek.* Compared to the Greek tongue spoken by the cosmopolitan citizens of Athens or Thebes, the Greek of the Macedonian court would have been considered either a fairly exotic dialect

---

* Alexander, like all Macedonian boys of his class, spent his early years with his mother and her household; in his case she was Greek. His tutors were also Greek; meanwhile, Macedon under Alexander's father was becoming increasingly Hellenized in culture. In the thick of battle, especially, Alexander was reported to have used the Macedonian tongue.

or, at the very least, the uncouth argot of a country cousin. The young man's culture—his gods, habits, customs, reading—was also Greek, but his home was Macedon, a rough, mountainous land at the edge of the Greek world. Babylon, and Mesopotamia in general, had entered a twilight with the rise of Cyrus's Persia two hundred years earlier. Now, it seems from later events, Alexander wanted to make Babylon the capital of a new empire. He would not see his home again.*

Alexander had left Greece at the head of his murdered father's armies three years earlier. Two centuries after Cyrus, the city whose gates Alexander now stood before was still the largest metropolis of the Orient, and indeed of the world.† Alexander needed Babylon. Its unrivaled size, wealth, and cachet were essential if he was to realize his dream of infusing into Asia the Greek culture of Aristotle, his boyhood tutor. And the city—not that it knew or cared—needed the success of this endeavor if it was to awaken from its lengthening torpor and once more become the pivot of the civilized world.

The huge walls that Herodotus had described a hundred years earlier must have appeared daunting as Alexander organized his troops into battle array before them. The invading army consisted of about forty thousand infantry and seven thousand cavalry.[2]

Alexander did not know what welcome or resistance waited behind Babylon's walls.

---

* There are numerous ancient sources for Alexander's life and characteristics. Plutarch (d. ca. 120 AD), a generally tertiary source himself, is always a pleasurable way to read about Alexander and many of the people around him. Plutarch claims to have seen, as well as written sources now lost, statues by Lysippus, "the only artist whom Alexander considered worthy to represent him." Arrian (d. ca. 150 AD) and Diodorus Siculus ("the Sicilian") (writing until about 30 BC) are the other two principal classical sources, both thoroughly readable. The mysterious Quintus Curtius (likely writing in the first half of the first century AD) is considered less reliable. Most details in this chapter that have not been specifically attributed come from Plutarch. Others come from Arrian especially. Where the differences are not material, I have not made a consistent effort to follow one author over another. As Arrian writes in his account of Alexander and the Gordian knot, which Arrian says the Macedonian either severed or undid by removing a peg, "Accounts of what followed differ . . . I do not myself presume to dogmatize on this subject." *The Campaigns of Alexander,* trans. Aubrey de Selincourt (London: Penguin, 1971), p. 105.

† Babylon's population at the time would probably have been between 200,000 and 300,000. Soon eclipsed in size by Alexandria in Egypt, Babylon was at the time of Alexander's arrival rivaled in size only by the northeastern Chinese city of Xiadu, the largest city of China's Warring States Period but one of more local importance.

He had spent the last three years campaigning through Asia Minor, Syria, and Egypt, then back through Syria, and finally into Mesopotamia. He had defeated the much larger armies of Darius III, heir to Cyrus's empire, three times in battle.

A few months later, in Susa, Alexander would be adopted by the mother of the Great King he had defeated. In return, Alexander adopted her as a mother. Undoubtedly well aware of Cyrus and his legend as promoted by Herodotus and Xenophon, Alexander frequently showed a Cyrus-like diplomatic touch. Alexander also often evinced a blood-thirsty, intemperate side that, in the case of Cyrus, only the steppe queen Tomyris is known to have remarked.

The early accounts of Alexander convey a sense that he was grateful for the relationship with Darius's mother. His own mother, Olympias, was a seductive virago. From the court at Pella, back in Macedon, she plagued her son with dangerous politicking and a ghoulish emotional importunacy that reached him across a thousand miles of Europe and Asia.*

By the time Alexander reached Babylon, he had won battles on three continents. At Tyre and Gaza he had successfully prosecuted sieges that the world had thought impossible. In these actions and in small engage-ments that must—even then, less than halfway through his extraordinary adventure—have seemed innumerable, Alexander had often fought in or near the front rank. Nobody counted the many times he was wounded in battle. He had already founded a city—Alexandria, in Egypt—that would eventually be the world's largest for perhaps two centuries, and he was to found sixteen more cities that bore his name and many more that did not.[3] Arrian, the most sober and analytical in tone of his ancient biographers, writes that Alexander was "the slave of ambition," driven primarily by "his nature," which was, "if he had no rival, to strive to better his own best."[4]

Alexander's father, Philip of Macedon, had been the greatest man of his day, a Greek Charlemagne or Bismarck of sorts. Philip had trained the Macedonians, his mountain countrymen, into masters of the phalanx, an ancient military tool that he had brought to near perfection.† On the

---

* Olympias moved back to her home court at Epirus in the next year, 330 BC, but her interference, and Alexander's frustration, continued.

† There are records of forebears of the phalanx having been used by the Assyrians and even Sumerians. In the classical Greek world the formation was perfected by Epaminondas

appropriate terrain, and properly supported by other arms, it could not be stopped by any enemy at the time. With this and other innovations, Philip's army was the best in the world. Having brought the Greek city-states, apart from Sparta, under his hegemony by force and diplomacy, Philip had been preparing to invade Persia at the time of his murder in 336 BC. From the Greek perspective this meant the conquest of "Asia."

While the intellectual flowering of the fifth century BC was Greece's greatest moment, and belonged mostly to Athens, the first half of the next century saw both Greece's greatest soldier and politician, and its greatest intellectual: Philip and Aristotle. It is not often remarked that each sprang from the poor and backward soil of Macedon. Aristotle was born in the Macedonian city of Stageira in 384 BC. Later that year, Philip destroyed Stageira and enslaved its citizens, and Aristotle eventually moved to Athens at the age of seventeen to study under Plato. In 343 BC, as Alexander reached his teens, Philip brought Aristotle home to Macedon with a promise, which he honored, to rebuild the razed city of Stageira and resettle its inhabitants.

At Philip's court, Aristotle taught Alexander subjects ranging from the natural sciences to rhetoric, from logic to the canon of Greek literature. But the most influential topic was political: the nature and meaning of the freedoms of Greek citizens. Aristotle taught the young prince that these freedoms made the Greek world civilized, and that the rest of the world was a land of tyranny and slaves. After the long wars of defense against the armies of Cyrus's heirs, this primarily meant the Persian East. Civilization, Aristotle taught, must be brought to the *barbaroi*, the "babblers" or non-Greek speakers.

The Greeks, like every other culture of that world, had slaves too. The difference in the Greek view was that among the *barbaroi*, everyone was a slave except for the king. Aristotle looked back on the repeated victories of free Greek citizen soldiers over the huge armies of Asia and

---

of Thebes, who used it to defeat the Spartans at the Battle of Leuctra in 371 BC. Philip of Macedon grew up in part at Epaminondas's court in Thebes, as a hostage. Philip's main innovation to the phalanx itself was to double the length of the spears, "out-reaching" the spears of opposing hoplites and allowing the first few ranks to present a near-impenetrable "hedgehog." Lewis V. Cummings, *Alexander the Great* (New York: Grove Press, 2004), p. 107. Cummings's five-page treatment of the phalanx is a tour de force well worth the reader's time.

argued that the Greeks, in the superiority of their liberty, must conquer and spread their light.

For Aristotle's pupil, then, the empire founded by Cyrus was the huge eastern land on which to shine the lamp of Greek humanism. It would also provide the forum for one of the greatest, bloodiest epics of megalomania in history. Alexander himself, like his father before him, was a king, but one elected by his citizens; in Macedon this meant by all the free men in the polity, which in turn was more or less synonymous with the army. So Alexander, by Macedonian law and convention, served at the pleasure of his troops.

Between 332 BC and his death at Babylon nine years later, Alexander conquered the Persian imperial world from the Nile to the Indus. In central Asia, Afghanistan, and western India, the Macedonian won victories much farther east than Cyrus and his successors ever had. Throughout this brief period, Alexander took great pains to spread Greek culture almost everywhere he went. He did it through migration, organized intermarriage, the education of leading Asians in Greek culture, and the integration of Asians into his army and administration.

Alexander founded city after city in which people of western and central Asia participated for the first time, in numbers, in what might be called a political class. They did this as Greeks did it, as citizens in the new cities, debating in the agora, the gymnasium, and the symposium, participating in demos, the Greek form of political life. The Macedonian empire, as a single entity, died with Alexander, but his legacy in Asia was to be far more profound and enduring than is commonly remembered. Greek Asia lived on for three hundred years, if by the end only in isolated pockets. Twelve centuries after Alexander, a Persian-Arab dynasty in Baghdad, the Abbasids, rediscovered the Greek learning he and his heirs had spread. They built upon it and passed it along for another rediscovery a few centuries later: the European Renaissance, which led to the birth of the modern world.

On that summer day in 331 BC, Babylon stood before Alexander as the last great gate through which he must pass to realize Aristotle's vision and his own ambitions. The Macedonian approached the city cautiously.

Known already for its decadence and eclipsed administratively by the Persians' twin capitals at Susa and Ecbatana, for well over two centuries Babylon had not possessed the vitality to generate another homegrown giant, a Hammurabi or a Nebuchadnezzar. But the city had provided many of the soldiers and most of the wealth with which the Persians had threatened Greece since the early fifth century.

Alexander came at the old metropolis with care, his army in battle order, with mounted scouts and skirmishers in the fore. But on near-ing the old and famous walls, Alexander and his men were surprised. Babylon had opened her gates. The figures whom the Macedonians had spied along the parapets were gawkers and well-wishers, not bowmen and slingers. "Not far from the city," wrote Arrian, a Greek soldier, scholar, and politician of the Roman Empire in Xenophon's mold, in the second century AD:

> He was met by the people of the place, who with their priests and magistrates came flocking out to bring him various gifts, and to offer to put the city, with the citadel and all its treasures, into his hands. He marched in accordingly, and instructed the people to restore the tem-ples which had been destroyed by Xerxes, in particular the temple of Bel, the god held by the Babylonians in the greatest awe.[5]

The prize that came with Babylon was once again the greatest on earth. Persia had risen with Cyrus, but the land of the Tigris and the Euphrates remained, with Egypt, one of the two centers of gravity in the Eurasian world.* Egypt, however, was isolated by its geography. Its culture had started slightly later and had developed for the most part along its own peculiar path. Mesopotamia, at the core and crossroads of global trade and ideas, was incomparably more important to the world at large.

The last version of the Gilgamesh book known to us today, which tells a story first written seventeen centuries before Alexander, had by this time been buried for three hundred years. The land between the rivers, considered ancient even in Cyrus's time, occupied in Alexander's day a place of near reverence among educated people. But the Babylon

---

* To take an example for context: the first imperial dynasty in China, the eponymous Qins, would not appear until 221, over a century later.

that Alexander entered that August day in 331 BC was still capital of the
Persian Empire's richest province and the religious center of Iraq.

———

Throughout Alexander's youth and into his manhood, his mother, Olympias, was fanatically committed to the rites of Dionysius and Orpheus.
Mystery cults, these were for initiates only. We cannot know for certain
what went on within them. The rites seem to have consisted mostly
of trance-induced orgies. Ostensibly the purpose of the cults was to
recognize, call forth, celebrate, and channel the atavistic, primal elements within humanity. This the cults did in ecstatic, intoxicated, highly
sexualized rituals that gave Greek society's marginal figures, such as
women, slaves, and foreigners, an opportunity to assert themselves. At
the "orgiastic rites of Dionysus," writes Plutarch,

> It was Olympias' habit to enter into these states of possession and sur-
> render herself to the inspiration of the god with even wilder abandon
> than the others, and she would introduce into the festal procession
> numbers of large snakes, hand-tamed, which terrified the male spec-
> tators as they raised their heads from the wreaths of ivy and the sacred
> winnowing baskets, or twined themselves around the wands and gar-
> lands of the women.[6]

Olympias herself has been described as vampish, vicious, sensual, febrile,
and semi-barbarous. Philip of Macedon had met her at a religious festival
when they were both in their twenties. Their mutual carnal attraction
appears to have been instant and overwhelming. For Philip, several more
wives, and children with at least six women, followed. The relationship
with Olympias quickly took on a poisonous, furious quality. They were
well matched, a pair to compare with Cleopatra and Julius Caesar.

Philip was the most consequential political figure in the history
of ancient Greece. Working the fractious Greek states under his
domination—aristocratic and high-spirited Thebes, quarrelsome Athens,
and all the others except for Sparta—he was bibulous, well educated, and
disputatious. Political life in Greece before Philip had been complex and

occasionally world historical. From Philip on, it would be occasionally complex but never important.

Alexander was born on a stormy July or October night in 356 BC.* Omens of a significant birth had been in place for almost a year. On the night before her wedding to Philip, Olympias had dreamed of a bolt of lightning flashing from the heavens and fizzing deep between her legs and into her belly. Shortly after, Philip dreamed that he had needed to stop up his wife's womb with a seal bearing the imprinted image of a lion's head.[7] The court seer duly pointed out that no one needs to stop up an empty vessel. As for lightning, that was a form Zeus often took when having sex with mortal women. Everyone knew this. So there was no reason for Philip or anyone else to doubt that on her wedding night with Philip, Olympias was already pregnant with the spawn of Zeus.

Shortly after Olympias dreamed of coupling with lightning, Philip saw her in bed with a large snake. The Zeus of Epirus, where Olympias came from, was equated with the Egyptian god Ammon—and Zeus Ammon frequently chose the form of a snake for his adventures with mortal women. So Olympias was once more in bed with Zeus. Plutarch relates that it was this discovery, "more than anything else, we are told, which weakened Philip's passion and cooled his affection for her."

As Olympias entertained snakes in bed and whirled through her Bacchic orgies, and as Philip took on younger new wives and consorted with countless dancing girls and courtesans, king and queen fell into conflict. Philip meanwhile was transforming Macedon into the greatest power the Greek world had yet seen. From soon after their marriage until Philip's death twenty years later, the witch and the conqueror were united only in a cycle of domestic and diplomatic warfare. Running free in his mother's quarters in Macedon's royal palace at Pella, their son, Alexander, spent his first six or seven years, as was traditional, almost entirely in the company of the women of the family and household.

---

* For Philip it was, if Plutarch is to be believed, one of the better evenings in the history of fatherhood. His army defeated the Illyrians (the Greeks' northwesterly neighbors along the coast of what is now Albania and the former Yugoslavia) at Potidaea, his wife gave birth to the greatest conqueror in history, and his horse won the race at the Panhellenic Games held every four years at Olympus. The omens for Alexander were not lost on Philip's soothsayer.

Alexander was a precocious boy. In his father's absence, at the age of ten or so, he entertained an embassy from the Great King in Persia. The boy so impressed the Persians with his questions—about the roads in their country, the numbers of troops commanded by their king, and so on—that they concluded that Alexander would be an even more serious challenge than his father. The boy was athletic and a fast runner, but when someone suggested that he enter the Olympic Games, he said, in effect, "Only if I am to race against kings."

Whenever Philip won another battle or persuaded another Greek city into his thrall, Alexander was said to regret to his youthful companions that Philip was leaving nothing—for young men of the Homeric tradition this meant no glory—for them. The story, related by Plutarch, is one of the early signs of the unusual role of boyhood friends in Alexander's view of life.

No other great man of history shows anything like Alexander's preoccupation with friendship. The mature Alexander's chief lieutenants, the "Companions," had been raised with him. They drank together in the tradition of Macedon's martial aristocracy, with a brutal, formal zeal. They grew into generals who won dozens of battles, conquered the known world at his side, and then established dynasties that lasted for centuries from Egypt to India. No other conqueror—except perhaps Genghis Khan, who also fought alongside his boyhood companions—has ever had such successful generals or been nearly so close to them.

Philip eventually removed Alexander from Olympias's clutches in the palace harem and sent him into the care of a Spartan-influenced relative of Olympias. This man, Leonidas, kept Alexander on a meager diet and made him wear thin clothes and sleep under thin blankets even in the cold winters. Perhaps as a result of this Spartan regime, Alexander grew up smaller than his friends. Later, through the greatest and harshest series of campaigns ever undertaken by a single leader, he was always seen as physically tougher than his men.

During his youthful years, we hear from the various sources, Alexander excelled at sports, became a good enough musician to appall his father, disdained professional athletes in favor of actors and other entertainers, and had the courage and empathy to tame the Thessalian stallion Bucephalus. The horse, according to Plutarch, was "wild and unmanageable," but so strong and beautiful that he was on sale for thirteen talents of gold.* As boy and stallion galloped back toward Philip and a crowd of other onlookers, the king was proud and tearful. "My boy," said Philip, "you must find a kingdom big enough for your ambitions, for Macedonia is too small for you."[8] Bucephalus would die at the age of thirty, in the Punjab with Alexander, who was the same age.[9]

When Philip sent for Aristotle—"the most famous and learned of the philosophers of his time," in Plutarch's words—Alexander was about fourteen.[10] Studying in the groves of the temple of the Nymphs at Mieza, one of Macedon's greenest and most beautiful villages, the prince and the philosopher became close. In shady lanes and on stone benches in the dry, fragrant air of vineyards and orchards in a region known as the Gardens of Midas, Alexander imbibed the secretive science of Aristotle's metaphysics. Alexander learned medicine from Aristotle, and later, on the campaign trail across much of Asia, would often serve as a field doctor. Aristotle most probably also taught him rhetoric, zoology, and geometry.

Those times with Aristotle in the Gardens of Midas must have been days of magic for a young man of Alexander's intellect and curiosity. What Plutarch would call a "violent thirst after and passion for learning" lasted through Alexander's life. Like Napoleon in Egypt, the young king brought scientists and philosophers with him on his campaigns. He diligently sent rivers of information back to Aristotle from the wildest and farthest reaches of the known world.

Alexander would have received a bracing, if informal, education in practical politics from the struggle between his parents. After the episode with Bucephalus, a thirteen-year-old Alexander had won further respect from his father by commanding the Macedonian elite cavalry at the great Battle of Chaeronea in 343 BC. There Philip, defeating the combined forces of Athens and Thebes, finally brought Greece together under his mastery.† Philip's philandering was meanwhile driving Olympias to become ever more "jealous and vindictive."[11]

At a wedding of Philip to an especially young new bride (his seventh; Olympias had been his fourth), a drunken uncle of the girl raised a toast to the prospects of, at last, a legitimate Macedonian heir to the throne.

---

* An ancient Greek talent was a unit of weight equivalent to about fifty-seven pounds.

† Chaeronea has aptly been called "one of the world's decisive battles . . . even in those days, recognized as marking the end of Greek independence." Cummings, *Alexander the Great*, p. 74.

Olympias, from Epirus, on the far side of the northern Greek peninsula, was an outsider, making Alexander only half Macedonian.

Alexander, eighteen at the time, threw his wine cup at the man, one Attalus, shouting, "Villain, do you take me for a bastard then?" Philip stood up from the banquet couch, tried to confront his son, and, "overcome with drink and with rage . . . fell headlong." Alexander asked aloud how a man could hope to conquer Asia who could not cross the banquet room. Then Alexander decamped with his mother from Philip's court at Pella for Olympias's home city.[12]

Estrangements and reconciliations flew between king and queen as Philip planned his assault on Persia at the head of the newly unified Greeks. Finally, in 336, when Alexander was twenty, Philip was murdered at the wedding of a daughter, by a courtier named Pausanias, with Alexander looking on. Who, if anyone, was behind the killing? The Persians never denied it. Alexander was ambitious and influenced by his mother. Olympias was capable of anything. Pausanias himself had a grievance against the king.* History has no answer, but Alexander, loved by Philip's army for the courage and leadership he had already shown in battle with them, was quickly elected the next king. He and Olympias saw to the elimination of any other children of Philip's who might threaten his crown.

It is hard to think of another great figure of history whose nature was so prefigured by his parents. Alexander inherited Philip's intelligence and toughness, and some of the feral Dionysian charisma of Olympias. His material inheritance was Philip's army, with Philip's priest-sanctioned plans for an invasion of Persia that would finally punish Cyrus's heirs for their pillaging and destruction in Greece a century and more before.

Philip's four great contributions to the art and science of war make him unrivaled to this day among innovators in that enterprise. The Macedonian

---

* The man being married, the same Attalus who at Philip's wedding feast had implied that Alexander would not be a legitimate heir to the king, had raped Pausanias in revenge for the latter's having insulted Attalus's lover, also named Pausanias. Philip had refused to punish Attalus for this. Of the various candidates, Alexander was the least likely. The murder occurred at a public, well-attended event and the difficult getaway exposed the killer to instant torture, and any plot to swift discovery. Olympias was at home in Epirus.

phalanx comprised tightly massed ranks of infantrymen carrying a fifteen-to eighteen-foot pike known as the *sarissa*. The basic unit within the phalanx was a square of sixteen files of sixteen men; sixteen of these *syntagmas* made a phalanx proper, and four of these bodies of 4,096 spearmen comprised a grand phalanx, 16,384 men, "the heaviest massed striking unit the world has ever known."[13] * The use in close order of a handheld weapon as long as the *sarissa* required so much discipline, coordination, and precision that the drill itself was guarded as a technological secret. The intensity of training required to execute the Macedonian phalanx led Philip to create what was probably the first full-time, professional, national standing army. As a fighting system, the phalanx was, in the context of the associated combined arms doctrine that Philip had developed, invincible in pitched battles in open country for two hundred years.

Philip was also one of the first generals to drill cavalry intensively. Building on this combination, he more or less invented the doctrine of combined arms, using his heavy infantry in systematic coordination with cavalry and skirmishers for what was probably the first time in the history of warfare. Philip also invented the siege train, a discrete, coherent suite of mobile siege weapons. This in turn used various forms of heavy artillery that Philip and Alexander personally worked to refine, such as mangonels and large catapults.

If ever a mighty legacy met a worthy heir, it was in Macedon in 336 BC. Following Philip's death in that year, the twenty-year-old Alexander moved swiftly to secure his control over this extraordinary machine. Philip's planned expedition against the Persians would proceed.

Discovering Philip's treasury to be insufficient to meet the needs of a long intercontinental war of conquest, Alexander borrowed money. Garrisoning Macedon with half of his own army, he gathered troops from the Greek city-states, hired Greek mercenaries, marched to Byzantium, and in May of 334 crossed the Hellespont.

At last Alexander was in Asia. He would never again show real interest in Europe, beyond the attention required to sustain an ongoing supply of fresh Macedonian troops. First he drove the Persians from the Greek cities of the Asian shores of the Aegean Sea—the Ionian cities of yore,

---

* As Cummings points out, the attrition of men meant that in practice the full complement was rarely achieved in active campaigning.

the same that had sparked the original Persian invasions of Greece. Doing so brought Alexander to Troy. There he and Hephaestion, his dearest friend since childhood, paid honor to Achilles and Patroclus by running a naked race around the twin tombs of the Homeric warriors. After the race Alexander and Hephaestion cut their long locks and laid a wreath together for the ancient pair. Before leaving, Alexander swapped his shield for one alleged to have belonged to Achilles.

No more than a few days later, perhaps fifty miles east of Troy at the Granicus River, Alexander won his first great victory against Darius's armies. The core of the Persian army was a contingent of Greek hoplite mercenaries, about twenty thousand in number, that was larger than the entire army, perhaps nineteen thousand strong, that Alexander brought to the battle.[14] Heavily outnumbered, Alexander won at the Granicus with a surprising dash across the shallow, wide river, where the enemy awaited atop a steep bank.

Shrewd, lucky, and reckless, riding the extraordinary inspiration that he elicited from his men, Alexander could be gripped by violent frenzies that were more reminiscent of his mother than his judicious father. At the Granicus, Alexander demonstrated all of these traits, which were to win him battles for the rest of his life. Twenty-two years old, he had routed the greatest power in the world. But Darius himself, underestimating the Macedonian threat, had left the campaign to his generals, and thanks to his absence, Alexander's victory was incomplete.

After a year of smaller victories, Alexander came to Gordium, in the Persian satrapy of Phrygia. Phrygia was just east of Lydia—central Turkey today—where 220 years earlier Cyrus, after defeating Croesus, had begun to show the diplomatic virtues Xenophon extols in the *Cyropaedia*. The work had become the leading "mirror of princes" of the classical world. It is likely to have been an important part of the education of Philip's son, and Cyrus would have been the most important model of good kingship in Alexander's notably studious youth.

At Gordium, the founding king, Gordius, had long ago hitched a wagon to a yoke using a famous knot.* Legend said that whoever could

---

* The legendary Gordius was the father of the legendary King Midas. Midas washed away his gift/curse of the golden touch in the river Pactolus, whose ore-rich sands were said to be the source of the wealth of Croesus.

untie the knot would rule Asia.[15] Alexander could not let this opportunity pass. Arrian, Alexander's most reliable ancient biographer, is unsure whether Alexander undid the knot by slicing it apart or by removing a peg at its center. Either way, Alexander sent a message about his plans. The smoldering drive to master Asia was clearly present, but officially his mission was more modest. As hegemon of the Hellenic League assembled by his father, Alexander's public goals in the East were to free the Greeks of Asia Minor and punish the Persians for their sacking of Athens and other depredations a century and a half previously. These Greeks of Asia Minor were now three hundred miles westward, to his rear.

In November 333, having marched north and south through what is now Turkey, Alexander found himself in trouble at Issus, in the far eastern corner of Anatolia's south coast. Darius had raised another army and marched from Babylon. With Alexander pressed against the sea, Darius had outflanked him, circling to the north of the Greeks, severing their line of communications that reached a thousand miles back to Macedon, and appearing behind them. Alexander now feared that Darius, possessed of famously great numbers, might also have left another army as an anvil of sorts to the south. Once again, at Issus Darius had more Greek hoplite mercenaries in his army than Alexander had infantry of any kind in his own: thirty thousand versus twenty-six thousand.[16]

Speaking to his rattled men, Alexander reminded them of the difference between them and the Asiatic armies whom the forebears of their Greek cousins had defeated so consistently in the Persian Wars:

> Our enemies are Medes and Persians, men who for centuries have lived soft and luxurious lives; we of Macedon for generations past have been trained in the hard school of danger and war. Above all, we are free men and they are slaves.[17]

Alexander then invoked the greatness of the prize that lay before them: "the sovereignty of Asia." Finally he reminded them of Xenophon, who with his Ten Thousand had fought through enemy territory from "the gates of Babylon" to the Black Sea. This famous Hellenic feat of arms against the Persians had taken place seventy years earlier.

After the speech, Alexander was mobbed by his men. They begged him to lead them into battle. As at Issus, Alexander attacked suddenly. He himself rode directly for Darius. Fighting swirled hand to hand around the two kings. The Persian fled the field. Darius's armies crumbled and the battle turned into another defeat of the Persians by the Greeks, the sixth in a row since Marathon in 490.

Three years earlier Alexander's mother had urged him to marry and father an heir before leaving Macedon. He had not done so. At this point in his career, apart from an intense mutual fascination with his mother, he had shown no interest in women. This changed at Issus. Darius had left behind in his flight his harem as well as his army and treasure. A Persian noblewoman called Barsine, famously beautiful, successively widowed by two Greek mercenary captains who had been brothers, was brought before Alexander after the battle. Her "beauty and noble lineage" turned his head. With her he finally lost his virginity, at the age of twenty-three.*

Darius's baggage train also brought three thousand talents of gold and Darius's own family: his mother, wife, two daughters, and young son. Upon discovering Darius's lavish campaign tent, Alexander commented, "So this, it seems, is what it is to be a king."

Luxuriating in Darius's tent the night after the battle, having failed to catch the fleeing Great King but eating off his gold and silver plate, presumably feeling fresh after washing off the day's blood in Darius's tub of gold, Alexander heard wailing nearby. He asked why women had been placed so close to his tent. He was told that the noise came from Darius's own family, in their own quarters, mourning what they thought was the death of their son, husband, and father.

Alexander sent word to the queen and queen mother that they were not to worry. Darius was still alive, and they had Alexander's word: they would enjoy safety and respect and keep their royal titles. The struggle with Darius, Alexander explained, was nothing personal. It was merely a matter of who ruled Asia.

---

* In the succession struggles following Alexander's death in 323 BC, a teenaged boy was produced, named Heracles, said to be a product of this affair. "Heracles of Macedon" was murdered in 309 BC.

The next day Alexander and Hephaestion went in to see the Persian women.[18] They were Alexander's spoils of battle. When the two Greeks walked in to introduce themselves, Sisygambis, Darius's mother, prostrated herself before the taller of them—Hephaestion. Quickly learning that she had the wrong man, she was embarrassed. "Do not worry, mother," Alexander told her. "He too is Alexander."

Darius's wife was possibly also his sister or half-sister, as was sometimes the Iranian and Zoroastrian custom. Called Stateira, she was said to be the most beautiful woman in Asia. Alexander's friends urged him to enjoy his rights. There were also the daughters and the boy. Under another conqueror, all would have gone to the beds of the victors. Alexander touched none of them. His relationship with Sisygambis, the old queen mother who must have been embarrassed by her own son's flight, would last until he died.

Alexander's only imposition on the young princesses was to order that they be taught Greek and be brought up henceforth in Greek culture. It was Alexander's first clear opportunity to implement the idea, associated with his tutor, of bringing Greek civilization to the East. Alexander was beginning to make clear his intentions about what a Greek Asia meant for him. Nine years later he would marry the elder of the two girls, called Stateira like her mother.

Plutarch attributes Alexander's conduct with Darius's wife to self-restraint. Alexander's sexual awakening with respect to women was happening at that very time, so a disinclination toward females was probably not the cause. "These Persian women are a torment for our eyes," the Macedonian is said to have remarked at the time.[19]

We cannot know if Alexander, in the unusual scenario before him, remembered the story of Cyrus and the Lady of Susa, but the circumstances are remarkably similar.[20] It is told in Xenophon's *Cyropaedia*.

Some two centuries earlier, Cyrus had defeated the Assyrians and their allies. The Lady of Susa, the most beautiful of many captives, had become his; her husband was captive too. Cyrus's officers had seen her nakedness as she tore her clothes in lamentation; truly, they thought, she was the most beautiful woman in all of Asia. But Cyrus had refused even to look at her. Romantic love, he said, was merely a form of slavery. He entrusted the lady to the care of one of his officers, but the man fell in love with her, and Cyrus was forced to banish him before anything

untoward could happen. After all of this, the Lady of Susa sent word
to her husband, commending Cyrus's restraint and care. Such a king,
she told her husband, was worth following. And so the husband came
to Cyrus's court, pledged fealty, took possession of his faithful wife, and
remained loyal to Cyrus unto death.

In the aftermath of Issus, Alexander thought that Darius might do
as the Lady of Susa's husband had done: see the victor's virtue and join
his cause. Whether Alexander's treatment of the Persian princesses was
pragmatic or humane is not the issue. More significant is that something important changed within Alexander at this stage. While he did
not assume Darius's title of Great King, from then on Alexander was a
Persian emperor in all but name.

Alexander's public goals in Asia, as hegemon of the Hellenic League,
had been fulfilled at Issus. There were also some more personal ones: the
Aristotelian urge to push the barbarian power over the eastern horizon,
and maybe vengeance for his father's murder. In the aftermath of Issus,
Alexander seems to have glimpsed a different kind of motive: one that
no longer obliged, but rather appealed. After a brief lifetime of constant
victories, here was something on a new scale. Suddenly possessing all
that Darius once possessed, the twenty-three-year-old from Macedon saw
what mighty kingship truly meant. Any reflections of Cyrus, inventor
of world empire, were clearer in the looking glass. Heady new horizons
beckoned.

Instead of continuing eastward to finish off Darius, Alexander changed
direction, heading toward the south, away from Persia, away from Darius
and the world of Asia's Greeks whom he had set out to free. He marched
down through Syria and the Levant, taking the rich city of Tyre after
a six-month siege. Seizing Egypt next, Alexander visited the oracle of
Zeus at Ammon, in the oasis at Siwa. This was the god who was Philip's
rival for Alexander's paternity. The young man wanted to ask about the
matter. Yes, confirmed the priest at the shrine, where the oracle was
at least as important as the Oracle at Delphi in the Greek world of the
day, Alexander was indeed the son of Zeus.[21] Ever thereafter Alexander
seems to have believed that the god was his father. Olympias had told
young Alexander so. Philip, believing it too, had called the boy a bastard.

Meanwhile Alexander continued, wittingly or otherwise, to emulate
Cyrus in much that he did. He retained the local administration in Egypt

while placing Macedonians in charge of the garrison. As Cyrus had done in Egypt and elsewhere, Alexander visited temples and worshipped the local gods. At Memphis Alexander assumed the powers—and for Egyptians, the divinity—of pharaoh, and performed the pharaonic sacrifices. Alexander restored local rites that previous conquerors, in this case Cyrus's successors, had abolished. In April 331, the son of Zeus founded his second eponymous city: Alexandria in Egypt.

With Olympian paternity confirmed and Egypt his, Alexander turned again to Asia, and to Darius with it, for the Persian was still at large. Asia was the great need for Alexander. From this point on there is a sense of *pothos*, of a burning desire that is close to obsession, pervading his actions.[22]

Alexander marched back up through the Levant and Syria. Then he moved east into northern Iraq. Darius now had a third army. As large as ever thanks to the vastness of Cyrus's eastern empire, the Great King's new levy comprised good cavalry and tough, if by Greek standards disorganized, infantry, both drawn from the tribes of Central Asia, Afghanistan, and northern India: famous warrior lands all. In October 331 Darius marched out of Babylon for the second time to meet Alexander.

Again, the Persian army was at least twice the size of Alexander's. Darius marched north for the final clash in the gentle country south of the highlands now known as Iraqi Kurdistan. Superior numbers, fifteen war elephants, the luck of the third try, some remaining Greek mercenaries, and fifty scythed chariots were not enough for Darius. At Gaugamela, near Arbela (contemporary Erbil), with Alexander in the thick of the fighting, the Macedonians and Greeks crushed a much larger Persian army for the third time.* Darius fled again, this time east into the Median hills. Three weeks later, Alexander arrived outside the walls of Babylon at last.

Other cities might resist Alexander, who now, after Darius's flight into the mountains, was "king of Asia."[23] Several did resist him over his career,

---

* The clash on the plain of Arbela was the last recorded time that Alexander used the phalanx, which was unsuited to the often broken terrain of his adventures farther east. Cummings, *Alexander the Great*, p. 108. Alexander's later battles were also often less of a classic "set piece" in nature.

despite knowing that to do so was never successful. Babylon was different. It was as if the gods had made Alexander and the city for each other. Babylon, the ur-metropolis, luxuriating on her centuries like a courtesan on a couch, could only love Alexander, the violent, cultured god-king, beautiful and yet slightly deformed from birth, somehow both man and child, as indulgent as he was temperate. It was a remarkable moment when the two met: Babylon, "the grand old wicked city," the fulcrum of the world; and Alexander, on his way to being something like a planet in a man, soon a living god from Egypt to India.

Alexander and his army entered Babylon in eddies of incense and rose petals. Persian rule there had turned sour in the two centuries since Cyrus. The old regime had been unpopular. Change was welcome. But in the surviving accounts there is a sense of something deeper behind this reception.

At Babylon Alexander moved into the six-hundred-room palace of Nebuchadnezzar.[24] If Darius's war tent had impressed the Macedonian after Issus, this must have made Philip's palace back at Pella, well-known in Greece for its splendor, seem utterly parochial. During the next month the Greeks relaxed. For those unsated by the decadent city's pleasure-loving populace in its famous hanging gardens and elsewhere, there were half-crocodile prostitutes, according to Strabo, the first-century AD Greek traveler, geographer, and historian.

A century after Herodotus, Alexander would have seen much of what his Greek predecessor described. The city walls, ten miles square, seventy-five feet high, enclosed a city bisected by the Euphrates. The walls were wide enough, according to the Father of History, for two chariots to pass each other on top. Fifty canals emanated from the river, said Herodotus, each one a commercial thoroughfare 150 feet wide. Upstream within the city walls, the huge palaces of Nabopolassar and Nebuchadnezzar, complexes already known as wonders of the world two centuries before Alexander was born, sat over the broad brown river. Downstream from these was the Esagila, Babylon's famous ziggurat, the 450-foot-high Tower of Babel that, like the city itself, had symbolized human ambition from the time of Genesis.

On campaign Alexander kept a copy of the *Iliad*, annotated by Aristotle, under his pillow with a dagger. For the Macedonian, the Trojan War was the wellspring of history. Those events far on the ringing plain of windy Troy had taken place nine hundred years earlier. This tower of Babylon that Alexander had just acquired peaceably was so ancient that it had been home to the great Mesopotamian gods for at least ten centuries before even the time of Hector and Achilles. By the time of the Trojan War, more than five hundred years had passed since Hammurabi had made Marduk, Babylon's city god, the preeminent god in the Mesopotamian pantheon. The city continued to be steeped in a pomp that only Rome would ever match as a center of the world. As in the time of Cyrus, according to local custom the only way to gain true kingship of this city was to take the hand of the god in the New Year celebration.

The megalopolis on the green and carefully watered floodplain then stood about a hundred miles closer to the head of the great southern gulf than it does today. The lower Euphrates was sufficiently navigable, and tied into the commerce of the world, that Alexander later made it a naval base. Now, in 331 BC, to a soldier from the wild Macedonian highlands, carrying his sixteen-foot pike and other equipment, it promised all the comforts and vices of the world.

The ancient sources—Arrian, Plutarch, Diodorus the Sicilian, and Quintus Curtius are the principal ones—do not tell us just how Alexander and his troops enjoyed the fruits of entry into Babylon.* But the dusty warriors must have enjoyed themselves. Herodotus had written that "the pretty girls" of the city were customarily sold off to provide for dowries for the "ugly or misshapen ones." Moreover, he wrote, "all girls of the lower classes" in the city worked as prostitutes, and every Babylonian woman had to serve as a temple prostitute at least once in her life.[25]

Alexander and his men seem to have drunk relatively peaceably from the perfumed trough of the holy city. Had there been any unusually spectacular debauch at Babylon, the festivities would almost certainly have been related in the ancient histories of Alexander. Dominated by the Athenians, who resented him, these texts are generally eager to emphasize the Macedonians' uncouth carousing. Alexander seems mostly

---

* Alexander's historiography is once or twice removed from the events themselves. As one translator of Diodorus reminds us, "the earliest of these [four ancient biographers of Alexander] belongs to the period of Augustus (d. 14 AD). Behind them lie the narrators of the early Hellenistic period." Diodorus Siculus, *The Library of History*, vol. 8, trans. C. Bradford Welles (Cambridge, MA: Harvard University Press, 1983). Arrian, the most sober and detailed, relied on Ptolemy, a firsthand participant in the events but not necessarily always an impartial one. Plutarch mentions at least fifteen sources by name.

to have rewarded his men by sharing out much of the treasure that the Persians had accumulated there since Cyrus's time.

Alexander worshipped at the shrine of Bel-Marduk. Then he paused, for the first time, to reorganize the administrative edifice of his expanding realm. In further reflection of Cyrus, Alexander kept the administrative framework of the Persians and retained Babylon's Persian satrap; Macedonians were placed alongside him to control the garrison and treasury. Retaining the conquered foreigners marked an important step in Alexander's larger project. Among the Macedonians there would have been grumblings. There would be resistance, with each additional step in the "Persophilic" or "Asiatic" strategy, as it has been called, that came to characterize Alexander's leadership during the remaining eight years of his life.

After a month in Babylon Alexander marched along the ancient Royal Road to Susa, three hundred miles to the east, and there took possession of the principal Persian treasury. The old Elamite capital had become the winter capital and, it seems, the main administrative center of the Achaemenid emperors. Arriving at Susa in mid-December 331, Alexander sat himself on the throne of Xerxes and Darius. The Macedonian was so much shorter than the Persian kings that his legs swung above the floor like those of a child. It was quite possibly from there at Susa, maybe from that very seat, that the order had come to murder Alexander's father.

In Susa, Alexander's men found a famous statue that had been much loved by the people of Athens. It depicted Harmodius and Aristogeiton, two teenaged lovers who in 514 or 513 BC had murdered their city's tyrant, Hipparchus, and then been killed by their victim's brother. The tyrannicides had been revered by Athenians ever since as martyrs to demos. After the Persian sack of Athens in 480 BC, Xerxes had taken the statue back to Susa with him. Given its semi-religious importance to the defeated Athenians, it was almost as if the regicidal lovers had been a pair of Sumerian city gods captured by one city from another.

There was a degree of irony in Alexander's liberating the statue of the Athenian tyrannicides. Alexander's relations with bumptious Athens were always troubled. His father, in uniting the Greeks under himself as hegemon, had personally ended the Greek city-state tradition after four centuries. The Athenians would later avenge their subjection to Macedon by writing much of Alexander's history, coloring large parts of his posterity with their scandalous accounts of his character. Alexander in turn never stopped indulging Athens, adoptive city of his mentor Aristotle.

Alexander left Susa in midwinter 331–330. Seven years passed before he returned. In May 330, about six months after their harmonious entrance into Babylon, the Macedonians burned Persepolis to the ground.* Darius was still at large at the time. The most positive accounts—for example, Arrian—relate that Alexander destroyed Persepolis as a measured act of "retribution for the destruction of Athens, the burning of the temples, and all the other crimes [the Persians] had committed against the Greeks."[26]

The gossipy Plutarch, writing some 430 years after the fact, voiced a common view of the matter by attributing the infamous event to a courtesan and a drinking party. Alexander, wrote Plutarch,

accepted an invitation to a drinking party held by some of his companions, and on this occasion a number of women came to meet their lovers and joined in the drinking.† The most celebrated of these was Thais, an Athenian, at that time the mistress of Ptolemy, who later became the ruler of Egypt.

As the drinking went on, Thais delivered a speech which was intended partly as a graceful compliment to Alexander and partly to amuse him. What she said was typical of the spirit of Athens, but hardly in keeping with her own situation.

She declared that all the hardships she had endured in wandering about Asia had been amply repaid on that day, when she found herself revelling luxuriously in the palace of the Persians, but that it would be an even sweeter pleasure to end the party by going out and setting fire to the palace of Xerxes, who had laid Athens in ashes.

---

* The ritual capital of the Persian kings was 435 miles southwest of Susa.

† Arrian writes of Alexander, "His drinking bouts, too, as Aristobulus says, were prolonged not for the sake of the wine, for he drank little wine, but out of courtesy to the Companions."

She wanted to put a torch to the building herself in full view of Alexander, so that posterity should know that the women who followed Alexander had taken a more terrible revenge for the wrongs of Greece than all the famous commanders of earlier times by land or sea.[27]

Soon after Persepolis, Alexander caught up with Darius about sixty miles south of the Caspian Sea. The Great King had been kidnapped and, finally, murdered, by three of his own satraps. Alexander's men arrived at Darius's final stop just in time to find the Persian breathing his last gasps, "lying in a waggon riddled with javelins."[28] Alexander covered the corpse with his own cloak before sending it to the royal women at Susa.

Alexander had now reached a crossroads. Persia was conquered, Persepolis destroyed, and Darius dead. The Ionian Greeks were long since liberated. Philip's murder had been avenged and his greatest ambition realized. Greece ruled Asia. Alexander's obligations in his old world had been fulfilled.[29]

———

Babylonia and Persia were familiar to the Greeks. Countless Greeks had traded, settled, and—like Xenophon—fought as mercenaries across much of the broad empire of the Great Kings for the past four or five generations. The lands to the east were different. This was new country for the Macedonians and Greeks, unknown and nearly fantastical.

During the coming seven years, Alexander's army crossed the steppes of Central Asia, scaled the Hindu Kush, and sailed down the mighty Indus. They fought battles large and small nearly constantly. High-blown ideals and epic mythologizing aside, it could also be seen as the wildly overgrown adventure of a tiny group of hard-carousing Macedonian noblemen, mostly in their late twenties, at the price of extraordinary bloodshed.

The story of the seven-year fling out of Babylon into the distant East and back was the story of Alexander's *pothos*, his deep longing for something—glory, immortality, power, blood, creation. The youthful king changed along the way.

Early in the Eastern adventure, two or three months after Darius's death, Alexander reached Parthia, in the northeast of today's Iran, near

Turkmenistan. "It was here," writes Plutarch, "that he first began to wear barbarian dress."[30] Alexander took to wearing striped purple-and-white tunics under his Macedonian cloak. Many of his companions began to trim their hats and capes in Persian purple, and adopted ornate Persian bridles for their horses. "Alexander came to allow himself to emulate Eastern extravagance and splendour, and the fashion of barbaric kings of treating their subjects as inferiors," writes Arrian—a supporter of Alexander's among the sometimes-skeptical ancient biographers, but not one of the outright panegyrists—of developments around this time. "Regrettable too," Arrian continues, "was the assumption by a descendant of Heracles of Median dress in place of what Macedonians have worn from time immemorial, and the unblushing exchange of his familiar head-gear, so long victoriously worn, for the pointed bonnet of the vanquished Persians."[31]

Around then the Persians started to bow before Alexander, as they customarily did before a king. To Greeks, *proskynesis*, bowing before a fellow mortal, was not only absurd but sacrilegious. In the human-centered Greek view of the world, a man abased himself only before the gods. And this he did rarely. A Greek, so little different from his gods, as capable of breeding with them as of being punished by them, mostly prayed standing, hands and face raised to the sky.

Alexander's principal officers had hunted boar and lion with him in the Macedonian hills since youth. They had wrestled and read Homer together and studied with Aristotle among the nymphs of Mieza. Now their childhood friend was Great King, *Shahanshah*, Basileus. Some were shocked at the Eastern ways that he began to adopt. But for the most part it was the older guard, Philip's men, who objected.

One of the many lingering questions about Alexander is whether, with his embrace of the trappings of what many around him saw as Oriental absolutism, he was allowing the success and power to corrupt him. Was his adoption of Persian ways the manifestation of some high-minded ideal of fusion? Or was it something else—vanity, grandiosity, pragmatism? The question is impossible to answer. There is evidence for each of these impulses in Alexander's character. Arrian, who elsewhere is critical of Alexander's adoption of what he describes as haughty, cruel, and luxurious Eastern ways, says also that it was "a matter of policy: by it he hoped to bring the Eastern nations to feel that they had a king who was not wholly a foreigner, and to indicate to his countrymen his desire to move away from the harsh traditional arrogance of Macedonia."[32]

Plutarch writes that Alexander "believed that if the two traditions could be blended and assimilated in this way his authority would be more securely established when he was far away, since it would rest on goodwill rather than force."[33] Macedon and Greece were now but a tiny part of an essentially Asian empire.

Within a year of Persepolis, Alexander was addressing the important Persians at his court as Kinsmen. This upset his Macedonian compatriots, whose leaders he called merely "friend." He brought Persians and other Asians into his bodyguard. He eventually added a Persian diadem to his evolving synthesis of Greek and Asian dress.

Driving obsessively eastward following a four-month stay at Persepolis, Alexander for the first time discovered or imagined plots against him. For their suspected treachery he executed a pair of lovestruck page-boys, a senior commander and his son, and others, including his court philosopher, a nephew of Aristotle and a partisan of the troublemaking Athenian camp back at home. Drunkenly, Alexander murdered a grizzled old Macedonian general who, after dinner one night, had spoken too well of Philip and too ill of Alexander's divine claims and increasingly Oriental ways. Meanwhile, the Macedonian army followed Alexander on foot across the mountains of Afghanistan in midwinter.

Along the way east he was leaving colonies of soldiers, founding cities, renaming towns, and naming settlements for himself, for his colleagues, and even for Bucephalus.* At some point in the third century BC, Alexandria in Egypt would supplant Babylon as the largest city in the region, and possibly the world, with a population that reached half a million. Alexandria's rise likely marked the first time that the largest city on earth was not in Iraq. Until well into the twentieth century AD, Alexandria would be a creative, lively embodiment of Alexander's dream, a mixed,

---

* Plutarch says Alexander also named a city after his dog, Peritas, but evidence of this is hard to find. Plutarch, *The Age of Alexander*, trans. Ian Scott-Kilvert (London: Penguin, 1986), p. 61.

heterodox Greek city in former barbarian lands. In the east, Kandahar in Afghanistan still bears the echo of his name, Iskander.

In 327, at twenty-nine, Alexander married for the first time. His wife, Roxana, was a princess from Bactria, the far eastern corner of the Iranian world, in what is now northeast Afghanistan and southern Tajikistan. This choice of a "barbarian" wife further alienated the Macedonian old guard. He also tried, unsuccessfully, to persuade the Greeks and Macedonians to perform the *proskynesis*. He trained thirty thousand Asian boys in the weaponry, and in the secret drill and tactics, of the Macedonian phalanx. He called these young Asians, who by the time he returned from India were old enough to join his army, the Epigonoi: his successors.

Eventually, at the Ganges in 325 or 324 BC, Alexander's weary and homesick army refused to go farther. Alexander marched them south along the Indus and at its mouth split the force in two. One part returned to Persia by sea, at the time a pioneering voyage for any fleet. The rest marched westward through a desert that had never been crossed by an army, the Gedrosian wastes of south Iran. Half of the men died among the towering sand dunes, while the rest went half mad with thirst. Emerging from these horrors, they celebrated with a weeks-long rolling orgy as they made their way through Carmania, now the Kerman region of southern Iran.[34] *

Arriving back in Persis proper, Alexander followed a custom of Cyrus's by distributing a gold coin to every wife or mother in the province.[35] Then he visited Cyrus's tomb at Pasargadae. Arrian writes, "Alexander had always intended, after his conquest of Persia, to visit the tomb of Cyrus." Finding the tomb desecrated, Alexander punished those he held

---

* Plutarch: "Alexander feasted continually, day and night, reclining with his Companions on a dais . . . the whole structure being slowly drawn along by eight horses . . . [Other] vehicles carried the rest of Alexander's officers, all of them crowned with flowers and drinking wine . . . Along the whole line of the march the soldiers kept dipping their cups, drinking horns, or earthenware goblets into huge casks and mixing bowls and toasting one another . . . while the whole landscape resounded with the music of pipes and flutes, with harping and singing and the cries of women rapt with the divine frenzy." Arrian, noting that Dionysus had enjoyed a similar progress "after his conquest of India," says that none of the credible original accounts of Alexander mention any such thing. Arrian, *Campaigns of Alexander*, p. 342.

responsible and ordered the gold coffin repaired. He inscribed in Greek on the tomb's exterior the words that were already there in Persian. These famously ended, "I am Cyrus who won the Persians their empire. Do not therefore grudge me this little earth that covers my body." Alexander and the army, making their way back to Babylon, stopped at Susa in early 323.

At Susa, Alexander married himself, eighty of his officers, and ten thousand of his men to women of the Persian Empire.[36] Here he himself finally married Darius's elder daughter, called Stateira like her mother. (He married Hephaestion to a younger sister.) The size, opulence, and theatrical nature of the huge ceremony left no doubt that this daughter of Persia would be Alexander's official wife. As for his intended heir, Macedonian kingship was not a matter of birthright, but Asiatic kingship was. A message at Susa was that any son of this marriage would be the natural king of Asia.

A project of synthesis, if perhaps only as a practical matter, could not be more real than this, especially following the quasi-Persian dress, the prostrations, the elevation of Asians to senior roles in government and army, the Epigonoi, and the allowing of Persians to call the king kinsman. Alexander had also introduced the Persian regiment of Immortals into his own bodyguard. He had brought Persian officers into elite Macedonian units. Among the ordinary Macedonian foot soldiers and the older officers who had served his father, the grumbling intensified.

In 324, the Macedonians mutinied at a place called Opis, near where the city of Diyala sits on the east bank of the Tigris today, north of Baghdad. Addressing his exhausted men, Alexander proclaimed the wars of conquest finished. Then he persuaded the Macedonians to join the Persians and other Asian nations of his army in a banquet. At this they would share a loving cup, a prayer to "concord and unity" among the races present, and an oath to uphold the same.

The extant text of this Oath (or Prayer, as it is sometimes called) at Opis most likely originated with the quasi-mythical "Alexander romances" that began to emerge as early as his own lifetime, remaining popular in numerous languages into medieval times. It bears echoes of Xenophon's funeral oration for Cyrus. But the oath as passed on in the romances does not stray far from the ancient descriptions of the banquet, including Arrian's: Greeks and Persians sitting together, sharing wine from the same bowl, and together following the lead of each other's holy men, "Greek seers and [Persian] Magi."[37] The only really glaring anachronism is the oath's reference to a single God. Plutarch wrote of Alexander at Opis that "the chief object of his prayers was that Persians and Macedonians might rule together in harmony as an imperial power."

There are no ancient recountings of the prayer itself. The version in the romances goes a step farther than the Cyrus Cylinder as perhaps the first major statement of interracial concord in history:

It is my wish, now that wars are coming to an end, that you should all be happy in peace. From now on, let all mortals live as one people, in fellowship, for the good of all. See the whole world as your homeland, with laws common to all, where the best will govern regardless of their race. Unlike the narrow minded, I make no distinction between Greeks and Barbarians.

The origin of citizens, or the race into which they were born, is of no concern to me. I have only one criterion by which to distinguish their virtue. For me any good foreigner is a Greek and any bad Greek is worse than a barbarian. If disputes ever occur among you, you will not resort to weapons but will solve them in peace. If need be, I shall arbitrate between you.

See God not as an autocratic despot, but as the common father of all and thus your conduct will be like the lives of brothers within the same family.

I, on my part, see you all as equal, whether you are white or dark-skinned. And I should like you not simply to be subjects of my Commonwealth, but members of it, partners of it.

To the best of my ability, I shall strive to do what I have promised. Keep as a symbol of love this oath which we have taken tonight with our libations.

At this stage, Alexander was on his way back to Babylon after conquests that had brought him to the outer edge of his world and back. He clearly seemed to be speaking of settling down. Henceforth, Alexander promised at Opis, there would be an era of comity in the new world he had built. Aristotle's urging to bring the Greek virtues to the East had relied on superiority to the "barbarians." At Opis, having done so much already to establish the Asians as peers, Alexander appears to have completed his evolution and gone beyond this.

As he made his way back to the mother city, there were worrying omens. Hephaestion died of a fever in western Iran, when the journey was almost complete.* Then, as the Macedonians approached Babylon, a delegation of Chaldean sages came out of the city and tried to warn Alexander away. Babylon would be his death, they cautioned, but if he insisted on entering the city he must do so from the west.

These priests of the city had failed to obey Alexander's command, eight years earlier, that they rehabilitate the great ziggurat temple, the Tower of Babel. Determined not to be caught in their perfidy, according to a plausible ancient interpretation of events, they sent Alexander in the direction that would kill him, through the fever-ridden wetlands west of the city. The story certainly has a Babylonian feel to it. Alexander tried to approach the city from the west as advised, but the swamps forced him back to the east. His fate was settled.

One day, in his palace in the city, he left his throne on some brief errand. A halfwit sat himself upon the throne. This was considered a deadly omen. Then, on a boat voyage down the Tigris, as Alexander eerily watched the tombs of ancient kings pass by along the riverbank, a gust of wind plucked off his hat. It was decorated in the Persian royal colors of purple and white. A sailor jumped into the Tigris, retrieved the hat, and swam back to the boat wearing the royal diadem on his head. Another bad augury. Alexander rewarded the man with a generous

---

* Hephaestion died at Ecbatana in October 324 BC, after he, Alexander, and the army had left Susa in the spring. The schedule, like so much else in Alexander's governance at this stage, follows that of the ancient Persians: winter at Susa, in the south; summer at Ecbatana, original capital of the Medes, in the hill country 280 miles north.

gift of gold. Then, depending on the account, Alexander had the man either scourged or killed.

Now Alexander's character starts to change in the accounts. To kill or whip a loyal, humble boatman is unlike the golden youth who attended to Darius's mother, wife, and children following the victory at Issus, and who performed myriad elegant acts in the early days of the grand adventure. The illnesses and wounds; the thousands and thousands of miles through mountain and desert; the betrayals and the executed companions; the countless victims of his own sword in battle; the gore, blood, and death all around him; the loss of friends and companions in battles that were all of his own making; the many debauches: all seem at this stage of Alexander's story to be leading to the death of Alexander the idea, if not the man. In the various ancient narratives, the godking's portrait, so to speak, seems to age on the very canvas during this period. Coins that Alexander minted for himself at Babylon during this period—he was the first Greek to commemorate himself in a likeness of any kind—show him with a thunderbolt, as if he were now Zeus.

Early in that summer of 323, Alexander arranged a throne for himself in the sacred garden of the palace of the kings of Babylon. Surrounded by censers filling the air with perfume and by his friends on silver-footed couches, he received embassies and began to pay attention to the governance of his huge empire. One can imagine the edifice swaying on its young, green foundations.

It was increasingly clear that Babylon, the geographical and historic center of an empire that was largely that of Cyrus, was his chosen capital. There his treasury was based, and there he paused to plan his next conquests. As he settled back in at Babylon, peoples from nearly every reach of his broader world sent gifts and emissaries. From the far west the Carthaginians and Libyans sent embassies. The Scythians sent Alexander a delegation from the northern steppe that lay above his eastern conquests. The Ethiopians paid their respects from the edge of Africa. Celts and various half-barbaric Italian tribes did so from darkest Europe. One people, if an obscure one, stood out by refusing to recognize his dominance: the Arabs.

Arrian indicates that perhaps even the small Italian city-republic of Rome, which had recently consolidated domination over central Italy, sent an embassy. There is a story that Alexander was so impressed with

The Empire of Alexander the Great, 323 BC

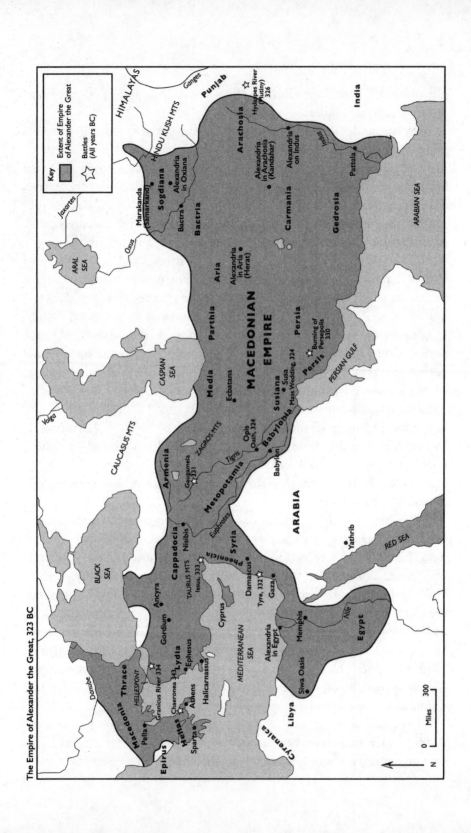

the modest dress of this insignificant group, and so taken with "the proud freedom of their bearing, their obvious devotion to duty and to order,"[38] that he knew instantly that they would enjoy a great future. Alexander would not have known that two hundred years later these Romans would keep the lamp of Hellenism lit in Europe and Asia for five centuries after the last of his own direct successors, the Seleucid kings, had died in 63 BC. In turn, the Roman Empire's eastern continuation, based in the "New Rome" of Constantinople, would carry on the Greco-Roman legacy for a further millennium after that. Rome was the ultimate inheritor of the Greek culture that Alexander evidently cared so much to spread.*

He started to rebuild Babylon. Construction began on a port for a thousand ships of war, along with dockyards to supply and build them. Like any great Mesopotamian king, Alexander set to work on new dikes and canals to control the two mighty rivers. Also like his Mesopotamian predecessors, he ordered the renovation of the great city shrine, the Esagila, where the ancient god Marduk continued to be worshipped atop a ziggurat inside the wide walls described by Herodotus.†

Alexander's world was more or less conquered, and his Oath at Opis, only eighty miles north, appeared to promise an end to the wars. All that remained was lightly populated Arabia. It would hardly be a major challenge after Egypt, Asia Minor, Persia, Central Asia, and western India.

Alexander attended to the administration of his many Alexandrias, the last of them in the south of Mesopotamia, near the marshes at the head of the great gulf below Babylon. He arranged the funeral of Hephaestion, his Patroclus. Reflecting Alexander's great joining, the monument for his friend would be Babylonian in shape—a stepped pyramid two hundred feet high—but Greek in decoration, with images of ships, battling centaurs, the hunt, bulls alternating with lions, and hollowed-out sirens through which singers could sing. The great wooden structure was designed to form a vast pyre. Much of it was gilded, most of the rest was scarlet or blue.

---

* The last directly Greek light in the East flickered out in the Punjab in around 10 AD.

† There is no record of Alexander's holding the people or priests accountable, on his return, for their failure to rebuild the temple. Plutarch speculates that the priests' desire to keep control over the temple wealth explains why they sent him into the city by the marshy route where he caught the fever that killed him.

By May of 323 Alexander had prepared his army for the invasion of Arabia. At the end of the month, word came that Hephaestion had been accepted as a demigod by the priests of Zeus Ammon at Siwa, in Egypt. This was the same Zeus Ammon who had allegedly taken the form of a snake to seduce Olympias, and who was therefore Alexander's own father. Alexander was already ill from his foray into the Babylonian swamps. Now, completing a drinking bout in celebration of Hephaestion's deification, he felt a pain in his stomach. Despite Alexander's many wounds in battle, it was said that this was the only time that he ever cried out in pain.*

After thirteen days of fever, Alexander died. "Babylon," writes Edwyn Bevan, an English historian of the Hellenistic period that followed, "which had seen the glories of the oldest conquerors remembered by man, saw the youngest conqueror die."[39]

Sisygambis, queen mother of Persia, queen of Asia, and Alexander's own adopted mother, locked herself in a room and starved herself to death.

---

* Arrian says it was a fever. Other sources claim poison—a favorite culprit in the non-violent deaths of the young until the nineteenth century. Plutarch, claiming that the story ultimately came from Antigonus, one of Alexander's successors, says that Aristotle himself procured the poison. Aristotle was supposedly angry at Alexander's treatment of Callisthenes, a great-nephew of the philosopher and the Asiatic expedition's official historian. The story is significant: Callisthenes had died in prison after criticizing Alexander's adoption of *proskynesis*, the Persian practice of bowing before more important people.

Chapter 6

The Hellenistic East

The Seleucids, 323–64BC

In the spring of 323 BC, the whole order of things from the Adriatic away to the mountains of Central Asia and the dusty plains of the Panjab rested upon a single will, a single brain, nurtured in Hellenic thought. Then God, as if trying some fantastic experiment, plucked this man away. Who could predict for a moment what the result would be?

—Ernest Bevan, *The House of Seleucus*, 1902[1]

On his deathbed, Alexander whispered with a last breath his intentions for the succession: *"Kratistos."* The word means "to the best." With no son nor any clear successor among his generals, it was a prophecy more than a testament. At any rate, however Persian Alexander had become, it was for the Macedonians to choose their own leader.

The ambition that Alexander had articulated at Opis did not immediately take hold. By the time of his death in 323 BC, a year had passed since the Opis oath and the mass marriage uniting Macedonians with "Persian" brides; a decade had passed since the personal defeat of Darius at Issus, with the capture of the Persian princesses and queen mother. Now, with Alexander gone, only one of his senior commanders kept the Persian wife that Alexander had chosen for him.* This man was Seleucus, once Alexander's head of the Companion cavalry, latterly chosen to lead

---

* Apama, "Persian" wife of Seleucus, was, according to Arrian, a daughter of the Sogdian chief Spitamenes. Sogdia was an Achaemenid satrapy based in Samarkand. The main Sogdian language was an Iranian dialect—an example of the "Greater Iran," extending deep into Central Asia, of ancient times.

the Epigonoi. Alexander left no heir: none in Macedon as Olympias had advised ten years before, nor any children among his Eastern wives and women. Darius's daughter was pregnant but not yet a mother.

With the word *"kratistos,"* Alexander was predicting great funeral games for himself.[2]

The world has never seen anything like the struggle that followed. The Macedonian armies clashed from Greece to India, fighting for the legacy of a king whose name is still spoken today in local languages across the entire vast theater. Twenty-one years of epic fratricide ensued between former comrades, many of them boyhood friends, who had grown into the most brilliant and experienced group of generals in the history of warfare. Most of them were in the prime of life. They fought with mighty tools: the confident, perfectly trained, infinitely hardened pieces of an army for the ages. The master may have gone, but the war machine, "the instrument with which he wrought," remained intact. "It was still only necessary to get command of that in order to rule the world."[3]

At the end stood two main winners. Only one of the nine contestants, Ptolemy, was to die in his bed. This general, bodyguard, and boyhood companion of Alexander's quickly seized the royal corpse and Egypt too. Both moves were master strokes. Alexander's corpse had great symbolic importance, and the deification that had begun in his lifetime only grew after his death. Egypt, rich and relatively self-contained, was a prize bastion in the brutal fraternal fighting of the Diadochi and their heirs. Ptolemy's dynasty ruled a Greek kingdom on the Nile until the last of its monarchs, Cleopatra, submitted to the Romans in 31 BC.

The other winner was Seleucus. He had been a prominent officer in Alexander's lifetime but never one of the most important. Before commanding the Epigonoi, he had led an elite infantry unit, the *Hypaspistai*, or shield bearers. By 321, after the first couple of years of jockeying following Alexander's death, Seleucus was able to persuade his fellow Diadochi, his colleagues and rivals, to make him satrap of Babylonia. It took Seleucus nine years of guile and fighting, on land and sea, to secure this position. In 316, after some reverses, he fled Babylon with fifty men. Over the following four years he traveled to Egypt and Lebanon, then back to Babylon through Syria, then to Egypt again, back to Syria and the coast of what is now Lebanon—Tyre to fight by sea, Gaza to fight on land—and finally back to Mesopotamia. He seized Babylon permanently in 312.

Over the following decade, Seleucus made all of Alexander's empire east of Syria his own. From 305 to 303 he fought in India, ultimately trading a daughter and Alexander's farthest satrapies for five hundred war elephants, which proved critical to his ambitions in the west. Seleucus then spent a further twenty-two years conquering the Levant and Asia Minor from his former brothers-in-arms.

———

In 305, Seleucus founded a new capital for his reassembled Asian Greek empire. He located the new city, Seleucia, carefully, at the point on the Tigris where that river and the Euphrates came closest to each other, about twenty miles apart in their courses at the time, forty-odd miles north of Babylon.* Seleucus now effectively ruled the empire of Cyrus, and his capital became the new Babylon. At its peak, under Antiochus IV (d. 164 BC), Seleucia may have been the largest city on earth, rivaled in the West only by Alexandria and perhaps Rome.

Seleucia-on-Tigris was so successful that Babylon itself withered and died two thousand years after it had been founded, in the time of Abraham. Seleucus forcefully moved much of Babylon's remaining population to his new city. He built it in part with a million and a half fired bricks that had survived from the time of Nebuchadnezzar, transported the forty miles southeast from Babylon.†

---

* In their present-day courses, the Tigris and Euphrates enter Iraq from Syria (having originated in Turkey) about 180 miles apart. Baghdad is on the Tigris, roughly where that river currently comes closest to the Euphrates, at a distance of about thirty miles. South of Baghdad and the site of ancient Seleucia, the courses diverge again until the rivers join at Al Qurnah, forty-five miles north of Basra, whence their waters, now called the Shatt al-Arab, flow together to the Persian Gulf. Al Qurnah is the legendary location of the Garden of Eden.

† Nebuchadnezzar II (d. 562 BC) is estimated to have used fifteen million bricks, stamped with his name, in his building schemes at Babylon. Many were used in the early construction of Baghdad, beginning in 762 AD—a millennium after Seleucus. Original Babylon bricks bearing the Nebuchadnezzar stamp can be found in the walls of houses in modern Hillah, the Iraqi city nearest Babylon.

A turn-of-the-twentieth-century history of the Seleucid dynasty has this to say about Babylon's finally submitting to fate: "Sennacherib had razed it to the soil, and it had risen again to new glory. Cyrus and Alexander had conquered it, and it was still the capital of the world. But Seleucus Nicator brought its doom upon Babylon at last."[4] The new city on the Tigris, with the Euphrates so nearby, was simply better for trade in the new world opened up by the Greeks.

In about 293 BC, the sixty-five-year-old Seleucus, married to a granddaughter of an old rival, Antigonus, noticed that his son was unwell. The king soon learned from his physician the real nature of the boy's sickness: the prince was dying of unrequitable love for his young stepmother. Seleucus gave his empress to his heir, who became Antiochus I. As Babylon wasted away, Antiochus moved what remained of its population to the new capital in 275.[5] Some population must have returned to the ancient city, however: numerous hints in the record, from Babylonian chronicles to the various histories that have come down from the Roman world, suggest that several Seleucid princes, including Antiochus, worshipped at Babylonian temples or walked with their gods at New Year celebrations as Cyrus had done.*

In deference to the huge eastern hinterland of this Greek empire, Mesopotamia's greatest city had now shifted eastward, from the banks of the Euphrates to the banks of the Tigris. The province of Babylonia would provide the early Seleucids with wealth and prestige as it had done for Cyrus and Alexander. "It was the richest country of Nearer Asia," writes Edwyn Bevan, "the seat of its oldest civilization, the natural focus of its life."[6]

———

The sole senior Macedonian to retain his Persian wife from the mass marriage at Susa was now master of what was essentially the great, original Achaemenid Persian Empire. In the west, Seleucus possessed Ionia, the rest of Asia Minor, and Syria. In the east, his writ was bounded by the Indus River, the Hindu Kush, and the southern edge of the Central Asian steppes.

---

* Antiochus IV later refounded Babylon as a Greek city, replete with "a Greek theatre, gymnasium, and city organization," but it did not last.

In 281, Seleucus, in his seventies, crossed from Asia Minor into Europe. He had recently defeated his last living rival among the Diadochi, Lysimachus, who controlled Macedon, Thrace, the southern Black Sea coast, the Ionian coast, and Asia Minor. So these broad lands, too, were Seleucus's now. After forty years of struggle, "the whole realm of Alexander," writes Bevan, "from Greece to Central Asia and India was fallen to Seleucus, with the one exception of Egypt."[7] And Egypt looked to be his for the taking: Ptolemy had died the previous year, Seleucus possessed the wealth of Xerxes with the army of Alexander, and Ptolemy's eldest son, one Ptolemy Keraunos ("the thunderbolt"), the "claimant to the Egyptian throne by right," had sought refuge at Seleucus's court.[8] As for Greece and Macedon, all Seleucus had to do now was travel there and take possession.

All in all, the achievement was greater than Alexander's: Seleucus began with nothing, and his opponents had the same tools that he had. He now planned something not often seen in great conquerors. He would retire—to Macedon, there to "be content for the remainder of his days with the narrow kingdom of his race."[9] As for Asia, Seleucus would settle that on his son Antiochus, still married to his own former wife.

In the summer of 281 BC, Seleucus crossed the Hellespont. He had not been in Europe since crossing in the other direction as a twenty-four-year-old with Alexander, back in 334. Now he was seventy-seven. Not long after landing on the European shore, the veteran general learned of something interesting nearby, a humble "pile of stones," said by tradition to have been "an altar raised long ago by the Argonauts."[10] Seleucus rode away from his army to have a look, accompanied by a few men, including young Ptolemy Keraunos. It must have been a poignant scene, the old man who—and the record still stands—had fought longer and more successfully than anyone in history, now on his way back to the land of his youth, pausing to hear legends of the heroes of his boyhood. As he did so, his ward, Ptolemy Keraunos, "came behind and cut him to the ground."

The Thunderbolt managed to have himself declared king of Macedon by Seleucus's troops and within a year was killed in a rash attack on the invading Galatians, Gauls who had recently "poured over the Balkans" into Asia Minor.[11] * By then Ptolemy Keraunos had married

---

* "Ancient Mediterranean civilization lived all its life on the edge of a great peril, which it forgot perhaps between the moments of visitation, but by which it ultimately perished. From time to time the forests and fens of Central Europe spilt upon it some of their

his half sister Arsinoe, widow of Lysimachus, after promising her that he would protect her two sons, whom he murdered on the morning of the wedding day. Arsinoe eventually returned to Egypt and found a degree of tranquility in the arms of a third husband, her full brother Ptolemy II. Meanwhile, under Seleucus's son Antiochus, a century of warfare—the Syrian Wars—between Seleucus's heirs and the Ptolemies of Egypt began in 274, seven years after the murder of Seleucus.

Coins and statues of Seleucus show a man with a long, straight, strong-bridged nose, grimly downturned mouth, and forceful chin. Alexander must have trusted him to put him in command of the Epigonoi, the greatest embodiment of the young king's dream. Many of these thirty thousand young men of Asia, trained up in the closely guarded complexities of the Macedonian phalanx, would have fought for Seleucus as he consolidated the core of Alexander's eastern empire. With his mixed army of Macedonians and Epigonoi fighting from Turkey to India over a period of twenty-eight years, and his children from an Asian mother creating a dynasty of Greek culture and mixed blood, Seleucus provided something extraordinarily close to a true achievement of Alexander's ambition.* For all the war and anarchy at his death, Alexander's *pothos* did not die without fulfillment.

The Seleucids ruled their Greek kingdom in Asia until 63 BC. For most of this time Mesopotamia was the center of their power. The cultural legacy of the Seleucids and the other Greek dynasties of Asia that followed Alexander is known as Hellenism. Essentially it was what Alexander seems, by his actions, to have contemplated, and something far more Asian than what Aristotle appears to have imagined. The Seleucid dynasty lasted a remarkable two and a half centuries yet is often

---

chaotic, seething peoples. They passed—wild-eyed, jabbering strangers—over a land not theirs, which they saw only as a place to devour and destroy . . . They were hordes of Gauls, or, as the Greeks called them, Galatians." Edwyn Robert Bevan, *The House of Seleucus*, 2 vols. (London: Edward Arnold, 1902), vol. 1, pp. 135–136.

* "Always lying in wait for the neighboring nations, strong in arms and persuasive in council, he [Seleucus] acquired Mesopotamia, Armenia, 'Seleucid' Cappadocia, Persis, Parthia, Bactria, Arabia, Tapouria, Sogdia, Arachosia, Hyrcania, and other adjacent peoples that had been subdued by Alexander, as far as the river Indus, so that the boundaries of his empire were the most extensive in Asia after that of Alexander. The whole region from Phrygia to the Indus was subject to Seleucus." In ca. 310–305 BC Seleucus gave up India and a daughter to Chandragupta Maurya in return for five hundred war elephants. Appian, *The Roman History*, vol. 1 (New York: George Bell and Sons, 1899), p. 55.

The Hellenistic World

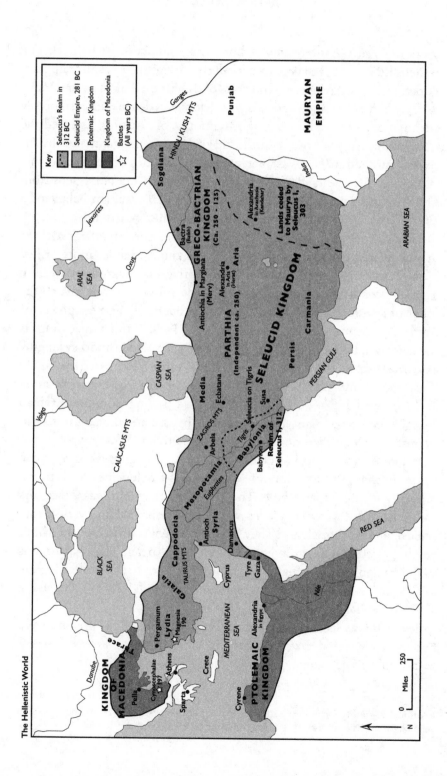

Key

- Seleucus's Realm in 312 BC
- Seleucid Empire, 281 BC
- Ptolemaic Kingdom
- Kingdom of Macedonia
- ☆ Battles (All years BC)

MAURYAN EMPIRE

Punjab

Ganges

HINDU KUSH MTS

Sogdiana

GRECO-BACTRIAN KINGDOM (Ca. 250 - 125)

Bactra (Balkh)

Alexandria in Arachosia (Kandahar)

Lands ceded to Maurya by Seleucus I, 303

Indus

ARABIAN SEA

Jaxartes

Oxus

ARAL SEA

Alexandria in Aria (Herat)

Aria

Antiochia in Margiana (Merv)

PARTHIA (Independent ca. 250)

SELEUCID KINGDOM

Carmania

Persis

PERSIAN GULF

CASPIAN SEA

Media

Ecbatana

Seleucia on Tigris

Susa

Volga

CAUCASUS MTS

ZAGROS MTS

Arbela

Tigris

Mesopotamia

Euphrates

Babylon

Babylonia

Realm of Seleucus I, 312

BLACK SEA

Cappadocia

TAURUS MTS

Galatia

Pergamum

Lydia

☆ Magnesia 190

Antioch

Syria

Damascus

Cyprus

Tyre

Gaza

RED SEA

Nile

KINGDOM OF MACEDONIA

Thrace

Pella

☆ Cynoscephalae 197

Athens

Sparta

MEDITERRANEAN SEA

Crete

Cyrene

Alexandria in Egypt

PTOLEMAIC KINGDOM

0   250

Miles

N

overlooked in the memories of both East and West. At its peak, the Hellenistic world in Asia covered modern Turkey, the Levant, Iraq, Iran, Turkmenistan, Afghanistan, and parts of Tajikistan, Pakistan, and India.

In 275, Seleucus's son Antiochus, who had succeeded his father smoothly but then encountered an enormous amount of fighting, defeated the Galatians in Asia Minor "with the aid of sixteen elephants sent by his general in Bactria."* It was an event that said much about the Seleucids: almost fifty years after Alexander, elephants were being sent from Afghanistan to defend the Hellenistic world in Turkey on behalf of a king, son of a Greek father and a Persian mother, based in Iraq.

The fifth Seleucid king after Seleucus himself, Antiochus III (r. 222–187 BC), recreated the Asian empires of Cyrus and Alexander more or less in their entireties in the course of a thirty-five-year reign that saw him, like Seleucus himself, fighting almost constantly from one end to the other of Alexander's domains. Had it not been for the new power of Rome, Antiochus III, who gave himself the Persian title Great King, as Alexander had done, would probably have succeeded in another lengthy extension of Alexander's project. In 206 BC Antiochus crossed the Hindu Kush. "Once more a Macedonian king at the head of his army stood at the door of India."[12] The next year he was sailing along the Arabian coast of the Persian Gulf. Four years later he embarked on his third war against his fellow Macedonian dynasts, the Ptolemies of Egypt.

In 190, Antiochus lost a major battle, at Magnesia in western Lydia, to the Romans. At the time of Magnesia, the Seleucids were strong, probably stronger than Rome. Their Macedonian vigor was intact, and six kings into the dynasty they were more robust than ever—a rare achievement in those lands. They possessed the wealth of the old Asiatic empire, stretching from India to the Mediterranean. The phalanx was still formidable; as a formation it had lost but once to the Roman legion, in a battle between the Romans and the Antigonid dynasty in Macedon at Cynoscephalae in northern Greece in 197.

The Romans seem mostly to have entered Asia Minor preemptively, because they feared that Antiochus III, after his huge successes in the east, would attack them next. At Magnesia, he was winning until his own

---

* Antiochus had five children with his former stepmother. The first of these, named Seleucus after his grandfather, was executed for rebellion in about 267 BC.

elephants panicked and broke the phalanxes.* The Battle of Magnesia, often forgotten, marked an important moment in history. Rome's victory over the Macedonians of Asia pushed the border between East and West well into Asia: from the Bosphorus into the highlands of Turkey. Severing the Seleucid connection to Europe, Magnesia initiated the gradual disintegration of Greek Asia. Ironically, the berserk pachyderms of Magnesia, an Asian importation from lands far to the east of even Persia, initiated the unraveling, in Freya Stark's words, of "the unifying dream of Alexander, which the Seleucid dynasty alone among the 'Successors' had, however imperfectly and perhaps unintentionally, prolonged."†

At the end, exhausted by the struggles with Rome, the Seleucid kingdom shrunk to a few cities in northern Syria. Antioch (now Antakya in southern Turkey), founded by Seleucus and named for his heir, was the Seleucid capital from 240 BC until the end. Over time, as the Seleucids receded, smaller Greek kingdoms emerged as far east as northern India. The Greco-Bactrian kings, who rebelled against the Seleucids in 250 BC, reigned until 125 BC. The Greco-Indian kingdoms, initially offshoots of the Greco-Bactrians, survived from 180 BC to about 10 AD; communities of Greeks survived in India for another two or three hundred years.

As Stark writes, the Seleucids "had kept the passage into farther Asia open as a bridge" from Europe. When the Seleucids finally fell, the Romans would close this passage. The bridge became a "frontier."[13] Under the Greek kings in Asia, a more or less constant stream of Greeks had flowed eastward, mostly from Ionia and Anatolia. For 260 years, from Syria to Afghanistan, founding new colonies and cities or joining those

---

* At Magnesia, Antiochus's experienced phalanxes were at least a match for the Romans. It was when a Roman ally directed his missiles at Antiochus's elephants that the beasts panicked and rampaged through the Macedonian phalanxes. The Roman general facing Antiochus the Great at Magnesia was Scipio Africanus, the conqueror of Hannibal. Hannibal, meanwhile, having finally been defeated by the Romans in 202 BC, had since 195 been an exile in the court of Antiochus, and later, in 190 BC, commanded a Seleucid fleet that was itself defeated by the Romans. Hannibal well knew by then the dangers of including elephants in one's order of battle.

† Despite the role of the elephants, Magnesia is generally taken as the watershed from which dates the gradual eclipse of the Macedonian phalanx by the more flexible "maniple" formation of the Roman legions.

laid down by Alexander and Seleucus, the Greeks and Macedonians east
of modern-day Turkey mixed gradually with the local populations. Typically, the colonists would be given land somewhere near a Greek city
such as Seleucia-on-Tigris. In return, they would promise military service to the crown. The colonies that particularly grew and prospered
were awarded the status of cities by the local Hellenistic kings, who
also founded cities of their own. There were at least twenty Seleucias
in what is now Turkey, Jordan, Syria, Iraq, and Iran.

Politically, in Hellenistic terms, the "city" meant something specific:
a formal status, established by the king, involving autonomous local
government by an electoral class of citizens. Among these polities there
were scores of smaller royal cities—local Alexandrias, Seleucias, and
Antiochs—but also larger metropolises old and new, such as a revital-
ized Susa, or Herat (founded as Alexandria-in-Aria, Aria being the old
Achaemenid Persian satrapy where Herat was located), which would
become the great Persian city in what is now western Afghanistan. The
Hellenistic cities incorporated such Greek features as the gymnasium,
the agora, the charter or constitution that made law the paramount
arbiter, and the accompanying political culture of debate and consent.

At the higher levels of politics, however, the Hellenistic cities were
members of states that were organized according to the Asiatic—to use
the classical expression—not the Greek, model. The Seleucids in Asia and
the Ptolemies in Egypt were the two lasting Macedonian dynasties. In
contrast to Macedonian traditions, these Asiatic monarchies were absolute: "these kings were the state" as absolutely as had been the Persian
or Egyptian monarchs before them. In contrast to life under Cyrus, Alexander, and the Roman emperors to come, for people in these personal
states of the Diadochi, no membership in a "national" or "imperial"
identity was on offer.[14]

Like Alexander, the Seleucids grounded their imperial administration
in the old Achaemenid system. They divided their realm into satrapies
and maintained the Persian roads and postal system. The Seleucids did
not install Persians as satraps to nearly the extent that Alexander had
done. Ultimately this, a departure from the policy that had seen their
own founder marry a Persian, contributed to their fall. Like Cyrus and
Alexander, the early Seleucids took care to support Babylonian traditions.
The use of cuneiform in local literature experienced a revival, Antiochus

I continued Alexander's work restoring the Esagila temple at Babylon, and in Uruk under Seleucus himself the worship of the ancient city gods was reestablished.[15]

The colonies and cities of the Hellenistic world quickly became commercial entrepôts. Growing and growing through five and ten generations and more, they offered hitherto unknown opportunities to the local people who chose to join them. The Hellenistic outposts were influential neighbors. Often, when the Seleucid colonies obtained land, the peasants, serfs, or slaves associated with the territory were immediately freed. Most of the time those who did not receive instant manumission were freed eventually. These people in turn fed their potential into the system, often becoming citizens or at least organizing themselves in emulation of Greek cities.[16]

With the maturing of the Hellenistic cities, significant intermarriage occurred in many of them. Alexander had settled his new cities with Macedonian or Greek colonists, frequently "broken soldiers" or retired veterans. As the Seleucid kings saw the value of the thriving city system, they attached more and more territory to the cities, whether by direct gift or sale of "king's land," or through forced transfers of feudal lands.[17] The people—Asian, Greek, and mixed—of this period of new freedoms and new energies, of a new Greek archipelago dotted across the eastern expanse, were in almost every way the grandchildren of Alexander and his men.

The Seleucids did not promote their Greek gods. Local religions carried on as before. Often the local faiths were encouraged, with their temples included in the street planning—as at Dura Europos in eastern Syria—or even built by the Hellenistic city governments. The local gods were frequently embraced by the Greeks and often became conflated with Greek deities, as happened also in many places with the deified Alexander and his ancestor Hercules. In other cases, it was the Greek gods that were embraced by the local people.

The Persian system that the Seleucids inherited from Alexander included vast areas belonging to many "temple states." In Iraq, these often had roots going back to Sumerian times. The priests managing these states may later have claimed descent from Hercules or some other Greek god-hero, but "the *system* had never changed."[18] Any imperative for it to change itself is hard to imagine. A high priest, a role which was usually hereditary, had complete authority over the peasants on these lands. They paid their taxes to him, and provided their daughters to him as "temple slaves, many of them sacred prostitutes." Once the temple prostitutes had fulfilled their duty, in Seleucid days as before, they returned to their peasant communities bringing prestige to their pious families.[19]

The Seleucid period in Iraq lasted from 312 until 129 BC, when Antiochus VII permanently lost Babylonia to a new wave of invaders, the Parthians. Seleucia-on-Tigris became the Parthian capital, but the city remained thoroughly Greek in language and culture. By the end of this period, the Greek cities of the east were predominantly local by blood, despite the near-constant flow of new Greek arrivals.

There was a high degree of artistic syncretism, if not of true synthesis, as Hellenistic art absorbed Asian traditions. In much of today's Afghanistan, northern Pakistan, and northern India—the lands of the Greco-Bactrian and Greco-Indian kingdoms—the Greeks tended to perceive an affinity of sorts with their Buddhist neighbors. The encounter led to the development of a Greco-Buddhist artistic form that was still thriving a millennium later when it was brought to a halt by the Muslim conquests of the late seventh century AD.*

In Syria, the Seleucid calendar—with its Year One at 312 BC, when Seleucus took Babylon for the first time—was used into the twelfth century AD. In Central Asia, Eastern Christian gravestones using the Seleucid calendar date to as recently as the fourteenth century AD.

Science was another element of the fusion that dominated Iraq and the world around it during the Hellenistic centuries. Alexander on his grand comet ride had assiduously sent back to Aristotle and others a stream of information relating to a variety of sciences, from zoology and botany to geography and ethnology. But his greatest contribution in this regard was probably his exposure of the Greeks to the achievements of Babylonian science.[20] The classical Greek picture of the heavens as divided into the twelve familiar houses of the Zodiac is pure Babylonian astrology, transmitted in the Hellenistic period. The five planets that are

---

* The destruction by the Afghan Taliban of the huge Greco-Buddhist statues at Bamiyan in 2001 was a development in this long clash of outlooks.

visible to the human eye as they travel across the heavens all originally derived their identities from the ancient Babylonian gods. Our planet Jupiter was known to the Babylonians as Marduk. The planet named after Ishtar, goddess of love, is the one we know today as Venus. The planet of Nergal, god of war, was the same heavenly body that we call Mars.

Meanwhile the Greeks improved calculations that the Babylonians had been making for centuries. The result of this combination was a flourishing of the mathematical sciences in Seleucid Iraq. A Hellenistic Babylonian working around 300 BC, Kidenas of Sippar, calculated the length of a solar year at three hundred and sixty-five days, forty-one minutes, and four seconds. He was five hours, seven minutes, and forty-two seconds short.[21]

Sparked by the "Chaldean" mathematicians of Babylon, the surge of Greek science and learning in Asia during the century after Alexander would be the greatest flowering of rational enquiry for the next thousand years. Then, in the eighth century AD, the rise of an Iranian-Arab dynasty, the Abbasids, in their new city of Baghdad—fifteen miles from Seleucia—led to a rediscovery of the genius of the ancient Greeks, including in large measure the Hellenistic Greeks. Through the geometry of Euclid (fl. ca. 295 BC), the physics of Archimedes (d. ca. 212 BC), and the mathematics and geography of Ptolemy (d. ca. 170 AD; the Greek geometer and geographer from Alexandria-in-Egypt shared a name with the dynasty that ruled there), Hellenistic science defined the physical world of the West and the Middle East until modern times.

In Iraq, while Babylon died with the rise of Seleucia, the ancient Mesopotamian culture as something discrete and more or less distinct died with it. Over a few generations Iraq, culturally, became mostly Greek. Even the gods were Hellenized. Marduk and Ishtar disappeared from view as Zeus and Aphrodite replaced them in the archaeological record. The new cities with their Greek freedoms simply had more power, more energy, more wealth, and more appeal than their local neighbors. So ancient Iraq perished with Babylon.

The extraordinary phenomenon of Hellenism affected daily life in Mesopotamia and the surrounding lands on many levels. In what is today Iranian Kurdistan, commercial contracts have been found from the Hellenistic period that were written in Greek between parties with local names; the Greek language was being used, for business at any rate, by indigenous people as well as by Greeks. In modern-day Georgia, Greek inscriptions exist from the period in areas where Greeks never lived, and to which they traveled rarely if at all.

In India, Greek was used on coins six hundred years after the death of Alexander. Susa, the ancient Elamite and Persian capital, became a Greek city until the Romans arrived at the end of the first century AD.

In the generations that followed Alexander, the Greek kings of Asia never softened into decadence. After two and a half centuries, the Seleucids died fighting, crushed between two rising powers. In the west it was Rome, entrenched in Asia since the defeat of Antiochus the Great at Magnesia in 190 BC. In the east it was the muscular new Iranian power known as the Parthian Empire.

By 129 BC, the Seleucids, severely weakened by their encounters with Rome, had lost Babylonia as well as western Iran—ancient Media in the north, Elam in the south—to the Parthians. The Seleucids then struggled on in Syria for a further seven decades. Of Seleucus's thirty successors in the dynasty that he founded, only one—Antiochus I, his son and immediate successor—died peacefully in his bed. And although Antiochus died quietly, it was still the fighting that killed him. He was worn out by nineteen years of "the task bequeathed him by Seleucus . . . typical of his house, indefatigably busy in keeping the unwieldy empire together, hurrying from one end of it to the other, fighting almost incessantly."

The only other quiet death in the dynasty was achieved by Demetrius III, the twentieth Seleucid monarch, who expired in captivity in Parthia in 88 BC. All of the others died in violence of some kind. At least twelve perished at war against outsiders. Three were killed by their wives.

By the time of the Seleucids' final demise, with the murder of Antiochus XIII at Roman instigation in 64 BC, Iraq had become in essence a Greek borderland between Parthia and Rome. Meanwhile Hellenism did not end with the Seleucids and Ptolemies. Rome looked to the Greeks for high culture, and "the Greece that taught Rome" was Greece not of the Classical age but of the Hellenistic period. To the extent that subsequent Western civilization was based on the ancient Greek culture via Rome, the inheritance was largely Hellenistic.[22]

Chapter 7

Borderland

Romans, Parthians, and Sasanians, 100 BC–630 AD

> On horse they go to war, to banquets, to public and private tasks and
> on them they travel, stay still, do business and chat.
> —Justinus, second-century AD Roman historian,
> on the Parthians[1]

The Parthians were originally Scythians: fair-skinned, flaxen-haired
nomads from the grasslands north of the Black Sea and Caucasus Mountains, modern-day Ukraine and southern Russia. Herodotus devoted
forty pages in Book IV of his *Histories* to the Scythians, these Parthian
ancestors, and the unsuccessful attempt of Darius the Persian to conquer
them.

According to Herodotus, the Scythian drank the blood of the first
man he killed, sewed a cloak from the scalps of his enemies, and drank
from their skulls.[2] He threw hemp seeds on the coals of his sauna, we
are told, "and howled with pleasure" from the cannabis smoke. A party
of young Scythians, hoping, perhaps, to breed the perfect warrior, once
seduced a group of Amazons on the shores of the Sea of Azov, and
settled with them a few days' ride inland.*

---

* Herodotus also has this to say about the Scythians: "The Scythians, however, though
in other respects I do not admire them, have managed one thing, and that the most
important in human affairs, better than anyone else on the face of the earth: I mean their
own preservation . . . A people without fortified towns, living, as the Scythians do, in
wagons which they take with them wherever they go, accustomed, one and all to fight
on horseback with bows and arrows, and dependent for their food not on agriculture
but upon their cattle: how can such a people fail to defeat the attempt of an invader?"

In about 680 BC, some of these blue- and green-eyed horsemen rode south over the Caucasus and from there moved east to what became the Achaemenid and Seleucid province of Parthia in northeast Iran. Parthia eventually became the Iranian province of Khorasan. When the proto-Parthians arrived there, the great powers of the world south of the Caspian and Black Seas were the Medes in the east and the Assyrians in the west. In the 630s BC, the ancestors of the Parthians forced the Medes into tribute, until a Median king murdered the drunken Parthian chiefs at a banquet. The Parthians then raided their way to Egypt and back and, in an alliance with the Assyrians, briefly helped to rescue Ashur-banipal's Nineveh from the Medes not long before the great city—and with it Sardanapalus, in Greek accounts—fell to the Babylonian-Median alliance in 612 BC. Some accounts say the Scythians had become a part of that alliance.

In power the Parthians reflected the Greek mood that prevailed in the East after Alexander. After driving the Seleucids from Iraq and Iran in the 140s BC, the first Parthian king appended to his name the official sobriquet *Philhellene*, "friend of the Greeks." His successors called themselves this for six or seven generations into the time of Christ. Plutarch relates a story about Orodes II, the Parthian king at the time of their great defeat of the Romans at Carrhae in 53 BC. Orodes was attending his son's wedding in Armenia when the battle took place. Orodes and the Armenian king, the brother of the bride, were watching Euripides's play *The Bacchae*, starring the Greek actor Jason of Tralles, when a messenger brought in the head of the Roman general Crassus—during the very scene in which Queen Agave arrives at court with the head of the son she has killed in a Bacchic frenzy. The trophy was put to use as the severed head in the play, "to the joy and acclamations of the Parthian company."[3]

In the centuries that followed, Iraq was to play a new role in history. Mesopotamia, and specifically the Euphrates, now formed the eastern part of what the Romans called the *limes*.* This was the limit, the frontier: the border between civilization, as the Romans saw it in a distinct echo of the Greeks, within the *limes* and barbarism without. The meeting

---

* In Roman Britain, the principal *limes* was Hadrian's Wall; in Continental Europe, the *limes Germanicus* mostly followed the Rhine and the Danube.

place, in the great scheme that has prevailed ever since Alexander, continued to be Mesopotamia. The land between the rivers both joined and
separated the region's two constantly warring empires of East and West.

Humanism retreats from the stage during most of this period. There
was the surface Hellenism of both the Parthians and the Romans; the
ethical ideals of Zoroaster went largely underground; the Jews of the
region were quiet; communities of scientists and Neoplatonist philosophers did their isolated work.

Meanwhile, at the forefront of events, the seven-century embrace that
now bound Iran and Rome was to prove uniquely intimate among the
great power relations of ancient history.* The Romans took Ctesiphon—
the Parthian and then Sasanian capital, originally a Parthian village next
to Seleucia-on-Tigris—five times. On several other occasions they fought
battles outside the city. But however frequently Rome marched into
central and southern Mesopotamia, Iraq remained essentially a part of
the Iranian empire of the day, and home to that empire's capital, from
shortly after the retreat of the Seleucids until the Muslim invasions in
the seventh century AD.

During the early centuries of their empire, it was not remarkable for
the Romans to find themselves negotiating a border or a treaty with a
Parthian warlord who was himself a Roman citizen, or for a consul of
Rome to be a grandson of a Parthian king. Parthian hostages in Rome
"soon became familiar sights, seated in the theatre or driven by Caligula
in his chariot." Pliny the Elder wrote that the Parthian nobility "smell
from too much wine" and put lemon pips in their water as an antidote.[4]

"Like the Achaemenian monarchs who moved from Susa to Persepolis
and again to Ecbatana," wrote Sir Percy Sykes, the Edwardian brigadier
whose *History of Persia* remains the best work on the subject, "the Parthian court spent the winter in Mesopotamia and the summer in Media
and Parthia. Its winter capital was Ctesiphon, built on the left bank of
the Tigris opposite Seleucia and a few miles from Baghdad."[5] It was a
measure of the ongoing strength of Seleucia through the Parthian period
that the Greek city fathers of Seleucus's original capital were able to
keep the Parthians out of their city. Ctesiphon was originally a nomad

---

* For Iran this meant first the Parthians and, after 224 AD, the Sasanian dynasty. For
Rome, the capital moved to Constantinople in 324 AD.

settlement that grew at the feet of Seleucia—just across the Tigris—took root, and eventually became a great city in its own right.[6]

Under the Sasanians, the dynasty that succeeded the Parthians, Ctesiphon was in turn to become the largest city in the world, and remain so until the Muslim conquest in 637 AD.[7] Strabo, the first-century AD Greek geographer, described Ctesiphon's village roots, even as an imperial capital:

In ancient times Babylon was the metropolis of Assyria; but now Seleucia is the metropolis, I mean the Seleucia on the Tigris, as it is called. Nearby is situated a village called Ctesiphon, a large village. This village the kings of the Parthians were wont to make their winter residence, thus sparing the Seleucians, in order that the Seleucians might not be oppressed by having the Scythian folk or soldiery quartered among them. Because of the Parthian power, therefore, Ctesiphon is a city rather than a village; its size is such that it lodges a great number of people, and it has been equipped with buildings by the Parthians themselves; and it has been provided by the Parthians with wares for sale and with the arts that are pleasing to the Parthians.

Babylon seems to have survived, temporarily, the prosperity of Seleucus's eponymous neighboring capital. The following description of a Parthian royal palace near Ctesiphon (at Babylon, in fact) is taken from the Roman historian Philostratus (d. ca. 250 AD):

The palace is roofed with brass and a bright light flashes from it. It has chambers for the women, and chambers for the men, and porticoes, partly glittering with silver, partly with cloth-of-gold embroideries, partly with solid slabs of gold, let into the walls, like pictures. The subjects of the embroidery are taken from the Greek mythology, and include representations of Andromeda and of Orpheus . . . You behold the occupation of Athens and the battle of Thermopylae and a canal cut through Athos . . . One chamber for the men has a roof fashioned into a vault like the heavens, composed entirely of sapphires, which are the bluest of stones, and resemble the sky in color.[8]

From the women's separate quarters, where the ladies of the harem were veiled, to the vaulted sapphire-blue dome, to the depictions of Athens and Thermopylae, it is hard to imagine a more evenly balanced fusion of the Greek and the Persian than this sparkling Parthian palace at Babylon. The great blue vault no doubt reminded the Parthians of their other inheritance: the wide warrior steppes of the north.

The Parthians' strong preoccupation, in Iraq and beyond, with the culture of Alexander was more than a manifestation of the substantial prestige of the Macedonian and his successors. Indeed it was more than simply a matter of the proven appeal of Greek civilization in its own right, an attraction evident in Iranian lands long before Alexander. In much of the Persian Empire, especially Iraq, the elite of the Parthians' towns and cities remained Greek. The Parthians required the cooperation of these rich and vigorous Greek communities in their centuries of struggle with Rome.

For the first four Parthian centuries, Seleucia-on-Tigris thrived and remained thoroughly Greek in the image that Alexander had encouraged. Hatra, a hundred miles north of Baghdad, was distinctly Hellenistic in style, its columns, arches, and plinths crude reflections of the Parthenon or Paestum.* Parthian royal palaces as far east as Turkmenistan were visibly Greek in style, and Greek plays and poems were produced for many a Parthian royal wedding, as The Bacchae was staged at the wedding of Orodes's daughter.

The Parthians ruled Iraq and Iran for almost five centuries, from 247 BC to 227 AD. The longest-lived of any of Iran's dynasties, they made little cultural contribution to the world apart from keeping a vestigial day-to-day Hellenism alive in their territories for two or three additional centuries. Not very much remains of the Parthians' buildings, their written works, or their plastic arts. What does remain, as at Hatra, is undoubtedly handsome but shows little that is new.

The Parthians were dramatic nevertheless. They were a dynasty of fratricides and parricides, of favorite queens who murdered their kings, of princely exiles to Rome who grew to manhood in the West and

---

* Hatra is the greatest Parthian city still to some extent standing in the early twenty-first century.

returned to the East to scheme and murder their way to the throne. Tacitus gives a nice insight into Parthian politics when he explains of a Parthian prince hostage in Rome that the young man had been sent there "not so much from dread of us [i.e., the Romans] as from distrust of the loyalty of his countrymen." Occasionally the Parthian dynastic tree was watered with strong new nomad blood from the vast prairies to the north.

The great Iranian dynasties that came before and after the Parthians were much more Persian in their origins or adopted identity than the Parthians were. Unlike the other major dynasties of ancient Iran, the Parthians did not bring the harem world of eunuchs and queen mothers into a significant place in their politics.[9] The only woman to figure significantly in their history was one "Musa, the Italian slave girl."[10] The Roman emperor Augustus sent Musa to the Parthian king Phraates IV (d. 2 BC).* After bearing her new master a son, Musa persuaded Phraates to send his four prior sons off to Rome, where they would be little better than hostages. Phraates then made the concubine his queen. His reward came when she conspired with their son to poison him. Musa then married the boy.† For two years, before he disappeared from history, the Parthian king was both son and husband to a Roman slave girl sent east by the subtle Augustus.[11]

Parthia's location ensured it a lucrative role as the bridge in the overland trade between China and the Roman world. The Parthians were not by nature unduly inclined toward trade. But they enjoyed the wealth it brought when they controlled it.

A fifth-century AD Chinese work known as the *Hou Hanshu*, the official annals of what became known as the Later Han dynasty (25–221 AD), tells a story, amusing in hindsight, of a Han emissary sent to try to reach the Roman Empire in 93 AD. Arriving at the head of the Persian Gulf near Susa, he wanted to continue toward Rome. The Parthians there told him this was their westernmost frontier, and that the only way thence to Rome was over treacherous waters. "The ocean is huge," they said, and

---

* Phraates, the Roman chroniclers relate, came to the throne by murdering his own father and kept it by murdering thirty brothers.

† Brother-sister marriages were not uncommon among the Parthian monarchs, as in all ancient Iranian dynasties, but a mother-son marriage was rare.

if you encounter winds that delay you, it can take two years. That is why all the men who go by sea take stores for three years. The vast ocean urges men to think of their country, and get homesick, and some of them die.

"When [Gan] Ying heard this," the history continues, "he gave up his plan."[12] The Parthians, of course, were lying to the Chinese. There was another route to Rome: the relatively easy overland route northward through Babylonia, via Palmyra to the Levantine coast, but the Parthians wanted to keep that for themselves.[13]

At Merv, just inside Parthia's eastern border, westward-bound Chinese caravans were forced to stop, unload their goods, and turn for home. Chinese silk went west in heavy brocade, and then was unraveled and rewoven into lighter weaves in the Roman Levant. The Parthians then sold the silk back to the Chinese, pretending that this more refined product had originated in the Roman Empire. The Han annals say of Rome, "The king of this country always wanted to send envoys to the Han, but Anxi [Parthia], wishing to control the trade in multi-coloured Chinese silks, blocked the route."[14]

A pioneering version of the Silk Road was opened in 115 BC, thanks to the first Sino-Parthian diplomacy. Sixty or seventy years later, Julius Caesar had silk curtains at his house in Rome.[15] Trade increased under Augustus's Pax Romana, and soon nostalgists of Rome's lost republican virtue, from Seneca to Pliny the Elder to old-fashioned senators quoted in the *Annals* of Tacitus, were bemoaning the wasteful love of silk among their contemporary countrymen: the sheer, smooth, clinging material, they complained, made matrons into harlots and men into women, denuding the Roman Empire of its wealth and the Roman family of its meritorious foundations.[16]

Chinese traders could buy other Roman goods from the merchants of Parthia: "much gold, silver, and rare precious stones, especially the 'jewel that shines at night,' 'the moonshine pearl,' 'the chicken-frightening rhinoceros stone' . . . and thin silk-cloth of various colours," according to a list that the Parthians provided to the Chinese at Merv.[17] For the forty years between 90 and 130 AD, the Han Chinese enjoyed a brief period of quiet in their far west after subduing the area around the Tak-lamakan Desert. With the Pax Romana at its peak, peace now reached "from North China to Rome, and conditions for trade were altogether more favourable than they had ever been before or were ever to be again until the establishment of the Mongolian Empire." That would be eleven centuries later.

The Parthians were as eager to intermediate easterly trade along the new Silk Roads as they were to control the trade flowing the other way from China. The *Hou Hanshou* reveals that the Romans "always desired to send embassies to China," but the Parthians would not allow it. "The An-Hsi [Parthians] wished to carry on trade with them in Chinese silks," writes the chronicler, "and it is for this reason they were cut off from communication."[18] Finally, in the year 166, the Roman emperor, one "An-tun" (likely Marcus Aurelius, second emperor of Rome's Antonine dynasty) dispatched an embassy by sea. That said, the chronicler notes that the alleged Roman offerings of "ivory, rhinoceros horns, and tortoise shell . . . contained no jewels whatever, which fact throws doubt on the tradition."

———

Century after century the ramshackle Parthian Empire went on, led by one warlike king after another struggling for survival atop a litter of contending vassals. A Parthian monarch would call himself Great King in emulation of the Achaemenids and Alexander, but an administrative empire, governed in the Persian tradition through military governors and appointed satraps, was beyond his capabilities and inclinations. Organized governance of this nature did not feature in Parthian times. Throughout it all, Iraq was little more than a bloody dance floor, and home to the capital at Ctesiphon, as the Parthian Empire lived its turbulent life, locked in the four-hundred-year waltz with Rome. The Parthians' easterly borders were comparatively quiet.

For all their disorganized shortcomings, if shortcomings they were, the Parthians possessed a unique and ineffable glamor. They wore boots and trousers in their glittering courts lest they ever forget that they were at heart horsemen of the open plains. When a prince who had grown up in exile at Rome returned home to rule as king, he provoked the contempt of his countrymen, according to Tacitus, "by his rare indulgence in the chase, by his feeble interest in horses."[19] Of the great Parthian general who won the epic victory over the Romans at Carrhae, Plutarch wrote, "Surena was the tallest and finest looking man himself, but the delicacy of his looks and effeminacy of his dress did not promise so much manhood as he was really master of, for his face was painted, and his hair parted after the fashion of the Medes, whereas the other Parthians made a more terrible appearance, with their shaggy hair gathered in a mass upon their foreheads after the Scythian mode."[20]

After one successful battle against the Romans, the Parthians made a shocking discovery: the Roman baggage train contained pornography and even stories of romantic adventure. The Vikings of the steppe were disgusted. They had been fighting against men "who were not able even in the time of war to forget such writings and practices."[21] And yet, says Plutarch, the Parthian general campaigned with "a whole Parthian Sybaris in his many wagons full of concubines." A Parthian army was "like the vipers and asps people talk of, all the foremost and most visible parts fierce and terrible with spears and arrows and horsemen, but the rear terminating in loose women and castanets, music of the lute, and midnight revelings."[22]

The Parthians appear to have disdained serious efforts at religion. Governing was similarly beneath them. Their art, originally Greek in style, focused on the hunt, the banquet, the field of battle.

Parthia's importance to Rome is difficult to overstate. For about three hundred years during Rome's most glorious days, the Parthians appear again and again in the Latin annals as the great power in the east against which Rome endlessly contends. In the west especially, different minor barbarian powers came and went, notably the scores of Germanic tribes along the Rhine and Danube. In the east, imperial Rome inhabited a world with one other player: Parthia. This great power was "a counterpoise to the power of Rome, a second figure in the picture not much inferior to the first, a rival state with Rome dividing the attention of mankind and the sovereignty of the known earth."[23]

The two empires were anchored too far apart geographically for either to hope to conquer the other, and the Parthians were far too disorganized for sustained offensive operations or occupations. But in their borderlands stretching from the Armenian highlands south through Iraq, Parthia and Rome fought again and again. The Romans saw themselves

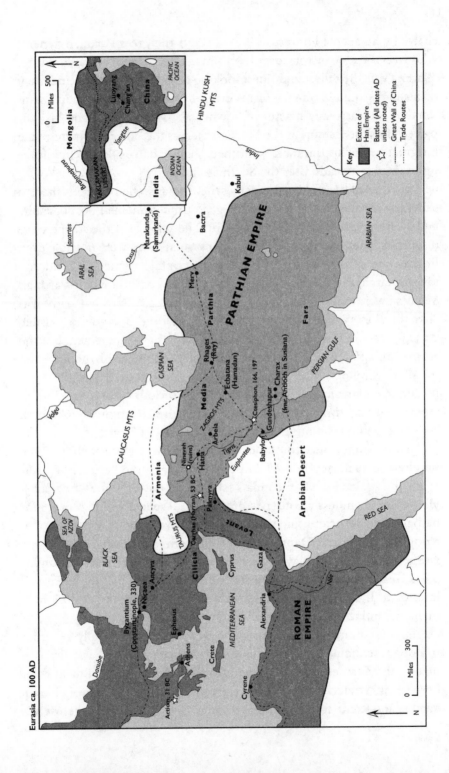

Eurasia ca. 100 AD

partly as successors to Alexander. The Parthians were rooted in the lands of Cyrus.[24] The clash was unavoidable. The casus belli usually arose in Armenia, but Mesopotamia was once again the key battleground for East and West.[25]

As the Persian Wars provided the defining crisis of ancient Greece, so the mood of Rome can be charted in the way that it responded to this great power of the East in their epic pas de deux. Later republican Rome, heir to classical Greece and with a swelling imperium of its own, inevitably faced the question of whether to resume Alexander's mission of bringing Hellenic civilization to the natural end of their world at the Indus. The Republic chose instead to set Rome's eastern border at the Euphrates. This was the relatively modest Rome, before the days of the emperors, eschewing entanglement in the East. Syria and what is now eastern Turkey, well inside the *limes*, were squarely of this Roman, Western world.

In the time of Julius Caesar (d. 44 BC), ambitious men and a wealthy state already grown imperial in size eroded Rome's republican restraint. The eastern adventure beckoned. Parthian Iraq would no longer be but a far-off frontier. It became a canvas for the ambitions of enterprising Romans.

The plutocrat Crassus, jealous of the military fame of his rival Pompey (Pompeius Magnus), was the first of these. Crassus was inspired, like many of the Romans who followed him into the East, by the success of Alexander: "He would not limit his fortune with Parthia and Syria," writes Plutarch of Crassus, "but . . . proposed in his hopes to pass as far as Bactria and India, and the utmost Ocean."[26] Crassus, however, met his death at the hands of the Parthians in 53 BC at the battle of Carrhae. The town the Romans called Carrhae was ancient Harran, the same northern Mesopotamian town where Abraham had stopped on the way from Ur to Canaan. Including the local Hellenistic settlers who augmented Crassus's army, there were about fifty thousand troops on each side when the Parthians met the Romans at Carrhae. With the mounted Parthian archers pouring arrows on top of the exhausted, thirsty, and less mobile

Roman legionaries, Crassus lost twenty-four thousand men and seven eagles. It was the worst Roman defeat since the days of Hannibal 160 years earlier.* In the thousand years of Rome's growth and greatness, Carrhae was the only defeat the Romans never managed to avenge by ultimately conquering their enemy.[27]

Crassus had famously made much of his fortune (it was perhaps the greatest in Roman history) in the slave trade, and by buying the land beneath burning buildings. After marrying his brother's widow, Crassus had been accused of becoming "too familiar with one of the vestal virgins." When an investigation discovered that Crassus had merely been trying to lay his hands on a valuable property of the virgin's, "his avarice, so to say, serving to clear him of the crime, he was acquitted." ("Nor did he leave the lady," notes Plutarch, "till he had got the estate.") In Crassus's own lifetime his cupidity was legendary even in the East. Cassius Dio, a Roman historian writing in the early third century AD, reports that after Carrhae the Parthians poured "molten gold" down the throat of his corpse.[28]

Julius Caesar, Crassus's colleague in Rome's first Triumvirate, was preparing his own invasion of Parthia when Brutus and the others murdered him in 44 BC. The plans had been drawn up, sixteen legions allocated, gold dispatched to the east, and an advance party positioned in Syria when the Ides of March came. Four years later, the Parthians raided deep into Roman Asia Minor and Syria. Four years after that, Caesar's lieutenant and co-consul Mark Antony tried his hand in the East. Inheriting Caesar's papers and with them the great man's plans for the eastern invasion, Antony assembled an army twice the size of that of Crassus.

Antony had spent much of the previous five years luxuriating with Cleopatra, last of the Macedonian *Diadochi*, in Alexandria; in 41 BC he had been in the East preparing an expedition of his own against the Parthians

---

* In the figure of Surena, the Parthian general at Carrhae, Plutarch gives an insight into the political culture that typified the Parthians. Surena was "in wealth, family, and reputation the second man in the kingdom, and in courage and prowess the first, and for bodily stature and beauty no man like him . . . and he had at least ten thousand horsemen altogether." The Surenas traditionally crowned the Parthian kings, and this Surena traveled with a thousand camels, and his concubines in two hundred chariots (Plutarch 1975, p. 664). This was the sort of vassal that a Parthian king had to live with. Surena's reward for Carrhae was to be executed soon after, "out of mere envy to his glory," according to Plutarch. *The Age of Alexander*, trans. Ian Scott-Kilvert (London: Penguin, 1973), p. 674.

when his fateful first encounter with Cleopatra postponed the project. Reading Plutarch's description of the meeting, one can only sympathize with Antony's decision to forsake, for a while, the blood-drenched sands of the *limes* for the palm-shaded terraces of the Hellenistic Egypt of the Ptolemies, whose inheritance from Alexander had been so much gentler than that of the Seleucids:

> She came sailing up the river Cydnus, in a barge with gilded stern and outspread sails of purple, while oars of silver beat time to the music of flutes and fifes and harps. She herself lay all along under a canopy of cloth of gold, dressed as Venus in a picture; and beautiful young boys, like painted Cupids, stood on each side to fan her. Her maids were dressed like sea nymphs and graces.*

When Antony finally unrolled Caesar's plans and invaded Parthia, it was a disaster almost as bad as that of Crassus. In 36 BC Antony marched into northwest Parthia, left behind and then lost his siege train on the way, unsuccessfully besieged the provincial capital of Phraaspa, and retreated back to the Syrian coast through a lethal winter. Antony had begun the adventure with an army of roughly a hundred thousand. It was said to be, "whether you consider strength and youth, or patience and sufferance in labours and fatigues," the finest a Roman general had ever assembled.[29] Invading Parthia he lost forty-two thousand of them and two eagles.[30] †
In 33 BC, looking for revenge, Antony invaded Armenia, garrisoned it with Roman troops, persuaded the king of Media into an alliance, and declared his own infant son Alexander "king of Armenia, Media

---

* It is impossible here not to quote Shakespeare's version, inspired by Plutarch (*Antony and Cleopatra*, Act 2, Scene 2):

The barge she sat in, like a burnish'd throne,
Burn'd on the water: the poop was beaten gold;
Purple the sails, and so perfumed that
The winds were love-sick with them; the oars were silver,
Which to the tune of flutes kept stroke, and made
The water which they beat to follow faster,
As amorous of their strokes. For her own person,
It beggar'd all description . . .

† Freya Stark points out that if Antony had had with him at Actium the magnificent army that he squandered in the East, the battle might have gone differently. If so, the new Rome would have been a Greek city in Egypt, and the Caesars the heirs of Alexander.

and Parthia—all the land from the Euphrates to India."[31] When Antony eventually returned west, Armenia and Media immediately reverted to the Parthian orbit and the new Roman garrisons were massacred.

After Octavian, adopted son of Julius Caesar, defeated Antony and Cleopatra at Actium in 31 BC, he became—as Augustus Caesar—the first Roman emperor. In the ashes of the Republic, Augustus decided that Rome and her dominions required above all else peace, stability, and good governance.* Reintroducing what Gibbon calls "a spirit of moderation" into Roman foreign policy, Augustus once more set the Roman world's eastern boundary at the Euphrates.[32] "Instead of exposing his person and his legions to the arrows of the Parthians," Augustus "obtained, by an honourable treaty, the restitution of the standards and prisoners which had been taken in the defeat of Crassus."[33]

Under Nero, the Roman forays across the Euphrates began again. Nero died in 68 AD, leaving behind him, as Caesar had done, plans for a major invasion of Parthian territory. But not until 114 AD did the century-long Pax Romana established by Augustus truly come to an end in the East. The emperor Trajan invaded Armenia, declared it a full province of Rome, and then invaded northern Mesopotamia the next year. In the spring of 116, having just sent a formal announcement to the Roman senate of the annexation of the two rich territories, Trajan could have returned home in glory. Instead he made his way farther east, across the Tigris, to Arbela (current-day Erbil), site of Alexander's great victory over Darius at Gaugamela and at that time capital of the Jewish kingdom known as Adiabene.

Passing by Nineveh, Trajan followed the Tigris south into Babylonia. "He was drawn thither by the reputation of Alexander," writes Cassius Dio, "to whom he performed funeral honours in the very place where he died." Again there is Alexander, towering over every imagination, almost five centuries later. But the land of Babylon was a disappointment to Trajan. "He found nothing that answered his expectation. There was nothing but Fables and Ruines."[34] The Roman took Parthian Ctesiphon after a siege of some sort and seems to have entered next-door Greek Seleucia unopposed. He then sailed down to Charax at the head of the

---

* Mark Antony and Octavian were brothers-in-law at the time of their clash at Actium, Antony still being married to Octavian's sister even after traveling east and falling in love with Cleopatra.

Persian Gulf, not far from present-day Basra. There, watching a mer-
chantman set sail for India, ruing that he was too old to follow Alexander
farther east, Trajan gave himself the surname Parthicus, and struck coins
inscribed with PERSIA CAPTA. Leaving behind him the fleet and a statue
of himself, he turned for home and the celebratory triumph that was
the yearning of every ambitious Roman.[35] *

Trajan died on the way, in Cilicia, on the Turkish coast in 117 AD, very
near where Cleopatra had presented herself to Antony and delayed for
years his own eastern fling. Revolts, especially among the Jews of the
eastern diaspora, were exploding along Trajan's trail, and his expeditionary army was now back in Syria. His successor Hadrian immediately
retreated back across the Euphrates as part of a broad settlement with
the Parthians.† Trajan's Mesopotamian adventure had achieved nothing
except to hasten the death of a brilliant emperor.[36]

When Rome and Parthia were not at war in this period, peace reigned
from east to west across Eurasia. Three of Trajan's successors followed
suit in marching against Parthia. Most of these conflicts brought Rome
little but distraction and expense. The thrusting conquistador projects
of the emperors Lucius Verus, Septimius Severus, and Caracalla are
poignant in hindsight: a succession of ringing imperial names bringing
their endless and costly campaigns beyond the *limes* of the Euphrates to
fight against a chaotic power that rarely attacked Rome, never succumbed
to her, usually lost to her, and occasionally defeated her spectacularly.

---

* On the way back from the Gulf, Trajan was forced to retake Seleucia from the previously
friendly Greeks. He had tightened tariffs in Babylonia, leading to a revolt as the Hellenistic
merchant culture of southern Iraq "crashed like a hailstorm around him . . . Seleucia
turned for the first time against the westerners." Freya Stark, *Rome on the Euphrates*
(London: John Murray, 1966), p. 212. Trajan sent two legions to retake the city, which
they burnt. It recovered fairly quickly.

† In an episode with echoes of Alexander and Darius, Trajan had captured at Susa a daughter of the Parthian emperor and a golden throne of some importance to the dynasty. As
part of his broad peace with the Eastern power, Hadrian had then returned the daughter
and promised to return the throne. The Romans never did return the throne. Following a
failed attempt by the Parthians to persuade them to do so in perhaps 139 AD, history has
little record of Parthian politics for the next decade or two. Rawlinson notes that Roman
history is equally spare during these years. A reflection upon this curious, brief moment
of historical quiet occasioned Gibbon's famous verdict on history itself: "little more than
the register of the crimes, follies, and misfortunes of mankind." George Rawlinson, *The
Sixth Great Oriental Monarchy* (London, 1873), p. 322; Edward Gibbon, *The History of the
Decline and Fall of the Roman Empire* (New York: Everyman's Library, 1993), p. 89.

The strange symbiosis did not always involve war. Sometimes Rome and Parthia supported each other, sometimes they stood apart but did not fight. At one point, in the 70s AD, "the Parthians being at war with other people and demanding succor of Vespasian," writes Cassius Dio, the Roman emperor "refused them, saying, that he did not concern himself with the affairs of others."[37]

In keeping with the ancient reputation of Babylon, sensuality and the lure of wealth were hallmarks of the Roman experience in the East during this period. The principal city of the Roman Orient, the key staging point for most of these wars, was Antioch (now Antakya in eastern Turkey, on the Syrian border), last holdout of the Seleucids until 63 BC.

Under the emperor Commodus, at the request of the Antiochenes, a festival known as the Maiouma had been established, devoted to Aphrodite and Bacchus. The rites, known as the Orgies, celebrating the mysteries of the two gods, comprised a "thirty days festival of all-night revels."[38] According to the French historian Ernest Renan, sometimes something of a fantasist, "troupes of courtezans swarmed in public in basins filled with limpid water. This fete was like an intoxication, a dream of Sardanapalus, where all the pleasures, all the debaucheries, not excluding some of a more delicate kind, were unrolled pell-mell."[39]

The Romans were well aware of all of this. Their sense of the East, going back at least to Antony's first encounter with Cleopatra, mixed danger with the hope of wealth and glory, and honey with blood.

The Romans took the Parthian capital at Ctesiphon three times in a little over a century, between 166 and 273, and sacked it twice. In 197 Septimius Severus enslaved one hundred thousand women and children of Ctesiphon, after a complete massacre of its men. Severus eventually abandoned the ruined city when his starving troops, forced to live on roots, succumbed to mass dysentery. Septimius Severus would call himself "Parthicus Maximus," as would three other Roman emperors.* The emperor Caracalla, obsessed with Alexander, raided his way to Ctesiphon and back in the years 215–217. On the way home to Rome, at the age of twenty-nine, he was murdered at Carrhae by a bodyguard while urinating at the side of a road.[40]

---

* Aurelian was the last to do so, after sacking Palmyra in 273.

For most of this time the *limes* remained the Euphrates. Any imperial territories beyond the river were never, after Trajan, full provinces of Rome. Standing watch over the border between East and West from their stations in Mesopotamia, the Parthian cataphracts, armored cavalrymen with lance and sword on huge armored horses, immortalized by numerous Roman authors, threw a stern and rather magnificent shadow over the Western memory.* They "shone like lightning in their breastplates and helmets of polished Margianian steel,"† Plutarch writes of the cataphracts at Carrhae, "with their horses covered with brass and steel trappings."[41]

The Seleucids and Romans, learning from the Iranian powers, developed cataphracts of their own, eventually leading to the mounted knight of medieval Europe. At the epic defeat of Crassus's Romans at Carrhae in 53 BC, the Parthian cataphracts with their long spears "ran through two men at a time, making large and mortal wounds."[42]

The Greeks of southern Iraq—Babylonia—could have been most helpful to the Romans in these wars, but Rome spurned the opportunity.

In 165 AD, Avidius Crassus, a general of the emperor Lucius Verus, arrived at the Parthian capital's Greek neighbor, Seleucia. A thriving city "of almost four hundred thousand," it "still retained its Hellenistic characteristics."[43] The Greeks of Seleucia welcomed the Romans, their cousins in Hellenism, into their five-hundred-year-old city, still one of the largest in the world.‡ The Romans burnt it to the ground. Where Trajan had merely called himself "Parthicus," Lucius Verus used the "Parthicus Maximus." A year later, Lucius Verus's far more famous co-emperor, Marcus Aurelius, assumed the title too. By 167 AD, both

---

* The specific historical origins of heavily armored cavalry, including the breeding of suitable horses, are not clear, but by about 1000 BC there are traces of the phenomenon emerging across the belt from northern Mesopotamia (Assyria) to northern Iran and western Central Asia.

† Margiana was a region northeast of Parthia, mostly comprising the eastern half of present-day Turkmenistan, with its principal city at Merv.

‡ Rome was the world's largest city at that time, with a population of around half a million; Alexandria rivaled Seleucia for second place.

were dead, from a plague—apparently smallpox—brought back from Iraq by the legions.*

When the Romans sacked Seleucia in 165 AD, it was the last great center of Hellenism in Iraq. Tacitus described the Greek city as something of an island in the Parthian ocean, "a powerful and fortified city which had never lapsed into barbarism, but had clung loyally to its founder Seleucus."[44] Of the period around 47 BC, during the reign of Caligula, Tacitus wrote that the city—which the Parthians had first taken in 141 BC—at one point withstood seven years of Parthian threats and sieges before capitulating. Seleucia would have regained its autonomy not long after, within the loose Parthian framework. Tacitus writes that Seleucia had remained fully Greek, with "a kind of senate, and the people have powers of their own." Seleucia was at this stage more or less a Greek city-state, strong enough to stand on its own as long as its people and senatorial class got along: "When both act in concert," wrote Tacitus, "they look with contempt upon the Parthians."†

Plutarch wrote of Crassus that the Roman's greatest mistake ("except, indeed, the whole expedition") was to winter in Syria before crossing the Euphrates when instead "he ought to have gone forward and seized Babylonia and Seleucia, cities that were ever at enmity with the Parthians."[45]

After the sack of Seleucia in 165 AD, the Greek language died out in western Asia, to be replaced as a lingua franca and elite tongue by Aramaic, the language of the surging new faith of the followers of the Levantine Jew Jesus Christ. Thus it was the Romans, the greatest of the heirs of Hellenism, who finally extinguished the last important lamp of Greek Iraq. But until at least the year 200 AD, Parthian kings took care to call themselves "Philhellene" on their coins.

---

* The Antonine Plague was perhaps the most impactful of Roman times, lasting several years, sweeping the entire empire, killing up to two thousand people per day in Rome itself, and causing manpower problems for the legions and food shortages due to a depleted countryside. It has been variously credited with creating spiritual conditions for the spread of Christianity within the empire and material conditions for allowing barbarian tribes to settle within the imperial borders and barbarian soldiers to be mustered into the Roman army.

† "As a fact," Tacitus added, "popular government almost amounts to freedom, while the rule of the few approaches closely to a monarch's caprice." Tacitus, *Annals and Histories*, trans. Alfred John Church and William Jackson Brodribb (New York: Everyman's Library, 2009), p. 203.

The Parthian monarchs, even as they styled themselves Philhellene and
basileus megas, or Great King, also borrowed the old Iranian formula
of Cyrus, the first *Shahanshah*, styling themselves King of Kings. The
message was that they too, like the Seleucids, were the heirs to both
Alexander and the Achaemenids.

The Parthians number among the great Iranian dynasties, but they
were not a Persian one. They had come from the northern plains, not
the Persian highlands. The province of Persis frequently allied with the
many local Greeks in resisting the imperial power. While physically the
Parthians resembled Norsemen, in religion they were, loosely speaking,
Zoroastrians, having absorbed the faith from the locals after arriving in
Iran from their Scythian homeland. The Parthians were content to live
alongside Jews, Christians, and others, and to encourage the temples
and shrines of these faiths in their towns. With their gentlemanly diffidence in religious matters and their chaotic domestic affairs, marked by
a thorough refusal or inability to establish anything like a government,
the Parthians never established the sort of divinely sanctioned imperial
state, relatively centralized in nature, that Cyrus's successors had made
a model for the future great Iranian dynasties.

In 224 AD a great man, Ardashir, emerged from the southwest Iranian
province of Fars more or less as Cyrus had emerged there almost eight
hundred years earlier. Ardashir rose up from roots as modest as those of
Cyrus to topple the Parthians and found a dynasty that lasted almost as
long as theirs: 430 years. Ardashir named his dynasty after an ancestor
called Sasan, as Cyrus had named his in honor of his ancestor Achaemenes, so we call them the Sasanians.

In a sense, name and family aside, the Sasanians represented a
resumption of the Achaemenid Empire, which had in essence survived
in Hellenized form under the Macedonians, after the long Parthian inter-
ruption. The Sasanians marked "a new and splendid epoch in Persian
history . . . Iran recovered its independence, instead of constituting one
of many provinces ruled by a Parthian King of Kings."[46] As Cyrus had

located his most important capital in Iraq, at Babylon, so this second Persian Empire would also have its capital in central Iraq, at the Parthian city of Ctesiphon, across the river from Seleucia-on-Tigris. The Parthians, too, had started elsewhere but eventually located their capital in Babylonia. As with Cyrus, Alexander, the Seleucids, and the Parthians in turn before them, for almost eight hundred years, possession of Mesopotamia was what made the Sasanians a truly great power.[47]

With the Sasanians, religion returned to the center of political life in the Persian dominions. "Ardashir began by restoring the Magi to their privileges and the whole nation rallied to the faith of Zoroaster."[48]

As the Parthians had been in a near-perennial state of conflict, hot or cold, with Rome, so the Sasanians and Romans were always either at war or between wars. But there was a difference. Where the Parthians were already in decline while dealing with a Rome at the peak of its power, the Sasanians settled into power while an older, corrupted Rome endured what is known as the Crisis of the Third Century. This was the period of barracks emperors that at one stage saw fourteen such figures—common soldiers mostly, from frontier legions—don the purple in thirty-three years. It was a Rome "whose decline," as Sykes put it, "had fully set in."

In 232, responding to Sasanian raids into Syria and eastern Anatolia, the Roman emperor Severus Alexander launched a campaign against the Persians that achieved little but a modest chastisement of Ardashir, and a full triumph at home in Rome.[49] In 238 Rome had its infamous Year of the Six Emperors, and Ardashir took advantage of the turmoil to take Carrhae and Rome's great border fortress at Nisibis (now Nusaybin, near Mardin on Turkey's eastern border with Syria). In 241, Shapur I, Ardashir's son and successor, launched a raid that penetrated all the way to the coast of the Mediterranean. He took Antioch along the way. In 243 and 244, a Roman army drove Shapur back across the Tigris and was threatening Ctesiphon when the vigorous and popular young emperor, Gordian, died in the field—either in battle or killed by traitors.

In 256, Shapur captured Antioch again. He sacked the city, seized its bishop, Demetrianus, and eventually settled him at a new town for captive Romans, built by their labor, called Veh Antiok Shapur ("Shapur's Better Antioch"). The name later became Gundeshapur, possibly a corruption of the Persian words for "fortress of Shapur." There the erudite Demetrianus "assembled his fellow Christians around him and established a new bishopric." Demetrianus was the first of many scholarly Christians who would make Gundeshapur a famous center of learning for centuries under the Persians.

In 258 or 259, the Roman emperor Valerian invaded Persia, only to be defeated and taken captive by Shapur, whose rock carvings at Naqsh-e Rustam and Bishapur show the Roman kneeling before his conqueror. Shapur's defeat of Valerian had taken place at Edessa, very near to Abraham's Harran and Crassus's Carrhae, at the northern tip of the Fertile Crescent.

In 283 and 298 AD, the Romans replied by sacking Sasanian Ctesiphon; they apparently did not harm its sister city of Seleucia. The latter year was the last time Rome took an Iranian capital. Galerius, the emperor who conquered the city in 298 AD, immediately swapped it for Armenia, Mesopotamian territories along the Euphrates, and thirty years of advantageous peace. In 337, the emperor Constantine, who had made Christianity legal in the Roman Empire in 313 and moved the capital from Rome to his "Nova Roma" at Byzantium in 324, died as the first Christian in history overseeing an invasion of the Persian East.* In 363, Shapur II broke the peace, and the emperor Julian—the Apostate, a nephew of Constantine and Rome's last real pagan emperor—marched to Ctesiphon and won a battle on its outskirts. Lacking siege engines, Julian failed to take the ancient capital. He turned back and died in battle along the Tigris. Meanwhile Seleucia continued to survive as a Greek city, alive and even lively despite its various sackings, burnings, and conquests, if diminished and isolated.

In 410, with the blessing of the Sasanian king Yazdegerd I, Seleucia was host to the Council of Mar Isaac, which organized what became known as the Church of the East. A year earlier, Yazdegerd, in "a political move . . . designed to break the traditional tie between the Christian subjects of the Persian empire and Byzantium,"[50] had officially opened the Sasanian realm to Christian worship. The Council established the bishop of Seleucia-Ctesiphon as Archbishop of All the Orient, with the

---

* The empire was not truly split into two, Eastern and Western, until 395, when, on the death of the emperor Theodosius, one of his sons assumed emperorship in the east and one in the west.

new Church adhering to the Nestorian doctrine of Christ's two distinct natures, human and divine.*

In early Christianity, as in Abraham's time and during the development of Judaism in the day of Cyrus, and as in Islam later, Iraq played its usual central role in the region's long conflict between humanism and the outlook of power. At the 410 Christian council in Seleucia, the Filioque clause, an addendum to the Nicene Creed of 325, was first advanced. The Filioque stated that the Holy Ghost proceeded from the Father *and the Son* (*"filioque"*). This role for the carpenter Jesus, as divinity rather than mere prophet, significantly elevated the stature of man at the heart of Christianity. The Filioque inevitably became a key distinction in the eventual eleventh-century schism between Latin Christianity—which embraced the clause and the Son's centrality, and thus the prestige of humanity and reason—and Orthodox Christianity, which did not.

In 395 AD, Huns from north of the Black Sea crossed the Caucasus and raided all the way south to Ctesiphon, "the royal city," before the Sasanians scared them off, liberating the Huns' loot and eighteen thousand captives.[51]

Procopius (ca. 500–560 AD), the last major historian of the Greek and Roman world, told the story of the eastern Roman emperor Arcadius in 401 AD appointing Yazdegerd, the Sasanian King of Kings, to be guardian over the Byzantine's infant son and heir, Theodosius. Yazdegerd, more likely as an excuse to interfere in Roman affairs than as an exercise in comity, honored the commitment after Arcadius's death. This initiated a brief "policy of profound peace with the Romans, preserving the empire for Theodosius."[52] The peace continued after Theodosius reached his maturity. In 440, after Theodosius had been on the throne for thirty-two years, the Sasanians took advantage of the growing distraction provided by Attila the Hun to attack the Romans of the eastern empire.†

As in the time of the Parthians, the peculiar intimacy of Sasanian relations with the Roman Empire could involve cooperation in the interstices between the bloodshed. There were cases of the Romans contributing to the Sasanians' wars and northerly defenses against the Huns; just

---

* The Nestorian Church had spread to China and India by the ninth century and was strong across most of Asia until the chaos following the dissolution of the Mongol Empire in the fourteenth century.

† Theodosius II, r. 408–450.

as often the Romans would pay off the invaders directly. In the East, "Rome" meant Constantinople.* There the Romans under the emperor Anastasius (d. 518), approached by the Sasanians for such a contribution, understandably thought it "inexpedient" to use their own money to strengthen "the friendship between their enemies."[53] The Persians promptly attacked the Romans as a result, and the five-year Anastasian War (502–506 AD) ended a peace that had endured since 440. The war ended with both sides exhausted and the frontiers little changed.

Around 540, the great Sasanian emperor Khosrow (Chosroes in Greek) sacked Antioch—then "in wealth and size and population the first of all the cities of the Eastern Roman Empire"[54]—and extracted from the Romans an annual tribute in gold, ostensibly that the Persians might "keep the peace secure for them," shouldering the burden of guarding the civilized world from the Huns.[55] Near Ctesiphon, according to Procopius, Khosrow built a new city for Roman captives and runaway slaves, with a "bath and hippodrome and other luxuries besides," where the Romans lived at his expense and were known as King's Subjects, a designation that offered them some protection from the locals. Having burnt the real Antioch to the ground, the Great King called this new city Antioch-of-Khosrow.[56]

Under the Parthians, the local, tangible, helpful gods of Mesopotamian culture had given way to monotheisms, principally Zoroastrianism but also Judaism and the surging faith of Christianity. This latest one-god religion combined elements of the other two with the Greek spirit of individualism, humanism, and man-worship still prevalent in much of the region. The Abrahamic traditions of the Jews, and the messianism and justice preoccupations that the Israelites had brought back from their captivity among the Zoroastrians of Babylon, found a potent fit with the Hellenistic emphasis on that which is distinctly human.

The Greek contribution would make the new faith very different from its two monotheistic ancestors. The religion of Zoroaster is so exclusive

---

* On moving the Roman capital east to Byzantium in 324 AD, the emperor Constantine renamed the city Nova Roma. In 330 AD, after massive reconstruction, he renamed it Constantinopolis.

that it does not accept converts. Judaism's remarkable "spiritual breadth" is paired in that religion with an "intense racial patriotism" that limits its universal ambitions; the Jewish God rules all the world, but He has made his special bargain with one tribe only, the people of Abraham.[57] The teachings of the Nazarene carpenter, Jesus, were different. These involved no chosen people or special bargain for one tribe or another. The conduct that he advocated was owed to all, regardless of faith. The eternal life he promised was available to all. He left earthly government to Caesar, so in the essential faith there was no question of conquest or worldly laws. He was himself human, so reason and natural law, the definitive human qualities, would balance divine will at the heart of his meaning. He, his apostles, his followers, and those who articulated the basic faith in the centuries between his death and its final definition in the Nicene Creed during the reign of Constantine were all from the Hellenistic world. Christianity would be the third universal idea to reach the region, after the empire of belonging posited by Cyrus and the concord of races raised by Alexander at Opis.

The Sasanians, true Iranians, were committed followers of the Zoroastrian religion. As the dynasty aged, its faith fossilized. By the late sixth century AD, Sasanian holy books were placing a complete focus on liturgy and form. Ethics, spirituality, and any intimate experience of God were not mentioned. The ever more arcane rites of the Sasanians were mumbled by their priests, the magi, in Avestan, the language of the prophet Zoroaster. The tongue was by then as dead as he. Like the Parthian kings minting coins with Greek letters that they could not read, a Sasanian magus in Mesopotamia of 600 AD did not know the meaning of the words that he incanted.

Beyond Christianity and Judaism, the One God vogue bred other compelling new challengers to the state religion in this second Persian Empire. In the third century, a group called the Manichaeans produced a synthesis of sorts, drawing on both Zoroastrianism, with its constant choosing between good and evil, and Christianity, with its messianic Christ figure. This combination held out the brief possibility of a friendly henotheism uniting the worlds of Abraham, Cyrus, and Alexander. The Sasanian state eventually crushed the Manichaeans in Iraq and the rest of the empire. The Mazdakites, who believed in the sharing of wealth and women, also met a swift and bloody end at the hands of the Iranian religious state. Gnosticism, mysticism, and secret cabals thrived in this repressive atmosphere.*

Zoroastrianism itself grew so ritualistic and arcane in the latter Sasanian centuries that in far-off Europe the words "magus" and "magi" came to be used to describe occultists, hence the term "magic." By the time the Islamic armies invaded the Persian Empire in 636, the Sasanian state was spending much of its remaining energy, after the grueling four-century conflict with Rome, on maintaining the theocracy. This is hinted at in an edict from the Sasanian king Shapur II in 340 AD:

> The Christians destroy our holy teaching, and teach men to serve one God, and not to honour the Sun, or Fire. They defile Water by their ablutions, they refrain from marriage and the propagation of children, and refuse to go to war with the King of Kings. They have no rules about the slaughter and eating of animals; they bury the corpses of men in the earth. They attribute the origin of snakes and creeping things to a good God.

The Sasanians ruled from Iraq, but they had an Iranian exquisiteness. They brought the great arch to a perfection rarely rivaled, and invented the dome-on-squinches, which allowed the circular footprint of a dome to stand upon the four walls of a square space. Centuries later, after a new empire emerged from Arabia to adopt much of its material culture from Persia, this was to become the defining element of Islamic architecture. A Sasanian ambassador brought chess back to Iran with him from India during the mid-sixth century. The painted miniature flourished.

When the Christian Roman emperor Justinian I closed the pagan Neoplatonic academy at Athens in 529 AD, the philosophers there came to the Sasanian emperor's court at Ctesiphon. Bringing with them to Iraq a chain of thought and argument reaching back unbroken eleven centuries to Socrates, the last of the Greek philosophers moved eastward to the Sasanians' academy of learning at Gundeshapur, next to ancient Susa.

Gundeshapur's Greek roots went back to the time of its founding by Shapur I, the Sasanian emperor who in 260 AD had defeated Valerian

---

* Mazdak "appropriated the richest lands and most beautiful females" to his own followers, writes Gibbon. The reformer also "enforced a vegetable diet." (Gibbon, *Decline and Fall*, vol. 4, p. 332.

at Edessa and used the Roman emperor as a mounting block. Shapur eventually married a daughter of Aurelian, the next Roman emperor but four.* The empress in turn brought two Greek physicians with her to Persia, and these joined Shapur's captive bishop of Antioch, Demetrianus, and taught Greek medicine in Gundeshapur. Under Khosrow I (r. 531–579), Gundeshapur's character—latent since its founding—as a center of Greek and Christian philosophy, medicine, and other sciences began truly to blossom. Bit by bit the medical school there "became a liberal school of poetry, philosophy, and rhetoric."[58] By then the language at Gundeshapur was the Syriac dialect of Aramaic, and most of the scholars there were Christians of various kinds, supported by the Persian crown. One of Gundeshapur's Christian expatriates, known as Paul the Persian, translated Aristotle's *Logic* for Khosrow.

The greatest of the Sasanian emperors, Khosrow was something of a Cyrus figure. As the Romans did with Caesar, subsequent Sasanian emperors dignified themselves by taking his name, which became "almost a synonym for splendour and glory," as a title.[59] An intellectual who looked east to India as well as west to the Greeks, he was seen by the Romans as something of an archetypal philosopher king, in the mold of a Marcus Aurelius, if more martial.

Khosrow claimed that his learned circle, searching for truth, "examined the customs of our forebears," but also "studied the customs and conducts of the Romans and Indians . . . We have not rejected anyone because they belonged to a different religion or people." Three hundred years later, when Baghdad under Persian, and nominally Muslim, rule became home to a great revival of Hellenistic thought, the Syriac-speaking Christian physicians of Gundeshapur became court doctors to the caliphs of Islam. Gundeshapur's Christian scholars would play an important role in the "translation movement" that saw many works of Greek antiquity translated into Arabic.

Eventually, the exiled Athenian philosophers who ended up at Gundeshapur in the time of Shapur I found their new home uncomfortable. Their disputatious nature sat ill with a strong and centralized state, and

---

* Aurelian's seizure of the purple in 270, followed by a series of victories over various barbarians, marked the end of Rome's Crisis of the Third Century, with its bewildering succession of barracks emperors. He called himself *Restitutor Orbis* ("Restorer of the World") on coins.

the Athenians went home as soon as they were allowed, some twenty years later. This left the local, Syriac-speaking Christians to continue their work. Back in the far west of Asia, in the Levant and Asia Minor, doctrinal squabbling and the orthodoxies imposed by the Byzantines would sap Christianity of much of its intellectual energy. North African and European Christianity would be for the most part similarly bereft, for some time. Henceforth, Greek philosophy lived not in the Latin and Greek West but in the Persian East.

This long process of the "eastward migration" of the Aristotelian legacy, begun by Alexander and continued under the Seleucids, was now complete.[60] Eventually, when the European West was ready to awaken to this legacy, it was in the wider Persian world that reclamation of these treasures would have its roots. But the great recovery was to come later. First came a storm, blowing from the southerly deserts, that found the great empires of Persia and Rome fatally sapped by their long centuries of war.

Chapter 8

Sword of Allah

Khalid ibn al Walid, 590–642 AD

> I was ordered to fight all men until they say, "There is no god but Allah."
> —The Prophet Mohammed, 632 AD[1]

In a dusty, quiet town in northwest Arabia, six hundred miles southwest of Babylon, a tall man, lean and dour, sat upon the floor of a modest house. All around him the sound of wailing welled up from the narrow streets. It made him furious.[2]

The town was known simply as Medina, "the city." The year was 642 AD. Medina's crooked alleys were filling with women and their keening as they beat their breasts in a communal ecstasy of sorrow. Men, too, gave their laments to the loud river of tears in that arid place, for a great and beloved member of the community of Islam had just died. The tall man fuming in his small house was the Caliph Omar. Commander of the armies of the young religion, Omar ruled over the spiritual and temporal lives of the people of a growing empire that stretched already from the Libyan desert to the Persian highlands.

Thirty-two years before that day of crying in the streets of Medina, an extraordinary story had begun that was to hold Mesopotamia in its grip ever after.

In 610 AD a merchant from the Arabian town of Mecca, two hundred miles south of Medina, had begun to tell his closest companions about fainting spells he was having in a quiet mountain cave that he liked to visit for relaxation. Mecca was home to the Kaaba, the principal shrine for local pagans. For centuries the town had been the major religious center of the Arabian subcontinent. Located near north–south caravan routes about fifty miles from the west coast of the Arabian Peninsula, halfway south toward Yemen and the mouth of the Red Sea, Mecca was also an important trading center for a regional population that included many Jews and Christians. Because of Arabia's poverty and the long, deep desert borders, the land had enjoyed few important connections to Mesopotamia in the nine centuries since the Arabs stood alone in not sending tribute and ambassadors to Alexander at Babylon.

During the fainting fits, the merchant reported, an angel came to him in the dark quiet of the cave. The angel's name in the Arabic tongue was Jibril. This was the same Angel Gabriel with whom the merchant's Jewish and Christian neighbors were familiar. Gabriel was an emissary frequently used by their deity, the one Almighty God of their patriarch Ibrahim, or Abraham. The Arabs called Abraham's deity al Lah: the God. Speaking to the swooning merchant, Gabriel revealed al Lah's exact words. This old God of Abraham began to describe a new faith, one founded on complete surrender to Him as mediated solely by the merchant. The Arabic word for surrender, or submission, was islam.

As the revelations continued, the merchant began to tell a widening circle of his friends and family. Eventually he took to preaching on the streets of Mecca. This Allah, as he became known, was the same God long worshipped by the local monotheists, the merchant explained. But the Jews had perverted their Scriptures. As for the Christians, they blasphemously believed that the one God had three equally divine parts, one of which was, scandalously, His own human son. As for the new faith, God was making it clear through the revelations that this would be only, and exactly, what the merchant said it was.

At first the townspeople ridiculed the merchant, one Mohammed ibn Abdullah ibn Abd al-Muttalib, of the clan of Banu Hashim in the tribe of Quraysh. Mecca's Jews and Christians, Arabs all, already had their al Lah, their one Almighty God. They derided this Mohammed son of Abdullah. How was this individual, whom they had known throughout his relatively unsuccessful life to that point, suddenly a prophet? It seemed preposterous and self-serving that he was now God's final and perfect messenger. They mocked what they saw as his clumsy reworkings of their ancient stories of Noah, Abraham, and other prophets.

Mecca's pagans, meanwhile, were content to worship their rocks and crude idols in the Kaaba, the shrine that brought the city so much trade.

The Arabian Peninsula, 630 AD

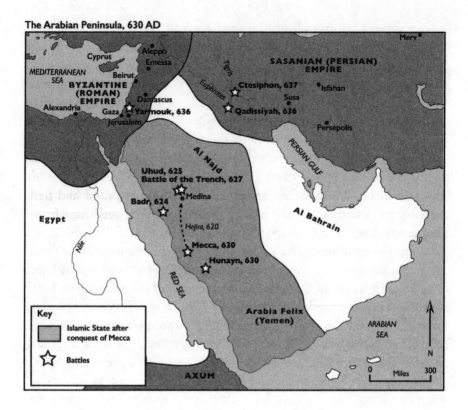

They, too, mocked the street preacher. Meanwhile the more senior clans of Mohammed's tribe, and the wealthy Meccan establishment in general, were comfortable with things as they were. Their current dispensation, however, would not last long. They were to fight Mohammed for ten years, and then, on the verge of losing to him, they coopted his revolution.

By the time Mohammed died in 632, twenty-two years after the first revelation in the cave, he ruled with a new and complete fusion of religion and government over the whole Arabian subcontinent. Behind him now stood the Meccan elite that initially had resisted him. Within two generations, their desert horsemen and their town-born leaders conquered most of the world from the Strait of Gibraltar to the Hindu Kush, subjecting all before them to the rule of Islam. The new empire's geographical form was much the same as that of Alexander's larger version of Cyrus's empire, with the considerable additions of Arabia and the Maghreb. Like Alexander's, the new empire's higher dream would die in Iraq.

The capital of this vast creation was Medina. Mohammed had fled there in 622 when at last the exasperated Meccans forced him from their community.

In 642, twenty years and a mighty empire later, the man who cursed the public lamentation as it filled his house in Medina, goading him to stand up to put an end to the public outburst of emotion, was the second *khalifa*, or successor, of the Prophet. As caliph, Omar ruled over what was at once a religious empire and an imperial religion. His great task was threefold: to continue the military expansion initiated by the Prophet Mohammed, to consolidate Muslim rule across the conquered lands, and to maintain the purity of the new creed as it fought to subject a diverse world.

The total surrender required by the faith demanded perfect obedience to a set of laws, known as *sharia* (the path), that had been conceived to regulate every element of human life. It was a formula that allowed no possible distinction between the spiritual and the worldly. It was, as the canonical compendium of Muslim law, the fourteenth-century *Reliance of the Traveler*, explained, a "unified system for human life"[3] or, as the brilliant twentieth-century Arabist G. E. von Grunebaum put it, "a complete system of thought and behavior."[4]

This same comprehensiveness meant that there could be no distinction between sharia and Islam itself. The merchant's law was the new religion, and the new religion was the merchant's law. The world would be divided into the *dar al salaam*, the house of peace, where Islam reigns, and the *dar al harb*, the house of war, where Islam has yet to conquer. (The Dar al Salaam would also be called the Dar al Islam, or House of Islam.) Everything that a man could do (the system addressed itself to men, touching on women and children where necessary in its legislation) would be either *halal* or *haram*—legal or illegal. Nothing was too small or too personal, or too great or too public, to be governed by the faith.

A doctrine of his new system held that the Prophet Mohammed did not smile or laugh. He abjured those who did so as frivolous, imperfect Muslims. Crying could be just as haram. On that evening of public weeping in Medina in 642, the Caliph Omar would have remembered the day of his own accession to the Prophet's mantle eight years previously. He had been appointed successor by his predecessor, Abu Bakr, the first Caliph of Islam following Mohammed's death in 632. It was Omar himself who had decreed, upon his ascension following Abu Bakr's death, that there must never be lamentation for the death of a good Muslim. If a believer is pious enough to be worth mourning, he is going to paradise. There is nothing to mourn.

In the green gardens of paradise, where rivers of milk, honey, and wine flow without cease, the faithfully departed will recline on "thrones encrusted with gold and precious stones," waited on by "young boys . . . as fair as virgin pearls . . . immortal youths." Attended by these boys, the pious will enjoy the attentions of "bashful, dark-eyed virgins, as chaste as the sheltered eggs of ostriches." There will be virgins upon virgins: "bashful virgins . . . virgins as fair as coral and rubies . . . virgins chaste and fair . . . dark-eyed virgins, sheltered in their tents . . . dark-eyed houris, chaste as virgin pearls." Even the houris, these busy "high-bosomed maidens" of paradise, were virgins all.[5]

The promise of this paradise after death was essential to the edifice. From its very beginnings in Medina, the project had relied on the commitment of its young men to *jihad*, the holy war that cannot end until the entire world has accepted Muslim rule. This struggle, then very much an offensive military one rather than a defensive or spiritual one, was the primary obligation of all believers.[6] The Prophet's vision was of a new order in which all were either Muslims, slaves of Muslims, or tribute-paying subjects of Muslims.[7] * The peace that the new faith imagined would be the peace of a world conquered entirely, a world in which all—believer and infidel alike—submitted to the comprehensive legislation of the sharia.

---

* The special tax, or *jizya* ("penalty"), based according to one theory on a Sasanian head tax on non-Zoroastrians, could be exchanged for military service. Richard N. Frye, *The Heritage of Persia*, p. 219.

Wealth today, bliss tomorrow, and endless sexual pleasure in both: these would be the rewards of the Holy War. As the invading Muslims told the Persian court in 637, "If you kill us, we shall enter Paradise; if we kill you, you will enter the fire."[8] To compromise the appeal of the hereafter, to allow that there might be something regrettable in the passing of a good Muslim, would be to undermine the very endeavor itself. And so in the small house at Medina in 642 AD, the Caliph Omar, master of an empire, was incensed at the clamor all around him.

To challenge the authority of a caliph was equally haram, or forbidden. Yet now much of Medina, the capital city itself, was defying Omar with this loud mourning. He raised himself from the floor where he sat and took his whip in his left hand.[9] As he made for the street, he heard a new voice amid the wailing. The voice came from next door, and Omar recognized it.

It was his daughter Hafsa. She had been the fourth of the late Prophet's thirteen wives. Hearing her voice, Omar turned away from the door. He gave up his whip and sat back down on the floor. The sound of his daughter's grief had changed the caliph's mind.[10] The people could weep.

Who was this who had just died, creating the lamentable grief? His name was Khalid ibn al Walid. Khalid had been the best loved and greatest of the original Muslim generals. During the bloody years of Islam's birth and expansion, Khalid ibn al Walid had earned the name *Saifullah*, Sword of Allah, for his many victories in large battles and single combats alike.

Loose in manner, not stern like the new religion, a freewheeling aristocratic spendthrift in a dour faith of merchants and nomads, Khalid had, like so many of the Meccan elite, been a latecomer to the Muslim cause. He converted in 629, at the age of forty-three, and then fought relentlessly for Islam and its rewards. In the Prophet's lifetime, Khalid had helped to conquer Arabia from reluctant fellow Arabs. When Mohammed died in 632 and the conquered Arabs revolted, Khalid crushed them. Starting with raids in Sasanian Iraq in 633, Khalid had done more than any Muslim to defeat the twin empires of Persia and Rome.

The latter now referred to the empire of the Nova Roma that the Emperor Constantine had established at Byzantium; it was known sometimes as the Second or Eastern Rome, but mostly just as Rome. Like a pair of ancient moldering corks, the Persians and the *Rumi*, as the Arabs called the Byzantines, had nearly kept the explosive new faith bottled in the Arabian Peninsula. Without Khalid, there would have been no Islam as the later world was to know it. Without his sword in particular, although Islam had other good generals, a faith that in those first generations spread only by the sword may hardly have spread at all. In 642, Khalid was to die peacefully as the second, after Alexander, of the region's great commanders never to lose a battle.*

Khalid had met his first defeat only four years before, but it did not come on the battlefield. It was political, at the hands of his own side, and eventually it would kill him. Omar was jealous of Khalid's success and popularity. A strict and ascetic character at the best of times, the caliph was rigid in his administration of Mohammed's system. The faith comprised a complete and final revelation to a perfect practitioner. It came from a God who demanded total obedience. The holy words themselves, being God's own exact syllables, were immutable. The entire system had thus been constructed with an unusual literalism and finality at its core. This suited a man like Omar. In a rule-based system that legislated all details of all aspects of human existence, from the believer's conduct in the privy to his relationship with the Almighty, it was easy enough for a leader to find occasion to punish a potential rival.

When Omar finally moved against Khalid in 638, the caliph's allegation was exquisitely appropriate to both accuser and accused. Khalid had allegedly been excessively extravagant in his generosity toward the sort of people he liked—poets, tribal noblemen, distinguished warriors from his battles—when instead he should have reserved the booty for good Muslim causes like the believing poor. Two years after Khalid's historic defeat of the Romans at Yarmouk in Syria, Omar dismissed his general and sent him into an impoverished retirement in a small provincial house at Emessa, present-day Homs in western Syria. There Khalid, the Sword

---

* Six centuries later Genghis Khan, whose grandson Hulagu was to sack Baghdad in 1258, would become the third.

of Allah, covered in the scars of battle and mortified at the prospect of dying in bed, would waste away and die.

"I die even as a camel dies," Khalid was to say in disgust from his Syrian deathbed. "I die in bed, in shame."

And then, in Khalid's final words, the old defiance returned. "May the eyes of cowards," spat out the expiring general who had vanquished two empires and never lost a battle, "never find rest in sleep!"

About thirty-five years earlier, maybe fifteen years before Mohammed received his first visit from the Angel Gabriel, two boys stood circling each other on a piece of flat ground in Mecca, the caravan entrepôt and pagan shrine town a couple hundred miles south of Medina. The boys' friends stood around them, watching. The two youths, maybe thirteen or fourteen years old, had already been rivals for years. Today they were wrestling. Both were tall, but one was an inch taller than the other, and left-handed. This was Omar. The other was Khalid.

The two boys were healthy and strong. Toughened by the Arabs' traditional boyhood training in the arts of war, they were already leaders among their peers. First cousins once removed, they looked so alike that they were sometimes taken for each other. Khalid, the more handsome, had a slightly pockmarked face. As the two youths warily circled each other and then closed for the first clinch, it seems unlikely that they would ever have imagined the glorious futures that lay ahead for themselves and their people, nor the extraordinary lifetime of conflict and rivalry that they would share.

The boys came closer. The grapple began. Khalid quickly levered Omar off the ground and sent him in a flail through the air. As Omar landed, his leg made an ugly cracking sound. He lay in pain on the ground. Khalid is said to have stared wide-eyed as his opponent grimaced in the dust.[11]

Khalid's father was the chief of their clan, the Bani Makhzum. The clan was part of a tribe, the Quraysh, that was the richest in Mecca, controlling the profitable pagan Kaaba shrine. The Bani Makhzum were the war leaders of the Quraysh, and the tribe's breeders and trainers of war-horses. Like any young nobleman of that world, Khalid had been taken from his mother while a baby and sent from town to live in the desert with Bedouin nomads of his father's clan. There he would spend his infancy and youth imbibing the purer atmosphere of the desert.

Khalid lived mostly among the horsemen of Arabia's desert steppes until he was fifteen or sixteen. During this time he learned that the sword, in the intimacy of its violence, was the most chivalrous of weapons. He also trained in the spear, the lance, and the bow. His kinsmen taught him to break a colt and school a war-horse. They trained him to fight on the fleet and hardy Arabian horse, to handle a camel for the long distances, to drink with his peers and the older men. He learned to recite the deeds and names of the twenty-nine generations of his paternal lineage that took him to the loins of Ismail, the first Arab, and to Ismail's father Abraham, founder of the monotheistic faiths of his neighbors, the Jews and Christians. Khalid learned of the next ten generations beyond, taking his paternity back to Noah, and of the final ten generations, making fifty in all, that connected him to Adam, the first man.*

Khalid, Omar, and their contemporary, the merchant prophet Moham-med, were born into a land that bordered Iraq physically. But in other ways their land was distant—on the edge, or even beyond the edge, of the Persian and Greco-Roman world. The subcontinent of Arabia was large, comparable in size to India or Western Europe. It possessed a handful of towns in which writing was known, but the great majority of its land was desert or dry steppe. Literate life, cities, and monumental physical culture; complex science, architecture, and engineering; gov-ernment beyond the tribal code: all of these were essentially unknown.

This does not mean that there had been no contact between Arabia and its neighbors on the northern land border, Iraq and Syria. The arid Arabian steppe, like the Central Asian plains, was prone to produc-ing periodic "eruptions of population," in the phrase of the historian Arnold Toynbee. These eruptions out of Arabia had provided the broader region with its various Semitic languages. Hammurabi's Akkadian, the

---

* At thirty years per generation, this would place Adam at about 900 BC, the time of the rise of Assyria and a thousand years or so after the "historical" Abraham.

Canaanite language spoken in Palestine and Syria during Abraham's time, and the Aramaic tongue of Jesus that was the principal language of Mesopotamia and the Levant during the coming Muslim invasions: each of these was ultimately descended from Arabia.

At a small number of oases such as Mecca, and in relatively fertile Yemen at the southern end of Arabia, communities of Arab merchants lived a simple form of town life during the time of Khalid, Omar, and Mohammed. Camel caravans brought trade with the Levant and Mesopotamia to the north, and with the small entrepôts of coastal Arabia, primarily Muscat in present-day Oman, that trafficked with India and beyond. Although many Arabians followed Abraham's God in Jewish or Christian form, most—like the Qurayshi tribe—were pagans. Many of these worshipped annually their sacred artifacts in the Kaaba at Mecca.

Beyond the towns, the *razziah*—the caravan or livestock raid—was the way of life. Often it led to tribal warfare. With his new formula adding jihad and unity to the time-honored booty imperative, Mohammed transformed this ancient Arab institution into an engine for world dominion.[12] As the Muslim war ambassadors were to tell Yazdegerd, the last Sasanian Persian emperor, at his palace at Ctesiphon while delivering their ultimatum in 637, five years after the Prophet's death: "We used to eat beetles of various sorts, scorpions and snakes, we considered this our food. Nothing but the earth was our dwelling. We wore only what we spun from the hair of camels and sheep. Our religion was to kill one another and raid one another."[13]

A near-complete historical darkness—essentially no written records locally, nor mentions in the writings of others, nor lasting buildings or other material legacy—had persisted in Arabia for almost three thousand years after civilization came to the adjoining lands of Iraq, the Levant, and Egypt. In the last decades of this period, events on Arabia's northern border had begun to encourage a sense of identity among the Arabians.

The Sasanian Persian and Eastern Roman Empires had endured three centuries of grinding conflict with each other. By the end of this era, in 628, the civilizations of Rome and Iran had been at war in Mesopotamia for seven centuries (682 years to be precise), since Crassus attacked the Parthians in 54 BC and had molten gold poured down his throat after the defeat at Carrhae. Fighting their final, most debilitating wars in the years 572–591 and 604–628, both the Byzantines and the Sasanians hired Arab tribes to fight as mercenaries against the other, primarily in southern Iraq. Thus, even as Rome and Persia bled each other nearly dead, they provided experience, money for arms, armor, and horses, and a nascent sense of common cause to the warlike but disorganized tribes to the south. The Arab warriors were mostly Bedouin from the subcontinental hinterland, led by the merchants of the few towns.

In 613 AD, Khalid was twenty-seven years old. Based in the prosperous shrine center of Mecca, in those easygoing heterodox days, the handsome and athletic young man with the scarred face would have enjoyed a life of caravan trading into Syria leavened with raiding and minor warfare against nearby tribes. Khalid's father was one of the richest men in town. Life, from various clues in the story, was good.

Three years earlier, Mohammed son of Abdullah had lost consciousness in his cave for the first time. The visitations from the Angel Gabriel were to happen again and again in various places over the following twenty-three years. The angel's verses comprised the gradual revealing of the original and only true holy book, the *koran* (literally "book"). This Koran, said the merchant, had existed in the same exact form since the beginning of time. Since then it had been corrupted by the Jews and Christians for their own Scriptures. Thus the Koran was replete with stories of Ibrahim, Musa, Issa, (Abraham, Moses, Jesus) and other prophets who had long been well known in Mecca.

But in the new Book, these stories had important differences, at first known only to Mohammed himself. Since the beginning of time, going back even before Ibrahim, and then later as first the Jews and then the Christians followed their corrupted versions of the book, God's authentic words had existed. Their revealing had simply awaited a suitably perfect messenger. Such a man would build a new and godly world according to these commandments that he alone would receive.

The first of the merchant's revelations from Allah had been a simple command: "Read."

"I do not know how to read," he had replied to the angel.[14]

After three years of this, Mohammed began to confide the revelations to his wife. Eventually he went to the streets to preach about his experiences. Mecca's religious atmosphere at the time was relaxed, as casual if not as cosmopolitan as that of a Greek city in Iraq under the Seleucids or Parthians. There was at first nothing alarming about yet another prophet accosting the townsfolk in alleyways or marketplaces with stories of his special truths.

But this prophet was different. Ridiculing the existing gods and holy books of his fellow Meccans, demanding a complete submission to God's will as revealed exclusively to him, Mohammed insisted that his neighbors and relatives were damned to hellfire if they ignored him. His preaching was pervasively concerned with the ideas of insider and outsider, of believer and unbeliever. This prophet was making demands like none before him in Mecca's long history as a town of faith.

Mecca's leading families, a merchant oligarchy dominated by Mohammed's own tribe of Quraysh, eventually took notice. Beyond the vitriol against their gods and ancestors, there was the matter of authority. This new version of the God of Abraham was so much more absolute and demanding, and his sole interlocutor lived right there among them, seething with criticisms of the social order.

It was a social order in which many, including this particular merchant, were faring poorly. Early-seventh-century Mecca was a society in flux. Commerce was burgeoning. The honor-driven tribal ways of the desert, complained those who sensed themselves left behind, were eroding. The chief qualities of the Meccan patrician of the day "were materialism and a plutocratic arrogance."[15]

Mohammed offered to address this. The message of his revelations was primarily that there was but one God, mediated by one Messenger, and that the pious must surrender completely to His rules. But there were social elements too in the commands that God was transmitting now: justice, equality, and charity among believers. For an enterprising and ambitious religion, it was an effective formula at a time of unsettling change. But however popular these themes might prove among those who were losing in Mecca, they were loathsome to Khalid ibn al Walid's peers and elders among the elite. This new Allah was inescapably political, and in an entirely new way.

As Mohammed castigated the mores of the day and called for equality and justice, a handful of followers began to gather around him. The first was a ten-year-old foster son and cousin, Ali ibn Abu Talib. Ali was

followed by a few close relatives and friends of Mohammed, and by
a growing number of poor townspeople who appreciated his leveling
message.

The Meccan establishment grew ever more alarmed. Khalid's wealthy
father emerged as one of the principal figures opposing the new movement. Known as Al Walid, "the unique one," for his singular wealth and
prestige, the old man was a pillar of the town's commercial order. "Is
prophethood to be bestowed on Mohammed," asked Al Walid, "while
I, the greatest of the Quraysh and their elder, am to get nothing?"[16]

The supreme leader of the reactionary elements was a similarly plutocratic figure called Abu Sufyan. As leader of the paramount clan of
the Quraysh tribe, Abu Sufyan had a natural ascendancy in Meccan
society. Mohammed's great-grandfather, Hashim, and Abu Sufyan's great-
grandfather, Abd Shams, had been brothers. By the time of Mohammed and Abu Sufyan three generations later, Hashim's family, the Banu
Hashim (the "tent" or house of Hashim), were still relatively poor, but
the descendants of Abd Shams, known as the Banu Umayya, had become
the richest and most powerful clan in Mecca. The Umayyad leader and
his ilk were accustomed to dominating the city and its commerce. Mostly
pagan, they were also accustomed to dominating the associated shrine
businesses. Now an upstart relative from a secondary clan was threatening this.

Mohammed's revelations from his time in Mecca, the early years in
his career as a prophet, are said to possess a beauty so ineffable in their
original Arabic that none but God Himself could have formed them.
In this passage from the Meccan period, as in much of the Koran, God
addresses Mohammed personally.

> By the light of the day, and by the dark of night, your Lord has not
>   forsaken you, nor does He abhor you.
> The life to come holds a richer prize for you than does this present life.
>   You shall be gratified with what your Lord will give you.
> Did He not find you an orphan and give you shelter? Did He not find
>   you in error and guide you?
> Did He not find you poor and enrich you?
> Therefore do not wrong the orphan, nor chide away the beggar. But
>   proclaim the goodness of your Lord.[17]

1. GENEALOGICAL TREE OF QURAYSH
THE PROPHET'S FAMILY

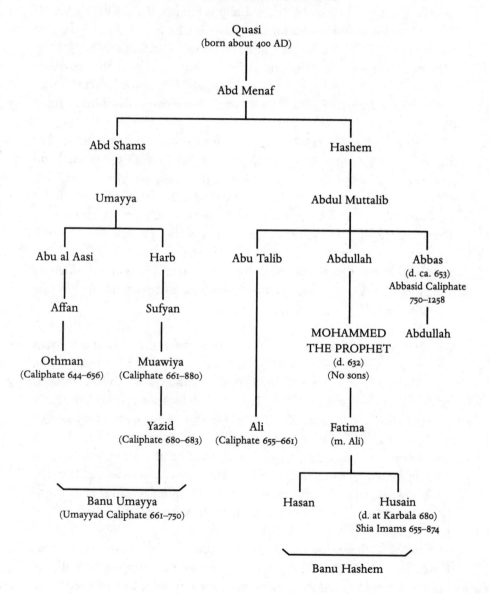

Quasi
(born about 400 AD)

Abd Menaf

Abd Shams

Hashem

Umayya

Abdul Muttalib

Abu al Aasi

Harb

Abu Talib

Abdullah

Abbas
(d. ca. 653)
Abbasid Caliphate
750–1258

Affan

Sufyan

MOHAMMED
THE PROPHET
(d. 632)
(No sons)

Abdullah

Othman
(Caliphate 644–656)

Muawiya
(Caliphate 661–880)

Yazid
(Caliphate 680–683)

Ali
(Caliphate 655–661)

Fatima
(m. Ali)

Banu Umayya
(Umayyad Caliphate 661–750)

Hasan

Husain
(d. at Karbala 680)
Shia Imams 655–874

Banu Hashem

Khalid's father was so prominent in opposition to Mohammed that Allah directed a few verses of His timeless revelation at the aging oligarch himself. "Leave to Me the man whom I created helpless and endowed with vast riches and thriving children," God tells Mohammed, in what is acknowledged in Islam to be a direct reference to Khalid's father. "I have made his progress smooth and easy: yet he hopes that I shall give him more . . . He pondered, and he schemed. Confound him, how he schemed!" fumes God. "He looked around him, frowning and scowling; then he turned away in scornful pride and said: 'This is but sorcery counterfeited, the utterance of a mere mortal!' I will surely cast him into the Fire."[18]

The highly personal quality of such revelations, so firmly located in time and place, might appear difficult to reconcile with the eternal and uncreated nature of the Koran, and with the Book's claims of transcendence and universality. On the contrary, said the faith. The specificity and foresight of these verses merely proved God's omniscience. The Koran, after all, had existed since the beginning of time. The Book's many personal verses, each of them improving minutiae of Mohammed's private life with awe-inspiring precision and timeliness, affirmed the completeness of God's plan and the unique importance of His one true Messenger.

Mohammed's adherents at this stage were few, possibly in the dozens. But the numbers were growing, not shrinking, and in the broader social context of the moment his message had potential. Abu Sufyan, Al Walid, and the other rich men of Mecca intensified their campaign against the insurgent preacher. They sent delegations to Mohammed's protector, an uncle called Abu Talib. "He abuses our gods," they said of Mohammed. "He vilifies our faith and the faith of our fathers." They even offered a favored son, Khalid's well-liked brother Ammarah, to Abu Talib in return for Mohammed, whom they would then execute. But Abu Talib refused to give up his nephew. A champion wrestler challenged Mohammed to a match, hoping to embarrass the preacher. Mohammed threw the man three times.

There was one thing the Quraysh would not do at this stage: break the tribal code. Even as they mocked the merchant prophet and abused his small band of followers, they would not murder one of their own.

Meanwhile Mohammed's following grew. The fortieth to join was Omar. Khalid remained aloof.

Through nine years of rising tensions between Mohammed's tiny band of followers and the rest of Mecca, Khalid and Mohammed shared the small town. There are numerous accounts of Khalid's father and Mohammed encountering each other during this time. There was the strange occasion of the Satanic verses, when Mohammed brought immense relief to the people of Mecca by proclaiming the legitimacy of certain pagan divinities of theirs, then later announced that the devil (shaitan) had made him speak this foul enormity. After Mohammed spoke the false verses, he prostrated himself alongside his followers; Khalid's father, Al Walid, is named as the only one present who did not prostrate himself with the prophet. Too old to bend down, the elderly tycoon simply leaned over a handful of dust that he had brought with him into the place of worship. On another occasion, Mohammed was so engrossed in lobbying the influential old man that he uncharacteristically ignored a blind man on the street. God revealed a verse about this episode too.

Later, Al Walid was appalled to learn that Mohammed was saying that not only the Meccans were destined for the fires of Gehenna, but also their gods. "Every god who wishes to be worshipped to the exclusion of Allah," said Mohammed, "will be with those who worship him"—in hell, in other words. In Mecca's habitually tolerant and diverse atmosphere, such threatening, exclusionary rhetoric caused fear and resistance.

The men of the Meccan establishment were practical. They were prosperous shrine monopolists and tough caravaneers with much to lose from any change in their community's leadership. Mohammed, meanwhile, was not inclined to compromise on his central requirement: the total submission due to the God whose sole Messenger he was. A clash could not be far away.

In the ancient Muslim accounts, Khalid's father and Mohammed saw each other on the streets, in the markets, even in the same house of worship. Al Walid sometimes mocked the preacher to his face. At other times the old man came to Mohammed's defense. The old chronicles, as these turgid events pile atop one another in the setting of the dusty little backwater that was seventh-century Mecca, give a strong impression of a small place quickly descending into claustrophobia under the unyielding pressures of a forceful preacher and his absolute truths.

Finally, twelve years after the first revelation in the cave outside of town, the Quraysh leaders decided to put an end to the threat. In July 622, they arranged to assassinate their fellow tribesman. The night before it was to happen, Mohammed, alerted to the plot, slipped out of Mecca with his chief companion, Abu Bakr. The Prophet's young cousin Ali stayed behind and slept in his leader's bed as a decoy to fool the attackers.

Mohammed fled two hundred miles north to the town of Yathrib, where for some time the leading citizens had been encouraging him to join them as an arbiter of sorts in their own disputes. Soon, about seventy of Mohammed's Meccan devotees followed him there. Mohammed's new town, inhabited then mostly by Jews, shortly thereafter became known simply as the City, Medina. There, to the surprise of many of the locals, Mohammed quickly established himself as their overlord. Now he had opportunities to express God's will in ways that had not been available in Mecca.

An important early step in Medina, after taking control of his new home, was the elimination of the city's Jewish population.[19] Medina's Jews had been established in the town for some centuries, perhaps since various Roman brutalities in Palestine during the first and second centuries AD, or even since the destruction of Jerusalem in 587 BC by the mighty Nebuchadnezzar of Babylon. The Jews themselves claimed that they had been in Medina since the time of Moses. Of the town's three main Jewish tribes, Mohammed drove one out in 624. These were mostly goldsmiths and craftsmen, and Mohammed's Meccan transplants took possession of their tools. He expelled the second of Medina's main Jewish tribes in 625, razing the date palms on which they relied. In 627, after what is called the Battle of the Trench, he liquidated the third main Jewish tribe, the Banu Qurayza, entirely. The Battle of the Trench had seen Mohammed's forces successfully hold Medina against a besieging Meccan force; the Banu Qurayza, having conspired to support the Meccans, eventually surrendered to Mohammed's forces after being besieged themselves.

Mohammed personally oversaw the physical elimination of these remaining Jews. "Some you slew," God reminded him in the Koran, "and others you took captive."[20] This refers to the beheading of the entire adult male population, perhaps six hundred in number after some had hastily converted to Islam, of the Banu Qurayza. After executing the men and those of the boys who passed an examination for the presence of pubic hair, Mohammed took pains to organize in detail the distribution of the Banu Qurayza's wealth. He also provided precise instructions for the enslavement of the Jewish females and boys. For the boys, girls, and younger women, this enslavement was largely sexual in nature.

Perhaps Mohammed eliminated the Jews of Medina because their fellow Jews in Mecca had been so scornful in rejection of the new prophecy, despite his many efforts there to placate them. Perhaps the new ruler of Medina wanted more spoils—the Jewish women, children, and chattels—for himself and his followers. The texts are proudly frank about his confiscating these as soon as he was able to. Perhaps Medina's Jews were conspiring with Mohammed's opponents back in Mecca. Perhaps, having been defeated by the Muslims, the hundreds of Jews beheaded at Medina simply made their own tragic choice, for the system allowed only three options for the Jews and Christians under its rule: convert, accept separate status as a tribute-paying underclass, or be killed.

For the decade of his government at Medina, Mohammed ruled with the powers of an absolute monarch. Enjoining charity and honesty among believers; dispensing wise judgments on matters of justice; punishing, killing, or exiling most who crossed him, he produced new revelations, legislating for an ever-wider range of daily life. Where there were gaps in the laws provided directly by Allah through revelation, Mohammed filled these with his own words and example. God Himself had said that Mohammed was the perfect Muslim. Everything that the Prophet did and said, no less than the Koran itself, must inevitably have the force of eternal law. In a total system, to differ was to blaspheme.

At Medina, with wherewithal at last, Mohammed's great idea became actual. He could now achieve complete integration of the religious, the social, the personal, and the political, all under his absolute personal direction. Originally, in Mecca, whatever had been happening among the Prophet and his followers had not yet been Islam. The subversive preaching of borrowed legends and reworked myths to a ragtag band of powerless followers; the vague promises of a fairer order; the poetic articulation of transcendent truths about God's unity and the inevitability of the Judgment Day: these hallmarks of the earlier years at Mecca did not, for Mohammed, contain the essence of the new faith that he would create. In strictly religious terms, nothing in the Mecca period had been new at all.[21]

The theocracy at Medina was something else. The complete submission of a community of people according to God's will: this was Islam. Thus it is from the year 622, the year of the *hejira*, the flight to Medina, that the faith dates its birth.

———

Three months after Mohammed's move to Medina, in Mecca Khalid was called to the deathbed of his father. Al Walid had three dying requests. One was the repayment of certain moneys owed to him; Mohammed was among the debtors. God now issued to Mohammed a timely revelation forbidding the payment of interest on debts such as his own: "Believers, have fear of God and waive what is still due to you as usury, if your faith be true; or War shall be declared against you by God and his Apostle."[22] The verse is widely accepted as having been directed specifically at Khalid and his claim to the money due his father. Ever after, Islamic finance would go to lengths to accommodate this implicit proscription against interest-bearing debt.

In the spring of 624—March, when the wildflowers are already dying in the Arabian heat—Khalid was away from Mecca, presumably with a caravan of spices or other goods on the Levant route. A small Meccan army came limping home while he was away. They were returning from a bruising battle with the Muslim forces from Medina. The clash is known as the Battle of Badr. It was the opening confrontation in what became a six-year war. Three hundred and thirteen Muslims, hoping to ambush a rich Meccan caravan from Syria, had instead encountered a force of over a thousand Quraysh and defeated them. The caravan was led by Abu Sufyan of the House of Umayya. "Go out and attack it," Mohammed had commanded the Muslims, "perhaps God will give it as a prey."[23] The Muslims killed seventy Meccans at the Battle of Badr and captured seventy more. One of the captives was a brother of Khalid.

Khalid had his revenge a year later, at the Battle of Uhud. This time the Meccans, personally led by Mohammed's perennial adversary Abu Sufyan, brought the fighting to the outskirts of Medina. It was springtime again. Mohammed almost always took an active, detailed role in the battles and raids of his jihad. At the mountain of Uhud, he positioned his archers just so, on a low hill, with instructions to concentrate their fire upon the enemy cavalry. Khalid was now actively supporting his father in the fight against Mohammed. The young nobleman commanded one of the two wings of the Meccan army. The battle began well for the Muslims, but even as the Meccan center crumbled Khalid stayed firm on his wing.

Seeing the disarray of the Meccans, Mohammed's men ignored his orders and stormed down from their higher ground, swarming into the Meccan camp. Khalid's moment had arrived. A secondary commander in an obscure tribal skirmish in a backward and forgotten corner of the world, he was about to discover the calling that would make him one of the great commanders in the history of warfare. At the head of his horsemen, Khalid charged onto the hill abandoned by the Muslims and then swept down and into their rear. They scattered before him.

Elsewhere on the battlefield, Mohammed had become separated from most of his troops and was coming under pressure. He had prepared carefully for combat, putting on two coats of mail. Now Mohammed fired arrow after arrow into the Quraysh forces. He accepted a challenge to single combat and slew his adversary with a spear, and then was wounded in the head with a rock. Bleeding from his lip, cheeks, and forehead, two teeth broken, Mohammed watched as an enemy shot an arrow into the buttocks of one Umm Eiman, an Ethiopian former slave who had been his nursemaid. Seeing the enemy bowman laughing, the ruler of Medina pulled an arrow from his own quiver and handed it to his best archer. "Shoot that man," Mohammed ordered. The arrow went through the Meccan's neck. God's Messenger laughed for one of the very few times in his career.

Meanwhile Khalid was cutting through the main Muslim force. As the Meccans surged, Mohammed was able to escape up onto the mountain of Uhud. Khalid himself was given the difficult task of taking the high ground. At that moment he and Mohammed came the closest they would come to fighting each other. As Khalid's small group of riders moved up the hill, Mohammed sent his own cavalry to block them.

Seeing the horsemen above, knowing that he could not beat them from lower ground, Khalid turned back. He saw that heading the Muslim detachment, facing him down from the heights, was an old friend: Omar.

During the next five years, Mohammed sent his army out from Medina on dozens of expeditions against the Meccans and others. The once-humble preacher was now called the Prophet of God, deemed such by Allah Himself in the ever-flowing revelations of the Medinan Koran. Sometimes Mohammed led the raids and battles himself, sometimes he delegated. At the oasis town of Khaibar in 629 he extirpated the remnants of the area's Jews, two years after he had beheaded hundreds in the trench near Medina. He had expelled the Jews of Khaibar from Medina in 625, and since then they had been conspiring to defeat him. With the Jews gone, and submission tendered by almost all of their neighbors, the Prophet's power in the Medina region was now virtually undisputed.

Wealth poured into the new community. As Mohammed and his followers conquered their neighbors, they confiscated their belongings. The women and children of the vanquished were taken into slavery. This was no accident or byproduct. The Koran, especially in its eighth chapter, titled "Al-Anfal" ("The Spoils of War"), provides a careful legal framework for this element. The Sunna, the great body of traditions recollecting Mohammed's deeds and words, mostly from the Medina years, provides more. According to the detailed system elaborated in the Koran and the Sunna, Islam itself—the Prophet and those to whom he disburses—must receive one-fifth of the confiscated wealth. The leader was also to select from among the newly enslaved women, some for their own protection. Other women he distributed individually to his friends. The humbler believer benefited too from the spoils as Islam swept through Arabia.

In Mecca, Khalid saw all around himself a world in which the momentum and the glory were on the side of the Muslims. He was forty-three years old, a young man no more. After his success at Uhud, he must have possessed a stimulating sense of his own ability in battle. He remembered how passionately Mohammed's warriors had fought on the other side.

"It is evident that . . . Mohammed is neither a poet nor a sorcerer, as the Quraish allege," Khalid eventually told his companions in Mecca in late May of 629. "His message is truly divine." Khalid decamped for Medina that night with his armor, weapons, and horse. When he arrived in the Muslim town, the optimism and the enterprising spirit intoxicated him.

At Medina Khalid saw Omar. They greeted each other cordially enough. But both knew that Omar was an early Muslim—number forty, no less—while Khalid had the blood of many Muslims on his hands after seven years of armed struggle against God's Messenger. It was an exciting time in Medina, and in this heady atmosphere a relaxed Khalid found himself making one of the many impolitic slips that were to compromise his career as a Muslim. One evening he visited the Prophet at the house of a wife. The woman, one of Mohammed's eight or so brides at that time, was an aunt of Khalid's. Khalid was present when a dish of cooked food arrived. The meal had been sent by a Bedouin supporter, a true nomad of the desert.

"O Messenger of Allah," asked this wife of the Prophet, "do you know what this is?"

"No," said Mohammed.

"This is roast lizard!"

"This meat I shall not eat," said God's Apostle.

Here Khalid interjected. Perhaps he was remembering the days when he had been sent to live with relatives in the desert as a youth. He had certainly learned to ride and fight and carry himself like a man; maybe he had also acquired a seemly Bedouin taste for roast lizard.

"O Messenger of Allah," he asked, "is it haram?"

"No," answered the Prophet.

"Can we eat it?"

"Yes, you may do so."

Khalid promptly ate the lizard meat with characteristic zest. It would never be forgotten that he had enjoyed what the Prophet had rejected.

Medina was full of hope and wealth then. Tribe after tribe capitulated to the spears and swords of Islam. Captive horses, women, girls, boys, and other booty flooded in. But Medina was a stern place, too.

There was far more to the new formula than sex slaves and loot. The Prophet was a man of modesty in material matters. Charity, integrity, and justice were expected between one believer and another. Allah was busy revealing laws for every aspect of life, and only that which was not haram was halal. The surrender demanded by the Prophet was complete. Any infraction was an affront to God Himself. The atmosphere in God's perfect community could not avoid a certain censoriousness. The anecdote of the lizard comes with a tone of foreboding for Khalid, the easygoing, good-looking nobleman who would never be truly convincing as a member of the austere new faith.

Three months after moving to Medina and declaring himself a believer, Khalid found himself fighting for the Prophet for the first time. It was an expedition into southern Syria. At Uhud, Khalid had inflicted on the Muslims the only military defeat that they were to suffer during the Prophet's lifetime. Now Khalid found himself beginning his Islamic career as an ordinary soldier, fighting in the ranks.

Early in the first battle of the raid into the north, the Muslim commander was killed. Khalid quickly emerged as the leader of the remaining band. Slaying the enemy all around him, he used nine swords, one after the other, on his way to victory. After this the Prophet dubbed him *Saifullah*, the Sword of Allah. For the next three years Khalid fought for Mohammed nearly constantly in the wars to conquer the Arabian subcontinent.

Khalid sometimes went too far even for the violent context of the moment. In 630 Mohammed and the Muslim army finally conquered Mecca, eight years after he had fled it with a sole companion in the dark of night. A series of military victories and a last-minute conversion by Abu Sufyan, chief of the Meccan commercial nobility, whose family was to benefit spectacularly from his switching sides when he did, had turned the balance. With the defection of Abu Sufyan and his ilk, Mecca was essentially delivered to Mohammed, although some resisters remained. The Prophet surrounded it with his troops. There were four entry points, and he divided these among Khalid and three others, charging them with entering the city by force if necessary. Their instructions were to kill only in self-defense. The sole violence of the day took place in the sector that Khalid commanded. On this and at least two other occasions, Mohammed rebuked him publicly for killing more than the jihad required. The rebukes, however, were minor. Khalid was the Prophet's best general.

———

Mohammed's rule at Medina lasted from shortly after the hejira in 622, with its official birth of Islam, until his death in June 632. A dramatic change took place almost as soon as this period began. At Medina the street preacher became a ruler. Passing along binding revelations from the Almighty, legislating for all eternity with every word and action, he alone was the source of law and he alone possessed the power of judgment.

Mohammed at Mecca had been a warner in the tradition of the ancient Jewish prophets, reminding the town's pagans of their error and of the Judgment to come. All the while he courted the town's Jews and Christians with a related message. As they submitted to Abraham's One God, so too did he; they were all People of the Book together. Had his fellow merchants of Mecca succeeded in killing him that night when he fled to Medina, Mohammed ibn Abdullah ibn Abd al-Muttalib would be remembered differently today. We would know him, if we knew him at all, as an obscure seventh-century mystic of great poetic power, slaughtered by a gang of his own illiterate pagan kinsfolk. But it was the youth Ali, not the Prophet Mohammed, whom the Quraysh found in the Prophet's bed before dawn on that fateful morning.

Then, starting in 622, comes Medina. There "the primal prophetic power goes slack."[24] The language itself changes, the Arabic rhymes become workaday, the grammar loose. The content, often transcendent at Mecca, becomes legalistic and practical, sometimes strikingly so.[25]

When charity was enjoined at Medina, it was cited not as a general principle, as it had been at Mecca, but rather as a specific prescription. The categories of individuals who were to receive the good works were carefully listed (orphans and the "traveler in need," for example), and they all had to be Muslim.[26] When a Muslim had polluted himself—by urinating, or by having sex with a woman—before prayer, the contamination could be removed with dust from a high place if there was no water to be had.[27] The degrees of relationship that made a woman available or unavailable for marriage, or the degrees of status that allowed the believer to force sex upon her, were detailed. If a wife was too young or too old to menstruate, the time to wait before divorcing her was not four months but three, during which time she had to be lodged well in the believer's own home and not harassed. Once the waiting period had expired, spoken testimony from two honest fellow believers was sufficient to effect the divorce. Hunting game while on pilgrimage was haram, as was eating carrion at all times except those of severe hunger. "Wine and games of chance, idols and divining arrows, are abominations devised by Satan."[28]

The Medina years also produced the many verses legislating for the military jihad, including its material benefits, as in the Anfal chapter. The famous verse about unbelievers that begins, "Make war upon them until idolatry shall cease," was one of scores of Medina references to the imperative of the Holy War. Hundreds of other instances set the tone for this obligation by referring to "unbelievers," "infidels," "idolaters," and "enemies of God."

With regard to the "kaffir," the unbeliever or infidel, the change in both substance and tone between the Mecca revelations and those from the Medina years is representative of the broader evolution in the message. In his second to last Meccan revelation, in 622, mere days before he was finally forced to flee from the town, Mohammed said,

> Be courteous when you argue with the People of the Book, except with those among them who do evil. Say: "We believe in that which has been revealed to us and that which was revealed to you. Our God and your God is one. To Him we submit."[29]

Here the message is for his followers to treat emolliently with the Jews and Christians. This is typical of the Mecca period, the early years when the believers were weak and outnumbered. An emulation of Christianity, suited to outsiders and underdogs, informed much of the prophecy then. Mohammed's twelve years of preaching in Mecca never garnered more than a few score of disciples. Then came 622 and the formal birth of Islam with the move to Medina, bringing earthly rule, the fruits of offensive jihad, and a widening community of believers.

With the Prophet governing absolutely and his armies beginning to conquer the rest of Arabia, the message was a new one. "Believers, take neither the Jews nor the Christians for your friends,"[30] said the penultimate revelation from Medina, while other Medinan verses repeated again and again God's commands to "make war on the Unbelievers"[31] and "slay the idolaters wherever you find them."[32] * The Prophet's truth was nothing if not absolute, and ultimately "there cannot be equality between those who have and those who spurn absolute truth."[33] † The superiority of the believer, in other words, went further than mere law. In a faith of government that soon became an empire, this would have important political implications later.

With the change at Medina, contradictions arose between earlier and later commandments. Settling any such conflicts, revelations now came establishing the principle of abrogation, whereby later revelations canceled earlier ones with which they differed.[34] Thus in the Medina period there is the all-abrogating command "When the sacred months are over slay the idolaters wherever you find them,"[35] whereas earlier at Mecca had been crafted the diplomatic "Be courteous when you argue with the People of the Book."[36]

Just after the arrival at Medina, while the tiny group of believers were new guests in what was still a largely Jewish town, mollifying the wary locals was a priority. A new revelation was announced: "There shall be no compulsion in religion."[37] The acquisition of earthly power was imminent, and this was one of the last of the Mecca-style revelations, encouraging tactful dealings with those in power.

Later, once the Medina theocracy took root, the "no compulsion" commandment was abrogated by a profusion of revelations mandating the martial jihad and detailing the choice to be imposed upon the conquered. The Jews and Christians, being People of the Book, had a third choice, besides conversion or death. They could keep their religion in return for accepting a subservient, tribute-paying, but protected status. "Dhimmis," as they became known, were exempted from military service and free to eat their pork and drink their wine in private, as long

---

* The Book sometimes uses the word "jihad" in reference to something that is not military at all, but rather an inner striving of sorts. Almost all of these usages occur in the earlier Mecca period. The ultimate message about the overriding necessity of making war upon the kaffir was emphasized in a comparatively larger number of verses produced during the subsequent Medina period. Chapters as diverse as numbers two, nine, forty-seven, and sixty-six, to select a few examples, repeat the message in a large number of different ways.

† This was pointed out by the great Viennese-born Arabist G. E. von Grunebaum, an escapee from Austria following the Anschluss in 1938.

as they accepted restrictions on their personal and public lives and paid the "jizya," the poll tax on unbelievers. But pagans, polytheists, and atheists were different. They did not believe in the One God of Abraham. They thus possessed no "religion" at all. So they could indeed be compelled. Unlike the dhimmis, the Abrahamic monotheists with their three choices, the pagans and the godless had only the first two options: conversion or death.*

"Mohammed is God's apostle. Those who follow him are ruthless to the Unbelievers but merciful to one another"[38] was typical of Medina's message in these matters. The Medina revelations account for about 80 percent of the Koran's text. In some cases, the divine messages took on a notable tone of convenience or pragmatism. At Medina, for example, God gave his Prophet a personal dispensation to possess more wives than other men were allowed, and wives who were closer blood relations.[39] Mohammed was permitted to start his Ramadan fast later than ordinary Muslims, and to end it earlier. When Mohammed found himself frequently visiting one especially alluring Christian slave woman, a jealous wife forced him to promise that he would stop. God commanded His Messenger to ignore the conjugal promise. "Prophet," He said, "why do you prohibit that which God has made lawful for you, in seeking to please your wives?"[40]

In this classic Medina situation, God also directly addressed two of Mohammed's other wives, commanding them to stop gossiping and harassing his Messenger; should they fail to do so, Mohammed could divorce them and "his Lord will give him in your place better wives than yourselves." When the Prophet developed a desire for his daughter-in-law Zaynab, and his adopted son quickly divorced her so that Mohammed might have her, the community was scandalized. Swiftly, the Almighty took pains to issue a series of revelations sanctifying the controversial deed.[41]

God gave his Prophet detailed dispensation to marry almost any woman he chose, saying, "This privilege is yours alone." Mohammed's wives were told that they must be more modest than the wives of other men. "You are not like other women," God reminded them through his

---

* Zoroastrians, encountered in the invasion of Iran, were not people of the Abrahamic book, but they were at least monotheists. Islam eventually offered protected dhimmi status to Zoroastrians too.

Prophet. "Do not be too complaisant in your speech, lest the lecherous-hearted should lust after you."[42]

Few opportunities to improve the Prophet's personal life appear to have escaped the Almighty's care in the Medina revelations. "Believers," reads one of these numerous instances, "do not enter the houses of the Prophet for a meal without waiting for the proper time, unless you are given leave. But if you are invited, enter; and when you have eaten, disperse. Do not engage in familiar talk, for this would annoy the Prophet and he would be ashamed to bid you go."[43]

Mohammed's favorite wife, the youthful and cheeky Aisha, was herself surprised at God's uncanny solicitousness. "I used to look down upon those ladies who had given themselves to Allah's Messenger," she recalled, referring in part to fellow wives who slept with her husband out of turn. But then Allah handed down to the Prophet a revelation explaining that he was welcome to sleep with any of them in whatsoever order he chose, whenever he pleased. "I feel," she said to her husband with characteristic impertinence, "that your Lord hastens in fulfilling your wishes and desires."[44]

Under the Prophet's vigorous military leadership, the armies of Islam subdued almost all of Arabia by the time of his death in 632. Sometimes, as at Hunain in 630, where Mohammed defeated a coalition of tribes and took six thousand women, children, and slaves, it was a pitched battle. Other times there might be a siege, as at Taif, or the Muslims might capture an enemy chief on a daring raid, as Khalid did at Daumat al Jandal. Often the tribes, with the tide of Islam well in flood, submitted before fighting was necessary.[45]

Mohammed died in his bed at Medina. He was sixty-three years old, and the flight from Mecca had been a dozen years earlier. By this time the essential project had been successful in his own land, if not yet in the broader world. For the next stage, the greater ambitions, men such as Khalid, Sword of Allah, would need to take Islam's sharp spears and swift ponies into Iraq and far beyond. The earthly rewards promised to the warriors of the faith were vast, and the distribution of these rewards was guaranteed in detail by the holy law of Medina.

As valuable, perhaps, as these worldly incentives was the full moral encouragement that Islam's desert horsemen received from their God, who now commanded them:

When the sacred months are past, kill the idolators wherever you find them, and seize them, besiege them and lie in wait for them in every place of ambush; but if they repent, pray regularly and give the alms tax, then let them go their way, for God is forgiving, merciful.[46]

"The trumpet of war he sounded was real enough" in the Medina period. "Red blood clung to the sword he wielded to establish his realm." Military expansion—"down-to-earth, matter-of-fact war"—would be the inheritance of the first caliphs who were to follow him, for "there was now no preference for peace . . . The struggle must go on until 'God's word is supreme.'"[47] *

At the end of August 632, Khalid ibn al Walid sharpened his sword and saddled his horse once more. The Prophet had died in June. Islam was facing the worst threat of its young life. From the coasts of Bahrain and Oman in the east to the Red Sea by Mecca in the west, from the greener highlands of Yemen in the south (called *Arabia Felix* by the Romans for its relative verdancy) to the dry steppe bordering fertile Mesopotamia in the north, the Arabs were rising against rule from Medina.

The Arabs had indeed sworn loyalty. But events were now making clear that this had been loyalty to a man, a ruler, Mohammed the war leader, Mohammed the sharer of spoils, rather than loyalty to his *al Lah* whose angel had spoken to the man in a cave. Other conversions, clearly, had been a matter of self-preservation or material possibility. Soon Islam's rule held in only three towns of the Arabian subcontinent. The embattled Muslims found themselves but "a small island of belief in an ocean of disbelief, a lamp shining in the darkness."[48]

Islam needed its finest soldier as never before. Apostasy, leaving the faith, was the single worst enormity of the many crimes in the Prophet's legislative religion. It was worse even than homosexual acts with an

---

* Ignatz Goldziher (d. 1921), author of these words, was a Hungarian professor who pioneered the field of Islamic studies. Goldziher's love of the faith extended to his some-times feeling that he himself was Muslim; in fact, despite these occasional moments, which occurred mainly while he was traveling in Muslim lands, he was a committed Jew dedicated to improving his own faith with the Islamic example.

adult, or the murder of a fellow Muslim male. Along with these sins it was one of the few crimes punishable by death. And now, with apostasy spreading through Arabia, the Muslims' subcontinental empire, with its bountiful tax harvests, had melted away. For a decade the believers had slaughtered their neighbors, enslaving the women and children and subjecting survivors to humiliating tributes or the rejection of their ancient faiths. Now the founder was gone, and the men in charge had much to fear.

Islam's new leader was Abu Bakr, Mohammed's companion on the hejira, the flight from Mecca to Medina ten years earlier. The father of Aisha, Mohammed's favorite wife, Abu Bakr had become the Prophet's first successor, or caliph. Abu Bakr was close to the Banu Umayya, the leading oligarchical clan that, like Khalid and his father, had resisted Mohammed for so long. Thus Abu Bakr's succession had been a blow to the hopes of members of Mohammed's own family, especially the Prophet's cousin and foster son Ali. But it was good for Khalid.

In August or September of 632, Abu Bakr formed eleven corps of fighters to begin the reconquest of Arabia. Khalid received the first of these commands, with orders to go into battle immediately while the rest organized. Inspired by Mohammed's success, additional enterprising prophets had arisen in Arabia. Khalid swiftly subdued these and others. First he brought to heel Tulaiha the Imposter, then the tribes of Banu Fazara and Banu Sulaim. He defeated the grande dame apostate Salma, who commanded her troops from "an armored litter atop her mother's famous camel."[49] Khalid forced Sajja, the rhyming Christian clairvoyant, to flee to Iraq. Then he defeated and executed her ally, Malik.

The night that he killed Malik, Khalid married the man's famously beautiful wife, Laila. Khalid could not help himself. Taking slave girls was one thing, but this was another matter. A dashing roué in the dour world of the complete faith, Khalid seemed always to have been close to trouble, and Laila was said to possess the finest legs in Arabia. In the morning, after the conquering hero had enjoyed his spoils, a pious Muslim galloped off to Medina to complain to the caliph about Khalid's behavior. Abu Bakr ordered the man back to his post. But Omar disagreed. Khalid, he demanded, should be brought to them in irons.

"O Omar," said Abu Bakr to the severe and pious man who would succeed him, "keep your tongue off Khalid. I shall not sheathe the sword that Allah has drawn against the infidels." Khalid was nonetheless called back to Medina to explain himself.

Khalid knew it meant trouble. But it was hard to repress this brilliant commander who had grown up the son of the greatest man in Mecca. Called to account by a man he must always have considered his inferior, the Sword of Islam appeared at Medina's mosque en dandy, with an arrow in his turban. Almost immediately, he saw Omar.

"You ought to be stoned to death," said Omar, grabbing the arrow and snapping it in two. Khalid knew Omar's power in Medina and turned away quietly.

Later that day, Khalid successfully came through his meeting with the more congenial Abu Bakr, an ally of sorts from the old Meccan elite. Confident, seeing Omar in the street again, Khalid called out to him boisterously, "Come to me, O left-handed one!"[50] Omar said nothing and went off to his house.

The closest document that Islam has to an official biography of its founder is Ibn Hisham's (d. 833) abridgement of the lost text of the *Biography of the Prophet of Allah*, by Ibn Ishaq (d. ca. 767). According to this venerated work, the Prophet "took part personally" in twenty-seven battles and raids during his nine years at Medina. "He actually fought in nine engagements," wrote the author, naming each. Mohammed had personally planned thirty-eight of formative Islam's original battles and raids.[51] The numerous executions and assassinations that he ordered were not counted.

For People of the Book, Mohammed's definitive injunction was, as God commanded in this all-abrogating verse from the very end of his legislating career:

> Fight against such of those to whom the Scriptures were given as believe in neither God nor the Last Day, who do not forbid what God and His apostle have forbidden, and do not embrace the true Faith, until they pay tribute out of hand and are utterly subdued.[52]

Under Abu Bakr the Arabs began their great expansion. To the north of Arabia lay the two great empires of Rome and Persia. Not nearly as strong as they had been, these were still spectacularly rich to the Arabs, and Abu Bakr turned to a tool that Mohammed had used effectively in building support on a smaller scale in Medina and then the rest of Arabia: "soliciting loyalty by rewarding it with opportunities for acquiring loot—for which the poverty-stricken Arabs had an insatiable appetite."[53] *

Mohammed had died in June of 632. By February or March of 633, the Apostasy was defeated. It was time to carry on the broader work that the Prophet had begun, and Khalid received the historic orders from Abu Bakr.

"Proceed to Iraq," the caliph commanded. "Fight the Persians and the people who inhabit their land."

It was a momentous instruction. The Sasanians had ruled for four centuries. Their empire was for the most part the empire of Cyrus, Alexander, Seleucus, and the Parthians. They were heirs to a culture that was the most splendid on earth. Babylonia and Assyria provided, as usual, the richest and most important provinces in the realm. The illiterate, nomadic Arabs were traditionally no more than a flea on the underbelly of this great Persian Empire, but Islam had given three crucial gifts to the Bedouin and merchants of Arabia: ten years of incessant warfare to sharpen military skills that were already impressive, a hard-won unity that they had never before enjoyed, and a system of belief that forbade their killing each other while rewarding them with slaves and other booty when they conquered others. With the tribes united following the crushing of the Apostasy, thirteen years after the Prophet's lonely escape from Mecca with Abu Bakr, the world was about to quake.

In the five years since Persia had concluded its last, twenty-four-year-long, war with the Romans of Byzantium, the Sasanian Empire had had nine kings. As Byzantine and Persian rule shifted east and west and back again in the Mesopotamian borderland north of Arabia, the decay of the ancient empires laid the ground for a new master.

---

* Hugh Kennedy points out that the Arab accounts and poems from the time of the early conquests refer very little to "martyrdom" and other otherworldly aspects of the faith. Instead they make reference mostly to tribal and Arab pride, glory-seeking, an ancient "delight in battle and slaughter . . . straight from the pre-Islamic world," and "desire for booty" as their motives. *The Great Arab Conquests* (London: Phoenix, 2008), pp. 62–64. Islam and its jihad were, for such warriors and their poets, a system for amplifying, and sharing out the rewards of, age-old traditions.

Mesopotamian life still went on in its ancient combination of scale and sophistication. The people were mostly Christian, and their language, Aramaic, was the tongue of their Redeemer.[54] Under both Byzantines and Persians, civilized life continued, "notwithstanding the vilest tyranny of sots, drunkards, tyrants, lunatics, savages, and abandoned women, who from time to time held the reins of government."[55] For all this, "Mesopotamia, Babylonia, and Syria contained enormous populations, huge canals and dykes were kept in repair, and commerce and architecture flourished in spite of a perpetual procession of hostile armies and a continual changing of the nationality of the governor."

Khalid sent riders across northern and central Arabia, calling for volunteers to plunder these soft lands to the north. The general's name was already great among the Arabs. The plunder and glory promised to be more than anything that arid Arabia had ever offered. Khalid's men would ride with God's blessing, and no good Muslim could ignore God's call to jihad: "God has purchased from the faithful their lives and worldly goods, and in return has promised them the Garden. They will fight for the cause of God, they will slay and be slain."[56]

In less than a month Khalid recruited eighteen thousand men. It was by far the largest Muslim army ever gathered. Before riding north into Iraq, he sent the classic Muslim submission formula to the Persian governor. This would have been familiar to Khalid from a decade of war in Arabia. It was now to be repeated countless times from Gibraltar to the frontiers of India over the next few generations:

> Submit to Islam and be safe. Or agree to the payment of the Jizya [the head tax on the kaffir], and you and your people will be under our protection, else you will have only yourself to blame for the consequences.[57]

Late Sasanian Iraq had a substantial Jewish minority. Nestorian Christians made up most of the population. Their Church of the East, as it was called, adhered to the Nestorian "radical Dyophysite" doctrine that Christ had two natures, divine and human, entirely separate. The "Son," the divine element, lived within Jesus, but Jesus himself was fully human. The Byzantines, rejecting this as heresy, held to the Chalcedonian Creed. Named for the 451 AD Council of Chalcedon that claimed to settle the question of Christ's divinity, this held that Christ had a single united nature, both human and divine.

Nestorianism put the people of Iraq at odds with the "Romans" of Constantinople. But as Nestorians, the Iraqis were Christian nonetheless, and their loyalty to the rigidly Zoroastrian state of the late Sasanians was not deep. Meanwhile Islam was still seen by many as a jury-rigged offshoot of Christianity, one that shared the Nestorian instinct that it was absurd to consider a flesh-and-blood historical figure, such as the Nazarene carpenter, to be in any way divine. The Nestorian Christian and the Muslim had this in common: their final prophets were men, not gods, to be followed, not worshipped. In addition to the general weakness of the Sasanian state after over four hundred years, much of it spent warring with either the first Rome or the second, this backdrop would be to Khalid's advantage in Iraq.

In his early days there, Khalid won numerous small battles, his fast desert horsemen slicing through the cataphracts, the renowned heavy cavalry of the Persians. During one of these clashes, the Persians' champion, one Hazar Mard ("Thousand Men"), challenged Khalid to individual combat. Khalid slew the man, ate lunch sitting on the corpse, picked up his own weapons again, and went on to win yet another battle. Eventually the Persians withdrew into their towns, leaving the desert and its margins to Khalid and his fleet cavalry. Then he was called back to Arabia to subdue a Christian revolt, and the Persians took the field again. Khalid returned, and the Sasanians retreated once more into Ctesiphon. Throughout the campaign, Khalid sent a river of dazzling booty back to Arabia.

In June of 634, Khalid received another message from Abu Bakr at Medina. "I appoint you commander over the armies of the Muslims," it read, "and direct you to fight the Romans." The Sword of Islam was to fall upon Syria.

For Khalid, it was splendid news. In Iraq, he had shown his superiority to the Persians; now was his chance to prove himself against another empire, and further immerse himself in booty and laurels.*

---

* The incentivizing effect of Islam's spoils system has been aptly compared to that of the prize money system in the British Royal Navy in its heyday.

In a heroic desert march Khalid brought part of his army into eastern Syria. On one especially merciless stretch, it is said, he had the camels drink their fill or more and then sewed their mouths shut so they could not chew their cud and digest the water. As they crossed the desert, Khalid slaughtered the beasts "one by one so his men could drink the water from their stomachs."[58] Appearing dramatically in eastern Syria after this historic crossing, Khalid marched toward the Mediterranean coast.

Syria was the fairest province of the Eastern Roman Empire. Compared to arid Arabia and flood-wracked Mesopotamia, its climate was gentle and generous. Damascus and Aleppo were the two leading cities between Rome and Ctesiphon. The ports of Tripoli, Tyre, Beirut, and Jaffa were thriving centers of far-flung trade.

The Byzantine position in Syria, meanwhile, had major weaknesses. In the Greek cities, loyalty to the Roman Empire and its official, Chalcedonian Christianity was strong. But in the Arab countryside and smaller towns, a heterodox Christianity called Monophysitism prevailed. This heresy stood at the opposite end of the Christological spectrum from the Dyophisitism of the Nestorians: while the Nestorian Christ was essentially human, the Monophysite Christ was essentially divine. From the Byzantines' Chalcedonian perspective, with Christ equally human and divine, both were blasphemies to be stamped out.

In the Arab-speaking Syrian hinterland, then, the Roman state centered at Constantinople was not only a foreign overlord but an impious one as well.[59] That the Persians had taken Damascus in 612 and held it for fifteen years also weakened Byzantine legitimacy in the province. Add to this the exhaustion of the Byzantine Empire after the long wars with Persia, and Syria was ripe for the picking when Khalid rode west from Iraq. Ultimately, however, the resistance of the "Romans" there, while doomed, was strong.

After a year of raids and battles across the country, the Arabs settled down to a siege of Damascus in the spring of 635. The city held out for six bitter months. When it fell that September, Khalid's army entered from the east, another Arab army entered from the west, and the two met in the middle of the city's famous Straight Street—where Paul, not long after the death of Christ, had been baptized. On the first day of October, Khalid wrote to Abu Bakr in Medina that Damascus was now his. It was the first city of stature to belong to the Muslims.

A few hours later, a messenger arrived to hand Khalid a letter. It came from far-off Medina, to which he had just sent news of his victory. It was from Omar, written nine days earlier. Abu Bakr had died. Omar was caliph now. He relieved the Sword of Allah of his command.

The humiliation of Khalid, it was said at the time, was Omar's first official act as Regent of God on Earth. Back in Medina, in the mosque where Omar read out the news of the decision, the listeners responded with shocked silence. Then a young member of Khalid's tribe stood up and challenged the new caliph.

"Do you dismiss a man in whose hand Allah has placed a victorious sword?" asked the man. "Allah will never forgive you, nor will the Muslims."

The next day, Omar, in the mosque once more, explained. Khalid, he said, "is wasteful and squanders his wealth on poets and warriors, giving them more than they deserve, which wealth could be better spent in helping the poor and needy among the Muslims."

Brutally demoted, Khalid could not stay away from battle. He remained in the field with the army in Syria, standing beside his replacement Abu Ubaida and coaching the man to one victory after another. The Romans reeled before Khalid as the Persians had done. Then, in 636, the emperor Heraclius gathered an army, perhaps fifteen to twenty thousand strong, to drive the Muslims from Syria once and for all.[60] * It was a pivotal moment. Roman victory would keep the Levant and Egypt Christian. Arab victory would unleash Islam's warriors across vast, soft tracts far to the west of their conquests thus far.

The great confrontation took place in August 636 at the Yarmouk River, a tributary of the Jordan that forms the western part of the border between the present-day states of Syria and Jordan. The Arab force was likely a little bit smaller than Heraclius's. For five days the Romans pounded the lighter Arab forces. The demoted Khalid, moving his elite cavalry from point to point to counterpunch wherever possible, gradually took charge from his less forceful and charismatic colleagues. By the end it was as if the Sword of Allah alone held the small Muslim army together.

On the sixth day, with both sides exhausted, Khalid concentrated his horsemen against the enemy's left flank, broke through their ranks, and

---

* The ancient Arab sources put it at a hundred thousand.

swept them into the steep gorge of the Yarmouk. It was an annihilation
from which Christianity in the Holy Land and surrounding regions was
never to recover. Khalid rapidly vanquished the remaining Roman forces
in Syria, mopping them up from Jerusalem to Antioch, still not losing
a battle. The gold and slaves streamed seemingly without end back to
Medina.

But Allah was sovereign over all, and now Omar wielded His power
on earth. No glory, no gold, no green provinces nor trains of human
chattel could avert the fall of the Sword of Allah.

In autumn 638, two years after the defeat of the Romans, Khalid had
recently been reprimanded by the Caliph Omar for using alcohol in his
bath oil. Now the Sword of Allah found himself the subject of another
letter from the Muslim capital. The general was in Emessa, present-day
Homs. It was one of Syria's richer cities, founded by Seleucus the Macedonian almost a thousand years earlier. The letter was addressed to Abu
Ubaida, Khalid's replacement as commander of the Muslim armies.

Once again, for at least the third time, Omar had been angered by
stories of Khalid's immoderate patronage of poets. This time, Khalid
had given ten thousand dirhams to one who had sung his praises. It was
a large sum, the same amount that the town fathers there in prosperous
Emessa had earlier offered to the Muslim invaders as payment for the
safety of the city.

A crowd gathered when the messenger from Medina arrived. The
people of Emessa knew something important was afoot. The crowd
needed its explanation, but Abu Ubaida, an old companion of Khalid's
from many a battle, could not bear to make a public spectacle of his
friend. Instead, one of the emissaries from Medina, a former slave from
Ethiopia called Bilal, played that role. Bilal stood up and loudly asked
Khalid whose money had funded the old general's extravagances. Had
Khalid paid for his generosity himself, or had he used the public purse?

The implication was preposterous. Khalid was dumbstruck. Bilal asked
again. Khalid could not reply. Bilal stepped up, removed Khalid's turban,
and used it to tie the general's hands behind his back. "From my own
pocket!" cried out Khalid at last. Bilal replaced the turban on Khalid's head.

Soon enough Khalid himself received yet another letter from Medina. This one was a summons. He hastened to appear before the caliph. Omar stripped Khalid of a quarter of his wealth and removed him from his remaining duties. Humiliated, Khalid bought a small house for himself and his family back in Emessa. He would never again see the dry and distant land that had produced him, Omar, their faith, and their God's beloved Messenger.

Four years later, as Khalid wasted away of humiliation and boredom in the provincial town, a friend from campaigning days came to his deathbed. Khalid showed the man first his own left leg and then his right. The two old companions agreed that Khalid had not a hand's length on either limb unmarked by scars from battle in the service of God.

"Do you not see that I have sought martyrdom in a hundred battles?" asked the dying general. His greatest wish had been to die the best of deaths, fighting the kaffir.

"Why could I not have died in battle?"

"You could not have died in battle," said Khalid's visitor.

"Why not?"

"You must understand, O Khalid, that when the Messenger of Allah, on whom be the blessings of Allah and peace, named you Sword of Allah, he predetermined that you would not fall in battle."

Khalid must have looked surprised. His friend continued.

"If you had been killed by an Unbeliever it would have meant that Allah's sword had been broken by an enemy of Allah. And that could never be."

Chapter 9

At War Forever:
The Bloody Schism in Islam

Ali and His Son Hussein, 626–680

I can but see life with such oppressors as tribulation,
And death as martyrdom.
                    —Hussein ibn Ali before his death at Kerbala, 680 AD

An hour before sunrise in southern Iraq, the eastern horizon is almost impossible to discern. The dusty plain, flat from one edge of the world to the other, is immersed in darkness. Above an invisible line in the direction of Iran, a bruised purple, soon to brighten into a livid red, seeps into the early sky. Soon enough, the reddening glow becomes a fiery orange.

On October 10, 680 AD, forty-eight years after the death of Mohammed, the changing colors of the horizon heralded, as ever at that time of year in this part of Iraq, a day of scorching heat. An unremarkable part of the dusty plain, at a place called Kerbala, thirty-five miles west of Babylon, was soon to be forever famous.

As dawn rose, Hussein ibn Ali said his morning prayers. Hussein was the surviving son of Ali, the Prophet Mohammed's foster son, favorite, cousin, and son-in-law. Hussein had with him thirty or forty members of his family, some of them women and children. He was also accompanied by seventy-two loyal warriors. Around them were their tents and animals. In the tragedy ahead, the story of Shiism would find its second chapter, after beginning with the disappointments of Ali following the death of the Prophet in 632.

Beyond Hussein's modest encampment, a force of four thousand soldiers from the nearby garrison town of Kufa faced them. The Kufans
were loyal to Yazid, the grandson of Mohammed's bitter foe and third
cousin, Abu Sufyan of the house of Umayya. The Umayyads had taken
control of the Islamic empire upon the murder of Hussein's father, Ali,
the third caliph, in 661. The family had then moved the capital to their
family stronghold at Damascus. Now Yazid, the second of the Umayyad
caliphs, ruled over the faith-empire from the old Greek city in Syria. For
nine days his Kufan troops, an Umayyad army loyal to the Syrian power,
had been there on the plain facing the Prophet's grandson.

Every adult present was obliged to pray that morning, including the
Kufans and the women of Hussein's camp, except for those who were
menstruating. The law, the all-encompassing rules of the faith, dictated
that they must perform the morning prayer between the first tinges of
dawn and the rising of the sun. The day before, Hussein had asked the
commander of the Kufans for one last night, saying that he wished to
weigh his options of surrender and resistance. The early Muslim chroniclers relate that in truth Hussein had wanted something different: an
opportunity to arrange his affairs before the battle that he knew would
be his end.

The story does not say whether Hussein was able to sleep that final
night, before the dawn came and with it the prayer that begins with the
first lines of the Koran itself, so mesmerizing in spoken Arabic: "In the
name of Allah, the Merciful, the Compassionate. All praise be to Allah,
the lord of the worlds, the all-merciful, the all-compassionate, master
of the day of justice." For Hussein and his devotees, who eventually
looked to that day at Kerbala as the moment of supreme iniquity that
would evermore characterize their Shia faith, God's day of justice was
never farther away.

"You only do we serve," continued Hussein. He may well have been
kneeling outside his tent as the eastern sky brightened and the mounts
of his warriors began to nicker and paw at the ground with their morning needs. "And You alone do we ask for help. Guide us on the straight
path, the path of those whom You have blessed. No wrath rests upon
them and they do not go astray."

Hussein's Kerbala calvary was the final scene in a drama that had begun with Mohammed's death in 632, forty-eight years previously. The Prophet died, like Alexander, without naming a successor. Hussein's death was the last major event in the ensuing contest for control of the Muslim faith and empire. The contestants had been the Prophet's own family, notably Hussein and before him his father, Ali, and against them, the traditional Quraysh elite. The latter were in essence the same Meccan commercial establishment that had fought Mohammed until the moment when, in 630, two years before his death, they finally allowed him back into Mecca.

The time of Mohammed's first four successors, lasting from 632 to 661, is known as the *Rashidun*, or Rightly Guided, period. For the orthodox mainstream, the Rashidun Caliphate is seen as a halcyon age. The four Rashidun caliphs had all been leading companions of Mohammed, as was proper; none of them were explicitly profane and two were pious indeed; and during their rule the faith spread immensely, with the commensurate worldly rewards as laid out by the holy formulae. Under the surface, however, this golden age was as replete with inner turmoil and bloodshed as any other era. Only one of the four Rightly Guided caliphs died peacefully.

For Hussein, the story began with his father, Ali, known to all Muslims, Sunni and Shia alike, as *Asad Allah*, the Lion of God. Ali was the first male follower of Mohammed, the strongest fighter and the kindest soul among the Prophet's companions, and, even more than Hussein, the sorriest figure in all of Islam.

There is no relationship in the saga of the early Muslims to match the extraordinary closeness of Mohammed and his young cousin Ali ibn Abu Talib. As a boy in Mecca, Mohammed had himself been orphaned and taken in by an uncle, Abu Talib, keeper of the pagan Kaaba shrine. Decades later, when an adult Mohammed was a merchant in Mecca, Abu Talib was an old man with a large, hungry family and a business ravaged by bad crops. Helping his former foster father through these difficult times, Mohammed took in one of Abu Talib's children, a five- or six-year-old boy called Ali who would become, at the age of ten, Mohammed's first male follower.[1] Twelve years later, in the summer of 622, Ali would risk his life for the Apostle of God by sleeping in Mohammed's bed to deceive the assassins on the night that Mohammed fled from Mecca to Medina.

Ali soon caught up with Mohammed in Medina, two hundred miles to the south. In the coming years, as the Prophet's rule burgeoned there, Ali grew into magnificent manhood. He led many of the raids that funded the growing Islamic government. In Mohammed's early wars to bring Muslim rule to his fellow Arabs, Ali was to prove himself in single combat time and again against the best individual fighters of the various enemies.

In the scores of battles, raids, and ambushes of the early theocracy at Medina, there was no hero like Ali. Adding up the various names of his victims and the counts of his slaughters in the Muslim chronicles, it is likely that Ali killed at least fifty people with his own hands during the Prophet's lifetime. When the arrows rained down and the other Muslims fled the field, Ali was the one to shield the Prophet. When the flow of battle ran against God's Apostle, Ali, by his example, would reverse the tide. It was to Ali that Mohammed presented the double-tipped sword thenceforth known as Zulfiqar, following a successful assault upon the worshippers of the wooden idol Manat. When an important battlefield offensive required a new leader after Abu Bakr and Omar had failed, Ali finally led the charge and prevailed. Ali wore armor in the Prophet's many battles, but never on his back.

The nearly unremitting bloodshed of those early days served only to purify Ali. Each battle against Arabia's pagans, Jews, and Christians made him an even greater embodiment of chivalry and Muslim tenderness. The angelic purity and honor of Asad Allah were qualities he had learned growing up as a beloved ward in the household of God's Messenger. Through the long story of Ali's endless heroism in the birth years of the faith, these attributes never failed to shine through. In single combat during one battle against the Jews, a vanquished foe spat on Ali just before the Lion of God was to deliver the final sword thrust. Ali simply walked away. He would not corrupt his killing with a personal motive.

God may have given his Prophet the gift of Ali, but Mohammed's fourteen wives and concubines gave him few children of his own: four daughters, none of whom survived him, and three sons, none of whom lived past infancy.

Within their clan, the Banu Hashim, Ali was Mohammed's clear heir. But family was not everything in the political life of the seventh-century Arabs. And the Hashemites were a weak clan within the Quraysh tribe. Apart from Ali and one son of a freed slave, of Mohammed's ten core Companions, as his innermost circle were known, eight were men from various other Quraysh clans. Among these individuals, the Prophet's other favorite was Abu Bakr, the first adult convert, the first Muslim outside of the Prophet's family, and Mohammed's most trusted political colleague. A close second to Abu Bakr was Khalid ibn al Walid's nemesis, the austere Omar. Also a Quraysh from an influential family, Omar had been the first to propose murdering Mohammed, during the early days in Mecca. Omar's eventual conversion had done much to deliver Mecca to the Muslims.

Both Abu Bakr and Omar would attempt to marry Fatima, the Prophet's favorite daughter.* Mohammed, however, gave the girl to Ali. At the wedding, a small and modest affair, the Prophet had taken a swig from the water jug, gargled in the back of his throat, spat the water back in the jug, and doused the heads and shoulders of the newlyweds. This was in 624 AD, the second year in Medina and thus year two of the Muslim calendar.†

Ali was ten years old when his foster father, so doting that he used to chew the boy's food for him, started to receive God's messages. Eventually, after encountering little but frustration and exclusion in the prosperous town that for the most part did not want to hear his message, Mohammed gathered forty relatives for a generous meal. Who among them, he asked, would support his revolutionary mission? Mohammed's invitation met with an icy reception. Only the young Ali spoke up to commit himself.

Ali had been born inside the Kaaba shrine, where his father, Abu Talib, was the keeper. Ali was the only person ever to be born there. It was said that he then kept his eyes shut for three days, until his mother removed

---

* According to Sunnism, Mohammed had four natural daughters, all with his first wife, Khadija; of these, Fatima was his favorite and the longest-lived, dying shortly after him in 632. According to Shiism, Fatima was the Prophet's only natural daughter, the others having been adopted.

† At the time of the wedding, Ali was twenty-four years old. Fatima's age is unclear. According to Sunni sources, she was born in 605, which would make her nineteen at the time of her marriage—unusually old for seventh-century Arabia. Shia sources put her birth at 612 or 615 AD.

him from that place of idols. With his eventual adoption of Islam at the age of ten, Ali was then unique in another way among Mohammed's companions of pagan background: he had never worshipped any pagan god. He had never mumbled blasphemies before a holy rock or bowed to a living god of clay like those inside the dark little structure built, according to local lore, by Abraham and his wild son Ishmael. Meanwhile the rest of the Arabs, apart from the pagans, were Jewish and Christian. Unlike these, Ali had never followed a revelation other than Mohammed's. He was uniquely unsullied.

When the Muslims finally took possession of Mecca in 630, after eight years in Medina, Ali entered the polytheistic sanctuary with the Prophet and stood upon his shoulders. There Ali swept the idols from the high shelves, shattering them in the dark and dusty room as his forefather had done in Ur twenty-five centuries before.

As a result of Ali's early commitment, perfect piety, success in the battles of the jihad, and special place in the heart of the Prophet, he remains, after Mohammed, the most versed about, the most attested in traditions, the most beloved, and the most important figure in Islam. Ali's children, Hasan and Hussein, were both said to resemble their grandfather Mohammed strongly. The boys were, according to the chroniclers, the delight of the Prophet's later years.

Mohammed affirmed Ali's unique importance with more than the sobriquet Asad Allah. "Ali is from me and I am from Ali," said the Prophet. "Ali is the guardian of every believer after me."[2] The Prophet also once said of his most beloved Companion, "I am the city of knowledge, and Ali is its gateway." But Islam, a government as much as a religion, needed more than guardians and gateways. It required a leader, and for all his love of the Lion of God, Mohammed never quite named Ali his successor.

The result of Mohammed's intestacy would be, upon his death, a swift and terrible loss of innocence within Islam. The original, core faith, given the martial nature of the text of the Koran and of the Prophet's own sacred and perfect personal example, would be forever in *jihad* until the time of peace, when all the world had submitted. Now the competition among the leading Mecca families, whose milieu Mohammed had both upended and spectacularly expanded, condemned the faith also to be forever at war with itself. The Sunni-Shia schism in Islam developed from the events that presently took place.

Eventually orthodox Islam, covering nine out of ten "Muslims" under its wide umbrella, would be known as Sunnism, because it follows the Sunna, the traditions of the Prophet himself. Shiism, named after the *shia't Ali*, the supporters of Ali, would be guided by something different: the personages, biographies, and teachings of Ali, Hussein, and their successors. Sunnism contends that Ali was not awarded the prize because Mohammed did not trust his foster son's political skills. Shiism says Ali was the victim of the evil men who thenceforth dominated the Sunni faith.

The Prophet's death left layers of challenges behind him. Numerous individual ambitions were left unresolved in the absence of clear succession plans. More fundamentally, there was the issue of what the *umma*, Mohammed's community of believers, really signified now that the founder was gone. If Islam meant earthly government, as the system indisputably insisted by the Prophet's word and example, the enormous question remained of how to bind the believers together under one rule. Mohammed had fused faith, politics, and warfare brilliantly, but his was a rare combination of personal qualities. Of the two principal contenders in the succession struggle, the Quraysh and Ali, the Quraysh were, by and large, politic but not pious, and Ali was pious but not politic.

Within Mohammed's inner circle another rivalry existed, between the men of Medina, who had embraced the outcast preacher and given him a supportive base when he had fled there, and those who had followed him there from Mecca. With Mohammed gone, the new faith-state faced a substantial intra-Meccan division as well: the divide between the *muhajirun*, Mohammed's early followers, and the Quraysh aristocracy such as Khalid and his ilk, who had opposed Mohammed for so long before opening the gates of Mecca to him in 630.

Mirroring all of this on a broader scale was another divide, between the Quraysh and the other Arab tribes. Late as they had been in accepting Mohammed, only two years before his death, Mecca's dominant tribe had successfully traded access to Mecca for a central role in the Prophet's young state. Soon enough they used this position to ride the powerful force of Islam to a wider hegemony. Arabs, with their traditions of independence, could not accept this easily.

The latter issue was more than merely a matter of which, if any, tribe was on top. Key parts of the new framework itself were strongly at odds with Arab ways. Mohammed's early preaching as a political outsider had defended certain time-honored local traditions against the grasping commercial nobility of Mecca. But now, after his years of legislating at Medina, the Arabs' ancient freedoms were challenged by the absolute, comprehensive, and centralized character of the Prophet's creation, this new phenomenon whose name meant "submission." As demonstrated in the Apostasy that Khalid had defeated in 632–633, most of the Arab tribes had seen their compelled oaths of fealty to Islam as merely pragmatic obligations that died with Mohammed.

Finally, completing the dizzying web of conflicts waiting to emerge after Mohammed's death, there was a divide of Quraysh versus Quraysh. Mohammed's own clan, the Banu Hashim, had historically been relatively minor within the Quraysh tribe. Led by the Prophet's direct kin—Ali, then Hussein—the Hashemite clan could attach itself to Mohammed's prestige in attempting to rise from weakness to control. If successful, this would see them ruling over the larger, richer, and more senior clans of their tribe. Such an aspiration was bound to lead to conflict.

This was all routine local politics, of no inherent interest to the world or posterity. What made these matters important were the energies unleashed by Mohammed's genius. His formula for unifying and incentivizing the Arabs would soon give their feuds intercontinental scope, even as his religion made compromise difficult for the believer. God's will was absolute, and His rules had now been revealed immutably.

Many of these legacies bequeathed to early Islam were to make even the Rightly Guided early days remarkably fraught and violent. Beyond these factors, certain underlying philosophical challenges within the system itself were also to contribute to the tragedy that was unfolding.

It was part of the system that Mohammed's own conduct was perfect in every way, and that in its perfection this example carried the weight of absolute law. The Prophet's personal story was thus to provide the key template for the pious. It was a template that placed not only politics, but an autocratic, centralized, coercive politics, and a considerable amount of personal violence, at the center of the story alongside benevolent concerns for equality among believers or for the welfare of women, animals, children, and the poor. The theocracy at Medina, no less than the Koran itself, made it clear that in the Prophet's true faith there could never be a leaving unto Caesar what was Caesar's.

The succession struggle between Mohammed's relatives and the Meccan oligarchy burst into the open as soon as he died.

Poisoned by a Jewish woman in revenge for his beheading of her father, uncle, and husband, Mohammed expired at his Medina compound in the bedroom of his favorite wife, Aisha, a daughter of Abu Bakr. It was not, however, their faction that took the first advantage in the new world without Mohammed. Barring Aisha and her family from their presence, the Prophet's close blood relatives promptly took control of Mohammed's body, washing it and preparing for the burial.

Whatever advantage this conferred upon the Banu Hashim did not last long. A momentous meeting was taking place not far away in the meeting hall of another clan, local to Medina, called the Banu Saida. The Medinans had welcomed the Prophet when he had fled to their town from Mecca twelve years earlier. For this they were known as the Ansar, or Helpers, of the Prophet. Then, in 630, Mecca had acceded to the faith, and the Ansar found themselves suddenly dominated by the same Quraysh clique that had been fighting them for the last decade.

For generations before that, the Quraysh had been the leading tribe of western Arabia. They had built upon their lucrative control of the Kaaba, Mecca's pagan shrine, to establish trade networks north into Syria and beyond. The wealth, connections, organization, and experience of the Quraysh made them stronger than any other Meccan tribe, and much stronger than any tribe in poorer Medina. Once the Quraysh entered Mohammed's tent, so to speak, they naturally overshadowed any rivals.

Now, with the Prophet's death, the Ansar, the leading men of Medina, hoped there was an opportunity to reassert themselves. They gathered in the hall of the Banu Saida to choose a new leader. It was not at all clear that the Ansar wanted a true replacement for Mohammed, someone to rule all Muslims. It was not even clear that they, or any of the Arabs, desired or expected any ongoing unity whatever. What they certainly did not want was to exchange the leadership of their late Prophet for rule by the Quraysh, led by the wily Abu Sufyan of the Banu Umayya.

The historic gathering of the Ansar at the meeting hall of the Banu Saida has been parsed in detail ever since. It seems to have been a somewhat chaotic scene. Chiefs, elders, and ordinary tribesmen jostled in the crowded room. Each of them had his own hopes for a favorable resolution to the vacuum Mohammed had left behind. Ali, representing the Prophet's family, loved by many for his own merit in Islam, and a valued counterweight for the Ansar against the Meccan oligarchy, might well have emerged from the scene as the new leader—had he been there.

The *shura*, or council, in the hall of the Banu Saida seems to have taken place mere hours after Mohammed's death. Correct as ever, Ali was initially with Mohammed's corpse, doing what the male next of kin did, cleansing the body and standing vigil. He later gathered with other members of the Prophet's family at the house of Fatima, presumably to plan their next moves while denying their prestige to the *shura*, scene of such hasty and overt politicking.

Abu Bakr, however, was at the meeting. Omar was with him, as was Khalid's old friend Abu Ubayda. Hearing of the gathering, they had rushed to be present.* Left to their own, the Ansar were likely to pass over the Meccans in the brewing leadership crisis; Abu Bakr and the other Meccans with him hoped that by being present they could forestall this and perhaps seize the Prophet's mantle for themselves.

In the milling about, Abu Bakr, by now a frail old man, delivered a short speech.

"The Arabs will not accept the rule of anyone but this tribe of Qureysh," he began.[3] "They are the most central of the Arabs in lineage and abode." With the Apostasy about to spread across Arabia now that Mohammed had died, the Arabs were not in fact inclined to accept the rule of anyone—neither person nor tribe. But that question was for another day. Abu Bakr was a Quraysh, as were Omar and Abu Ubayda.

"I am satisfied with either of these two men," Abu Bakr continued, taking them by the hand. It was a deft piece of politics: making tribal status, rather than kinship with the Prophet, the basis of the decision. Once Abu Bakr had established this, it meant that he himself, by far the most prominent Quraysh present, was in the lead position. Omar, a prominent

---

* They had with them a small number of unimportant supporters and retainers, fellow Meccans.

Companion of the Prophet but widely disliked for his severe demeanor, was a lesser figure whom no Medina crowd would ever acclaim. Abu Ubayda was a straw man at best.

The time had come for Omar to play his role.

"No indeed," Omar shouted out. He addressed Abu Bakr but was in reality speaking to the crowd. "The Prophet, when he was ill, named you to lead the prayers. We swear allegiance to you."

Omar then grabbed Abu Bakr's hand and swore the oath of loyalty. The other Meccans in the room, few as they were, joined in the acclamation of the old man. The men from Medina, a trickle at first, agreed. Momentum swelled in the room. Soon the acclamation was complete, if far from unanimous. Abu Bakr, the candidate of the rich Quraysh of far-off Mecca, was proclaimed the *khalifa*—the successor—of Mohammed.

Many of those who did not acclaim Abu Bakr that day, and some who did, would have chosen Ali had he been there. Many others would have preferred no one at all. It was not a convincing start to Islam's life without the Prophet.

Ali, outmaneuvered for the first time in what would become a pattern of failure—or rank injustice, from the Shia perspective—did not swear loyalty to Abu Bakr for a further six months. By then his wife Fatima, the Prophet's favorite daughter, had herself died following a miscarriage. The loss of Fatima further weakened Ali politically, and he now had no choice but to submit to the demands of the triumphant Aisha–Abu Bakr group. Having at last given his promise of fealty, Ali kept himself apart from the affairs of government and power during Abu Bakr's two-year reign.

Led in the field by Khalid ibn al Walid, the Quraysh crushed the Apostasy by the summer of 633. They could now turn their attention to the world outside Arabia. Khalid himself spent the year raiding the rich marches in Persian Mesopotamia.

———

Abu Bakr died in 634 at Medina. Sixty-one years old, he had caught a cold after a bath. The next three of the four Rashidun, or Rightly Guided, caliphs would not die so peacefully.

The First Two Islamic Caliphates, 632–750 AD

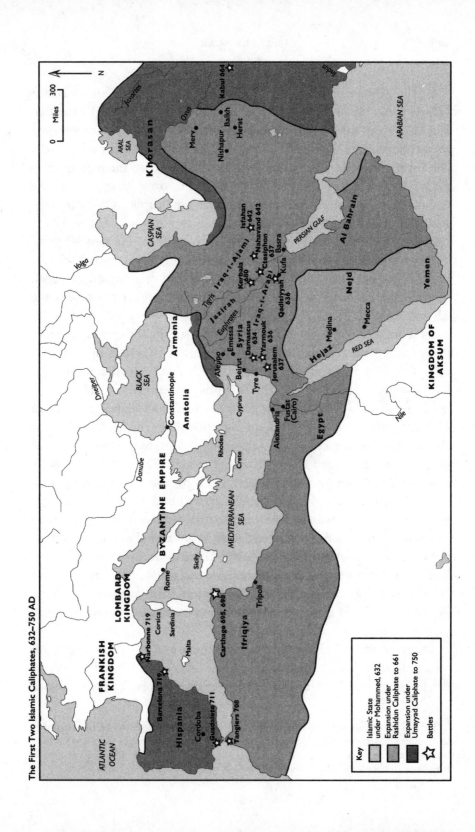

Key

Islamic State
under Mohammed, 632

Expansion under
Rashidun Caliphate to 661

Expansion under
Umayyad Caliphate to 750

☆ Battles

Unlike Mohammed, Abu Bakr took care to nominate his successor before dying. His choice, of course, could never have been Ali. The two had been rivals for Mohammed's ear and trust throughout the years of the Prophet's rise. Each had vied to be chief acolyte to the new apostle, chief warrior of the new conqueror, chief minister in the new government. Abu Bakr had wanted the Prophet's favorite daughter, but Ali had married her. Abu Bakr's daughter was the Prophet's favorite wife, Aisha. Ali had been the first Muslim after the Prophet, Abu Bakr the first person outside the Prophet's family to embrace the new religion. The two men were linked by their destinies, but they were not friends.

Adding a personal bitterness to what would otherwise have been mostly a power struggle, a poisonous episode had occurred between Ali and Aisha.

In about 623, ten years previously, Aisha, still in her teens after marrying the Prophet at six, had been traveling with a Muslim army on one of the Prophet's many campaigns in Arabia.[4] * Realizing that she had dropped a favorite necklace "with onyx beads from Zafar" while urinating some way back along the trail, Aisha had slipped away from camp unnoticed and gone back on foot to look for the necklace. When she returned to the camp, the caravan had departed, so she wrapped herself in her cloak and lay down on the ground. There she was met by one Safwan, a young warrior hastening on his camel to catch up with the Muslim column. Eventually Aisha arrived back in Medina the next morning riding Safwan's camel, led by the dismounted young man.[5]

Many a dusty eyebrow was raised about what had happened during those missing hours under the lonely desert moon. Aisha was feisty, and famously capricious. She was married to a moralizing disciplinarian sixty years of age who produced few offspring from his fourteen wives. What, in fact, had Aisha been doing, risking her modesty with a dashing young warrior? The scandal was great.

When Mohammed asked his foster son what should be done, Ali recommended divorce. Ali had always been sincere, often to his political detriment; maybe here he thought he was simply providing good advice

---

* Aisha was nine or ten years old at the time of the consummation of her marriage to Mohammed. The Muslim chronicles tell us that after his conjugal visits she and the Prophet used to while away gentle hours playing with her toys. W. Montgomery Watt, *Muhammad: Prophet and Statesman* (Oxford: Oxford University Press, 1961), p. 102.

to his cousin and leader. Or maybe Ali's intention was to weaken the girl's father, his rival Abu Bakr. Regardless, the rancor between Aisha and Ali would be significant for the rest of Ali's life. The relationship between Ali and her father, Abu Bakr, was never good thereafter.

Forever since, with every new tragedy in what developed into the never-ending Sunni-Shia struggle, the world would feel reverberations from these disagreements between two obscure seventh-century mercantile families deep in the Arabian Peninsula. But for Mohammed himself, the Affair of the Necklace was quickly solved. Almighty God, Mohammed told his followers a few days later, had sent him a fresh revelation proclaiming Aisha's innocence. "Why," asked God about Aisha's accusers, "did they not produce four witnesses? Since they produce not witnesses, they verily are liars in the sight of Allah."[6]

Aisha herself was impressed that Allah took care to intervene on her husband's behalf. "I considered myself too unworthy to be talked of by Allah with something of my concern," she later recounted.[7] * As a result, subsequent generations of Muslim women would be obliged to provide no fewer than four male witnesses to substantiate an accusation of rape. Without these, any Muslim woman making the accusation against a man was herself a criminal, a self-implicated fornicator or adulteress. This was the paradoxical legacy, for countless women in centuries to come, of Aisha's absolution.

---

* In Mohammed al Bukhari's (d. 870) famous collection of *hadith* (the "traditions," or sayings and doings, of the Prophet, passed along by his circle), there is a detailed account by Aisha of the entire affair. A brief section, modestly edited, gives a flavor of the narrative character of much of this corpus of holy writ. Mohammed comes to a distraught Aisha ("I could never sleep till I thought that my liver would burst from weeping"), apparently in the house of her parents, after not visiting her for a month: "I never thought that Allah would reveal about my case Divine Inspiration that would be recited forever . . . but I hoped that Allah's Messenger might have a dream in which Allah would prove my innocence. But the Divine Inspiration came to him. So there overtook him the same hard condition which used to overtake him . . . The sweat was dropping from his body like pearls though it was a wintry day and that was because of the weighty statement which was being revealed to him. When that state was over, he got up smiling, and the first word he said was, 'O Aisha! Allah has declared your innocence!'" Bukhari, hadith no. 2661. www.sunnah.com.

Abu Bakr's choice for his own successor as caliph was Omar, his accomplice from the acclamation in the hall of the Banu Saida. Far from the most liked of the Prophet's early Companions, Omar was, after Ali perhaps, the most pious. Thanks to the generalship of his lifelong foe, Khalid, and others, Omar was to oversee a decade of imperial conquest that rivaled the achievement of Alexander.

When Omar assumed the caliphate in 634, Islam had resubjugated Arabia only a year previously. By the time of his death in 644, the hybrid religion-state ruled an empire that reached west along the Mediterranean littoral through all of rich northern Egypt to Libya; north through Iraq and Syria to eastern Anatolia, Armenia, and the southern Caucasus; and east through Iran and deep into the Greater Persia of southern Turkmenistan and western Afghanistan and Pakistan.

Of the two historic empires that for so long had kept the Arabs inside their huge and arid peninsula, Omar's expansion conquered all of the Persian and roughly two-thirds of the Roman during those years. Between August and November in the extraordinary year of 636 alone, with Khalid ibn al Walid's defeat of the Romans at Yarmouk in Syria, and the comparably important victory at Qadissiya in southern Iraq against the Persians, Omar's armies won two of history's pivotal battles.[8]

In April of 637, Omar arrived at Jerusalem to accept the surrender of that city following a six-month siege initiated by Khalid. After five centuries of exclusion by the Romans, the Jews were allowed by Omar to return to their holiest city and worship there freely. A thousand years had passed since Cyrus sent them home from Babylon with funds to rebuild their temple. When the Christian Patriarch of Jerusalem, Sophronius, invited Omar to pray at the Church of the Holy Sepulchre, the caliph declined the offer. To subject their church to future Muslim interest as a mosque, declared Omar, would dishonor his agreement with the city's Christians.

Omar was no Cyrus, however. Nor was he an Alexander. He did not achieve the epic expansion of Islam's empire through diplomatic charm, personal magnetism, or courage in battle. Nor did he do it through the desire of new peoples to take part in his project. Where former foes as disparate as the Babylonians and the Bactrians had willingly marched with Cyrus, and the sons of Persia and Transoxiana had studied the secrets of the Macedonian phalanx under Alexander and Seleucus, none but Arabs marched in Omar's armies. Strictly devout, unstintingly modest in his dress and affairs, he dispensed his rule barefoot from the small house at Medina while generals such as Khalid fought the unbeliever across thousands of miles. When the success of Khalid and others made them rivals to him, or rivals to God as Omar framed it, the caliph demoted them.*

Omar strove as zealously to recreate the pure and simple days of Mohammed's Medina as he did to expand the empire and improve its administration. Of the four Rightly Guided leaders of Islam following Mohammed, Omar was particularly concerned to honor the literalism so firmly encoded into the faith from its founding. He thus became the principal Sunni hero among the caliphs of Islam.

The second caliph's personal austerity and ostentatious modesty provided the dusting of charisma that his otherwise uninspiring personality could not. Omar owned no shoes. He possessed a single shirt and patched its holes with pieces of animal skin. He ate what the common folk ate. "Prisoners of war brought to Medina expected to see palaces and imperial pageantry such as they had witnessed in Constantinople or Ctesiphon," wrote the English Arabist Sir John Glubb.† "Instead, in the glaring, dusty square of a little mudbrick town, they would find a circle of Arabs sitting on the ground. One of them, a tall, lean man, barefoot and wearing a coarse woolen cloak, would prove to be the world's most powerful emperor."[9]

Unusually among the Prophet's circle, Omar was literate. A gifted administrator, he organized the Muslim army into a standing body. Hitherto it had been little more than an informal collection of whichever Arab tribesmen were currently inclined to participate. The Prophet understood that "the survival of my community rests on the hooves of its horses and the points of its lances."[10] He had frequently worried that the jihad might suffer from the temptation of its warriors to settle down

---

* Omar's replacement for Khalid as military chief was Abu Ubayda, a former subordinate of Khalid's. The story goes that at Damascus in 636, at the very same time that Khalid stormed the eastern gate of the city, Abu Ubayda persuaded the defenders of the western gate to capitulate peacefully. Unlike Khalid, Abu Ubayda was an early convert to Islam, one of the original emigrants who first went to Medina with Mohammed, and a fighter for Islam in the early battles in Arabia before the late conversion of Khalid and other representatives of the traditional Meccan elite.

† "Glubb Pasha," as he became known, served with the Arab Legion, eventually the army of Jordan, from 1930 to 1956, commanding it for the last seventeen of those years. He authored twenty-one books, mostly of Arab history.

on the richer lands they conquered. Omar worked to counter this by instituting a record of the names of the Muslim warriors and the moneys owed to them from the conquests.[11] Omar also worked to put Muslim jurisprudence on a relatively systematic basis. By limiting governors to two-year terms, he tried to address nepotism and corruption.

The great exception to this effort was the rich and vital province of Syria, then comprising current-day Palestine, Lebanon, Syria, and parts of southeast Turkey. There the Umayyad family was allowed to establish itself in effective autonomy, governing the province amid the wealth and sophistication of the ancient Hellenized and Romanized city of Damascus. Two of Abu Sufyan's sons, Yazid and Muawiya, had been senior commanders in the conquest of Syria. Yazid was appointed governor of the province by Omar in 639; when Yazid died of the plague that same year, Omar replaced him with Muawiya. Ascending to leadership of the Banu Umayya following the death of his father, Muawiya was to rule from the Greek-speaking city with increasing independence from 639 until he himself became caliph in 661.

Syria in the coastal strip dominated by Damascus was a wealthy, cultured, Hellenistic, Mediterranean land. It was far from Arabia in every way. The consolidation of Umayyad power in Syria underscored the strategic brilliance of their acceptance of Mohammed into Mecca in 630. As the dominant family within Mecca's Quraysh nobility, the Banu Umayya had demanded a high price for their ostensible capitulation to Mohammed, including two of the Prophet's four daughters and the installation of Muawiya, the Umayyad heir apparent, as Mohammed's personal secretary. With this, the Banu Umayya effectively took over management of the Muslim enterprise. Two years later, Mohammed was dead and their friend and kinsman Abu Bakr was caliph. A dozen years after that, with the accession of Othman following Omar's death in 644, the Banu Umayya ruled an empire larger than Alexander's.

In the final year or two of Omar's caliphate, he reined in the armies and focused Islam's energies on consolidation and administration. He had recently overseen the conquest of Egypt, and the effort to subdue Persia was ongoing. The manpower of the Arab occupation in these lands, and in Syria and Iraq, numbered perhaps a hundred thousand strong in Omar's time. This put the Muslims at a roughly fifty-to-one numerical disadvantage relative to the local populations.[12]

Ruling the non-Muslim subject peoples of Islam was a challenge. Converting them was not desirable: a free kaffir in the House of Peace paid the special tax on infidels, the jizya, and this in turn supported the privileges of the Muslim occupation and paid for its arms. Thus the kaffirs in the occupied lands were not encouraged to convert. They did not begin to do so in large numbers for a couple of hundred years after the conquests. There was also the problem of temptation and softening. The worldly ways of the Byzantines and Persians could only corrode the warlike spirit of the desert nomads.

In the conquered lands, Omar segregated the Muslim occupiers into cantons of their own. In Iraq he established bases at Kufa and Basra, flat and unpleasant places that he hoped might contribute to maintenance of the proper perspectives, away from the decadence of the Persians.[13]

With Islam's conquering drive mostly suspended by Omar toward the end of his rule, the rivers of slaves and gold dried up. The Arab tribesmen had traded in their poor but free existences and in return had received adventure, status, and glory. They had won booty, human and otherwise, beyond anything their ancestors could likely have imagined. Now they passed their days under the rule of a dour theocrat who had a divinely mandated claim to regulating every element of their lives. They lived behind mud walls in fly-bitten cantonments in far-off places like flat and humid Iraq and Egypt. After Omar, they would be doing so for little purpose other than the aggrandizement of a rival Arabian tribe, the Quraysh. It was a state of affairs that the Arabs would never have accepted at any other stage in their history. Nevertheless, while the pious Omar lived, hypocrisy was not yet a problem.

Omar oversaw the absorption of the Roman tax-collection system in Syria and the Persian system in Iraq, laying the foundations of a true imperial administration that would last for almost four hundred years. All that Omar did for the Islamic empire, he did in the single decade of his rule, 634–644. In temporal terms, he was easily the greatest figure in the history of Islam. Of those who ruled after Mohammed, Omar was also the most serious in his faith. Sunni Muslims see Omar as the best Muslim and greatest conqueror among the four Rightly Guided caliphs. Shias see him as the second, after Abu Bakr, of the usurpers who for twenty-four years denied to the tragic Ali his rightful leadership of the faith.

In 644 in Medina, a Christian slave from Iran fatally stabbed Omar with a poisoned sword. It was revenge for the Muslims' ongoing conquest and subjugation, then in its third of nine bloody years, of a reluctant and cultured land. Another potential succession crisis was at hand.

Omar's rigid religiosity had seemed to favor Ali as next in line. Among other factors in choosing a successor, Omar insisted upon "merit in Islam." It was a test that included the promptness of the individual's embrace of the faith during its difficult early years, as well as his later piety and contributions to the jihad. All of this boded well for Ali. Furthermore, "merit in Islam" also would seem to exclude the Umayyad family, and most of the rest of the Quraysh elite. Omar's showy personal austerity was itself a public challenge to the rich Quraysh families such as Khalid's, to well-heeled clans such as the Banu Umayya, and to the rest of the Meccan establishment, all of them gorging themselves on the new wealth.

From Omar's point of view, Ali and the Hashemites appeared as natural allies in the anti-Quraysh cause. Ali shared Omar's desire for a return to Muslim modesty. He shared Omar's respect for the rules and examples set by the Prophet in his lifetime. Omar had therefore tried to strike up an accord with Ali, emphasizing their common preference for the early Companions over the late-converting Meccan plutocrats.

Omar's efforts with Ali were doomed. Ali was never one to compromise, and rarely made the right political decision. In the face of Omar's approaches, Ali remained adamant that the proper basis for being caliph was the one thing that Omar lacked and that Ali possessed: close kinship with the Prophet. This was not "merit in Islam." And so Ali had never truly participated in Omar's project. Otherwise, a smooth succession to rule by Mohammed's Hashemite house may well have been arranged.

From his deathbed in Medina, Omar named a *shura* of six prominent early Muslims, including Ali, to gather in the town and choose a new caliph from among themselves. As the group gathered, it was clear that Ali was, from a purely Islamic perspective, peerless among them. Of the others, only one, Othman ibn Affan, had been an important Companion of the Prophet. Othman was a handsome and affable old man who lived in famous grandeur at Mecca. He had substantial prestige as a rare early convert from the ranks of the Quraysh. But Othman was no Ali. With Abu Bakr and Omar already in their graves, any true rivals to Ali based on merit in Islam or on the Prophet's regard had ruled and died by then. Ali's time, it seemed clear, had come at last.

The other members of the six-man *shura* were all Quraysh. Othman and one of the others were married to daughters of Abu Bakr. This made them brothers-in-law of Aisha, Ali's old adversary from the Affair of the Necklace. Othman had also secured for himself a daughter of the Prophet, a reward for his early conversion.*

Ali would once again find himself outmatched. The deliberations of the *shura* dragged into a third or fourth day. Ali agreed to the selection of one of the council's lesser members to make a final decision that would be binding upon all of them. When this man polled the group, Ali refused to vote for himself. Few outside Ali's camp would have been surprised by the result. Othman, the quintessential Umayyad plutocrat, was chosen as the third caliph.

In November 644, Othman's supporters announced his selection in a crowded mosque at Friday prayers. In such a setting, argument was impossible. The required acclaim—nothing extravagant, but enough— was secured from the crowd. Ali appears to have been present in the mosque. For the third time in the twelve years since Mohammed's death, he had no choice but to announce to the world his acceptance of a caliph other than himself. His excuse for acquiescing was Muslim unity. Ali's agreement to Othman's accession nonetheless raised a crippling question. If Ali knew himself to be God's rightful choice, why did he not struggle harder for the outcome that God desired? The Prophet himself had spent the final decade of his own life fighting. Either Ali did not truly believe that he was God's choice, or else his submission—in this case, accepting God's will and the struggles that came with it—was incomplete.

In any event, Ali had now compromised himself too many times. Victimized or indecisive, self-sacrificing or unfit, tragic or merely hapless: the two sides—Shia and Sunni—would ever after say opposing things about Ali. None could deny his record of consistently being on the losing end of politics in an endeavor that made politics its business. With the accession of Othman, the Banu Umayya had secured its triumph over the other players in the Prophet's funeral games. Ali was to have a

---

* This marriage to a sister of Fatima made Othman also a brother-in-law of Ali.

brief and troubled moment on the throne after Othman died, but this would prove a minor interregnum as the House of Umayya, starting with Othman's caliphate, ruled Islam for the next century, until 750.

These very same people—the wealthiest and most powerful Quraysh clan, led by Mohammed's nemesis Abu Sufyan—had been the Prophet's principal foes throughout his career. As a result of their victory, the Prophet's original uplifting appeal in Mecca, his call to the outcast and the dispossessed, was to be forgotten by Islam's leaders within a generation. Mohammed's later call, articulated at Medina, for equality within a community of followers supported by taxation and slavery imposed upon the kaffir, quickly gave way to the victory of the people he had tried to replace.

The Prophet had re-entered Mecca only fourteen years before Othman became caliph, having made the bargain with Abu Sufyan, his family, and their allies. At the time, the town—the great prize in their narrow world—was a benighted backwater in the bleakest of desert lands. Now, as Othman eased himself onto the glittering throne in Mecca of 644 AD, the House of Umayya controlled an empire like few the world had seen. Continuing to expand under Othman, its realm soon stretched from Libya to Afghanistan. The empire grew further under the Umayyad Caliphate, as the coming period of rule from Damascus would be known.

In religious terms, it was the victors in these succession struggles following Mohammed's death who came to be known as the Sunnis. The losers, supporting the unsuccessful claims of the Prophet's direct family —first Ali and then his son Hussein, followed by their descendants— would be the Shias. Much later, profound theological differences would develop between the two sides.

In 653, after almost a decade of Banu Umayya rule, Ali finally began to speak out against Othman.

For nine years Othman and his family had been celebrating with gleeful rapacity their victory over the Hashemites. Taking full advantage of the new, imperial scale and wealth of the prize, the Umayyads appointed themselves to the top governorates, generalships, and other lucrative posts in the Dar al Islam. Eschewing the modesty of Mohammed and his

first two successors, Othman built himself a sumptuous new palace at
Medina. He imported marble for the columns and chefs for the kitchens.[14]
Under Othman, the practice began of shortening the title "Deputy of
the Prophet of God" (*khalifat rasul allah*), used by Abu Bakr and Omar,
to the simpler but more ostentatious "Deputy of God" (*khalifat allah*).

The promise of the Prophet seemed all but over. There would be no
new social equality within the *umma*, the community of believers. With
the Banu Umayya in charge, there was little prospect of government
by true Islamic precepts, including the just distribution of the spoils of
conquest. Othman did some important Islamic work, continuing the
expansion of the empire and standardizing the Koran for all future generations. But by the end of his reign, he had little support except perhaps
in Syria, second home of the Umayyad family.

The Arabs had been free and poor. Now they were richer and subjected. The eight years of Mohammed's Medina theocracy, and the twelve
years of the caliphates of Abu Bakr and Omar after him, had been like
green springtime: a beautiful moment that comes only once in the cycle,
and all too briefly, before the desert returns to its harsher ways. When
Ali finally spoke out against the rapaciousness of the Umayyads, this was
where he found his metaphor. "Othman shrugs his shoulders arrogantly,"
Ali said in response to one instance of Umayyad corruption, "and his
brothers stand with him, eating up the property of God as the camels
eat up the spring-time grasses."[15]

In 653 or 654, Othman's half brother Walid, governor of the central
Iraqi garrison town of Kufa, vomited drunkenly on the pulpit of the
local mosque while leading the morning prayers.[16] The greed and brazen
nepotism of the new rulers were matched by their arrogance. Walid had
previously dismissed the local criticisms of Umayyad venality as nothing
more than "a goat's fart in the desert plains of Idam." His successor
would incite near riots by referring to Iraq's rich, irrigated lands as "the
garden of the Quraysh."[17]

The Iraqis themselves, Walid had said, were but a "provincial riffraff."[18]
By "Iraqis" he was referring not to the indigenous Iraqis living under the
new Arab Muslim overlordship, but to the Arab occupiers. With ever
more Arabs seeking opportunities in the rich and ancient lands of Iraq
and Egypt, and with enslaved women—some local and some brought
from elsewhere—numbering in the scores of thousands, a population

boom occurred. The towns of the Arab occupiers, of which Kufa and Basra in fertile Iraq were by far the empire's largest, became "breeding factories for a vastly expanding population."[19] As a result of sexual slavery on this scale, the Arab population had risen threefold in the previous thirty-odd years.[20] Conquests were slowing, and what funds remained were increasingly pocketed by the Umayyad clique. The southern Iraqi towns with their growing populations of mestizo Muslims—sons of Arab fathers and their female slaves—became seething centers of discontent.

In early 656, the twelfth year of Othman's caliphate, incensed by their governor's behavior, the Kufans sent a delegation to Medina to seek remonstrance with the caliph. There Othman mocked them for finding support only with Aisha.[21] Ali and Aisha, the two individuals who during the Prophet's lifetime had been most important to him on a personal level, now briefly found themselves on the same side for the first time since the Affair of the Necklace about thirty years before. Outraged at the Umayyads, Aisha wrote an open letter calling on "true Muslims to defend Islam against injustice and corruption."[22] Soon contingents of rebellious warriors had marched from Iraq and Egypt to Medina, where they camped threateningly outside the city.

True to his oath of loyalty, Ali tried for weeks to mediate between the caliph and the rebels. Eventually Othman was attacked with a hail of stones as he tried to lead prayers in the Medina mosque. Ali then put himself forward as the guarantor of an arrangement between the insurgents and the chastened caliph, who promised that he would address their needs if they returned to their garrison towns in Kufa, Basra, and Egypt.

The shaky détente was not to last. On their way home to Egypt, the rebels intercepted a messenger from Othman's headquarters. The rider was carrying an order, bearing the caliph's own seal, instructing the governor of Egypt to arrest the leaders, cut off their beards, and lash them. The provincial warriors turned back to Medina and besieged Othman's palace. Ali sent his sons Hasan and Hussein to help protect the old man.

It was not clear that the rebels initially intended to kill Othman. But the tensions grew and grew. The eighty-two-year-old caliph, who for all his venality had strictly abjured non-judicial violence against or among Muslims, was murdered as he read the Koran with his Syrian wife in his opulent new palace. Like Omar before him, the third of Islam's four Rightly Guided caliphs was stabbed to death. The man who struck the first blow was Abu Bakr's eldest son, a stepson of Ali. Blood soon covered the walls of Othman's room, his carpet, and the holy Koran that he had been reading.

The Muslim shedding of Muslim blood at the end of Othman's reign made a profound change within Islam. It was the first time that this had happened in the young history of the faith; the assassins of Mohammed and Omar had been infidels. The dreadful descent to Kerbala could now begin in earnest. "For twenty-five years," wrote English soldier and scholar Glubb Pasha, "the Muslims had lived in a dream. God had chosen them to conquer and rule the world, after which they would pass into the unimaginable joys of paradise. The dream had suddenly evaporated and they found themselves once again surrounded by war, violence and bloodshed."[23]

With the murder of Othman in 656, Ali's time came at last. Five days after the rebels from Iraq and Egypt hacked Othman to pieces, the Lion of God was acclaimed caliph by the people of Medina.

The trouble that bedeviled Ali's short and frustrating reign began almost immediately. Othman's killers were still at large and Ali's rivals, knowing that he sympathized with the rebels in their criticisms of the corrupt Othman, insisted that the new caliph find and punish them. The real issue was power. In this, Ali's adversaries had not changed. The Umayyad family was still implacably against him. So, despite their recent alignment in proclaiming outrage over Othman's death, was Aisha. The Prophet's forty-two-year-old widow could not bear to see her longstanding opponent succeed her husband and father at last. The Umayyads from their stronghold in Damascus would use all their ample wealth and skill to ensure that the Hashemite interregnum was as brief and ineffective as possible.

Even before the people of Medina had a chance to celebrate Ali's accession, Aisha was stirring Mecca into a fury of indignation over Othman's murder. No matter that she more than anyone had encouraged the mob that had slaughtered him. This daughter of Abu Bakr, late prince of Mecca's Quraysh elite, with her own longstanding quarrel with Ali, could not help heating up the old antagonisms: Mecca versus Medina, late converts versus Ansar, Quraysh versus Hashemite.

As soon as Aisha heard the news of Othman's murder, she went to the Kaaba, now a Muslim shrine. "People of Mecca," she called out. "The mob from the garrison cities and the tribesmen and slaves have conspired. They charged Othman with defeat, nonetheless he attempted to pacify them. When they could then find no real argument they showed their hostility openly. They spilled forbidden blood, they violated the sacred city, they appropriated sacred money."[24]

As the crowd cheered her on, Aisha took the next step. This would contribute substantially to a conflict that was to be fatal for countless people over the centuries, and for the faith itself as it had been envisioned by her late husband, the Prophet.

"By Allah! One of Othman's fingertips is better than a whole world of their type," Aisha cried out with extraordinary gall. "Save yourselves from association with them. Let them be punished." She did not name Ali, but few in the crowd would have doubted that he and his family were the target of her call to arms.

Aisha's hypocrisy was remarkable. Despite his deep objections to Othman's plutocratic style and the injustice of his policies, Ali had sent his own sons to protect the caliph from the baying mob. As an interlocutor between the two sides, Ali had worked to prevent the shedding of Muslim blood in the turbulent scenes outside Othman's palace. All the while Aisha had been inciting the crowd. Now, six months after Othman's murder, after Ali had at last attained the caliphate, she and her brothers-in-law were leading their own rebel army in open revolt against him.

A clash between two Muslim armies, one led by the Prophet's favorite wife and one by his foster son and grandsons, would mark another step in the disintegration of Mohammed's formula. The collapse of the House of Peace—the Dar al Salaam, that place of tranquility for believers—may have been inevitable given the system's attempt to manage fundamentally unpredictable worldly affairs. But the inevitable seemed to be coming on with dreadful speed. The ancient chroniclers describe the impending battle between Ali and Aisha not with their characteristic tone of martial triumphalism but rather with a sense of building catastrophe. Soon the two armies faced each other a few miles from Basra.

A series of characters in the chronicles voice unease with the looming disaster of *fitna*, meaning dissension, chaotic division, civil war. A wise old early Companion called Abu Musa chose a powerful analogy. "Fitna," he said, quoting the Prophet himself, "rips the Community apart like a stomach ulcer."[25] And, said the old man, it would be endless. Like a wildfire, "it dies down for a while," but will always reappear. Abu Musa called on the Muslims gathered with him to sheathe their swords, snap their spears, cut their bowstrings, and let the hot blast of the *fitna* blow over them.

A man carrying a letter from Aisha to the people of Kufa knew the truth. Avoid the eternal curse of *fitna* now? They might as well "turn the Euphrates back on its course," he said.[26] Both men were all too correct. Muslim civil war would thenceforth be as much part of the landscape of Iraq as the ever-flowing Euphrates. Like Abu Musa's wildfire, the flames might sometimes die down in one place, but eventually they would resurface somewhere else in the land.

On the humid plain southwest of Basra in 656, at a featureless spot that is visible more than thirteen centuries later from the straight roads that cut through the oil installations there, the forces of Ali and Aisha, of the Medinans and the Meccans, of the people who had joined Mohammed early and those who had withstood him as long as they could, faced each other for a week. In retrospect, it was an eerie prelude to the battle at Kerbala, twenty-four years later and two hundred and fifty miles to the northwest.

Abu Musa entreated the opposing forces, "Be the ones all Arabs look to! Sheathe your swords, remove your spearheads, shelter the oppressed until this *fitna* is over!"[27] Another Muslim called out that "he would prefer to be a mutilated Ethiopian slave pasturing nanny goats with lopsided udders on some mountain top until the day he dies than for a single arrow to be shot between the two armies."[28]

When the fighting finally started, Aisha watched from a camel. The bloodshed was greater than any in the Prophet's time. It was worse even than in Khalid's battles of the Apostasy, when the Arabs had rebelled after the death of Mohammed. The chronicles relate that three thousand Muslims died in the Battle of the Camel. Ali and his sons prevailed over Aisha's Quraysh rebels. Appalled, fair even in victory, Ali buried his foes with full Muslim observance. Then the last of the Rashidun, the four caliphs of Islam's brief golden age, sent Aisha home, silenced at last, to a quiet and respectable retirement in Mecca.

———

From Damascus, meanwhile, the Umayyads, too, were pressuring Ali to identify and punish Othman's killers. As the crowds in Medina gathered to celebrate Ali's accession, the shirt in which his predecessor was murdered was being spirited to Syria. Wrapped in a bundle with the blood-caked, tattered garment were the hacked-off fingers that Othman's wife had lost as she tried to protect him from the assassins' knives.

The Umayyad governor of Syria, Muawiya, had ruled there for twenty years, largely unmolested by interference from Medina. A second cousin of Othman, he was the son of Abu Sufyan, leader of the Quraysh opposition to Mohammed in the early days. Muawiya controlled a huge and rich area comprising much of southwest Turkey and all of the Levant from the Mediterranean to the Euphrates River and the Iraqi border, reaching far south and west through the rich trading cities of Palestine to the border of Egypt. He lived like a true Umayyad, in a Damascus palace that was even more extravagant than Othman's in Medina.[29]

In 656, Ali, newly acceded, called the empire's various governors to Medina for a pledge of fealty. Muawiya alone refused. After decisively winning the Battle of the Camel against Aisha, Ali summoned Muawiya again, more sternly. The Umayyad threatened war. Ali backed down, but then made his own threat, moving his troops north from Basra near the Arabian border to Kufa, deep inside Iraq and closer to the Umayyad cities of Syria. Ali never returned to Medina. Iraq was thenceforth the base of his power, and would inevitably become "the cradle of Shia Islam."

Muawiya now led the calls for Ali to bring Othman's killers to justice. Ali refused. When Ali sent a messenger to Muawiya demanding a statement of allegiance, Muawiya replied elusively but threateningly that Othman's "murder was a hideous act . . . and no master or arbiter will be found for it but I."[30] Muawiya paid an army of poets to unsheathe their pens and stir the public into a call for justice. No caliph could safely ignore this kind of challenge. Ali failed to respond. Muawiya sent a letter declaring war on him.

"Ali," wrote Muawiya, "to each caliph you had to be led to the oath of allegiance as the camel is led by the stick through its nose." Othman's murderers, said Muawiya's stunning missive, were Ali's people, and until Ali surrendered them, "the people of Syria" would fight him. And even if Ali did hand over the killers of Othman, wrote the Umayyad, then the people of Syria would choose the next caliph.

For Ali, the battle against the Umayyads, when it finally came, was another sorry affair. It was fought in June or July of 656 at Siffin, on the northern Euphrates in Syria. At one point, the Syrian arrows fell so thick that Hasan and Hussein had to cover their father with their shields. Earlier, before the fighting began, Ali had offered Muawiya the opportunity to save many lives by deciding the matter in single combat. Muawiya declined, stating truly enough that "I have not been made a fair offer. He has killed everyone whom he has challenged to combat."[31]

On the morning of the third day of fighting, Ali's Iraqi army was everywhere advancing against the Syrians. With victory imminent, the men in Ali's forward positions suddenly saw something they had never seen before. The Syrian cavalry were holding their spears aloft, and from the sharp tips white sheets of parchment were fluttering.

The Syrians were calling out to their Iraqi foes, "Let the word of God decide!" Ali's men realized that the pieces of paper were pages from the Holy Koran. The clear message: nobody could argue with the word of God. The experts must sit down and patiently decide the struggle according to Islam itself, according to the words of the God who provided rules for everything.

The idea, of course, was risible. Muawiya did not care a whit about Islam, and the armies knew it. Ali tried to rally his men, but many of them felt they could not fight against the Book. Against this tide of muddled piety, Ali was powerless. The soldiers on both sides stopped fighting.

Muawiya had outwitted Ali. The Syrian governor had moved the conflict from a sphere where Ali always won, physical battle, to one where Ali always lost, and where the Umayyads excelled: arbitration, deal-making, politics. Six months passed before the arbitration council met, in January 658. For Ali, caliph and leader of Islam, it was six months of grossly compromised rule. His world saw him kept waiting for a meeting he had not sought, over a dispute he had not wanted, with a mere provincial governor. Muawiya was a patently impious man with no connection at all to the Prophet. He was a common rebel, a near apostate, and a traitor to the vice-regent on earth of God Himself. Waiting half a year for others to decide the fate of such a man did not help Ali's standing.

The six months wore on. In their barracks at Kufa, elements of Ali's army that had betrayed him at Siffin boiled with discontent. Their grievance was the arbitration itself, the same arbitration that they themselves had forced upon Ali just when he was winning the battle. Only God could choose the leader of Islam, said the malcontents now. Who were men to arbitrate in these matters? How could Ali, God's rightful caliph, take this decision from God's hands?

The dissidents became known as the Kharijites (from *khariji*), the Outsiders or Rejectionists. The arbitration council, when it finally took place, lasted for two weeks and ended in another humiliation for Ali. The *shura*, after dirty dealings by Muawiya's representative, declared that the Umayyad in Damascus was in fact the rightful caliph. The Kharijites now rose against Ali. For the third time, the most pious man in Islam was forced to take the field against his fellow Muslims. Ali's forces slaughtered thousands of Kharijites at a place called Nahrawan, near the spot where Baghdad was to rise a century later.

Three and a half years passed. In January 661, a Kharijite attacked Ali with a poisoned sword as the caliph walked into the Kufa mosque to pray on a Friday morning. The wound was fatal. The rebel shouted out, "Judgment belongs to God alone, Ali! To God alone!"[32] But God was not to be the beneficiary of Ali's martyrdom. Muawiya, so contemptuous of Islam that the Kharijites had killed Ali merely for negotiating with him, was promptly acclaimed the new caliph. The son of the Prophet Mohammed's most implacable enemy in Mecca now ruled as a secular king over the empire.

Twenty-nine years after Mohammed's death, the office of caliph had been transformed. The Rightly Guided golden age was over, and the caliphate had become a conventional family dynasty.[33] It never went back to anything that the Prophet would have recognized as Islamic. The caliphate had been founded to give ongoing expression to Mohammed's vision, the complete unity of state and religion in the service of God. But only Omar's decade of rule, from 634 to 644, ever truly exemplified this. Instead, for the coming thirteen centuries of its survival, the caliphate would be, almost entirely, that most profane of things: the worldly tool of a succession of ambitious individuals and their descendants.*

In 680, at Kerbala in southern Iraq, as Hussein ibn Ali's tenth dawn on the dry plain warmed into morning, the Prophet's grandson arranged his warriors and their families for the destiny that awaited. Surrounded by the army of almost four thousand men from Ali's former capital at Kufa, less than ten miles away, Hussein's fighters numbered forty on foot and thirty-two on horseback, plus the men among the thirty relatives who were with him. Overnight, Hussein had commanded them to dig a ditch behind their tents and to fill it with firewood and dry cane. Now he arranged his fighters with the tents and baggage at their rear and the women and children among the tents. With the trench fire wall ready to be lit behind the tents, protecting their rear, they waited for their fellow Muslims to advance upon them.[34]

As the Kufans prepared to move forward, Hussein sent his tiny band a clear signal of the fate into which he would lead those who stayed with him. Stepping into a tent erected for the purpose, he anointed himself with musk perfume. A Muslim corpse was often prepared for burial in this way.[35] Hussein's followers understood the message. As two of them vied to be the next to anoint himself, one said, according to the account of the chronicler Abu Jafar al Tabari (d. 923 in Baghdad), "I feel happy for what we shall soon meet, for, by God, if all there is between us and the maidens of Paradise is that these people should come against us with their swords, then I want them to come against us."[36]

Duly anointed, Hussein mounted his horse. He put a copy of the Holy Koran in front of him on the saddle. The Kufans began to advance. Hussein ordered the fire ditch behind him to be set alight. Seeing the

---

* The main office of caliph continued until 1924, when, as shall be seen later, it was abolished by the new Turkish Republic following the fall of the last sultan of the Ottoman Empire in 1922. Numerous secondary "caliphates" have been declared. These include fairly major ones like the Shia Fatimid dynasty in Egypt (909–1171) and the Umayyad "Caliphate of Cordoba" (929–1031) in Spain. Tiny self-declared territorial "caliphates" have been numerous in various Muslim lands over the centuries; an example is the one declared in 2014 by the Islamic State in Iraq and Syria (ISIS). Al Qaeda has articulated the goal of a reestablished global caliphate, but unlike ISIS it has not been a territorial entity or declared a living caliphate.

flames, a member of the Umayyad cavalry shouted out to him, asking whether he was going to the fires of hell even before the Judgment Day. The Prophet's grandson shouted back that the man was the "son of a goatherdess." Refusing to allow his own men to start the fighting, he called out to the Kufans to be quick about their work. His own daughters and sisters were shrieking and crying. He sent men to silence them.

"Trace back my lineage and consider who I am," Hussein shouted to his foes. And who, he continued, were they?

"Am I not," he cried, "the son of the daughter of your Prophet?"[37]

To slaughter a grandson of Mohammed, the son of the Prophet's favorite child, would be a wrenching act for the still-forming world of Islam. The *sharia* enjoined believers to murder any kaffir who rejected tribute or conversion, but to kill a fellow Muslim was a heinous crime. Citing the legal framework of the faith, Hussein called out to the Kufans, "Tell me, are you seeking retribution from me for one of your dead whom I have killed, or for property of yours that I have stolen, or for a wound that I have inflicted?" All of these acts were punishable by violence when perpetrated by one believer against another.

Nobody in the caliph's army answered him. How could they? Hussein responded to their silence with the offer that, in terms of the embryonic religious schism, would put his blood on the hands of the Sunnis.

"People," he called out, "since you dislike me, let me leave you for a place in the land where I may be safe.

The Kufans replied that Hussein must first submit to the authority of Yazid, the caliph. Yazid was of course the head of the Umayyad family that had consistently outmaneuvered Mohammed's family for the imperial prize. Yazid's court at Damascus was infamous for its impious decadence, its wine and song, and its contempt for the austere faith of Medina. Indignantly, Hussein refused the suggestion of submitting to such a character.

The Umayyad force advanced. "People of Kufa," Hussein called out to them, "we are still brothers in one religion and one faith as long as the sword does not strike between you and us."

Hussein was reminding them that among fellow Muslims they were protected by the Prophet's law. Fully able to stand down safely, they had it in their power that morning to redeem the faith. They could honor this inheritance of one religion, or they could compromise Islam and divide it forever. For "when the sword strikes," Hussein warned them, "the protection will be cut asunder. We will be a community and you will be a community."

These were the last words of importance uttered by a Muslim in a world in which there was any prospect of living up to the promise of the House of Peace. The first to attack his fellow Muslims on the plain of Kerbala was the commander of the Umayyad forces. Fifty-eight years had passed since the founding of the faith. Now, with that first arrow loosed toward Hussein's tiny force, the brief era of something approaching true Islam was over forever. Never again would there be any real hope of a world of Muslims living at peace with each other, saving their violence for the holy war against the kaffir as the Prophet had commanded, governed in all matters by one law administered by a single pious leader.

"By God, I was anxious to make jihad against the polytheists," called out a supporter of Hussein's, according to the ancient account of Tabari. As the Kufan arrows whistled in upon Mohammed's family, those far-off days of the faith's early conquests must indeed have seemed happy. "I hope that making jihad against these people," the man continued, "who are attacking the son of the daughter of their Prophet, will be no less rewarded."

The little band loyal to the Prophet's family sent a warrior forward for individual combat. He won. As the morning went on, more such challenges were made. They tended to favor the outnumbered and more motivated partisans of the Banu Hashim. Eventually the leader of Yazid's troops ordered an end to this and sent his forces to attack the Hashemites. Hussein's horsemen, so few that they could hardly be called cavalry, counterattacked. They put the Kufans to flight wherever the two forces met, but eventually the Umayyad arrows took their toll. Soon every horse on Hussein's side had been wounded. His surviving men continued the fight on foot. As the Kufans set fire to the tents where the women and children of the Hashemites cowered, every loss among Hussein's dwindling band seemed to make a difference. But however many Kufans they killed, it seemed to have no impact on the numbers of their attackers.

The sun hit its zenith over the parched and bloody scene. A break was called for the midday prayer. But the respite was brief.

When almost all of Hussein's warriors had been slaughtered, including most of his male family, he briefly entered the fight. He stormed onto the battlefield "like a raging lion" and chopped off an opponent's arm at the elbow.[38] His sally did not last long. Returning to his nearly deserted lines, Hussein carefully placed the corpse of a nephew next to the bodies of one of his own sons and various other close relatives who had died in the fighting. He then sat himself by the bodies, hunched under a thick hooded cloak.

For much of the afternoon, none of the Umayyad soldiers dared to attack him. Eventually one of them slashed Hussein on the head through the wool hood. Weakened and exhausted, a turban now wrapped around his bleeding head, Hussein took in his hands an infant son. The boy was promptly hit with an arrow. The dying child's blood filled Hussein's hand. The Kufans overran their camp. Hussein, wracked by an appalling thirst after many hours in the sun, tried to make his way to the Euphrates. He was blocked by the Kufans. Then they shot him through his parched throat with an arrow. Again his hands filled with blood. The soothing waters of the river were beyond his reach. Near mad with thirst, Hussein began once more to hurl himself at the enemy. Again they refused to fight him man to man.

The afternoon stretched on under the relentless sun. The end was surely near. Hussein dressed himself for death. The theater of martyrdom had begun with his morning anointment that same day. It would be a specialty of the Shia faith thenceforth. Now Hussein changed into a pair of precious trousers edged in glittering Yemeni cloth. Knowing he would die in them, he ripped them open where the two legs met, that the trousers might be worth less to whoever took them from his corpse. A follower suggested that Hussein wear an undergarment, but he refused. Exposed, he launched himself first at the Kufans to his right, then at those to his left. All melted away in front of him, "as the goats retreat when the wolf comes upon them."[39]

The end seems to have come suddenly. For a long time in the heat of the afternoon, the Umayyad soldiers continued to refuse to touch him. "Each," the chronicler tells us, "hoped the other would kill al-Hussein."[40] Then one of them struck him on the left shoulder. As Hussein staggered about, another Kufan stabbed him with a spear. Others rushed in with their swords, hacking and stabbing. Finally, one of their number, Sinan ibn Anas, leaned down and delivered the fatal cut. Then he decapitated the son of Ali.

On the corpse of the martyr were the marks of thirty-four blows and thirty-three stab wounds. His lower body was left naked as his trousers of Yemeni cloth were stripped away for spoils. The "turmeric, garments and camels" in his camp were plundered, as were the "womenfolk of al-Hussein, his baggage, and equipment."[41] The women were dragged away naked. The Shia would never forget. Hussein had been the third of their twelve Imams, after his father, Ali, and elder brother, Hasan.

Hussein had one surviving son, a twenty-one-year-old too ill to fight in the battle. The Umayyad army carted him off to Damascus with the women, who were made slaves. Zayn al Abidin, as the young man was known, would keep the bloodline of Ali and Hussein alive for future martyrdoms.

In early 661, five days after his murder, Ali was buried at Najaf, ten miles from where he had been killed. Hussein's martyrdom at Kerbala in 680 took place a day's march to the north. Thirteen centuries later, the two cities would receive ten times as many pilgrims as Mecca annually.[42] *

---

* Sunnis outnumber Shias by about ten to one globally, but the proximity and large population of Iran, predominantly Shia, added to the roughly twenty million Shias of Iraq, provide Najaf and Kerbala with their huge numbers of pilgrims. The annual pilgrimage to Mecca is almost entirely Sunni.

Chapter 10

The Umayyad Caliphate
and the Abbasid Revolution

661–750 AD

The ascendancy of the Persians over the Arabs, that is to say of the conquered over the victors, had already for a long while been in course of preparation. It became complete when the Abbassids, who owed their elevations to the Persians, ascended the throne.
—R. H. P. A. Dozy, *Histoire de L'Islamisme*, 1879

After the murder of the tragic caliph Ali in the mosque at Kufa in 661, his eldest son was proclaimed leader of Islam by the *shia*, or supporters, of the family. It was never quite a true caliphhood for Hasan, who from the start lacked acclamation and acceptance beyond the adherents of his late father. After six months Muawiya, the head of the Umayyad family, persuaded Hasan to retire to a modest provincial life. In return, Muawiya had promised that he would rule according to Islamic justice and never establish a family dynasty. Thirteen Umayyad caliphs followed Muawiya. Only one of them, Omar II (r. 717–720), can be described as recognizably pious.

On the temporal side of the faith-empire's mission, the Umayyad Caliphate was a stunning success. The early Umayyads, starting with Muawiya, nearly doubled the size of the empire, conquering Iberia, North Africa from Libya to Morocco, most of modern Afghanistan and Pakistan, and tracts of southwest Central Asia. Wealth flowed to Damascus. The traditional Muslim narratives of the conquests exaggerate the numbers, but they nonetheless give a flavor of the achievement and its priorities: "Musa took 300,000 captives from North Africa, one-fifth of whom he forwarded to the caliph, and from the Gothic nobility in Spain he captured 30,000 virgins; the captives of one Moslem general in Turkestan alone numbered 100,000."[1]

Much had changed since the conquests of Khalid ibn al Walid in the generation after the Prophet. Ruling from Damascus for nearly a century, the Banu Umayya paid the nonmaterial elements of Mohammed's faith little more heed as four-continent emperors than they had as small-town oligarchs in Mecca. After wresting the faith-empire from the Prophet's family with humiliating ease in the years following Mohammed's death, the House of Umayya mostly ruled as an old-fashioned Quraysh clan writ large: as Arabs, in other words, not as Muslims. The Umayyad court was infamous for its wine, music, and sexual license, even if the presence of its many slave girls and concubines enjoyed full sanction in the holy legislation.

One of the greater Umayyad achievements was in the field of law. Law had been indistinguishable from Islam itself in Mohammed's system, but a century or so had passed since the earthly paradise of his rule at Medina. Muslim law now faced the challenge of translating the perfection of the Prophet's brief local theocracy into a body of working legislation for an empire.

For the first century after Mohammed, customary Arab law, Roman law from Syria, and Sasanian law from Iraq, as well as elements of rabbinic, Talmudic, and Canon law, all inflected the emerging Islamic jurisprudence. This was the period when a "new society" was being built, a Muslim way of life that unified enormous stretches of the world that previously had had little in common with the Arabs whose culture created the faith.* Politically, the Umayyads ruled as an Arab clan concerned with dynasty and empire. Administratively, the Umayyads understood that Islam was all that might unite their huge dominion. In the law governing daily life, in matters of family, inheritance, slavery, and contract, no less than in

---

* Unbelievers, insofar as their acts did not bring them into conflict with Muslims, were allowed to continue with their own legal systems, although subject to Islamic taxes and restrictions.

the rules of war or the rituals of observance, there was now a need for a framework that worked as well in Samarkand as it did in Cordoba. This would be the faith of Medina, applied with Umayyad pragmatism.

While the Arabs before Mohammed had been extraordinarily free— free of any state, lord, king, or written code—they were very much bound by the long-standing practice of their people. Lacking government and letters, in legal matters the Arabs had immemorially looked to tradition and precedent. Their word for this unwritten corpus was *sunna*, meaning, most literally, the "path."* Mohammed's personal legislation in his decade as an absolute ruler at Medina included much that reflected traditional Arab Sunna.

Mohammed had been followed by his four successors of the Rashidun Caliphate: Abu Bakr, Omar, Othman, and Ali. The imperial expansion achieved by the first three of these brought sudden, close encounters with sophisticated civilizations, while internally the Rightly Guided time had been one of civil war and murderous faction. With the accession of the Umayyads in 661, the internal turbulence of the Rashiduns' "golden age" of piety was followed by ninety years of religious disinterest and political peace on the home front. The old Arab freedoms gave way to an imperial state, built on the Persian and Roman foundations of the conquered lands. Such a state required law, at least for the believers; the kaffirs of the Dar al Islam were largely left to themselves in legal matters as long as they paid the jizya. Thus, following the Umayyad consolidation there was both more need and more leisure for creating a coherent Islamic approach to legislation and judgment.[2]

The year 722 marked the turn of the first century of Muslim history. Around this time, what became known as Islam's "ancient schools of law" began to grow roots in Kufa and Medina primarily, but also elsewhere in Iraq and Arabia, and to a lesser extent in Syria.† These "ancient

---

* The desert- or wilderness-born idea of a "path" or "way" guiding the believer through the dangerous wastes is key to the Islamic vision. *Sharia*, the word for Muslim law, also means "path," "road," or "way." The Prophet Mohammed is frequently called the Guide, and the principal compendium of Islamic law is called the *Reliance of the Traveler*.

† Throughout this period, writes the late Professor Joseph Schacht, "the non-Muslim subject populations retained their own traditional legal institutions . . . This is the basis of the factual legal autonomy of the non-Muslims which was extensive in the Middle Ages, and has survived in part down to the present generation." P. M. Holt et al., *Cambridge History of Islam* (Cambridge: Cambridge University Press, 1970), vol. 2, p. 548.

schools" were made up of lay specialists using their personal discretion according to the guidance in the Koran but also other sources: primarily the customs of the community and the inherited practice of the Sasanians and Byzantines.[3] Early Umayyad law had the distinctly cosmopolitan, businesslike quality that typified the dynasty. Over the following century there would come the transformation of these practices into a more systematic and truly Islamic framework. Iraq in particular would be home to these developments, which shaped the orthodox faith and provided its name, Sunnism, ever after.[4]

Two competing centers of legal thought emerged within the faith-empire during the Umayyad period. One of these was the Hejaz, the western strip of Arabia, along the Red Sea, that is home to Mecca and Medina; the other was southern Iraq, especially Kufa but also Basra. The work of both was to fill in the gaps left by Mohammed when his legislative career ended with his death in 632. The Hejazi legal schools, based in the cradle of the faith, a land where the traditions of Sunna had long been the basis for law, claimed to find their solutions in the traditional practice of the Muslim community. The Iraqi schools, based in a Hellenized world, were said to focus more on *ijtihad*: individual opinion, based on reasoning and analogy.[5]

The great innovation of the Iraqi schools was to begin to cite, as the basis for their judgments, not ordinary Arab Sunna but rather the "Sunna of the Prophet," Mohammed's personal way. The school of law at Kufa, in particular, led a broad process to project current law backward onto the earliest days of the faith, giving the prevailing jurisprudence an imprimatur of Islamic precedent.[6]

Now took place the most significant development in orthodox Islam after Mohammed. It was a development that is rarely given sufficient attention. Once the Sunna of the Prophet had been established as the basis for law, there followed an inescapable pressure to ground any individual statute or ruling in a specific reference to Mohammed's own words or practice.

The fundamental character of Mohammed's mission had been to create a legal framework that legislated for all of human life, marrying the immutable words of an all-disposing One God to the exemplary power of the Prophet's perfect life. The Umayyads may have been contemptuous of the new religion, but these tenets at the heart of their empire could not be ignored forever. But what in fact was this "way of the Prophet," and what, precisely, had Mohammed said and done in various situations? And how was one to understand his equally legislative silences and forbearances? Such information was now recognized as the only truly Islamic basis for law and judgment, but little was known about the Prophet's daily history. A century had passed since his death. For any law or judicial decision, an incident from Mohammed's biography now had to be produced.

Soon enough, detailed biographical anecdotes began to appear, each claiming to be a literal report from a witness to the Prophet's actions. These anecdotes were known as *ahadith* ("traditions"). Each individual hadith included a detailed claim first of its origins, always in the recollection of an identified Companion of the Prophet, and then of its oral passing along by a chain of named and dependable individuals.[7] A few of these Traditions had existed since the period shortly after Mohammed's death. Now, starting in the second Islamic century, in the 720s or so, thousands more hadiths emerged. A hadith follows a standard form: "A (the last narrator) says he heard it from B on the authority of C who said this on the authority of D that the Prophet of God said . . . , and so on."[8] By the turn of the third Islamic century, the hadiths numbered in the hundreds of thousands.

With the supremacy of Sunna, a basic change in the nature of the law occurred. Law was now something to be memorized, not understood. The Traditionists, or Sunnis, "disliked all human reasoning and personal opinion, which had become an integral part of the living tradition of the ancient schools."[9]

The body of law that exists within the Sunna came to be known as *sharia*. This word, also long used in traditional pre-Islamic Arabic law, was something of a synonym of *sunna* in its literal meaning: the "path" or the "way," with roots in the culture of the desert raider and caravaneer. Eventually, the sharia was to force aside scholarly interpretation— *ijtihad*—and the teachings of the "ancient schools." As a result of this process, mainstream Islam is known as Sunnism.

The Arab conquest of Iraq from the Sasanian Persians had begun a decade after Mohammed's death and taken ten years, 642–651. Once again, Iraq was the richest province on earth. During the Umayyad heyday of the late eighth century, Iraq was contributing four times as much income to the imperial treasury as Egypt, and five times as much as Syria with its rich port cities of Palestine.[10]

The Arabs ruled the great prize from the military outpost that they had established in the south of the country at Kufa, less than ten miles from Najaf and the resting place of the martyred Ali, and twenty miles south of where Alexander had died in his fever at Babylon. In Iraq as elsewhere in the Muslim empire during its first century, the Arab invaders kept themselves apart from Islam's conquered peoples. This included those who had converted to the faith. The Arab occupiers lived, as the Caliph Omar had intended, in fortified enclaves like the one at Kufa, exempt from most taxes.

By the middle of the eighth century, significant numbers—if still a minority—of the empire's conquered peoples had professed the new religion. Conversion could secure safety and exemption from the jizya, but it could not secure equality. In his last sermon at Mecca a year before his death, the Prophet had promised that "every Muslim is the brother of every other Muslim. All of you are of the same equality." As H. G. Wells put it in 1920, this resulted during the early years in "a society more free from widespread cruelty and social oppression than any society had ever been."[11] * But the Umayyads were not really Islamic. They cared little for the faith, generally, and less for its stipulation of equality among believers. Under Umayyad rule, converts from Islam's subject races found themselves excluded from many of the privileges of the Arab occupation. These victims of the internal apartheid were known as *mawali*, or clients, of the Arab Muslims.

A maula (the singular form of "mawali") male in the time of the Umayyad Caliphate was not allowed to marry an Arab girl or woman. Despite embracing the new religion, he would have been denied, on account of his non-Arabic race, the right to live, or even to worship, in the same places as an Arab. Nor did he have quite the same tax preferments that he may have hoped would privilege him over the kaffir. He had little hope for office and other governmental spoils of submission.

---

* This would refer to Arabia itself during roughly the time between the elimination of the Jews of Medina in about 622–623 to the end of the Rightly Guided Caliphate with Ali's death in 661.

Despite the requirement that the believer follow in detail the day-to-day practice of the Prophet, even Arab dress was at times banned for many of these non-Arab Muslims, including Iranians, Iraqis, Turks, Egyptians, and others. By the 740s the mawali comprised a majority of believers in every part of the empire save Arabia itself.

The garrison character of the latest empire to come to Iraq was in profound contrast to the previous great external idea to visit Western Asia's pivotal land. In the Hellenistic East, religion had played no role in political life, except insofar as tolerance was reckoned a tool of diplomacy and governance. The Seleucids had frequently followed Alexander, as he had followed Cyrus, in supporting local faiths. The very notion of subjugation, taxation, or death on the basis of religion would have endangered the Hellenistic enterprise. It would have been equally unwelcome under Cyrus. In Greek Asia, peasants previously tied to the land had been freed in large numbers by the burgeoning new centers of trade. The self-governing political form of the Greek *polis* had been copied and freely adopted in many a town where the population was largely local rather than Greek.

A system that harvested slaves and tributary taxes had strong economic incentives to discourage conversion. In the conquered lands, every convert was one slave or tribute payer the fewer. This had roots in the Prophet's example. He had "left his immediate achievements within his Arabian sphere as a testament for the future of his community: to fight the unbelievers, to extend not so much the faith as the territory dominated by the faith . . . The warriors of Islam had as their immediate concern the subjugation, rather than the conversion, of the unbelievers."[12]

Omar II was the eighth of the fourteen rulers of the Umayyad dynasty. Perceiving that eventually the relatively small number of Arabs would struggle to rule over the more numerous subject peoples, Omar worked to reestablish Islam itself, rather than the prevailing Arab overlordship, as the legitimating force of the empire. He reigned from September 717 to February 720.

In his time on the throne, Omar II made it a priority to give all Muslim men the equality that the Prophet had intended.[13] Infidels became believers, taxpayers became tax receivers, and the treasury suffered. An Umayyad official in Egypt wrote to Omar at the capital in Damascus in about 719, "If things continue in Egypt as at present, the Christians will, without exception, embrace Islam, and the state will lose all its revenues."[14] After Omar's brief caliphhood, the Umayyads turned their attention back to the Arab tribes and away from Islam.

It was thus not a failure but a success of the faith's imperial project that, for at least the first century of the Islamic empire, fewer than 10 percent of the people in the House of Peace were Muslims. This was despite the financial advantages of conversion and the lamentable condition during the eighth century of the neighboring alternatives—the calcified state Zoroastrianism of the late Sasanian Persian Empire and the obstruse and doctrinaire Eastern Christianity of the Byzantines of the day.

In 739, an Umayyad governor in Iran, Nasr ibn Sayyar, found himself dealing with a restive province that was home to "thirty thousand Muslims who had been paying the *jizyah* and eighty thousand polytheists who had been exempted from the *jizyah*." This was the opposite of how things were supposed to work in the House of Peace. Nasr swiftly "imposed the jizya on the polytheists and removed it from the Muslims."[15]

That year, 739, was the fifteenth year on the throne of the Umayyad caliph Hisham. His reign proved to be the high-water mark of the dynasty, its peak in strength and splendor. Hisham, tenth of his house to be caliph, was the tenth to die peacefully. There may be only one other dynasty in the region's history, the Ottoman Turks, that can match half of this record. Upon Hisham's death came the one-year reign of Walid II, the most decadent character in a dynasty notable for its degenerate reputation in Islam. Walid, killed in a coup, was the only Umayyad caliph apart from the fourteenth and last to die of violence. (The death of the fourth Umayyad, Marwan I, was attributed by some to an insulted wife; that Marwan died in his sleep is not disputed.) The contrast to the four pious Rightly Guided caliphs who followed Mohammed, three of whom died by the blade, is striking. After Walid II, the final three Umayyad caliphs were successively seated within seven months in 744.

In 740, a grandson of Hussein led an anti-Umayyad revolt at Kufa. Like Hussein's uprising sixty years previously, this one was abandoned by the locals who had promised to support it and then crushed by the forces of the Umayyad caliphs. Zayd ibn Ali, the revolt's leader, was a great-great-grandson of the Prophet. At Kufa Zayd was shot in the head with an arrow that lodged in his skull. When the arrow was removed, he died "screaming" in the house of a supporter. The location was revealed by a Sindhi slave. When the Umayyad forces found Zayd's corpse, they beheaded and crucified it.[16]

With events like Zayd's doomed rebellion and tragic demise, Shiism under the Umayyads was continuing along its path of gradual articulation from political party to rebel sect to, eventually, its own creed. The term *shia* originally meant "partisans" and referred to the *shia't Ali*, the supporters or partisans of Ali in the early succession struggles after the Prophet's death. Islam's greatest historian, the early tenth-century Persian polymath Tabari, used the word *shia* to refer to members of the movement throughout his accounts of the Umayyad years.

The great and pious Ali, most beloved by far of the Prophet's companions, had seen the more worldly House of Umayya turn his own promising career into a misery and ultimately a failure, leading to his murder. After the Umayyads had finally, officially seized power in 661, their army had then defeated and beheaded Ali's son, Hussein, at Kerbala in 680. The phenomenon had continued. In 713 Hussein's first son, and then in 732 that individual's first son, were poisoned to death by order of the caliph. It continued to happen until 874: the first sons of the line of Ali and Hussein, poisoned at the behest of the caliph of the day, one after another for eight generations.

The Shia tradition calls these martyrs the Imams ("leaders" or "models"). Sunnism, while disputing some of the historical account of the Imamate and accepting other parts of it, uses the term "imam" simply for a mosque's prayer leader. Mainstream, or "Twelver," Shiism maintains that in 874 the twelfth and last of the Shia Imams was occulted, meaning that he supernaturally disappeared, shortly after his predecessor was poisoned to death. This twelfth Imam is a messiah figure, called the Mahdi, whose return will bring justice and peace. Until then, all earthly rule is corrupt and unjust.

As the tragedy of the Imams unfolded through the Umayyad years, the Shia religious identity was gradually developing among the partisans of Ali's line. The heritage of Medina made the political inescapably religious, so that every time the wrong person was assassinated or enthroned, it was a religious event too. These events, meanwhile, made the party of the Prophet's family a natural home for those who were, in the imperial setting, more generally excluded and aggrieved. Just as the Shia Imams were denied power by the Umayyads of Damascus, so too were the indigenous people of Arab-occupied Iran and southern Iraq who believed in these Imams. A tale circulated among the colonized Iranians asserting that the principal wife of the Imam Hussein had been a daughter of the last Sasanian king. The claim would make the Shias' Imamate an imperial Iranian bloodline.

In these early days Shiism was especially strong around Kufa and Kerbala, where Ali had been based and where he and Hussein met their martyrdoms. This was not far from where the Hebrews had encountered Zoroastrianism and become Jews during their exile by the waters of Babylon. Links to Iran's Indo-European civilization had long been stronger there in the south than elsewhere in Mesopotamia. As the nascent sect developed into something more freestanding, it would be shaped, in conscious contrast to the faith of the Arab invaders, by the ancient Perso-Hellenistic culture of Iran.

Throughout the Umayyad years, the proto-Shias in their traditional stronghold of southern Iraq continued to agitate for the political claims of the descendants of the Prophet. The Byzantines, still known as the *Rumi*, or Romans, occasionally roused themselves into considerable opposition. The skills and tools of imperial administration had to be borrowed, learned, and copied from these Romans and Persians. Observant Muslims periodically fought back against what they saw as the wine-soaked corruption of the descendants of Yazid in their ancient Greek and Roman city of Damascus. Meanwhile most of Islam's subject peoples continued to resist conversion, and the humiliations and tributes imposed on the kaffir brought additional strata of tension. Until 744, a year of four caliphs that presaged the coming end of the dynasty, the practical Umayyads managed all of these challenges.

The dynasty faced danger from the frustrations of the mawali, the inevitable reassertion of Iran's natural weight in the regional balance, and the resistance of the people of Iraq to the Syrian soldiery in their midst. But none of it was quite enough for a revolution. The Arab power in Damascus was still formidable, and the chaotic year of 744 had ended with the emergence of an organized and militarily experienced caliph, Marwan II.

The mawali of the eastern Islamic empire were beginning to develop bonds with the growing new identity of Shiism. If these principal elements of opposition to the Umayyads were to effect a revolution, it was going to require sophisticated leadership. The pathetic collapse of the Zaydi uprising in Kufa in 740 had underscored the chronic haplessness and failure of the mainline Shia effort in terms of worldly power. Fatally for the Umayyads, a better-organized cause existed, quietly working in the background for many years, and the Zaydi fiasco served to channel the revolutionary energies toward it.

Living in ostensible tranquility on a farm in deep rural Syria (at Humayma in present-day Jordan) was a family called the Abbasis. Like the Shia imams, they were related to the Prophet. Unlike the Shia imams, they possessed cunning, political drive, and a talent for organization. The founder of the house had been an uncle of the Prophet Mohammed's, called Abbas, a rich merchant who died in 653. Abbas converted to Islam so late (probably in 630, just before the Quraysh struck their bargain allowing Mohammed back into Mecca) that Mohammed, only three years his junior, called his uncle the Last of the Muhajirun, meaning in essence the last of the true converts.

The rivalry between Mohammed's clan and the House of Umayya had ancient roots in Mecca predating even the Prophet's own revolution a century previously. Once the Umayyads had settled themselves in power, Abbas's descendants fell afoul of them. The Abbasis eventually retreated in quasi-exile to their estate at Humayma. The family possessed no particular power or prestige, although they had some wealth, as Abbas, a successful trader in spices, had owned the Zamzam, the lucrative well next to the Kaaba in Mecca, and had passed this on within the family. The Abbasis' assets were ambition, a grievance against a ruling family that had many other enemies, a family connection to the Prophet and thus tenuously to the Shias, and an extraordinary multigenerational quality of patient, focused cunning.

Starting in 721, the Abbasi family began to send secret emissaries to disaffected mawali elements. As Arab, Syrian, Umayyad rule chafed ever more across the empire through the 740s, the shadowy House of Abbas carefully pulled together the various strands of opposition. The Abbasis' secret agents, as they worked quietly to build their revolution in the last decades of the Umayyad Caliphate, did not emphasize that among all of Mohammed's circle of relatives, friends, and associates, Abbas had been the latest convert and the most reluctant Muslim. Instead, the Abbasi propagandists emphasized the vague *Ahl al Bayt*, or "people of the house," meaning the family of Mohammed.

In a remarkable cloak-and-dagger saga, the *dawa* ("call") of the Banu Abbas, their underground effort of propaganda and mobilization, went on for twenty-six years (721–747). The Umayyad intelligence apparatus discovered and killed many of the family's agents over the long years of secret revolution, but the profane Arab overlords in Damascus continued to create new enemies, and new recruits kept the revolt brewing. It did not matter that the Abbasis were no more pious than the Umayyads, or that both were Arabs and at equal removes from the mawali ethnically. What mattered was that Umayyad rule produced inevitable foes, and that the Abbasis were adept at overstating their Shia sympathies and links to Mohammed.

The quarter-century *dawa* of the Abbasis was a tale of secret missions to Khorasan and back, of hidden letters, fake pilgrimages, and fortunes sewn into the linings of cloaks. There were tense encounters in the desert and murmured moonlight conversions as caravans laden with dinars, dirhams, and musk traveled through the stony wastes to avoid the caliph's security network. Funds shuttled back and forth with the mysterious revolutionaries between Kufa, the Iranian hinterlands, and the shadowy headquarters in the Syrian countryside. Toward the end, new whispers spread through the east: the Savior, the Promised One so dear to the Iranian outlook since the time of Zoroaster, was coming.

———

On a June day in 747 near the northeast Iranian city of Merv, capital of the large and rich province of Khorasan, a twenty-eight-year-old warrior raised a black banner before his gathered troops. Small in stature and grim in temperament, he bore the mysterious nom de guerre of Abu Muslim. His followers numbered perhaps a few dozen.

Black was the color of the Prophet and his family. For Abu Muslim and his men, Iranians all and many of them also dressed in black, the flag signified rebellion against Arab rule. The black flag also represented a holy cause: the rebels hoped to replace the Umayyad voluptuaries in far-off Damascus with a new caliph from the *Ahl al Bayt*. Mohammed himself, in simpler and purer days, had flown a plain black standard. Whispered prophecies of the imminent coming of the Messiah were now sweeping the Persian-speaking lands of the eastern empire. Black flags were said to be the sign of the Chosen One.[17]

By the next day, fighters were streaming to join Abu Muslim from across the vast and wealthy province of Khorasan. Some arrived in groups of hundreds; others came alone. Three weeks later the heads of a handful of local foes decorated the gates of Abu Muslim's camp.

Within a month and a half, Abu Muslim's insurgent army numbered seven thousand.[18] The "people of the house" in whose name they rebelled were the Banu Abbas. At this point, almost a hundred and fifty years had passed since the death in 653 of their ancestor, Mohammed's uncle Abbas. The revolutionaries who cited the priority of this unimportant figure did not care that, in the Prophet's lifetime, Abbas had rejected the faith of his nephew until almost the end. The slogan fed to the rebels was that they were fighting for *Ahl al Bayt*. Believing that this referred to Ali and Hussein, the budding Shia communities within the empire quickly signed up to the cause. Only after their sacrifices for the Abbasi revolution did the Shia understand that these "People of the House" had nothing to do with Ali, Hussein, and descent from the Prophet himself. The Abbasis would soon enough prove to be, in their early years in power, worse enemies to the Shia than even the Umayyads had been.[19] For the Shia, their naïve co-option in service of the Abbasi family's gambit was yet another tragedy, another case of the endless injustice of earthly affairs.

When Abu Muslim raised the black flag of revolt in 747, imperial Islam was at its geographical apogee. The House of Peace under the later Umayyad Caliphate stretched from Gibraltar to the marches of China. The caliph in Damascus, the tough and capable Marwan II, fifty-six years old, ruled from the deserts of Sudan to the foothills of the Armenian mountains. Marwan was the successful veteran general of foreign wars against the Byzantines and the nomadic Turks and Alans. At home he had prevailed in a time of vicious and complex dynastic infighting, becoming the third new caliph to be sat in 744 after the debauched Walid II was overthrown and killed by a cousin in April of that year. What Marwan seems not to have known is that for the past twenty-six years, the Abbasis had been secretly organizing the revolution that now burst forth in their name.[20]

Abu Muslim and his men conquered the Muslim empire for the Banu Abbas within three years. On that June day of the black banner in 747, his rebel troops were still in Khorasan, their homeland. Comprising most of today's northeast Iran as well as the historically Iranian parts of what are now Afghanistan, Tajikistan, and Uzbekistan, Khorasan is by far the largest province of historic Iran, or greater Persia. The Arabs had conquered this land, which corresponded more or less to ancient Parthia, exactly one century before, in 647. There, as everywhere else in the empire except for Arabia, they remained a small minority of the population. In Christian Syria and Palestine in 638, five years after the Muslim conquest, Arabs comprised about 2 percent of the population.[21] In far-flung Khorasan a century later, the Arabs are unlikely to have been more than 5 or 10 percent of the total.

Khorasan was large, distant from the Arab homeland, and wealthy in human and material resources. It was home to some of the richest cultural centers of greater Iran. The Khorasani city of Merv, in what is now southeast Turkmenistan, was the leading Iranian metropolis of the time. A former regional capital under the Seleucids, called first Alexandria-in-Margiana and then, in the Hellenistic period, Antioch-in-Margiana, Merv had been a significant place for at least a thousand years. Both Zoroastrianism and Nestorianism continued to be popular in the province. A "vigourous Hellenism" continued to thrive there.[22] By the time of Abu Muslim, even the Arabs of Khorasan, much assimilated with the local landowners, had for decades barely acknowledged the writ of the Banu Umayya in their distant Syrian capital. The creole nobility of this rich and isolated province, the largest in the empire, had its own aspirations.

Almost none of the Khorasani revolutionaries would ever so much as see a member of the far-off Arab family in whose cause they fought.[23] Yet

The Revolt of Abu Muslim and the Early Abbasid World

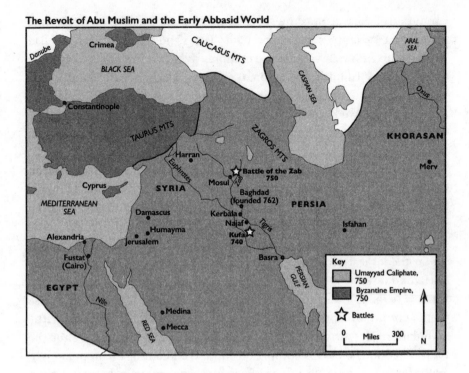

it was mostly through the Khorasanis that the Hashemite clan, through its Abbasi branch, now wrested back power from the Umayyads a century after the struggles over Mohammed's succession. The Abbasid revolution was a racial revolution too: the inevitable revolt of Persian against Arab. Abu Muslim's orders from the Abbasi family commanded him to "see that there is not one left in Khorasan whose tongue is the tongue of the Arabian."[24] The Abbasis themselves were Arabs, not Persians, but they understood the power of this anti-Arab message for the people who would do their fighting.

The caliph, Marwan II, was known as Marwan the Ass for his hardiness on the campaign trail. Marwan was no embarrassment to his house, but by then the Banu Umayya had too many enemies, the Abbasis had done too well mobilizing the Iranians and Iraqis for the "people of the house," and Khorasan had developed too far along its own path. As Abu Muslim moved against Marwan, the drama shifted westward from

Khorasan to Iraq. Throughout the story as told around a century and a half later by the Persian historian Tabari, it was a clash between the "Khorasanis" and the "Syrians." Iraq was once more the battleground of East and West in a world-historical struggle. The Umayyads in their Hellenistic capital city of Damascus, with their administration and even much of their art and architecture borrowed from the "second Rome" of Byzantium, were heirs of the Greeks and Romans; the Khorasanis were the Iranian power of the day.

Two years of Khorasani advances, replete with a pious plethora of crucifixions and beheadings on both sides, culminated in late 749 with fierce small battles at Kufa and then Basra. In January 750, Marwan marched south from Harran, stopping just below Mosul for the decisive clash with Abu Muslim. Repeatedly disobeyed by his men, who finally dissolved before the Khorasanis and tried to flee across the Zab River, Marwan eventually took flight. He cut the ropes of his pontoon across the Zab behind him. Of Marwan's forces, "more were drowned that day than were slain in battle."[25]

The last Umayyad army had been destroyed, but the Caliph Marwan himself escaped with two sons. The booty was disappointing for the Abbasi army: "They found many weapons and much wealth, but they found no women except a slavegirl of Abdallah bin Marwan."

Marwan fled through Damascus to Palestine and then on to Egypt, where the Abbasis at last brought him to ground. The final hiding place of the fourteenth Umayyad caliph was a church near the oasis town of Faiyum, south of Cairo. Marwan's sons escaped to "the land of the Abyssinians," according to Tabari, where one was killed. The other seems not to have been heard from again.[26]

The Battle of the Zab was another of Iraq's history-shaping battles. Within three years of Abu Muslim's raising the black banner in 747, the Khorasani armies fighting for the House of Abbas toppled an empire that reached from the Atlantic Ocean to Central Asia. With Abu Muslim's victory over the last Umayyad caliph, the Arabs' brief and bloody moment in the sun was over. Arab importance on the world stage had begun in the period after the Prophet's passing, with the dazzling conquests by Khalid ibn al Walid and the other great generals of the Rashidun Caliphate. Now, with the fall of the Umayyads, the collective relevance of the Arabs in the strategic affairs of the region, outside of a narrow sphere, had ended after a hundred and ten years and would not return until the petroleum age thirteen centuries later.

———

The first of the Abbasids to rule, one Abul Abbas, proclaimed himself caliph in the mosque at Kufa in 749, the year before Abu Muslim's decisive victory over Marwan at the Battle of the Zab. Tabari writes that Abul Abbas had "curly hair, and was tall and white skinned, with a hooked nose and a handsome face and beard."[27] After defeating Marwan and the Umayyad armies in 750, Abul Abbas began in earnest to earn his self-assigned moniker of As Saffah. The Abbasids took regnal names in the form of adjectives that they found expedient or flattering, and "As Saffah" meant both "the Generous" and "the Bloodshedder." Mostly in "circumstances of inhuman cruelty and revolting treachery,"[28] the Abbasids hunted down and slaughtered the male members of the Umayyad family wherever they could find them. Even Mecca and Medina provided no sanctuary. At Damascus, the Abbasids invited eighty male members of the Umayyad family to a dinner to celebrate their pardon, and massacred them before the food arrived. The corpses were heaped in the banquet hall, covered in leather, and used as a table. The Abbasids destroyed the tombs of all thirteen Umayyad caliphs who had preceded Marwan, except for that of the pious Omar II.

Swimming across the Euphrates after fleeing Abbasi agents in Damascus, a single Umayyad prince, the nineteen-year-old Abd al Rahman, escaped the bloodbath. He made his way through hostile Egypt to North Africa and the land of the Berbers, the people of his slave-girl mother. After a peregrination of five years, Abd al Rahman crossed to Spain in 755 and within a year had united, through conquest and diplomacy, the various Arab tribes there, present since the original Muslim conquest of Al Andalus (Muslim Iberia) in 711. The emirate that he established at Cordoba would follow mainstream Sunni norms in all legal matters, from dhimmitude and apostasy to marriage and sexual slavery.[29] * Abd

---

* In 929, a successor, Abd al Rahman III, declared himself caliph in the West while reuniting Muslim Spain after generations of internecine splintering. Christians and Jews prospered during the following century in Cordoba, which at the turn of the millennium was the largest and most sophisticated city in Western Europe.

al Rahman is remembered as the Falcon of Spain, and a fine statue commemorates him at Almuñécar, near Granada, where he is thought to have come ashore from Africa.

As an Umayyad prince setting himself up in a wealthy Western caliphate of his own, Abd al Rahman was a threat to the usurping House of Abbas. Nonetheless, the second Abbasid caliph, the great Mansour, who founded Baghdad, gave the Falcon of Spain one of history's more elegant encomia, probably in the early 770s:

> The falcon of Quraysh is Abd al-Rahman . . . who after wandering solitary through the deserts of Asia and Africa, had the boldness to seek his fortune without an army, in lands unknown to him beyond the sea. Having naught to rely upon save his own wits and perseverance, he nonetheless humiliated his proud foes, exterminated rebels, organized cities, mobilized armies, secured his frontiers against the Christians, founded a great empire and reunited under his scepter a realm that seemed already parcelled out among others. No man before him ever did such deeds [and] Abd al-Rahman did it alone."[30]

In 752, two years after their victory at the River Zab, the Abbasis moved the capital of faith and empire five hundred miles east, from Damascus to Kufa in southern Iraq. It was the same Arab garrison town that had been Ali's capital during his short and troubled reign. Damascus was too imbued with the Umayyad atmosphere, and too associated with their rule, for the new dynasty. Moving the capital eastward, moreover, served to mollify the Persian mawali and the Shia of southern Iraq and to invest them in the new order.

Almost as soon as the Abbasids and their supporters had overthrown the Damascus caliphate, pro-Umayyad revolts began in Basra and central Mesopotamia. It was as if Iraq were a pendulum that could neither be pulled for long all the way toward the Arabs or the Persians nor ever find the peace of equilibrium between the two. But like Alexander from the West and the various great Iranian dynasties, the Abbasids understood that south central Mesopotamia was the region's pivot, and that is where the new dynasty, soon to represent Islam's storied pinnacle, committed itself.

The departure from Damascus marked a watershed. The Mediterranean world of the Levant was left behind. The new location of Islam's capital reflected the Iranian and Iraqi origins of the new order. The results of this, in terms of inflections toward either East or West, are perhaps surprising. A great irony was at work. It was in the east (Iran and Iraq) that vestiges of Hellenism still prospered, while in the west (Syria and Turkey) the classical Greek legacy was busily being expunged. The old Greco-Roman city of Damascus, Islam's most recent capital, sat within the orbit of eighth-century Byzantine Christianity, with its stifling atmosphere of orthodoxy, its obsession with petty doctrinal feuds, and its loathing of rational and humanist antiquity. Thus, when the Islamic capital moved east from Damascus to Kufa, it was to a milieu—the Persian-dominated Orient—in which the more liberal legacy of the ancient Greeks was far stronger than it was in the Byzantine west.

Even in its better days, Eastern Christianity had held a deep distrust of pagan classicism and of the humanist spirit of free will embodied in the vision of the Classical Greeks and their heirs in Asian Hellenism. Al Masudi, the tenth-century historian who was also a noted traveler of his day, understood this:

> From the days of the ancient Greeks through Byzantine times, scientific knowledge continued to grow and develop. Learned men and philosophers were held in great esteem, and investigated the human body, reason and the soul . . . The sciences were financially supported, honored everywhere, universally pursued . . . Then the Christian religion appeared in Byzantium and the edifice of Greek learning was obliterated.[31]

In Umayyad and then Abbasid times, Iraq and Iran were home to numerous communities, Christian, pagan, and Zoroastrian, that were still steeped in the world of Aristotle and Alexander.[32] Eventually, through the Iranian bridge, the Arabic-speaking world would make contact with this Hellenism that lived on beyond the grasp of Orthodox Christianity at the time of Western Europe's so-called Dark Ages. In 1892, the Scottish Orientalist William Muir described with clarity the underlying forces behind the developments that now unfolded:

With the rise of Persian influence, the roughness of Arab life was softened and there opened an era of culture, toleration, and scientific research. The practice of oral tradition was also giving place to recorded statement and historical narrative, a change hastened by the scholarly tendencies introduced from the East. To the same source may be attributed the ever increasing laxity at Court, of manners and morality and also those transcendental views that now sprung up of the divine imamate, or spiritual leadership, of some member of the House of Ali, as well as the rapid growth of free thought.

The links between Iran and the eastern Mediterranean world were incomparably stronger than any connection that either of these places had with Arabia. The Prophet's faith and culture were never truly to take root in the lands of greater Iran. Instead, the old Persian-Greek cross-pollination, under a layer of Islamic nomenclature, would grow into something wildly fertile. The Arabs, in losing their empire to a revolution whose Iranian roots would increasingly define the new dynasty, had now supplied the Perso-Greek culture with a single canvas from east of the Indus to the Atlantic Ocean. Within fifty years, the Abbasid revolution ushered in a period of three centuries in which the lands conquered by Islam became home to a shared, distinct, and spectacular early medieval civilization.

In 754, As Saffah, the Bloodshedder, first of the Abbasid caliphs, died of smallpox. He was succeeded by a brother, who took the regnal name of Al Mansour, "the Victorious." In 755, Mansour summoned Abu Muslim from Khorasan to Iraq, called him into his tent and had his throat slit. Abu Muslim's stature among the Khorasanis, whose troops had won the battles against the armies of the Umayyads, made him a threat to the new dynasty. The chief of the House of Abbas then threw into the Tigris the corpse of the man who had won them a world.[33]

Abu Muslim's devotion to a family whom he hardly knew had been extraordinary. He was an elusive character, described by a French historian as an *"homme sombre et dur,"* a man whom the pleasures of this world hardly touched.[34] His career persuaded much of the Iranian nobility finally to embrace Islam; until then they had retained their Magian faith alongside the considerable wealth and political privileges that they had been able to maintain under the rule of the thinly spread Arabs. Some considered Abu Muslim the true Imam, returned at last to bring justice to the world. His death unleashed messianic cults associated with Zoroaster and the martyred Shia saints. In Iran the two religious currents were increasingly intertwined as their adherents discovered common ground in their principal themes of justice and the coming savior.

Later in that same year of 755, an enraged follower of Abu Muslim launched a rebellion in Iran. Imperial troops murdered sixty thousand of his supporters.[35] Apart from the men whom Abu Muslim and his troops killed in battle, this gnomic and gloomy character reckoned that he had himself ordered the execution of a hundred thousand souls.[36] Al Tabari put the number at six hundred thousand, "in cold blood."[37] Abu Muslim was the single indispensable element in the success of the Abbasid revolution, but he appears never to have sought anything more than the opportunity to serve the cause of the cynical Banu Abbas. Alongside the deception of the Shia and the slaughter of the Umayyads, Abu Muslim's murder and its aftermath soaked the new caliphate in treachery and blood.

In 762 the caliph Mansour inaugurated a new capital. The location was ninety miles north of Kufa, on the site of an obscure Persian village called Baghdad. Twelve years had passed since the Abbasids had left Damascus for southern Iraq. Baghdad, at the point on the Tigris River where it comes closest to the smaller and more westerly Euphrates, was fifty miles from Babylon. The new city was less than twenty miles from Seleucia-Ctesiphon, also on the Tigris in the "neck" where the two rivers come closest, just east of the center of the country. Mansour called his new capital *Madinat al Salaam*, the City of Peace. For many, this must have had an ironic ring from the start.

For the Arabs, the 762 move to Baghdad represented the culmination of the process of political marginalization that had begun with the mawali-driven Abbasid revolution itself. The people who soon replaced the Arabs in government were largely Persians, with a few Jews and Christians. As Al Masudi was to write in the tenth century, Mansour, the founder of Baghdad, was the first Caliph to employ his clients and freedmen as provincial governors or tax collectors and delegate to them authority, preferring them over Arabs; subsequent Caliphs in this line followed this example. The commanding position of the Arabs was thus abolished, their leadership came to an end, and their high rank vanished.[38]

At the time of the anti-Umayyad revolution, a large majority of Muslims in the empire were mawali. The revolution, in terms of most of its supporters and soldiers if not of its Abbasi puppet-masters, had been an initiative on their part to equalize the status of all Muslims, regardless of race. This was not so much a social justice movement as it was a power-seeking project on the part of excluded Khorasanis and others. But it would nonetheless carry profound importance across the wider lands of Islam. Berbers, Kurds, Copts and other Egyptians, black Africans, Iberians, Levantines, Arameans, Afghans, Turks, and more: the empire's great non-Arab majority was diverse and far-flung. The revolution of the mawali, for all that it delivered power to yet another Arab family, now brought the races of the empire under one roof as far as faith was concerned. The formal distinctions were ended.

The change in regime thus fulfilled for a time some of Islam's early promise, so long ignored amid the imperial and economic energies unleashed by other parts of Mohammed's formula, of the equality of all believers before God. This set the scene for large-scale intermarriage between Arabs and indigenous Muslims throughout the conquered lands. No longer associated with an occupying race, the Arabic language also spread. As a result of these developments that began with the passing of the Umayyads, "Arab" has become the word used to describe the ethnicity of most of the people from Morocco to Iraq.

A hundred and eighteen years after the Prophet's death, the Abbasid accession marked the loss for all time of another definitive part of his system. Faith and state would not again be one. From the moment the Banu Abbas seized the empire, it began to break apart. Al Andalus was immediately lost to imperial control forever. Central sway in Africa became sporadic and patchy at best, and then evaporated entirely.[39]

Within a decade, other pieces started to split off. Twelve centuries then passed before the Arabs ruled even themselves again.

The Abbasid Caliphate, as it came to be known, lasted from 750 until the Mongols rode in to sack Baghdad in 1258. In its coming five centuries as Islam's capital, Baghdad would provide an epic of creativity, curiosity, reaction, extravagance, war, murder, and vice. The mighty Harun al Rashid, grandson of Baghdad's founder Mansour and the greatest of the Abbasid caliphs, played a starring fictional role in the fantastical tales known as the *Arabian Nights*. The true story of medieval Baghdad makes these tales of Ali Baba and the forty thieves, of Aladdin's magic lantern and Julnar the Mermaid—she of the coal-black eyes, heavy lips, slender waist, and luscious thighs—seem pale and prim by comparison.[40]

Chapter 11

High Noon

Caliph Mamoun, Abbasid Baghdad, and the Battle for the Faith, 786–833

Blessed be the site of Baghdad, seat of learning and art;
None can point in the world to a city her equal;
Her suburbs vie in beauty with the blue vault of the sky;
Her climate in quality equals the life-giving breezes of heaven;
Her stones in their brightness rival gems and rubies;
Her soil in beneficence has the brightness of amber;
The banks of the Tigris with their beauteous damsels surpass the
    city of Cathay;
The gardens filled with lovely nymphs are not below Kashmir;
And thousands of gondolas on the water
Dance and sparkle like sunbeams in the sky
            —Auhad-uddin Ali Anwari, twelfth-century Persian poet

One of the two men, standing before the other, had a light complexion, a long, straight nose, and a long beard. This was forty-three-year-old Abdullah ibn Haroun al Rashid, known by his regnal name of Al Mamoun, or "the Trustworthy": twenty-fifth Caliph of Islam and seventh of the Abbasid dynasty. The faith-empire still stretched, as it had in Umayyad days, from the Strait of Gibraltar to the Hindu Kush.

The other man was seated on a throne. He had reddish-white skin and a high forehead atop bushy eyebrows. This was Aristotle.

The year was perhaps 830 AD. Alexander's tutor had been dead for eleven and a half centuries. The Prophet Mohammed had died two hundred years earlier. Mamoun, the Prophet's distant successor, now styled the Commander of the Faithful, was speaking to the Greek philosopher in a dream.

The city of Baghdad in central Mesopotamia had been founded about seventy years previously, in 762, by Mamoun's great-grandfather Mansour. Five hundred miles east of Damascus, in the heart of what was now known as *al Iraq Arabi* ("Arabian Iraq"), Baghdad had quickly become the largest metropolis on earth, with a population of over two million.[1] Ctesiphon, former capital of the late Sasanian Persian Empire, was merely a day's walk to the southeast, and the new city was very much in the orbit of greater Iran.

Only two days' ride away from where Alexander had died, here was a new pupil of Aristotle's, even more devoted, ruling much the same empire. Al Mamoun's fourteen years as caliph in Baghdad (819–833) may well have been the most cultured and intellectually productive reign of any individual anywhere, ever. In his story of the dream of Aristotle, Mamoun would say that he was the first of the two men to speak.

"Who are you?" inquired the Commander of the Faithful. The other man was bald but handsome, with dark-blue eyes.[2]

"I am Aristotle," replied the Greek from his throne.

The caliph later described himself as "filled with awe" at this. Aristotle was his philosophical hero. Mamoun had undertaken a personal struggle to transform Islam into a humanist faith, and Logos—the classical Greek concept of reason and formal logic—was at the heart of the project. For Mamoun, the effort was as risky as it was ambitious. The clergy, the "ulema," stood squarely against him. So, overwhelmingly, did the teachings of Medina. So did the traditions of the Arabs, who had made of Mohammed's faith a world empire.

Mastering his sense of wonder, the Commander of the Faithful asked, "O philosopher, may I ask you some questions?" Told to proceed, Mamoun began.

———

The son of an Iranian mother, Mamoun had taken power in Baghdad by overthrowing his Arab half brother in a vicious war during the years 810–813. The odds had been against Mamoun. He ruled as a viceroy of sorts in Iran and the eastern empire, but his half brother Amin was caliph and held Iraq. The land between the rivers was once again, as under Cyrus, Alexander, Seleucus, the Parthians, and the Sasanians, the wealthiest province of the empire and home to its capital.[3]

After two years of fighting, Mamoun forced his brother to retreat into Baghdad. A nightmarish siege began. Both sides razed neighborhoods to improve the fields of fire of the mangonels that rained their missiles into the various parts of the smoldering city. Food ran out. Proud women resorted to prostitution or "exposed their ankle bracelets" in flight, according to the Persian chronicler Tabari. Amin stripped the gold from the roof of his palaces as his troops deserted him. Soon all he had left were "people from the prisons, riffraff, rabble, cutpurses, and people of the market." The armorless guerrillas from the slums, carrying on the desperate fight, were known as "naked ones." Gangs "despoiled anyone they were able to lay their hands on—men, women and infirm people from the ummah and non-Muslims" alike.[4]

Launched into the city from the siege engines beyond the walls, naphtha brought flames from above. On the ground Amin's concubines picked through the ruins to find him water to drink. In Baghdad's earlier days, "the world's breasts yielded abundantly to her inhabitants." Now, "their gardens have been defiled with blood— Desolate and empty! Dogs howl in them."[5] The City of Peace had been founded fifty years before. Its "fall from grace" took one year.[6]

For six years after this dreadful victory, Mamoun ruled the empire from his home in deepest Khorasan. When he at last moved to the conquered capital, he brought with him his Persian court and Persian wife. Once in Baghdad, Mamoun would try to impose green, the traditional color of the Sasanians, the last of Iran's pre-Islamic dynasties, as the compulsory color for the dress of courtiers. Black was the traditional color of the family of the Prophet, as Abu Muslim and the early Abbasids had recognized, and Mamoun's attempt failed. Mamoun also tried to nominate as his successor Reza, the eighth Shia Imam in the line begun by Ali and Hussein. A near insurrection resulted. Mamoun finally removed the old man with a poisoned bunch of grapes. Thus another of Shiism's twelve saints was martyred, poisoned like the others, this time by one of his own. Meanwhile, the caliph's Iranian and crypto-Shia tendencies put him constantly on the edge of a renewed civil war.

———

Having successfully seized a world empire from his own brother, perhaps Mamoun did not perceive a need for political advice from a long-dead Greek. But the usurper needed something else: validation. Now here was Aristotle before him, ready to answer the biggest question of all.

"What is good?" asked Mamoun.

"Whatever is good according to reason," answered the Greek.

By the very nature of Mamoun's position—Caliph of all Islam—this account of the dream of Aristotle is at least in part propaganda. Here was the leader of the Muslim world using the greatest of the ancient Greek humanists as a mouthpiece. Mamoun's message was that the paramount principle did not lie with God Himself. Nor did it lie with the truth revealed by any prophet, including Mohammed, God's last and perfect Messenger. Instead, it lay with Reason.

The claim was explosive. Advanced by the caliph himself, it was clearly at odds with any traditional notion of Islam. What was best lay not in total surrender to the Almighty, as the faith called Submission insisted. Rather, it lay in a human quality that admits no chains at all and whose rules are beyond the reach of divine will.

Few believers in Mamoun's contemporary audience would have missed the parallels. The Prophet Mohammed's teachings, too, had also claimed to be messages received from on high while he was unconscious. Now here was Mamoun playing Mohammed, with Aristotle in the place of God. Philosophy would be the new religion, and its foundation stone was Logos, the formal logic of classical Greek reason. Mamoun had launched nothing less than an intellectual war for the future of the faith. Were he to succeed, the twenty-fifth caliph would be a new Prophet, but with an altogether different message.

Falsafa—philosophy—is a bad and foreign thing in the traditional faith. The word itself is a pejorative and a condemnation. To find and explain the truths of the universe through the human intellect is a threat to the supremacy of God. Allah, master and creator of all, can be rivaled by nothing. He can accept no law other than His own will. He can be constrained by nothing. There is no power of action, nor any principle, rule, or explanation, apart from His divine caprice.

But reason follows laws of its own. The same was true of the related Aristotelian fields of science and ethics.

In terms of guidance for everyday life, believers already possessed all they needed. The system was complete. Every facet of human existence was covered. As for keeping track of which was which, halal or haram, there were of course gaps in the sharia. But these were easily enough filled, according to the clergy and traditional believers, by the use of *qiyas*, or analogy. The gaps were certainly not to be filled using reason, that foreign, God-usurping tool of the Greeks.

As Aristotle spoke, Mamoun was eager to hear more from his hero. The Greek had, after all, tutored Alexander, the last great emperor before Mamoun to attempt what Mamoun was now undertaking, the fusion from central Mesopotamia of the energies of Greece and Iran.

"Then what?" the caliph asked the philosopher. After reason, what?

"Whatever is good according to sharia," replied Aristotle.

The caliph, then, did recognize a role for religious law. The Christian word for this conflation of God and humanity was that same word at the heart of Aristotle's achievement: Logos.[7]

"Then what?" asked Mamoun. The caliph's question-and-answer method, with its overtones of the Socratic and the dialectical, was itself decidedly Greek. "Whatever is good according to the masses," answered the tutor of Alexander. Political calculations were important, but they must come third after reason and religion.[8]

"Then what?" asked the caliph.

The question was perhaps superfluous, rhetorical. What else could guide a man in Mamoun's position other than intellect, religion, and politics?

"Then," replied Aristotle, "there is no more 'then.'"

A century earlier, the conversation would have been unimaginable. In the Prophet's day, only seventeen members of the tribe of Quraysh had been able to read and write.[9] * The faith's founding generation had likely never heard of Aristotle. It is doubtful that they had heard

---

* Al Waqidi (ca. 748–833), one of the earliest and most authoritative historians of Islam's founding days, lists these individuals by name. Ali, Omar, Othman, and the Umayyad chiefs Abu Sufyan and Muawiya are among them. Edward Granville Brown, *A Literary History of Persia*, vol. 1 (London: T. Fisher Unwin), 1902.

of Logos. Had they known about Aristotle, it is improbable that they would have imagined that one day a Successor of the Prophet might discuss the highest questions of philosophy with the man's shade. That the caliph should be doing so in a new, eastern, quasi-Iranian capital, Baghdad, would likely have been equally inconceivable.

Mamoun was caliph in a dynasty whose power had come from Iran. He himself was largely Persian. Forty-five years after Baghdad's founding, he had come to the city as the victor in, effectively, an Arab-Iranian civil war for the caliphate. The Persian infusion that Mamoun embodied, bringing an embrace of Greek learning, with contributions from the Hindu and Chinese cultures to the east, would transform the world inhabited by Islam during this, the third caliphate, into a great civilization in its own right.

The process had begun under the second Abbasid caliph, Mansour (714–775), founder of Baghdad, great-grandfather of Mamoun, and murderer of the loyal Abu Muslim. Mansour initiated what became known as the translation movement, a project to translate the practical works of foreign science into Arabic.

As the Umayyad milieu had been Greco-Roman, the early Abbasid milieu was by and large Sasanian. The Zoroastrian "imperial ideology" of the Sasanians had held that the works of Greek science were originally a part of the Avesta, the holy work revealed to Zoroaster.[10] They had been lost, according to Iranian legend, when Alexander torched Persepolis, and now existed almost solely in Greek translations. A more Islamic gloss on the same story, recorded by Mamoun's court astrologer, a recent convert from Zoroastrianism, held that the Greek works had originated not with the Persians but with the Babylonians, right there next to Baghdad.

From caliphs to merchants making the most of the new technology of paper that had arrived from China around the turn of the ninth century, the translation movement flourished under rich patrons throughout the Abbasid world, reaching its height under Mamoun's sponsorship. Families from the Christian "science city" established by the Sasanians at Gundeshapur provided the caliphs with their doctors

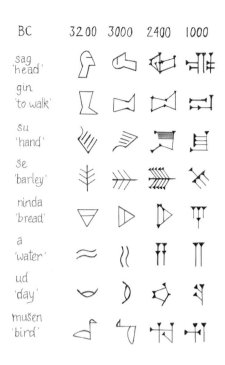

BC	3200	3000	2400	1000
sag 'head'				
gin 'to walk'				
su 'hand'				
še 'barley'				
ninda 'bread'				
a 'water'				
ud 'day'				
mušen 'bird'				

Bulla and contents from Susa in southwest Iran, ca. fourth millennium BC.

The evolution from pictographs to late cuneiform, 3200–1000 BC.

"The Lady of Uruk," discovered by the German dig at Uruk in 1939, is the oldest known accurate representation of the human visage. Looted from the Iraq Museum in April 2003, she was recovered from a farmyard near Baghdad.

The "Flood" fragment of the Gilgamesh epic discovered by George Smith in the British Museum in 1872.

An Assyrian image of Gilgamesh subduing a lion. His long beard and hair are signs of his physical perfection.

The ziggurat of Ur outside the southern Iraqi city of Nassiriyah. First excavated in the 1920s and 1930s, it was partially rebuilt under Saddam Hussein in the 1980s.

Sumerian devotional statuary,
late third millennium BC.

The Death of Sardanapalus, by Eugène Delacroix (1862).

An Assyrian king blinds captives and leads them away by the nose. From the palace of Sargon II at Khorsabad, ca. 700 BC.

Cyrus, King of Kings, from a bas-relief on his tomb at Pasargad.

The tomb of Cyrus the Great at Pasargad, Fars Province, Iran.

Columns at
Persepolis.

Marble bust of Alexander the Great,
thought to be from Alexandria in
Egypt, first or second century BC.

The Macedonian
phalanx,
ca. 350 BC.

An early Buddha from Gandhara, now eastern Afghanistan, in first or second century AD, showing distinctly Greek characteristics of dress and form.

A coin of Strato II, last of the Indo-Greek kings (d. ca. 10 AD).

Parthian ruins at Hatra, Nineveh Province, Iraq.

The "Sassanian arch" at Ctesiphon opened into the largest unsupported vaulted space in the world. With a height of 121 feet, it was 164 feet deep, compared to the seventy-one foot radius of the Pantheon in Rome.

The Great Mosque in Damascus shows notable Greco-Roman influences. It was built by Al Walid (d. 715), the second Umayyad Caliph, on the foundations of the city's former cathedral, itself occupying the site of a former temple of Jupiter, which had replaced an Aramaean temple.

Abbasid-era Arab scholars study at the feet of Aristotle, from the mid-eleventh century *Sayings of the Philosophers* by Abu al Wafa al Mubashshir ibn Fatik, a Damascus-born polymath living in Fatimid Cairo.

A gold imitation dinar struck in Britain during the reign of King Offa of Mercia (d. 796).

A tenth century Abbasid astrolabe.

A Persian painting of medieval Baghdad.

A leaf from a 1224 Arabic translation of Dioscorides' *Materia Medica*.

The mausoleum of the Seljuk Sultan Sanjar at the ancient Iranian city of Merv, formerly Alexandria-in-Marghiana and original seat of the Caliph Mamoun, in current-day Turkmenistan.

Suleiman the Magnificent, by Melchior Lorck, a German artist who was part of Ogier de Busbecq's embassy to the Grand Turk.

Roxelana, *La Sultana Rossa.* Captured in a slave raid in the south of present-day Ukraine, the daughter of a Ruthenian priest, she ascended through a crowded imperial harem to become the influential wife of the most powerful man alive, Suleiman the Magnificent.

Ogier de Busbecq in Constantinople, by his colleague Melchior Lorck.

Shah Ismail (d. 1524), founder of the Safavid dynasty.

Safavid Isfahan, ca. 1650.

View of the City of Bagdad.

View of Baghdad as it would have appeared to a nineteenth-century visitor.

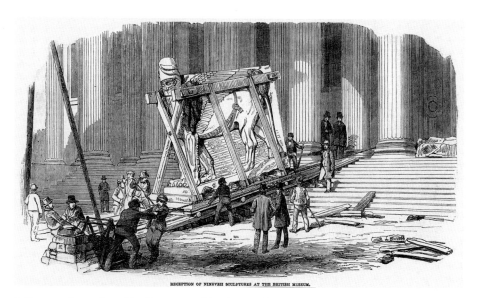

RECEPTION OF NINEVEH SCULPTURES AT THE BRITISH MUSEUM.

A "lamassu" or winged bull excavated by Austen Henry Layard enters the British Museum, 1852.

Rashid Pasha (d. 1858), Ottoman grand vizier, author of the Rose Garden Edict, and architect of the Tanzimat reforms.

The Red Sultan, Abdul Hamid II (d. 1909).

Sir Sassoon Eskell, known as Sassoon Effendi. A graduate of Baghdad's Alliance Israélite Universelle, knighted by George V in 1923, he was one of two Iraqis to attend Churchill's 1921 Cairo Conference that chose Faisal of the Hijaz as future King of Iraq.

G. H. Q. — BAGDAD — G. Q. G.

The British Residency in Baghdad, 1917; note steps down to the Tigris at right.

Faisal I, T. E. Lawrence, and the Hejazi delegation at the Paris Peace Conference, 1919. The man at upper right is a slave.

The bar, Basra Airport, 1935.

A gentleman in the day of the
dictator: King Faisal I of Iraq with
Reza Pahlavi, Shah of Iran, 1932.

"The Boy King": Faisal II of Iraq, photographed in Baghdad
by Cecil Beaton in 1943.

for many generations, and these medical dynasts were major sponsors of the translations of medical works.[11] An eleventh-century Arabic library in Egypt contained eighteen thousand volumes translated from the Greek.[12]

Throughout the Hellenized world of the eastern Muslim empire, communities still existed where Greek science and philosophy were living forces. At Harran, where Abraham had stopped at the far north of his Fertile Crescent journey, an "obstinately pagan"[13] community continued to use Greek as their liturgical language; at Merv in far Khorasan, where the black flags of the Abbasids first rose, the dominant faiths of Zoroastrianism and Nestorian Christianity were both heavily Hellenized at the time; and so on in numerous other places.

The individuals carrying on these traditions in Greek were speakers of Aramaic, Persian, and Arabic, depending on their circumstances. Across this archipelago of multilingual Hellenistic learning, scientists and philosophers throughout much of western and central Asia now found themselves enjoying the umbrella of a single unified world: the Pax Islamica, "united politically and administratively." These learned individuals traveled, corresponded, and knew each other. Under the Umayyads and early Abbasids, this culture had no intolerant religious orthodoxy to stifle it.[14] Pursuing a centralizing, anticlerical agenda, sympathetic to his own Persian roots, and apparently a sincere humanist in his own right, Mamoun would take up the translation initiative, amplify its scope, and give it an intentionally revolutionary new meaning.*

When he was not at war with the Byzantines, Mamoun would from time to time write to their emperor in Constantinople requesting works from the Greek libraries. The collections of the ancient community at Harran were perhaps the greatest source of the Abbasids' Greek originals.[15] † These books would then be translated in Baghdad, always

---

* The notion of the formal, large-scale, or official translation of works from prestigious earlier cultures had likely originated in Iraq, with the translating of Sumerian works by the newly arrived Semites of Akkad and Babylon starting in approximately the twenty-third century BC. Dimitri Gutas, *Greek Thought, Arabic Culture: The Graeco-Arabic Translation Movement in Baghdad and Early Abbasid Society* (London: Routledge, 2005).

† The great scholar of Persia Edward Granville Browne (1862–1926) relates the story that in about 830, as Mamoun was passing through Harran on his way to fight the Byzantines, he asked the oddly dressed locals whether they were "people of the book." To those who were not, in accordance with Islamic law, he offered the choice of death or conversion to

by kaffirs—mostly Syrian Christians, with some Jews and Harranian pagans—or recent converts.[16]

While the Abbasids revered the classical Greeks, Byzantine Christianity in these days looked on the pagan world of Herodotus, Xenophon, and Aristotle as an embarrassment. For the Byzantines, "Hellenism was the defeated enemy, to be treated with contemptuous indifference."[17] Here was an Orthodox Christian version of the Sunni Muslim notion of *jahiliyya*: the time of ignorance and idolatry before the arrival of the true faith.

For the Caliph Mamoun in particular, there was an added resonance when his Byzantine foes rejected their pagan Greek heritage. Coming to power as he had, it was important for Mamoun to do more than merely centralize power and religion in the Sasanian tradition. He had to go beyond his attempt to rein in the old-line clergy theologically. He needed to rally the empire more broadly, to bring it together around a common cause. This he did with an aggressive posture against the Byzantines.

In anti-Byzantine polemics, the Basra-born essayist Amr ibn Bahr, an ally of Mamoun's known as Al Jahiz, argued that these "benighted and inferior" *Rumi* were unfit modern-day heirs of the noble language of classical Athens. They spurned their own inheritance.[18] And their Christian faith was absurd. The Christians, Jahiz reminded his readers, ridiculously worshipped a mortal who urinated and defecated just like the rest of us. A typical Abbasid cleverness, of which Jahiz was an exemplar, was working here. The ultimate target of his salvoes was usually the enemy at home, Mamoun's true foe: the same forces of Sunna who were confronted in the dream of Aristotle. The real message in Jahiz's anti-Byzantine writing was that an Islam shunning reason was no better than the ridiculous religion of their enemies.

For some centuries after the death of Mamoun and Jahiz and the defeat of their project within Sunni Islam during the second half of the ninth century, a surviving minority would write about how Christianity

---

Islam, Judaism, or Christianity. Those who preferred not to convert paid for the advice of a local Muslim scholar, who counseled them to tell the caliph that they were "Sabaeans," as the Koran refers to a mysterious people of that name who were People of the Book. Mamoun left them in peace, and died fighting the Byzantines before he was able to return to Harran and check on their status. Browne, *Literary History of Persia*, vol. 1, p. 302.

was stifling science and philosophy, while true Islam carried the torch.[19] It was a coded way of saying, long after the struggle had been lost, that their way was the "true Islam."

A "House of Wisdom," a state repository of ancient books, many of them Greek works in Arabic and Persian translations, flourished under Mamoun after receiving its start as part of the translation initiative launched fifty-odd years earlier. The House of Wisdom is often described as a hive of philosophical and scientific output. It seems to have been more of an archive or library of translated works; it may not have been a single building or location at all. Institutions of this type had been known under the Sasanians, with their claim that the contents were in fact originally Persian.

At his court, Mamoun invited debates between believers and kaffirs. "Advance thine arguments," he urged his guests at the beginning of one of these sessions, "and answer without fear, for there is none here that will not speak thee well. Let everyone speak who has the wisdom to demonstrate the strength of his religion."

This open-mindedness did not endear Mamoun to the Baghdad "street." Unbelieving or intellectually dangerous guests sometimes needed a military escort to travel to and from his palace. With urbane Abbasid wit, Mamoun came to be known by opponents as the *Amir al Kafirin*, or Commander of the Unfaithful.[20]

In 833, four months before his death, Mamoun instituted an inquisition of sorts, the *mihna* ("trial"), for prominent officials, scholars, and religious figures. On pain of imprisonment, these men were required to profess their belief in the "created" Koran, the unorthodox doctrine that Mamoun made his litmus test. This theory held that God had formed the Book at a point after the beginning of time. Orthodox dogma, by contrast, insisted on the "uncreated" Koran: a book that was coeternal with the Almighty. Mamoun's doctrine was radical enough that it would eventually be known as "secession," or *mutazila*.[21] He and his followers are known as Mutazilites.

The most famous victim of Mamoun's inquisition by far, and the leader of the popular opposition to Mutazilism, was a scholar called Ahmad ibn Hanbal (d. 855). Born in Baghdad, to which he ultimately returned after spending years traveling and collecting hadiths, Hanbal was famous for refusing to eat watermelon on the grounds that Sunna had no mention of the Prophet eating it.[22] * The question that Mamoun's inquisition posed was "Do you agree that the Koran was created in time?" Of the several hundred or so individuals subjected to the *Mihna*, most who disagreed were able to evade the question with clever answers such as "The Qu'ran is the word of God, and God is the creator of everything."[23] A handful of individuals were imprisoned for refusing to acknowledge the created Koran, Hanbal most prominent among them, and a few were punished physically.

Mamoun's inquisition may have been mild, but the implications of its question were great. The conflict calls to mind the bitter Christological disputes of fourth-century Christendom, the mind-boggling feuds of Patripassionists, Ebionites, Arians, and others; as abstruse as they were vehement, these disagreements may seem like hairsplitting madness but in fact they expressed deeply different views of the very nature of God. Similarly for Mamoun and his opponents, a holy book created in time expressed a fundamentally different outlook from one represented by a book that had always existed alongside the Almighty.

For Mamoun and the Mutazilites, the coeval book, existing in parallel with God from the start and therefore independent of Him, was a threat to the most fundamental Islamic principle of all: *tawhid*, God's unity.[24] If God was all and created all, how could something else, especially something of equal religious perfection, have been present when He Himself began? A "created Koran," by contrast, posed no such problem. Formed by Allah at the time of its revelation to Mohammed, the created Koran was born of a moment in human events and, being produced by God Himself, presented no competition with the Almighty.

For the orthodox, on the other hand, the created Koran presented a fundamental threat. Inextricably connected to events in time, made for a living and mortal man, a created book is of this world. Being of man and of this world, it is subject to context and interpretation, which implies the exercise of human faculties. It eventually means freedom—the opposite of submission. A book open to interpretation and subject to reason could be questioned. Perhaps it could be improved upon. Such a

---

* The Hanbali school of Sunni law, developed largely in the generation after Hanbal's lifetime, remains the school of Sunnis in Saudi Arabia and along much of the Persian Gulf. It is followed by most Salafi ("originalist") Muslims, including Al Qaeda and the Islamic State.

book confronted mightily the very notion of the Sunna, of "tradition" in the Islamic sense. The Prophet himself had said that the Koran was uncreated. Now, with the caliph's blasphemy, even Mohammed was compromised.

Mamoun and his Mutazilite followers also claimed that the human individual possessed free will. Followers of the Sunna derisively called them *Qadiriyya*, or "Free Willers." An inevitable corollary of the created Koran, this claim of human agency was equally dangerous. With their created Koran, the Mutazilites saw themselves as pious Muslims above all else, defending the paramount principle of God's oneness. Their doctrine of human agency was also, in their view, a defense of Islam rather than an attack upon it. They were saving God Himself. People do bad things, after all, and according to the Koran are punished in the hereafter. A God who directly determines all human action is thus responsible for the evil with which the world is replete, so He cannot be good. And one who punishes although He alone is responsible is also not just.

So there could be a God of pure and unfettered will, or there could be a God of justice and human choice. The Sunnis chose the powerful God, the capricious despot, and considered this not insult but humble piety. The Mutazilite Almighty was the prime mover, not the only mover: people were responsible for their own actions.

The disagreement was the same in the physical realm of nature and science. The Medina, or orthodox, version of the faith holds that God's will is responsible for all things in an immediate and literal way. In trying to understand the physical world, the Mutazilites aimed to replace the conservatives' divine law with the scientific law of cause and effect, developed by Aristotle in parallel with his rules of logic fourteen centuries earlier. The deductive reasoning embodied in the Greek syllogism ("Only humanity possesses reason; I possess reason; therefore I am human") is the equivalent in logic of observed physical causation in the natural world. This is why Aristotle, the third great philosopher after Socrates and Plato, was also the first true scientist; it is why Alexander took "natural philosophers," meaning scientists of the day, with him deep into Asia so they could send back to the master their information about the natural world along the way. While Mutazilism flourished or at least lingered on in some strength, so would science in the Dar al Islam.

Sometime after he had moved his court from Khorasan to Baghdad in
819, Mamoun gathered three young men before him. They were brothers,
known as the Banu Musa, the Sons (or House) of Moses. They were
named after their father, Musa, a former highwayman who had become
an astronomer at Mamoun's court in Khorasan.

The caliph had a question for the young men. Was the circumference
of the Earth really twenty-four thousand miles, as the Greeks had said?
(Eratosthenes had first made the calculation in about 240 BC.)[25]

Certainly, the brothers replied. They too were scholars of the classics.
They were confident that the old method had been sound. Mamoun,
however, was not so sure of the Greek calculation. Or perhaps he wanted
to prove the ancients right. Perhaps he wished to experience the thrill of
participating directly in the empirical tradition founded by his paragon,
Aristotle.

"I wish you to use the methods described by the ancients," said the
caliph, "so that we can see whether it is accurate or not."

To repeat the calculation that Mamoun had studied, an expanse of flat
land was needed. So the Sons of Moses inquired, and found that such a
place existed below the mountain of Sinjar, northwest of Baghdad, not
far from the ruins of Nineveh near Mosul.

The Banu Musa brothers organized an expedition there, to what is
now known as the Nineveh Plain. Finding the ground flat as described,
they took an elevation of the Pole Star. Then they walked due north
until the star's elevation had risen by precisely one degree. A degree,
ever since the Sumerians had invented the notion, probably around
2400 BC, is 1/360 of a full circle. The distance that the young men had
walked north through the desert was 66⅔ miles. Multiplying this by the
360 degrees that make up the heavenly sphere, the brothers calculated
that the circumference of the Earth was indeed 24,000 miles.*

The Sons of Moses then went to the caliph and declared that the
ancients had been correct. Mamoun asked them to repeat the experiment somewhere else. They went to Kufa, to the large, flat plain where

* The exact circumference of the Earth at the equator, where the planet bulges, is 24,902
miles.

Hussein had met his end a century and a half previously, and there found the same result.

———

On waking from his dream of Aristotle, Mamoun would have turned himself to the daily affairs of state for a Caliph of Islam in the first half of the ninth century AD. Mamoun brought uniform standards to the empire's mints and coinage, and centralized Baghdad's control of the armed forces. The Byzantines had to be fought frequently, a duty that Mamoun accepted with enthusiasm and some success. There also were revolts in various parts of the empire, including Egypt and Sindh, which Mamoun managed to suppress. The empire had shrunk in the west, but Mamoun's armies extended the Dar al Islam into most of Afghanistan and strengthened imperial rule over parts of Iran and Central Asia.

Under the indifferent Umayyads, the clergy, or ulema, had effectively amassed all religious authority. The ulema also constituted, in essence, the empire's judiciary. The first six Abbasid caliphs had done nothing to reclaim this power. Now Mamoun, the half-Persian caliph from Khorasan centralizing in the Sasanian style, wanted it for himself.

The typical Muslim cleric of Mamoun's time was a Traditionist, a mnemonic virtuoso deriving his status from verbatim mastery of Sunna and Koran. In ninth-century Baghdad politics, any threat to the sanctity of canon was a threat to the clergy, and vice versa: any caliph who wanted to tackle the overweening ulema would have to address the primacy of canon. Rote memorization was a crude tool available to any village troublemaker, and by the cosmopolitan standards of Mamoun's Persified Abbasid court, such a figure was generally a provincial and uncultured individual. The usurper from Iran would replace Sunna with something that the caliph possessed and that a truculent plebeian clergy of Arab inclinations did not: the Hellenistic methods of his own cultivated mind.[26]

———

Mamoun died in 833 while traveling north to fight the *Rumi*. The next two caliphs were his brother Mutasim (r. 833–842) and nephew Wathiq (r. 842–847). Both carried on Mamoun's tests for Mutazilite conformity and continued to support the translation movement. Under the next caliph, Mamoun's other nephew Mutawwakil (r. 847–861), the Sunni backlash set in.

Upon assuming the caliphate, Mutawwakil immediately ended the *Mihna*, Mamoun's inquisition based on the "created" Koran, and unleashed in its place something far harsher. The conservative counter-revolution began as a "reign of terror . . . in which Shiah, Mutazilite, Jew and Christian suffered alike."[27] Partisans of Mamoun's old adversary Ibn Hanbal terrorized Baghdad. Mutazilism became punishable by death. The writings of the Mutazilites were destroyed wherever the caliph's men could find them. It was a "fearful beginning" to a long history of religious strife in the City of Peace.[28]

In Baghdad, the Sunnis confiscated the library of the philosopher Yaqub al Kindi. a classic Abbasid polymath who produced works on Archimedes, Ptolemy, Euclid's theory of perspective, the astrolabe, Hippocratic medicine, cryptology, and a variety of other topics such as "glass manufacture, swords, and music."[29] With his famous treatise *On First Philosophy*, relying heavily on Aristotle, Al Kindi had established himself as the first philosopher to work in the Arabic language. Arguing that "religion commands the study of philosophy," Al Kindi was a leading figure in the House of Wisdom and employed his own group of translators.*

The conservative "street" had never accepted Mamoun's foreign ideas, and Mutawwakil's men whipped Al Kindi with sixty lashes in front of an appreciative crowd.[30] In 861, Mutawwakil ordered the Cypress of Kashmar, a huge tree in a Zoroastrian sanctuary in Khorasan, said to have been planted by Zoroaster himself, to be chopped down for use in one of the twenty-odd palaces that he built for himself.[31] Remembered as the "Nero of the Arabs," the drunken and epically lecherous Mutawwakil, as devoted to pornography as he was to the Sunna, was murdered in 861 by his Turkish guards before the tree arrived.[32]

Their orthodox foes had another name for the Free Willers or Secessionists: "Magians," a reference to the Magi, the priests of the Zoroastrians. This insult branded the Mutazilites not only as kaffirs—or worse,

---

* Mamoun appointed Al Kindi tutor to his brother and heir, Mutasim, who in turn made Al Kindi tutor to his own son.

apostates—but also as foreigners, Persians, non-Arabs.* It was also, in theological terms, rather true.

After Mutawwakil, no other Abbasid caliph attempted to revive Mutazilism. In terms of the worldly power of the Abbasids, Mutawwakil's caliphate (847–861) marked the end of the beginning, so to speak. After him, the power of the caliphs eroded significantly. But Mutawwakil's religious victory, his triumph over the attempted humanist coup d'état, his annihilation of Mutazilism within orthodox Islam and within the principal loci of power, was complete.

The violent Sunnite reaction under Mutawwakil put into context the strong connection between the Hellenistic intellectual culture of the High Abbasids and their personal roots in pre-Islamic Iran. The Iranians and the Greeks possessed, in their distant origins, a shared Indo-European heritage of blood and language. More recently, as separate peoples, their complex intercourse had gone on since the time of Cyrus. It had continued through Alexander's day and the 250 years of the Seleucids, a house founded with a Persian queen. Given Rome's partly Hellenistic nature, the relationship had carried on in ways with the extraordinary eight centuries of violent intimacy between Rome and first Parthian and then Sasanian Iran.

The ideas of Zoroaster stood in strong contrast to the submission-based framework of the Abrahamic power god. The ancient Iranian religion had its founding emphasis not on obedience but on right and wrong, Zoroaster's prescription of "good thoughts, good words, good deeds." From this the rest rolled out: the Iranian eschatology, the judgment that all receive in the hereafter as a consequence of free choices while alive; absorption of this Zoroastrian message during the Exile at Babylon turning the Hebrews into Jews; and Christianity's emergence as a Judaeo-Hellenistic synthesis, showing once more the iterative, complementary relationship between ethical monotheism and classical humanism in the region.

The two great Indo-European systems were very different from the outlook of the Hebrews and Arabs. Might was paramount in the religious culture of these descendants of the Semites whose Babylon had eclipsed

---

* Sunni participants in the ongoing wars of the Apostasy in Iraq and Syria today frequently call their opponents *Majous*, or Magians, for the same reason: to condemn supporters of Shia or quasi-Shia regimes as un-Islamic, non-Arab, quasi-Persian.

Ur long ago, possibly driving Abraham from his home. Anything other than might was an insult to the unquestionable God of pure will, and the powerful Aristotelian trident of reason, science, and ethics was the most threatening insult of all.

There were other commonalities between the two cultures, the Persian and the Hellenistic, that informed the medieval Muslim humanists. In contrast to seventh-century Medina, both were highly literate. There was also Persian culture's claim that the leading works of Greek science had in fact first appeared in the Zoroastrian holy texts, only to be appropriated by the Greeks when Alexander came to Persia, before the originals were lost when he burned Persepolis. The assertion, while untrue, was an undeniable endorsement not only of the content of these works but also of the intellectual method and outlook embodied in them. With this claim, the Iranians placed the objective, rather than the relativist or power-driven, view of the natural world near the heart of their own religion.

Of all the mighty conquerors whose armies had raised the dust of the Mesopotamian flatlands of axial Asia, only Cyrus and Alexander, the Persian and the Greek, had attempted, in their flawed and complex ways, a vision that might be called universal. The system of Medina desired universal dominion, but with its requirement of either enslaving, taxing, or killing the kaffir, it did not concern itself with universal appeal. The Dar al Islam would one day achieve global mastery, God willing, but within this House of Submission, the believer reigned over the infidel.

For Mamoun, fighting against the Arab side of the debate as represented by the brother he had defeated in Baghdad's gruesome siege, Aristotle was not only an intellectual inspiration, and a part of his ancestors' faith, but a political ally as well. It is no surprise that in the caliph's shocking dream, Aristotle, bald and frank like some old Sumerian god, was treated with an intimate reverence.

———

Abu Hasan al Masudi, who described the death of pagan classical Greek science and philosophy in the eastern Mediterranean following the arrival there of Christianity, had something similar to say in the ninth-century

Islamic context. One of the truly magnificent travelers and intellectuals of the tenth-century Islamic world, Masudi noted the thorough reversal of official intellectual culture when Mutawwakil succeeded to the caliphate:

> He ordered the abandonment of investigation and discussion and debate and everything which people had enjoyed in the days of Mamun, Mutasim and Wathiq. He ordered submission and the acceptance of tradition. He ordered the senior scholars to expound the traditions of the Prophet and teach the sunna and generally accepted opinions.[33]

From around the time of Mutawwakil's accession, the House of Wisdom disappears from the annals. In 850, Mutawwakil reinstituted Islam's dhimmi laws, which had largely lapsed in the generally liberal atmosphere of Mamoun and his two predecessors and two successors. Mutawwakil required Christians and Jews to wear yellow on their clothing, barred the renovation of their churches and synagogues, forced their rich to wear yellow hoods and ride with humble wooden stirrups, and more.[34] In an empire as broad as that of the Abbasids, the application of these laws was inconsistent, but the tendencies were clear.

In 851, Mutawwakil razed the tomb of Hussein at Kerbala and forbade the locals to visit the site. At court, the jester performed with a pillow strapped to his belly and the caliph called him Ali, for the first Shia Imam had been known to run to fat in his later days.

The attack on Greek logic and formal reasoning, the reinstatement of the Sunna, and the greatly heightened persecution of dhimmis were of a piece. So were the insults to the memories of Ali and Hussein, and a proposed move back to Damascus and away from the Iranian influences to which Iraq was prone. It did not matter that Mutawwakil was an infamous drunk who would eventually be killed in his cups. It did not matter that he was "a voluptuary, a perfidious scoundrel, a monster of cruelty." Mutawwakil possessed the orthodox faith, and as caliph he made the extermination of the nonconformists, through torture and execution where necessary, his business.[35]

In 846, thirteen years after the death of Mamoun, Mohammed al Bukhari, a Persian scholar from Bukhara in Central Asia, produced what has ever since been the definitive hadith collection.* To do so, Bukhari spent sixteen years traveling across much of the eastern Pax Islamica, collecting Traditions of the Prophet and studying their authenticity. He found six hundred thousand narrations and reduced these to twenty-six hundred. For Sunni Muslims, Bukhari's hadith compilation is second only to the Koran as a source of Islamic authority.

The hadith corpus undoubtedly expressed various broadly held priorities of the ninth-century umma, or Islamic community. From a textual or secular perspective, there is little question that by and large, even as winnowed by Bukhari over two hundred years after the Prophet's death, it represents "one of the greatest and most successful literary fictions" of all time.[36] In orthodox Islam, the memorization of these Traditions would become the leading field of learning ever after.

Medina was, generally speaking, the winner in the great clash. From Mutawwakil's time onward, it would be inconceivable that one day a week at the court of a pious caliph would be reserved, as it had been under Mamoun, for debates about religion, literature, science, and philosophy.† Thanks to the large populations conquered in East and South Asia, in future centuries followers of the Sunna would account for perhaps 90 percent of all those who identified themselves as Muslim. The heirs of Mamoun would account for most of the remainder, and in Iran and Iraq, as well as some smaller countries, their numbers would dominate. Shiism was to develop numerous strands over the coming centuries, but its essentials remained by and large Mutazilite.[37]

It was probably inevitable that the vast and profound force of Iranian culture should refuse the Arab idea. The land of Cyrus eventually pulled together its own Zoroastrian legacy, Mamoun's revival of the long Persian relationship with Greek learning, the rebel memory of a bitterly conquered land, and a form of rage over the frustrated succession claims of Mohammed's family. From these, Iran wove something both old and new in the centuries to come. This would be Shiism. In the time of the

---

* The first hadiths had begun to be recorded under Othman almost two hundred years earlier. The real surge in hadiths did not begin until the second Islamic century.

† There would, many centuries later, be Ottoman caliphs of humanist inclinations, but their piety was another matter.

martyrs Ali and Hussein, it had been a political faction. In the time of Mamoun and the Mutazilites, it was a theological deviation within the one faith. Over the coming centuries the heresy became its own religion.

In southern Mesopotamia, scene of the founding martyrdoms and land of the greatest Greek and Iranian capitals, the Perso-Hellenistic religion, with its saints and syllogisms, its ethics and eschatology, all cloaked in the story of the Prophet's true heirs, found fertile ground. Thus Iraq, the low alluvium between the plateau of the Arabs and the highlands of the Persians, the place where the two races met and mixed, would eventually find itself home to two distinct faiths claiming to be the true Islam and accusing each other of apostasy, the very worst of enormities.[38] The schism would not become fully realized until the wars of two later dynasties, the Ottoman Turks and the Safavid Iranians, beginning in the sixteenth century, seven hundred years later.

Chapter 12

The Abbasid World

750–1258

> We ought not to be embarrassed of appreciating the truth and of obtaining it wherever it comes from, even if it comes from races distant and nations different from us. Nothing should be dearer to the seeker of truth than the truth itself, and there is no deterioration of the truth, nor belittling either of one who speaks it or conveys it.
> —Yaqub al Kindi (d. ca. 870)

On a hot summer day in ninth-century Baghdad, a servant or a fly on the wall of a royal palace in Baghdad might have seen the Caliph of Islam in a bare and carpetless room, its door left open for the breeze. A silver bowl was on the floor. Inside the bowl were rosewater, saffron, and perfumes. A eunuch brought in seven slave girls. He undressed them and they put on tunics that had been dipped in the bowl's fragrant liquid. There were seven chairs for the young women, with the seats pierced and incense burning beneath. When the concubines had sat on the chairs long enough for their clothes to dry, the pleasures of the caliph's afternoon rest hour would begin.[1]

Outside the walls of its twenty or more palaces, the City of Peace could be a sinister place during this Abbasid high noon, replete with sights that might have been taken from disturbed fantasies.

Imagine a Hindu merchant visiting Baghdad from one of the prosperous cities of Sindh founded by Alexander's Greeks, or perhaps an Arab mathematician from Cordoba in the far-off land of Al Andalus, where the Umayyad descendants of Abu Sufyan and Muawiya still ruled. Making his way through Baghdad's noisy streets one morning during these years, the visitor might see a parade of captured conspirators, their lacerated backs black with dried blood, led through the streets sitting backward upon the donkeys of water-sellers. He might see the head of a rebel general paraded by his own soldiers on one of the sticks used by bakers to shift bread in their ovens. Down a dusty boulevard, maybe he would spy a rebel being led to his execution on the back of an elephant. A train of fair-haired, half-naked Greek human chattel shuffling to market could have been interrupted by a drunken troop of Turkish slave-soldiers on one of their periodic eruptions of looting and rapine.

Even a royal palace—any one of the twenty or so, depending on the precise moment in the century, offered little sanctuary. Mansour, Baghdad's founder and the second Abbasid caliph, died peacefully in his sixties on the *hajj* in 754. Over the remaining five centuries of the dynasty there were thirty-five more Abbasid caliphs. Seven of them lived to see their fiftieth birthday, most of these having been deposed and blinded well before dying. The average age at death of these thirty-five Baghdad caliphs after Mansour was forty-four years; half of those who died in Baghdad died peacefully. During a dynasty in which the world of the court gradually became ever more cut off from life outside, the palace was often not so much a ruler's paradise—center of power, grove of pleasures—as it was a claustrophobic satellite planet of blood and fear.

Poetry, beauty, learning, and irony were the avowed values of this turbulent, racy, and hugely productive civilization. But inside the palace was a potentially deadly labyrinth of blocked doors, narrow corridors, and treacherous servants, a nightmarish world spun upside down in which bathhouses became prisons, and where the pet lions turned hungry in a siege.

"The story of the City of Peace," wrote Baghdad's English biographer Richard Coke in 1927, "is largely the story of endless war; where there is not war, there is pestilence, famine and civil disturbance."[2] The City of Peace was only fifty years old when it suffered its first civil war, Mamoun's attack on his half brother in 812. The ensuing two years of siege warfare marked the loss of an innocence that Baghdad never regained. This poem, written by an anonymous Baghdadi in 812, the first year of the siege, manages to convey the feeling with a hauntingly elegiac tone:

I wept tears of blood over Baghdad when I lost the ease of a pleasant life.
We have been given sorrow for joy,

A dearth instead of plenty.
The eye of the envious has afflicted Baghdad
And made its people die by the mangonel.
Here are people who have been overcome and burned by flames,
There a woman mourns a drowned man,
Here, a beautiful, dark-eyed woman
In a perfumed shift
Flees from the fire into the looting
While her father flees from the looting into the fire.

Call on someone to take pity, but there is none to take pity.
Here are people who have been driven from their shelter
And their property is being sold in every market.
Here lies a stranger from home,
Headless in the middle of the road.
He was caught in the middle of the fighting
And no one knows which side he was on.

Reading these gossamer, maudlin lines, it is hard not to be reminded of Biblical passages about the same land, and much the same subject matter, that have a very different tone: "Call together the archers against Babylon, all them that bend the bow; encamp against her round about; let none thereof escape," said the Old Testament prophet Jeremiah.[3] "Woe to the bloody city! It is all full of lies and robbery . . . there is a multitude of slain, and a great number of carcases; and there is no end of their corpses," said the prophet Nahum about Nineveh.[4]

To shed the blood of the mighty was considered inauspicious in Abbasid times. So caliph after caliph was poisoned, strangled, or suffocated. The last of the Baghdad caliphs died when the Mongols rolled him in a carpet and rode their horses over him. The great Haroun's brother and predecessor was killed by a slave girl who sat on a pillow atop his face as he slept. Perhaps the relative clemency and, knowing the Abbasids, even the indecent irony of this method were due to the fact that the order to kill came from the victim's own mother.

The Abbasid Caliphate was as imaginative a time in murder as it was in more edifying spheres. The military and security chief of Mamoun's two immediate successors, a brutal Turkish former cook called Itakh, was killed, depending on which account one reads, either by being crushed to death by chains or by being slowly parched to death. The Abbasid chronicles are full of lethal perversities, with crucifixions, flayings, immurements, live burials, crushing of testicles, and fathers punished by being forced to kill their own sons.

Although it was rarely achieved, there was an ideal of just rule in Abbasid times: a pious and benign caliph from the family of the Prophet governing through an enlightened and energetic chief minister, or vizier. The office of the vizier was a Sasanian and ultimately Achaemenid legacy. Idealized in Islamic posterity, burnished subsequently by the Ottomans, the arrangement came to represent the perfect Muslim monarchy.

The world of the Abbasids was global to the very limits of the known cultures of the day. It was a time when a Central Asian "Turk," working as an officer in the army of the Arab caliph, might farm his estates in southern Iraq to a local Iranian landowner who would in turn pay the dinars to the Turk's Jewish secretary. The caliph's mother might be Greek or Berber or perhaps Armenian, Iranian, or African. One Bukayr ibn Mahan, a prominent figure in the days of the Abbasid revolution against the Umayyads, came from Kufa in Iraq, fought the Persians on the shores of the Caspian Sea, was left estates in Sindh (now southern Pakistan) by the death of a brother, traded perfume in Syria, made rebellion in Jordan against the Banu Umayya of Damascus, and visited the Central Asian steppes of Khorasan.[5]

In 751, an Abbasid army halted the westward expansion of Tang China at the Battle of Talas, where the Tien Shan mountains meet the Kyrgyz steppe, not far from the capitals of present-day Uzbekistan and Kyrgyzstan. Chinese prisoners from that battle divulged to their Arab captors the secrets of making paper, a skill that the Arabs then brought to Europe through Muslim Spain and Sicily.* Four years after the victory at Talas, with the Abbasids and Tangs now allied, four thousand Arab soldiers

---

* This is the most widely related story of the origins of papermaking in the Islamic world. It may be apocryphal; a definitive account has not been established. Regardless, paper's advent in the Muslim lands came during Mamoun's reign and the literary and philosophical achievements of the Abbasids would have been "inconceivable" without

sent east by Mamoun recaptured the Tang capital in central China on behalf of their new allies. Now the art of papermaking traveled in the other direction, enabling even private individuals across the Muslim world to accumulate substantial libraries, helping to fuel the massive intellectual renaissance to which the Abbasids gave their name. Trade bloomed between Asia's two great powers. The remains of a ninth-century Arab merchant ship found off the Indonesian island of Belitung in 1998 include over sixty thousand Tang-era Chinese ceramic, gold, and silver objects.

The Abbasids' material dealings with Latin Europe could be just as lively as those with Asia, although the Europeans had far less to offer than did some of the lands to the east. Cut off from the Mediterranean following the seventh- and eighth-century Muslim conquests in North Africa, Southern Europe, and the Levant, Western Europe was becoming relatively poor, isolated, and backward. Abbasid currency was important even in the benighted backwaters of forest and bog beyond the Mediterranean littoral. At the end of the eighth century, King Offa of Mercia, in the English Midlands, minted a gold coin that was a direct, nearly contemporaneous copy of an Abbasid coin minted by Mansour three thousand miles away in Baghdad. The English king's coin shows his name in Latin, OFFA REX, accompanied by Arabic script.* The Arabic writing on the coin is upside down, evidently copied from the original by an engraver who could not read the original. This piece of gold minted into an imitation dinar by a regional chieftain on a primitive and mist-bound North Sea island announces that the original had been struck in the Islamic year 157 (773–774 AD).[6]

The Abbasids and Europeans traded fruitfully and possessed a common enemy in the flourishing Umayyad caliphate in Spain. Diplomacy reflected these mutual interests. Between 797 and 809 no fewer than five embassies, and possibly more, passed between Charlemagne and Haroun al Rashid, Mamoun's father. A chess set, brass water clocks, and an elephant went west during these diplomatic exchanges. "Aaron, King of the Persians," as the Franks knew Haroun, received gifts of a presumably far simpler nature from the illiterate Carolus Magnus.

---

it. Hugh Kennedy, *The Early Abbasid Caliphate: A Political History* (London: Croom Helm, 1981), p. 36.

* The coin is in the permanent collection of the British Museum.

The Khorasani poet Anwari wrote of Baghdad in the early twelfth century: "The banks of the Tigris with their beauteous damsels surpass the city of Cathay." With the reference to China, these words immortalized the Abbasid fact of inhabiting one great world from the Atlantic to the Pacific. Baghdad, founded by Mamoun's great-grandfather in the shadow of Seleucia and Ctesiphon, built on layers of Sumerian, Babylonian, Persian, and Hellenistic cultures, brought together Arabs, Iranians, Greeks, Turks and others from Central Asia, Levantines, Africans, Circassians, Armenians, and more. It was a true "melting pot" city.

———

While gore and anxiety drip from the political annals of the Baghdad caliphate, another hallmark of the Abbasid ambience was how it married the darkness to the light. It did so with, among other things, an epic four-century-long celebration of the pleasures of the flesh. Consistent with Mamoun's bequest, the atmosphere was culturally Persian and intellectually Greek.

"The evening parties of the wealthy were always of a high standard," wrote Glubb Pasha.

> After the day's work, people would change into clean clothes of bright and cheerful colours. The guests reclined on low couches, spread with cushions and carpets and scented with musk, myrtle and jasmine. Behind a screen, an orchestra of slave girls sang and played the violin, the lute or the guitar. The conversation was lively and intellectual and would often include the recitation or the improvisation of poetry.

The War of Bread and Olives; *Adultery and Its Enjoyment*; *Stories about Slave Boys*; *Stories about Women*; *Masturbation*: such were the titles of some of the books written by one Ibn al-Shah al-Tahiri, a mid-tenth-century Abbasid courtier from an Iranian family. Upon the death of the Yemeni wife of Mansour, the ruler's consolation gift was a hundred slave girls, virgins all. Mansour's grandson, Haroun al Rashid, famous father of Mamoun, was said to have had over two thousand singing and servant girls in his harem. The ordinary concubines were without number.

Mutawwakil allegedly possessed four thousand concubines and bedded every one of them during the five thousand–odd days and nights of his reign. Kurdish and Greek slaves were especially prized in such roles. So too, as would later be the case with the Ottomans and other sex-slave cultures of the region, were the girls and young women of Circassia and the wider Caucasus.

That the best singing girls came to Baghdad via Medina, city of the Prophet and the dour Caliph Omar, was an irony typical of a culture in which the greatest courtesans, such as the Restless Butterfly, a Greek slave of Mansour's, achieved lasting fame for their skills and beauty. There are Abbasid accounts of girls so prized that even the caliph of the moment could not afford to buy them from their merchant or landowner master. (That the caliph could not simply seize what he desired is also notable.)*

As the Abbasid state and court culture grew more decadent in the later ninth century, and the caliphate fell ever deeper under the sway of Turkish soldiers imported from the steppes, these Central Asian horse-men brought an uncouth and threatening element to the streets.† Partly as a response, the Iranian custom of purdah, or separate living places for women, became more pronounced in the city's life. The caliphal palaces became cities within the city. Their inhabitants lived at a remove from the life of town and empire.

Within the palaces, these strange and nervous islands of hothouse luxury, the lives of even the most powerful women were increasingly restricted as the harems grew ever larger and more separate. But the royal mothers had substantial power, if only through influence over their sons and control over the money set aside for the harem. In 918, out of a state budget of over 2.5 million dinars, 743 thousand were allotted to the caliph's mother, wives, concubines, sons, and eunuchs.[7] That same year, 51,000 dinars were allocated by the state to buildings and repairs across the empire.

---

* Another Abbasid refinement that could cost significant sums was the love of trained pigeons, especially white ones, which were compared to European slave girls. Prices could reach five hundred gold dirhams. Baghdad's pigeon market today is near to the old Abbasid palace in the Rusafa district. Fuad M. Caswell, *The Slave Girls of Baghdad* (London: I. B. Tauris, 2011), p. 17.

† There would not be Turks in Anatolia until the Seljuks conquered it from the Byzantines and then occupied it and settled there in numbers following the Battle of Manzikert in 1071.

For the last 450 years of the Abbasid dynasty, almost no caliphs married.[8] The Arab mother of Mamoun's half brother Amin had been a full-fledged wife of their father, Haroun. But Mamoun's mother, the "Persian," who like Alexander's Roxana hailed from the hills of Afghanistan, was a slave. Mamoun himself married, but when he eventually tried to divorce his childless wife, the clergy would not allow it. His successors heeded the lesson. Mamoun was the first of twelve caliphs in a row born to non-Arab mothers, every one of them a slave.[9] The writ of Medina's dispensations for sexual slavery, so powerful as incentives in the faith's early military explosiveness, made it easier that way. Having a mother who was a slave and a non-Arab, be she blonde Slav or dark-skinned Abyssinian, had little effect on the status of a potential caliph or of anyone else. In the conventional Muslim understanding, women were merely "vessels for your seeds," as a son of Mansour reminded his father.

All the while, Sasanian traditions of elaborate court culture combined with the wealth of the empire to produce, in Abbasid Baghdad, a civilization of spectacular extravagances. A Byzantine embassy visiting the city in 917 was led on a tour of twenty-three palaces, according to an account written a century later but more or less corroborated by three others. These Baghdad palaces contained lions, elephants caparisoned in satin, large gardens of citrus and dates, and—it was said—thirty-eight thousand curtains woven in gold brocade. A House of the Tree in one palace contained a mechanical tree worked in silver and gold, with jewels for fruits and gold and silver birds to eat them.

Extravagant feats of generosity were a defining value of the Abbasid court civilization. When Mamoun married, his mother scattered a thousand pearls over the new bride. At a party, guests might receive a ball of musk with a piece of paper inside it naming their gift: a valuable horse, girl, or estate.

Arab poetry and musical culture reached their historical heights during this first century and a half of the Baghdad caliphate (ca. 762–910). Often the truly staggering prices of the great slave girls—thousands or even tens of thousands of dinars, when a thousand dinars contained almost 150 ounces of pure gold—had as much to do with their learning or their talent at extemporaneous poetry as with their physical charms and skills. The annals contain many stories such as that of Inan, a beauty from eastern Arabia, who in improvising poetry at parties was a match for Abu Nuwas, the great poet of the day. On two different occasions Haroun himself could not afford to buy her. He had two thousand others.

Love poetry, often about boys, abounded in this High Abbasid world.

> A boy of beckoning glances and chaste tongue.
> Neck bowed enticingly, who scorns the rein.
> Proffers me wine of hope mixed with despair,
> Distant in word and deed yet ever near.
> His face a goblet next his lip looks like a moon lit with a lamp;
> Armed with love's weaponry, he rides
> On beauty's steed, squares up eye's steel—
> Which is his smiles, the bow his brow,
> The shafts his eyes, his lashes lances.

When an Abbasid princess grew truculent, a courtier might appease her by arranging a visit from a famous poet, such as Abu Nuwas. The poetry itself, as the lines above hint, reflected the elaborate, sometimes overheated, intellectual activity of a court culture deeply concerned with its own intelligence and refinement. Most of Abbasid Baghdad's sponsorship of the arts and of intellectual life in general came from private individuals, households, and families. The salons of the rich and cultivated were populated with grammarians, translators, mathematicians, scientists, philosophers, astronomers, and literary critics. In Baghdad most free adults, male and female, were literate, as was many a slave, at a time at least three centuries before most European monarchs could read.

Unhappy love, showing off the sensitivity of the lover, was fashionable in the poetry of such an environment. Irony, paradox, and contrarianism also marked the intellectual tone.[10] The poet Ibn al-Rumi compared a rose to "the anus of a defecating mule." On the morning after his marriage to the bride whom his mother showered with a thousand pearls, Mamoun himself wrote a poem about how during the previous night the "stallion" had gone in with its "spear outstretched" to draw blood but had been prevented by blood from another direction.

The Islamic world's medieval cultural glory floated on a river of wine. Half the adventures, seductions, crimes, and feats of intellect, libido, and virtue in the annals of the period seem to involve wine in one way or another. For all the refined skills of the elite singing girls, most of the establishments where they performed were little more than brothels where the drink flowed as freely as the bawdy ditties. For homosexuals and men simply seeking to binge in a secluded environment, the numerous Christian monasteries served as welcoming retreats.[11] The liquor trade in Baghdad, as in much of the Arab world, was dominated by Christians.

Sometimes the wine was part of the Abbasid celebration of life, of imagination and companionship. At other times, as in some of the works of the poet Abu al Atahiya, Abu Nuwas's rival for the title of greatest Abbasid poet, wine was used to reflect upon mortality and the fleeting nature of worldly pleasures in a world so devoted to them:

> Men sit like revelers o'er their cups and drink
> From this world's hand, the circling wine of death.[12]

After all, Mutawwakil himself, champion of the Sunna, was assassinated in an intoxicated stupor in his palace. Hanbal, the persecuted jurist of Mamoun's reign who was such a key part of the Sunni reaction and ultimate victory, was a close friend of the poet Ibn al Jahn, who wrote of a favorite singing girl's house, "Ask and you will not be refused . . . The house is yours so long as your gifts are aplenty and you are replete with the honeyed wine."[13] The poet Abu Nuwas appears frequently in the *Arabian Nights* stories as the "rogue and jester" companion of the mighty caliph Haroun al Rashid. One of Abu Nuwas's poems describes three young men setting out for an inn one evening. They persuade the ostelress—"in whom remained a trace of youthful bloom"—to let them in for a drink.

> "Come in," she said, "a welcome visit.
> You're fine young blades and brainy with it!"
> "Pour by the book," said we to her.
> "Full bottles bring, no less no more."
> She brought fine wine like the sun with rays
> Like stars, fair wine in glass ablaze.

When the young men cannot afford the price she names, the poet persuades her to accept him for the night instead.

————

Mamoun's friends, the Banu Musa brothers, were exemplars of the Abbasid intellect. They had come with Mamoun to Baghdad from Khorasan in 819, and upon the death of their astronomer father, the caliph had made himself their guardian. Growing up in Baghdad under his guidance, the brothers received the best education the caliph could obtain. As adults, they wrote perhaps twenty or more books, including works on geometry, astronomy, mechanics, and history. Voracious collectors of the more scientific works of the ancient Greeks, the Banu Musa brothers invented numerous machines and built many exquisite small mechanical devices of their own design. At least nine of their books, including *On the Motion of Heavenly Spheres* and *On the Construction of the Astrolabe*, related to the study of the heavens. Their seven known works on mathematics and geometry include the *Book on the Measurement of Planes and Spherical Figures* and the *Book on a Geometric Proposition Proved by Galen*. Wealthy in their own right, they paid three men five hundred gold dinars per month each for full-time translation work. Five hundred High Abbasid dinars contained almost seventy-five ounces of pure gold.

The Banu Musa brothers' *Book on a Geometric Proposition Proved by Galen* referred to Claudius Galenus (129 – ca. 200 AD), a Greek-speaking Roman from Pergamon, in Hellenistic Asia Minor. Galen would be but one example of the role the Abbasid translations were to play in preserving and passing on important parts of the classical learning that ultimately fueled the Renaissance in Europe.

Galen of Pergamon was the preeminent empirical scientist of classical times. He received the Greek classical education typical for a Roman patrician of his day, a curriculum much like that of the young Mamoun, or of the Banu Musa boys under his direction, in Baghdad over six centuries later. Much of it would have been familiar to Alexander too, almost five centuries previously.

Galen went on to study medicine at Alexandria, where he made a name for himself by carving apart and reassembling a dead ape. At twenty-eight, he was made physician to the gladiators of the senior Roman high priest in Asia. Using the wounds of dead gladiators as "windows into the body," since Roman law proscribed dissection of human corpses, Galen studied human anatomy as best he could. Called eventually to Rome, he became personal physician to three Roman emperors, including the philosopher Marcus Aurelius. About three million words of Galen's writings survive, on topics medical, scientific, and philosophical.*

Galen's works would go on to dominate European medicine until fifteen centuries after his death. Well into the Renaissance, they served as a body of formal medical learning so complete and unchallengeable that "Galenism" has become a byword for suffocating intellectual orthodoxy. Galenic theories on curative bleeding dominated entire fields of medicine well into the nineteenth century. Cataract surgery is said to still follow directly in the path that he developed with his patients. Galen's conclusion that the brain directs the muscles through "cranial and peripheral" nervous systems, a theory based on his experiments with nerve connections, conforms with our modern understanding of the human nervous system.

More than six centuries after Galen's death, a professional translator working for the Banu Musa translated 129 of his works into Arabic. All in all, it is reckoned that the Abbasids translated into Arabic the entire corpus of Greek "philosophy, medicine, and the exact sciences" still extant in the late Hellenistic period.[14] The first translation of Euclid into Arabic was dedicated to Mamoun himself.

The books that the Abbasids translated ultimately began to be discovered again by Europeans when Sicily and parts of Spain and southern France were reconquered from Islamic rule during the eleventh and twelfth centuries. Many of the Greek works translated by the Abbasids would have been lost forever had they not entered the great Arabic libraries and private collections. Original Arab works also benefited from this process. The writings of Al Kindi, for example, which began to be translated into Latin in twelfth-century Spain, in many cases survived only in that language.[15]

---

* The 1821–33 compendium of 122 of Galen's works by Karl Gottlob Kuhn of Leipzig amounted to twenty-two volumes comprising more than twenty thousand pages. Kuhn's index was 676 pages long. The extant works are thought to represent less than a third of Galen's production.

The Banu Musa brothers made other contributions to what could be called the Great Transmission. Their *Book on the Measurement of Planes and Spherical Figures* was used by Francis Bacon, the seventeenth-century Englishman who in pioneering inductive reasoning became the father of the basic methodology of modern science.* Another major figure in European science who referred to the work of the Banu Musa centuries after they had died was Leonardo Fibonacci (ca. 1170–1250), the great Pisan mathematician. Fibonacci traveled to North Africa with his merchant father as a boy in the 1170s and 1180s. He learned to appreciate the number system in use there, which he called "the art of the Indians' nine symbols," now known as Arabic numerals. In 1202, Fibonacci published the work that was to catalyze the global success of this "modus Indorum." The *Liber Abaci* (*Book of Calculation*), as it was called, offers a direct view into an extraordinary moment in history. Here at sunrise in Latin Christendom's great awakening was the physical transmission of the medieval Arabic legacy to Western Europe.

This particular transmission, of an Arabic borrowing from India in this case, took place in Abbasid Algeria, at a port city called Bugia that had especially close ties to Pisa. Fibonacci's book introduces the new method as follows: "The nine Indian figures are: 9 8 7 6 5 4 3 2 1. With these nine figures, and the sign 0, which the Arabs call zephyr, any number whatsoever is written."[16] The coming golden age of European trade and finance would almost certainly have been the poorer if conducted in Roman numerals.

The thousands of Greek works translated into Arabic in the High Abbasid civilization were pragmatic in nature.[17] Ptolemy's astrology aided the Abbasids in their practice of the old Sasanian tradition of political astrology.[18] Aristotelian logic helped the Abbasids to reply to Christian critiques of their religion, or to argue with each other about such issues as the created Koran. Greek, Babylonian, and Hindu achievements in mathematical fields contributed to Abbasid trade and engineering. Galen

---

* Inductive reasoning proceeds from observation to broader conclusions; deductive reasoning, taking the form of the syllogism, works the other way around. Bacon's inductive reasoning is often described as a rejection of Aristotle, but Aristotle acknowledged a major if not equal role for induction in natural science, writing in the *Nicomachean Ethics* (chapter 4, section 3) that science "proceeds sometimes through induction and sometimes by syllogism."

the doctor and Euclid the geometer were of immense interest to the sponsors of the Christians, Jews, pagans, and recent Muslim converts who did the translating. The iambs of Homer, the statues of Phidias, and the plays of Sophocles were of no interest at all. No literature was translated.[19]

While the Abbasid translation movement died within fifteen years of Mamoun himself, on the periphery of Islam, especially in the lands of greater Iran, the work of the Mamoun-era translators would be used to fuel an ongoing intellectual flowering in the wider Abbasid world.

A colleague of the Banu Musa in the House of Wisdom, so to speak, was the mathematician Al Khwarizmi (ca. 785–850). He seems to have come from Khwarazmia, the part of ancient Iran, north even of Khorasan, that is mostly southern Turkmenistan today. Drawing on Babylonian, Greek, Hindu, and Persian sources, "the Khwarazmian" was, like so many of the major intellectual figures of the Abbasid era, a remarkable polymath. Al Khwarizmi would give his name to the algorithm, but he was also a cartographer, an astronomer, and an engineer of measuring devices. The term "algebra" is taken from his *Kitab al Jabr w'al Muqabala* (*Book of Completion and Balancing*), the title of the treatise in which he more or less invented algebra as a discrete discipline. (*Al jabr*, "completion," referred to the shifting of a negative term from one side of an equation into a positive term on the other side.) Al Khwarizmi, like Al Kindi, helped to popularize decimal places, zero, and Hindu numerals in the Abbasid world.*

Rhazes (*Al Razi*, d. 925), a Persian who died almost a century after Mamoun, added Iranian and Indian medical works to the Arabic-language canon that was being built upon the Greek foundation. Ibn Sina (d. 1037), another Persian who lived a century later, came from Bokhara on the northeast marches of the Iranian world, in what is now southern Uzbekistan. Avicenna, as he became known in Europe, was easily the greatest intellectual figure in the history of the Islamic lands, writing over four hundred books and treatises on philosophy, medicine, mathematics, formal reasoning, alchemy, and many other topics. One of his main works

---

* He, not Fibonacci, is sometimes credited as the individual mainly "responsible for the introduction into the West of the Arabic numerals." There are also hints that Al Khwarizmi took part in Mamoun's effort to calculate the Earth's circumference, and even speculation that he was in fact the eldest of the three Banu Musa brothers. Philip K. Hitti, *The Arabs: A Short History* (Washington, DC: Regnery Publishing, 1996), pp. 146–147.

was an extensive proof of the existence of God using the rigorous rules of classical logic. The effort calls to mind that of St. Thomas Aquinas and his five proofs of God, but without Aquinas's final admission that, for a true believer like himself, proofs were beside the point. Aquinas studied Avicenna closely.

The work of the scientist-philosophers writing in Arabic in various parts of the Abbasid world has been excluded from orthodox Islamic culture since the latter part of the ninth century. But in Europe, these writings became fundamental to the birth of a new world, as much of the Renaissance's rediscovery of classical learning came via the Great Transmission. *The Canon of Medicine*, Avicenna's synthesis of Galen's opus, was the main text for young doctors in Western European universities as recently as the middle of the seventeenth century. Al Khwarizmi's *Book of Completion and Balancing* "was translated into Latin and used until the sixteenth century as the principal mathematical textbook of European universities."[20] The study of Arabic, considered a classical language, was required of all students pursuing their Master of Arts at Oxford during that century.[21]

It was no coincidence that the Abbasid Empire, the last world power to be based in Mesopotamia, was also the last of the important Iraq-based states to maintain the agricultural and irrigation resources of the *jazira*, the fertile but flood-prone belt between the two great rivers.[22] Once the early Abbasid strength had waned, much of Mesopotamia eventually regressed to a flood-wracked semidesert, able to "support nothing more than small-scale principalities."[23] The thirteenth-century Mongol invasions ravaged what remained of the irrigation networks. After the Abbasids, Mesopotamia would not again be the treasury, breadbasket, or center of anything notable until the birth of archaeology there in the nineteenth century.

Chapter 13

Slave Girls and Reason

Abbasid Baghdad, 750–1258 AD

> You may hate a thing although it is good for you, and love a thing
> although it is bad for you. God knows, but you know not.*
>
> —Koran 2.216

Amr ibn Bahr al Basri was born in Basra around 776, the dark-skinned
grandson of a slave of African descent. As a boy, young Amr sold fish
along a Basra canal. Swept along in the Abbasid intellectual explosion
that was fueled partly by the advent of papermaking from China, he
was able to read widely as a youth and young man. At the feet of a local
teacher who appreciated his potential, he studied not only the Koran
and hadith but also Persian histories and the Classical and Hellenistic
Greek corpus, especially the many Neoplatonic works then attributed
to Aristotle.

Basra was the birthplace of Mutazilism. The young Amr ibn Bahr
attended the lectures of eminent Basra intellectuals and gathered with
other youths in the city's main mosque for debates. Eventually acquiring
the name Al Jahiz ("the goggle-eyed"), he was considered exceptionally
ugly in an age that made great virtues of both ugliness and beauty.
Inevitably Jahiz made his way to Baghdad. There he lived by his pen,
attracting the attention of Mamoun and writing hundreds of works. Jahiz
died at ninety-three, crushed by an avalanche of books in his library at
home in Basra. He was the greatest of all Arabic prose writers.

---

* Full quote: "Fighting is obligatory for you, much as you dislike it. But you may hate a
thing although it is good for you, and love a thing although it is bad for you. God knows,
but you know not."

Probably around the year 825, Jahiz wrote his *Epistle on Singing Girls*, the most trenchant and important work in a prolific career that made him "the propagandist-laureate of Mamoun and his Mutazili successors." A student of the works of the ancient Greeks since his youthful days in Basra, Jahiz was closely associated with the House of Wisdom. Mamoun had appointed him as tutor to his children, it was said, but they were put off by his peculiar looks.

In *On Singing Girls*, the worldly, sardonic Jahiz offers one of the best windows into the elite culture of the time. Pulling back the robe for this prurient glimpse, Jahiz also brings his reader into the thick of Mamoun's struggle for the nature of the faith. Jahiz wrote works on animals, on noted misers of the day, on the superiority of black people over whites, on Mutazilism and other politico-religious topics dear to his caliph, and on many other topics. However, it was in the *qiyan*, the Abbasid-era singing girl, that Jahiz found his definitive subject. She was the ideal subject for a classic Abbasid mix of raciness, irony, gossip, and politics.

If the Baghdad caliphate were a film, the *qiyan* would be its star. She was as titillating and dangerous as a triumphantly lewd civilization could possibly make her. She was a slave, but she enslaved. She was chosen for her wit as well as her looks, and her learning and sexuality transported her into a world of agency. If she managed to earn enough money for herself, or for an owner whose sympathies she succeeded in cultivating, the singing girl might be able to buy her own freedom. If she bore him sons whose situation might benefit from a free mother, he might one day manumit her.* By seducing and scheming her way up a ladder of ever-wealthier owners, she had genuine opportunity to climb the social hierarchy.

The *qiyan* was a slave, but the dismal position of other women in Abbasid society meant that she was freer than her female counterparts in any other position, free or enslaved. In a culture in which freeborn women found themselves ever more incarcerated in the stifling harem, the singing girl was courted by the most prominent men in her world. The *qiyan* could cultivate arts and perform them in public. The successful *qiyan* could have a career and her choice of lovers, in a world where

---

* If a slave woman of any kind bore a child to her owner, then Islamic law forbade him from selling her on to someone else.

neither a free woman nor an ordinary concubine could have either. The "free" sister or daughter of a man in this Abbasid world spent the cloistered days and nights "in a dark, loose-fitting cloak," with no males outside her close family permitted to see her face. The qiyan was, as a slave, not veiled.

The qiyan was usually far more educated, and current with politics, the intellectual debates of the day, and the goings-on of the world than her unenslaved counterpart. A modern chronicler of this feature of Abbasid life cites the opinion of the Frères Goncourt that "only the woman of the world is a woman—the rest are simply females." The comment expressed the view of a deeply prejudiced age, and Abbasid society would have agreed with it. By this standard the successful Abbasid qiyan was undoubtedly a woman of the world. The typical "free" woman of the early medieval harem in Baghdad or elsewhere in the Abbasid orbit was not.

But Jahiz's work On Singing Girls addresses another, different issue. Couched as a defense of the widespread qiyan phenomenon on impeccable, Sunna-citing Islamic grounds, Jahiz's slim treatise, disarmingly humorous and titillating, is in fact a dangerous work of high politics. For Jahiz, the singing girl herself, who according to the tropes of the time is sexually dominant and infamously lustful, has been trained to enjoy too much a life that grossly offends basic decency. Financially, too, according to these tropes, she is predatory and insatiable. Her pimp, of course, is worse. For Jahiz, the very thing that makes this wretched institution legally possible is also what makes it acceptable in the corrupt culture all around him: the Sunna, or true path.

Mutazilism has been described as "the enduring protest of sound human understanding against the tyrannical demands which the orthodox teaching imposed upon it."[1] Even the Arabic prose in which Jahiz wrote On Singing Girls is imbued with this clash. His language contains numerous words and inflections, many of them Persian in origin, that postdate the Koranic lexicon of Mecca and Medina. The Mutazilite message of Jahiz's diction would have been clear at the time, for the devotees of Sunna demanded that the only proper Arabic vocabulary was the one used by the Prophet. The system of the originalists, the theological foes of Jahiz and Mamoun, could not allow ethics or "natural law." In a religious outlook of pure power, there was only halal or haram, licit or illicit. Moral law, by contrast, like the other Aristotelian pillars of reason and science, established truths that were beyond the reach of any power, including God's. Thus *On Singing Girls*, using irony to argue for basic ethics over canonical tradition, is a polemic in support of Mamoun, a Free Willer's broadside.

Jahiz mentions an "Abyssinian girl" who sold for 120,000 dinars. Other singing girls might come from the green valleys of Armenia, the rugged Atlas Mountains of North Africa, the broad Turkish steppes, or the Greek slums of Aleppo. Around them wafted the Abbasid civilization's rich world of poets, merchants, emperors, pimps, and viziers.

The huge sums frequently paid for the *qiyan* demonstrate the extraordinary wealth of the Pax Islamica in the Abbasid heyday. The cunning of the businessman who owned her, like the artistry of the intrigues in which she engaged, shines a light into the overripe quality—cruel, clever, self-absorbed—of this most velvet of epochs. The extraordinary monetary value stored in those elements of the singing girl that might be called "culture," in her knowledge of poetry, songs, and the techniques of enchantment, is a society's boast of its own refinement. The substantial influence that her owner wielded among even the most powerful men speaks of what currencies their civilization held dear. And the impunity of her ghastly owner, Jahiz argues in his light and urbane way, reflects the corruption of the world that they all inhabited.

As the Islamic empire was shrinking from the very time of the Abbasids' founding, conquest was no longer a source of young boys and girls for the beds of the Successors of the Prophet. With war spoils largely an anachronism already, the faithful were left to pay for their slaves. The marts around the empire's borders provided a plentiful harvest throughout the year. Africans and Indians were mostly used as domestic staff for the kitchens and elsewhere. Fair-skinned European girls, including Greeks from Asia Minor, were mostly preferred for the bedroom. Poor families burdened by daughters would give the girls away, or sell them if possible. The slave traders bought them young, if they showed *qiyan* potential, so that they could grow up to sing and recite their poetry in good Arabic, and thus command much higher prices.

One Abu Uthman the Broker ("al Dellal") said that "assuming good stock for a start," ideally by the age of nine—when the Prophet first consummated his marriage with his favorite wife, Aisha—a girl would be sent to Mecca to spend three years learning the secrets behind the "good looks" of the slave girls there. Then she would go to Medina for a further three years, to pick up the "tenderness" of its slave girls, before coming to Baghdad for "sophistication."[2] With the known world contributing to the menu, this part of the Abbasid feast was as refined as the rest. "The Berbers for procreation, the Byzantines for service and the Persians for good behaviour," reflected one connoisseur.

An auction catalogue listing national characteristics praised the Indian for her "good figure," the Berber for her sexual "energy," and the Byzantine for her "straight blond hair, blue eyes, obedience and amiability." The Abyssinian was known to be "useless for singing or dancing." The Armenian, though full of "rude health and strength," suffered from "monstrous legs." Ibrahim al Mawsili, a prominent music master who was an early Abbasid pioneer in the development of qiyan, set a lasting fashion in his world by avoiding completely the "yellow-skinned Chinese, the dark-brown Indians and Sindis, and the black Africans."

———

Jahiz addressed On Singing Girls to a wide enough audience: "unto ignorant and boorish folk," he said archly in his preamble. Of course his true audience was Mutazilite sophisticates and well-heeled society wits and gossips. Ostensibly the object of his withering pen was "the owner of singing girls."

Combining elements of the pimp and the racehorse trainer, this man bought the future temptress when she was a child. He housed, fed, and clothed his asset as she grew up and learned the skills that would enhance her value. Investing substantially in the girl's education, the pimp expected a good return. A eunuch perhaps, or maybe a retired qiyan, taught the girl to read and write, that she could pen and reply to the love letters of seductions to come. The pimp and his people trained her intensively in song and poetry, for public performances of these would set her apart from ordinary slave girls. Decent flesh could be bought at livestock prices in any dusty provincial town square.

What the young singing girl was not trained in was religion or chastity. In the "ten thousand verses" that she would learn, Jahiz tells us, "there is not one mention of God." Indeed, he writes, the verses of her valuable repertoire "are all founded on references to fornication, pimping, passion, yearning, desire and lust."

Growing up in this way, she developed into a notably sexual individual. But the *qiyan* was not to blame for her voluptuous ways. "How is it possible for her to be chaste?" Jahiz asks. "It is in the very place where she was brought up that she acquires unbridled desires."

So Jahiz evinces some sympathy for the *qiyan*. But it is not the kind of sympathy that we may have expected from this grandson of a slave. His concern for the girls is not that they are chattel. After all, the *qiyan* in her silks and jewels had it easier than the common concubines of the Islamic world. Rather, the problem here for Jahiz—or so he writes—is that in such a setting of seduction and carnality, a natural licentiousness runs amok. The pimp, the flesh peddler, corrupts the girls and bankrupts the lust-maddened customers. In their mutual contempt for ordinary ethics, abetted as they are by canon, girls and pimp together stand in for Jahiz's true target: revealed law.

The relationship with her owner makes the girl not only wanton but also "insincere, and given to employing deceit and treachery." The end to which *qiyan* and owner work is simple: "squeezing out the property of the deluded victim and then abandoning him." The dupe, the lover of this cruel and carnal woman, with her cynical pimp behind the scenes, finds himself writhing in psychic pain from their well-choreographed wiles. One well-known Abbasid poet wrote of the sensation:

> A slave girl with wobbling buttocks filling the anklet and the bangles
> I moan to God for what ailed me
> from the love of her
> and the loathing of her master[3]

The devil himself could not find a worse "snare" or "temptation," writes Jahiz. But of course, as he goes on to say, this is not "any criticism of them but the highest praise." Jahiz mocks his opponents here by unearthing, as they would, a line from revelation to defend on religious grounds what is indefensible on moral grounds: "For we find in *sunna*," he writes, "'The best of your women are the charmers and deceivers.'"

———

After years of investment, the owner of the *qiyan* is ready to claim his profit. He invites a group of men to his house. Or perhaps he brings a few girls with him as he visits the house of an associate; they might sing after dinner, or amuse the men with poetry and bons mots. For the client—the mark—here is the moment of danger.

"As soon as the observer notices her," writes Jahiz, "she exchanges provocative glances with him, gives him playful smiles, dallies with him in verses set to music. Then when she perceives that her sorcery has worked on him and that he has become entangled in the net, she redoubles the wiles."

When this first evening is finished, *qiyan* and dupe find themselves back under separate roofs once more. Passionate letters start to fly, and new facets of her owner's investment begin to show their value. "She corresponds" with the dupe, "pouring out . . . her infatuation for him, and swearing that she has filled the inkwell with tears and wetted the envelope with her kisses."

A fantasy must be maintained: that of the girl's desire to escape to her lover from beneath the repressive roof of her master. "She puts the letter in a sixth of a sheet of paper, seals it with saffron, ties it up with a piece of lute-string, declares it to be concealed from her guardians," and finds a way—enabled by the very owner she claims to fear—to convey the missive into the hands of her suitor.

Soon the mark returns to the "pimping house" for another evening of wine and poetry. Darting secret glances at her admirer, she performs. He thinks it is all for him. Of course, as Jahiz points out, there could well be several other such fools there, reclining before her with the other gentlemen, goblets in hand. As she sings, perhaps the dupe is thinking of her letters:

Many a missive telling the heart's secret, charming in its melodious eloquence, has come when my heart has been sore because of the long time I have waited for it; I laughed when I saw it, but wept when I read it; my eyes saw unpleasing news and the tears started up unbidden to my eye. You tyrant of my soul, my life and death are in your hands.

The girl's owner is at this stage in a position better even than that of the Caliph of Islam. Caliphs "give more than they get," Jahiz notes. Fonts of wealth, advantage, and position for other men, they receive little in return. The owner of singing girls, by contrast, gains materially from those who pay him court. Men send him "presents of all sorts, in the way of food and drink." In this high civilization of the Abbasids, the happy pimp is not only solvent but also endowed with the greatest of gifts, the regard of his fellow men. "He is always met with the greatest respect, is called by his formal name when addressed, and is spoken to with all the polite phrases; he is favored with the choicest titbits of news."

Knowing that "the conquest of the loved one tends to hasten the dissolution of the passion," that when the admirer has finally possessed his beloved sexually "nine tenths of his ardour disappear," the pimp keeps the unrequited passion groaning along for as long as he believes the dupe can afford the ceaseless stream of emoluments.

After the evening with company at the pimp's house, the furtive, passionate letters continue. The dupe will feel fortunate to arrange a private visit to the pimping house as the young woman keeps up her pretense of desiring only to outwit her owner in the pursuit of true love. The owner "abandons surveillance of the girls (though choosing his spies well), accepts the room rent, pretends to doze off before supper, takes no notice of winkings, is indulgent to a kiss, ignores signs, turns a blind eye to the exchange of billets doux."

The squeeze continues for as long as there is anything to extract from the victim. If the man is influential, the pimp avails himself of his influence. "If the customer is rich but not influential, he borrows money from him without interest." Whether there is any consummation at the end is beside the point. Eventually the dupe, impoverished, is abandoned. It may all seem dreadful, but it is not the girl's fault, says Jahiz toward the end of *On Singing Girls*, or even the pimp's. There is in fact no fault at all. The phenomenon is to be welcomed, for it is perfectly righteous. "Everything which is not prohibited in God's Book and the Sunna of the Prophet," Jahiz reminds his reader, "is a matter indifferent and free."

Jahiz later lived through the reign of Mamoun's righteous nephew Mutawwakil, said to have possessed four thousand slave girls and to have had sex with each of them. "Will anyone but an ignorant fool," asks Jahiz at the end of *On Singing Girls*, "shrink from availing himself to the full of what is legally permitted?"

And there, with this final faultless appeal to faith and law, ends the work that began, "In the name of God the Compassionate the Merciful."

The ninth-century confirmation of Sunna's hegemony was ultimately "the result of such tendencies within the community rather than the cause."[4] The underlying culture of seventh-century Arabia was what it was, and the holy book produced by this culture said what it said. But while Sunna's victory may have been inevitable, the proximate cause of this victory was above all the work of one man, Abu Abdullah Muhammad ibn Idris al-Shafii. A contemporary of Jahiz, Shafii would be the great intellectual counterweight to the ugly man from Basra.

Shafii was one of countless Abbasid characters whose movements over a lifetime reflected the cosmopolitan nature of the world of the Baghdad caliphate. Born in Gaza in 767 to a Yemeni mother and a father who died in Syria, Shafii was taken to Mecca at the age of two. There he memorized the Koran by the time he was seven. In his twenties, Shafii moved to Medina to continue his studies. By the age of twenty-eight, he had acquired a reputation as a brilliant legal scholar. He moved to Baghdad, and thence back to Mecca. There he lectured in the Grand Mosque to students who included Ahmed ibn Hanbal.*

Shafii returned to Baghdad in 810 and left it forever in 814, the year after the city fell to Mamoun. The caliph offered Shafii a judgeship, but the disapproving Sunni refused it. Agreeing to Mamoun's "created Koran," the crystallizing Mutazilite notion that was the stipulation of Mamoun's inquisition, would have been impossible for Shafii.

Shafii went to Egypt, dying there in 820. His greatest work, known simply as *The Epistle*, or *Al Risala*, was a product of the Cairo years. In *Al Risala*, Shafii provided what came to be accepted as the "definitive methodology for Islamic law."[5] In Baghdad, a young Shafii was said to

---

* Shafii's route from Baghdad to Mecca was much like Abraham's from Ur to Palestine: beginning in Iraq, he followed the Fertile Crescent north to Harran, then south through Syria. Majid Khadduri, translator's introduction to *Islamic Jurisprudence: Shafii's Risala* (Baltimore: Johns Hopkins University Press, 1961), p. 13.

have discussed "Greek medicine and philosophy in their original language"[6] with the mightiest of all Abbasid caliphs, Mamoun's grandfather
Haroun al Rashid. But by the time of Egypt and *Al Risala*, Shafii was a
different man. Now he was known as the Upholder of the Traditions.
He would not allow theology to be discussed in his presence. Theology,
after all, was Logos applied to faith.

Shafii's idea was simple. Hadith, being the words or behavior of the
Prophet himself, overrode all else except the Koran. *Ijtihad*, personal
opinion based on logical reasoning, could have no role at all. The mere
exercise of intellect "had to be restricted to making correct inferences
and drawing systematic conclusions from the traditions."[7]

An example is supplied by the treatment of women who happen to be
married at the time of their enslavement. Under ancient Arab custom,
all captured women were eligible for slavery regardless of their prior
status; it was not of consequence to the pre-Islamic Arabs whether their
female war booty had been married or not. Now, with Islam, there was
an empire, and it was an empire of religious laws. So these matters had
to be codified. In the Prophet's day and during the great expansion under
his Rightly Guided successors, the old Arab custom had been observed.
Midway through the second Muslim century, the two main legal per-
suasions had emerged, one based at Medina and one in southern Iraq.
The Medinese tended to side with the Prophet and Arab custom; the
Iraqis held that as captivity and marriage were different matters, there
was no good cause for one to impinge on the other.

For most Muslims, Shafii's argument from Mohammed's perfection
was impossible to refute. The Traditionists soon enough became known
as *Ahl al Sunna*, "the people of the Sunna," and their triumph was effectively complete by the time of Shafii's death in 820.

From shortly after Shafii's death, Sunni law would resolve itself permanently into four schools, as they are known. These would be named
after Shafii, Hanbal, and two other jurists: Malik ibn Anas (d. 759) and
Abu Hanifa (d. 767). All four schools are Shafiite, following his framework
with equal devotion, and each considers the others valid. Such was the
sweeping nature of Shafii's victory over Mamoun, Aristotle, and Jahiz.

The four schools are "identical in approximately 75% of their legal
conclusions," with the variances resulting merely from "methodological
differences in understanding or authenticating the hadiths themselves."[8]

Here is one such, from the *Reliance of the Traveler*. Among the things that "invalidate" one's Ramadan fast are "allowing phlegm or mucus at the back of the mouth to be swallowed when one could have spat them out."[9] So say the Shafiite, Hanbali, and Maliki schools. The more liberal Hanafi school, however, concludes from hadith that swallowing one's mucus "does not break the fast even if it is intentional."

The triumph of Tradition was achieved relatively early in the Abbasid period. Over the next hundred years, work on the details would continue. By the end of the third Islamic century, the experts of the four schools "felt that all essential questions had been settled." This meant "the closing of the gates of ijtihad," as it is known, sometime between the years 900 and 950. It was "the end of independent reasoning in Islamic law." Henceforth, "all future activity would have to be confined to the explanation, application, and, at the most, interpretation of the doctrine as it had been laid down once and for all."[10]

———

In about 914, most likely in Baghdad, another great Abbasid figure had a famous dream. It happened during Ramadan. The dreamer was Abu al Hasan al Ashari (d. 936), a well-known Mutazilite theologian who came originally, like Jahiz, from Basra. Ever since Mutawwakil, the caliphs had been Sunni, but Mutazilism was still a force, if only in the rarefied world of scholars. The man on the street was solidly Sunni.

Ashari spent his youth as the leading acolyte of Basra's top Mutazilite theologian of the day. When the man died, Ashari was passed over as his replacement. Now, in the dream, when Ashari was forty-one, the Prophet Mohammed himself appeared before him.

"You must support only that which comes directly from myself," said the apparition.

Ashari, like his erstwhile hero Mamoun after his dream of Aristotle, immediately understood what the dream meant. But the message was the opposite. Twice more during that Ramadan came the dreams of Mohammed advocating Tradition. The Free Willer was converted to the path of Medina.

Ashari devoted the rest of his life, twenty-two years, to taking the dialectical skills he had learned as a Mutazilite and turning them against his former colleagues. He became a robust defender of Sunna, informed by Shafii's innovation of the all-conquering hadith. The *Encyclopedia Islamica* calls Asharism "the most important theological school in Sunni Islam."[11]

Most powerfully, Ashari developed a metaphysics known as voluntarism. Asharite voluntarism starts with God's transcendent omnipotence. Given this, every human act is purely and simply an expression of God's will at that given moment. So is every fact or event in the natural world. To take a time-honored Sunni example, the arrow speeds forward not because the bow shot it, but because at every sliver of time along the way, God wills an entirely new reality in which the missile is a little bit nearer its target. With no earthly causation in the physical world, nor any agency, morality, or responsibility in the human world, truth, reality, and right are merely whatever the strongest want them to be. All is relative. It was the natural juncture of the paths of chaos and power.

The Hanbalis, hardest of the Sunna's medieval hard core, would reject Asharism for its use of theological methods. Just as Hanbal himself had refused to eat watermelons because the Prophet had not known them, so it was with theology: anything with *logos* in it had not been part of the Prophet's framework. Theology, indeed, was worse than watermelons, for in its very nature it contradicted the model of pure power and absolute tradition. Asharism, despite its application of Greek reason to questions of the faith, nonetheless led to the same conservative endpoint as the purer literalism of the Hanbalis, and the two were thenceforth the twin orthodoxies of the Sunni world. On the more liberal side of Sunnism, a school known as the Maturidis, who accepted that the human intellect could divine certain moral truths without the aid of revelation, became popular in the northern and eastern fringes of the Muslim world, especially among followers of the Hanafi school of law.

By the early twelfth century, when the last of the great orthodox Islamic thinkers, the Asharite theologian Al Ghazali, died in 1111, development of Sunni theory would be finished. If any tiny crack had been left open in "the gates of ijtihad" when they were shut in the late tenth century, the closing was now complete. All was settled.

Chapter 14

Mayhem from the Steppes

Turks, Tatars, Mongols, 1000–1400

For he shall wear the crown of Persia
Whose head hath deepest scars, whose breast most wounds
—Christopher Marlowe, *Tamburlaine*, Act II[1]

In 833, making his way north to fight the Byzantines, the Caliph Mamoun died, at the age of forty-seven, of a fever after swimming in a cold stream at the foot of Anatolia's Taurus Mountains. He was succeeded in Baghdad by his half-brother Mutasim. Where Mamoun had been fond of dialectics in the salon, Mutasim was a pure warrior. From western Anatolia to Persia, he fought throughout his nine-year reign.

As a young prince, Mutasim, ten years Mamoun's junior, had chosen martial pursuits over the divans and libraries of High Abbasid life. Around 815, long before he would have expected to assume the Prophet's mantle, Mutasim began to buy male Turkish slaves in Baghdad and drill them into a disciplined private army. Later, he bought his men directly from the slave markets of Central Asia.[2] At about the same time, the swells of the Abbasid court developed a taste for what was to become, alongside the *qiyan*, a classic Abbasid creature: the *ghulam* ("youth"). An almond-eyed Turkic boy in his early teens, the *ghulam* was as slender and handsome as he was vicious and tough, at once "slave, guard, muse, and bedfellow to his master."[3] *

Shortly after Mamoun moved from Khorasan to Baghdad in 818, Turks began to take on an increasingly important role in the imperial army of

---

* The word *ghulam* seems also to have been used quite frequently to denote the Turkish slave-soldiers in general.

the Abbasid Caliphate. The habits of rapine and drunkenness that they brought from the steppes quickly alienated the people of the capital. "They were rough-mannered barbarians," wrote the chronicler Tabari, "who used to ride through the streets and roads of Baghdad, knocking down men and women and trampling children underfoot."[4]

By the time Mutasim became caliph in 833, the presence on the streets of this rough foreign soldiery was leading to public calls for their removal. Tabari reported that the Turks, known as mamluks (from the Arabic *mamlūk*, "slave"), often found their colleagues assassinated in the barracks. The growing number of Turks began to crowd Baghdad. In 836, Mutasim decamped with his mamluks to a new capital that he built at Samarra, on the Tigris eighty miles north of Baghdad. The land at Samarra was bought from a Christian monastery for five hundred dirhams, according to a report in Tabari's chronicle; there were said to be eight monasteries in the area at the time.[5]

The move to Samarra, where the royal palaces were surrounded by the quarters of the mamluks, was not a success. Feeling their power, the Turks soon overshadowed the caliphs. In 858, Mutawwakil tried to move the capital back to Baghdad, but the soldiers prevented him. Three years later they murdered him in his Samarra palace, replacing him with his eldest son.

The Turks of palace and army were now de facto rulers of the empire. They eventually killed three more of their captive caliphs. The rise of these Central Asian praetorians marked another of Iraq's watersheds in wider history: "the end of the rule of Muhammad's family as despotic emperors of the world's greatest empire."[6] For four centuries, from the time of Mutawwakil's murder until the Mongols ended the Baghdad caliphate forever in 1258, the Abbasid caliphs mostly lived the nervous lives of caged nightingales in the gilded and perfumed halls of their palaces.

Mutawwakil's assassination by his Turkish guards marked the end not only of the Abbasid caliphs as a political power but of the caliphate as a territorial empire. In the nine-year period of domestic anarchy that followed Mutawwakil's murder, the Iranian, Syrian, and Egyptian provinces fell away. By 870, when there was a brief restoration of stability in Iraq, the empire was gone. The Dar al Islam as a state, assembled under the Rightly Guided caliphs who followed Mohammed, then ably administered by the Umayyads from Damascus and governed by the mighty early Abbasids from Baghdad since the city's founding in 762, had lasted about 235 years. The caliphs in Baghdad, with a few brief exceptions, now served as little more than religious figureheads, "sometimes cajoled and conciliated, but more often coerced or ignored" by Iraq's true rulers as power passed among more vigorous hands, from one dynasty of foreigners to the next.[7]

The first of these was the Buyids, a clan of Shia warriors from the southern, Iranian, coast of the Caspian Sea. The Buyids took power in Baghdad in 945 and lasted there until 1055, never controlling more than most of Iraq and southern and western Iran. While the Buyids kept the peace by giving Iraq's Sunnis and Christians a relatively loose rein, their reigning atmosphere was self-consciously Iranian and Shia.*

The Buyids adopted the old title of *Shahanshah*, or King of Kings, used by great Persian emperors from Cyrus to the Sasanians. It was in Buyid times, in Baghdad, that Shiism completed its evolution into an explicit and well-defined religious tradition of its own. The Buyids instituted the Muharram, the Shia festival of grief commemorating the martyrdom of the Imam Hussein at Kerbala, and promoted Shia pilgrimages to that city and Najaf. They fostered silverwork and painted miniatures that, in their depictions of human figures in lush gardens surrounded by plants and animals—images traditionally not allowed in Sunni art—harked consciously back to Sasanian, pre-Islamic Iran.

Language and poetry were a part of the Buyids' cultural-ideological line of Persian revivalism. For centuries after the Muslim conquest, the occupiers and their heirs had barred the Persian tongue from public use in Iran. Writing over the course of forty-three years (977–1010) at the height of the Buyid period, the Khorasani poet Ferdowsi produced a poem called the *Shahnameh*, or *Book of Kings*. Four times the length of the *Iliad*, it is Iran's national epic. Ferdowsi's creation of the *Shahnameh* was a conscious act of cultural rescue and regeneration after the centuries of Arab dominance. Writing in his native tongue, Ferdowsi strenuously purged Arabic influences from the Persian language of the time. Doing so, he established in this one long poem the Farsi language as it has, in

---

* Mutannabi, a poet from Kufa whom the Buyids encouraged, gave his name to the Baghdad street that is still the city's center for booksellers.

essence, been spoken for the last thousand years. Ferdowsi's disdain for
the Arabs was clear:

> O Iran! Where have all those kings . . . who decorated You with pomp
> and splendour gone?
> From that date when the barbarian, savage, coarse Bedouin Arabs sold
> your king's daughter in the street
> And cattle market, you have not seen a bright day, and have lain hid
> in darkness.

The Buyids, originally founded by three sons of a Caspian Sea fish-
erman called Buya, were not so much a dynasty as a confederacy of
related clans. Inevitably they fought with each other as well as with their
neighbors. Politically their period was chaotic. They presented themselves as the protectors and sword arms of the caliphs in Baghdad but,
like the mamluks of Samarra, were essentially their captors. An insight
into the state of the caliphate in the Buyid years is provided by a note
from the caliph Al Muti (d. 974) to the Buyid prince of the day, who had
asked for support in the fighting against the Byzantines:

> The Sacred War would be incumbent on me if the world were in my
> hands, and if I had the management of the money and the troops.
> As things are . . . all I have is a pittance insufficient for my wants, and
> the world is in your hands . . . All you can claim from me is the name
> which is uttered in the khutbah [prayer] from your pulpits as a means
> of pacifying your subjects.[8]

In 1055, an illiterate Turkish chieftain, Tughrul Bey of the House of
Seljuk, entered Baghdad on horseback after alighting from a barge at a
gate on the Tigris. The Turk had defeated the Buyids in western Iran
and northern Iraq, opening the way to Baghdad and driving away the
caliph's Shia captors. Now Tughrul rode to the caliph's palace and dismounted. The exterior of the building may well have been quite plain.
Inside would have been at least one large courtyard lined with vaulted
arches resting on rounded pilasters. The walls and arches were probably

covered in colored stucco and arabesque carvings, the floor marble if not tiled.

After 110 years of chaotic rule by the Buyids, Baghdad in 1055 offered more prestige than power to Tughrul Bey. By the time he took the city, "the once-worldwide Arab Empire," in the words of the Orientalist S. B. Miles, the British Resident in Baghdad in 1879, had "so dwindled and sunk into so low a condition of impoverishment, degradation, and decrepitude that it was at death's door."[9]

On foot, surrounded by the leading noblemen of his own nomadic warrior court, all of them disarmed, the Turk entered the palace.[10] The long path that had taken these men to Baghdad, especially through rich Khorasan, had afforded them pillaging of historical proportions. In Mesopotamia, it was said that the Turks raped every woman they could find.

In front of Tughrul and his Seljuk lieutenants, the twenty-sixth Abbasid caliph sat on a golden throne. His name was Al Qaim: "he who carries out the will of God." A screen of hanging textiles partly shielded the caliph from the eyes of the barbarians. On his shoulders was the black mantle of the Prophet Mohammed. In his right hand Al Qaim carried the Prophet's staff. High functionaries around him may have been wearing the Abbasid black; others would have been wearing silk clothes of probably any color except saffron, considered garish in Abbasid high society, and yellow, associated with dhimmitude since the laws of Mutawwakil.

Tughrul, a great conqueror already, "approached the sacred presence on foot and unarmed."[11] Gibbon, with characteristic archness, here refers to the Turk as a "shepherd." Tughrul was at that stage a shepherd who had in twenty years elevated his tribe from bandit herdsmen to masters of an empire little different geographically from Cyrus's at its peak. The shepherd strongman wanted the caliph's prestige; the caliph, usually little more than a hostage in his own city, wanted Tughrul's armed might. Both Tughrul and Al Qaim had strong Sunni views at odds with the Shia leanings of the Buyids.

Seeing the Caliph of Islam for the first time, Tughrul Bey fell to his knees and kissed the ground. Then Tughrul was led to a throne of his own near Al Qaim's. Gibbon called the ceremony "a solemn comedy . . . the triumph of religious prejudice over barbarian power." But it may just as well have been an expression of the enduring religious importance of the office of caliph. These great conquerors, after all, would later prove themselves again and again to be zealous true believers. As for Tughrul,

> A decree was then read, appointing him the Viceregent of the Successor of the Prophet and Lord of all Moslems. Seven robes of honor and seven slaves were then bestowed upon the Seljuk to symbolize the seven regions of the Caliphate; a rich brocade scented with musk was then draped over his head, surmounted by twin crowns to signify kingship of Arabia and Persia.[12]

Tughrul and Al Qaim made a bargain. The Seljuks would destroy the principal Shia political power of the day, the Fatimid dynasty in Egypt, and restore the Sunni empire under the spiritual authority of the caliph. Al Qaim would confer upon the Seljuks the blessings and bona fides of the caliph of Sunni Islam. But in the ensuing years of fighting it was the Shia Fatimids who took Baghdad, in 1058, rather than the Sunni Seljuks who took Cairo, and the caliph Al Qaim was made a captive of the Shias once more. In 1060 Tughrul took Baghdad again and demanded the hand of the caliph's daughter. The Seljuk duly received her troth. Apparently, however, it was never completed, this beguiling union of a product of the perfumed, secluded hothouse that was the Abbasid harem with a blood-soaked Turk of the great northern prairie, a seventy-year-old man hardly separable from his horse. Tughrul died on campaign in 1063.

In 985, on the banks of the Jaxartes River in what is now southern Kazakhstan, Tughrul's grandfather Seljuk Bey (d. ca. 1009) had converted himself and his tribe to Islam. For the next century at least, the Seljuk dynasty sustained the zeal of the recently converted. Since Umayyad times, and through the worldly Persianate centuries of the Abbasids thus far, the temporal leadership of the Muslim world had been relatively indifferent to the timeless requirement of offensive jihad. The frequent border fighting with the Byzantine neighbors during this period was not expansionist. But the Seljuks were different: fervent Sunni Muslims, frontiersmen with the habit of holy war against the infidel, nomads of the harsh open spaces, reminiscent of the first soldiers of the faith. The

Seljuks were, as H. G. Wells wrote in his perceptive 1920 two-volume *Outline of History*, "Moslems of the primitive type, men whom Abu Bekr would have welcomed to Islam."[13]

The Seljuks were the first of the great Turkish dynasties that thenceforth dominated the broader Fertile Crescent until the early twentieth century. The Seljuk revival of Sunni Islam would in many ways shape the Middle East ever after. For roughly the century on either side of the year 1100, the Seljuk Turks ruled over much the same basic footprint as the Iraq-centered Asian empires of the Achaemenids, the Macedonians, the Parthians, the Sasanians, and the early Abbasids. Mutawwakil's murder by his own Turkish slave-soldiers in 847 had initiated two centuries of petty, feuding dynasties. Now, under the Seljuks, a single Muslim family held sway once more from the frontiers of India to the eastern Mediterranean.

When the Seljuks arrived in the Fertile Crescent, the region was still largely Christian. In the four centuries since the time of the conquests that followed the death of the Prophet, most local people in the Dar al Islam had not converted. Formal Islam's restrictions on the dhimmi were largely ignored in the centuries after the first Muslim generation died out, and with the lucrative era of Muslim conquests long gone, the incentives to abandon the old faiths were minor. Now, under the more observant rule of the Seljuks, dhimmitude became less attractive as the strict old rules of early Islam were dusted off. The process of mass conversion began.

The caliph Al Qaim accepted Tughrul Bey as his sultan (a title literally meaning "power"). With this, the office of sultan, a political ruler sitting in parallel to the spiritual figurehead of the caliph, had come to Islam. It started well, as Tughrul Bey "took the government into his firm grasp" and reinvigorated the empire. "The dismembered provinces were once more brought back together, order and prosperity took the place of tumult and decay."[14]

Tughrul died in 1063. His successor, nephew Alp Arslan, was a famous archer, a tall man with "such long moustaches that they had to be tied up when he shot."[15] His name, meaning "conquering lion," was well deserved. In the east, Alp Arslan conquered western Afghanistan, where the principal city, Herat (once Alexandria-in-Aria), has ever been a part of the Iranian world. In the west, recalling that his uncle had retaken Baghdad from the Shia Buyids, Alp Arslan's principal priority was the chastisement of a much greater Shia power. Based in Cairo since they had founded it in 969, the Fatimids, so called because of their descent from Ali and his wife Fatima, controlled an empire from Sicily to the Syrian coast and most of the way down both shores of the Red Sea. Alp Arslan seized Mecca and Medina back from these North African apostates whose namesake, Mohammed's daughter, had been born in one of these holy cities and married in the other.

The Conquering Lion also took seriously the duties of the jihad, with immeasurably more impactful results than Tughrul had had. For the *Rumi* of Constantinople, the Seljuks were the greatest threat they had seen for four hundred years.[16] Khalid ibn al Walid, Sword of Allah, had been the last menace of their caliber. From 1068 to 1070, Alp Arslan sent armies to invade Byzantine Anatolia three times. The emperor Romanus IV Diogenes repulsed each invasion, forcing the Turks back across the Euphrates. Finally, in 1071, at Manzikert near Armenia in the far east of the Byzantine possessions, a jealous courtier catastrophically betrayed Romanus in the midst of battle, and Alp Arslan beat the *Rumi* at last. It was a historic victory.

"In this fatal day," wrote Gibbon of the great battle at Manzikert, "the Asiatic provinces of Rome were irretrievably sacrificed."[17] Manzikert changed the Anatolian heartland from Christian to Muslim, permanently shifting the balance of power in the lands north and west of Iraq.

Within a decade, the Byzantines themselves were widely acknowledging the Battle of Manzikert as the beginning of the end of the Roman Empire. Alp Arslan's victory at Manzikert was, for the eastern Romans, "the greatest disaster suffered by the Empire in the seven and a half centuries of its existence" up to then.[18] In the battle's aftermath, the Conquering Lion famously asked Romanus what he would have done had the roles been reversed, now that the battle was over.

"Perhaps I would kill you, or exhibit you in the streets as a prisoner," said Romanus.

"My punishment is far heavier," the Turk answered him. "I forgive you and set you free."

After this ritual humiliation, Alp Arslan treated his conquered foe with great respect, hoping for peace on the northwest frontier so that he could focus on the war with the Fatimids. Romanus's own people did not treat him so well. He ended his days stinking like a corpse as he wandered on a donkey, blinded by his enemies in Constantinople, his face a crawling mess of worms.

Manzikert was a watershed in history, but Alp Arslan's greater concern was the ongoing conflict with the Shia apostates of Fatimid Egypt. He imposed a manageable tribute on Romanus, allowed him to keep Anatolia, arranged marriage between two of their children, and sent the emperor home to Constantinople with gifts and an ostentatious escort. Most of Romanus's army survived too. But civil war soon followed the weakened Byzantine emperor's return to his capital, and Rome's eastern frontier had been pierced. Turks of various stripes, Seljuk or otherwise, flooded Anatolia, never to leave. By 1080, nine years after Manzikert, the Turks had occupied thirty thousand square miles of the Anatolian hinterland, lands that since the seventh century had been the core of the Eastern Roman Empire.

Alp Arslan died in 1072. His tomb at Merv, in present-day Turkmenistan, bore an epitaph, a model, perhaps, for that of Percy Bysshe Shelley's apocryphal Ozymandias:

Thou hast seen Alp Arslan's head exalted in the sky
Come to Merv and see how lowly in the dust that head doth lie[19]

Alp Arslan's son Malik Shah, in his twenty-year rule, brought the Seljuk Empire to its brief apogee, conquering Bokhara and Samarkand in the east and most of Egypt and Syria in the west.[20] With Syria came Jerusalem, where in 1073 the Seljuks celebrated the capture of the city from the Fatimids with a spasm of religious violence, slaughtering three thousand of the city's Shia and Christian inhabitants.

"They robbed and murdered and ravished and pillaged the storehouses," according to a Jewish poet in Jerusalem at the time, who had also seen the Turks invade Fatimid Egypt in the same campaign. "They were a strange and cruel people, girt with garments of many colours, capped with helmets black and red, with bow and spear and full quivers.

They burned the heaped corn, cut down the trees and trampled the vineyards, and despoiled the graves and threw out the bones."[21]

The Turks' "spirit of native barbarism, or recent zeal," as Gibbon put it, led to significant new oppression for Jerusalem's native Christians, and for the pilgrims from Latin Europe who made the arduous voyage to the holy city. The Seljuks dragged Jerusalem's Orthodox patriarch through the streets by his hair and threw him into a dungeon. "The pathetic tale" of the Christians in Jerusalem, wrote Gibbon, "excited the millions of the West to march under the standard of the cross to the relief of the Holy Land."[22] By 1074, three years after Manzikert, Pope Gregory VII was issuing the first call for a European army to march east and "take up arms against the enemies of God and push forward even to the sepulchre of the Lord."[23]

The call in Europe swelled for twenty years, until Pope Urban II preached the First Crusade at Clermont and then across southern France in late 1095. An embassy had come from the Byzantine emperor in March of that year, pleading for assistance in the face of mounting Seljuk conquests.[24] *

Throughout the Seljuk period Baghdad remained the seat of the Abbasid caliphs. But for the men who actually ruled, the city had otherwise lost its importance. Alp Arslan and Malik Shah, the two sultans representing the Seljuk peak, visited the city a single time between them. Their capital was Isfahan, and the four other capitals that later Seljuks had were all in Iran too. Malik Shah died in 1092, at the age of thirty-nine. After him, the dynasty collapsed into the usual fratricide.

———

In 1098 and 1099 the European Christians of the First Crusade, after fighting their way through Seljuk Anatolia, conquered a string of important cities of the Syrian littoral. First came the former Seleucid capital of Antioch, a largely Christian city. Syria had always enjoyed a voluptuous

---

* Percy Sykes argues that when, in 1010, at a time of increasing Western European pilgrimages to the Holy Land, "the mad Fatimite Hakim Biamrillah . . . destroyed the buildings of the Holy Sepulchre . . . the Crusades became inevitable, although eighty years were to elapse before the movement gained sufficient strength for action." Sir Percy Sykes, A History of Persia, 3rd ed. (London: Macmillan, 1963), vol. 2, p. 43.

reputation among the Greeks and Romans. Gibbon noted that once there, the Crusaders, engaged as they were in a holy war, might have been expected to lead "a sober and virtuous life." Instead, the Franks outside Antioch displayed "such scenes of intemperance and prostitution" as would have been notable even in an ordinary secular conflict.[25]

The Crusaders' desperate nine-month siege of Christian Antioch led to extraordinary scenes of starvation, famine, and desertion among the invaders. The count of Flanders was reduced to begging for lunch. Godfrey of Bouillon had to borrow a horse.[26] Farther down the coast, at Maarat al-Numan, a contingent of starving peasant Crusaders welcomed the new year, 1099, by feasting upon the locals. "I shudder to tell that many of our people, harassed by the madness of excessive hunger," wrote the chronicler Fulcher of Chartres, "cut pieces from the buttocks of the Saracens already dead there, which they cooked, but when it was not yet roasted enough by the fire, they devoured it with savage mouth."[27]

Another Frankish chronicler recalled that the Crusaders at Maarat "boiled pagan adults in cooking-pots, impaled children on spits and devoured them grilled."[28] Tripoli, Beirut, Sidon, Tyre, and Haifa submitted in turn to the Christian warriors. Finally, on July 13, 1099, the Crusaders took Jerusalem. The sack began immediately. Soon the horses of the Frankish knights were up to their knees in blood, according to a Christian chronicler who was present. "Jews were burnt inside their synagogue," according to a modern history of the Crusades, and "Muslims were indiscriminately cut to pieces." As a silver lining, noted one Jew who survived, after this particular siege "the Christians did not rape their victims before killing them as Muslims did."[29]

Small groups of Muslim refugees made their way to Baghdad, bringing accounts of the Christian massacres and pleading for revenge. The victims of the Crusaders found no sympathy among their fellow believers. The caliph was powerless to help them had he cared to, which he did not. The feuding Seljuk princelings ignored the refugees, and so did the ordinary people of the *umma*. In regional terms the Frankish appearance on the Syrian coast played out mostly as an intervention in feuds between the Shia Fatimids, the Sunni Seljuks, and various local powers. It had no impact farther east, in Iraq. And in Persia, where resided the true weight of affairs for the Muslim world of the day, "no one took any political notice of it."[30]

The Crusades, responding in part to the disruptive new phenomenon of the Seljuks' bellicose Sunni orthodoxy, coincided with a major shift in Islamic history. The great Muslim powers preceding the Seljuks had borrowed hungrily from the West. The Umayyads had taken what they could from the Hellenistic Romans of Byzantium and Damascus, in fields as varied as administration and architecture. The Abbasids, with their translation movement and more, had extended this deep into the intellectual realm. Seljuk pusillanimity, based on a revivalist, originalist view of the faith itself—a view eschewed by both Umayyads and Abbasids—slammed this door shut. Under Abbasid rulers such as Mamoun, the ongoing fighting with the Byzantines had, like the wars between the ancient Greeks and Persians, never precluded a fruitful cultural exchange. Any such diffidence in the jihad ended under the Seljuks.

With the Seljuk closing of the Sunni world by the turn of the twelfth century, it was as if, in the orthodox faith, the ultimate defeat of Mamoun had finally come. Bernard Lewis points out the irony of the timing: "This self-containment of Islam was completed at the time of the Crusades, just when the Western world, in spite of all its fundamental opposition to Islam, was largely becoming receptive to the oriental civilization it encountered, not only in the Holy Land, but also in Spain and southern Italy."[31] These were the lands where the Great Transmission, the passing to Europe of elements of the classical Greek legacy from Arabic-speaking lands during the Abbasid Caliphate, had its start in this period.

For the lands around Iraq, the later eleventh century, roughly the generation from the death of Tughrul in 1063 to the death of his grandson Malik in 1092, would prove to be the last golden age for almost five hundred years. While Alp Arslan and Malik Shah quelled revolts, rebuffed incursions, and extended the borders, a single man administered the Seljuk Empire through both reigns: the great vizier Nizam al Mulk (1018–1092). Twenty years after the illiterate Tughrul had abased himself before the powerless caliph Al Qaim in Baghdad, Nizam, one of the greatest administrative figures in Muslim history, ran a state of such efficiency that it was said he "paid the boatmen on the Oxus by bills on Antioch . . . and they were readily cashed."[32] One result, no doubt, of the grand vizier's flashy act was the fostering of a sense of "knowledge of, and pride in, the Empire."[33]

Al Mulk was no less ardent a Sunni Muslim than were his Seljuk masters and their fathers. The numerous theological colleges that he founded, known eponymously as Nizamiyyas, provided the model for the madrassah, the Muslim school where Koran and hadith are memorized alongside other elements of Sunni learning such as grammar, classical Arabic, and the knowledge tools of commerce and war. Nizam al Mulk opened the most famous of his schools of Sunna in Baghdad in 1067. There the archconservative theologian Abu Hamid al Ghazali, a protégé of the vizier's, wrote his most influential work, the *Tahafut al Falasifa*, or *Incoherence of the Philosophers*. The twenty-chapter work would be known by the Franks and Romans as the *Destructio Philosophorum*. In it, Ghazali, like his intellectual predecessor Ashari, turned the intellectual tools of the Mutazilites back against them. Ghazali is often described as the most important Sunni thinker of all. By Seljuk times, however, two centuries of Sunna's triumph, beginning with the conservative caliph Mutawwakil's crushing of the Mutazilites, had made his intellectual rebuttal of the philosophers barely necessary.

The *Incoherence*'s vehemently Sunni conclusions notwithstanding, as a matter of method—reasoned argument using the rules of classical logic— Ghazali's great work was a fundamentally Hellenistic undertaking. This presented a paradox. It was the same problem that the Hanbalites had found with Shafii, who had worked so hard to provide their simple truth with a theology. The author of a book like Ghazali's would never be truly at one with the laws of seventh-century Medina, however strenuously he might exert the tools of Aristotle in their defense. By the end of the eleventh century, during a decade-long retreat from the world, studying mysticism and seeking a satisfactory approach to his faith from Jerusalem to Mecca to Khorasan, Al Ghazali ultimately found himself foreswearing hadith and advocating that the pursuit of mystical inner states comple- mented a true adherence to the sharia.[34] In works like his *Deliverance from Error* (also known as the *Path to Sufism*), he would advocate instead a return, as he saw it, to spirituality in Islam. It was an approach that became Sufism: a direct, unmediated communion with the Almighty.

Mysticism within Sunni Islam had existed before Al Ghazali. But it took Ghazali's stature, Ghazali's brilliance, to bring it inside the perimeter walls of the orthodox faith. There Sufism would enjoy an established but inescapably subversive position evermore. Coming from Islam's Destroyer of the Philosophers, here was a second enormous accom- plishment. The historian Arnold Toynbee called this feat, the validation of Sufism as a part of Sunni Islam, a "tour de force," without which "the Sunnah might have failed to gain a hold on human hearts."[35]

Late in the Seljuk period, at Cordoba, capital of far-off Umayyad Spain, a lone Arab thinker was fighting the last great intellectual action in the doomed service of reason's place in the orthodox faith. The Andalusian polymath Ibn Rushd, remembered in the West as Averroes, wrote upward of sixty works of philosophy and science. His *Incoherence of the Incoherence*, produced in 1180, was a strong, targeted refutation of Ghazali aimed at an orthodox audience. "Truth does not contradict truth," Averroes wrote in defending philosophy's ability to coexist with Islam. The widespread making of paper and the hungry adoption of the printed word in the Muslim world of this period meant that the ideas of dueling intellectuals like Averroes and Ghazali could receive wide attention. By the time of Averroes, the libraries of the major cities of the Islamic world were the largest on earth—bigger than those of China and much larger than anything in Europe outside of Constantinople.

In his case against Ghazali, Averroes cited physical causation as a primary example. The humanist tradition had not forgotten its founding link between science and philosophy. Like Aristotle, the great Abbasid intellectuals were scientists as well as philosophers and saw no difference between the two. The hallmark of the High Abbasid intellectual world, a cultural moment that was still strong during much of the Seljuk political period, was that each side in the great conflict, humanists and Sunnis alike, understood this.

Ghazali took the classical Sunni view of physical causation: that it did not exist. This was Asharite voluntarism, the metaphysics at the heart of theological (as opposed to hadith-based) Sunnism at the time when the gates of *ijtihad* were slammed shut. God causes everything. Physically as much as morally, we live in a world of His pure will. In the *Incoherence of the Incoherence*, Averroes writes:

Ghazali says: "According to us the connexion between what is usually believed to be a cause and what is believed to be an effect is not a necessary connexion . . . e.g. the satisfaction of thirst does not imply drinking, nor satiety eating, nor burning contact with fire, nor light sunrise, nor decapitation death . . . and so on for all the empirical connexions existing in medicine, astronomy, the sciences, and the crafts . . . on the contrary it is in God's power."[36]

This was indeed how Averroes's opponents saw the world. We cannot understand it, we cannot influence it, we can only submit. Averroes disagreed, but he was no liberal revolutionary. He was in many ways a straightforward Sunni jurist of the Maliki school who repeated mainstream jurisprudence on almost all topics dear to conservatives. He undoubtedly believed. Among his arguments for Islam's superiority is the claim that its rewards in the afterlife, so desirable and so material, "are far more conducive" to the virtuous life than the purely spiritual rewards of other faiths.[37]

The works of Averroes mark the culmination of the Hellenistic intellectual tradition in the Arabic-speaking world, but they also mark its swan song. His attempt to make room for reason and causation was the last gasp to claim the faith for humanism and science as the Mutazilites had tried to do early in the Abbasid period. Three centuries after Mamoun, Averroes was too late. By the late twelfth century, after Ghazali's coup de grace, the triumph of Sunna was complete. The earlier victory of Shafii, Hanbal, and Ashari would never be overturned, and the writings of Averroes sank almost without a trace in the Dar al Islam. Their dreary and obscure demise would be the final episode in a story that had begun with the Syriac scribes scribbling translations of Galen and Plotinus in the House of Wisdom in far-off Baghdad during the time of Mansour and Mamoun.

In Catholic Europe, however, the Andalusian's influence changed the course of the world. Averroes was translated first into Hebrew by impressed Spanish Jews, especially the great Maimonides (d. 1204), and then into Latin by Cordoba's Christian intellectuals. Averroes's work then made its way to the universities emerging in Northern Europe, in particular at Paris and Oxford.[38] There, his commentaries on the works of Aristotle almost singlehandedly placed Greek philosophy at the heart of the emerging European intellectual tradition. For the next four hundred years or more, when a student read Aristotle at a Western university (all did, philosophy being required in every curriculum), the chances were that he read it with Averroes's commentaries on the facing page. The Arab was known simply as the Commentator, while the Greek, Aristotle, was the Philosopher.

As the modern Western mind was born over the coming two centuries, the Philosopher and the Commentator stood as twin pillars. This was already true by the time of Thomas Aquinas (d. 1274), who studied Averroes closely in developing the reconciliation of reason with his faith. Averroes's great contribution to the world of Latin Christendom was in effect to make "a sharp division between religious and scientific truth."[39] This meant that God and science could coexist. If scientific law did not clash with God, neither did logic, reason, or "natural" (i.e. moral) law. law. Ironically, Averroes's attempt to rescue Islam, his contention that objective truth and the human mind were no enemy of the faith, rescued Christianity instead. The Cordoban Muslim's updating of Aristotle for the monotheistic context, intermediated by Aquinas, was unsurpassed as an intellectual factor in making possible the surge of Europe into the Renaissance and beyond.

In 1193, the Sunni city fathers of Cordoba expelled Ibn Rushd from the city of his birth. Two centuries earlier, Cordoba, capital of the Umayyad mini caliphate in Al Andalus, had been a model of open-mindedness. Averroes was perhaps thinking of the cosmopolitan sophistication of this lost world when he defended the Koran's divine origins by saying that no mortal, especially not an "illiterate" from "a primitive, bedouin milieu," could have written it.[40] In 1198 the Sunnis banished Averroes from Spain altogether. He moved on to North Africa and died that year. A bonfire of his books lit the central square of Cordoba.*

———

The crucial influence of the Seljuks in the formation of what would become the modern Middle East receives little recognition. By the time of their advent in the mid-eleventh century, Sunni Islam was in potentially terminal trouble. All of the key lands of the original Islamic empire were now in "apostate" Shia hands. Apart from Arabia, which had been

———

* This was not limited to Cordoba. A thirteenth-century Moroccan historian described watching horse-loads of Averroes's works arrive in Fez to be burned.

barely consequential since Umayyad times except as a place of pilgrimage, all that remained to Sunni rule was Spain, parts of North Africa, and Anatolia. The Shia Fatimids ruled Egypt and the Levant, claiming the universal caliphate for their own. The Shia Buyids dominated Iraq and held the Sunni caliphs prisoner at Baghdad. Persia and the east were a vast nest of Shia sectaries. Then came Tughrul Bey and the Seljuks. Thanks to these Turks, from 1055 Baghdad would be a Sunni-ruled city for the next 950 years.

"They caused a great revival of vigour in Islam," wrote H. G. Wells of the Seljuks, "and they turned the minds of the Moslem world once more in the direction of a religious war against Christendom. A sort of truce had existed between these two great religions after the cessation of the Moslem advance and the decline of the Umayyads. Such warfare as had gone on between Christianity and Islam had been rather border-bickering than sustained war. It became only a bitter fanatical struggle again in the eleventh century."[41]

In the Levant, Seljuk fanaticism contributed importantly to a key turning point in Latin Europe's awakening from the Dark Ages. While cut off by Islam from the Mediterranean in Southern Europe and the Levant, Western Europe was a benighted afterthought in world affairs. With the reopening of the Mediterranean thanks to the Crusades and the *Reconquista* in Spain and Sicily that they inspired, Europe's revival began. The Sunni zealots of the Seljuk Empire may well have contributed as much to the eventual European rebirth as did the Hellenistic Abbasids.

In greater Iran, the influence of these Central Asian believers was far more direct. In terms of religion, the Seljuks tried unsuccessfully to scourge Persia, and a Mesopotamia that at the time had become little more than a Persian backwater, of its heretical native tendencies. In terms of governance and culture, however, the Seljuks did the opposite. They allowed local governors a more or less free hand in ruling the Iranian provinces. More important, the Seljuks voraciously embraced Iranian material culture, to which in return they contributed a salutary vigor. Pondering the perfection of a Seljuk masterpiece (the smaller dome chamber of the Friday Mosque at Isfahan, built during the reign of the great Malik Shah) that he encountered while visiting Iran in 1937, the English traveler Robert Byron put it well:

> One wonders what circumstance at that moment induced such a flight of genius. Was it the action of a new mind from Central Asia on the old civilisation of the plateau, a procreation by nomadic energy out of Persian aestheticism? The Seljuks were not the only conquerors of Persia to have this effect.[42]

At the time of the Seljuk arrival in the middle of the eleventh century, almost four hundred years had passed since the completion of the Muslim conquest of Iran in 654. During the Rashidun and Umayyad caliphates, Iran had been under Arab domination. Even the heavily Persified early Abbasids had ruled in Baghdad as Arabs, in Arabic. When the Abbasid caliphs in Baghdad slid into a four-century figurehead status with the murder of Mutawwakil by his Turkic praetorians in 861, Iran had, like Iraq, entered a confused period of minor rulers and dynasties that was cleared up only with the advent of the Seljuks. Now, under the successors of Tughrul Bey, Iran became a significant power again.[43]

Elements of this development were contradictory, for the Seljuks were originally Turks, not Iranians, and, from the Persian point of view, the rankest of barbarians at that. Their aggressive Sunni orthodoxy was fundamentally at odds with Iran's Zoroastrian, Hellenistic ethical and intellectual culture, expressed through the developing faith of Shiism. Perhaps stimulated by these tensions, Seljuk Persia became home to a spectacular cultural flowering that included many of the highest achievements of the greater Abbasid epoch. The Seljuks made Persian their language of government from early on, and Arabic retreated from the inroads it had made in Central Asia and greater Iran.

Nizam al Mulk, the great Seljuk vizier, was the patron of Omar Khayyam, who is remembered in his native Iran as a mathematician more than a poet. Khayyam, the first person to lay out general solutions to the cubic equation, fixed the Iranian calendar to an accuracy of one day in about four thousand years.* Not for a further four centuries would

---

* The effort to solve cubic equations, which involve polynomials with a cube root, had stymied mathematicians of all the great cultures of the world—Indian, Chinese, Greek, Persian—since Babylonian times.

The Seljuk Empire and the Crusades, ca. 1100 AD

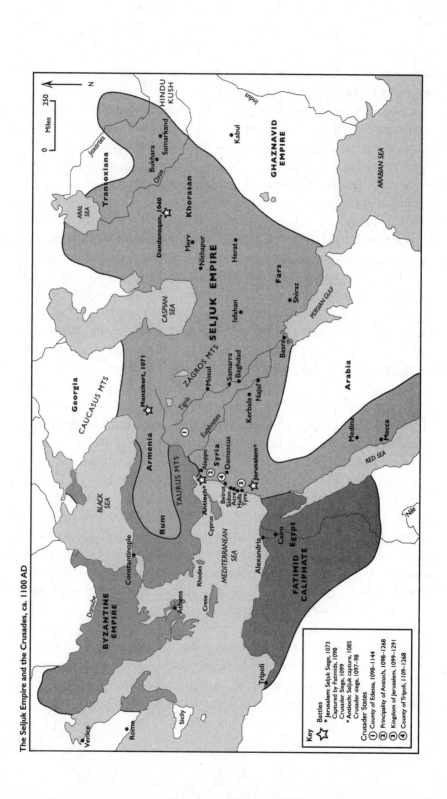

Key

Battles
* Jerusalem: Seljuk Siege, 1073
  Captured by Fatimids, 1098
  Crusader Siege, 1099
* Antioch: Seljuk capture, 1085
  Crusader siege, 1097–98

Crusader States
① County of Edessa, 1098–1144
② Principality of Antioch, 1098–1268
③ Kingdom of Jerusalem, 1099–1291
④ County of Tripoli, 1109–1268

Europe develop and adopt the Gregorian calendar, with its error of one day every three thousand–odd years.

A rival of Nizam built the large domed chamber of the Friday Mosque at Isfahan, a room where the play of soaring physical space and infinite decorative geometry can quite literally take away the breath of a visitor seeing it for the first time. Looking at it a millennium after it was built, one is not surprised that the same culture produced the mystical, almost trancelike poetry of Omar Khayyam.

Looking back on these centuries of the glory of medieval Islam, roughly 850 to 1150 AD, one can say that much of the phenomenon represented evolutions, sharings, and appropriations of an older Iranian civilization. Even in the distant bookends of the Islamic world, Mogul India and Umayyad Spain, this was the case. Of all the bloodlines visible in the Taj Mahal or the Alhambra, the Persian is essential. The world of Islam's extraordinary contribution to global culture in the half millennium after Mohammed consisted largely in serving as the transmitter of the Iranian genius outward from Baghdad to Andalusia, to Samarkand, to Hindustan. The medieval Turks, first the Seljuks and then their grandchildren in the west, the Ottomans, were responsible for at least as much of this transmission as the Arabs had been in their brief primacy. Even classical Ottoman art and architecture of the sixteenth century, as in the great mosque of Sultan Suleiman the Magnificent on the Golden Horn, would be at its best a marriage by Turks of the Persian to the Greek.

In philosophy and poetry, there is a strong current of liberal humanism, much of it likely deriving ultimately from Zoroaster, in the immense contribution of Iran to a medieval world in which Baghdad was more often than not the leading light. Abu Nasr Mohammed al Farrabi (d. 951), who wrote about Plato's "virtuous city" and produced the first system of philosophy in the Islamic world (he was known as the Second Master, after Aristotle), as well as writing about physics, mathematics, astronomy and much more, hailed from the Persian milieu of Khorasan but spent his working life in Baghdad. There were many of these remarkable characters in the long Abbasid world of which the Seljuk period occupied the central century. Where Farrabi and the others touched on religion, a Mutazilite or Shiite inclination is usually detectable.[44]

Seljuk rule, outside of Anatolia, collapsed in the late twelfth century. In Baghdad, the thirty-fourth Abbasid caliph, Al Nasir, was able to shake off three and a half centuries of dynastic torpor and dominate most of Iraq and some of southwest Iran. Much as Nasir's predecessor Al Qaim had done in recruiting the Seljuks to rid him of the Buyids a century and a half earlier, Nasir now called in a new Turkish power from north of the Oxus, the Khwarazmians, to rid him of the later Seljuks. In 1194, the shah of Khwarazm defeated Tughrul III, last of the Seljuks, in battle at Rayy in north-central Iran. The Seljuk's head was sent to Baghdad, where Al Nasir displayed it outside his palace.

Then, in 1219, a new storm arrived over the northeast horizon of the Iranian world and the Fertile Crescent beyond: Genghis Khan and the Mongols. Across a span of almost fifty years, until the death in 1265 of Genghis Khan's grandson Hulagu, the Mongols would subject western Central Asia, Khorasan, much of Iran, and Iraq to some of the greatest mayhem in the history of the world. In the systematic destruction of Baghdad, Merv, Nishapur, Herat, and other cities, the Mongols slaughtered hundreds of thousands at a time. In both the Persian uplands and the Mesopotamian floodplain, they destroyed irrigation systems across vast stretches of the landscape. Starvation and famine killed uncounted millions. In Iraq, the demolition of the irrigation systems had the additional effect of exposing the flat landscape once more to its endemic floods. With the floods returned the twin scourges that the rise of civilization under the Sumerians had largely banished three millennia previously: pestilence and salination of the soil.*

Hulagu approached the Iraqi frontier from northwest Iran in late 1257. He received numerous envoys from the caliph, Al Mutasim, seeking relief from the impending tempest. "Having come so far," Hulagu told one such emissary, he, the Mongol leader, "could not well go back without an audience of the Caliph."[45] Supporting Hulagu's attack upon the seat of the caliphate were many Shias from southern Iraq. A larger

---

* In Iran, it would take seven centuries—until the mid-1900s—for the size of the population to recover from the Mongol devastation and its consequences. Sandra Mackey, *The Iranians: Persia, Islam and the Soul of a Nation* (New York: Plume, 1996), p. 71. Iraq, as far as we can tell, was not much different. Only then was a new system of dykes and channels built in Iraq. These used engineering plans drawn up by yet more invaders, this time the British.

part of his army—almost half by some estimates—comprised Christian cavalry from Georgia.[46]

The destruction dispensed by the great Mongol conquerors of the thirteenth century was not conducted randomly or for pleasure. It was a tool of war, methodical and judicious. Those who accepted vassalage were left to pay tribute in peace. Some of these, including the northern Crusader state of Antioch, saw their territories increase under Mongol rule. Al Mutasim could have chosen this path when the Mongols arrived before Baghdad in 1258. Instead, the last Abbasid caliph listened to his Shia vizier, who advised him that the Mongol army could be driven away even by women, throwing stones from the city walls. The Mongols, guided by their shamans, more successfully sought their guidance in the burned shoulder blades of a sheep.

The City of Peace fell after a siege of almost a month. Breathless Persian accounts of the ensuing week of ceaseless looting and slaughter claim that up to two million inhabitants were put to death.[47] Eight hundred thousand is a more realistic estimate. One Mongol horseman, a lonely sentimentalist in a coldhearted horde, found forty motherless suckling babies in an alley and ended their misery himself. In the caliph's harem alone, seven hundred girls and women were hacked to death, alongside a thousand eunuchs.

The Mongol conqueror's mother was a Christian, as was one of his wives. The Christians of Baghdad were to see their churches and families spared the depredations of the largely pagan and Buddhist invaders. In the massacres of the city's Muslim civilians, the Georgians and other Christian troops of Hulagu's were said to have "greatly distinguished themselves."[48] Baghdad's Shias, like its Christians, were spared. The Jews, however, had fought hard for the caliph and suffered alongside the Muslims in the prodigious rapine.[49]

"Mountains" of gold, silver, jewels, and other booty piled up around Hulagu's tent outside the ravaged city. It was said that the waters of the Tigris ran black with the ink of books from the city's libraries, looted by the barbarians of the steppe. Nasir al Din al Tusi, the last great Abbasid intellectual, who produced the definitive Arabic versions of Euclid, Archimedes, and Ptolemy even as he wrote works of philosophy, theology, and biology, reportedly moved four hundred thousand manuscripts out of Baghdad before the Mongols could destroy them. In an emblematic case of the Fertile Crescent's long history of "the desert and the sown," of warrior peoples from open places conquering and then being civilized by those of the rich settled lands, Al Tusi was to end his days as astronomer and science minister to Hulagu.

Al Mutasim's death at the hands of the Mongols brought to an end half a millennium of Abbasid caliphs in central Iraq. There are several versions of the last caliph's demise. Some accounts relate that Hulagu personally slaughtered the caliph. Echoed in Marco Polo's accounts written forty years later, another telling has Hulagu ordering a platter of gold to be brought to the caliph. "Eat!" commanded the grandson of Genghis Khan.

Mutasim answered that gold could not be eaten. "Then why did you keep it," asks the Mongol, "and not use it to pay your soldiers?"[50] In Europe a related story was told. Hulagu, it was said, starved the caliph to death by locking him in a room with nothing but gold and silver to eat:

Then said Halcon to the Calyf of Baldach; 'because that thou art master and techer of Mahometz laws, we shall make thee fede of these precious tresour and richesses that thou hast loued so moche in this lyfe'. And then Halconcommaunded that the Calyf sholde be put in a close chamber and that some of his tresour sholde be layd before hym, and that he sholde sate of it yf he wolde. And in the same manner the wretched Calyfe ended his lyfe, and nouer sythe was Calyfe in Baldache.
(From a sixteenth-century translation for the third Duke of Buckingham of a history of King Hayton II of Armenia, a vassal of the Mongols)[51]

The most accepted story has the Mongols, to avoid shedding royal blood, rolling Mutasim's body in a carpet and trampling him to death under the hooves of their horses.

The Mongol tide in the Middle East peaked in coastal Syria. Most of the Levant, including Aleppo and Damascus, fell to them quickly in early 1260. A handful of Crusader castles on the northern coast stood out as an island in this sea, although other Crusaders swiftly accepted Mongol vassalage. To the north, the Seljuks of Rum, masters of Anatolia, acknowledged Mongol suzerainty and survived. There was now one last remaining Islamic power of significance anywhere on earth: the Egypt-based Mamluks, who would eventually drive the Crusaders from the Syrian coast at the end of the thirteenth century. Like the Turks who had murdered Mutawwakil, ending the worldly power of the Abbasid Caliphate three centuries before, the Mamluks of Egypt had originally been slave-soldiers—in this case Turks and Circassians from the northern and eastern shores of the Black Sea—who had seized power from their by then effete Arab masters.

In 1260, at a place in southwest Syria called the Spring of Goliath (Ain Jalut, in what is now Palestine), the Mamluks dealt the Mongols their first significant defeat. The Mongol general was a Nestorian Christian. Syria was far from the broad grasslands to which the mounted hordes were accustomed, and Hulagu now gave up on the province. Behind it, Egypt was safe, and with it, Islam. It is a measure of the damage wrought on the faith by the Mongols, and of the importance of the battle at Goliath's Spring, that as Baghdad now slipped swiftly into the status and size of a "small provincial town," in the aftermath of Hulagu's devastation, Cairo would thenceforth emerge as the principal city of learning, religion, and culture in the Muslim world.[52]

This movement of Islam's cultural center of gravity eight hundred miles west, to a location that was almost on the Mediterranean, would prove a boon to an awakening Western Europe. But Cairo's importance in the Muslim world, like that of Umayyad Damascus before it, would never come close to that of Baghdad in its heyday.[53]

A lasting contribution of Mamluk Egypt to the Muslim world was the publication in Cairo in 1368 of the *Reliance of the Traveler*. The twelve-hundred-page *Reliance*, with chapters on topics such as fasting, inheritance, and justice, became the definitive compendium of Sunni law ever after. The book, immediately accepted as conclusive, set a final seal on the conservative victory in the great debate launched by Mamoun, Jahiz, and the other Mutazilites in Baghdad five centuries previously. Sunnism, like any other great religious tradition, would have myriad variants, offshoots, and heresies over the centuries. But the orthodox faith, the version with the direct line to the perfection of seventh-century Medina, would be the one set down in the *Reliance of the Traveler*.

The *Reliance* was a simple codification of the work of the school of Shafii in the ninth century. No change in the creed had occurred in the intervening five centuries. The *Reliance* states, "The good is not what rea-son considers good, nor the bad what reason considers bad. The measure of good and bad . . . is the Sacred Law."[54] The statement was a reflection of the debates from the time of Mamoun and the Mutazilites. From the orthodox Sunni point of view, applying intellect or Logos to religion continued to be worse than almost any other sin. It implied a human sovereignty, in effect a parallel God. This in turn threatened tawhid, the paramount Islamic principle of divine unity. Worshipping a rock, twig, or clay statue was the only thing worse: "For a servant to meet Allah with any other sin than idolatry," read the manual of Sunni law, directly quoting the words of Shafii himself five and a half centuries earlier, "is better than to meet Him guilty of anything of scholastic theology."[55]

The texts had numerous injunctions about the importance of seeking knowledge, but the law was clear that this meant not science or philos-ophy but "sacred knowledge" from its two sources, Koran and hadith. This was material to be learned, not understood or explained: the correct performance of ablutions and prayers; the prohibitions on apostasy and sodomy; the treatment of slaves, animals, children, and women; the rules for wills and divorces; "what is permissible and what is unlawful of food, drink, clothing, and so forth." Certain topics were specifically banned: "Unlawful knowledge," according to the *Reliance*, includes "philosophy, magic, astrology, [and] the sciences of the materialists."[56]

Hulagu died in 1265. His descendants ruled Mesopotamia and Persia, and a declining number of neighboring territories, until about 1350. Known as the Ilkhans, or "sub-khans," denoting an increasingly nominal fealty to the Great Khan in China, the Mongol rulers of Iraq and Iran devoted themselves to culture with some seriousness, although much less than had the Seljuks before them. Thanks to the investiture in Baghdad in 1282 of a Sunni son of Hulagu, the Ilkhans were Muslims, but they possessed none of the Seljuks' Islamic fervor.

At Soltaniyeh in northwest Iran, the Ilkhan ruler Oljeitu built him-self a mausoleum, completed in 1313, that is a fine example of the creative power that flowed into Persian architecture from the periodic injections of "Central Asian virility" of which the Mongols were one.[57]

Rumi (d. 1273) and Saadi (d. 1291), two of the three or four poets seen as
defining post-Muslim Iranian literary civilization, lived in the lands under
Ilkhan sway. Rumi, like Omar Khayyam in the previous century, was a
representative of the broader period's rich tradition of liberal mystical
poetry written in Persian. Rumi became known in Persian as *Mawlana*,
the Master, and his son founded a Sufi order named after him called
the Mevlevis, or "Whirling Dervishes," based at Konya in present-day
Turkey. Certain later Ottoman sultans were said to be closet Mevlevis,
despite their status as caliphs of mainstream Sunni Islam.*

Oljeitu's mausoleum at Soltaniyeh, built 1302–1312, has a double-shelled
dome. It was the largest such dome on earth at the time. Arthur Upham
Pope (1881–1969), an architectural historian of Persia, writes of Soltaniyeh:

> Here grandeur and tranquility both dwarf and magnify; man is both
> diminished and ennobled. There are larger enclosed spaces—the 17th
> century Gol Gunbad in Bishapour (India), the Pantheon in Rome—
> but perhaps none that combines in such transparent unity, power,
> repose and sovereign beauty. It is the visible realization of the poet's
> dream: "a palace as massive as the mountain, resplendent as the stars,
> wide as the land, lifting itself into the sky."[58]

From the start, the Ilkhans existed in a condition of fracture and
decline. Their Iranian chroniclers considered it remarkable when a chief
minister died naturally in office. By 1340 the Ilkhans had lost Baghdad
to a local dynasty, also Mongol, called the Jayalarids.

While the Ilkhans controlled Iraq, the Mamluks of Cairo ruled neighboring Syria. Friction between the two was almost constant. With the
Crusaders perched on the Syrian coast, this Ilkhan-Mamluk rivalry gave
the Mongol rulers of Iraq and Iran common cause with the powers of
Christian Europe. The Christian king of Cilician Armenia (an Armenian
enclave on the eastern Anatolian coast) and the Crusader prince of Antioch
had fought on the Mongol side in the defeat by the Mamluks at Ain
Jalut in 1260. Many Mongols were themselves Christians, followers of the
Nestorian Rite prevalent among Christians in the East during the sixth

---

* Rumi lived mostly in Anatolia; hence his name, "the Roman." There the Seljuks of
Rum continued to be largely independent while acknowledging the suzerainty of the
Mongol khans of Persia.

to fourteenth centuries. The greatest of the Ilkhans, Ghazan, was raised a Christian, converted to Islam upon assuming the throne, and practiced Mongolian shamanism in private thereafter. His brother and successor, Oljeitu, was also raised a Christian before converting at a wife's behest to Sunni Islam, apostatizing to Shiism, and eventually returning to Sunnism.*

The charms of a wife who was a daughter of the Byzantine emperor Andronicus failed to return Hulagu to Christ. Missionaries from England also failed. The Ilkhans swapped embassies with Philip IV of France and Edwards I and II of England, and corresponded with popes and other European princes, all with a view to an alliance against the Mamluks, the Mongols' fellow Sunnis.

Baghdad, meanwhile, was showing some resilience economically, if not culturally or politically. Fifty years after Hulagu sacked it, the Western emissaries to the Mongol's successors would have found a city at least somewhat reminiscent of its Abbasid prime. The most famous dancing girl of Oljeitu's time, known as the Spring of Life, gave the khan "a wonderful gondola on the Tigris, with magnificent star-decorated sails, a curtained canopy in white, and a specially fitted fountain and dancing stage."[59]

A *Pax Mongolica* across the great landmass, from Beijing to Baghdad and Kiev, now provided Silk Road trade with its "best conditions since the early second century AD."[60] For the Crusaders and their supporters in Europe, this sympathetic Mongol power on the far side of the Mamluks gave rise to the legend of Prester John, the Christian savior who would ride from the East to rescue the Holy Land. The Ilkhans and Franks made numerous plans for joint operations in Syria during the last decade of the twelfth century, but nothing came of these hopes. In Baghdad, the seventy years of the Ilkhans after Oljeitu were marked by a bewildering succession of uprisings, assassinations, plagues, and calamitous floods.

———

In 1384, disaster from the eastern steppes returned to the world of the Fertile Crescent. Timur the Lame, a Turkic-speaking warrior from what is now southern Uzbekistan, became known in Europe as Tamerlane.

---

* It is also said that in his first Muslim phase, a thunderstorm nearly converted Oljeitu to paganism. Roger Stevens, *The Land of the Great Sophy* (London: Methuen & Co., 1965), p. 25.

Claiming descent from Genghis Khan, he was in fact the son of a senior minister to one of Genghis's sons. Timur would eventually surpass both Alexander and Genghis in the extent of his conquests. Unlike his predecessors—the various Turkish and Mongol leaders who before him had led their horsemen south across the Oxus and down through Iran's inviting, grassy northeast corridor of conquest—Timur came from literate, sedentary folk. His warriors, however, were still horsemen of the steppe.

Timur's defeat of the Ottoman Turks in 1402 at Ankara, not far from the Byzantine border, earned Christian respect. His spectacular individual gifts and his stupendous embellishment of a new capital at Samarkand appealed to the ambitious, expansive spirit of the European Renaissance, and he impressed himself more strongly upon European culture than had any foreigner since Cyrus. But the Tamerlane persona was altogether bloodier than that of Cyrus. At Isfahan in 1387, Timur commissioned from his warriors a group of pyramids—twenty-eight, in one account—built from the heads of the city's slaughtered residents. The skulls numbered seventy thousand. The incident was characteristic of Timur's behavior from India to Syria. At Tikrit, north of Baghdad, in 1394, the piles were described as "minarets," not pyramids.[61]

Far more than his hero Genghis, Timur evinced an unmistakable joy in the slaughter and destruction that he lavished upon his world. Unlike Genghis, Tamerlane was appreciative of culture—when suitably appropriated to his personal grandiosity. The Mongols had generally been tolerant of, and often sympathetic to, the many Christians in their realms. Timur, calling himself the "sword of Islam" and "scourge of God," professing an "ostentatious Sunni piety," ravaged Christian communities wherever he found them.[62] Christianity effectively disappeared from the region during his time.

The majority of Timur's victims were fellow Muslims. It is doubtful that anybody has caused more harm to individual believers than did the self-proclaimed Sword of Islam. Near Delhi in 1398, Timur flayed alive the captured Hindu troops of his opponent, but merely slit the throats of the Muslim troops who had fought alongside them. At Damascus in 1401, he enjoyed learned theological debates with Sunni scholars before sacking their city.

Samarkand, in present-day eastern Uzbekistan, is located in the far northeast of greater Iran. There, Timur collected the greatest craftsmen and artists of the lands of his wide conquests, from the Black Sea coast to the Indus Valley, and built himself a magnificent Persian city. The Arabs were now a far-off memory. So was their former Baghdad-based empire. Mesopotamia remained a near-irrelevance, although since the Mongol devastations of the thirteenth century, the former Abbasid capital had regained a sizeable population to go with its hoary prestige.

In mid-July of 1401, Timur stormed the City of Peace after a six-week siege. Tough Baghdad, standing up to Genghis Khan for a month and Timur for a month and a half, was different than sultry Babylon had been in ancient times, serenely opening her gates to new gods depending where the power lay. Timur's assault on Baghdad's city walls took place during a July so hot on the scalding Mesopotamian plain that "birds fell down and died, and the soldiers in their cuirasses might be said to have melted like wax."[63] There was sadism even in Timur's choice of the hour of his midsummer assault on baking Baghdad: noon. On pain of death, Timur's ninety thousand soldiers were not allowed to return to camp from the defeated city without at least one head each. Only mosques and hospitals were protected from the devastation inside the city walls. Where the barbarian Hulagu had spared Baghdad's Christians and left the city with an imperial administration, the civilized Timur spared nobody and left the corpse of the city to rot. His was the true calamity from which Baghdad never fully recovered.[64]

Unlike Alexander and Genghis, Timur left no government behind him when he died. Also unlike those two, Timur engendered a distinct artistic flowering, known as the Timurid Renaissance. It scattered pearls of beauty across Central Asia, from mausolea, mosques, and public spaces, as at Samarkand and Herat, to countless miniatures and illustrated manuscripts. Timur's descendants, wrote Robert Byron in his *Road to Oxiana*, "recognized no law of succession. They murdered their cousins, and boast among them one parricide. One after another they drank themselves to death. Yet if pleasure was the object of their lives, these princes believed the arts to be the highest form of pleasure, and their subjects followed their example."[65]

Timur died in 1405. In his aftermath, Iraq was dominated successively by two rival groups of Turkish horsemen from Armenia and northern Mesopotamia, first the Black Sheep and then the White Sheep. The former were Shia and the latter Sunni. Its irrigation long ago destroyed, its cities in ruins, the birthplace and pivot of world civilization was now, by 1402, little more than a large pasture. It was a poor pasture at that: dry, denuded, deluge-prone, depopulated.

In Richard Coke's words, from his history of Baghdad: "The land that had once figured as Paradise in all the holy books of the Semitic religions, now turned into an arid, treeless desert, across which swept every storm with irresistible force, upon which fell alike the pitiless heat of summer and the lingering floods of winter, fed by the errant waters of the great rivers, now for the first time since the great inundation of Noah freed from all human direction and control."[66]

Chapter 15

Shadows of God on the Earth

Suleiman the Magnificent and Shah Tahmasp of Persia

1555

I, the sultan of sultans, and the strongest ruler, the loftiest king who defeats the kingdoms around the world, and the shadow of Allah on the Earth, am the son of Sultan Selim who is the son of Sultan Bayezid, Sultan Suleiman, Caesar of Rome, the sultan of the Mediterranean Sea and Black Sea, and Thrace, and Anatolia, and Karaman and the City of Dulkadir and Diyarbakir and Kurdistan, and Iran and Damascus and Aleppo and Egypt and Mecca and Medinah and Jerusalem and the whole Arab land and Yemen and many more lands that our lofty ancestors conquered with their crushing powers and I conquered with my fire-scattering sword.

—Sultan Suleiman the Magnificent in a
letter to Francis I of France, ca. 1562

In May of 1555, in the hilly northern Anatolian town of Amasya, a Flemish man about forty years old watched from a nearby hill as a feast was served in the garden of a Turkish pasha. The landscape in that part of Anatolia is exceptionally green in spring. A large fortress sat above the town, which was about halfway between the Persian frontier and the Ottoman Turks' capital at Constantinople. The weather was already warm enough for the inhabitants to eat, and even sleep, on the roofs of their clay houses. These reminded the Fleming, Ogier de Busbecq, a newly arrived ambassador to the Ottomans, of houses in Spain.[1]

Busbecq was not invited to the feast, and four months later, having accomplished little on this embassy to the Turks, he was back at the court of his employer, Ferdinand of Austria. Busbecq's Hapsburg master was also king of Bohemia, Hungary, and Croatia, and younger brother of Charles V of Spain, whom he would soon succeed as Holy Roman Emperor. Safely home in Vienna, Busbecq showed a hint of jealousy as he described that May afternoon in Anatolia, with one succulent dish following another for the Sultan's guests while they reclined on their divans in the shade of an awning, not far from a burbling stream. The Hapsburg ambassador's description of this scene is one of many vignettes in a series of four lengthy "letters," known together as *The Turkish Letters*, describing the seven years Busbecq was to spend among the Ottoman Turks.

A new era of writing had arrived in the greater Mesopotamian world. Forty-five centuries had passed since Gilgamesh, King of Uruk, had become the hero of the world's first written epic. Thirteen centuries previously, Arrian had adapted Ptolemy's 350-year-old memoirs of Alexander's campaigns. Seven hundred years had elapsed since Bukhari had sifted through more than two centuries of politicized hearsay to record his definitive collection of the hadiths. Long before that, Herodotus had actually traveled to some of the places that he wrote about, but the history he wrote was all secondhand. Xenophon's *Anabasis* was a firsthand account, but while it told the story of an extraordinary feat that said much about the larger picture, the events it described were not themselves important in the historical scheme. Now, in the middle of the sixteenth century AD, Busbecq's *Turkish Letters* provide the very first personal account, intimate and direct, of great events in the history of the lands of the region.

Busbecq's observations occurred at a key historical moment. Like every other European of his day, it would seem, Busbecq read this moment wrong. He believed he was witnessing Islam's imminent overwhelming of Christian Europe. Instead, what he described happened to be the very time when Muslim and Asian power crested, and a new surge of European power began. The developments revealed by Busbecq portended great changes for Iraq and its environs. His *Letters* provide a rare glimpse of a world at dawn, in this case the political Middle East as it was at the time of Suleiman the Magnificent and as it would remain, essentially, until the First World War.

Busbecq's *Letters*, based on private missives he had originally written to a friend and fellow diplomat, were first published in 1581. By the year 1700 the work had been published in seven languages. During that time, more than twenty editions of it appeared from Glasgow to Leipzig. The popularity of the *Letters* is a measure mostly of the fear, and later the fascination, that the Ottoman Empire inspired in Christian Europe in the sixteenth and seventeenth centuries. The popular success of the *Letters* was also a testament to Busbecq's lively eye, so representative of the vigorous new spirit of curiosity that had risen in Europe during the Renaissance. Busbecq's accounts provided an enchanting story of a tiny cog—Busbecq himself—in the machinery of statecraft, contending, far from home and usually alone, with the mightiest and most frightening power on earth.

The family of Suleiman the Magnificent—the Ottomans—took its name from a forebear called Osman. In 1288, Osman had succeeded to the leadership of a tribe of nomads who had been pushed westward into Anatolia by the Mongols. In Anatolia, Osman's tribe found themselves on the marches where Islam bordered the Byzantines and other, lesser, Christian entities. Constantinople, the Second Rome, was now in its tenth century. It had been weakened badly by the Fourth Crusade, which saw Catholic Christians of Western Europe sack Constantinople in 1204 and occupy it for fifty-seven years. Osman's bands, fighting the Christians, became successful ghazis, or border warriors of the jihad. His success attracted recruits from other Muslim Turkish tribes. As the Ottomans rose, the Byzantines' resistance to the jihad on their frontiers grew weaker and weaker.

By 1346, the position of the Ottoman Turks was strong enough that Osman's son and successor, Orhan, could marry the Byzantine emperor's sixteen-year-old daughter, Theodora Cantacuzene. Within a decade Orhan had established the Turks' first permanent territorial foothold on the European shores of his father-in-law. During that same year, the Ottomans began expanding east into the neighboring Muslim lands of central Anatolia. By the end of the 1370s, Bulgaria and much of Serbia were Ottoman possessions. The Muslim armies were now more than four hundred miles into Europe.

By the turn of the fifteenth century, the Ottomans had reduced the Byzantines to little more than an enclave on the European side of the Bosphorus. In the famous year of 1453, the Ottomans' twenty-one-year-old sultan, Mehmed II, later known as the Conqueror, took Constantinople. The desperately hard-fought fifty-three-day siege very nearly destroyed the Ottomans, who prevailed on what was likely the very last day that Mehmed would have been able to keep his army fighting. Not for over another century, until the siege of Malta in 1566, the year of Suleiman's death, would they lose a significant land battle to any Christian foe.

For more than seventy years after the conquest of Constantinople, the Ottoman writ was limited to southeastern Europe and western Asia Minor, mirroring the later Byzantine Empire that it replaced. Then, under Suleiman's father, Selim, known later as "the Grim," the Ottoman regional state became an empire.

Selim the Grim came to power in 1512 and spent a year killing his brothers and nephews. In 1513, he slaughtered forty thousand Shias in western Anatolia. In 1514 he secured from his clergy numerous fatwas declaring it his Muslim obligation to chastise the broader world of Shia "heretics." The issue had become acute. In Persia a strong new leader had emerged in 1501, Shah Ismail of a family called Safavi. Ismail made Shiism the key rallying cry of the new Iranian empire that he was reconstituting on the Ottomans' eastern border.* Later in 1514, Selim the Grim defeated Shah Ismail at Chaldiran in northwest Iran. In 1516 Selim marched south against the Cairo-based Mamluks, defeating them in Syria that year and in Egypt the next.

In August of 1514, the Ottomans had been little more than the Turkish-speaking owners of the small and largely Christian corpse of the late Byzantine state. By January of 1517 they were the leading power of the Islamic world. The Ottomans' old capital, at the Balkan city of Adrianople until 1453, had been in Europe.† Their new capital, Constantinople, was

---

* Shah Ismail named every one of his six sons, including Suleiman's great adversary Tahmasp, after heroes of Ferdowsi's *Shahnameh*. For the arriviste Safavids, eager to Persify themselves and leave their Turkish origins behind, this national epic poem, fleshed out and put into consciously "pure" Persian language by Ferdowsi in Buyid times, was a potent tool.

† Adrianople is known today as Edirne, at the junction of Turkey's present-day borders with Greece and Bulgaria.

also a European city. Now, quite suddenly, with the conquests of Selim the Grim, the area ruled by the Turks was two-thirds Arabic-speaking and Muslim. Possessing Mecca and Medina, Selim took over the Mamluk title of "Servitor of the Two Holy Cities."* Suleiman, his heir and eldest son, went on to add most of Iraq and Hungary as well as much of the North African coast between Egypt and Morocco.

Ogier de Busbecq had arrived at Amasya in the spring of 1555 following a thirty-day journey from Constantinople. Six weeks later he passed through the Turks' capital again. He would ultimately spend the better part of seven years in the city on the Bosphorus. His tone on initially describing the enemy capital was positive:

> As for the site of the city itself, it seems to have been created by nature for the capital of the world. It stands in Europe but looks out over Asia . . . From the centre of Constantinople there is a charming view over the sea and the Asiatic Olympus, white with eternal snow. The sea is everywhere full of fish . . . such large and densely packed shoals that they can sometimes be captured by hand.

At Amasya, Busbecq had a distinct assignment. He was to secure, if possible, a peace with the Turks in the Transylvanian borderlands of Hungary. Beyond this, merely to meet the Ottoman emperor, the mighty Sultan Suleiman, and to return to Europe with personal impressions of the man and his realm, was also valuable.

The first half of the sixteenth century is unique in history for the grandeur and *virtu* of the princes playing leading roles on the world

---

* The term "caliph" had long since "lost its original meaning" by Selim's time. He coined a new title of Exalted Caliph, denoting an overlord of the Islamic lands deriving legitimacy from rule and from ghazi war against the infidel—rather than from descent from the Prophet's family as in the Abbasid Caliphate. Later, as the Ottomans declined, they adopted a more Abbasid-type role for the caliph, as a religious figurehead for the umma. In the eighteenth century, the Ottomans would invent a story saying that the office of caliph had been formally invested in Selim by Al Mutawwakil III, last of the Abbasid "shadow caliphs" maintained in Cairo by the Mamluks since 1260, following the death of the last Baghdad caliph in 1258. Holt et al., *Cambridge History of Islam*, vol. 1, pp. 320–323.

stage. In a single decade at the end of the previous century, a remarkable group of future sovereigns had been born. Shah Ismail of Persia, founder of the Safavid dynasty that would be Suleiman's great nemesis in the east, was born in 1485. Henry VIII of England was born in 1491, Francis I of France in 1494, and Suleiman himself in 1495. Charles V, king of Spain and Holy Roman Emperor, brother and imperial predecessor of Busbecq's Hapsburg employer, was born in 1500.

As William Stubbs, the founder of modern history studies at Oxford, wrote in 1904, "There may have been greater sovereigns than Charles, Henry, Francis, and Solyman, but there were never so many great ones together, of so well-consolidated dominion, so great ability, or so long tenure of power."[2] Born into this cohort of giants, Suleiman was the most powerful and feared man of his day. Known in Europe as the Grand Turk, and later as the Magnificent, Suleiman was called by his own people *Kanuni*, the lawgiver.*

"Soleiman stands before us with all the terror inspired by his own successes and those of his ancestors," Busbecq wrote about Suleiman. "He overruns the plain of Hungary with 200,000 horsemen; he threatens Austria, he menaces the rest of Germany; he brings in his train all the nations that dwell between here and the Persian frontier."

Busbecq had journeyed to Amasya from Vienna to treat with this fearsome figure. But the feast that the Hapsburg ambassador now beheld, with apparent envy, he watched from afar. The celebration was in honor of another ambassador: the representative of Tahmasp, shah of Persia. This was not good news for a Christian diplomat who believed that only Persia stood between Suleiman and a helpless Europe:

> Persia alone interposes in our favor; for the enemy, as he hastens to attack, must keep an eye on this menace in his rear. But Persia is only delaying our fate; it cannot save us. When the Turks have settled with Persia, they will fly at our throats supported by the might of the whole East; how unprepared we are I dare not say!

In 1524 Tahmasp had succeeded his father, Shah Ismail. Their dynasty, the Safavids, would be at war with the Ottomans, on and off, until the

---

* It marked a connection to the Abbasids of yore that this, Suleiman's principal appellation among his own subjects, came from the Greek word *canon*.

Safavids fell in 1736. Now the two sides were signing a peace whose main import was to ratify Suleiman's conquest of Iraq from the Persians in 1534. The peace ended what came to be known as the First Ottoman-Safavid War, which had gone on, in three phases, since 1532.* Iraq's eastern border never meaningfully moved again.

———

Having conquered Baghdad from the Persians, Suleiman stayed there for four months, from November 30, 1534, until April 1, 1535. S. H. Longrigg, a one-time British colonial administrator who in 1925 published a scholarly and sympathetic history of Ottoman Iraq, *Four Centuries of Modern Iraq*, wrote that Suleiman's new provinces "lay now long ruined by callous oppression, wild, desolate, and disordered from the rock fortress at Mardin to the Shatt ul 'Arab."

Of all Suleiman's major subject cities, Baghdad, with its quasi-Persian history, was by far the most vulnerable to Shiite tendencies. In 1508 Shah Ismail had razed the tombs of the Abbasid caliphs and the important Sunni scholar Abu Hanifa. Suleiman rebuilt them; he had managed, he announced, to find Abu Hanifa's body in a state of perfect preservation in the ruins of the man's sepulcher. The Sultan also funded the reconstruction of various Shia shrines in Baghdad and Najaf.† He extended his tolerance to Jews and Christians. Many of the latter made their way to Baghdad to escape from persecution in Iran. Suleiman made Baghdad the capital of a new, eponymous province and took pains to reform local laws and administration. Iraq was backward and poor by then, but Suleiman took care of it like no other place in his wide domains.

Baghdad would not then have impressed a visitor as the most prepossessing prize in the sultan's orbit. An Englishman of the 1590s described

———

* Twice more after his 1532 conquest of Baghdad, in 1548 and 1553, the Grand Turk marched against the Persians. Suleiman usually defeated them tactically, but he was never able to maintain himself in their principal territories for long enough to force Shah Tahmasp into a decisive battle. Tahmasp repeatedly retreated before the Ottoman armies, scorching the earth behind him.

† In a letter to Francis I of France, Suleiman would make note of his visit to the Shia holy cities. Caroline Finkel, *Osman's Dream: The History of the Ottoman Empire* (New York: Basic Books, 2005), p. 126.

the city much as it would have been in Suleiman's time, as "a towne not very great but very populous, and of great trafike of strangers, for that is the way to Persia, Turkie, and Arabia." The two sides of the city, on the east and west banks of the Tigris, were connected by a "bridge of boats tyed to a great chaine of yron, which is made fast on either side of the river."[3]

Longrigg wrote of Baghdad at the time of Suleiman's conquest, "The most pretentious buildings were the palace and barracks of the governor, the public baths and mosques, and the roofed bazaars. The rest was of shabby, huddled, one-story houses, with windowless walls on the narrow winding alleys. Dates and rice came from lower Iraq, wool from the grazing tribes, wood from Kurdistan, grain from Mosul. Indian goods were brought from Basrah, Levantine from Aleppo, . . . Persian from Karmanshah."

The City of Peace that Suleiman captured in 1534 was a backwater, but far from a ghost town. "Learning was not entirely dead," wrote Longrigg, "security fair within the walls, government venal and capricious, craft and industry at their lowest level, the phrases of religion, as ever, on every lip."[4]

As for Iraq itself, in the first half of the sixteenth century, Longrigg wrote, "Few lands of ancient renown have faded before the eyes of the later world to more obscurity than that spread over the Tigris and Euphrates valleys in the early sixteenth century." For Europeans, even trade had begun to abandon Iraq in the new world of sea routes to the Indies, and Iraq's value as the "land-bridge joining Mediterranean to Persian waters" had much diminished.[5]

Fly-bitten and forgotten as the city may have been, possession of Baghdad was important to Sultan Suleiman. Memories of the Abbasid Caliphate lent valuable prestige to the Ottomans, a dynasty with relatively recent roots on the fringes of the Islamic world. The city was also important to Suleiman's foe, the Persian shah. Iraq's location continued to be strategic. Despite the new sea routes of the Portuguese navigators, Mesopotamia's two great rivers continued to provide an important trade link between India and the Mediterranean.[6] Forty years after Suleiman's death, Ralph Fitch, the leading English merchant traveler of his day, was still calling Baghdad "the way to Persia, Turkie, and Arabia."

In the south of Iraq, a visitor traveling in a marsh boat "along willow or date-lined streams ever dividing and reforming, saw rare patches of sown maize and barley, herds of buffaloes, reed-matting villages of the marshmen, and black tents of the shepherd tribes forced by drought from steppe to river-side." Basra was a place where "Portuguese and Persian and the Arabs" competed for dominance.* Farther north, above Fallujah and Samarra, where "silt gave place to gravel and rock, flatness to undulation, signs of mineral wealth appeared. For the few cultivators, waterwheels and the more copious rain replaced flood-channels and . . . mud-huts the tent or reed-hut."7 At Mosul, "base for the cities of central Kurdistan," a state of "shabby disrepair" reigned inside the impressive city walls. Kurdish merchants traded in gall nuts, raisins, and gum.

"Trade was brisk, agriculture in constant danger of drought and locusts. The quarrels of Christian sects outdid in bitterness the chronic factions of the Mosul families."8

As for the people of the country, "in race Iraq was never an Arab country. From Sumerian to Mongol, wave after wave of conquest had added new elements to its blood, which in the dawn of history was neither Arab nor Semitic. Its Arab nationality was partly of recent date, preserving the memory of but one of many conquerors."

Eight centuries after the Arab conquest, the country remained diverse in the time of Suleiman the Magnificent.

Persians were domiciled in the Holy Cities, Indians and negroes at Basrah. The "Sabaeans"—quiet silversmiths in river-side villages—were scattered over southern Iraq. Kurdish and Turkish families were long settled in Mosul and Baghdad, where Jews in thousands also plied the trades of their race. Christians were of many sects and origins. In Mosul they formed a great part of the townspeople, and their populous villages covered the low hills to the north . . . Jabal Sinjar and hill-tracts north-east of Mosul held the fierce Yazidis, their hand against all men and every government.9

---

* Portugal was an important player in the Persian Gulf during the sixteenth century. In 1515 the Portuguese captured Hormuz, at the entrance of the gulf into the Indian Ocean; they held Hormuz until 1622. The Portuguese held Bahrain from 1521 to 1602. In 1623 the Portuguese were granted permission to establish a *feitoria*, or trading and customs post, at Basra.

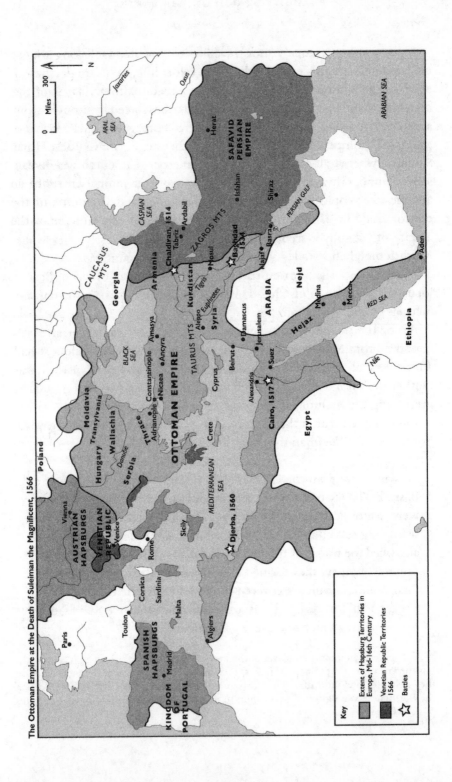

The Ottoman Empire at the Death of Suleiman the Magnificent, 1566

Key

Extent of Hapsburg Territories in Europe, Mid-16th Century

Venetian Republic Territories 1566

☆ Battles

KINGDOM OF PORTUGAL

SPANISH HAPSBURGS

Madrid ● ● Paris

Toulon ●

Corsica
Sardinia
Malta ●
Algiers ●

Rome ●

AUSTRIAN HAPSBURGS

Vienna ●

VENETIAN REPUBLIC

Venice ●

Sicily

MEDITERRANEAN SEA

Crete

☆ Djerba, 1560

Poland

Moldavia
Transylvania
Hungary
Wallachia
Serbia
Thrace
Adrianople

Danube

BLACK SEA

Amasya ●
Constantinople ●
● Ancyra
● Nicaea

OTTOMAN EMPIRE

TAURUS MTS

Cyprus

Beirut ●

Alexandria ●

☆ Cairo, 1517

Egypt

Nile

CAUCASUS MTS

Georgia

Armenia

☆ Chaldiran, 1514

Tabriz ●
● Ardabil

CASPIAN SEA

SAFAVID PERSIAN EMPIRE

● Herat

● Isfahan

Shiraz ●

ZAGROS MTS

Kurdistan
Mosul ●

Tigris

Euphrates

☆ Baghdad 1534

Aleppo ●

Syria
● Damascus

Jerusalem ●
☆ Suez

Najaf ●

Basra ●

PERSIAN GULF

ARABIA

Nejd

Hejaz

Madina ●

● Mecca

RED SEA

Ethiopia

Aden ●

ARABIAN SEA

ARAL SEA

Jaxartes

Oxus

N

0   Miles   300

In 1550, five years before the meeting at Amasya, Suleiman had commissioned Mimar Sinan, the greatest of five centuries of Ottoman
architects, to build a magnificent new mosque in the Turks' capital,
overlooking the deep, curling harbor known as the Golden Horn.
Suleiman's eponymous mosque, completed in 1557, combined Byzantine domes with Ottoman minarets. Above its principal entrance an
inscription proclaimed Suleiman "Possessor of the Kingdoms of the
World, Shadow of God over All Peoples, Sultan of the Sultans of the
Arabs and the Persians."

Each of these claims involved hyperbole, but the final one, that Suleiman was sultan of "the Persians," was not accurate at all. Iran had by
then reemerged as a great power and would present a far greater challenge to Suleiman than Busbecq's Hapsburg employers. For the three
centuries after Iran's rebirth with the Safavid founding in 1501, the key
counterweight and preoccupation for the Ottomans was to be not Europe
but Iran. This of course merely mirrored the ancient pattern, with Iraq
as ever the *limes*.

At the turn of the sixteenth century, in the time of Suleiman's grandfather, Iran had not had indigenous rulers for the full eight and a half
centuries since the time of Khalid ibn al Walid and the Muslim conquests
under the Rightly Guided caliphs.[10] It is a painful record unmatched by
any of the world's other great civilizations: an incalculably rich and
sophisticated land ruled by wave after wave of barbarians, many of them
nomads—first the Arabs, followed by the Seljuks, Mongols, and Tatars
from the eastern plains. Then, during the reigns of Suleiman's father
and grandfather, the third and last great imperial Iranian dynasty, the
Safavids, had risen.

Even these Safavids were originally Turks. The Safavid emergence
began in 1501, when a thirteen-year-old Turkish boy from Ardebil in
northeast Iran declared himself shah, the classic Iranian formulation
for king. Four or five generations of his fathers before him had been
holy men—first Sufis, then Shias—in the borderlands where the eastern
marches of the new and growing empire of the Ottomans met the lands
of the Mongol and then Turkic rulers of Iran. The family, descended
from the seventh Shia Imam in the line begun eight centuries earlier by

Ali and Hussein, were called Safavi.* The boy's mother was a daughter
of the late leader of Iran's rulers at the time, the White Sheep.†

The boy was called Ismail. Said to possess supreme charisma, he was
thought by many to be the Mahdi, the long-awaited Shia messiah. Hardened Turkish warriors from neighboring eastern Anatolia flocked to his
banner, casting aside the Sunni suzerainty of the Ottoman sultans far
away to the west. Fanatical and violent, the Qizilbash ("red heads," after
their red turbans with twelve folds, one for each of the Imams), as these
Shia Turks were called, conquered most of Iran within eight years. Ismail
had now grown into manhood, "fair, handsome, and very pleasing . . . is
as brave as a gamecock and stronger than any of his lords," reported a
Venetian visitor.[11] In 1508, then twenty years old, Ismail conquered Baghdad from his mother's people, the White Sheep Turcomans. There, in
his Shia fanaticism, he destroyed the tombs of the Abbasid caliphs and
slaughtered Sunnis, Jews, and Christians.

Percy Sykes, in his *History of Persia*, tells a story about Shah Ismail
and the Uzbeks, Mongol descendants who had taken Khorasan from
Ismail's White Sheep forebears. When Ismail sent the Uzbeks an embassy
requesting a halt to various depredations, they replied that if he wanted
his inheritance he could have it, and sent him a beggar's bowl and staff.
Ismail sent in return a "spindle and reel," for weaving. "Words," Ismail
signified, "were a woman's weapons."[12]

Across Iran, Ismail's Qizilbash enforced conversions to Shiism. Officials
of the new regime paraded in the streets carrying axes and shouting out
insults to Mohammed's first three Rightly Guided caliphs, men near-
sacred to the Sunnis: "Cursed be Abu Bakr! Cursed be Omar! Cursed
be Uthman!"[13] Anyone in earshot who did not show approval of these
insults faced death. The Iranian populace seems mostly to have accepted
this new state religion that was so deeply rooted in their old, pre-Muslim
faith. The idea of the Mahdi's eventual return, bringing the new age of
righteousness, found a deep-rooted sympathy in the land of Zoroaster,
which had given birth to the very notions of the messianic savior and

---

* The name is said to come either from "sufi" or from "safi" (meaning purity of religion).
Stevens, *Land of the Great Sophy*, p. 27.

† This Turcoman chieftain, one Uzun Hasan, was a vigorous ruler whose hopes of
defeating the Ottomans had been credible enough for far-off Venice to form an alliance
with him.

the End of Days.[14] Among the more recalcitrant ulema, or Sunni clergy, many fled or were killed.[15]

Ogier de Busbecq understood the political importance of Shiism to the Safavids. "The Persian King," he wrote, "was conscious that his dynasty had not long been established and had based its claim to rule on the pretence of religion."

In such a context, Busbecq asked, "who could be certain that among the many peoples over whom they ruled, there were not many who disliked the existing regime?" A new, distinctly Iranian state would unite them, especially through religion, and the early Safavid state was a genuine theocracy.[16] The Buyids had overseen Shiism's crystallization into a formal faith in the tenth century, but in comparison to the Safavids, they had been small, fragmented, and comparatively diffident. The Safavids made Shiism a state religion for the first time, and an aggressive one, marking a major development in Islamic history.

Soon enough the Turkic roots of the new shahs were forgotten. By the time that Busbecq encountered their embassy at Amasya, the Safavids were maturing into what has ever since been seen as the quintessential Iranian dynasty. Iraq, so long the borderland between Persia and the successive great powers of the eastern Mediterranean, was now also a fault line between two imperial religions.

When Ogier de Busbecq watched the Ottoman-Persian peace festivities from his Anatolian rooftop in 1555, one of these great powers was the foe of his master in Vienna, the other a potential ally in a complex geostrategy that saw an Ottoman-French alliance on one side and Ottoman conflicts against the Hapsburgs, Portuguese, and Persians on the other. Before the rise of Safavid Iran, Sunni and Shia had never met as equals.

Leading up to Amasya, mainstream, orthodox Sunnism had settled into its long stability. The gates of ijtihad had been closed for five hundred years. The *Reliance of the Traveler* had been published in Cairo almost two centuries earlier, with its final statements of Sunnite literalism and submission to the God of pure power.

Shiism had by now developed into a deeply articulated religious tradition that was in significant opposition to all of this. The twelve Imams of the Shia, each a historical figure of flesh and blood, are venerated in shrines like so many saints.* Each of these perfect men left behind him his own corpus of holy words and example. The *Al Kafi* is the principal book of Shia hadith, compiled around the year 920. It is a pillar of the Shia faith, according to the *Al Kafi*, that "all the Imams are infallible just like the Prophets." At the same time, the compiler of the collection observed that any such work of compilation must be subject to human error; so the Imams—all twelve of them—were perfect, but there is no absolute claim to know what they said and did. The Shia approach to canon was, in other words, effectively anti-canonical in nature. The opposition in outlook with Sunna was unmistakable.

Shia jurisprudence was to be divined from this multitude of sources along the lines suggested in Aristotle's answer to the Caliph Mamoun: according to reasoned argument using the rules of Aristotelian logic (*mantiq aristu*). Shiism, true to the Mutazilite element of its origins, holds that God has endowed mankind with the capacity of reason, that individuals are obliged to exercise this sacred capacity in the realm of belief; and that if believers are not persuaded on a point of religion, they do not have to believe it. If believers think that one teacher makes more sense than others, they should follow that guide.

Saints of flesh and blood prayed to as if divine, the discovery of God's will not through sacred revelation but instead through the quintessential human faculty of reason, subjecting the Almighty to the competing sovereignty of the Greek syllogism, the requirement that God's followers must be rationally persuaded rather than simply surrender: each of these was an enormity against the orthodox system of Medina.

In these fundaments the Shia religion, now so much more than a sect and often sharing with Sunnism little more than the Imams' descent from Mohammed and the claim to be "Islam," had by this time evolved into something closer to Christianity than to Sunnism.† This is not surprising, as Shiism and Christianity were both half Greek in their roots, while Shiism's other half was Zoroastrian and Christianity's other half

---

* The historicity of the occulted twelfth Imam, the Mahdi, is debated.

† The largest current of Shiism by far is "Twelver" Shiism, following the twelve Imams. Next in number are the Ismaili Shias, who follow Ismail, a son of the sixth Imam, and are thus also known as "Sevener" Shias. Zaydi Shiism, the smallest of the three main Shia sects, follows Zayd, a son of the fourth Imam; they are also known as "Fiver" Shias.

had Zoroastrian roots via the Judaism of the Babylonian Captivity. The strength that gave the Safavids priority over the Hapsburgs at Amasya in 1555 was, ultimately, a victory of sorts for the Mutazilites of ninth-century Baghdad. Shiism, under the strong Persian dynasty founded by Shah Ismail, had come into its own both as a political power and as a separate creed.

———

In rebuilding the Iranian nation with a Shia identity, the Safavids were carrying on a longstanding project that had begun under the Buyids. For the Ottomans, the threat of a burgeoning apostate Persia was soon too dangerous to ignore. Suleiman's father, Selim the Grim, had marched against Shah Ismail in 1514, setting off three centuries of intermittent Ottoman-Iranian warfare. Selim's victory at Chaldiran in the first year of the conflict pushed the Ottoman border with Iran to a position that, just north of Iraq in a region mostly Kurdish in population, has ever since marked the frontier between Turkey and Iran. It is the oldest national land border in the world. Behind it, the Safavid state became the Iran that we know today.

The Ottoman-Safavid Wars had one other lasting result: the loss of Iraq to the Sunni Ottomans in Suleiman's time. Poor as Iraq was after the Mongol and Tatar depredations, its change in ownership would nonetheless be significant. For the Ottomans, Baghdad's tattered glamor burnished their eventual claims to the caliphate, the spiritual leadership of the Sunni world. Iraq also gave the Turks access to the Persian Gulf, a valuable asset for an empire that was fighting the Christians, in particular the Portuguese, as far away as present-day Ethiopia and Indonesia. For most of Iraq, in the simplest religious terms, what the Ottoman conquest meant was Sunni rule over a largely Shia land from the sixteenth to the twentieth centuries. In 1624 the great Shah Abbas, Tahmasp's grandson, took Baghdad. The Persians withstood two long Ottoman sieges over the next fourteen years, but the 1639 Treaty of Zuhab essentially confirmed the Amasya agreement of 1555, and Iraq remained Ottoman until the First World War.

———

At the time of Busbecq's first travels among the Ottomans in 1555, Christian Europe had been enjoying a twenty-three-year respite from the attentions of the Grand Turk. Suleiman had unsuccessfully besieged Vienna in 1529; somewhat like Shah Tahmasp in coming years, Emperor Ferdinand refused to take the field against him. Another Ottoman attempt on Austria, in 1532, also failed. At that point the Possessor of the Kingdoms of the World turned eastward, launching his first campaign against the shah in that same year. The celebrations witnessed by Busbecq at Amasya came more than twenty years later, after Suleiman had launched two more draining campaigns against the Persians.

At Buda, in Ottoman-held Hungary, soon after crossing from Austria into Suleiman's domains, Busbecq had his first encounter with the Janissaries, the Ottomans' crack troops. Culled as promising boys from Christian families in the Balkans, raised and trained as committed Muslim warriors, the Janissaries were the most feared infantry of their day. Busbecq mentioned that one of the principal duties of these elite soldiers, "who carry such terror wherever they go," was to protect Christians and Jews against the local Muslim populations. When Busbecq met his first Janissaries, they entered his dining room in pairs, rushed up to him, made as if to kiss the hand or hem of their distinguished visitor, and pressed upon him bunches of hyacinths and narcissi.

Busbecq, who has been credited with introducing the lilac and especially the tulip to Europe after his Ottoman travels, later noted a love of flowers that resided in the "fierce heart of the Turk, who hates all nations." Ordinarily frugal and spartan in their ways, the Turks apparently thought nothing of paying large sums for a single "fine blossom." Rose petals could not be allowed to drop to the ground in Suleiman's dominions, according to Busbecq, for the first such flowers sprang from the sweat of the Prophet himself. As for colors, the aging Sultan preferred green, like the Prophet in his older years.

The topic of wine occurs frequently in the *Letters*. Busbecq explains that the drinker of wine receives his punishment in the Islamic hereafter, and that this punishment (he does not say what it was) will be the same whether the believer has imbibed greatly or very little. So, when the Turks drank, they drank deep—and "count their drunkenness as all to the good." The *Letters* reveal details about the preservation of grapes, the making of wavy patterns in mohair, and the cost of various foodstuffs.

Busbecq discovered birds unknown to European science, procured a two-headed tortoise, and explained the distinction between jackals and hyenas.

Thrilling to the "traces of antiquity" that surrounded any visitor to Anatolia, Busbecq collected Greek and Roman coins. At Ankara he spotted a lengthy inscription in Latin and Greek on the walls of a Roman building. This, he recognized from his knowledge of Suetonius, was a record of the achievements of the reign of Augustus. Busbecq made a transcription.* At Niš, Busbecq spent the night in a building where he believed the Council of Nicaea had sat in 325, there to limn Christianity for all time with its Nicene Creed. A nearly intact Roman statue of a soldier with his weapons was discovered while he was there and "mutilated by blows of hammers" at the hands of local Turks in an act of pious iconoclasm; Busbecq's protests were met with accusations of idolatry. At Libyssa, nearby, he passed through the death place of Hannibal.

Most important, Busbecq recorded how the great and intimidating empire of Suleiman the Magnificent really worked. At the base of it all were the ordinary, hardy Turks themselves. They were thrifty and mostly sober. They always fed their horses first. "If they have bread and salt and some garlic or an onion, and a kind of sour milk," wrote Busbecq, "they ask for nothing more."

Busbecq remarked repeatedly on the Ottoman army's extraordinary discipline, exemplified in silence even in camp. Ottoman society, Busbecq reported admiringly, was a strict meritocracy. On the approach to Constantinople, he noticed beautiful young women in the fields. The women must, he thought from their looks, have been the products of fine breeding. Indeed, he learned, so they were. But they were married to "ploughmen and shepherds." Such was the unimportance of birth among the Ottoman Turks, concluded Busbecq, himself the illegitimate son of a minor country noble.

---

* The original text, of which the inscription on the building at Ankara was a copy, was written by Augustus himself as a record of the achievements of his rule. Sections dealt with topics such as public works and military achievements. Other copies of the text, known as the Res Gestae Divi Augusti, have since been found, but the one at Ankara (the "Monumentum Ancyranum"), first noticed by Busbecq, is the most complete. To this day, the Res Gestae remains the most valuable single source for the history of the golden age of the Roman Empire. Before Busbecq, it was entirely unknown to scholarship.

At the Sultan's busy court, Busbecq observed: "In all that great assembly no single man owed his dignity to anything but his personal merits and bravery . . . This is why the Turks succeed in all that they attempt and are a dominating race and daily extend the bounds of their rule." Even the Sultan's chief minister had his start as a swineherd. "Our method," Busbecq observed pointedly, "is very different."

As for the Shadow of God, Suleiman the Magnificent himself, this descendant of Osman the ghazi warrior kept his bow and arrows by the side of his divan. "His dignity of demeanour and his general physical appearance are worthy of the ruler of so vast an empire." The Grand Turk was "frugal and temperate . . . , a strict guardian of his religion." Suleiman conducted himself with a stern majesty, although there was sadness, too, in his mien.

Weakness was also there. The Possessor of the Kingdoms of the Earth was now so old that he wore "a coating of red powder" on his face before foreign emissaries, to give an impression of vigor. And Suleiman's "undue submission to his wife" had resulted in the execution of his most promising son. More generally, "the position of sons of Turkish Sultans is a most unhappy one." Any brother who did not succeed to the sultan's throne had to be murdered.

Nothing—not Busbecq's delight in "picking up shells and watching the shoals of dolphins, while the waves played upon the shore" on the Sea of Marmara, nor his embarrassment among the berobed Turks at the unseemly bulges in his tight European leggings—ever made him forget the threatening, militant nature of the realm into which he had ventured. "The Turkish armies," he wrote, "are like mighty rivers swollen with rain, which, if they can trickle through at any point in the banks which restrain them, spread through the breach and cause infinite destruction."

Within a month of the negotiations at Amasya, it was time for Busbecq to return to Vienna. On his way back, he passed a slave caravan. "We were met," he writes,

> by wagon-loads of boys and girls who were being brought from Hungary to be sold in Constantinople. There is no commoner kind of merchandise than this in Turkey; and, just as on the roads out of Antwerp one meets loads of various kinds of goods, so from time to time we were met by gangs of wretched Christian slaves of every kind.[17]

Busbecq's second letter came ten months after the first. Where the first missive had been written from a secure respite in Vienna, the second was written under conditions of house arrest in Constantinople. Busbecq now wrote in response to the reader's "astonishment at my allowing myself to be induced to revisit regions so notorious for the barbarity and savagery of their inhabitants."

By July of 1556, a darker tone appears in the ambassador's hitherto cheerful pages, a new element of anxiety and fear. Busbecq's first trip had been partly successful. Shortly after watching the Turks and Persians celebrate their peace in the pasha's garden at Amasya in May of 1555, he had managed to secure a six-month truce for the Hapsburgs, allowing him to leave for Vienna in June. Now, a year later, Busbecq had been back in Constantinople for eight months.

When Ferdinand had "ordered" Busbecq back to Suleiman's capital— "anything but good tidings"—the ambassador had had no choice but to go. "Since I could not find a substitute, I had to yield to necessity," he wrote nine months later from his confinement on the Bosphorus. The Hapsburgs were at war with the Ottomans again, now that Busbecq's Amasya truce had expired. He called his return "putting my head again into the lion's mouth."

Busbecq had arrived back at Suleiman's capital carrying a dangerous message for the sultan: Ferdinand did not intend to give up the rump of Hungary that he still possessed. At this, "the Sultan and the Pashas and the Turks in general," said Busbecq, were "fiercely and unreasonably angry." Initially the Ottoman courtiers refused even to present the message to Suleiman. "How many heads, they asked, did we imagine that they possessed, that they should venture to usher us into the Sultan's presence with such an answer?"

Busbecq's interlocutors now reminded him of Suleiman's success against the Persians, with Baghdad and the rest of Mesopotamia now Ottoman. The Shadow of God over All Peoples sat secure upon his throne, his army replete with victory. "What better could he wish for" than to feast his troops on the carcass of Hapsburg Hungary? Busbecq was told that his companions would be "thrown into a filthy dungeon" while he was to be sent back to Vienna without his nose and ears. Instead,

Busbecq and his retinue were restricted to their lodgings, treated "as prisoners instead of as ambassadors."

Prevented by Suleiman from seeing the great city that hummed so temptingly outside his door, Busbecq instead turned to the family life of Suleiman himself. In his first letter, Busbecq had told the story of Suleiman's murder of his most capable son, the popular Mustapha, strangled by burly mutes in the sultan's tent after bravely obeying an ominous command to join his father's side during a campaign against the shah. Mustapha, the son of a Circassian or Albanian concubine, was the innocent victim of the machinations of Suleiman's wife, Roxelana, a former Polish slave girl who was promoting her own son. Throughout the *Letters*, Busbecq argued repeatedly that Suleiman was unduly under her sway; at one point he said Suleiman's susceptibility to her was the sultan's only flaw as a leader.

Throne of my lonely niche, my wealth, my love, my moonlight
My most sincere friend, my confidant, my very existence, my Sultan,
   my one and only love
The most beautiful among the beautiful . . .
My Constantinople, my Caraman, the earth of my Anatolia
My Badakhshan, my Baghdad and Khorasan
My woman of the beautiful hair, my love of the slanted brow, my love
   of eyes full of mischief . . .

    —A love poem written by Suleiman for his wife Roxelana, ca. 1540.
      The Sultan uses the pseudonym *Muhibbi*, or "Sweetheart."

At the end of this brief second letter, eight pages long, all Busbecq could muster for his worried reader was a promise that he would seek consolation "with those old friends my books, who hitherto have never failed me, but always render me loyal and attentive service day and night."* And there he bid a simple "Farewell."

---

* The first letter is fifty pages long; the second, eight; the third, fifty-five, and the fourth, forty-nine.

In June of 1560, Busbecq had been in Constantinople for four years, more or less incarcerated for much of that time by a sultan who was displeased with the ambassador's masters in Europe. Ferdinand of Austria had succeeded his brother Charles V as Holy Roman Emperor. Busbecq was still there, waiting for conditions to be right for a new peace treaty.

"My colleagues have left me a long time ago and I have remained here alone," Busbecq wrote now, at the start of his third letter.

His mood is as gloomy as it was at the end of the second letter. "When my colleagues," he wrote, "saw that we had already spent three years here in vain and that no arrangements had been made for peace or a truce of any duration, and there seemed only a vague and distant hope of making any progress in the future, they began to exert all their efforts to obtain leave to depart." The Constantinople of the Grand Turk proved much more difficult to leave than to enter. Suleiman preferred to keep him there.

The importance of Busbecq's work was a factor for both him and the sultan. When the rest of the Hapsburg embassy had left for home three years previously, in August 1557, Busbecq was eager to accompany them. But he loyally concluded that to do so would mean "throwing open a window whereby war might enter." If he stayed, on the other hand, "the prospect of peace was unimpaired."

In addition to their lands in Central Europe, the Hapsburgs ruled Spain, the Netherlands, large parts of Italy and France, outposts in North Africa, and vast parts of the Americas. It is a measure of Suleiman's greatness that, having recently conquered Iraq and most of North Africa, he was strong enough to make even this European power tremble. To the east, meanwhile, Safavid Iran stretched from the mountains of Afghanistan to the shores of the Indian Ocean and the Caspian Sea.

A new phenomenon had arisen, a new near-global complex of great-power relations. The combinations of alliances and rivalries in the sixteenth century were remarkable. In Constantinople, Busbecq found his efforts frustrated by an alliance between the Ottomans and Francis I, one of France's greatest kings. In 1543, an Ottoman fleet had joined the French navy in besieging Hapsburg-held Nice.

The Ottoman fleet spent the following winter as guests of their French allies at Toulon. The next year, Francis sent French artillery to Hungary to fight alongside Suleiman's forces against the Hapsburgs. This was reminiscent of the Crusader Levant in the twelfth and thirteenth centuries, when the interminably feuding local Franks and Muslims fought as allies as often as they fought each other. Apart from Suleiman and Francis, the Hapsburgs' great concern at the time was the epic turbulence of the Reformation in Germany. There, Suleiman reached out to Protestant leaders, urging them on against Ferdinand and the Pope and promising that when he invaded Germany, he would leave them in peace. Hulagu had done so with Baghdad's Christians in 1258.

In Africa, Suleiman allied with a Somali princeling to fight against Ethiopia's Emperor Galawdewos. In league with his Portuguese fellow Christians, the Ethiopian also fought Suleiman at Diu on the east coast of India as well as at Suez, Aden, Muscat, Hormuz, and elsewhere. The year after Suleiman's death, his navy fought the Portuguese at Aceh, in present-day Indonesia. With the shahs of Iran squeezed by two great Sunni powers, the Ottomans in the west and the Mughals in the east, and Henry VIII of England aligned with Suleiman's ally Francis against the Hapsburgs and their Persian allies, sixteenth-century Eurasia could be a deeply intertwined world.*

––––––

Clearly the stakes of diplomacy were significant in this remarkable time of such mighty princes. Suleiman and his capital were in the very center of a new international system made of empires whose possessions now circled the globe, and Busbecq found himself near the heart of the whole vast story, playing an active role in its outcome. And yet, in the third letter, confined by his hosts and left behind by his colleagues, he seems

---

* The Sultana Roxelana, the daughter of a Polish priest and originally enslaved by Crimean Tatars, left behind two extant letters to the king of Poland—with whom the Ottomans enjoyed good relations—in the West, and embroidery, allegedly from her own hand, that she sent to Shah Tahmasp in the East. Her correspondence with these rulers was a part of Suleiman's diplomacy.

to want nothing more than to go home. Suleiman's grand vizier, a powerful character called Rustem, with whom Busbecq clashed repeatedly over the years, tried two tactics in attempting to persuade the Hapsburg ambassador to remain in Suleiman's capital.

The first was a personal appeal: the grand vizier himself wanted Busbecq to stay behind and see to it that a peace was concluded. The grand vizier feared that if the aging Suleiman, now sixty-five years old, went off campaigning in the Hungarian borderlands, the sultan's sons might try to seize the throne. Such worries would have been out of place, if not inconceivable, during Busbecq's earlier letters. Evidently the sultan was losing his grip as he aged. Here again, Busbecq was proving his value as an observer: not until Napoleon would another individual strike such fear into the nations of Europe, and yet here was this same Suleiman unable to lead his armies abroad without risking his own throne.

Another, unwitting, message reveals the weaknesses that are beginning to appear in what was supposed to be the awe-inspiring Ottoman might. Implicit in Rustem's fear is the presumption that there could be no offensive campaign without the personal presence of the sultan himself. Such was the time-honored way of the House of Osman. Or so it was through the time of Suleiman. This tradition of sultans leading from the front ended with Suleiman's death and the accession of Selim II, "the Sot."

Rustem's second argument was more conventional. The vizier claimed that only he and the senior women of the harem, notably Suleiman's wife and mother-in-law, were keeping the sultan from rampaging into Hungary. The tiniest Austrian provocation might set Suleiman off. Rustem and the other lovers of peace among the sultan's circle were "clinging to the hem of his raiment," in Rustem's metaphor. Busbecq had to remain in Constantinople and not wake this "sleeping lion."

Again Busbecq gives precious insights into truths about the otherwise invisible weaknesses of an older Suleiman. These are also insights into the evolving system that the sultan had come to embody. In the old days, as the dynasty grew from local ghazis to world-shaking emperors, the harem had not had a meaningful influence on the statecraft of the sons of Osman. Now Roxelana herself, with her palace scheming, was choosing the next sultan.

The reign of her son Selim the Sot was to initiate a turbulent period of transformation that extended more or less from Busbecq's embassy through the Ottoman defeat and significant territorial losses in the Wars of the Holy League (1683–1699). After this conflict, also known in Europe as the Great Turkish War, the empire experienced a century-long plateau during which the administration ossified somewhat, decentralized significantly, and showed remarkable resilience as a broadly flexible and tolerant approach successfully managed the challenges presented by countless religious and ethnic identities on three continents. In 1683, an Ottoman army was once more at the gates of Vienna—if again unsuccessfully—but in general the true offensive threat of Ottoman power to either Iran or Europe was over after Suleiman.

Of the twenty-two Ottoman sultans who followed Suleiman, only two possessed the original ghazi spirit. The situation described by a Venetian ambassador in 1582 was not unusual during the centuries that began with Suleiman's later years: "The wife . . . with the queen-mother governed everything . . . one had to depend on them, or at least not have them against you."[18] Perhaps, after the generations of expansion beginning in the 1300s, this was just what was needed. Under the approach that developed after Suleiman, the empire lasted for another three and a half centuries. Without the European-driven conflagration of the First World War it, would almost certainly have endured much longer.

In the summer of 1560, as Busbecq wrote his third letter, he had been "enclosed within the four walls" of his house for two years. But he appeared to have settled into his existence in this fascinating world that yielded more and more to him the more he inhabited it. The demands of diplomacy were intermittent. Reports to Vienna, and instructions back to him in Constantinople, would have taken six weeks or more to reach their destinations. Two or three times a year, a message arrived from Ferdinand that required Busbecq to pay a visit to the sultan's palace.

Fifty centuries after the birth of civilization in Iraq, this was the moment when the weight of history in Eurasia shifted to Europe from the Fertile Crescent and the lands around it. Perhaps the very fact of Busbecq's *Letters*, and their popularity for centuries across many European countries, is the most important message embedded within them. The

Ottoman and latter-day Persian Empires had been founded in the early sixteenth century. By the mid-nineteenth century their world would be politically dominated by Europe. Between these developments, hundreds of embassies traveled back and forth between the courts of Europe and those of the Ottomans and Iranians. Thousands of merchants, artists, and travelers did the same, although, as with the embassies, far more visited the East from the West than vice versa. There would eventually be many European Busbecqs leaving written accounts of one kind or another. There would hardly be a single Ottoman or Persian equivalent during the period.

Ottoman engagement with Europe at the time was of a different nature, and Rustem, for all his toughness with Busbecq, happened to be an example of it. Rustem, born in the Ottoman Balkans in about 1505, had come from a Christian family and been trained up, like countless other Christian boys of the empire, into the Ottoman administrative system. Of twenty-six Ottoman grand viziers in the sixteenth century, twenty-two were born and raised as boys in the Christian faith within the empire; it was not very different at other administrative levels. Others of Christian background, mostly Italians, entered the Ottoman service through the slave trade conducted by the Barbary corsairs. In 1598, an Ottoman fleet appeared off the Sicilian coast, only four years after a vicious sacking of nearby Reggio. The Sicilians were alarmed, but in fact the Ottoman admiral, the *kapidun* pasha, one Cagaloglou Sinan Pasha, merely wanted to visit his mother in Messina. He had been born Scipione Cigala, son of a nobleman of Genoa, and captured by the Barbary corsairs as a boy. The two previous grand admirals of the Ottoman fleet had also been Italians, from Calabria and Venice.

When a local revolt was launched the next year, 1599, against Spanish rule in Calabria, its leaders tried to coordinate their rising with the *kapidun* pasha, their erstwhile countryman. The Turkish fleet did not appear at the promised time and the revolt failed, but one of its leaders, the Dominican friar Tommaso Campanella, kept a portrait of Mehmed III, the Ottoman sultan of the day, on the wall of his prison cell. Campanella's quasi-mystical prison masterpiece, *The City of the Sun*, described a paradisiacal utopia with many similarities to other depictions of Ottoman society in European writings of the day. At a time when the Spanish Inquisition would torture a "heretic" like

Campanella for forty days straight, Ottoman Constantinople in that generation after Suleiman, as it would for the next three centuries until the fall of the last sultan, peacefully accommodated an astonishing mix of religions and communities. There were ongoing "rhetorics of crusade and jihad" on both sides, just as the enslavement of Muslims by the Knights of Malta (with a large slave market at Messina itself) matched the enslavement of Christians by the Muslim corsairs. But the borders of faith and culture were far more porous and fluid than much of the bombast would suggest.[19]

In the winter of 1557–1558 Busbecq was called to see the sultan at Adrianople (Edirne today, on Turkey's Bulgarian border), where Suleiman liked to go for falconry and the "far more bracing" seasonal climate. On the journey, Busbecq found that the members of his Janissary escort were surly. They resented his quick pace and the muddy road. When he discovered that they enjoyed his cook's special pudding of wine, eggs, sugar, and spices, he made sure that they were served it every day for breakfast. Apparently, even among the elite troops of the High Ottoman jihad, Islam was not always as literal or severe as the original version.

Back in Constantinople, having achieved the signing of a seven-month truce, Busbecq tried to persuade the Turks to allow him to rent a house of his own. At first they were enthusiastic about this. It would save the sultan four hundred gold pieces per annum. The wealth of the Grand Turk, like the might and martial perfection of his armies, was supposed to be beyond all reckoning, yet here again was an early inkling of constraint. Busbecq's minders eventually decided to keep him in the former caravanserai that the sultan was renting for him. Its rooms all looked inward to the courtyard in which merchants of old had loaded and unloaded their burdens. This would spare the pious locals the scandalous sight of a Christian living in their midst.

In the caravanserai, Busbecq created a zoo. The numerous small, stable-like rooms arranged around a courtyard were ideal for housing a menagerie. On four feet there were wolves, bears, fallow deer, mules, lynxes, mongooses, martens, sables, and a pig that appalled the Turks. Busbecq's birds included "eagles, crows, jackdaws, strange kinds of ducks, Balearic cranes and partridges." A friend compared the scene to Noah's ark.* Waiting to take the ambassador to freedom and the pleasures of Vienna were well-bred horses from Syria, Cilicia, Arabia, and Cappadocia. Camels were there to carry his baggage when the day came, and to delight his master Ferdinand as gifts.

Indeed, Busbecq kept everything at the ready for the journey home. The Turks' looming "civil war between the princes," as Busbecq put it, made a peace with the Hapsburgs ever likelier, or so the ambassador hoped.

After recounting an "offer" by the grand vizier that he convert to Islam, Busbecq found an indirect way to illuminate a bit more about the eastern strategic picture, that question of great import to his employers back in Vienna and to fellow Europeans in general.

Rustem expressed surprise that Charles of Spain could be at war with a coreligionist such as Francis of France. "What right have they to wage war against one another," asked Rustem, "when they are bound by religious ties?"

"The same right," replied Busbecq, "as you have to go to war with the Persians."

Busbecq, it turns out, provided as valuable a window into the Ottomans' geopolitical affairs as into their domestic and dynastic matters. He went into some detail on the methods that the Ottoman armies used in places such as western Iran, where provisions were sparse. Suleiman took forty thousand camels on campaign, and almost as many mules, especially when he went to Persia, because the Persians "lay waste and burn everything, and so force the enemy to retire through lack of food." These methods showed "with what patience, sobriety, and economy" the Turks waged war. European warcraft, by contrast, was for Busbecq marked by sloppiness and decadence:

---

* One thing missing from the ark was a hyena, a species that had caught Busbecq's attention during his journey across "Asia" (Anatolia) from Constantinople to Amasya described in the first letter. Busbecq relates that in his time at Constantinople, there were two hyenas in the city. He tried to buy them but the owner refused, needing to keep them for the "love charms and magic arts" practiced upon Suleiman by the sultana, the powerful Roxelana.

On our side is public poverty, private luxury, impaired strength, broken spirit, lack of endurance and training; the soldiers are insubordinate, the officers avaricious; there is contempt for discipline; licence, recklessness, drunkenness, and debauchery are rife; and, worst of all, the enemy is accustomed to victory, and we to defeat.

"How different are our soldiers," he wrote, "who on campaign despise ordinary food and expect dainty dishes (such as thrushes and beccaficoes)." Frightened by the contrast, Busbecq continued:

I tremble when I think of what the future must bring when I compare the Turkish system with our own; one army must prevail and the other must be destroyed, for certainly both cannot remain unscathed. On their side are the resources of a mighty empire, strength unimpaired, experience and practice in fighting, a veteran soldiery, habituation to victory, endurance of toil, unity, order, discipline, frugality, and watchfulness.

Returning to the details of Ottoman life, Busbecq discussed in turn the dress and armor of Suleiman's soldiers, the kindness of the Turks toward animals, "and the high standard of morality which obtains among the Turkish women." Busbecq explained that the Turkish women were locked up all day, and that if they did need to leave their houses they were "so covered and wrapped up that they seem to passers-by to be mere ghosts and specters." Among the wealthier Turks, a condition of marriage, said Busbecq, was "that their wives shall never set foot outside their houses, and that no man or woman shall on any pretext whatever be admitted to visit them." A man, despite his concubines, did have to spend Friday nights with his wife, Busbecq related.

As for the domestic life of Suleiman himself, Busbecq explained that the beguiling Roxelana had cleverly manipulated Islam's laws providing for the sexual enslavement of women. By bearing Suleiman a child, Busbecq reported, Roxelana had automatically become as free as the sharia allowed an unwed woman to be. According to Muslim law, Suleiman could no longer force sex upon her at will. The sultan could insist on sex with Roxelana only if he married her—so marry her he did. Suleiman's capitulation stunned the world around him, for Ottoman sultans, enjoying the sharia's provisions as much as the Umayyads and Abbasids had done before them, had no need to marry and thus never did.* Reading Busbecq it is clear that to a European of the late Renaissance, these Islamic arrangements were exotic and somewhat titillating.†

Eventually the Turks invited Busbecq to a military camp not far from the capital. He went, and was detained there for three months. He was again impressed by the discipline of the Ottoman army: the "complete silence . . . entire absence of quarelling and acts of violence . . . the utmost cleanliness . . . Moreover you never see any drinking or revelry or any kind of gambling."

Busbecq continually picked up information of value for contemporaries and historians alike. Suleiman's succession drama continued. After Roxelana had arranged, as revealed in Busbecq's first letter, the murder of Suleiman's son Mustapha, two princes remained: the martial and popular Bayezid and the "gluttonous and slothful" Selim. Somehow, Selim defeated Bayezid in battle. Bayezid was forced to flee with his army to Persia, there to seek the protection of the shah.

As Busbecq said, "the fortunes of Bajazet and our interests are closely connected." In this entirely new phase in the Fertile Crescent's history, when far more than even in the time of the Romans the region was part of an intercontinental political framework, an Austrian family controlling an empire from Cuzco to Vienna was following minutely the fate of a young Turkish man in the Persian highlands. The shah's treatment of Bayezid would indicate whether the Persian state was a friend or an enemy to Suleiman. This mattered to Busbecq and the Hapsburgs, for the better Suleiman's relations with the Safavids, the more he could turn his aggression against Christian Europe. As it happened, the Persians, after initially welcoming Bayezid, imprisoned the young prince and eventually

---

* Busbecq attributed the Ottomans' custom of eschewing marriage to an earlier sultan's pain at the "affronts to which his wife was subjected before his very eyes" after the defeat at the hands of Timur at Ankara in 1402. Busbecq pointed out that under Islamic law the children of concubines enjoy the same rights as those of wives. This, combined with a woman's gaining additional rights by marriage, meant that there was usually little point in a man's choosing to marry.

† During a disquisition here that also touches on Ottoman dueling, divorce, cavalry training, and archery, Busbecq remarks on the louche habits of the people of Mingrelia, an Ottoman province on the agreeable Georgian Black Sea coast: "Where there is so much leisure and food is so abundant, the standard of morality is not high and chastity is rare."

handed him over to be garroted by Suleiman's personal executioner. The inducements for the Persians' doing so, fortunately for the Europeans, were large gifts of money from Suleiman, rather than any burgeoning Ottoman-Safavid friendship.

Busbecq continued to relate details that he did not realize were signs of the incipient change among his hosts, as the Ottomans began their maturation from a terrifying offensive threat into an extraordinarily adaptable and durable status-quo power. He told an anecdote about Rustem equipping one of Suleiman's cavalry squadrons with muskets. The story ended with the weapons so badly maintained, and the proud Turks so "offended" by the sooty powder and the "clumsy powder-boxes and pouches hanging down" from their waists, that the experiment was abandoned. The troopers "resumed their bows and arrows."*

Busbecq pointed out that the Turks refused to allow the printing of books, for these would compete with the scripture of Medina. Public clocks too were shunned. Like the Aristotelian reasoning of the philosophers and scientists of Abbasid Baghdad, the clock, that cold and rational dictator of the day, implied a freestanding set of rules that threatened God's omnipotence. And yet the Turks, said Busbecq, would not put to sea in springtime without a blessing of the waters by Greek priests.

The sense of stress at the seams also made itself felt in Constantinople itself, dread capital of the Grand Turk, whence Baghdad was ruled. Suleiman's capital was "a city which is almost falling to pieces, and of whose former glory nothing remains except its splendid position."

Even some of Busbecq's observations of Suleiman's army carry hints of the coming change. When Busbecq's servants found themselves in an altercation with a group of Janissaries, the grand vizier himself sent a message to the ambassador instructing him to avoid at all costs quarrels with these local soldiers. At times of war, such as they found themselves in, the Janissaries "were masters to such an extent that not even Soleiman

---

* More generally, the Ottomans had been using firearms to good effect for some time; at Chaldiran in 1514, as we have seen, their muskets and artillery were decisive against Shah Ismail's forces. Busbecq does allow that the Turks are quick "to adopt the useful inventions of others."

himself could control them and was actually afraid of personal harm at their hands." In general, Busbecq perceived, Suleiman's grasp on his own best troops was uncertain. "There was nothing which the Sultan so much dreaded," he wrote, "as that there might be some secret disaffection among the Janissaries."

Immediately afterward, Busbecq gave the lie to Rustem's conceit of Suleiman as the "sleeping lion" prevented only by his vizier and harem from ravaging a helpless Europe. An emissary from Ferdinand arrived at the Ottoman court, bringing gifts: "a number of gilt cups and a clock of ingenious workmanship, which had the form of a tower mounted on an elephant's back." Suleiman was eager that Busbecq present these to him "in camp in the sight of the army . . . as a proof that no military operations were impending on the part of the Christians."

Busbecq's fourth and last letter, written in late 1562, began by accepting his reader's congratulations, for he had at last returned safely to Vienna.

The Turks had won a significant naval battle—off Djerba on the North African coast, in 1560—against Ferdinand's nephew, the new king Philip II of Spain. In its aftermath, Busbecq ransomed Christian prisoners in Constantinople, bought the beaten Spanish admiral's captured standard from a Turkish officer, and endured a mocking crowd outside his door.

"This defeat of the Christians at sea," wrote Busbecq, "made one very anxious that the Turks should become more arrogant, and therefore less accommodating." By then, Ferdinand's ambassador had been among the Turks for most of seven years. The aging Suleiman was becoming ever stricter in his Islamic observance. He had given up the boys' choir that used to charm him. He had committed to flames the musical instruments of his players, instruments "ornamented with fine work in gold and studded with precious stones."

Suleiman had also banned the importation of wine into his capital. This, claimed Busbecq, who was clearly attached to his tipple and perhaps somewhat melodramatic on the subject, presented a grave health danger to an already enfeebled household. "Disease and death," without question, would result from the absence of wine, claimed Busbecq. Fortunately the crisis passed without tragedy. Busbecq's diplomatic skills enabled him to persuade Suleiman's ministers to allow a single, secret shipment of wine to be unloaded at Constantinople's docks one night and quietly carted to the former inn where the ambassador lived with the lynxes, stoats, lizards, purebred horses, and other animals of the zoo that he continued to keep for personal amusement in the stalls of his caravanserai.

Through the vicissitudes of diplomacy, Busbecq maintained his sense of delight in the world around him. He managed to remove himself for three enchanting months to Prinkipo, a small island—then, as now, "wonderfully quiet, quite free from crowds and noise"—of Greek fishermen in the Sea of Marmara. There he had a measure of freedom at last, "to wander where I liked and to sail about among the various islands as I pleased." Accompanied on local adventures by a Franciscan monk who had joined him from a monastery at Pera on the European mainland, Busbecq enjoyed the lavender and the myrtle. The milieu was reminiscent of the seaside idyll of Siduri, Gilgamesh's divine barmaid, if with a prelate for company instead of an enchantress. In Prinkipo's "transparent shallows," Busbecq fished with a trident for lobster and crab.

After Busbecq had returned from the island to Suleiman's capital, the plague took hold. Twelve hundred people were dying every day. The Turks forced Busbecq to remain in his "plague stricken house of death." The sultan himself, reported the grand vizier, had asked of Busbecq, "Did I not know that pestilence is God's arrow, which does not miss its appointed mark?"

Fatalism reached far down below the sultan. Busbecq later told of Turks so resigned to God's supreme will that they wiped their faces with the sweaty "garments and linen in which plague-stricken persons have died." As a result, said Busbecq, "contagion is spread far and wide, and sometimes whole families are exterminated."

———

Toward the end of Busbecq's time in Constantinople, the ambassador became more optimistic. Peace between Spain and France had strengthened the Hapsburg negotiating position. A peeved Suleiman wrote to Francis, his erstwhile ally in Paris, to remind the French king that "old friends do not easily become enemies, or old enemies friends."

Meanwhile the vizier Rustem, "always gloomy and brutal," had died. His replacement was Ali Pasha, "a kind and intelligent Turk if ever there was one," formerly the vizier in Egypt and soon to be a friend of Busbecq's. The role of men like them, Ali Pasha told Busbecq, was to guide princes in the right direction. The best peace, said the new grand vizier, would be one that satisfies both parties. "The minds of princes," he said, are like mirrors. They "present as it were a clean surface to receive the impress of the ideas which are presented to them." And so Busbecq's peace negotiations began at last, after eight years, to sail smoothly forward.

"Our position indeed was excellent," Busbecq reported, "and the desired result seemed to be in sight . . . Eventually, the terms of the peace, which had already been settled, were adhered to."

Given three fine horses by Ali Pasha, "a box of antidote to poison of the finest quality from Alexandria," and a bottle of precious Egyptian balm, Busbecq set off for home. "I started on my long-desired journey," he wrote, "taking back as the result of my eight years' mission a truce for eight years."

Busbecq pointed out proudly that his truce provided for easy extensions. It lasted less than three years.

Chapter 16

Mighty Ruins in
the Midst of Deserts

Austen Henry Layard and the Search
for Mesopotamia's Past, 1800–1900

A deep mystery hangs over Assyria, Babylonia and Chaldaea. With these names are linked great nations and great cities dimly shadowed forth in history; mighty ruins in the midst of deserts, defying, by their very desolation and lack of definite form, the description of the traveller; the remnants of the mighty races still roving over the land; the fulfilling and fulfillment of prophecies; the plains to which the Jew and the Gentil alike look as the cradle of their race.
—Austen Henry Layard, *Nineveh and Its Remains*, 1848[1]

In April of 1841 a twenty-three-year-old Englishman, Henry Layard, found himself at Aleppo.* Soon enough he would be in Iraq. With another young Englishman, he was on his way overland from Kent to Ceylon (present-day Sri Lanka). There Layard was to take up work as a lawyer.

"I had traversed Asia Minor and Syria," he wrote seven years later, "visiting the ancient seats of civilisation, and the spots which religion has made holy."[2] He visited Jerusalem. He saw Tarsus, Antioch, and Mount Carmel and carved his name—as in a sense Gilgamesh had too—on a cedar of Lebanon. Riding alone through Bedouin country to see Petra, he was robbed of all he had with him; this would happen at least a dozen times in his life.

---

* He would later add the name Austen to his prenames, in honor of a rich uncle, and would be known as Austen Henry Layard.

Undoubtedly, the eastern sites of the classical Greek and Roman world interested Layard, as they would have interested any educated Englishman of the mid-nineteenth century. But for Layard, while the relatively familiar Greco-Roman antiquity of the Levant and western Turkey had its appeal, another, farther land truly compelled him. This was Iraq, the land of greater age and deeper mysteries just over the sunrise horizon of his own Western civilization. Looking eastward from Aleppo, Layard felt himself overtaken by what he called an "irresistible desire." It was the desire, as he wrote in his brilliant first book, Nineveh and Its Remains, "to penetrate to the regions beyond the Euphrates, to which history and tradition point as the birthplace of the wisdom of the West."

At the time of these travels, Layard was an impecunious young man. The book in which he wrote these words would lead him to fame, influence, and riches. Published in the era of Thoreau, Marx, Mill, and Emerson, Layard's classic was one of the most popular and lasting non-fiction books of the mid-nineteenth century and has rarely been out of print since.

For a European in 1841, Iraq's history was semi-mythic. Over the previous five hundred years, perhaps a few dozen European travelers had produced published reports on the local legends that placed the Biblical cities of Nineveh and Babylon in the Land of the Two Rivers. In 1826, the widow of Claudius James Rich, who for most of the period 1809–1820 had been the British East India Company's official Resident at Baghdad, published her late husband's memoir, describing in part his visit to "Nineveh," near Mosul. The account included a plan that Rich had drawn of the locale.*

But with no proof, only the talk of locals and a tradition among foreigners, Nineveh's location—and even existence—was still no more than a legend. The same was true of the other quasi-fabulous cities of Iraq. From north to south, the flat brown country was dotted with vast mounds called tels. Nobody knew for sure what, if anything, really lay beneath them. As Layard wrote in 1849, "a deep mystery hangs over

---

* In a sign of how things had changed vis-à-vis Europe and the Ottomans, James Silk Buckingham, a traveler to Baghdad in 1825, was to write, "Mr. Rich was universally considered to be the most powerful man in Baghdad; and some even questioned whether the Pasha himself would not shape his conduct according to Mr. Rich's suggestion and advice rather than as his own council might wish." James Silk Buckingham, Travels in Mesopotamia (Cambridge: Cambridge University Press, 2012, first published in 1928), vol. 2, p. 200.

Assyria, Babylonia and Chaldaea. With these names are linked great nations and great cities dimly shadowed forth in history." The "mighty ruins in the midst of deserts" were ultimately cyphers in their "desolation and lack of definite form."

The question of the truth of these legends mattered. The middle third of the nineteenth century was a time of a nascent crisis of faith in Christian Europe. Darwin's *On the Origin of Species* would not be published until 1859, but already intellectuals were driving new cracks in the edifice of Latin Christianity. With David Strauss's 1832 *The Life of Jesus, Critically Examined* and other work of Germany's "Tübingen School" that led ultimately to what is called the Higher Criticism, modern scholarship, both historical and linguistic, was casting doubt upon the claims of the Bible. In England, George Eliot translated Strauss's *Life of Jesus* into English in 1846. Matthew Arnold and Samuel Coleridge also took up the cause of Biblical skepticism.

Regardless of Iraq's special appeal to Layard, the young man was headed there anyway. His job in the law awaited at Ceylon, and he had decided to make his way to India overland. The land route was, even then, almost unheard-of for travelers from England to the East Indies. It took Layard from the Levant to inland Syria, and from there—Aleppo— he would have to cross first the Syrian desert, then "Turkish Arabia," as Iraq was often called at the time, and then the Persian Empire. Iraq still belonged to the Ottomans, while in Persia yet another dynasty of Turkic origins, the Qajars, ruled.

From Aleppo, the next major stop on the journey east was Mosul. The trip typically took two or three weeks' riding. Fifty miles east of Aleppo lay the storied Euphrates, the Roman *limes* of East and West, as Layard would well have known. Beyond the Euphrates was Mesopotamia, all the way to the Tigris, with Mosul on its banks.

"After a journey in Syria," Layard wrote, "the thoughts naturally turn eastward; and without treading on the remains of Nineveh and Babylon our pilgrimage is incomplete."[3] As he prepared to head east from Aleppo, across the *limes* and the Syrian desert, Layard's plans for Ceylon seemed to disappear from the page. He described Iraq not as a place he needed to cross, but as the destination.

Syria at the time belonged to Egypt and its strongman Mehmed Ali Pasha, nominally a vassal of the Ottoman sultan in Istanbul but in fact an increasingly independent power. The Ottoman vigor was waning almost everywhere. The frontier between Mohammed Ali and Abdulmejid I, the thirty-first Ottoman sultan, was east of Aleppo, essentially along the age-old north–south line between green, western, Mediterranean Syria and the poor, dry country inland. This frontier now stood between Layard and Iraq. To arrive at the land of his dim but powerful dreams, Layard would have to cross the desert borderlands, the lawless country between pasha and sultan, where the Arab tribes were raiding and looting at their leisure.

Riding first with a caravan for safety, and then on their own, Layard and his traveling companion, a fellow Englishman called Edward Mitford, made the trip from Aleppo to Mosul in twenty-three days, arriving on April 10, 1841. Mitford would write of Mosul, this "ill-constructed mud-built town," that in the shadow of its crooked minaret, the rotting corpses of camels and cattle bred disease among the "mean and dirty" bazaars.[4] Over the coming decade Layard traveled to Mosul four more times. On his last visit, in 1851, the man who had first arrived so poor that his possessions fit onto his saddle would be one of the most famous men in Europe.

Layard's *Autobiography* was published by his widow in 1903, and probably written in the decade or so before his death in 1894. In it, his earliest memories are of journeys and wonder: of his family traveling to Italy, sent there for the climate by the doctor of his asthmatic father; of holding a lion cub, to the alarm of his nurse, as a three-year-old in Paris. In Geneva, the boy Layard, to protect his eyes, watched a solar eclipse through its reflection in a bucket of water. From Italy, images of "the piles of grapes and figs that were heaped up on the roadside stalls" still stuck in his mind's eye sixty or seventy years later, youthful visions undiminished despite a long subsequent life of almost unimaginable richness and color.[5] At the age of eight, in England once more, Layard found himself sent "like a parcel" alone from Ramsgate to Mougins in the south of France.[6] Along the way, he took a shine to the pretty daughter of the landlady of his Paris hotel, accompanied the girl on rambles about the city, and landed his father with a bottle of champagne on the hotel bill.

At Mougins, the eight-year-old Layard met a youthful Benjamin Disraeli, then an author traveling on the Continent. Always a devotee of the female sex, at Milan the young Layard inhaled "with the greatest interest the letters of Lucretia Borgia."[7] At Florence his father rented the main floor of the Rucellai palace; Layard slept every night with a Filippino Lippi altarpiece above his bed.* In the daytime he would snoop around the palace with a manservant who had served with Napoleon at Waterloo or haunt the picture galleries with his father and idle at the feet of the bedraggled wizard-bearded painter and black-magician Seymour Kirkup, who knew Shelley, Keats, and the Brownings. Other friends of Layard's parents in those days included Edward Trelawny, an intimate of Byron's who in his days fighting the Turk in the mountains of Greece was said to have purchased a harem of a dozen women.

Above all, young Layard spent hours and hours with the tales of the *Arabian Nights*. These he read "stretched upon the floor" of the dusty palazzo, "under a great gilded Florentine table." These tales of Abbasid Baghdad had Layard utterly bewitched. "I thought and dreamt of little else but 'jins' and 'ghouls' and fairies and lovely princesses," he wrote many years later, "until I believed in their existence."[8] These stories ultimately had a greater impact on Layard than any other part of his superb, if exotic, education. "To them," he would write, "I attribute my love of travel and adventure that took me to the East."

Such was life for the son of an impecunious but unusually cultured English gentleman, wandering in Europe on doctor's orders, in the generation after Waterloo, at perhaps the height of the Romantic period—a time whose atmosphere would do so much to color Layard's later life. Layard then found himself back in England at the age of twelve. There his schoolmates, disgusted with his speaking of Italian, called him an "organ grinder."[9]

---

* "Now in the National Gallery," Layard notes in his *Autobiography and Letters*. The editor of Layard's memoirs adds in a footnote that the painting "still bears the traces of a wound inflicted by the heel of Henry Layard's shoes, flung at his brother in a childish quarrel." Austen Henry Layard, *Autobiography and Letters from His Childhood until His Appointment as H.M. Ambassador at Madrid* (London, 1903), vol. 1, p. 27.

Mosul in 1841 was a fly-bitten backwater that generally typified the neglect and torpor of Ottoman Iraq at the time. Almost four centuries had passed since the Ottoman Empire's heyday in the time of Suleiman the Magnificent.

The trading town was, with Damascus and Cairo, one of the three leading cities of the empire after Constantinople. Mosul was richer than Baghdad or Basra, but its old Silk Road wealth had ebbed with the development, since the days of the Portuguese navigators in the time of Suleiman, of the sea route between India and Europe. In Layard's day, the house of a typical rich Moslawi would from the outside have been quite anonymous, mostly modest walls along dusty alleys or narrow streets; within, four sides, possibly arcaded, would typically have surrounded a courtyard, perhaps with a fountain. Quite a few of the old houses of Mosul were home to significant and ancient wealth. To the visitor's eye, however, the city was an unprepossessing sprawl of anonymous mud brick.

Layard was in Mosul for about five days in April 1841. He had nothing to say about the city on this, his first visit. Already, his thoughts seem to have been consumed by the lost world whose ghostly mounds dotted the flat landscape nearby. Just across the Tigris from Mosul, on the river's east bank in sight of the city, were the mounds said by residents to be "the remains of ancient Nineveh," as Layard reported. He made sure to visit these.

He also made his way to a couple of sites farther south. One of these was known locally as Nimrud. This Layard associated with the character of Nimrod, "the mighty hunter" of the Old Testament. Nimrod, according to Genesis, had been the great Assyrian king who built Nineveh. Layard quoted the Genesis passage in a footnote: "He [Nimrod] went out into Assyria and builded Nineveh, the city Rehoboth and Calah, and Resen, between Nineveh and Calah; the same is a great city."[10]

Layard and his little party were worried about being attacked by the horsemen of the desert and felt safest in what he called "the jungle" that then lined the banks of the Tigris. The pasha of Mosul, the Ottoman sultan's provincial chief, had provided Layard's group with an armed individual escort known as a "cawass." Scared by the wild state of the local tribes, the man abandoned his charges "in the wilderness" twenty miles or so south of Mosul and ran for home. On the way he promptly "fell a victim to his timidity," and was murdered by the locals: a soldier of the

Turkish overlord, killed by the Arabs. As long and stable as the region's
Ottoman centuries appear from a remove, throughout the nineteenth-
century accounts there is a sense that the Turks in Iraq were little more
than occupiers. Two centuries after Ogier de Busbecq, Turkish Iraq was
a place of predatory tax collectors, imperial administrators from far
away, and rapacious or embattled soldieries.

Comparing an account in Xenophon's *Anabasis* to Nimrud's physical
position just south of where the Zab River meets the Tigris, Layard was
certain that the Athenian had stopped there with his Ten Thousand in
401 BC. Apparently mistaking some form of local name for the Greek
"Larissa," Xenophon had noted people on a nearby "pyramid of stone"
that sounds, from the Greek's description, like the remnants of a ziggurat.[11] "A day's march of eighteen miles," wrote Xenophon, brought him
and his men up the Tigris to a "city called Mespila," with its own ruins
nearby.[12] The latter city was clearly Mosul, Layard surmised correctly,
and he was impressed that the reputed site of Nineveh, which "the
Greek general saw twenty-two centuries before," had been even then,
in Xenophon's account, "an *ancient* city" (emphasis Layard's).

From the Old Testament to Xenophon: these mysterious places at
Mosul's doorstep were, if local legend and Layard's reading of the Greek's
account was correct, at the heart of this traveler's cultural ancestry. All
he had read and seen as a boy in the darkened, half-deserted Florentine
palaces of his youth—all that had started here, one way or another.
Layard's goal was to prove this to the world.

Mosul's apparently dead mounds had a living quality of sorts for local
people, too. "Strange figures carved in black stone," according to the
Arabs of the vicinity, occasionally appeared in the mound at Nimrud.
On that first, fleeting visit in 1841 Layard and his companions spent a
day scrabbling over the surface and "searched for them in vain." Meager
flocks of the local Arabs grazed over the site, which was "covered with
grass and flowers."[13] The old stories had said that Nineveh, "one of the
most famous and magnificent cities of the ancient world had perished
with her people, and like them had left no wreck behind." Layard found
nothing during this brief visit. He knew he must return.

To the naked eye, the ruins left behind by the ancient Mesopotamian
civilizations are simple humps on the flat landscape, with its drab palate
of medium browns. Not so for Layard.

"These huge mounds of Assyria," he wrote in *Nineveh and Its Remains*, "made a deeper impression upon me, gave rise to more serious thoughts and more earnest reflection, than the temples of Balbec and the theatres of Ionia." (Layard also confessed that the "ruin" of classical buildings likely impressed him more than the originals would have done.)

Even nature was conspiring against the imaginings of the traveler in Iraq. Whereas in the Mediterranean world the traveler would find "the graceful column rising above the thick foliage of the myrtle, ilex, and oleander," in Mesopotamia there was only "the stern shapeless mound rising like a hill from the scorched plain, the fragments of pottery, and the stupendous mass of brickwork occasionally laid bare by the winter rains." When the traveler saw a Greek ruin, its pristine white columns wreathed in blossoms, "overlooking the dark blue waters of a lake-like bay," he could rebuild it easily enough "in his mind's eye." In Iraq, the imagination is at a total "loss to give any form to the rude heaps."

And what of the people who built these civilizations, whose ruins Layard suspected lay before him under the shapeless mounds? Here was the greatest mystery of all. They had "left no visible traces of their civilization, or of their arts: their influence has long since passed away."

The greater the mystery, the greater the appeal. And yet one could not be sure these people had even existed at all. Just as one could not imagine their art, one had no idea what their stories were, except a haunting intuition that they were one's own. To someone brought up without Layard's deep art-historical education, the impulse to answer the questions posed by the Iraq he found may not have been strong enough to pursue the matter. These people, to whom Layard sensed he owed so much, had left no vouchsafe of their existence.

For three hundred years, the Assyrians had terrorized the world around them. Then, as Delacroix's painting of Sardanapalus's imminent incineration with his women, horses, slaves, and jewels reminds us, the Medes and Babylonians joined forces to crush the Assyrian Empire forever. That was in 612 BC. Nineveh apparently lay empty after its destruction, a tiny village thenceforth, if not an outright wasteland. In 401 BC, Xenophon mentioned one or two local spots, as Layard noted, but he did not mention Nineveh. This is curious, as not much later the stories of Sardanapalus's decadence and fiery demise—and of King Ninus, the city's founder in the Greek tradition—had most definitely entered the Greek cultural lexicon.

As with Xenophon earlier in the broad Greco-Roman period, so with the Latins later. The geographer Strabo, who died in 24 AD, did not mention Nineveh, even though he himself had visited Babylon, not very far south. Another six centuries on, when in 627 AD the Eastern Roman emperor Heraclius defeated the Sasanian Persian emperor Khosrow near Mosul on the east bank of the Tigris, the imperial account does not mention the ancient city. The battle, however, was eventually remembered as the Battle of Nineveh.[14]

Lucian, the popular satirist, novelist, and essayist of the second century AD, wrote in Classical Greek. In his *Charon*, the ferryman of the underworld comes up briefly to the surface world of the living. There, from the vantage of a great mountaintop, the god Hermes gives Charon a tour d'horizon of worldly life. Nineveh is one place the god cannot point out. "As for Nineveh," says Hermes to the ferryman, "it was wiped out long ago. There's not a trace of it left, and one can't even guess where it was." The god then points out Babylon, "over there . . . with great towers and a huge wall around it—but before long it will be just as hard to find as Nineveh."[15] Lucian was using Nineveh to speak, like Herodotus six centuries earlier, of the transience of power and the caprice of worldly affairs.

Local lore ultimately never forgot the city of Sardanapalus. In the Arab period, following the Muslim conquests in the seventh century AD, Ibn Battuta and others referred to the mounds opposite Mosul as "Ninawi" or some variant. In the Ottoman period, "Nineweh" was the official locator used in any property deed or transfer in the area across the river from what one historian describes as the "sleazy trading town of Mosul."

For later European travelers, some of them undoubtedly relying on local traditions, there seems to have been little doubt, when passing through Mosul or its environs, that the remains of ancient Nineveh lay nearby. The first known account since Xenophon is that of Benjamin, a rabbi from Tudela in Spain, who traveled east in the 1160s and reported on the Jewish communities of the Orient.[16] Mosul was by then, Benjamin wrote, a "large and ancient city."* Across the Tigris, Nineveh itself was a ruin dotted with villages, while Mosul boasted synagogues built by Jonah and Nahum. It was, of course, Jonah who had persuaded the Ninevites to mend their ways, buying some time before their ultimate destruction, and Nahum who prophesied the city's ultimate fall.†

The English soldier of fortune Sir Anthony Shirley, passing through on his way to the Safavid court in Persia in about 1599, certainly believed that Nineveh lay under one of the Mosul mounds. Layard, in his second book, *Discoveries in the Ruins of Nineveh and Babylon*, quoted Shirley: "Nineve (that which God himself calleth that Great Citie) hath not one stone standing, which may give the memorie of the being of a towne." Shirley noted that just a mile away was Mosul, "a small thing, rather to be a witnesse of others' mightinesse, and of God's judgment, than of any fashion of magnificence in itselfe."[17]

In 1766, the German explorer and cartographer Carsten Niebuhr, returning to Europe from an expedition to Yemen, stopped briefly at Mosul. The map he reproduced in his travel memoir shows the mounds across the river from Mosul, and one of these, wrote Niebuhr, was home to a contemporary village whose name he rendered as "Koindsjug"—the same "Kuyunjik" that Layard used a century later for the name of the entire Nineveh mound itself.[18] Niebuhr also mentioned a mosque, sitting atop a part of the more southerly mound, that was said to rest upon the site of the grave of the Biblical prophet Jonah.‡

A Biblical "gazetteer" written in 1813 by one Elijah Parish, Congregational minister at Byfield in Massachusetts, provides probably as good a summary as any of conventional wisdom as it stood when Layard arrived at Mosul twenty-eight years later. Noting that Jonah sized the city's circumference at a three days' walk, that Strabo had (rightly) said it was larger than Babylon, and that Diodorus the Sicilian had written that the city walls, two hundred feet high, were wide enough for three chariots abreast (Layard would "confirm" this, as he put it, on his own

---

* Mosul itself, wrote Benjamin of Tudela, was "Assur the Great, and here dwell about 7,000 Jews."

† Jonah's tomb is at Nebbi Yunus ("Tomb of Jonah") outside Mosul, and Nahum's is twenty-five miles north of Mosul in the Christian hill town of Alqosh.

‡ Well into the twenty-first century, the northern and southern mounds are known by these same names, which were also current in Layard's time: Kuyunjik and Nebbi Yunus.

rides), Dr. Parish stated: "Modern travellers say, that the ruins of ancient
Nineveh, may still be seen on the eastern banks of the Tigris, opposite
to the city Mozul." Parish quoted an unnamed traveler from 1300 who
had written, "Nineveh is totally laid waste, but by the ruins it appears
to have been the greatest city in the world."

Parish clearly detected the trend, since Benjamin of Tudela, of Europeans hearing from the locals that ancient Nineveh lay under one of
the mounds opposite Mosul, either Nebbi Yunus or Kuyunjik. And yet
uncertainty remained, for Parish also wrote, "The dispute at the present
time respecting the scite [sic] of this city is a wonderful fulfilment of
prophecy." For this Massachusetts clergyman in the period just before
Layard, the ongoing mystery of Nineveh served to confirm the holy
books. Symbol of man's wickedness and God's anger: Xenophon had
blamed it on Zeus, a different god, but the message was the same—
Nineveh, in its destruction, the emblem of divine wrath and retribution.

For Layard, then, the location of Nineveh in the environs of Mosul
was fairly well established, in his own Western canon as in the enduring
tales of people in the area. Where exactly it was, and whether anything
remained to prove that the fabled city of Scripture and the Classics had
indeed existed at all, were for him to discover.

A week or so after Layard's first cursory visit, in April 1841, with a solic-
itor's desk in Ceylon still beckoning and his inquiries around Mosul finished for now, the young man was floating onward to Baghdad aboard a
raft on the Tigris. Passing over a cataract that had been formed, according
to Layard's Arab bargeman, by the mighty Nimrod himself, the Englishman remarked that such vestiges of the ancient irrigation systems had
been considered very old even in the time of Alexander. Layard wrote
of "falling asleep as we glided on toward Baghdad," his boatman telling
tales of the ancient kings.

It was the final inflaming of his imagination as his youthful life took
a dramatic turn. "The river was a history book,"

with pages slowly turning as the raft drifted along. Each picture spoke
of past magnificence and present decay: the solidly built Sasanian

wall, standing alone; the shattered, early Islamic stone latticework; the decaying, corkscrew tower of the Great Mosque at Samarra . . . built by the Abbasside caliphs.[19]

Drifting slowly south on his raft, reclining on a bed-like platform "roofed with cane and felt," Layard now determined that one day he must be back for a thorough investigation of the "ruins of Nimrud."

Smaller rafts made the trip downriver from Mosul to Baghdad in three and a half days at that time of year. Larger ones took twice the time. The raft that Layard shared with his English companion was relatively comfortable, floating on fifty inflated goatskins. At Baghdad the wood would be sold for a profit, and the skins packed up to go back to Mosul. As Layard's coming discoveries were to reveal, these rafts had been used on the Tigris since the days of the Assyrians at least.[20]

Eventually, "sweeping round a bend in the river," wrote Layard of his arrival at Baghdad, "we came in sight of the city rising majestically on its banks." From that distance, the metropolis of domes, minarets, and palaces "seemed to be all that I had pictured to myself of the city of the Caliphs and the sojourn of Haroun al-Rashid."[21] Up close, however, Layard was to find mid-nineteenth-century Ottoman Baghdad a far cry from the city of his boyhood dreams. "A series of corrupt Turkish governors had allowed it to become a mass of ruins and a sinkhole of filth. Its common people were half-starved, and many of the once lovely houses of the rich were empty, falling apart, their owners dead."[22]

But the city was fascinating. Layard, enjoying the company and physical comforts at the British East India Company's official residence, studied Farsi and rode out hunting antelope and birds or exploring the great Sasanian vault that still stood at Ctesiphon. The City of Peace was now in its eleventh century.

Over the next year, Layard traveled eastward from Baghdad, but not to Ceylon. He fell in with the Bakhtiaris of Persia, joining them, Byron-like, for a while in their fight against the Persian crown. He then made his way farther south in Iran before heading back into "Turkish Asia" and reaching Basra. There he arrived "without a farthing in the world and with scarcely a shirt to my back, having been plundered some half a dozen times and exposed to the vicissitudes of war," as he wrote from Baghdad to an uncle. Nor had the vicissitudes ended at Basra. Layard

went on to report: "Between Busrah and Baghdad I was plundered by
the Arabs three times!" Layard arrived at the capital again to introduce
himself to the British Resident there wearing only a shirt.* Layard's
shoes having been robbed from him along with almost everything else,
"it was some time before he could walk again without pain."[23]

It was still 1841. Trouble was brewing yet again between the Ottoman
sultan and the Iranian shah. At Baghdad, Layard wrote home to his
mother to say that he was coming home. One senses from his letters
that duty made him say this, and that to leave the land of the lost cities
would not have been his choice. Layard would not in fact return to
England until 1848.

In June of 1842, nine months after arriving at Baghdad, he was still
there, having made three more trips into Persia. He now intended to sail
home from Beirut, but the British Resident at Baghdad, impressed with
Layard's Persian peregrinations, prevailed upon the twenty-five-year-old
to return via Constantinople. Queen Victoria's embassy to the "Sublime
Porte," as the sultan's ministry was called, was the headquarters of British
interests in the Near East, and Layard was dispatched there to provide
intelligence from his travels on the Turks' far Persian frontier. War was
brewing there once more.

———————

Along the way from Baghdad to Constantinople, Layard was able to
pay a second, fleeting visit to Mosul. He had tried and failed, during his
travels since his first visit there a year before, to attract English support
for more serious investigations of its mounds. Now he arrived at Mosul
to make a dramatic discovery. The new French consul there, Paul-Émile
Botta, supported by the government in Paris, had begun digging on a
nearby mound.

For most people in Layard's position, this would have been crushing news. For a year, he had been sending messages home and to the
embassy in Constantinople, pleading the cause of investigations into
the Mosul mounds. All of his pleadings had been rebuffed or ignored.

———————

* Another account has Layard and his companions robbed of, "quite literally, the shirts
off their backs." Arnold C. Brackman, *The Luck of Nineveh: Archaeology's Great Adventure*
(New York: McGraw-Hill, 1978), p. 92.

Now someone else, backed by the financial and diplomatic support of a rival world power, was in situ nearby. In the few days that Layard spent with Botta there at Mosul, they nonetheless became excellent friends.

Botta was the son of a well-known Italian historian exiled to France for his revolutionary opinions. When Layard met him at Mosul, the thirty-seven-year-old Botta had worked as a botanist, physician, and diplomat in Yemen, China, Syria, and Egypt. From 1826 to 1829 Botta had sailed around the world as ship's doctor with an expedition of the Jardin des Plantes in Paris. Serving in the Sudan as physician to the Ottoman governor of Egypt, he had "collected no less than 12,000 insects."[24] In his 1830 doctoral dissertation at Paris, Botta advocated the use of opium "in treatment of diseases like *nymphomania* and *satyriasis*."[25]

An infamous lotus-eater who had returned from China with the opium habit, Botta tried, when not taking Layard around his haphazard scratchings on the Kuyunjik mound, to interest the Englishman in the narcotic. Layard tried it once, with "the result, happily," that he "suffered from so severe a headache, accompanied by violent sickness," that Botta's further blandishments of a pharmacological nature went nowhere.

Fueled liberally with Botta's arak, the two men spent seventy-two hours talking of the mysteries of the ancient mounds, and much else besides, in "Italian, French, and English."[26] The Frenchman, sometimes gloomy with his opium, was even in this short period "despondent" at the task of searching, in the Mosul *tels*, for "the proverbial needle in the haystack."[27] Layard, then and later, never stopped encouraging Botta.

Layard was to spend the years 1842 to 1845 at Constantinople, working as an unofficial aide de camp of sorts to the august British ambassador to the Sublime Porte, Sir Stratford Canning, who towered in the Middle Eastern affairs of the day. Canning initially sent Layard on an undercover mission to rebels in Serbia, where the last Ottoman garrison had left in 1830. Canning later deployed Layard as covert envoy to a reform faction in Constantinople and sought his advice on the border dispute at the head of the Persian Gulf that had nearly brought the Ottomans and Persians back to blows. Canning eventually invited Layard to live with the ambassador's own family in Constantinople and tried hard to secure for him a proper position credentialed and paid by London.

The geopolitical alignment of the time placed Britain and her long-standing Ottoman ally at odds with Russia and her eastern ally, Qajar

Persia. As the Foreign Office in London was bent on appeasing Russia, and Canning and Layard took the opposite view, London constantly refused any paid, official position for the young man.

Layard eventually turned to paid newspaper work, writing for the *Morning Chronicle* in England and for the *Malta Times*, a respected publication that served as the key English paper in the Levant and broader Near East. Despite his penury, there was also time for a "merry . . . somewhat reckless and riotous" bachelor's life in the ancient city on the Bosphorus, so full of the intrigues, danger, and color that he loved. When not representing Canning in secret midnight meetings with reform-minded Turks, Layard studied Turkish, and also "Hebrew, Chaldee, and Syriac," to help him with the discoveries he hoped to be making soon enough. He walked in the hills, conducted a risky flirtation with a mysterious and beautiful young noblewoman who turned out to be a sister of the sultan, and never forgot the mounds of Mosul.[28]

But Layard's situation under Canning was frustrating. The work was unofficial and remunerated only occasionally, with personal dispensations from the ambassador. As Layard chafed at Constantinople, Botta dug fruitlessly around Mosul. The two proto-archaeologists wrote each other frequently, Layard encouraging his friend through the bouts of despair that alternated with the succor of the pipe.

In early 1843, still making no progress with his desultory dig at Kuyunjik, Botta received word from a local peasant that there were "sculptured stones" at a *tel* known as Khorsabad. Botta eventually transferred his efforts there, and immediately hit pay dirt. His very first trench uncovered what would be the first of "a hundred or so chambers, halls, and corridors." Almost all of them were "lined with exquisite sculptured bas-reliefs representing gods, kings, battles, sieges and religious ceremonies."

The palace turned out to be the ancient Dur Sharrukin, named after Sargon II, a ruler in the eighth century BC. Layard noted later that the early Arab geographers called it "Saraghoun"—sixteen or seventeen centuries after its founding.[29] Like the other archaeological mounds of Mesopotamia, the countless *tels* that look like simple rounded hills in the flat Mesopotamian landscape, here the many centuries of windblown sand, dirt, and dust, plus the detritus from the crumbling of the buildings themselves, had buried what remained of the structures.

The reliefs and inscriptions lining the ancient walls beneath Botta's Khorsabad mound were carved in alabaster, a form of gypsum. This had been transformed into crumbly, unstable lime by the fire that destroyed the original city at some ancient moment.*

The walls at Khorsabad would generally disintegrate when Botta's local diggers exposed them to air, but Botta managed to make drawings of numerous inscriptions and reliefs before they disappeared. The Frenchman's letter to Paris announcing the discovery traveled via Constantinople, where a delighted Layard was one of the first to read the news.

Eventually Botta's images of the reliefs and massive winged and human-headed bulls and lions began to arrive in Paris, causing a sensation. "The astonished French," writes a historian of Assyriology, as Mesopotamian archaeology came to be known, "found themselves presented with a seemingly endless succession of pictures" showing what these Assyrians, "a people til then remote and half-mythical," looked like, how they lived, and how they made war.

The French had originally sent Botta to Mosul in response to Claudius James Rich's work at Babylon and elsewhere. Botta had a diplomatic role as consul, but his main job was to win a victory in the nascent conflict for archaeological glory as mighty empires once more competed on Iraq's flat soil. Now, with Botta's stunning discoveries, the French government turned the taps of support open even further. The well-known draftsman and orientalist Eugène Flandin was commissioned to copy the images on site. More funds came Botta's way. A firman, a document commanding support from local officials, was arranged for him at Constantinople in the name of the sultan.

For Layard, the contrast between this French activity and his own frustrations was intense. But he and Botta kept up their warm friendship, with Botta detailing his developments to Layard, inviting Layard back to Mosul, and urging Layard to publicize the finds. The Malta Times enjoyed several scoops as the popular story unfolded.

"With a generosity and liberality rare among discoverers," Layard wrote many years later, Botta "allowed me to see his letters to his official

---

* It was later established that the destruction had come in 614 BC at the hands of the Medes, on their way to destroying Nineveh itself, with Babylonian help, two years later.

superiors in France," and the drawings and cuneiform copies that went with them.[30] Layard shared these treasures with Canning as the information passed through Constantinople on the way to Paris. One can imagine that the excitement of seeing this historic material firsthand was a factor in Canning's decision, soon thereafter, to pay from his own pocket for Layard to pursue the Mosul dream.

Botta believed he had found the main prize: Nineveh itself. Layard did not agree. Khorsabad was too small and too far from the Tigris, he surmised. From Constantinople, Layard wrote to Botta encouraging the Frenchman to try instead the mound at nearby Nimrud. Botta, however, apparently found the location "inconvenient."

"The success of M. Botta had increased my anxiety to explore the ruins of Assyria," Layard later admitted. "It was evident that Khorsabad . . . did not represent ancient Nineveh, nor did it afford us any additional evidence as to the site of that city."[31] Botta's discoveries and surging fame only deepened Layard's own desire to find Nineveh itself. But he had no money to go back to Nimrud and start digging, and nobody would listen to his exhortations.

The Constantinople in which Layard found himself in the years 1842–45 would have looked, smelled, and sounded little different from Ogier de Busbecq's city of three centuries before. But the air of Ottoman invincibility had been reversed. Behind the timeless muezzin cries from the minarets, and the growls of the city's famous empire of neighborhood dogs, a hundred thousand or so strong, behind the walls of divan, seraglio, and kiosk, it was a time of immense change.

In November of 1839, in a rose arbor—the Gulhane—in the grounds of the Topkapi Palace, the sixteen-year-old Sultan Abdulmejid had issued an epochal proclamation. Spurred by the British, whose support he needed against the breakaway Mehmed Ali Pasha of Egypt, the Gulhane Edict sent the Ottoman Empire a bold message of reform. It "called for the abolition of tax farming, security of life, property, and honour for all, universal conscription, fair public trials, and equality for every subject before the law."[32]

Abdulmejid's father, Mahmoud II, had ruled for fifty-four years, dying in 1839. It was a wrenching period for the Ottomans, coming to terms with both their own decay and the boisterous expansion of an industrializing Europe. Sultan Mahmoud's response had been a project of Europeanizing and modernizing reforms known as the *Tanzimat*, or restructuring.* A legend had it that Mahmoud's mother had been one Aimée du Buc de Rivéry, captured by Barbary corsairs as a girl and eventually given or sold on to the sultan in Constantinople. Mahmoud's reforming urge has been credited to love for his French mother, but the concubine in question was probably in fact a Georgian or Circassian, and her son had no choice but to try to catch up with Europe.†

The Gulhane Edict was in a sense merely a formalizing of the *Tanzimat* spirit of the young sultan's late father, who had died three months before. The edict's announcement of equality among the empire's creeds was especially controversial. Equality before the law meant equality before the tax man, and if a believer was now to pay the same as an infidel, then either infidels had to pay less—which the Porte could ill afford, especially with its new European tastes in everything from gunboats to palaces—or believers had to pay more. Presenting a further challenge were certain tenets of orthodox Islam, the largest faith in the empire and the faith of which the sultan, whatever his personal beliefs at any period, was caliph. The traditional creed of Medina accepted no equality at all, on three principal levels, as an Ottoman historian pointed out: "believer and unbeliever, master and slave, male and female."[33]

For the Ottomans in this first half of the nineteenth century, the external challenge was primarily the "Western Question": dealing with the increasingly predatory behavior of Europe's Great Powers.‡ For the Europeans, it was a matter of the hugely complex "Eastern Question": how to respond to an Ottoman Empire that seemed to be falling

---

* Mahmoud II disbanded the Janissaries in 1826, after they mutinied in response to his plans to establish a more formalized, European-style army based on conscription.

† The last four Ottoman sultans were all sons of Abdulmejid, from among his forty-four children. Of his nineteen official wives, all were from the Caucasus except one, who was from Bosnia.

‡ The great powers in the Concert of Europe international system following the fall of Napoleon in 1815 were Austria, France, Prussia, and the United Kingdom.

apart, when almost every episode in the decline opened opportunities for one of the European players to gain an advantage over the others.

Napoleon's brief seizure of Egypt in 1798 had been a harbinger, followed by Russian advances in the Caucasus early in the nineteenth century. Greece was the first Ottoman province to gain independence, rebelling in 1821 and becoming a kingdom under a son of the king of Bavaria, in 1832. In 1830, the French seized Algiers, an Ottoman city since 1529. The Russians were making incursions in the Balkans and eastern Anatolia throughout. Mehmed Ali Pasha of Egypt, long since set up as a "provincial dynast," was by 1838 trying to make himself entirely independent.[34]

Britain, fearful of an assertive Russia that would among other things threaten India, had decided that her interest lay in an Ottoman Empire as whole and healthy as possible. By far the leading global power, Britain could usually secure what it wanted in Constantinople, and by the time Layard arrived in 1842, his host Canning was uncontested as the most important foreigner in the Ottoman Empire. To the extent that some cynics at the time saw the Ottoman state as almost a British protectorate, Canning was nearly its viceroy. Within the sultan's court, the *Tanzimat* reform program was controversial. In the far-flung provinces, as Layard's subsequent return to Iraq would teach him, it was often nonexistent.

For "Turkish Arabia," or Mesopotamia, the long eighteenth century had been a time of local dynasties only loosely answerable to Constantinople. In the two southern provinces of Baghdad and Basra, a dynasty of Mamluks—originally Georgian slave-soldiers—had held sway from the City of Peace since the 1720s. In the northern Mosul province, encompassing Iraqi Kurdistan as well as the city and its *tel*-dotted plain, a family called the Jalilis, also originally Christians, did the same. The period shortly before Layard's arrival in Constantinople would see both Baghdad and Mosul return to more direct Ottoman rule, but as Layard soon discovered, the rest of the *Tanzimat* reforms would largely pass Iraq by.

Finally, in 1845, as Canning prepared a return to England and Botta— with continued support from the French state—was growing in fame, Layard managed to persuade his friend and sponsor to partner with him personally in funding a dig at Mosul. Competition with the French was clearly a factor in the ambassador's decision to support the young man. "Without his liberality and public spirit," wrote Layard later of Canning's support in countering the threat from Paris, "the treasures of Nimrud would have been reserved for the enterprise of those who have appreciated the value and importance of the discoveries at Khorsabad."[35] The Macedonians and the Achaemenids, the Romans and the Parthians and the Sasanians, the Ottomans and the various Persian dynasties, and now Britain and France: Iraq was once more cockpit of the world's principal imperial rivalries.

Canning's personal support was meager compared to Botta's funding from the exchequer in Paris. But at last Layard had means to pursue his dream. He was accustomed to doing much with little. After securing the usual letters and travel documents from the Ottoman authorities, Layard took a steamer from Constantinople to the eastern Mediterranean. From there, he wrote, "I crossed the mountains of Pontus and the great steppes of the Usum Yilak as fast as post-horse could carry me, descended the high lands into the valley of the Tigris, galloped over the vast plains of Assyria, and reached Mosul in twelve days."[36]

Layard arrived at Mosul to witness a near caricature of the later Ottoman Empire's encounter with nineteenth-century Europe. The well-known description of the sultan's realm as the "sick man of Europe" would not gain currency for another couple of decades, but as the rickety Ottoman edifice struggled to reform and modernize, the empire was showing the signs of its extraordinary age.

The Ottoman official charged with the Mosul vilayet, or province, in 1845 was called Mehmed Pasha. As this individual's previous service to his sultan had taken place on Crete, he was known in his new province as the Cretan. Having arrived at Mosul, Layard duly presented to the Cretan his documents from Constantinople, where both the Sublime Porte and the British embassy had provided him with letters.

"Nature had placed hypocrisy beyond his reach," wrote Layard of the Cretan. "He was short and fat, deeply marked by the small-pox, uncouth in gestures and harsh in voice."[37] The pockmarked pasha was unlikely to have been particularly successful at the sultan's court; Mosul, for all its ancient trading wealth, was hardly a plum posting in the Ottoman constellation. On the way to take up his position on the banks of the

Tigris, the Cretan, wrote Layard humorously, had "revived many good old customs and impositions, which the reforming spirit of the age had caused to fall into decay." One of these anti-reforms by the pasha was the reintroduction of an old Ottoman practice known as *dish-parasi*, or "tooth money." This was charged to every village "in which a man of such rank is entertained, for the wear and tear of his teeth in masticating the food he condescends to receive from the inhabitants."

Mehmed Pasha had arrived at Mosul shortly before Layard to find many of the town's leading men absent. The Cretan's rapacious reputation had clearly gone ahead of him. So he sent out comforting promises of "friendship and protection" to the city fathers, persuading them to return to Mosul. Once they had returned, the pasha promptly slit their throats. By the time Layard arrived, it was late October or early November of 1845. "The population was in a state of terror and despair."[38]

Layard now found himself the unwitting agent of yet more misery for the city's inhabitants. Whispers soon spread that this arrival of an Englishman from the embassy at Constantinople portended a coming change in governor. The Cretan's end, or so the Moslawis began to tell each other, had at last arrived. Hearing of this from his spies, Mehmed Pasha pretended to fall mortally ill. "General rejoicings" broke out among the locals. Suddenly, the Cretan "appeared in perfect health in the marketplace." Those few Moslawis of means who had survived his earlier predations were now beggared once and for all by the representative of their sultan.

Out in the villages and steppes it was the same. The pasha encouraged his tax agents to harvest as much money as they could. Their motto, he insisted: "Go, destroy, eat."* The result was chaos in the countryside, with the Arabs plundering every caravan they could find, travelers robbed and killed, and the farmland laid waste. "The villages were deserted, and the roads were little frequented and very insecure."[39]

Back in Mosul for the third time, Layard now had to make his way to Nimrud, twenty miles south across the lawless countryside. Twice before, Layard had come to Mosul and left empty-handed, his dreams unfulfilled and his intuitions about its gloomy brown *tels* still unproven. Now he could not let the pasha get in the way.

---

* Layard writes in a footnote: "To eat money, i.e., to get money unlawfully, or by pillage, is a common expression in the East." Layard, *Nineveh and Its Remains*, p. 13.

Nobody, least of all the avaricious Cretan, would believe that someone could be interested in old rubbish, or "mere stones," as Layard put it. If the Englishman was to dig, everyone would assume it was for gold. With the Cretan nearby, gold meant trouble. If, on the other hand, Layard was perceived to be seeking statues and friezes thousands of years old, this would not have been much safer than gold. The faith bore a deep antipathy for everything—especially gods—from the *jahiliyya*, the time of ignorance before the true religion was revealed to Mohammed.

And so, good Englishman that he was, Layard explained that his interest in the region was entirely of a sporting nature. He was off boar shooting. With an armory of "guns, spears, and other formidable weapons," he and a Mr. Ross, merchant of Mosul, accompanied by a manservant and Layard's Ottoman minder, boarded the raft that Layard had commissioned and pushed off into the Tigris to float south to Nimrud on November 8, 1845.

Seven hours on the river, the sun setting on his right hand and the late-year countryside cool, flat, and brown all around him, brought Layard to the ancient, partly submerged dam that local legend attributed to the hand of Nimrod himself, the "mighty hunter" of the Old Testament.

The tiny party alit in the gloaming and made their way on foot to the local village. It was empty, deserted, a "heap of ruins," without even the dogs that Layard was used to seeing in Arab villages. Then, through "the entrance to a miserable hovel," Layard saw the glow of a small fire.

Inside the ruined house was a sight typical of the devastated country around. An Arab family—a father, three wizened wives, some half-naked children, and "one or two mangy greyhounds"—had taken shelter in the abandoned village. When Layard entered, the family cowered, thinking he and his party were "Osmanlis." Seeing that the newcomers were not Turks but Europeans, the Arabs relaxed. Layard heard their story from the father. "Plundered by the pasha," their sedentary tribe had dispersed across the countryside. This family had taken refuge alone in the abandoned village.

The man of the family was called Awad. He impressed Layard immediately. The Englishman, there in the half-lit hovel, explained what he hoped to do at Nimrud and asked his host to recruit the necessary workmen and oversee them. Awad offered to set off that night to procure the men. Layard accepted.

Layard was twenty-eight years old now. In five years he had ridden from the Syrian coast to Baghdad and then into Iran. He had lived with the Bakhtiaris and fought with them against the Safavid crown, and made his way to Basra and thence on foot—possessing only a shirt—to Baghdad. He had ridden to Constantinople, and there engaged in midnight intelligence work for his queen, and he had conducted secret missions in the Balkans before riding back to Constantinople and onward, once more, to Mosul. Looking back on that evening near Nimrud with his companions and Awad and the man's miserably poor family, Layard laconically summed up the seasoning he had provided himself for the revelations ahead. "Such scenes and companions," he wrote, "were not new to me."

Layard could barely sleep. "Hopes, long cherished," he wrote, "were now to be realised, or were to end in disappointment." The anticipation had a feverish quality as he lay in the dark hut. "Visions of palaces under-ground, of gigantic monsters, of sculptured figures, and endless inscriptions floated before me."

Packed on the mud floor by the ebbing embers with ten other souls and the mangy dogs, Layard found himself in a febrile dream. After successfully extracting the long-secret treasures of the mound, he was "wandering in a maze of chambers from which I could find no outlet." Then suddenly the treasures were buried again, and he was out of the maze, and now the springtime grasses of the mound as he had first seen it five years before were beneath his feet in the fresh air. And then at last, he was falling asleep. And just as he did so, he heard Awad's voice, rousing him. The day, Layard's big day, had already dawned, and his new friend had returned as promised. The Arab had six men with him, ready for work.

Layard stepped outside the hut. There, in the morning light, "the lofty cone and broad mound of Nimrud rose like a distant mountain in the morning sky."[40] This *tel*, unusually large, was almost a mile and a half square. All was brown now, in November, "a parched and barren waste." The turmoil between the Ottomans and the Arabs had denuded the area of human life. "No signs of human habitation, not even the black tent of the Arab, were seen upon the plain."

The Nimrud mound was twenty minutes' walk away. Once there, Layard and his team set to work rummaging over the surface. But where to start? The *tel* at Nimrud covers almost nine hundred acres. Layard appears simply to have taken his team where his instincts told him to go. That first morning, he was thrilled when one of his workmen brought him a "fragment of a bas relief." The stone itself was, excitingly, much like "the burnt gypsum of Khorsabad," where his friend and rival Botta had enjoyed his stunning success.[41]

Then Awad showed Layard a corner of alabaster sticking out of the ground. Apparently it was part of a much larger block of stone, for the visible piece could not be budged. To prove that his lost city was indeed there, Layard needed buildings: the remains of major edifices buried in this bump on the flat plain. But really he needed something else. At Khorsabad, Botta had found impressive statues, human-headed winged bulls fourteen feet high, weighing twenty-eight tons. Made of single blocks of alabaster, they were so huge that they had to be sawed into pieces for the trip to Paris. Massive sculptures like these, spectacular objects to bring home, there to inflame the imaginations of a younger civilization, were the stuff of fame, fortune, and further funding. Could Layard find something similar? That first day on the mound at Nimrud, he dwelled repeatedly on the notion of statues. Far more than tombs, throne rooms, altars, or city walls, they were the gold for which he truly searched. "My chief aim," Layard wrote, "was to ascertain, as soon as possible, the existence of sculptures."[42]

After uncovering Awad's exposed piece of alabaster sufficiently to discover that it was "the upper part of a large slab," Layard and his team swiftly discovered a dozen more of these slabs. They appeared to form a rectangular room. "It was natural," he wrote, "to conclude that sculptures were still buried under the soil." A few days later, back in Mosul, he hired local agents to commence explorations on mounds closer to the city, hoping there "to ascertain the existence of sculptured buildings."

By the end of that first day, Layard had not in fact proven much. He had not found the large carved figures that he especially needed. But he had discovered enough to make what must have been an intoxicating conclusion, one that would keep him digging for his treasure. "It was now evident that the remains of a building of considerable extent existed in the mound."

On the second day, digging down toward the floor of the chamber they had found, Layard and his companions discovered fragments of ivory objects, with flakes of gold leaf still attached. Awad, the trusty superintendent, "who had his own suspicions of the object of my search," now grew excited, wrote Layard.

"O Bey," said Awad. "Your books are right, and the Franks know that which is hid from the true believer. Here is the gold, sure enough, and please God, we shall find it all in a few days."

Awad counseled Layard to keep the discovery a secret from the Arabs of the plain, lest they inform the grasping Mehmed Pasha in Mosul. Layard was interested in a different kind of buried treasure. He gave Awad the meager gold they had collected. If more was discovered, he promised, Awad and his crew could keep it.

After five days at Nimrud, Layard galloped the three hours back to Mosul to tell the pasha what he had been doing. The Cretan had just pulled off his gambit of feigning deathly illness only to recover miraculously and extort the men celebrating his imminent demise. Layard "congratulated him on his speedy recovery."[43] They then discussed the fanatical qadi, or chief Sunni prelate of the town. An English merchant had bought a warehouse, and the qadi was trying to cause riots with a claim that the Franks were attempting to buy up "the whole of Turkey." The Cretan explained that when he had been pasha at Siwa, in Egypt, the ulema there had objected to his encroaching on a Muslim burial ground.

"I took every gravestone and built up the castle walls with them," the pasha proudly told Layard.

Now it was time to talk about Layard's "boar shooting expedition." Layard explained what he had really been doing. The Cretan "feigned ignorance" before producing a dirty scrap of paper. "An almost invisible particle of gold leaf" lay in one of its folds. An "informer," apparently, had brought it from the dig. Layard invited the pasha to send a man to watch over the proceedings and secure any gold these proto-archaeologists might find.

Returning to Nimrud on November 19, Layard increased his crew to thirty men and set about "opening long trenches at right angles in various directions," crisscrossing the mound. "The soil," wrote Layard, "mixed with sun-dried and baked bricks, pottery, and fragments of alabaster, offered considerable resistance to the tools of the workmen."

The region, in this disordered time, was roiled by ongoing violence among the local tribes; meanwhile Mehmed Pasha in Mosul seemed to have plundered every village. The insecurity in the countryside forced Layard to move around from one deserted hamlet to another. He finally settled in an abandoned village three miles from Nimrud. There he shared a roofless house with "beasts of the plough" and used a table of his own construction to shelter from the rain when he slept.

This latest empty village had belonged to Turcomans: "descendants," as Layard wrote, "of tribes brought by the early Turkish Sultans from the north of Asia Minor." The sultans had imported these Turkic kinsmen as loyalists in a region marked by endless violence of one kind or another—ethnic massacres, foreign invasions, political strife. All around him, Layard heard the lapping of the various human tides in this turbulent sea of Mosul and the Nineveh Plain: Arab tribes in the steppe and desert, Turcomans, Kurds, and Yezidis in the rich plains east of the Tigris; "Chaldean and Jacobite Christians" in Mosul and surrounding villages.

There were also Christians in the mountains, Layard's hardy Nestorians, whose fathers had taken to the hills for "refuge from the devastating bands of Tamerlane."[44] Of all of these peoples, the Chaldean (former Nestorians communing with the Catholic Church in Rome) and Jacobite (Aramaic-speaking Orthodox) Christians, said Layard, were "probably the only descendants of that great Assyrian people" who twenty-four centuries previously had ruled the civilized world from Cyprus to Central Asia.

Soon after Layard had settled into his new home, he received a visit from a man who could become either an important new ally or a scourge: Daoud Agha, local chief of the bashi-bazouks, as the Ottoman irregular cavalry were known in certain lands of the empire.

In a nearly half-page footnote in *A Popular Account of Discoveries at Nineveh* (1851), Layard explained this feature of late Ottoman rule, the bashi-bazouks. "A man known for his courage and daring" would be named the chief of a unit of a few hundred to a thousand horsemen.[45] He would then recruit "all the vagrants and freebooters he can find." The chief often forced his irregulars to buy their horses from him, withholding their pay until he had sufficiently reimbursed himself. The housing and feeding of the bashi-bazouks was the responsibility of whichever village they happened to fall upon, to "plunder and ill treat as they see fit." The more successful chiefs of these bands would travel from province to province of the Ottoman Empire, renting themselves out to the local pashas for the plunder of their districts.

In much of the empire, in this age of reform, the unruly and somewhat outdated bashi-bazouks had been banned entirely. Their continued existence at Mosul was a sign of what an afterthought the city had become—this, and the fact that they were said to have been paid considerably less in the Mosul pashalic than elsewhere.

On November 28, digging at the southern end of the mound, Layard discovered a new slab. It was "unsculptured" on the side initially uncovered. The other side, however, revealed a fine carved relief, by far the most exciting find to date.

The Old Testament had given Nineveh a unique role. Where Babylon represented vice and decadence, and a degree of arrogant power, Nineveh was something else: the exemplar of violence and pure might, and of evil's ultimate end in degeneracy and flaming ruin. "Woe to the wicked city . . . there is none end of their corpses," Nahum had written. "Nineveh is laid waste: who will bemoan her?"[46]

In that age of cracks appearing in the European edifice of belief, Layard faced a major question alongside his personal quest, whether he acknowledged it or not. How true was Scripture? Was the historical Nineveh—if in fact it had existed—the place of epic, overweening violence and cruelty that the Old Testament described? Along with a neighboring slab, these latest finds would presage what Layard was to discover about the nature, and ultimately the identity, of this lost world.

On its sculptured side, the new slab showed a double-horsed chariot carrying three archers, their bows at full stretch. "Beneath the chariot wheels," wrote Layard, "were scattered the conquered and the dying, and an archer, about to be trodden down."

A lower panel on the same slab showed a walled city, or castle, besieged. As an attacker mounts a ladder against the walls, defenders shoot arrows, throw stones, and load their slings. A long-haired woman raises her hand "as if in the act of asking for mercy."[47] A defender tries to burn a catapult brought up to the walls by a ramp, while "an Assyrian warrior, bending on one knee, and holding a torch in his right hand, was setting fire to the gate of the castle."[48] Another Assyrian pries stones from the castle walls. Between these two besiegers, a wounded defender falls "headlong from the battlements" above. On a nearby slab, a woman "stood on the walls tearing her hair in grief."

Layard, who at the age of twelve had been able to "distinguish between the paintings of such minor artists as Carlo Dolci and his daughter Agnes," was impressed artistically.[49] He seemed pleased to note that in its general composition, in the "elegance and richness of the ornaments, the attempt at a faithful delineation of the limbs and muscles," the sculpture he had just found was superior to the finds of M. Botta.

Back in camp that evening, Layard did something that he often made time to do. He "meditated," to use his word, on the meaning of it all. The reverie was interrupted by the arrival of Daoud Agha, the leader of the fearsome bashi-bazouks, with news from Mosul: Mehmed Pasha had ordered Layard to stop his digging at once.

The next morning, Layard rode to Mosul to speak to the pasha. First the Cretan said he had ordered no such thing. Then he helpfully promised Layard a firman. Finally he explained to Layard that unfortunately the mound was covered with Muslim graves; the dig would have to end.

Layard suggested that the pasha handle the local religious authorities with the same firmness he claimed to have shown in similar circumstances in his previous posting at Siwa. The pasha replied that there in Egypt he had had true, civilized "Mussulmans to deal with and there was tanzimat."

"Here," lamented the Cretan, "we have only Kurds and Arabs, and Wallah! They are beasts."

"You are my dearest and most intimate friend," explained the pasha to Layard. "If anything happens to you, what grief should I not suffer." The life of his English friend, after all, was so much "more valuable than old stones."[50]

When Layard returned to Nimrud, his ally Daoud Agha had a confession to make. On the orders of the Cretan, during Layard's absence in town the bashi-bazouks had been hauling Muslim tombstones to the mound, to give substance to the pasha's false claim. "We have destroyed more tombs of the true believers," said the pasha's official bandit, "in making sham ones, than you could have defiled between the Zab and the Selamiyah. We have killed our horses and ourselves in carrying those accursed stones."[51]

Layard decided to keep digging, but more discreetly and with a smaller crew. This went on for three weeks, with Layard discovering a lion carved from black basalt, "a pair of gigantic winged bulls," and other interesting objects.[52] *

One night, Daoud Agha rode in with two wounded troopers and an Arab prisoner—a member of a raiding party that had hoped to plunder Layard's camp. The neighborhood was growing increasingly lawless. With Christmas approaching, Layard decided to rebury his treasures, leave the mound, and make for the comforts of the British Residence at Baghdad, 220 miles away. With no gold of significance to be found, plundering would not be an issue.

Layard must have been immensely proud, writing at this juncture to Canning at the embassy in Constantinople. The ambassador had been not only a friend, if a cool and somewhat Olympian one, but a partner in this venture. Now Layard had done his job, and the results were strong.

"There was no longer any doubt," wrote the young man, "of the existence not only of sculptures and inscriptions, but even of large edifices in the interior of the mound of Nimrud." They had found the traces of an ancient civilization, and it would indeed prove to be Nineveh. Now Canning could secure a firman, the sultan's all-important imprimatur, clearing local obstacles. And money, hopefully, would at last come from England.

Over the coming decade, Layard made discoveries there at Nimrud and elsewhere in the Mosul vicinity, and to a lesser degree at Babylon, that rewrote the history of the world. As Layard did so, the remarkable generosity of spirit between him and Botta continued. "His feeling that Nimrud was surpassing Khorsabad was shared by Botta," writes a historian of the great early Assyriologists, "who in several letters expressed

---

* Two of Layard's bulls from Nimrud—possibly those he mentions here—he gave to Lady Charlotte Guest, a young married relative to whom he was very close; they eventually were bought by John D. Rockefeller, who gave them to the Metropolitan Museum of Art in New York, where they stand to this day, over ten feet high and ten feet long. "Human-Headed Winged Bull (Lamassu)," The Met website, https://www.metmuseum.org/art/collection/search/322608.

his delight in Layard's discoveries, which appeared to him to be of such importance that his own contribution was quickly being reduced to being one who led the way."[53] Layard's efforts, combined with those of the geniuses—the Irishman Edward Hincks, the Englishman Henry Rawlinson, the German Julius Oppert, and others—who were soon to crack the code of cuneiform translation, confirmed in detail the historicity of swathes of the Old Testament. The work of Layard and Botta, and quite a few others who followed, would show the world, for the first time ever, the very chambers and walls where divine stories of many of their own origins had played out.

Layard himself, with the success of his writings, became a famous and powerful man: a member of Parliament, a cabinet member, founder of the successful Ottoman Bank, a director of London's National Gallery, an owner of Venice's Murano glassworks, and Queen Victoria's ambassador in Madrid. In 1877, now Sir Austen Henry Layard, he was sent back east—by none other than his old friend Benjamin Disraeli—as ambassador to Constantinople.

One wonders what emotions he must have had, returning as ambassador, rich and celebrated, to the Ottoman capital where as a young man he had worked for Canning in unpaid penury. Perhaps the stories of the *Arabian Nights*, which had inspired Layard in his youth, still occasionally gave him pleasure. He had long been a "great man" of the Victorian scene when he wrote, late in life in his autobiography, "I can read them even now with almost as much delight as I read them when a boy." Layard died, after many years in a palace on Venice's Grand Canal, at the age of seventy-seven in 1894. He had not only become a genuine "legend in his own time," but had also achieved his share of immortality.[54] Layard had achieved this in ways that were uncannily connected to the immortality of Gilgamesh. There was adventure, writing, and Nineveh itself, in whose mounds the ancient cuneiform tablets bearing Gilgamesh's story were soon uncovered. Layard's discoveries prefigured a great surge of archaeological interest in Iraq that itself mirrored an emerging broader European engagement with the land between the rivers. He was a harbinger, of sorts, as Iraq's sleepy latter Ottoman centuries gave way to an intensive reengagement with the West. With this would come a renewal of the age-old role of Mesopotamia as a pivot or crux of civilizations.

Chapter 17

Raw Sunlight and Hurrying Storms

King Faisal I and the Making of Iraqi Independence, 1900–1932

Accompanied by several British administrators and officers, a thirty-eight-year-old son of the sharif of Mecca emerged from the serai, Baghdad's old Ottoman administration building, with its arched recesses surrounding a central courtyard, at precisely 6:00 a.m. on August 23, 1921. The hour early because of the intense heat at that time of year. Wearing a khaki uniform, the man made his way over a "long path of carpets" to a temporary wooden dais, thirty inches high.[1] Gertrude Bell, the English Orientalist who helped to form the Iraqi state out of the Ottoman wreckage in those first years, would write home a few days later, providing the main account of the morning: the enthronement of Faisal I, first king of a newly independent Iraq.*

Faisal was unusually endowed with qualities for the job. He was intelligent, dignified, physically tough and brave; bred and raised amid power; experienced in politics tribal, imperial, and international. Contemporaries who described Faisal in writing mentioned his mesmeric presence. Field Marshal Lord Allenby, conqueror of Ottoman Damascus, Aleppo, and Jerusalem in 1918, offered a typical observation: "Tall, graceful; handsome

---

* Bell was an accomplished mountaineer (with ten Alpine first ascents to her name) and desert traveler. She wrote about, among other things, a remote Arabia, "dark with hurrying storms, glittering in raw sunlight, an unanswered question and unanswerable doubt hidden in the fold of every hill."

to the point of beauty—with expressive eyes lighting up a face of calm dignity."[2] *

Faisal was a warrior, the hero of the Arab Revolt that had seen an army of tribesmen rise against the Ottomans from the Hejaz through Syria during the years 1916–1918. The revolt had been paid for with British gold and led in the field by Faisal and his brothers under their father, the sharif of Mecca. Today Faisal looked, Bell wrote, "very dignified but much strung up." Faisal spoke beautiful classical Arabic, but the Iraqi dialect was foreign to him. He had come to Iraq for the first time exactly two months previously.

Fifteen hundred people, led by Iraqi "Provisional Government" ministers in European suits, with local notables in turbans and robes and British officials and soldiers in uniforms and medals, thronged the great courtyard of the serai. The most important stood facing the crowd on the dais where Faisal's new throne awaited him.

The throne was a severe, high-backed, simple affair in dark wood, said to be "on the model of that at Westminster."[3] According to Gerald de Gaury, an Englishman who intimately observed Iraq's monarchy through its thirty-seven years, the royal seat had been "hastily knocked up from packing case wood that still showed the signs of its origin," namely "'Asahi Beer,' a Japanese product." People watched from rows of seats facing Faisal, or stood leaning against the wood railings of the building's porticoes, the mud-brick arches festooned with the new flag of Iraq.

All stood when Faisal approached and sat when he sat. A distinguished Iraqi Sunni, one Seyid Hussein, like Faisal a descendant of the Prophet, read out a declaration. Prepared by the British high commissioner, it announced that "Faisal had been elected King by 96 per cent of the people of Mesopotamia." There had been a plebiscite in July, and while 96 percent in fact referred to caucus results rather than individual votes, not many of the chroniclers, apart from the waspish de Gaury, seem to have doubted that a respectable majority of the country supported Faisal. The 1919 Versailles peace conference had made a provisional country from the Ottomans' former Mesopotamian provinces, with a population of three million. After World War I there was no going back to the

---

* Faisal's slenderness appears to have made him seem taller than in fact he was. The king was, according to the records of his London tailor, "five feet nine and a half inches." Gerald de Gaury, *Three Kings in Baghdad* (London: I. B. Tauris, 1961), p. 40.

sultan's empire, and their own constitutional, parliamentary monarchy had suited Iraq's British sponsors well enough.

For Iraq, on that morning of its first coronation, the constitution could come later. As to who would be king, anyone local would have been far too divisive. Meanwhile Faisal's prestige—both personal, from his leadership of the desert war against the Turks, and familial—was peerless among Iraq's Muslims, Sunni and Shia alike.

"Long live the king," concluded Seyid Hussein, and with that the crowd stood as one, saluting the new monarch. Between the raising of a national flag at a flagpole by Faisal's side and a twenty-one-gun salute by a British battery, a military band (this, too, was British) struck up the chords of "God Save the King." As Gertrude Bell noted in her letter home, "they have no national anthem yet."

The flag that broke out by Faisal's side on the dais, and that fluttered from the arches of the old serai that Baghdad morning, had a red triangle against the pole, and three horizontal stripes: black, white, and green. The red signified Faisal's family, the traditional rulers of Mecca, and the desert fight they had recently led against the Turks. The three stripes reached farther back, to the moments of Arab greatness. Black was for the Abbasids—and the Prophet Mohammed. Green was for his nephew, the martyred imam and hapless caliph Ali, and was the color of the Fatimids, greatest of the medieval Shia dynasties in the Arab world. White was for the Umayyads.

The Umayyads, of course, had been Sunni and based in Damascus, and the Fatimids Shia and based in Cairo. The Abbasids had been a bit of each but ineffably of Iraq. As for the Kurds, they were there, in the new country, in Mosul province, occupied by the British and disputed by the Turks; but there was nothing Kurdish in this new flag of a new nation. The 1916–1918 Arab Revolt had been organized and paid for by the British, and Faisal's flag was based on a design, meant to rally the Arabs against the Ottoman overlord, drawn up by the Englishman Mark Sykes. Faisal and T. E. Lawrence, his British liaison, had fought under it in the desert. Now, only slightly modified, it fluttered over Baghdad.

Faisal would be dead, essentially from exhaustion, in thirteen years, at the age of forty-eight. His dynasty lasted a further twenty-four years, two more kings with a regent in between. These were Faisal's son, nephew, and grandson. A generation after his enthronement, Iraq was the freest and most prosperous country in the Arab world. The epilogue would be an ill-starred story of political assassinations, increasingly thuggish military juntas, and finally, in the latter decades of the century, a monstrous dictator reminiscent of the Ashurbanipals and Tiglath-Pilesers of yore.

What went wrong? All the suspects in this murder mystery were present on that Baghdad summer morning in 1921: the foreigners, the nationalist Arab officer class, the confected monarchy in a newly embordered state, the supremacy of power in the perfect teachings of Medina, the sheer variety of religions and ethnic groups sharing histories of bloodshed on a small patch of soil. The whole rogues' gallery was present there with Faisal at Baghdad's Ottoman serai, facing the slender newcomer.

Faisal ibn al-Hussein al-Hashimi was most likely born in 1883, in the month of May and therefore at Taif, the summer hill station of the Meccan elite, about seventy miles southeast of the holy city.* His mother's father and all four of his father's brothers had been emirs of Mecca, local princes under Ottoman sovereignty. From 1908 until 1916, when he made himself King of the Hejaz, Faisal's father, Hussein, also occupied the post.† The family were sharifs, descendants of the Prophet through Hasan, son of Ali and Fatima, elder brother of the martyred Imam Hussein.

Since Umayyad times, local political leadership in Mecca had mostly been in the gift of whichever Muslim dynasty controlled Arabia at the time. The various far-off suzerains would appoint a local notable as emir, and from 968 until the end of the practice in 1916 this emir was a member of the Banu Hashim, the clan of the Prophet and his family. To Europeans, these local rulers of the holy city and its environs were known as the Sharifs of Mecca.

From the Abbasid period onward, Mecca was usually more or less an appanage of Egypt. Thus the Sharifate was generally in the gift of whoever ruled at Cairo. The Abbasids had lost control of Mecca to

---

* Taif continues to be the summer residence of Mecca's rulers.

† The Hejaz is the western part of the Arabian Peninsula, along the Red Sea, encompassing Mecca and Medina, and is relatively developed and populous compared to the rest of modern-day Saudi Arabia.

the Shia fanatic Qarmatians in the mid-tenth century, whereupon the caliph in Baghdad called upon his vassal in Egypt to return Mohammed's birthplace to the fold. Then Egypt fell to the Shia Fatimids, who controlled Mecca for eighty-five years. The Seljuk interlude straddling the eleventh and twelfth centuries meant, for Mecca, intermittent and somewhat loose rule from Isfahan while the emasculated caliph, still an Abbasid, remained at Baghdad. Control from Egypt resumed with the Mamluks in the mid-fourteenth century. In 1517 the Ottomans defeated the Mamluks, taking Egypt and with it the Hejaz. The Ottomans in turn administered Mecca and the rest of the Hejaz from Egypt for the next four hundred years.

In 1801, a Sunni fundamentalist sect from eastern Arabia, the Wahhabis, took the holy city. The following year twelve thousand Wahhabi warriors sacked the tomb of the Imam Ali at Kerbala, killing several thousand Shias and returning home with a caravan of four thousand camels' worth of loot. The Wahhabis' religious differences were not with the Shias only, but also with the Ottoman Sultans themselves, whom the Wahhabis, not without reason from a strictly orthodox perspective, accused of laxity in their application of the true faith.

In 1811, Mehmed Ali Pasha, ruler of Egypt and still a somewhat loyal Ottoman vassal at that point, launched the reconquest of Mecca and Medina. It took him and then the Ottomans seven years to defeat the Wahhabis. At the end, in 1818, the Sultan Mahmoud II transported Abdullah ibn Saud, the Wahhabi leader, to Constantinople, beheaded him, and threw his head in the Bosphorus.

In 1827, Mehmed Ali appointed the first sharif of Mecca to come from Faisal's own clan among the broader Sharifian line of Hashemite Arabs. Faisal's direct family then held the sharifate until the eastern Arabian house of Al Saud, with its Wahhabi allies, drove them from the Hejaz in 1925. It is a little-noticed irony that the same Wahhabi-Saudi alliance that eventually seized Arabia from Faisal's family was the one that had indirectly led them to the sharifate in the first place, a century previously.

Mehmed Ali, essentially independent in Egypt through the 1820s, conquered Syria from the Ottomans in 1831–33. He defeated the Sultan again at Nizip, in the far south of Turkey just north of Aleppo, in 1839, sparking the "Eastern Crisis" that led to the European—largely British—pressure on the sixteen-year-old Sultan Abdulmejid to issue his reformist Gulhane Edict, formalizing the *Tanzimat*, the reforms of his father. In 1840, at the Conference of London, Britain and other European powers, eager to prop up the Ottomans, forced Mehmed Ali to return Mecca to Ottoman central authority.

In the early 1880s the British made Egypt an informal British protectorate, under Ottoman suzerainty that was once again largely nominal. Ensconced at Cairo, the British began to brute the idea of administering Mecca too, as other possessors of Cairo had done. Queen Victoria, the British pointed out, had four times as many Muslims in her empire, looking to Mecca for religious guidance and as a place of pilgrimage, as the Ottoman sultan had in his. As Winston Churchill repeatedly stated much later, in the period shortly after the First World War, the British Empire was "the greatest Mohammedan power in the world."[4] From the late nineteenth-century British perspective, a disproportionate number of Queen Victoria's better troops in her prized Indian possession were Muslim, and they cared about the hajj. Their hosts, so to speak, when they arrived in the Hejaz were Faisal's forebears of the Banu Hashim.

This Sharifate of Mecca provided the inescapably political family context into which the Hashemite prince Faisal ibn al Hussein was born in 1885. He came into a world dominated by a single overriding feature, which was the same one that Austen Henry Layard's patron Sir Stratford Canning confronted decades earlier: the challenge of the Ottoman Empire in adapting to a world in which Europe had raced ahead in might, energy, and wealth even as the empire found itself fighting internal decay three centuries after its peak under Suleiman.

Greece, with British, French, and Russian help, won independence in a war lasting from 1821 to 1829. The Ottomans lost Algeria to the French in 1832. Egypt slipped into the hands of Mehmed Ali during the 1820s and 1830s. Serbia, Bulgaria, Romania, and Montenegro broke away in 1876, leaving only Macedonia, of the Christian Balkans, under Ottoman sway, as well as Muslim Albania and Bosnia. In 1881, two years before Faisal's birth, the French took Tunisia, an Ottoman province since 1574. A year after the loss of Tunisia, the British effectively took control of Egypt. The process of Ottoman dismemberment, as Iraq would soon enough experience for itself, went on well into the twentieth century. Libya fell to an Italian invasion in 1911.

The First World War and an alliance with Germany's losing side saw the Ottomans' final territorial retreats. The Hejaz declared itself an independent kingdom, with British support, in 1916. The same year, orchestrated by the British, Syria and parts of Arabia rose up in the Arab Revolt. In March 1917, a British Indian army of fifty thousand men drove the Turks out of Baghdad. That same year, the British invaded Palestine from Egypt. Three years later, in 1920, the victors in the Great War formally settled the partition of the empire. 1920 would be a year of bloody uprisings across much of Iraq, initiated by a small number of Sunni nationalists and largely taken up by the more numerous Shias of the southern and central districts, against the British and the League of Nations "mandate" under which they controlled the region.

In 1922 the last Ottoman sultan, Mehmed VI, thirty-sixth of his line, left Constantinople on a British battleship bound for Malta. The Turks abolished the sultanate a week later. The forty-two-year-old general Mustafa Kemal, hero of Gallipoli and victor of the War of Independence (the "independence" being from Greece, which had fought its own War of Independence against the Turks a century earlier), founded the Turkish Republic in 1923.

Faisal spent the first seven years of his life in the traditional way, in the desert among his family's Bedouin relatives, for "hardening," as T. E. Lawrence was to put it.[5] As a boy, Khalid ibn al Walid had done the same twelve and a half centuries previously. Following a sojourn in Mecca, Faisal then grew up in Constantinople from the age of ten. Faisal's father was developing a reputation for independent-mindedness and the sultan wanted him there, firmly at heel and useful as leverage against the incumbent sharif at Mecca. "It had long been Ottoman practice," wrote de Gaury, "to bring to the capital, to a gilded cage, as it were, close relatives and possible rivals of the Sherif ruling in Mecca."[6] The Ottomans did this with notable families from the rest of the empire too, to Turkify them and knit them in with the life of court and Porte.

Faisal's was a youth, coming of age, and early manhood thoroughly dominated by the peculiar figure of the Sultan Abdul Hamid II, twenty-seventh of Osman's house to wear the Prophet's mantle. Paranoid and tyrannical, Abdul Hamid reigned from 1876 until 1909, dominating the long years of his reign until the 1908 revolution. As no sultan had done since the time of Suleiman, Abdul Hamid exercised a strong, if usually indirect, personal influence on the affairs of Iraq.

The Abdul Hamid period both exemplified and belied the theme of Ottoman decay. Infamous in Europe as the Red Sultan because of his massacres of Christians, Abdul Hamid was so afraid for his own life that he forbade the empire's newspapers from mentioning assassination. The American president William McKinley died of anthrax in 1901, according to the Ottoman press, "and the King and Queen of Serbia simultaneously of indigestion in 1903."[7]

The sultan was a solid traditionalist, reminiscent in ways of the ghazi sultans of ages past. All thirteen of his wives hailed from the western Caucasus, as was proper, and he was said to have banned the book *The Swiss Family Robinson* (published in 1812 and apparently still popular, although the story may be apocryphal) because the dog was called Turk.[8] Abdul Hamid's reign represented thirty years of repression on the political front, but in the central provinces, which decidedly did not include Iraq, in seemingly every facet of daily and economic life, there was exuberant, even frantic action. His goal was to Europeanize whatever might keep the empire alive: industry, schools, hospitals, ports, administration.* A poll tax was introduced. Bismarck's Germany trained and equipped the sultan's army.

Political modernizers and liberals had put Abdul Hamid on the throne, after declaring his brother and predecessor insane, but the new sultan was not what they expected. Abdul Hamid's first major political act, in 1878, was to suspend the constitutional, parliamentary government extracted from him by the Young Ottomans party that had made him sultan a year previously. His last major act, in 1909, was to attempt a coup against the Young Turks party that formed the empire's next such government. The glowering individual energy of this one man had kept the two democratic moments apart for a full thirty-one years, while the world around was liberalizing rapidly. For three decades Abdul Hamid

---

* This was reminiscent of the Abbasid hunger for only those works of classical Greek antiquity that were seen to be of practical use.

fought on every possible front to fend off the rising tide of constitution-
alism and reverse the political reforms of the *Tanzimat*.

The sultan's gloomy and paranoid personality made his reactionary
project seem all the darker. The death of Murad V, the brother whom
Abdul Hamid replaced on the throne, was announced in 1884; in fact
the man lived on, incarcerated in his Ciragan Palace, which he haunted
until 1904.* Abdul Hamid, almost never leaving his own serai, "reigned
among night terrors and revolvers," obsessively telegraphing orders to
the provinces, for relaxation taking "coffee in a mock-up of a real street
café whose other tables were staffed with his own bodyguard."[9]

As part of Abdul Hamid's administrative reforms, the provinces of
Mosul and Basra gained vilayet status in 1879 and 1884 respectively.[10]
A vilayet was the highest level of Ottoman province. The new Mosul
vilayet was made by carving off the three northerly sanjaks, or districts,
of the old Baghdad province: Mosul, Kirkuk, and Sulaymaniyah. With
vilayet status, each of Iraq's three historic parts—southern, central,
and northern—now had a full provincial governor of its own, with the
heightened local apparatus, and enhanced status back in the imperial
capital, that this entailed.

That the three sanjaks of the new Mosul province had long been
part of the Baghdad administrative unit was important later. In the
early 1920s, that fact was to provide Iraq and the British with a strong
argument to answer the new Turkish Republic's assertion of a claim
to Mosul. In the longer term, Baghdad's historic administration of the
Mosul province gave the lie to eventual claims that the Iraqi nation in its
modern borders was somehow a false or arbitrary creation of ignorant,
high-handed Europeans during this postwar period.

———

The Ottoman Empire had lost most of its European majority-Christian
territories by 1876. The Balkans and Romania were gone, while tenuous
footholds in Bulgaria and Macedonia remained. In 1878, the Congress

---

* The name of the Ciragan Palace comes from a word, originally Persian, for torch. The
palace's location, known as Ciragan, had traditionally been the scene of torchlit royal
parties on the Bosphorus.

of Berlin ratified this. Sultan Abdul Hamid now found himself atop a shrunken dominion that was proportionally more Arab than it had ever been, and more Muslim than at any time since the fifteenth century. Before the loss of the Christian territories, the reformers of the *Tanzimat*, seeking a unifying idea for the sultan's domains, had lit upon "Ottomanism." This was a notion that the empire's disparate subject peoples shared an identity as people of the ancient realm and subjects of the man at Constantinople—Sultan of Sultans, Khan of Khans, Commander of the Faithful, Caesar of Rome.

Then came the 1878 conference at Berlin, confirming the loss of 20 percent of the empire's people, most of them Christian. With the Christian provinces now mostly gone, Ottomanism was the answer to an outdated question. Henceforth, for Sultan Abdul Hamid, there would be a new emphasis: Islam. In what remained of the empire, the faith would be promoted as the binding identity.[11]

The position of caliph continued to reside with the sultan in Constantinople, as it had done since the early sixteenth century, during the reign of Suleiman the Magnificent's father, Selim the Grim. The Prophet's black woolen mantle still lay in the Topkapi Palace, where it remains. Through the twenty-four reigns between Selim and Abdul Hamid, Islam had not usually been a priority for the Ottoman sultans. A new sultan would begin his reign with public affirmations of his role as defender of the faith, but his status as caliph rarely featured in the politics of the day. This changed in 1878, with Berlin and the loss of the great majority of the sultan's Christian subjects.

Austen Henry Layard, now sixty years old, was present in Constantinople with a front-row seat to witness these developments. In 1877 Layard had arrived back in the Ottoman capital as the second most important man in the Middle East, like Stratford Canning before him: Her Britannic Majesty's Ambassador Extraordinary and Minister Plenipotentiary to the Sublime Porte. Layard observed later that Abdul Hamid "considered his position as caliph superior to that of sultan."[12] There is little record of personal religiosity in Abdul Hamid's career, but the sultan "saw no other way of saving the empire" than invoking Islam.[13]

In 1908, the Young Turks arranged an army mutiny against Abdul Hamid, forcing the sixty-five-year-old sultan to accept a reinstatement of the liberal constitution that he had suspended in 1878. Faisal's father, Hussein, after decades of politicking at Constantinople, at last achieved his goal. He was returned to Mecca and made sharif.

The Young Turks held elections for an imperial assembly. For Faisal, "with the advantage of good looks and the incentive of being only a third son," political ambition had become second nature.[14] In 1912, now twenty-nine years old, he was elected to the Ottoman parliament as member for Jeddah, principal port of the Hejaz. He had married a cousin in 1904 but saw her infrequently until she came to Baghdad twenty years later, bringing their four children.

Six months after Faisal was elected to the parliament in Constantinople, a brutal conflict known as the First Balkan War broke out between the Ottomans and the Balkan League, comprising Bulgaria, Serbia, Greece, and Montenegro.* By May 1913, almost all that remained to the Ottomans of their European possessions—Macedonia, Albania, Bosnia—was lost. Now the empire comprised two parts, in the most simple terms: Anatolia, home of Turks; and the rest, home of Arabs. Numerous minorities were scattered across each. As the Great War loomed, the Arab part of the empire comprised the traditional Fertile Crescent—Iraq plus Greater Syria, including the Levant—and the Hejaz with its prestigious holy cities.

At the age of eight or so, Faisal returned from the tribes of the desert to live with his family at Mecca. There he studied the conventional syllabus of Koran, Arabic grammar, and calligraphy. By the age of ten, in 1893, shortly after the sultan called his father to Constantinople, Faisal had mastered by heart a quarter of the Koran. He remained in the imperial capital until the age of twenty-six.

Faisal's life up to the age of ten had been different in no important regard from that of any other noble young Arab of Mecca during the past millennium and more. The cotton in the clothes he wore may now have been woven in Madras or Liverpool, not Mosul (which gave its name to muslin), but little else had changed. Even in the Prophet's day

---

* In the Second Balkan War, later in 1913, Bulgaria turned on its allies. Romania, sensing an opportunity, then joined the latter and attacked Bulgaria.

the merchant cities of the Hejaz had been connected to trade routes stretching to China and the Indies.

In 1893, Faisal sailed north from Jeddah to Constantinople, accompanied by two brothers and thirty-four relatives and retainers, to join his father. The ten-year-old Faisal was embarking on a life that would eventually see more event, variety, and change than had been experienced by any single Arab since the time of the Muslim conquests. Much of this would happen in Iraq, but even that chapter in Faisal's life did not begin for another quarter century. Making his way on a paddle steamer through the Suez Canal, built by the British and French thirty-four years previously, the boy from Mecca most likely never imagined that he would ever so much as visit *Iraq Arabi*, as Arabs referred to the empire's listless and fly-bitten Mesopotamian provinces. Passing through Suez, Faisal saw another remarkable sight: unveiled women out of doors.[15]

In the coming Constantinople years, Faisal gained an education in politics as he helped his father secure the emir's job in Mecca, watched Sultan Abdul Hamid try desperately to save his empire and his throne, saw the Young Turks launch a revolution, and sat in their parliament. The Byzantine ambience—many Arabs still knew Constantinople as *Roum*—on the Bosphorus is where Faisal came of age. "The refinements of the Court," wrote de Gaury, "the bland approaches and shadowy retreats of diplomacy, the snares of generosity, were subjects in which Faisal was schooled by his father in the old capital."[16]

Photographs from the period show the hilly green banks of the Bosphorus, their fields lined in cypresses, dotted with white palaces and summer houses: the famous "string of pearls." In the fabled harbor, innumerable slender rowboats—the long-prowed double-ended skiffs known as caïques— carried passengers on their daily business. The caïques jostled with square-rigged merchant ships, paddle steamers, and lateen-rigged fishing vessels with their triangular white sails. The streets and wood-floored bridges teemed with men in dress timeless or modern, from white robes to the black "stambouline" frock coats popular since the 1820s, when Mahmoud II began to Europeanize the military and civil service. Almost all of the men wore the fez, another sumptuary reform of Mahmoud II, dating from shortly after his bloody abolition of the Janissaries in 1826. Donkeys, European landaus, horse-drawn trams, traditional lace-curtained carriages hiding concubines or high-born ladies plied their way in the shadows of the four minarets of Suleiman's great mosque; under the burnt column of Constantine, which still stands on Janissary Street; and outside the gates of Sultan Abdulmejid's white rococo Dolmabahce Palace, completed in 1856 with gas lighting and British plumbing.

The Chemins de Fer Orientaux had cut its way along the Marmara shore, right through the lower gardens of the Topkapi Palace. In June of 1889 the first full journey of the Orient Express, originating at the Gare de l'Est in Paris, had arrived. The young Faisal ibn al-Hussein al-Hashimi would have seen his first railway there in old European Constantinople. Twenty-five years later, the Hejaz Railway, which the Ottomans eventually constructed to link them to Mecca and Medina, would play a key part in the fighting that made Faisal for a time a charismatic leader of the Arab world.

———

Faisal was twenty-five in 1908, when the Young Turks of the so-called Committee of Union and Progress, or CUP, imposed the constitutional restoration on Sultan Abdul Hamid. By then the Red Sultan was a wizened old recluse, poring late into the night over the endless reports of his secret police. Where the aging sultan had attempted to use Islam to unify what remained of the empire, the Young Turks, almost all of them Freemasons, were secularists and ethnic nationalists. In Islamic lands, nationalists have a strong secular bias. To define political power by ethnicity or nation-state, rather than faith, is to contradict the very project of the Prophet's Islam. The Young Turks' idea of unity was a stronger Turkish fist. They worked to centralize control over their Arab dominions, including the Hejaz.

Just as the CUP saw themselves as Turks, in the new cafes and academies of Damascus, Baghdad, and Beirut, speakers of Arabic were beginning to see themselves as Arabs. The notion of an Arab had not heretofore existed in any political sense. The term itself had long been somewhat pejorative. It was used to signify, from the speaker's perspective, an uncouth Bedouin type, rather than, as it came to mean, a native speaker of the Arabic language. Blood-and-soil nationalism was an entirely new notion. No one had ever been a "Turk" or an "Arab" before, just as in Europe until recently nobody had ever been an "Italian" or a "German." Now the Young Turks were in charge of the Ottoman government, installing Faisal's father as sharif at Mecca. The anti-Arab Turkish nationalism of the CUP, allying itself with the kaiser's aggressive new Germany that was promoting these new concepts, was the force with which Faisal's family now had to contend.

In 1914, Faisal was busy representing the interests of his father and the Hejaz in Constantinople, where the seat in parliament gave the young man a "perch" useful to the family.[17] A global conflict was brewing, and many knew it. The Ottoman government was going to have to choose a side. Since the time of Abdul Hamid, Germany had been sponsoring as much of the modernization as possible in the Ottoman Empire, from the military schools to the railroads. The Prussians had been remaking the Ottoman army since Helmuth von Moltke worked for Sultan Mahmoud II as a young captain in 1835.

These same builders of the new Ottoman military were also the inventors of the new ethnic nationalism that soon would roil the Middle East. Germany as a state had been created in 1871, when Prussia, having won a stunning string of victories against its neighbors over the period of 1864 to 1870, crowned its Hohenzollern king the German emperor.* Otto von Bismarck was the architect of this breathtaking achievement. The empire of his kaiser, Wilhelm I, comprised the lands of twenty-six neighboring German-speaking kingdoms, grand duchies, principalities, free cities, and the like, all of them formerly sovereign.† The new state, cloaking Prussian ambition in the innovative notion of ethnicity as the basis for nationhood, was now the strongest in Europe. The principal countries aligned against it were Britain, France, and Russia, known collectively as the Triple Entente.

Possessing deep overseas imperial histories, which newly minted Germany did not, the Entente powers looked on the dying Ottoman Empire

---

* The forces of Bismarck and the kaiser defeated Denmark in 1864; Austria, Bavaria, and various smaller local states in 1866; and France in 1870.

† Wilhelm's self-proclaimed empire had no overseas territories at this point. Including Prussia, the empire was formed from four kingdoms, seven principalities, six grand duchies, six duchies, and three republican Hanseatic cities. The empire's twenty-seventh and last constituent entity was Alsace-Lorraine, ceded by France in 1871. The first overseas possession was acquired in New Guinea in 1884.

with vultures' eyes. They also had live strategic reasons—France in Syria, Britain in India, Russia in the Caucasus and along the Black Sea—to desire pieces of the Ottoman Empire for themselves. Germany's interest lay in an Ottoman Empire kept whole, as a counterweight to the British, French, and Russians. Viewed from Constantinople, moreover, the Second Reich was the rising power, "virile," as many comments of the time suggest. The kaiser's anxious authoritarianism suited the Young Turk outlook, as it had suited Abdul Hamid before them. So did that same "blood and soil" spirit, absent in Britain, France, and Russia, that had driven the very creation of Germany over the previous few decades.

For the Ottomans, World War I began in late October 1914, when two German cruisers, reflagged as Ottoman and commanded by a Prussian admiral who had hastily been made commander in chief of the Ottoman navy, attacked Odessa, Sebastopol, and other Russian ports on the Black Sea coast. These were intentional provocations organized by the CUP leader Enver Pasha and his German allies to bring a reluctant Porte into the conflict. The war in Europe had begun a couple of months earlier. By the time the Ottoman Empire was involved in the hostilities, Faisal had made his way back to the Hejaz and his father's side. "I knew Sharif Faisal well," Liman von Sanders, the German inspector general of the Ottoman army, later wrote, "from the summer of 1914. He was the type of an Arabian grand seignior [sic]. He had a European education and spoke English. Mutual interest in sport had brought us together in various places, and we had visited each other at our homes. The harsh Arabian policy of the Turkish government made him its bitterest enemy."[18]

Faisal himself was no revolutionary at this stage, but around him the idea of Arab identity and Arab rights within the Ottoman Empire had been gaining strength over the past few years. Arab secret societies sprang up in the years before 1914, largely in Mediterranean Syria, the most developed of the Arab provinces, but also in Iraq. The Sharifian family of Mecca and Medina was inevitably of interest to the nascent Arab nationalists, and in 1915 Faisal, appointed emissary by his father, visited Damascus.

"In April 1915 I arrived in Damascus en route to Constantinople," Faisal recalled eighteen years later. "At Damascus I met with a great number of intellectuals, among whom were Bedawin, notables of Damascus, Syrian *ulema*, and officers of an Arab division belonging to the Ottoman army . . . They all assured me that they were prepared to start the revolution and begged me to raise the standard of revolt."[19] These officers of the "Arab division" in the sultan's army happened mostly to come from the Mesopotamian provinces. In 1913 they had formed an underground group called Al Ahd, "the Covenant," with the idea of forming an independent Arab state in Iraq and eventually Syria, with a son of the sharif of Mecca as king and themselves as the power behind the throne.

Faisal was a shrewd and cautious man. He was also conservative, and then still loyal to the empire, if not to the Young Turk junta with its ill-starred Prussian intoxication and contempt for the sultan's Arab subjects. In 1915 Faisal declined the proposals of the revolutionaries of Damascus. In 1933, shortly before his death, looking back on those discreet meetings with the secret societies of Damascus early in the Great War, Faisal would recall, "I was a moderate in those days!"[20] Phrased differently, this child of Byzantine politics was playing both sides.

Turkish repression of the rebellious Arab notables, intellectuals, and officers in Syria followed later in 1915 and early 1916. The brutality did much to turn Faisal's heart against Constantinople, as he was to call the city until he died. There had also been, in late 1914, the encouraging landing of a strong British Indian Army at Basra. Finally, and most important for Faisal's father, the sharif in Mecca, there were direct British inducements to rebel, including money, commitments of military support, and a written promise ultimately of "independence for the Arabs in all the regions lying within the frontiers proposed."[21] The pledge came with a strong presumption that the Sharifian family would lead any such Arab nation.

The British were also negotiating with the French the exact opposite: an arrangement in which France would control Greater Syria and Mosul, and the British Iraq, Palestine, and the Persian Gulf.* There was a third potentially contradictory British promise in the same period. The Balfour Declaration of November 1917 pledged a Palestinian homeland

---

* In 1915 Sir Mark Sykes, the erratic English Orientalist who gave his name to the ill-fated agreement, had visited Mosul. "By night robbers stalk untouched from house to house," he reported, and the darkness was full of "the cracking of pistols and confused cries of strife. By day, drunkenness and debauchery are openly indulged in. The population is rotted by the foul distemper, corrupted and rendered impotent by drink, stupefied and besotted by vice. Tales are whispered of dark and hideous sorceries." Mark Sykes, *The Caliph's Last Heritage* (London: Macmillan, 1915), p. 338.

to the Jews, while the correspondence with Sharif Hussein appeared to commit Palestine to the Arabs. The sharif of Mecca received his British promise of Arab independence from Sir Henry McMahon, British high commissioner in Cairo. The parallel, conflicting commitment to a Franco-British carve-up is known as the Sykes-Picot Agreement, after the two diplomats principally responsible for it.

In June of 1916, at Mecca, the sharif announced the Arab Revolt against the Ottomans. Faisal, the sharif's most capable son, would be its chief commander in the field. T. E. Lawrence was the foremost and, after his discovery by the American journalist Lowell Thomas, the most self-promoting, of numerous British officers who worked with Faisal and the Arabs in the field, fighting the Turks. Sykes-Picot, Lawrence said when he learned about it, was a "shocking document" and a "fraud."[22]

Sykes-Picot was ratified at London and Paris in May 1916, but it was never to be more than a putative sketch of the future. The British prime minister, David Lloyd George, had little enthusiasm for the agreement, and events rendered it a dead letter well before the end of the war. It seems unlikely that the sharif and his family placed significant credence in their promises from the British. If anyone in the Middle East was steeped in realpolitik in 1916, with no excuse for naiveté, it was the sharif of Mecca. Ultimately the Sharifians did well from the war, thanks to the British, and if they were not handed the entire Arab world, the loss was theirs alone. None of these actors had ever asked the Arabs themselves, much less the many religious and ethnic minorities of the region, whether they wanted to be ruled in a unified new caliphate, or imperial entity of some other kind, by the sharif or anyone else. It is this that gives the final lie to claims of perfidy when arrangements after the Great War fell short of a single Arab state under the Sharifian family.

———

The British Residency in Baghdad had been the principal European presence in Mesopotamia since at least the time of the Resident and Babylon explorer Claudius James Rich around the year 1810. A significant military presence for the British began with the Basra landing of Indian Army forces in 1914. The objective of the landing was to secure the head of the Persian Gulf, and especially the oilfields of neighboring southern Persia. A march north to Baghdad was not initially intended, but the mission expanded as the Turks vigorously defended southern Iraq. At Kut, a hundred miles southeast of Baghdad, in the course of a four-month Turkish siege that ended in April 1916, the British Indian Army lost twenty-three thousand dead, eight thousand captured, and many more wounded. Historians have called Kut "the most abject British capitulation in British military history"[23] and "the worst defeat of the allies in World War I."[24]

The British turned their fortunes around under the command of Sir Stanley Maude, who first won a new engagement at Kut in February 1917 and then continued marching north with a reinvigorated army. In March of that year Maude became the first Western conqueror of Ctesiphon, the ancient capital of the Parthian and Sasanian Empires, since the Roman general Galerius in 298 AD. Five days after capturing Ctesiphon, something the Romans had done five times themselves, Maude entered Baghdad.*

In 1919 the British shifted their reins in Iraq from military to civilian and set to work on administration and civil life. British activity brought such matters of astonishment as printing presses for newspapers, primary schools for girls, and smooth-chinned young men who tried to make the customs regime work.

Within the British context, this was the style of the Government of India, to which the Baghdad Residency then reported. Delhi's vision for Iraq was Britain in India, not Britain in Egypt: "direct rule" rather than a strong presence and suasion. The opposing view, in the British context, was that of the wartime Arab Bureau, based at Cairo. The apostles of this outlook were Gertrude Bell, T. E. Lawrence, and lesser lights of their ilk: the Arabists who seemed to know the name of every dry *wadi* in the desert and the genealogy of every minor tribal chief and his favorite brood mares and stallion too. These were the people who had, perhaps romantically, hoped for and promised "independence"—if that was the right word for the implied Sharifian rule—for the Arabs after the war.

---

* Eight months later, still on campaign, Maude died of cholera. Gertrude Bell wrote in a letter home from Baghdad a few days later, "There is a splendid sentence in Ammianus Marcellinus' history of that other conqueror who was mortally wounded, N.E. of Ctesiphon, the Emperor Julian, and 'praised the Almighty God that he should die in the midst of glory fairly earned.'" *Selected Letters of Gertrude Bell* (London: Penguin, 1953), p. 227.

For now, in the first year and a half after the war, the men of India were ascendant in Iraq. The "imperial school," as it came to be known during the ensuing debate at Westminster, saw Iraq as an "outright colony."[25] The style was managerial, not political, and hardly sympathetic in tone. Sir Arthur Hirtzel, in charge of the India Office's Political Department, and thus of political affairs in Iraq, said in 1920 that the Arabs were "no more capable of administering severally or collectively than the Red Indians."[26] The gentlemen of the imperial school did not speak Arabic. Their clerks were Indian. A provisional government of Iraqi ministers had been appointed, but it sat at the pleasure of Delhi.

"Little was done to render the machinery of government easy or acceptable to its public," wrote S. H. Longrigg, reflecting on the initial British period.[27] Even to travel "from the West to Iraq," wrote de Gaury, at the time an English officer seconded to local levies in Iraq, "was still by ship to Bombay, and then by another slower one up the Persian Gulf."[28]

During the two years of India Office rule, Longrigg wrote, the British Raj in Iraq "mixed little tolerance with its uncomfortable and not always desired justice, and was pitiless to long-familiar laxities."[29]

For Iraq on the international stage, the three years from the end of the war to Faisal's enthronement were dominated by a series of international conferences whose consequences would create huge challenges for Faisal and his partners over the coming decade and more. First, leading to the treaty signed at nearby Versailles, came the great gathering at Paris. There, in January 1919, the thirty-six-year-old Hejazi prince and his entourage arrived by the boat-train from London. At the Paris conference, Faisal had a widely acknowledged role as the voice of the Arabs.

"I came to Europe to defend the Arabs and demand our rights," Faisal wrote to his father from Paris. The powers from whom he would demand these rights were Britain, France, and the United States. "I ask the powers not to determine anything that concerns my land, except after the opinions of the people of the lands of whom the Arab army is composed are taken into account."

Faisal defined those lands as, effectively, reaching from the southern border of Turkey to the Indian Ocean. His father's independence in the

Hejaz had been recognized since 1916, the British were in Iraq, the Zionists held much of Palestine, and Faisal's own ramshackle "Arab army" was at Damascus with British troops from Palestine.

The United States, President Woodrow Wilson had declared, would make national self-determination its key principle at the Paris conference. Britain, meanwhile, having promised Syria and Mosul to France through Sykes-Picot, and full Arab independence to the Sharif Hussein through the McMahon correspondence, now possessed Mesopotamia from Basra to the Kurdish highlands. From Delhi, the influential British voice of the Government of India pressed for its preferred imperial outcome while an exhausted and bankrupt London preferred a shallower and more temporary "tutelary" arrangement. Over the western border of the Mesopotamian provinces, France thought Syria was hers. There was a history, if a tenuous one, reaching from Raymond IV of Toulouse in the First Crusade through Napoleon; later in the nineteenth century, French interventions in Syria occurred ostensibly on behalf of the Catholic Maronites of the Lebanese coast. These had led to romantic plans even before the Great War of a *Syrie Française*. For the Paris Peace Conference generally, dealing with the ruins of Europe, these abstruse questions about the former Ottoman Empire were mostly a sideshow at best.

The British and French reached an agreement at Paris promising British support for "French demands in the Ruhr," Germany's industrial heartland, in return for discarding the 1916 Sykes-Picot map and allocating Mosul and Palestine to the British, as had been London's preference all along. France also received a promise of a share in Mosul's oil.[30] The British were already the force on the ground in Mosul, having aggressively pushed north under General Maude's successor to seize it in the waning days of the war.*

As far as the Middle East was concerned, the Paris conference was a matter of the former Ottoman lands only. In Iran the Qajars had ruled since 1789 with little involvement in Iraq, solidly Ottoman as the latter had been since the 1639 Treaty of Zuhab and its reaffirmation of the 1555 agreement at Amasya. Iran sent a delegation to the 1919 Paris conference,

---

* The British occupied Mosul city on November 14, 1918—two weeks after the Armistice of Mudros ended hostilities with the Ottomans, and three days after the armistice in Europe.

but the British denied accreditation on the basis that Iran had not been a belligerent in the war.

In Paris, Faisal was something of a phenomenon. Staying sumptuously with a Countess Kellermann, who trotted him around society, he made a memorable impression. David Lloyd George, British prime minister at the time, recalled, in his *Memoirs of the Peace Conference*, Faisal and Lawrence "arrayed in the robes of dazzling white in which they were appareled when they led their mounted warriors to battle against the Turks."[31] Faisal's "intellectual countenance and shining eyes would have made an impression in any assembly," Lloyd George wrote. Others had the same response. "Here was a man whom nature had chosen to be a leader of men," wrote Robert Lansing, American secretary of state during the Paris gathering.[32]

Faisal had a single opportunity to speak to the leaders of the conference. These were Wilson, Lloyd George, the French prime minister Georges Clemenceau, and others of what was called the Council of Ten. When Faisal did so, they were "spellbound," according to an Arab companion. "The signs of astonishment," at Faisal's eloquence and charismatic presence, "were clearly on their faces."[33] But it did not matter. The British were compromised, little could budge the French desire for Syria, and Wilson did not care. A week earlier, the great powers had decided on a status of "mandates" for the former imperial possessions of the defeated Axis powers. The formerly Ottoman Arab lands would be assigned to Britain and France, directed "to guide and counsel the new states towards genuine independence."[34] This independence, should it come, would occur only when the League of Nations extended membership to the new country.

The affairs of the world's nations, which had arguably begun among the city-states of Sumer five thousand years previously, had never been a central control system before. The League of Nations documents that framed Iraq's aspirations through the 1920s make strange, almost farcical, reading. But a new global leader had emerged from the European self-immolation of the Great War. This was the United States. There the group in power had recently picked up, directly from the example of Bismarck's *Kaiserreich*, a centralized and managerial view. For the smaller nations of the world, with the American government in the hands of Berlin-inspired "Progressives," the League of Nations emerged from

Paris as if, in terms of ideas, the kaiser had won the war after all. Now there was a system, and this kind of system had to be written down.

According to Article 1 of the League's Covenant: "Any fully self-governing State, Dominion or Colony" that was not an original member could become one "if its admission is agreed to by two-thirds of the Assembly." It was of course the mighty, the authors of the Paris peace that proved so disastrous by the 1930s, who assigned to themselves the disposition of membership. With the blindness to irony of the truly arrogant, they had chosen, as the signing place for their schemes, Louis XIV's palace at Versailles: the European Persepolis, Western civilization's emblematic monument to its own worst tradition of statist hubris.

Article 22 of the League's Covenant was the key. It dealt with "those colonies and territories which as a consequence of the late war have ceased to be under the sovereignty of the States which formerly governed them and which are inhabited by peoples not yet able to stand by themselves under the strenuous conditions of the modern world." In these cases, continued the League of Nations Covenant, "the well-being and development of such peoples form a sacred trust of civilisation." To make good on this sacred trust, "the tutelage of such peoples should be entrusted to advanced nations . . . who are willing to accept it." These relationships would be known as Mandates.

The Mandates were divided into classes, with Class A denoting Iraq and its Arab neighbors that had belonged to the Ottomans: "Certain communities formerly belonging to the Turkish Empire [that] have reached a stage of development where their existence as independent nations can be provisionally recognized . . . until such time as they are able to stand alone." Alongside Iraq in this category were the four pieces of Greater Syria: Lebanon, Syria proper, Palestine, and "Transjordan." The first two would be mandated to France, the latter two to Britain.[35] *

---

* The Class B Mandates were Berlin's former possessions in Africa. These were less fortunate with the gods of Paris. "Other peoples, especially those of Central Africa," wrote the latter, "are at such a stage that the mandatory must be responsible"—responsible, full stop. No eventual independence was mentioned for these former German colonies that were now Ruanda-Urundi (latterly Rwanda and Burundi) and British and French Togoland (the former eventually becoming part of Ghana, the latter becoming independent as Togo). For these there was only the need for supervision as to more "public morals" and less trading in arms, people, and liquor.

T. E. Lawrence eventually called the two and a half months that he and Faisal spent at Paris the worst experience of both of their lives. But Paris taught Faisal much about the ways of the world beyond the Ottoman horizon. When the conference was over he sailed to Beirut.

In March 1920, the Arab nationalists of Damascus proclaimed the Arab Kingdom of Syria. The events were largely driven by Faisal's former officers of the Arab Revolt, the so-called Sharifian officers. These were the same men, graduates of the Ottomans' German military academies, who as officers in the sultan's "Arab division" had founded the Covenant secret society. Now Faisal, his hand somewhat forced by these individuals who had served with him in the desert, accepted an offer by their Syrian Arab Congress to be king. On the same day, a similar Iraqi nationalist organization in Baghdad proposed to offer a kingdom of Iraq to Faisal's brother Abdullah.

Faisal for a throne in Syria, Abdullah for a throne in Iraq, and their father already king in the Hejaz: T. E. Lawrence had been promoting this "Sherifian Policy," as it was known at the time, since 1918.[36] The Covenant circle had been scheming for something very similar since 1913. It is possible that Lawrence came purely by coincidence to a conclusion so similar to theirs; it seems as likely that the policy was first suggested to him by the Iraqi officers of the Covenant while they were fighting together in the desert with Faisal.

Four months after its birth, the Syrian kingdom collapsed, defeated in the field by ten thousand Senegalese and Moroccans of the French Army of the Levant. Faisal left Damascus on a night train headed south. In Iraq, the British and their appointed Iraqi cabinet continued to govern.

————

In April 1920, the British and French gathered at San Remo in Italy to flesh out the Middle East roles assigned to them at Paris a year previously. "The High Contracting Parties," read the resolution at San Remo, "agree that Syria and Mesopotamia shall, in accordance with the fourth paragraph of Article 22, Part I (Covenant of the League of Nations), be provisionally recognized as independent States, subject to the rendering of administrative advice and assistance by a mandatory until such time as they are able to stand alone." The boundaries of these "provisional" states of Syria and Mesopotamia were left for later.

In Iraq, in the late spring of 1920, San Remo's enshrining of the Mandates on April 25 struck the first nationalist sparks in a tinderbox that erupted that summer. In Syria, Faisal sat precariously on the throne he had accepted from the Syrian National Congress in March. His ultimatum from the French to fight or leave would come on July 20, and the defeat of his army by the *Armée du Levant*, at the Battle of Maysalun, four days later.

For the Iraqi elites of the former Ottoman period, the Mandate notion was both threatening, in that it seemed to signal British rule that would override their customary privileges, and insulting, in that it belittled their capabilities. The preeminence of the Sunni elites had done little for anyone else, and not much more for themselves, over the Ottoman centuries in Iraq. But in the new context there were elements of their stance that could be turned into a wider popular emotion. An alignment of political interests began to take shape.[37]

May 1920 saw rising tensions. In the Shia holy city of Kerbala, the lead ayatollah issued a fatwa banning his followers from working in the British administration. In Baghdad mixed mass meetings alternated between Sunni and Shia mosques. Winston Churchill, then in charge of the British military effort as Secretary of State for War and Air, wrote at the end of that brutal summer,

> It is an extraordinary thing that the British civil administration should have succeeded in such a short time in alienating the whole country to the extent that the Arabs have laid aside the blood feuds that they have nursed for centuries and that the Suni and Shiah tribes are working together.[38] *

In the summer of 1920, Sunni Arab nationalists in Iraq fanned the uprising that was mostly taken up by the Shias of the south and center of the country. The British spent forty million pounds quelling the

---

* Churchill's reference to the Sunni and Shia "tribes" indicates a limit on how far these cultural interests went for him at this stage.

three-month 1920 rebellion against the Mandate, more than they had spent on the entire 1916–1918 Arab Revolt. The British Empire's cost in blood included five hundred dead. Less than two years after the Great War, this was unacceptable to the British public. "How much longer are valuable lives to be sacrificed," wrote *The Times* of London in an August 1920 lead editorial that typified the mood, "in the vain endeavour to impose on the Arab population an elaborate and expensive administration which they never asked for and do not want?"[39]

In August 1920, with central and southern Iraq in ferment, came a conference at Sèvres. The powers met at this Paris suburb aiming to address the various international questions, from borders to finances, brought forth by the new status of Turkey. There the last, powerless Ottoman sultan, Mehmed VI, continued to reside with his five wives in the Dolmabahce Palace at Constantinople, where he had been born. A Grand National Assembly dominated by Mustafa Kemal—later to be known as Ataturk—sat at Ankara.* According to the Sèvres treaty, the Kurds of Turkey would receive "a scheme of local autonomy," and the Turkish border with Mesopotamia would be set at the "northern boundary of the vilayet of Mosul."[40] Mosul, in other words, would belong to Iraq.

Sèvres contained a wide range of other humiliations for the new Turkish state. Greece was assigned Smyrna, on the Turkish mainland. France would have pieces of eastern Anatolia to go with Syria. Turkish taxes, budgeting, and customs duties would come under the oversight of the Allies. The Turkish army would be limited to fifty thousand in number, there could be no air force, and so on.

It might have worked in the late Ottoman days, but power in Turkey now resided with Ataturk at Ankara. Sèvres represented a misunderstanding of the man with whom the Allies were dealing. They should have known better since Gallipoli at the latest. Sèvres swiftly became a dead letter. Greece refused to sign. In Turkey the nationalists found the terms so humiliating that they launched the Turkish War of Independence. Upon winning this conflict, Ataturk abolished the sultanate, declared the Turkish Republic, annulled Sèvres, and revoked the citizenship of any Turk who had signed it.

---

* Kemal would take the name Ataturk, "father of the Turks," after promulgating his westernizing Surname Law in 1934.

The Iraqi uprising of 1920 persuaded London that a new approach was needed. With the revolt raging in mid-July, London's Commander in Chief of the General Staff, working under Churchill, noted in his diary the receipt of "a wild wire from Winston about Mesopotamia and expense." Throughout the 1920 crisis, Churchill was "concerned above all with economy," according to his biographer Martin Gilbert, and took "a lead in urging a policy of withdrawal and disengagement."[41]

At the end of August, Churchill drafted a letter about Iraq to the prime minister, Lloyd George, who since 1916 had been sponsoring Churchill's political revival after the failed 1915 Dardanelles campaign. Churchill never sent the letter, but it reveals his outlook as the man who oversaw Iraq's creation.

"There is something very sinister to my mind in this Mesopotamian entanglement," Churchill wrote. "It seems to me so gratuitous," he continued,

> that after all the struggles of war, just when we want to get together our slender military resources and re-establish our finances . . . we should be compelled to go on pouring armies and treasure into these thankless deserts. We have not got a single friend in the press on the subject, and there is no point of which they make more effective use to injure the Government. Week after week and month after month we shall have a continuance of this miserable, wasteful, sporadic, war-fare.[42]

In October 1920, stung by months of costly rebellion, the British reinstated as high commissioner Sir Percy Cox. As chief political officer under the British military administration, he had been Gertrude Bell's superior in Baghdad in 1917. Cox calmed the various players, mostly Shia tribal leaders and clerics, and went on to become a widely admired figure among all sides. With Cox's arrival, the colonial men of Calcutta began to give way to the Arabists of London and Cairo.

"The task before me was by no means an easy or attractive one," Cox was to recall, writing to Gertrude Bell's mother after Bell's death in 1926. The job that began in late 1920, Cox continued, involved "a complete and

necessarily rapid transformation of the façade of the existing administration from British to Arab." Cox pointed out that it was not merely a
matter of the façade, but of the underlying structure too. There was to
be "a wholesale reduction in the numbers of British and British-Indian
personnel employed."[43] Cox represented a welcome change as the atmosphere of the violent summer of 1920 ebbed. The future King Faisal,
upon arriving in Iraq nine months later, would nonetheless have to deal
with a legacy of fighting and resentment as he and the British worked
to start afresh.

By the time of Faisal's enthronement in August 1921, the British had
been there long enough to be a disappointment. Maude's army had
entered Baghdad in March 1917 and by May of that year a breathless
Bell, busy helping to build the new administration, was writing home,
"It's the making of a new world."[44] Three years later came the eruption
of 1920. "Few indeed could deny the improvement . . . over the familiar
Turkish standards," wrote E. H. Longrigg, looking back in 1953, but "no
golden age had arrived."[45]

"I pray that the people at home may be rightly guided," Bell wrote
to her father in January of 1920, with the clouds of the summer storm
starting to gather. She hoped that the men in London would "realize
that the only chance here is to recognize political ambitions from the
first."[46] The Iraqi ambitions she referred to were those for independence.

In January 1921 Churchill was removed from the war ministry in London and put in charge of the Colonial Office, where the Iraq file was
sent over from the India Office and where, as Churchill had proposed, a
Middle East Department was created. Churchill and his new department
now had responsibility for Iraq policy. The British needed a regional plan
for the longer term, and Churchill gathered his team at the Egyptian
capital in March. There, at the Semiramis Hotel, with Bell and Lawrence
in the fore among his advisors, Churchill decided on the basic outline of
London's Middle East posture for at least the decade to come.* Churchill repeatedly articulated two priorities at the Cairo conference: first,

---

* During a camelback visit to the Pyramids with Bell, Lawrence, and others, Churchill
fell off his mount. Bell compared the performance to "a mass of sliding gelatin," while
Churchill's wife, Clementine, famously observed, "How the mighty have fallen." Warren
Dockter, "Flying in a Hurricane: Winston Churchill and T. E. Lawrence Shape the Middle
East," *Finest Hour: The Journal of Winston Churchill and His Times* 170 (Fall 2015).

to reduce Britain's expenditures in the region; second, to advance her various interests such as oil and the India link.

Cairo's major outcome for Iraq was the embrace by Churchill of the "Sherifian solution" advocated by Lawrence, whereby Iraq and "Transjordan" would be kingdoms and sons of King Hussein of the Hejaz would sit on their thrones. Faisal's simpler and rougher older brother Abdullah had originally been earmarked for Baghdad, but Lawrence knew Faisal was better suited to Iraq's greater importance and complexity. So Abdullah was reassigned to Jordan, as Palestine east of the Jordan River became known, and Faisal to Iraq. Iraq's British-appointed provisional government had two representatives at the Cairo conference. These duly asked for Faisal, of whom very few Iraqis had likely heard at that point, to be their king.

Three months later, in late June 1921, a Royal Navy vessel, HMS *Northcote*, took Faisal to Basra. He spent six days making his way up to Baghdad through the Shia south. Many Iraqis along the way, as would soon happen at Baghdad, were already proclaiming him king. But on the whole Faisal's reception in the south, among the Shia tribes and in the holy cities of Kerbala and Najaf and elsewhere, was mixed. The 1920 revolt had been strongest among the Shia of the central and lower Euphrates, and many of the rebellion's Shia leaders took refuge with Faisal's father in Mecca. Some of these now supported Faisal as a matter of course. Some were to predicate their support on the degree of independence that Faisal could secure from the Mandate. Others wanted to see an elected body emplaced first, to nominate Faisal as king.

The British advisor at the provisional government's interior ministry, St. John Philby, a committed republican despite his job, persuaded many of the Shias along Faisal's way north to dampen their enthusiasm.* But it seems not many doubted Faisal was the right man personally. His skills at tribal democracy, at sitting and talking with the men of steppe and desert, had been honed since boyhood. He was a fighter and a horseman,

---

* The instinct reached a culmination when St. John's son Kim Philby became the leading figure in the Cambridge Five communist spy ring in the 1950s and '60s.

and a descendant of Ali. His forefathers had ruled Mecca for a thousand years. The British had a weakness for the Sunnis of the desert, to whom they attached romantic notions of chivalry and honor, and Faisal was the personification of this ideal. There were Shias, secular ones, among the Arab nationalists. For these Faisal was the heroic field leader of the Arab Revolt, and the former king at Damascus of the first Arab state.

In Baghdad, when Faisal first arrived there in 1921, his reception was altogether different from the muted tones of the south. His train into the capital, arriving from Hilla next to Babylon, was late, and the crowd at the station swelled through the hot afternoon of June 29.[47] "The whole town was decorated," wrote Gertrude Bell, "triumphal arches, Arab flags, and packed with people. In the street, on the housetops, everywhere. At the station, immense crowds."[48] Bell found the enthusiasm to be "cheering," as "we don't want Feisal to come in through a coup d'etat of the extremists—we must have something much more constitutional than that." The "extremists" to whom Bell referred came generally from the relatively recent Sunni urban middle class, and in particular from among the Sharifian officers. These hoped to succeed in Iraq, building up a state where they provided the military muscle and received many of the spoils, where they had failed in Syria the previous year.

In contrast to Bell, Faisal himself was "bitterly disappointed" at what he saw as a generally tepid welcome in Iraq, according to de Gaury's recollection of conversations with Kinahan Cornwallis, the wartime chief of the Arab Bureau who became Faisal's leading British confidant in Baghdad. Faisal's arrival in the capital was nothing like Cyrus's welcome to an ecstatic Babylon twenty-four centuries earlier. In de Gaury's account, the king-to-be concluded from his "cool reception" that the priority must be to create, in his words, "a real feeling for independence and unity among the people of Iraq."

To do so, Faisal turned to the only Iraqis he knew, the Sharifian officers, his lieutenants from the Arab Revolt.[49] These were in many cases members of the same Covenant Society that since 1913 had been plotting Arab independence in an Iraq where they themselves, under a Hashemite monarch, would pull the strings. They had been the first to suggest such a monarch for the new country. They were the ones whom, in early 1921, the British had put in charge of its army—well before Faisal even saw his new country for the first time. From a certain perspective,

including perhaps their own, it was these individuals, rather than Faisal
or the British, who ultimately were the key players, from start to finish,
in the story of Iraq's 1921–1958 monarchy.

In the years after 1921 these individuals would serve well enough, and
sometimes too well, on the independence front. As Sunni Arab nationalists with mostly contempt for the Shias and Kurds, the Sharifian officers
did not, as things unfolded, do so well for their king and country on
the unity front. With the Shias representing perhaps two-thirds of the
national population, and the Kurds roughly equal to the Sunni Arabs
at a little bit less than 15 percent, this would develop into a problem.

On reaching Baghdad, Faisal now had mostly Sunnis, Jews, and Christians to meet. The Sunni Arabs had provided most of the ruling order
under the Ottomans, and among this minority there were three main
groups: the old upper class of landowners and "urban notables," the
newer professional class of the late Ottoman era, and the tribes.

The former of these Sunni Arab groups, the traditional elite, had
come into its own under a foreign ruler, the Ottoman Turks, and had
prospered for centuries under such a situation. They knew nothing of
nationalism generally, or "Iraqiness" specifically, and saw the British as
more orderly and efficient than the Turks; they were prepared to accept
Faisal as a British-style constitutional monarch in this context. The latter
of the three groups, the tribal as opposed to urban Sunnis, had been
strongly cultivated by the British and saw themselves as British allies;
they made clear to Faisal that their support for him was conditional
upon his continued acceptance by the British Residency.

The friction was to come from the third Sunni category, the relatively
recently minted middle class. These men came from the late-Ottoman
world of Sunni dominance, characterized in military and administrative
affairs by the rising importance of men like them, all of it inflected with
the new racial-authoritarian view imbibed from the late Sultan's Prussian
sponsors. The new men could work with Faisal while interests were
aligned. Many of the more prominent, including the Sharifian officers,
would be loyal to Faisal and the new monarchy personally. But as a class
what they and their children wanted was power.

Twelve days after Faisal's arrival at Baghdad, the cabinet of the provisional government passed, with British pressure, a unanimous resolution
that he should be king of Iraq. The resolution stipulated that the coming

government be "constitutional, democratic, representative and limited by law."[50] The British did not want the nationalists, Bell's "extremists" who had sparked the 1920 uprising, running away with any coronation. Faisal himself knew that he would need popular sanction, and the "plebiscite" of 1921 was called. There were no voter rolls, nor any election law, so the affair would be more of a canvassing of districts and communities through their leaders.

In Baghdad Faisal had a successful visit to the Shias' Kadhimain Shrine.* The Sunni religious leader of Baghdad, the elderly Naqib, organized a banquet. There were events in schools and gardens, and such endless speechifying that Faisal confided to Bell that in this, at least, Iraq was likely to be even worse than Syria.[51] At a skeptical gathering of the pro-British Sunni tribes west of the capital, "under the steep edge of the Syrian desert were drawn up the fighting men of the Anazeh, horsemen and camel riders, bearing the huge standard of the tribe." Introducing himself, Faisal spoke, as Bell recalled in a letter home, "in the great tongue of the desert, sonorous, magnificent . . . as a tribal chief to his feudatories."[52]

To the Christians, who were most numerous in Mosul, Faisal emphasized the importance of Britain's role. "We must not hurry and err," he said. "Let not our hot blood and nationalist sentiments boil over precipitously."[53] Here, again, was the concern that the Sunni Arab "extremists" would hijack the whole business.

At a banquet provided by Baghdad's chief rabbi—"a wonderful figure, stepped straight out of a picture by Gentile Bellini"—there were "thirteen speeches and songs interspersed with iced lemonade, coffee, tea and cakes and ices," wrote Bell.[54] With fifty thousand in Baghdad, the Jews were at their numbers from the late Captivity, before Cyrus sent many of them home. In the capital they were now almost as numerous as the Sunnis, "and exceeded the Christian, Persian, and Turkish minorities combined."[55] Baghdad was presently, in other words, almost a Jewish city as much as it was anything else.

---

* The event was organized by Seyid Mohammed Hussein al Sadr, a leading Shia cleric, and Abdul Hussein al Chalabi, a prominent Shia merchant. Descendants of these two individuals, bearing the same family names, would work together closely at the beginning of the next century, during the next attempt by a Western power to build up a new Iraqi state.

That morning, the unifying idea of Ottomanism was long dead, and the new spirit—short mustaches, long boots, uniforms for clerks—was afoot throughout the Middle East. Bell noted "the anxiety of the Jews lest an Arab government should mean chaos." When the Jews of Baghdad met Faisal on that July morning, the Sharif of Mecca's son was clearly the opposite of the recent Sunni type whom they feared. While the lemonade went around, Bell noted their "gradual reassurance, by reason of Faisal's obviously enlightened attitude."

The Hebrews of the Captivity had been the elite of Judah when Nebuchadnezzar first sent them off to Babylon. There, under Babylonians, Persians, Greeks, Turks, and others for two and a half millennia, they had in general done well, although every city, town, and large village in Iraq was said to possess Jews among its "poorest and most backwards elements" too.[56] Arrived in their Captivity, the Hebrews of Babylon had received a letter from the prophet Jeremiah exhorting them to settle down and prosper.* "Build houses and live in them," wrote Jeremiah to the Jews at Babylon,

> plant gardens and eat what they produce. Take wives and have sons and daughters; take wives for your sons, and give your daughters in marriage, that they may bear sons and daughters; multiply there, and do not decrease.[57]

The Jews of Iraq did indeed build houses, plant gardens, and multiply. After severe flooding of the Tigris in 1926, King Faisal lived in one of these houses, belonging to the immensely rich Menachem Daniel. Faisal's first house in Baghdad, in the summer of 1921 before he became king, had also belonged to a Jew. A Jewish traveler of the mid-nineteenth century, Israel Joseph Benjamin, who like Benjamin of Tudela seven hundred years earlier reported on far-flung Jewish communities, wrote of Baghdad's Jewish population, "in no other place in the east have I found my Israelitish brothers in such perfectly happy circumstances." The Jews were almost 20 percent of Baghdad's population through this period.[58] Much like the Muslims around them, Baghdad's Jews married

---

* Jeremiah also passed along a promise from the Lord to bring them back to Jerusalem in seventy years, which is when Cyrus sent them back.

their daughters off young, between the ages of eight and twelve, and required women to wear veils. The yeshiva was schooling sixty rabbis at a time in Rabbi Benjamin's day.[59]

Jeremiah admonished the Jews of the Mesopotamian exile to contribute to their new land: "Seek the welfare of the city where I have sent you into exile, and pray to the Lord on its behalf, for in its welfare you will find your welfare."[60]

The first finance minister of Iraq, in the provisional government established by the British before Faisal's arrival, was Sassoon Eskell, a nephew of Menachem Daniel. One of the three or four principal figures of Faisal's reign, Sassoon had been educated at Baghdad's French-Jewish school, the Alliance Israélite Universelle. He went to Constantinople in 1908, representing Baghdad, as Faisal represented Jeddah, in the Young Turk parliament. There Sassoon chaired the budget committee. He would be one of the two Iraqi representatives at Churchill's Cairo conference as it chose Faisal and a kingdom for Iraq. Knighted by the British in 1923, Sassoon Effendi (as he was widely known) served seven times as finance minister before dying in Paris in 1932.

Iraq's Sunni Arab nationalists were initially fairly favorably inclined toward the Jews, as they would always be toward the local Christians. While not quite Arab, as many of the Christians were, the Jews were at least Semitic. They were not Turkish or Persian. Later in the 1930s, as Arab nationalism in Iraq, Syria, and Egypt took on its ultimate national-socialist complexion, this would change for Mesopotamian Jews, now representing over a quarter, and in some accounts a full third, of Baghdad's population.

———

In the summer of 1921 as Faisal sought the support of Iraq's communities, he mostly had it, from Shias to Sunnis to Jews to Christians.* The Kurds of Sulaymaniyah did not participate in the plebiscite. The Kurds of Kirkuk voted against Faisal, by a small margin. The aggregate result was the "96 per cent," referring to the proportion of gatherings that

---

* The term "Sunnis" in the context of Iraqi politics is generally used as a shorthand referring to Sunni Arabs. Iraq's Kurds are mostly also Sunni by religion, but the most common breakdown of Iraq's main groups refers to "Sunnis, Shias, and Kurds."

reportedly voted in favor of Faisal. De Gaury recalls the impression of a British political officer involved in the proceedings: "many of the illiterate people in the north had thought that they were voting, not for a King, but for more sugar."[61]

Bayaa was the Arabs' immemorial tradition of "giving a binding allegiance."[62] There was no tradition of the referendum, the secret ballot, the formal count. *Bayaa* represented as deep a source of legitimacy as anything else. One way or another, Faisal achieved his *bayaas* up and down the country over those two hot months in 1921. He was new, the communities needed their protections from each other, and this novelty of a kingdom could not be allowed to be a stalking horse for an endless League of Nations "tutelage" or for British imperialism. So the *bayaa*, like any expression of fealty to a man without power, came with its stipulations.

An ayatollah of the Kadhimain shrine, a man at first suspicious of a foreign Sunni king propped up by the British, agreed to endorse the project. To "his high majesty Faisal the First," proclaimed the Shia cleric at a meeting, "we give our allegiance, to be king over Iraq"—on the proviso that there be a "constituent assembly, separate from the power of the others, independent alongside him."[63] Here "the others" meant the British. The Jews of Baghdad gave their *bayaa*, as did the Christians of Mosul. The Sunnis had already given it too, at their main shrine, with no stated conditions at all.[64]

Faisal's first cabinet was formed on September 1, 1921, a week after the enthroning. The sitting prime minister and others of the outgoing provisional government, all but two of them Sunni Arabs, took their jobs anew. With prime ministers quitting or being sacked by Faisal, and with the king, the various cabinets, and the British constantly feuding, there were three more ministries by the time the first elected parliament sat in 1925, and nine more before Faisal died in 1933.

Faisal's grand strategy domestically was to unite the new "urban nationalists" with the old elites and provide the British with the proofs of order and progress that League of Nations accession would require.[65] But it was not easy to persuade the grandee families to work with, and increasingly under, the relatively recent Ottoman "effendi" class of professionals and functionaries.* Meanwhile there were the Kurds, and the

---

* "Effendi" ("sir" or "lord") was an honorific used for respected officials in Ottoman times.

large Shia majority. During Faisal's reign and for some time thereafter, the education ministry was reserved for Shias, the finance ministry was reserved for Jews, and the rest of the government was Sunni Arab. Iraq's first education minister was able to write only in Persian, according to de Gaury.[66]

The effort of managing and balancing these various groups was Sisyphean in nature. Eventually it would wear Faisal down. The modern notion of a nation-state had been established among Europeans at the Peace of Westphalia in 1648: formally recognized borders, with full sovereignty domestically and in external relations. Nothing like this had ever existed in any Arab, Turkish, Persian, or Kurdish land.

———

The Mosul Question, as it came to be called, was emblematic of Faisal's many challenges at this point. The British were in possession of the province, the Turks wanted it and were already claiming that all Kurds were Turks, and Iraq considered its oil necessary to a solvent future. Mosul city was mostly Sunni and Christian. Its surrounding mountains and Nineveh Plain were home to the most dazzling diversity of small and ancient minorities on earth—Yezidis, Chaldean Christians, Assyrian Christians, Shabaks, Turcomans, and more. Most of the rest of the Mosul province was Kurdish. These Kurds had rebelled in 1919 and were mostly Sunni.

If the former Mosul vilayet was indeed to be a part of Iraq as Sèvres had intended, in the new state the Shias would see their four-to-one majority halved by the Kurdish inclusion. Mosul's Kurds, for their part, were wary of joining a country that would be at least 80 percent Arab, and the Kurds remaining within Turkey's borders had a dream of independence and Kurdish union that had been lit by Sèvres.

At Lausanne over the winter of 1922–1923, the various powers tried again to settle the outstanding issues in a treaty.* Where Sèvres had been clear about Mandatory Iraq's border with Turkey, Ataturk's victory in the War of Turkish Independence meant Turkey could try to claw back

———

* Among the Allied Powers, the United States had never been at war with the Ottoman Empire and was not a party to Sèvres or Lausanne. The new communist state in Russia dealt with the Turks separately in the Treaty of Brest-Litovsk in March 1918.

ownership of the Mosul province. Thus Lausanne stipulated merely that "the frontier between Turkey and Iraq shall be laid down in friendly arrangement to be concluded between Turkey and Great Britain within nine months." Should the two sides be unable to agree, "the dispute shall be referred to the Council of the League of Nations."[67]

The Treaty of Lausanne was signed in July 1923. The Turkish Republic had replaced Mehmed VI and the sultanate eight months previously, just before Lausanne began. With the sultanate gone, the matter of the caliphate remained. Ataturk's parliament appointed a first cousin of Mehmed's to the office as the Lausanne gathering began. Abdulmejid II, fifty-five at the time, had, as was customary by then, grown up not leaving the palace until the age of forty, and was a fairly good painter. When he requested an increased allowance, Ataturk allegedly wrote back, "Your office, the Caliphate, is nothing more than a historic relic. It has no justification for existence. It is a piece of impertinence that you should write to any one of my secretaries!"[68]

Under Ottoman rule, the Baghdad, Basra, and Mosul vilayets had not quite been a single administrative unit. Mosul's three sanjaks, as noted, were part of the Baghdad vilayet originally, but when Mosul achieved full vilayet status, it, like Baghdad and Basra, then answered directly to Constantinople. For historical and geographical reasons, however, the three provinces inevitably formed a loose Mesopotamian grouping in the eyes of Constantinople, of other capitals, and of themselves. The Ottoman Sixth Army Corps, based at Baghdad, was responsible for all three provinces and no others. Basra felt the "gravitational pull" of Baghdad more strongly than did Mosul, but Mosul was more in the orbit of Baghdad than it was of anywhere else besides the Ottoman capital.[69]

Now, in the fledgling country of Iraq, the Sharifian officers wished to "consolidate their power as a class using hard-knuckle politics, intimidation and the propagation of a strident Arab nationalist rhetoric."[70] If Mosul and its Kurds were to be included in Iraq, the Sunni Arabs would at least not be the country's only large minority. Mosul thus presented the Sunnis with a conundrum. Without the province, the country where they had nearly exclusive possession of power—high officialdom, the officer corps, and all of the "sovereign" ministries except finance—would be too Shia.[71] But to secure Mosul, the Sunnis would need British support, at odds with their nationalist message. This was Faisal's tightrope too.

Iraq, where the Imam Hussein had died in a hail of Sunni arrows in 680, where the Mutazilite caliph Mamoun had reigned, where some of the Shia holy men still spoke only Persian, was the sole Arab land that was largely Shia in population. Thus there was another concern at work for Iraq's Sunni political class. Arab nationalists still cherished, in many cases, geographically broader dreams of a new, secular Sunni "caliphate." An Iraq unified with other Arab lands in a single nation, joined up with Transjordan and Syria, maybe even Egypt—the new Arabia of the Wahhabi family of Al Saud, who had thrown the Sharifians out of Mecca in 1925, was out of the question—would bring back Sunni greatness. The Arab nationalists who surrounded King Faisal were not religious at all, nationalism and Islam being fundamentally at odds. They were Sunni chauvinists, not Sunni zealots: Umayyad, not Rashidun.

For the nationalists, attacking the British was the quickest route to political credibility, at least among their own almost exclusively Sunni Arab political circle. But the British did not want a colony. Nor, engaged in a global retreat with the reduction of expenses always at the fore, did they want a new imperial possession. They especially did not want one in Iraq, that "ungrateful volcano" of Churchill's, "out of which we are in no circumstances to get anything worth having."[72] What the British needed was two things: an Iraq that was quiet and functional, so that London could escape the Mandate as quickly and cheaply as possible; and an Iraq that desired a strong British presence as bilateral treaty partner and principal ally. These British goals could be achieved through either compulsion or choice. No money or will existed in London for compulsion.

———

When Faisal walked down Gertrude Bell's "long path of carpets" to his simple throne under his new flag at Baghdad in 1921, a clear, specific target lay ahead of him whose achievement would signify national independence and an easing of domestic stresses: admittance to the League of Nations.

No League membership would be granted to Faisal and Iraq until the British could at least pretend that Iraq was ready, in the words of

Versailles, to "stand alone." Nobody had articulated what this would mean in practice, but two things were certain. The country would have to be relatively orderly, peaceful, and secure within its borders, and the Mandatory power would need so to vouch.

In the United Kingdom, the 1920 rebellion had had a lasting influence on public opinion. Calls for a complete withdrawal from Iraq ("bag and baggage," as the saying went) were at the heart of the 1922 British general election campaign.[73] Arguing that Britain could not afford to play "the policeman of the world," the Conservative politician Andrew Bonar Law became prime minister by fighting and winning the election in part on a promise that his government would "at the earliest possible moment consistent with statesmanship and honor . . . reduce our commitments in Mesopotamia."[74]

The League, meanwhile, was not inclined to allow independence, or to acquit the Mandatory powers of their obligations, prematurely. For the Iraqis and British, among other issues was that of France. Despite the old dreams of *Syrie Française*, Paris was not making in Syria the investments toward "standing alone" that Britain devoted to Iraq after the 1920 revolt. Embarrassed by the contrast, France would use any excuses it could to deny Iraqi nationhood should Britain and Iraq launch their League push too soon.

At first Iraq had no constitution and thus no parliament, and all formal authority lay with the Mandatory power. Faisal's ministries initially came out of consultations between him and Percy Cox, the high commissioner. In Faisal's day-to-day work, he had two main elements to deal with. On one side were the British and on the other was the Iraqi government. All three constantly played off against each other: Palace versus Cabinet versus Residency versus Palace. The various ministries were constantly torn between the British purse string, nationalist sentiments, and the many Iraqis who believed the British would protect them from a return to centuries of Sunni minority rule. The cabinet and the British, not the king, had to work together on the day-to-day governing of the country. This usually left Faisal free to whip up support for himself and the monarchy, flogging his government as British lapdogs, excoriating the British as high-handed imperialists.

All the while the people of Iraq, and whichever parliamentarians were not at the moment in government, were militating for conflicting outcomes. The Sunnis, broadly, pressed for more and faster independence in a state they expected to control; the Shias and Kurds, adding up to a large majority that was mostly excluded from the administration and the armed ministries, pressed for a slower path and more safeguards against the strengthening Sunni Junker class of Baghdad. These safeguards could come only from the British.

The decade following the 1921 enthronement was Faisal's crucial period. The transition being undertaken was without precedent in the region: from long-forgotten imperial province to an independent country using the conventions for borders and other elements of sovereign statehood as established for Europe at the Peace of Westphalia in 1648, The very process of achieving the strange new definition of sovereignty, League of Nations membership, would subject Iraq's monarchy to extraordinary stresses while the more fundamental work of building a nation and a state struggled forward.

Faisal made clear from the beginning that he was implacably opposed to the League of Nations Mandate. The Iraqis detested the League's imperious creation, but had no power. The British did not like the Mandate either, but were bound by it. Meanwhile, if the Iraqis and British were to bring Iraq to a place where the League would lift the Mandate, they needed agreement between themselves on how to work together. Bilateral treaty relations with the British were thus a very different matter from the Mandate. Each side, Iraqi and British, had things the other wanted, and strong reserves of goodwill often obtained between key individuals. Most important, a treaty, if one could be achieved, would be signed by both sides.

Negotiating an Anglo-Iraqi treaty would be the first milestone for the new monarchy. The Iraqis wanted a document that avoided any acknowledgment of the Mandate. The British could not sign something pretending the Paris problem did not exist. As the Anglo-Iraqi negotiations proceeded through the summer of 1922 toward an agreement that could not avoid recognizing the Mandate, Iraqi popular opposition rose. Faisal aligned himself with the nationalist opposition. Cox, the high commissioner who was one of Faisal's early sponsors, now called him "crooked and insincere."[75] If Faisal kept up his antics, wrote Churchill to Cox in Baghdad, "I am sure that the cabinet," meaning the British cabinet, "will order an immediate evacuation." Churchill continued, "Faisal should be under no

delusion in this matter. He will be a long time looking for a third throne."
(This was a reference to Faisal's brief kingship in Syria in 1920—the year of
San Remo, with its finalizing of the Mandates, and the first Iraqi revolt.)

In August 1922 local hostility to the emerging Anglo-Iraqi pact mounted
into a near insurrection, almost a 1920 redux. At this point it is more than
possible that Faisal would have lost his crown, perhaps to the nationalists
but more likely to the British. Then, in the most fortuitous turn of his
career, Faisal developed appendicitis.[76] His English doctor later recalled
the unsettling experience of removing the offending organ under the
glowering eyes of heavily armed tribesmen from the Hejaz. Percy Cox
took personal control of the country. By the time Faisal recovered, the
high commissioner had stamped out the brewing revolt, using a far firmer
hand than he had in 1920 but with similar results.[77] A recuperating Faisal
turned cooperative, promulgating the treaty to the Iraqi public under
his own signature in October of 1922.

Soon enough came "triumphant tours" for Faisal in both north and
south, among the Kurds and Shia. Elections proceeded, disgruntled Persian divines decamped for Iran never to be missed, and in March 1924
Faisal formally welcomed the Constituent Assembly, a preliminary parliament. After two months of jockeying, and much last-minute midnight
nail-biting, the new body ratified the Anglo-Iraqi Treaty in June. With
sixty-nine of a hundred members present, the two-thirds quorum was
barely met. The vote was "37 for, 24 against, and 8 abstentions."[78] Clearly
passage was not easy. The prime minister who delivered it for Faisal and
the British was Jafar al Askari, one of the king's former comrades-in-arms
from the Arab Revolt. Jafar Pasha, as he was known, would eventually
be remembered as the "father of the Iraqi Army."

One of Jafar's earliest acts, as Iraq's first defense minister in the infant
government of 1921, had been to recruit, as the officer corps of the new
army, six hundred Iraqis who had served in the sultan's forces.[79] They
were, of course, all Sunni Arabs. With Jafar Pasha installed by the British
in the defense ministry of the new provisional government, his brother-
in-law Nuri Pasha had been serving as the first Chief of the General
Staff since February of the same year. Faisal, the future king, would not
lay eyes on his new country for another four months.

By 1922, Iraq's Kurds could see that life was not going to be very free for their cousins under Ataturk's state across the Turkish border. They helped the British to press the Turks back from incursions into Mosul province. The Assyrians, Nestorian Christians of the Mosul region claiming a direct lineage back to the Assyrians of Sardanapalus's day, also provided troops to help the British defend the northern border. The British organized the Assyrians, a minority with a martial history of defending themselves, into "Levies" that provided London with effective local forces in Iraq over the coming years. Writing privately about the Assyrians, Gertrude Bell said that "British officers 'constantly reminded the Levies that they're good British soldiers and not dirty little Arabs.'"[80]

At Mosul in 1923 and at Kirkuk in 1924, the Assyrian Levies rioted and killed scores of Muslims. The cause, says Longrigg, was in part "the fierce indiscipline, folly, and disunion" of these children of Nineveh.[81] The result was a "legacy of bitter anti-Assyrian feeling" adding to the myriad open sores with which Faisal already had to deal.[82] As it was for many Kurds and Shias, and for the Sunni tribes whom the British had long cultivated, so it was for the Assyrians and other small minorities: London was their only guarantor against the likely predations of a Sunni Arab state run by the new type of man who had served with Faisal in Syria.

In 1924, with an Anglo-Iraqi Treaty secured, the still-festering Mosul Question loomed as the country's biggest open issue. Ataturk's Turkey was on the rise and coveted the province, known to be rich in oil. The Baghdad assembly, upon ratifying the 1922 treaty in March of 1924, had taken pains to single out Mosul: "This treaty," read the parliamentary motion, "shall become null and void if the British Government fail to safeguard the rights of Iraq in the Mosul Vilayet in its entirety."

In January 1925, the League sent an Enquiry Commission to the disputed region. In July the commission submitted its report, recommending that the international frontier be set where the interim border already was, at the northern boundary of the old Ottoman vilayet.* This would give Mosul to Iraq. In December the League adopted the recommendation.

---

* Known as the Brussels Line, it had been drawn, slightly to the south of the maximal British position, at a meeting held in Brussels under the League Council's auspices in October of the previous year as the British and Turks bombarded Geneva with telegrams containing "mutual charges of frontier violation." Longrigg, *Four Centuries of Modern Iraq*, p. 153.

The Turks were furious but both sides had agreed to submit to the League's decision.

In 1925 Iraq held its first full parliamentary elections and the new parliament polished and ratified a constitution. This confirmed the monarchy and established a bicameral system of elected four-year parliaments, based on universal male suffrage, and an appointed senate.* Ten parliamentary elections would occur over the course of Iraq's constitutional monarchy, from 1925 to 1958.

By 1926, the midpoint of Faisal's critical decade, every ministry was in "effective Iraqi control." The various departments mostly were, too, including "Health, Education, Agriculture, Posts and Telegraphs, Government Accounts, Police, Prisons, the Census." Within these, a few dozen Britons remained. Their numbers were steadily falling, but there were "many," in Longrigg's words, who ultimately "offered years, twenty or more, of quiet efficient service to Iraq."[83] In the justice system, using primarily the old Ottoman codes, an Englishman sat as president of the civil court of appeals until 1934. On the criminal side, "unsuccessful efforts were made to form a Bar Association," writes Longrigg, "for the body of excitable, ill-disciplined advocates, into whose numbers the Law School poured annual recruits."[84]

The Iraqi Army was built up to seventy-five hundred in number by 1925. British ground forces were reduced from thirty-three infantry battalions and six regiments of cavalry in 1921 to none at all in 1929.[85] Churchill is credited with the insight, in 1920, that the RAF could do the work more cheaply from the air, which it did.† The Assyrian-dominated local Levies were also a factor; trained, funded, and partly officered by the British, they essentially belonged to the Residency.

1926 started well, with the new constitution and the conclusion of the League's process for Mosul. In January, Faisal secured a second

---

* Iraq achieved female suffrage in 1948.

† During the 1920 revolt Churchill had at one point also argued for the use of "mustard gas, which would inflict punishment on recalcitrant natives without inflicting grave injury upon them." David Freeman, "Midwife to an 'Ungrateful Volcano': Churchill and the Making of Iraq," *Finest Hour, The Journal of Winston Churchill and His Times* 132 (Autumn 2006).

Anglo-Iraqi Treaty, committing the British to a major step forward for his country. "At intervals of four years," the new treaty stated, His Britannic Majesty would "take into active consideration . . . whether it is possible for him to press for the admission of Iraq into the League of Nations."[86] In 1924, the British had confirmed the Iraq Mandate formally with the League of Nations, for a period of twenty-five years. Now, in the favorable new treaty of 1926, Faisal secured a mechanism for shortening the horizon of independence from twenty-five years to as little as four. In March of 1926, the British affirmed as much in a letter to the League.

The ratification of 1922's Anglo-Iraqi Treaty had required two years, the suppression of a near revolution, aggressive cajoling and vote buying, and a knife-edge parliamentary margin. In a measure of the better atmosphere of 1926, and of the popularity of the four-year provision secured by Faisal in that year's treaty, the Iraqi parliament ratified the second Anglo-Iraqi pact five days after it was signed.

By August 1926, the fifth anniversary of his enthronement, Faisal's borders were settled. He had a fair and modern constitution in place. The ally, Britain, present under a popular new treaty, was experienced, democratic, and weary of empire. Faisal now had a clear and official path laid out for eventual independence, four years in which to prepare for making the final date with sovereignty. Of a Baghdad evening, in between the exhausting politics, the king enjoyed games of bridge or chemin-de-fer at his residence or Gertrude Bell's. He smoked cigarettes almost constantly. De Gaury remembers a garden party where Faisal, sprinkling his Arabic with French bridge expressions, played cards with him and a couple of others in order to avoid speaking to the guests; on the way out there was "a curtsy to the ground from Miss Bell."[87]

Faisal undertook expeditions after wildfowl in the early hours of daylight, allowing him to indulge his greatest love of all these outdoor pleasures: horses. The British had introduced polo to Faisal's army, there was now racing at Baghdad, and from time to time the pleasures of a learned discussion of the lineage of purebred Arabian horses, always the prerogative of a gentleman's son of the desert, presumably provided solace too.[88]

Faisal must occasionally have looked south to Arabia, land of his birth. The contrast would have been striking. There, through 1924 and 1925, his family was losing a kingdom. King Hussein of the Hejaz, succeeded briefly by Faisal's brother Ali, had been locked in a bloody struggle with the House of Al Saud and its Wahhabi partners. Medina fell to the Saudi-Wahhabi alliance in December 1925. Later that month, a defeated King Ali departed Jeddah on a British minesweeper bound for Aden, much as the last Ottoman sultan had sailed out of Constantinople for Cyprus three years previously.

After a millennium of nearly uninterrupted rule, the Sharifian family had lost control of Mecca, Medina, and the rest of the Hejaz.[89] The family continued to sit enthroned at Baghdad and in the smaller Emirate of the Transjordan. Given the inability of the Hashemite royal family to hold on to their own western Arabian homeland, it was not a terrible return on the promises of Lawrence and McMahon. From the perspective of the British, who for years had paid equal subsidies to both sides in the fight for Arabia—to the Al Sauds and to Faisal's father—relatively friendly rulers still occupied all three thrones.*

With the fall of the Hejaz, Faisal's wife and his only son, Ghazi, twelve years old and small for his age, came to Baghdad. A four-year period of domestic quiet, in the absence of his family, now ended for Faisal. In the emotional tensions that soon developed, as seen in the letters and memoirs of the period's English-speaking observers (there are no Arabic firsthand sources), there is a sense that the hopeful days of the first few years, the days of hard work and of promise, were starting to give way to something more uneasy.

In Mecca, there had been talk of young Ghazi having a mild mental disability. Faisal took the boy's condition to heart. A courtier and minister of those days, the Arab nationalist Sati Al Husri, would later recall finding Faisal in the palace one day, "slumped in a chair," quietly repeating, "I love my son, but I love my kingdom more than anything else . . . I have to carry out my duty towards it, more than anything else."[90]

In his wife's absence, Faisal had garnered a reputation for affairs with various European women of Baghdad. He enjoyed partnering at bridge with the wives of British officers and administrators, and it was said that on his annual summer trips to the spas of Europe, he disported himself

---

* Given the nature of Wahhabi Islam and its long partnership with the Al Sauds, an argument can be made that Britain's biggest mistake in the Middle East in the 1920s may have been its hefty subsidies to the Al Saud family as it fought the more moderate Hashemites for control of Mecca and Medina.

under the nom de guerre of "Prince Usama."[91] In Baghdad, there was in particular a Mme. Shafwat. On coming to Baghdad, the queen promptly banned her from the palace.

Mme. Shafwat also had a daughter, living in Syria. Gertrude Bell hoped to bring the young lady to Baghdad for the king, "to place before him" like a macaroon. Miss Bell saw no reason why Faisal should not have a second wife, nor, presumably, more sons. Monogamy was no more the traditional way than was primogeniture, and Bell tended to take the Arabist point of view. Her scheme, however, was "nipped in the bud" by the queen's arrival and instant state of war with Bell. So, at any rate, wrote Henry Dobbs, high commissioner at the time, in a letter home to his wife. Faisal's kissing Bell on both cheeks in front of his wife did not help. On being banned from the palace, the Shafwat contingent accused "the Queen's handmaidens of carrying on with the military guard," according to Dobbs. Also flaring up was the matter of "little Ghazi's" fury at the removal of "some black page boy" whom he favored. The "domestic squabbles" caused Faisal, seasoned politico of Constantinople and Paris, a "nervous breakdown," in Bell's words. The world-famous desert warrior fled to his country estates.[92]

"I think the King is fearfully bored at their coming," Gertrude Bell had written about the impending family arrivals from Mecca, "but as he is away for another week yet, the evil moment is still to come."[93] Bell, as a leader among the "Arabists" whose policy of an increasingly local government had eventually prevailed in London, had been an important member of the British policy-making and administrative cadre in Baghdad in the years immediately after Faisal's arrival. By now she was out of the Residency and mostly attached to the palace, as an unofficial "queen bee" figure for Faisal.

Her plans for an additional queen scuppered, and Faisal's actual queen now present in Baghdad, Bell busied herself with the existing queen's wardrobe and son. At Mecca, Bell lamented, Ghazi had "been very much neglected in a household of slaves and ignorant women." She persuaded Faisal to send the boy to school at Harrow in England. In those weeks before her death in Baghdad from an overdose of sedatives, she seems to have considered the school an improvement over the atmosphere on the banks of the Tigris. On leaving Harrow well before his time there was up, Ghazi threatened to return with his army and burn the place to the ground.[94] He would at least have been living up to his given name, "Holy Warrior."

Faisal did love the boy. Bell wrote about the two of them, "the other day when I was sitting in H.M.'s garden, going off to pray hand in hand when the sunset prayers were called."[95] In this period, 1925 to 1927, Faisal, always slender, became so thin that courtiers thought he might waste away altogether. He was discovered, in 1927, to have amoebic dysentery. The accounts hinted that there was more, that the various tensions, through which he would smoke his way, while hardly eating, were eroding his health.

———

In June 1926 more good news arrived on the political front, contrasting with Faisal's personal trials: a tripartite treaty with Britain and Turkey, formally settling the Mosul Question on a sovereign basis after the League had handed down its verdict at the end of 1925. Turkey's acceptance of the League's decision was sweetened with a 10 percent stake in the Mosul-area oil revenues for the next twenty-five years.[96]

"The King is radiant over the Turkish treaty," Bell wrote to her parents. He gave her a bust of himself from a visit to London. It was to go in the Baghdad Antiquities Museum, later the Iraq Museum, that Faisal and Bell had inaugurated in a dedicated new building that year. Earlier in 1926, Faisal had visited Ur, and at the museum in the capital he and Bell had opened the Babylonian Stone Room. Now Faisal and Bell celebrated the Turkish treaty over dinner and bridge with the elegant Rustum Haidar, Faisal's French-educated Lebanese Shia consigliere, and Kinahan Cornwallis, Bell's tragically manqué love interest. After his evening with these good friends, Faisal set off to take the waters at Vichy for the summer.

In Iraq there were floods, pestilence, and locust plagues to deal with, schools and colleges to establish, oil fields at Kirkuk to inaugurate. The Sharifian officers were grabbing estates and farms. In the schools, despite Shia education ministers, other Sunni nationalists were imposing encomia to the Umayyads, and denigrations of the Imams Ali and Hussein, upon a largely Shia populace. The Shias, finally starting to press for a real role in government, nearly revolted. And always, underneath the crisis of the day, there festered the diabolical "balancing act" of the king's position between the nationalists and the British.[97] "I am going to see Faisal tomorrow morning," High Commissioner Dobbs wrote home to his wife in a typical comment, "but I fear he is eluding my grasp."

If Mosul was the emblematic issue of the first half of Faisal's decisive decade, the question of the Iraqi army played that role in the second half. Conscription was the key. By 1927, Faisal wanted to increase the size of the army to twenty thousand men. This was problematic enough, for the wary Kurds and Shias as well as the British. But Faisal also had an ambition of making service in his new army obligatory. He and others hoped a sentiment of unity would be achieved by shared national conscription; others, distrusting the Sunni officer class, saw it the other way around. In any event, without compulsion the state would not be able to afford the new soldiers.*

With sovereignty likely within a few years, according to the understandings surrounding the 1926 treaty, Faisal had good reason to fixate on the question of his military. Iraq's borders were largely hostile. To the north, Ataturk's Turkey was ill-disposed, assertive, and increasingly strong. To the south, in Arabia, the Al Sauds had just conquered Faisal's father and brother and were sponsoring Wahhabi raids into Iraq. To the west, the French in Syria had every interest in Iraq's failure before the League. And in the east, Iran's Reza Khan, a former Persian Cossack Brigade officer declared shah by his country's parliament in December 1925, was setting himself up as a thuggish Persian Ataturk.† In the Kurds,

---

* De Gaury reported that among certain Sunnis there was another theory of the economics of conscription: "At a party . . . rather late in the night," writes the Englishman, a minister told him that "the Jews would be the first to be called to the Colours, and they would all pay for exemption to the tune . . . of some five hundred thousand pounds; so conscription would pay for itself." De Gaury, *Three Kings in Baghdad*, p. 98.

† In 1920, Soviet and British forces had both been present in Iran since the Bolshevik Revolution of 1917, with the Soviets attempting to shore up their southern flank and the British trying to weaken the new Communist government while defending India from the Russians. Ahmed Shah, seventh and last ruler in the Qajar dynasty, sat on the throne in Tehran, but his government controlled little but the capital. In 1921, Reza Khan, forty-four, having risen through the ranks to command the Persian Cossack Brigade, came to effective power in a British-backed coup that saw him take command of the army. The Iranian parliament made Reza minister of war in that year and prime minister in 1923. Ahmed Shah, having acceded to these appointments, left for Europe with his family in 1923 and was formally deposed by the parliament and declared an exile in October 1925, two months before Reza Khan was declared shah.

Ataturk had a potent source of trouble-making for Baghdad. In the Shia, Reza Shah had the same.

In mid-1927, Faisal's prime minister was again Jafar al Askari. Son of an Ottoman colonel, Jafar was a stout and vigorous character with the common touch and a flair for languages. Educated at the Ottomans' German-run military college in Baghdad, and then in Constantinople and Berlin, he won the Kaiser's Iron Cross during the 1915 Gallipoli campaign. Captured by the British in Libya, Jafar agreed in 1916 during his confinement at Cairo to go over to the Arab cause. The British released him and he joined Faisal in the desert.[98] Iraq's first minister of defense, Jafar would be defense minister four more times and prime minister twice.

Another of these figures was Nuri al Said, from a similar background in Baghdad's Sunni middle class that emerged in the time of Sultan Abdul Hamid's modernizations of the late nineteenth century. Nuri had fought alongside Jafar against the British in Libya early in the Great War. The two were incarcerated together at Cairo. Nuri then fought in the Sharifian Army beside Jafar, Faisal, and Lawrence in Syria. Nuri and Jafar eventually married sisters. With many of the other top players in Iraq's political scene, and almost all of their fellow officers of the desert revolt, the two men had been members of the Arab nationalist "Covenant" secret society, plotting against the Turks just before the Great War. The two military paragons of the *effendiyat* were known throughout their Iraqi political careers by Ottoman, rather than Arab or British, monikers: Nuri Pasha and Jafar Pasha. Behind Faisal on the stage at public events, they would frequently speak quietly to each other in Turkish.[99]

In Iraq, as the countdown to independence began in 1926, this circle, the men who had welcomed their old commander to Iraq half a decade earlier, now had a fine prize in reach: dominance of a new state. But they had no indigenous resources to help them secure it. They were not members of "the historic notable families." Nor did they possess "roots in the tribal, religious or mercantile families."[100] As de Gaury wrote, "Men like Nuri al Said and Jaafar al Askari, unlike the members of the . . . older families had more to gain and less to lose in politics."

Some amongst the new men were, as exemplified by Nuri Pasha, sympathetic to the British. Others made political hay from constant, loud militating against the Mandatory power. Regardless of differences in the public arenas, as a class they shared an underlying outlook. It was a foreign outlook and novel in the land, but it had a muscular quality that resonated in Iraq. If the delicate project represented by Faisal were ground down too far, it might one day be determinative. The worldview in question was that of Potsdam: race primacy, the parade ground, the superintendence state. This is what the young officers had learned in the military schools of the Second Reich during the late imperial days of the Red Sultan, Abdul Hamid. The alternative was another foreign outlook, with Faisal working under his British-style constitution whether he truly believed in it or not. Now, as the 1920s gathered pace an ancient Iraqi tradition, reminiscent of Abbasid Baghdad and many other periods, had something of a revival: political murder. Whispers of assassinations now surrounded Jafar and Nuri.[101]

Nuri, Jafar, and the other Iraqis of the Covenant secret society had been talking about an Iraqi state under their own dominance since 1913, when they were young men in the sultan's army. Now, in 1927, the brothers-in-law had swapped their usual roles. Jafar Pasha was prime minister and Nuri Pasha was defense minister. In June 1927, Jafar sent to the parliament's speaker a draft bill for obligatory conscription in the expanded army that Faisal, too, desired.

The move alarmed the British. They feared that an expanded Iraqi army commanded by Arab nationalist Sunnis would unsettle the country. They also did not want any local threat or rival for their own forces. The conscripts would come mostly from the Shia masses, who did not want their sons taken like young Janissaries, stolen and used as the foot soldiers of their own repression, and from the Sunni tribes, who, unlike the strutting urban Sunni effendi class, were key British allies.[102] For the Shias of Iraq, the armed overlord had been Sunni since the time of Suleiman the Magnificent. Now, despite all the promises of Faisal and the British, with conscription it would be as if the sultan was gone but his henchmen were back. By November 1927, resistance to the conscription plan was strong enough that Jafar and Nuri, with Faisal's support, suspended it.

"There is little doubt that Nuri Pasha really wanted an army of this size," High Commissioner Dobbs wrote to the Colonial Office in London, "for the purpose of enabling him at some future date to make a coup d'etat in favour of Faisal and declare him an absolute monarch."[103]

Dobbs generally could not abide Faisal. When not gossiping in his letters home to his wife, the Englishman frequently boasted about his scolding of the king. "Faisal is really being very naughty and foolish," Dobbs wrote characteristically at one point in 1927, "and I am going to give him as stern a talking to as I can manage tomorrow."[104] Regardless of Faisal's relationship with this particular high commissioner, constitutional government was hardly in Iraq's bloodlines, or in Faisal's after a millennium of Hashemite rule at Mecca. There was likely truth in it when Dobbs wrote the Colonial Office that "both Faisal and Nuri chafe constantly against constitutional restraints."[105]

Outside of Iraq, contributing to the impatience of its leaders with "constitutional restraints," the day of the uniformed dictator was dawning. Ataturk provided the shining example over the northern frontier. On the eastern border Reza Shah used the dynastic name Pahlavi in a nationalist reference to the ancient Persian language spoken before the arrival of Islam. In China, Chiang Kai-shek's Nanjing Decade had begun in 1927. In 1930, Haile Selassie crowned himself King of Kings in Ethiopia. That same year, in Rome, Faisal commissioned an equestrian statue of himself during a smitten visit to Mussolini.

1927 and 1928 were not good years in Iraq. The tone of the country had become angry. Border disputes, Wahhabi raids, and the usual waves of flood and disease in the countryside added to the increasing strains. In 1927 another Anglo-Iraqi Treaty was signed. It offered nothing new and felt to Iraqis like a step backward. In Baghdad the press was intemperate and the coffers were nearly always almost empty. British financial support had nearly dried up and a weak state with little economic activity generated few taxes. The Sharifians were entrenching themselves. Kurds and Shias chafed against this, and the nationalists chafed against the British as politics descended into spiteful struggles between a high-handed Residency and a merry-go-round of ministerial governments. Faisal spent two days a week with his divan deluged by humble petitioners. At other times he was seen feather-dusting his desk or shifting the chairs around his office.

Then events turned again. In March 1929, a new British high commissioner arrived. As director of intelligence in the Arab Bureau at Cairo, Sir Gilbert Clayton had worked with Faisal in the Arab Revolt, and the two were friends. Even Dobbs, the outgoing high commissioner, knew the change might help. He wrote, "It may be easier for the British Govt to give way and make it up with the Iraqis when they have got a new man here."[106]

Clayton arrived in Baghdad with a proposal that Britain would support Iraq's League of Nations ascension in three years, meaning 1932. Britain, under the Clayton proposal, would also accept Faisal's suspended conscription initiative. Clayton's superiors in London were not pleased with the accommodations that the new high commissioner had presented. Faisal, however, had someone he could work with. The 1926 treaty had promised "active consideration" every four years, and now Clayton was proposing to make good on this at the early end. Another round of disputatious negotiations with London began, this time with the Residency on Faisal's side.

In 1929 Faisal enjoyed another piece of good fortune, one for which the hard work had prepared him nicely. A new government came to power in England after a hung election in May of that year. Clayton was now able to persuade London to make a promise. The British government would indeed "recommend unconditionally" to the League that Iraq should accede in 1932. It was significant news. Britain's formal step with the League had not yet come, but it was now London's public policy to take that step. The gifted and popular Clayton had done fine work with Faisal in bringing things to this point. He died in Baghdad in September 1929, following a polo match, the day after the telegram arrived from London announcing his accomplishment.

Clayton's successor as high commissioner in Baghdad, Sir Francis Humphrys, worked with the Iraqis to write a new treaty.[107] The Anglo-Iraqi Treaty of 1930, achieved in a brisk three months and implemented in 1932, "gave Faisal most of what he wanted: Britain's recognition of complete independence for Iraq; Iraq's responsibility for preserving internal order and external defence; and the withdrawal of British forces from Iraq with the exception of two remaining air bases."[108] The British would have a twenty-five-year alliance between the two countries, precedence for British ambassadors, and British "equipment and training" for the Iraqi armed forces.[109]

The 1930 treaty, as much as the underlying circumstances of development that led to it, placed Faisal's young kingdom in a uniquely advanced position among Arab countries. French Syria, a largely Mediterranean country, had entered the 1920s in a greatly more developed condition than Iraq and then gone nowhere. Faisal, with his family's longstanding notion of leading a broader post-Ottoman Arab nation, was well aware of the prominent spot in which his and British efforts had placed Iraq.[110]

In 1931 the British informed the League that London would be recommending independence for Iraq. Eleven years had passed since Faisal's enthroning, and the League asked for a report on the progress made and "Iraq's admissibility under the mandate criteria."[111] Various French "delaying tactics" were overcome and the League's "Committee VI.A" ("Mandates") advised acceptance.[112] On October 3, 1932, the League of Nations, in its thirteenth annual assembly, informed Iraq that it had been accepted.

With parades, speeches, and "entertainers, songs and festivities lasting through the night,"[113] Faisal and his people celebrated independence on October 6.

Chapter 18

Independence

1932–1958

On Iraqi Independence Day in 1932, a prosperous merchant or lawyer of Baghdad would have found himself wearing a suit, shirt, and shoes like those of his colleagues in Chicago or Berlin. He may have bought himself a celebratory new tie at a French shop on Al Rashid Street. Perhaps he visited his banker at the Ottoman Bank, which Austen Henry Layard had founded in 1856. He may have done the same at the Sassoon family's Eastern Bank or the Imperial Persian Bank of Baron Julius de Reuter. Then maybe he enjoyed a stroll around the Royal Pavilion. Electric streetlights lit the capital's still-unpaved main streets. Over three million outpatient cases had been registered at Iraqi hospitals in 1930, a not unusual year. Among other Baghdad hospitals where the gentleman could have an X-ray or a rabies shot was the still-independent Jewish hospital of Mar Elias.

Proud of his new country's heritage on this momentous day, a respectable member of the growing bourgeoisie would perhaps stop in at the museum, founded six years previously by Gertrude Bell with enthusiastic support from the king. She had died of an overdose four weeks after it opened. In 1932, the Baghdad Antiquities Museum's new building had artifacts streaming in from the "eleven expeditions of five different nationalities operating simultaneously."[1] The museum now boasted "a library, photographic section and laboratory."

Thirsty from the virtues of perusing the museum's collections, a man-about-town hopefully had time to refresh himself at the bar of one of Baghdad's several modern hotels, or of the city's several clubs, "both British and Iraqi."[2]

Out in the field, archaeologically, the Germans had arrived to join the British and French in the imperial scramble for prestige and insight beneath Iraq's dusty soil. American archaeologists had also come, well funded by their rich universities, notably those of Pennsylvania and Chicago. At Uruk, the Germans were uncovering Gilgamesh's walls. At Ur, Leonard Woolley finished his famous six-year dig that same year, 1932. At Layard's Kuyunjik mound by Mosul, twenty-eight-year-old Max Mallowan was in the midst of sending down a seventy-foot shaft that brought up layers reading like a history of old Iraq: the Assyrian, then the Babylonian, Akkadian, and Sumerian levels, and on through levels even more ancient, from a time when humanity had existed without civilization at all. Treasures from all these digs were already in the Iraq Museum.

Outside of Baghdad, too, the work of the twentieth century was proceeding: in irrigation, agriculture, roadworks and the mail system, river navigation and ports and channel dredging and railways. Faisal ran a model farm on his estate 120 miles northeast of Baghdad at Khaniqin. Unsuccessful attempts were made to turn the country's floodplains to cotton.

Above all, in business, crude oil was now advancing "from the conference room into the open."[3] Oil had been known in northern Iraq since at least the time of the "fiery furnace" of Nebuchadnezzar in the stories of the Babylonian exile Daniel. The strategic potential of Mosul's clearly plentiful oil had been recognized since the early years of this new century. In 1912 there were four groups—one German, one American, and two British—vying at Constantinople for the "Mesopotamian oil concession."[4] In what became known as the Foreign Office Agreement, signed at London in March of 1914, they had come together to form the Turkish Petroleum Company, the TPC. At this early date, oil was already important enough that, even as the Great War loomed, the Germans and British could engage in this final attempt at cooperation.

The TPC's ownership was 75 percent British, comprising the Anglo-Persian Oil Company at 50 percent and Royal Dutch Shell at 25. The remaining 25 percent belonged to the Deutsche Bank. From Shell's portion the Armenian dealmaker Calouste Gulbenkian received a nonvoting economic interest and a moniker that was to confer a degree of immortality, "Mr. Five Per Cent." In June 1914, the sultan's grand vizier agreed in a letter to the TPC that the combine would enjoy an exclusive lease on oil in the Mosul and Baghdad vilayets. Two months later, the Great War broke out.

In 1919, as Britain and France negotiated anew over the Mosul vilayet that Sykes-Picot had secretly assigned to France in 1915, the French demanded "an equal share with Britain"[5] in Mosul's oil. At San Remo, the British and French agreed to assign France the German stake held by the Deutsche Bank. The United States was insisting on an open-door policy that would see it included in the Middle East oil game. America had not been a belligerent with the Ottoman Empire in the Great War, was therefore not a party to San Remo, and so was in danger of missing out altogether on the new oil rush in the former Ottoman lands. But Washington had other leverage with her former allies, and Anglo-American negotiations in 1920 ended with an offer to the Americans of 20 percent of the TPC. Then came the Turkish War of Independence and its obviation of the Sèvres treaty, casting Mosul's future into doubt. In need of American support at the upcoming 1922–1923 Lausanne conference, the British increased their offer to 24 percent.

Once the League had confirmed in 1925 that Mosul would belong to Iraq, the Iraqi government signed an agreement with the TPC, based on the 1914 letter from the old Ottoman government, granting the company seventy-five years' exclusivity over two dozen eight-square-mile exploration blocks of its own choosing. Sassoon Effendi insisted that the royalty be payable in gold, a provision that paid handsomely when the pound sterling devalued during the Second World War. Annual auctions for additional blocks were to commence in 1929, assuaging American concerns at being left out.

At Baba Gurgur, near Kirkuk in the northeast, the eternally burning oil pits were an obvious place for exploration. When the first well struck there, in 1927, the ninety-foot geyser of crude petroleum was seen for miles. The city of Kirkuk was nearly flooded, and the main dam to protect it was hastily built a full fifteen miles away from the gusher. A year later, an American group led by Standard Oil of New Jersey took over half the Anglo-Persian stake, and the next year the TPC was renamed the Iraq Petroleum Company. There never were any auctions of additional exploration blocks. With the Americans now included in the IPC, the consortium and its subsidiaries would have exclusive rights throughout Iraq.

It took ten days to bring the wild geyser of crude oil at Baba Gurgur under control in 1927. Between 1932 and 1934 the IPC built a pipeline to bring the oil to the Mediterranean. To satisfy London and Paris, the line branched at Haditha northwest of Baghdad and continued by halves to Haifa in Palestine for the British and Tripoli in Lebanon for the French and Americans. Now there would be money, real money, for Baghdad for the first time since the Abbasids. With the pipeline due to open in 1934, the IPC and the Iraqi government signed a new agreement providing for immediate payments as an advance on the coming royalties. Having contributed nothing to this point, oil provided almost 20 percent of the Iraqi state's revenues in 1931–1932. The fledgling state, born in perennial penury, was now solvent.[6]

A country at last, on October 6, 1932—a brand-new country in a very old land.

It was eleven years since Faisal ascended the wooden platform in the courtyard of the old Ottoman serai. Much had been achieved since this foreign prince of Mecca sat himself on a throne of beer crates in Baghdad and then left the stage to the tune of a British song played by a British band.

S. H. Longrigg, an exemplar of the British administrative cadre in Iraq in that period, provided the best summary of where Iraq stood. An excellent speaker of Arabic, Longrigg went on from Iraq to serve in Libya, Somalia, and Eritrea. He would gain a doctorate at Oxford, work for the Iraq Petroleum Company in Saudi Arabia, write numerous books about the Middle East, and teach at Columbia. Longrigg served as Iraq's Inspector General of Revenue from 1927 to 1931, when, as had already happened some time before with most other functions in the administration, his post was at last filled with an Iraqi. During these years in Iraq, Longrigg wrote the definitive history of Ottoman Mesopotamia, *Four Centuries of Modern Iraq*. In 1953 he looked back at Iraq as it stood on Independence Day, 1932, and saw promise.

The territorial limits of the country had been settled. They followed almost perfectly the age-old Ottoman outer boundary for the three Mesopotamian provinces, which together were little different from the

The Hashemite Kingdom of Iraq at Independence, 1932

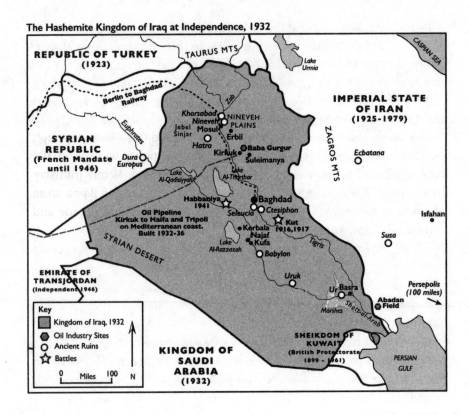

overlapping cores of the Akkadian, Babylonian, and Assyrian Empires before them, or the Mesopotamian satrapies of Cyrus, Alexander, the Seleucids, and the Parthians. The British had carved off Kuwait from the Basra province in the south, but that was the only major change from the *Iraq Arabi* of the Ottomans in the long centuries when Mosul had belonged to the Baghdad vilayet.

Statehood had been achieved and was, as Professor Longrigg wrote, "world-recognized."[7] The country's foreign outlook was generally positive. Of Iraq's three "independent neighbours," meaning Turkey, Saudi Arabia, and Iran, two had invaded Iraq during the 1920s: "Turkey in 1922, until repelled by the British, and Saudi Arabia between 1926 and 1929, when also stopped by Britain."[8] Now, with the Iraqi state taking root and surviving, the predations had ended and relations with Ataturk and

Ibn Saud were in a "firm and friendly" condition. The United Kingdom of 1932, constrained as it was, was a singular asset.

Iraq's people in this year of independence, wrote Longrigg, "were in no way below the average of humanity in moral qualities, and above it in intelligence." The country "had abundant space, great rivers, famous fertility, a healthy if severe climate, and the certainty of increasing population." The Mesopotamian Railways line reached from Basra through Baghdad to Baiji, near Mosul.* The courts and the police were good, the army small and well-behaved. The ministries worked. While industry already looked like it would not prosper, the date farms of Basra were the finest in the world and other farming was modernizing. Trade and communications were on a footing to grow with the country and the world. Petroleum was already contributing money and was poised to contribute more.

A system of representative democracy had been established, to provide governments managing the country under the constitutional monarch. Parliament, monarchy, and constitution all had shallow roots in Iraqi soil, although for the population of the countryside there were parallels in the immemorially democratic ways of the Arabian tribes. Flawed as Iraq's new way of government may have been, any other would have been even more tenuous. As Longrigg wrote, there was "no alternative." Iraq would never "consent to a patriarchal tyranny" in the Arabian style of the Al Sauds to the south. Iraq was too diverse for that and, after the long latter Ottoman centuries, too accustomed to loose and distant rule. For similar reasons Iraq was also "no Persia or Turkey, which could throw up an efficient military dictator."[9] Instead, for Iraq there were elections, and electoral rolls and electoral laws. In religion, in the press, in the right of protest, there was near-complete freedom.

Finally, Longrigg wondered whether there was, regardless of the extraordinary endowments that Iraq enjoyed in 1932, "a sound and benevolent authority in the state itself, with a political life based on stable foundations."

Faisal himself was indeed sound and benevolent. But his role was limited. Sovereignty was vested in the law and the people through their

---

* In 1936, Iraq would purchase the Mesopotamian Railways company from the British, rename it Iraq State Railways, and commence work on filling in the last gap to eastern Syria and thus to Turkey and the Syrian coast. This work would be completed in 1940.

national assembly. The ministry of the day governed, and political life expressed itself mostly through the factions in parliament.

"In 1932," as Longrigg wrote, "the Government of Iraq consisted of a façade of democratic forms." The "small ruling class" that ran the country behind this façade had no worse a balance of the talented and the ignorant, the selfless and the venal, the patriotic and the factional, than anywhere else. It was conceivable that Iraq would overcome its immense challenges. To master these the country needed time. The one who could buy that time, moderating the factions, cutting off the strongmen, comforting the communities, providing a symbol, was Faisal. On October 6, 1932, Independence Day, he was forty-seven years old.

In August 1933 trouble was brewing with the Assyrians in the north, who were requesting an independent enclave now that independence seemed to signal an eventual end to their protection by the British. In July 1933 a band of six hundred Assyrians, well armed, had tried to cross into Syria, there to seek asylum, but were turned back by the French. This led to clashes with the Iraqi Army units stationed near the Syrian border. In these confrontations the Iraqis came out significantly the worse. The Iraqi Army colonel in charge in the Mosul province, Bakr Sidqi, responded with an initial massacre of several hundred unarmed Assyrian men and a handful of women and children. More atrocities followed under Sidqi's leadership, punishing this martial minority of Nestorian Christians long cultivated by the British. Local Kurds and Yezidis joined in the killing, rapine, and looting. The final tallies are impossible to sift accurately from the various reports, but the toll was likely thousands of Assyrians slaughtered and scores of villages destroyed.

Faisal was in Switzerland at the time, taking a rest cure from heart trouble, and the decisive actions of Bakr Sidqi made the king look weak. The nationalists accused Faisal of being soft with the Assyrians, even though he had loosed local tribes upon them. The British accused the king of allowing the Christians to be slaughtered. Colonel Sidqi's initiative and aggression in Mosul unavoidably called to mind a young Ataturk or Reza Shah. Upon returning to the crisis in the exhausting heat of August, Faisal went days without sleeping or eating, instead smoking constantly and drinking coffee. All sides accused him of hiding or of inventing his illness.

At Baghdad, "delirious crowds" came out for the returning troops. This was the Iraqi army that Faisal had created and wanted more of. It was the army that his officers from the old Sharifian Army of the Arab Revolt had shaped, after they themselves had been shaped in Berlin and in the Prussian military schools of the late Sultan Abdul Hamid. The massacre of the Assyrians was the Iraqi Army's first major act.

When Colonel Sidqi himself returned four days later, fifty thousand people appeared at the aerodrome to welcome the plane of the conquering hero. With Sidqi and the army parading before him, as the nationalist crowds cheered wildly for the colonel but stayed silent for the true warrior, their wan and hollow-cheeked king, "Faisal stood at his balcony to salute the victorious officer."[10]

Faisal, whose illness had kept him from public view during the crisis, then flew to Cairo and on to Switzerland to rest and see doctors. He died of a heart attack at Bern five days after leaving Baghdad. He was forty-eight years old.

Ghazi, Faisal's troubled son who became king at age twenty-three upon his father's death, was the Sharifian Caligula. A soldiers' favorite as a boy, he grew up to be a drunken lout, much loved by the thuggish younger army leadership. Ghazi shared various sympathies with the brutish and "singularly unattractive" Colonel Sidqi.[11] *

In 1936, with Ghazi in the third year of his reign, Bakr Sidqi launched the Kingdom of Iraq's first military coup, murdering Jafar Pasha, the two-time prime minister and paladin of the old guard who was now defense minister for the fourth time. King Ghazi lent the coup quiet support; he had disliked Jafar at least since the days at Harrow, when Jafar, then ambassador in London, refused to send him a new car.[12] It was at the

---

* De Gaury paints his initial encounter with Bakr Sidqi in sinister tones: "In a cool, half-underground room" in a small Baghdad hotel by the Tigris, "I saw a middle-aged Iraqi sitting alone drinking whisky. The back of the head was flat, the neck thick, the lips sensuous, the face and expression vulgarly brutal. It was the face of a man born to be a criminal." De Gaury, *Three Kings*, p. 87.

wheel of a sports car that Ghazi died, in a midnight single-vehicle crash on a Baghdad bridge in 1939, after six years on the throne. The 1936 coup that he supported was the most significant event of his reign.

After King Ghazi's death, his son Faisal II became king at the age of four. An uncle, Crown Prince Abdulillah, a quiet man who loved horses and seemed unsuited to the increasingly noisy and hoodish times, became regent. For fourteen years, Abdulillah served in essence as the third of four Hashemite monarchs of Iraq. The regent proved a credit to the family, wielding the scepter successfully in Iraq, as de Gaury pointed out, for "longer than Faisal I or Ghazi and in more difficult times."[13]

Nuri Pasha continued to be the leading political figure of the country and would endure in that role until he died with the monarchy in 1958. Nuri was pro-British, as was the ostensibly apolitical regent. But many army officers sympathized with Germany through the latter 1930s. Baghdad became a nest of Nazi spies, led by the affable archaeologist Herr Doktor Fritz Grobba. The former Grand Mufti of Jerusalem, an anti-Zionist ex-Ottoman officer expelled from Palestine in 1937, was also in Baghdad, working on the Nazi side to secure German sympathies, and hopefully an eventual rising against the British, wherever Sunni Muslims could be found. The mufti, who had come to his office with no religious credentials to speak of and who had his own pack of gunmen in Baghdad, was a "notorious and long-standing sworn enemy of Britain."[14]

In September 1938, in Ghazi's last year on the throne, an Iraqi delegation participated in Hitler's rally at Nuremberg.[15] A year later, following Hitler's invasion of Poland, the British declared war on Germany. When Dr. Grobba was expelled from Iraq, his network remained, based in Baghdad at the Italian Legation.

France's defeat in July 1940 and subsequent establishment of a pro-Nazi government at Vichy delivered neighboring Syria into Axis hands. Here, alongside Nazi allies inside Iraq, was another asset in the German designs on Mesopotamia. German possession of Iraq would unlock its oil for Hitler, threaten British India and the British oil at Abadan in Iran, and envelop British Egypt, with its command of the Suez Canal.

In Vichy Syria in 1940, two Syrians founded a political movement called the Baath, meaning "resurrection" or "rebirth."* The two, Michel Aflaq

---

* They initially used the Arabic term "Al Ihyaa," a synonym.

and Salah al-Din Bitar, had met as students at the Sorbonne in Paris in the early 1930s. There, in the rainy passages and walk-up garrets of the Latin Quarter, these two sons of prosperous grain merchants from sunny Damascus became Communists. Eventually the Baath became a formal entity called the Arab Socialist Baath Party. Back home in Syria later in the 1930s, Aflaq and Bitar learned that Communism in the time of Stalin made little room for a parallel project of Arab national greatness. Then, in 1940, Syria became effectively a German province. Aflaq and Bitar moved on in their statism from the purer Marxism of the Sorbonne, grafting upon it the preoccupation with identity that had been present among Arabs of cafe and barracks since shortly before the Great War. Syria's new masters, the Nazis, claimed to have done the same, marrying the twin, original collectivisms that their own land had given the world: socialism and nationalism. The Baath thus called their party "Arab Nationalist" as their models in Germany called theirs "National Socialist."

On April 1, 1941, four Iraqi generals known as the Golden Square, led by one Rashid Ali al Gaylani, launched a coup in the capital. The regent made his way to the American embassy dressed as a woman. From there, under a rug on the floor of the ambassador's car with a pistol in his hand, he escaped to the British air base at Habbaniya, forty miles west of Baghdad, and thence on to Basra by plane. HMS *Cockchafer*, a British gunboat, took him to safety in the Gulf.[16] King Faisal II, a month before his sixth birthday, was sent with his English nanny to a small palace in Kurdistan.

Iraq was now in the hands of a Nazi-backed junta of local officers. As a counter the British had hopes of "raising the tribes," their allies since Faisal I's early days. But it was already early summer, when the tribes were habitually inclined to keep to themselves. The British sent forces from India to Basra, but spring floods hemmed them in. This left Palestine as a source of British relief, and a relatively defenseless Royal Air Force outpost at Habbaniya in Anbar province as the sole British military asset in Iraq itself.

In Egypt, base for the British fighting Germany's Afrika Korps, a tall twenty-five-year-old nationalist officer called Gamal Nasser was planning a rising against the British and the local monarchy. British intelligence in Cairo had learned that as soon as the anti-British revolt in Iraq proved successful, Egypt's Free Officers, as the Nasserites called themselves, would make their move. For the British in North Africa, engaged in the famous hair's-breadth struggle with the German commander Erwin Rommel, a significant Egyptian uprising would likely have been lethal. On the far side of Egypt, in the Libyan desert with his aggressive eyes on Cairo, Suez, and the vast oil fields beyond, Rommel had so little fuel that what he did have was often flown in from Italy. The British facing him had plenty of fuel, thanks to King Faisal I's pipeline from Kirkuk to the port of Haifa in what was then the British Mandate of Palestine. Construction of a refinery at Haifa had begun in 1938, and its refined petroleum product supplied the British through the war despite repeated Axis bombings.

A case can be made that in all its long history Mesopotamia had never mattered more than it did now, during the first half of May 1941, when the pro-German junta of Rashid Ali fought a small British force at the Habbaniya air base west of Baghdad. Yet the numbers of men fighting in the Habbaniya battle were minute; almost nobody else noticed at the time, and history hardly remembers the episode.

Less than a year after the French capitulation, almost all of Western Europe belonged to Hitler and his allies. To the east, the Soviet Union was a much weaker force than Germany and still Hitler's ally, supplying Germany with large quantities of oil and food every month.* In the United States, isolationism, with pro-German sympathy in powerful quarters, temporarily kept the free world's greatest power out of the war. Pearl Harbor was seven months away. All that stood in Hitler's path was Britain, its Empire, and its Commonwealth.

At the time, the Royal Navy was still the largest in the world, although reductions following World War I had left it small for a war that would soon include Japan, too, among Britain's enemies. On land, Britain had only partly reversed its post–World War I disarmament. Australia, Canada, and New Zealand contributed to Churchill's stand, but India was what

---

* In 1940, Stalin supplied Hitler with "900,000 metric tons of crude oil, 500,000 metric tons of manganese ore, 100,000 metric tons of chrome ore and a million tons of fodder to feed Germany's horse-drawn army." Len Deighton, *Blood, Tears and Folly: An Objective Look at World War II* (London: Jonathan Cape, 1993), p. 435.

allowed Britain to compete in a global conflict. Meanwhile Nazi Germany had been working for years to lay the groundwork of a rising wherever the British were present in the Muslim world, from Arabia to India.

At this crucial moment, Adolf Hitler could have turned south and southeast, taking Suez, the Levant, and Mesopotamia. Instead, he turned east, invading Russia on June 22, 1941. He did so with 153 divisions. By contrast, German strength in North Africa at the time numbered a total of four divisions. In terms of manpower, the "desert war" between Rommel and the British was so closely balanced that Archibald Wavell, commander of the British troops in the theater, staked his job on rejecting orders from Winston Churchill to redirect even a few thousand troops east to help counter Germany's moves toward Iraq. But in terms of materiel, there was a gross imbalance against the Germans. By the time the Afrika Korps lost to the Allies at El Alamein in November 1942, 80 percent of Rommel's transports were vehicles he had captured from the British. Of that pivotal battle, Rommel's successor commanding the Afrika Korps, General Hans Cramer, would later say that it was "lost before it was fought. We had not the petrol."[17]

A Wehrmacht division had almost thirteen thousand men. Even an additional division or two deployed to North Africa, instead of the 153 deployed to the Soviet Union, and a tiny portion of the fuel and airplanes devoted to Operation Barbarossa, would have tilted the balance to Rommel. In May, a month before launching the attack on Russia, Hitler invaded Crete with about two divisions' worth of men and hundreds of aircraft. Crete had an important role in any "Mediterranean Strategy" that would have made so much more sense for Hitler than Barbarossa at that stage, but Hitler was not pursuing a Mediterranean Strategy. Instead of Crete, had Hitler sent these relatively modest resources to Iraq through friendly Syria at this point in 1941, they may well have won him the war.

The stakes in British-dominated Iraq in 1941 were far more significant than almost anyone at the time seems to have realized. This leads to an intriguing counterfactual placing Mesopotamia once again at the very fulcrum of long-term world developments for a couple of months in that year.

By imposing a second front on Commonwealth forces that could barely contain Rommel as it was, Nazi success in Iraq would have doomed the

British in North Africa. Seeing a Nazi victory in Iraq, Nasser and the other Egyptian Free Officers would likely have activated their planned revolt against the British in Cairo, further tipping the North African balance in favor of the Germans. Most important to the fate of Egypt and North Africa in 1941, the Iraqi oil piped overland to Haifa fueled the British war effort there, and indeed in most of the Mediterranean. With Germany in possession of this oil, there was little question that the British in North Africa would have folded. Iran, under the German-leaning Reza Shah, would likely now have joined the German camp, ending Hitler's fuel shortages entirely and putting him on the border of India. Over the course of the war, Iran produced 8.6 million tons of petroleum annually for the British, and Iraq 4.3 million tons.[18] Turkey's pragmatic neutrality would almost certainly have swung Hitler's way too at that point. With no oil of its own—none from Iraq, none from Iran, and the Atlantic infested with U-boats—Britain's continuance of the war would have required an altogether bigger commitment from the United States than Franklin Roosevelt could likely have provided at that point.

With Britain out of the war, Hitler would have been free to turn his attention to Russia. Uncontested elsewhere, he would have had none of the shortages in oil, equipment, and men that ultimately doomed Barbarossa and with it the Third Reich. Not requiring the oil of the Caucasus, Hitler may have desired Stalingrad but he would not have needed it.* The Russians, meanwhile, would not have had the supply route through Iran that was to contribute about half of the Allies' mostly American material assistance to the Soviets during the war: five thousand airplanes, seven thousand tanks, perhaps one hundred fifty thousand trucks, and fifteen million pairs of boots.[19] With Britain defeated, the United States would have been unlikely to initiate a new European conflict.† Alternatively, had Britain somehow managed to keep fighting, with North Africa in German hands, the Allied invasion of Sicily and subsequent opening of a major front in Italy would have been impossible. With the German resources defending Italy (365,000 men in mid-1944, many taken from

---

* Hitler would also now have had access to the Caucasus oil fields from the south. Turkey and Japan would, furthermore, likely have opened new fronts against Stalin.

† On December 11, 1941, four days after Pearl Harbor, Hitler declared war on the United States, which responded with its own declaration later that day.

the Eastern Front) allocated to Normandy, a successful D-Day is hard to imagine.*

Instead, a few dozen flying instructors and student pilots at RAF Habbaniya fitted its slow and outdated training aircraft with jury-rigged bomb racks, successfully defended themselves against the army and air force of the Berlin-backed Golden Square putschists, and likely helped change the course of the war.

RAF Habbaniya lacked almost completely in defensive arrangements. Its villas, golf course, polo field, and fifty-six tennis courts sat placidly beside a lake long used by flying boats on the England-to-India route. Overlooking the facility rose a two-hundred-foot-high escarpment. Here Rashid Ali's forces began to gather days after his takeover in Baghdad at the beginning of April. By the end of the month, ten thousand regular troops of the Iraqi Army, fifty pieces of artillery, and numerous tanks loomed over Habbaniya. On the British side, the ground forces comprised twelve hundred Assyrian Levies, four hundred men of a British regiment from India that had been flown north from Basra, an armored car company, and a pair of retired howitzers rescued from decorative duty outside the officers' mess.

The principal action in the brief and vicious fight at Habbaniya was in the air. The Iraqis had fifty modern fighting aircraft, including "American bombers and fast Italian fighters."[20] Flying superannuated training aircraft—Gladiator biplanes, plywood-shelled Oxfords, and others— the British had thirty-nine pilots, including students. Only three of the instructors were classified as possessing "operational experience." All three of these individuals were at Habbaniya because they had been designated elsewhere as not "medically fit for ops"[21] and sent to Iraq to recuperate. In the first day of the battle, during the daylight hours of May 2, 1941, the British lost a quarter of their pilots; on the third day they lost four of the twenty who remained. From the start, however, using

---

* Similarly, by not wiping out the British in the Middle East and North Africa in 1941 when they stood alone and doing so would have been easy, Hitler ultimately had to devote much greater resources there to protect Europe's southern flank from the Americans. More German troops surrendered in North Africa (102,000) in May 1943 than at Stalingrad (90,000) at the end of January 1942. I. S. O. Playfair, *The Mediterranean and Middle East*, vol. 4, *The Destruction of the Axis Forces in Africa* (Uckfield, UK: Naval & Military Press, 2004), p. 460; and Andrew Roberts, *The Storm of War: A New History of the Second World War* (London: Allen Lane, 2009), p. 343.

the bombing equipment they had bolted onto their training aircraft, they attacked around the clock. After five days, "the well-equipped Iraqi Army . . . completely demoralized . . . fled, routed, never to reappear and fight."[22]

Air reinforcements arrived from British Palestine. Soon enough No. 4 Flying Training School, having sent the Iraqi Army fleeing, had "mopped up" the modern Iraqi air force.[23] At Berchtesgaden on May 11, Adolf Hitler secured an agreement with Admiral Darlan, chief of the French government at Vichy, for German planes to stage into Iraq from French Syria. When the Luftwaffe finally arrived at Mosul, it was too late, and the reinforced Flying Training School "mopped up" the Germans as well. Flying low over Baghdad on his arrival, Hitler's incoming military envoy was killed by friendly fire, shot through the neck by an Iraqi guard on a bridge who had not noticed the Messerschmitt's false Iraqi colors.*

On May 23, the Führer issued Directive 30, Middle East, stating,

> Whether and how the English position between the Mediterranean and the Persian Gulf will be brought to destruction will be decided only after Barbarossa.[24]

With this, the German push for Iraq was over. Four days after *Führerbefehle 30*, British troops were back in Baghdad. Rashid Ali and the Grand Mufti fled to Iran.† Iraq's six-year-old king, Faisal's grandson Faisal II, arrived back in his capital from Kurdistan with his English nanny, "spotlessly turned out in white shirt and shorts, immaculately ironed."[25] ‡

In the aftermath of the Iraqi Army's Nazi coup of 1941, humiliatingly defeated as it was by a handful of British trainee airmen and convalescent

---

* The German was a son of Feldmarschall von Blomberg, who, in a famous Nazi scandal, had been German defense minister until being forced to resign when confronted with pornographic photographs of his young wife, registered as a prostitute in seven German cities. Hitler was a witness at the wedding, and Hermann Göring the best man.

† When the British and Russians seized Iran in August, Rashid Ali and the Grand Mufti moved on to Italy and thence to Germany. There Hitler welcomed Rashid Ali as leader of an Iraqi "government-in-exile," while the Grand Mufti helped to recruit a Bosnian Muslim division of the Waffen-SS.

‡ Len Deighton, in his World War II history *Blood, Tears and Folly*, writes, on the basis of a personal letter he received, that in Palestine the British "recruited Iraqi Jews to penetrate and spy upon the Rashid Ali organization" (p. 295).

flying instructors, two events occurred that would have important reverberations later. First, Regent Abdulillah and Nuri Pasha ordered almost all of the coup's leaders to be rounded up and executed. When the next generation in the army's national-socialist, Arab nationalist tradition finally succeeded in destroying the monarchy seventeen years later, they would not forget the lesson that it could be lethal to allow a coup's victims to survive.

Second, a week after Hitler called off the Nazi push for Iraq, anti-Jewish riots verging on a pogrom erupted in Baghdad. On June 1 and 2, 1941, in Baghdad, Jewish shops were looted and burned, at least one synagogue was destroyed, and as many as eight hundred Jews were killed, although most sources put the toll at about two hundred. The regent and Nuri Pasha responded vigorously and the restored government killed hundreds of the rioters on the second day, the machine guns "sweeping the streets." Known as the *Farhud* ("forced dispossession"), the events did not yet spark a mass Jewish emigration, and many Iraqi Jews found a confirmation of their community's status in the government's response. But Ezra's handwriting on the wall was there at last. The end of the feast would come soon enough.

———

Immediately after World War II, optimism rose in Iraq. Faisal II showed promise. Ten years old in 1945, he was already quite unlike his father. The boy king was lively, restrained, polite, and intelligent. In contrast to Ghazi, Faisal was "a happy and successful Harrow schoolboy," wrote Longrigg.[26] "The boy king," according to de Gaury, "seemed to typify our hopes and the hopes of Arab youth."

Faisal spent the remainder of the war in England. In 1945, on his way back to Iraq, the boy king landed at Beirut to a warm welcome from Arabs at the docks and on the streets.[27] At Damascus he received a good welcome too. On reentering his own country, Faisal had to inspect so many dusty parades that his asthma, gone in England, returned.

The Iraqi Army was relatively weak after the war. It had not recovered from Habbaniya, and Nuri Pasha, with memories of the 1936 and 1941 coups, and various smaller crises and plots in between, preferred it that way. As the British pulled back following the war, however, they determined that their ally needed a more substantial military once again, and the Iraqi Army was rebuilt.

By 1948, Iraq's army was in a position to force upon the country a most inauspicious year. A new treaty with the British was signed at Portsmouth in January. The treaty's upshot was a continuation of Britain's role in Iraq, if on a slightly reduced basis. The Iraqi leadership, visiting England for the purpose, thought the document fairly harmless and successful. But in Baghdad it was seized on by an opposition that had taken on an increasingly malignant complexion. In Iraq's climate of ever-rising and more vitriolic Arab nationalism, here was an occasion for rebuffing the relatively pro-British political establishment.

The usual fevers were whipped up. The weak postwar economy had already soured the public mood. Strikes were called. Police shot and killed hundreds of protestors. Corpses floated once more down the Tigris through the City of Peace. The crowds chanted "Death to All Enemies," "Free Lands for All," and "Destruction to All Foreigners." The regent had to back down, and a week after its signing abruptly foreswore the new treaty that his political allies had negotiated. The prime minister of the moment—Salih Jabr, Iraq's first Shia head of government—eventually abandoned the agreement altogether, then stepped down, fled to his boyhood home in the south, and moved on to exile in London.[28]

Iraq's political leadership had negotiated the 1948 Portsmouth Treaty with the backing of only a narrow group domestically. The opposite had been the case with Faisal I's politically successful 1930 treaty, of which the 1948 document was essentially an update. Now, having forced the government to reverse course, the forces of illiberalism and violence in Iraq, growing busier and louder all the time, knew their strength.

The British, too, had lost their touch. The 1920s and early '30s, with the fifty-six tennis courts at Habbaniya and the seasoned advisors speaking perfect Arabic in every Baghdad ministry, had in a sense been for the British in Iraq the tail of a long nineteenth century. The tenor changed with the Labour government that swept Churchill from power in 1945. The new foreign secretary, Ernest Bevin, was the former general secretary of the Transport and General Workers' Union. In Baghdad, the Oriental Counsellor of the diplomatic mission was "sent as Colonial Secretary to Barbados." At the Foreign Office in London, "the head of the Eastern Department was sent as Minister to Iceland." The man in charge of the Iraq treaty negotiation was "posted to the Berlin Control Commission" before the 1948 treaty was announced. "The official in charge of the Iraq Section was sent as Head of Chancery to Rangoon." The days of Bell and Lawrence and the many others who deeply knew the Arab lands and their cultures, histories, and people had gone the way of the Hittites and the Mamluks.

In the days following May 15 of the same ill-omened year, 1948, the Iraqi Army joined an Arab invasion of Palestine, to confront the new Jewish state of Israel that had declared its existence when the British Mandate there ended at midnight of May 14. Egypt, Jordan, Syria, and Lebanon were the other principals in the invasion.* The Arab armies, including Iraq's, performed dismally, and Israel concluded the conflict in possession of almost 80 percent of the former British Mandate. The conflict is known by Arabs as *Al Nakhba*, the Catastrophe. At home in Iraq, three years of anti-Jewish purges began. By 1951 almost no Jews remained in Iraq. Twenty-five centuries had passed since Cyrus the Great had sent many of their forebears on the same route from the waters of Babylon home to Jerusalem.

Across the Middle East, starting in 1948, violence ensued from the same cohort of military nationalists who had long been bridling in Iraq. These groups, calling themselves Free Officers like their brothers in Egypt, were very much of a type, in country after country: midranking army officers; scions of a small bourgeoisie frustrated in the oligarchical societies of the post–World War I monarchies; Sunni by background, secular by dint of their quasi-atheistic higher creeds.

In Yemen the dynastic ruler and three of his sons were murdered in 1948. In Syria, military coups occurred in 1948 and 1949. In 1951, a Palestinian murdered King Abdullah of Jordan—older brother of Faisal I of Iraq—at the Grand Mosque in Jerusalem; Abdullah's crime had been to open talks with Israel. There were other major political assassinations in Jordan, Syria, Egypt, Lebanon, and Iran. Generally the targets of Free Officer violence were "elder statesmen," and the aim was "to make

---

* The Emirate of Transjordan, a British protectorate established in 1921, achieved independence in 1946, becoming the Hashemite Kingdom of Transjordan. It was renamed the Hashemite Kingdom of Jordan in 1949.

treating with Britain or her friends tantamount to a sentence of death."[29]*
In July 1952, a group of Free Officers, led by Gamal Nasser, deposed
King Farouk of Egypt. The Nasser clique had its own inspirations in the
Iraqi coups of 1936 and 1941. These had been the first in the Arab world.

In Iran the new strongman was not a mustachioed colonel of the
right but a languid and scholarly gentleman of the left. The socialist
aristocrat Mohammad Mosaddegh took his most important meetings
in bed. In 1951, as prime minister, he nationalized the oil fields. Iranian
production dropped by 96 percent within a year and Mosaddegh took
on emergency powers. In 1953 he called a referendum on replacing parliament with his personal rule. The "Yes" vote was 99.94 percent. After
suspending parliament, Mosaddegh was in turn removed by the forces
of his Shah as American and British agents helped to whip up large and
furious crowds in Tehran and elsewhere.

Egypt, with its size and vigorous Soviet backing amplified by Nasser's
personality, and Iraq, with its oil, relatively efficient administration, and
bustling modernity, had emerged as the two leading Arab powers. The
Cold War now dominated all international questions, and these rivals
for leadership of the Arab world were on opposite sides of the global
antagonism.

In 1953, Iraq seemed to receive a reprieve from the sense of gathering
crisis. Faisal II reached his majority at the age of eighteen and took over
from his dutiful uncle, the Regent. Forty-year-old regents stepping aside
at the height of their success and power were not a noted feature of
statecraft in the Fertile Crescent. It says much about the project of the
1920s that this feat of constitutional maturity happened in Hashemite
Iraq. On May 2, 1953, when the handover of responsibilities was celebrated in Baghdad, Crown Prince Abdulillah, as regent, had deposited
"the barque of State, after long and oft-times stormy passage, safely in
harbour."[30] In 1951, two years earlier, S. H. Longrigg had written:

> The Iraq of 1951 is a country which, with an increasing though still
> imperfect sense of unity and nationhood, neither has any reasonable
> claims or grievances against any other, nor is itself the subject of oth-

---

* The last Free Officers coup sponsored by Egypt's Gamal Nasser took place in Yemen
in 1962.

ers' demands. Its boundaries are fixed, its climate healthy, its people increasing and progressive. It possesses abundance of fertile land and controllable water, and the certainty that these together can produce, as they did in earlier ages, great material wealth; and it has a well-exploited mineral resource of exceptional richness to provide funds, meanwhile, for works of development and for social services.

Iraq's population had doubled since the turn of the century and now stood at almost five million.[31] About a third of the country's teachers, in secondary school as much as in primary school, were women, and girls had the same rights to attend the schools as boys did. In the cities the veil was increasingly rare. Iraq now boasted an engineering college, an agricultural college, an Institute of Fine Arts, and various schools like nursing and pharmacy at the Royal College of Medicine.[32] Eighty hospitals had been built, twenty of them in Baghdad. (The Jewish hospital of Mar Elias was still open, but after the Arab-Israeli War of 1948 and the departure afterward of almost all of Iraq's Jews to Israel, it was the only one left.) Hookworm, malaria, tuberculosis, and typhoid were still present, but the once-ubiquitous "epidemic diseases"—plague, cholera, smallpox—were under control. Some of them had now not been seen in Iraq for twenty-five years.[33]

Iraqi Airways, founded six years previously in 1945, was flying from Baghdad to Basra, Mosul, Cairo, and Damascus. A large radio tower at Abu Ghraib was taking in signals from Europe and beaming out to all of Iraq. Automatic telephone exchanges were enjoyed in Basra and Baghdad, and the telephone and telegraph had become "familiar or indispensable to all classes save the most backward."[34] There were sixty cinemas in the country. At Basra, reported Longrigg, "an Iraqi Port Director was a probability in the near future."[35]

Exports of crude petroleum, from Kirkuk to the eastern Mediterranean, had risen to seven million barrels a year, from slightly over four million during World War II. They would double from there within a few years. Oil revenues flowed directly to a technocratic Iraq Development Board (established in 1950), there to be devoted to capital improvements—irrigation schemes, bridges, and the like. The government's operating budget in 1951, the year of Longrigg's review, went 30 percent to the Iraqi Army and the Royal Iraqi Air Force. The next largest item was education at 16 percent; 8 percent was allocated to health.[36] By 1955, as the oil revenues began to outstrip what normal government department operating budgets would require, the Iraq Development Board was allocated 70 percent of oil revenue.[37] In parliament and in the economy, a small number of families seemed to dominate all, and their names would show up again in the following century: Pachachi, Ghailani, Al Sadr, Chalabi, Al Hashimi, Al Suwaidi, and others.

In the army, the most junior officers were good, said Longrigg, but the others were not. "There had been, in the ten years since the Golden Square, no sign of repeating the coups . . . or of imitating the Syrian Dictator-Colonels of the day." Nonetheless, he concluded, "the danger was real." Faisal II's promising youth was bearing fruit. "Unlike his father, he had regular habits, usually going to bed at eleven o'clock and reading for two hours."[38] Faisal had grown into a good shot and swimmer. He played chess well. His favorite drink was Pepsi. He was likable, responsible, "exceptionally able," and gracious. All of this was, as the regent's British advisor de Gaury pointed out, exactly what one wants in a constitutional monarch.[39]

For Faisal II's coming-of-age celebrations and the attendant handover ceremonies, diplomatic guests came to Iraq from around the world in May 1953. "The people of Baghdad," wrote de Gaury, "were in a seventh heaven of happiness." The various government ministries paraded a series of floats through the capital. The Department of Archaeology presented members of the king's guard dressed up in a *tableau vivant* of Assyrians on a war chariot. That night, "in the poorer quarters there was drumming and dancing until near dawn."[40]

The rising sandstorm, however, was engulfing, blinding, and loud. Young Faisal inherited the best-organized and most dynamic state of the post-imperial world in 1953. But he inherited too the Cold War, Nasser, and the insistent examples of Reichstag and Politburo.

Soon after Nasser assumed Egypt's presidency in June 1956, his Soviet support dwarfed anything Iraq was receiving from abroad. He began to dominate the region. Nasser pumped near-hysterical propaganda into Iraq, through his regional Voice of the Arabs radio station and his proxies in Iraq's free and hyperactive local press. In Iraq, the regent and Nuri Pasha, with their Western backers, were blamed as "the cause of every imperfection imaginable" as temperatures rose on the Baghdad street.[41]

In 1955, Iraq provided headquarters for the new Baghdad Pact, a group formally known as the Middle East Treaty Organization. With Turkey and the Shah's Iran, as well as Pakistan and Britain, the Baghdad Pact provided a pro-Western counterweight to the Soviets and their client in Egypt. In July 1956, Nasser seized the Suez Canal from the British and French who had controlled it since digging began in 1859. President Harry Truman in Washington vetoed his allies' moves to reclaim the canal, but not before Nuri al Said in Iraq had expressed his support for London and Paris. Nuri Pasha's position only contributed, domestically in Iraq, to a growing sense that the Hashemite monarchy was a weak lapdog when compared to the vigor and Arabism of Nasser. The Egyptian caudillo, with Moscow behind him as he controlled the trade route from Europe to Asia, now stood unquestioned over the Middle East.

But Iraq had its strengths. By 1957, Iraq's oil revenues approached a hundred million pounds sterling annually. The ministries poured forth plans for new bridges, and irrigation projects to bring back land unfarmed since the Mongols came in 1258. The Kurds of the former Mosul vilayet were relatively quiet. The young king was well liked. Red double-decker London buses crisscrossed the busy capital. In the heart of every city, the roads were now well paved, there was piped water, and the streetlights worked. The Iraqi monarchy had shed first the League of Nations Mandate, and then the 1930 Anglo-Iraqi Treaty, and was at last sovereign and well funded.

The expectations and pace of change of the 1950s brought a new anxiety in the land. It was different from the age-old problems of sect, tribe, ethnicity, and overlord. Since the 1920s, Iraqis had been told that what they had was democracy. They were told that this new thing—"grafted artificially into a society which was feudal in nature and theocratic in spirit"[42]—would bring happiness for all. They were told that they would have this happiness as soon as tomorrow. But what they had was not really democracy. This shortcoming was not a matter of the monarchy, which was constitutional and parliamentary. The deficit lay elsewhere in the system. In the parliament itself, and in the departments that ran their daily affairs, what Iraqis had was oligarchy: rule not necessarily by the rich, but by the political insiders, by a tiny active and connected elite spinning its way through the ministries.

A party-list voting system, whereby voters voted for a party rather than an individual member of parliament, meant there was no connection between people and their representatives in the assembly. The names never changed, merely alternated; the game felt rigged. The stakes were factional power and advantage, not a competition of policies and ideas. The rhetoric became ever more febrile and bitter. This was not "genuine democracy," feared Longrigg. In "an age when Government can be seized and held by a dominant armed minority," Iraq would need the public to be far more "loyal and politically integrated" with the state than it was.[43]

Thus there was the dangerous paradox of Iraq early in the second half of the century. Just when things were much better than ever, and improving every day, what would not long before have been excellent was now not good enough. No material change could match the expectations. Although Iraq's people had never been freer, they did not feel free enough. The popular villain for these disappointments was the same constitutional dispensation, British partnership, and liberal outlook that had brought things this far. Meanwhile the other, competing European system of thought lurked, with the huge figure of Nasser giving it a regional face.

Writing at more or less the high-water mark of optimism, in his 1951 review Professor Longrigg noted the potential for positive comparisons between Iraq and "the stark economic misery of Israel, the tragic self-destruction of Persia, the brief dictatorships of Syria, the corrupting wealth and now failing ruler of Saudi Arabia, the menace of over-population and the mob-brutality of Egypt."[44] In such lights, Iraq's future looked rosy. And yet, said Longrigg, "there was an alternative and less pleasing probability." The elements that had made Iraq so unstable over the previous twenty years "might not after all be surmounted."

Abroad, an "unholy alliance of Iraq's enemies," ranged up against Baghdad: Nasser in Egypt, his clients in Damascus, and the Soviets themselves.[45] At home, the Communists and the Free Officers found common cause in the anti-monarchical, anti-Western statist nationalism. In May 1957, an Egyptian military plot, hoping to topple the two Hashemite monarchies together—Iraq and Jordan—was foiled. Nasser's aim, with this and several other attempts against Faisal's throne, was "the strengthening of the relations of the Ba'ath Party with the Communist Party. It had the blessing of the Soviet Union."[46]

In February 1958, there was alarming news for Iraq as Nasser's Egypt, encouraged by Moscow, combined with Baathist Syria to form a new United Arab Republic. Syria's ruling Arab Socialist Baath Party had effected, in essence, an Anschluss of itself by Egypt, inviting Nasser, the Arab nationalist colossus, into a situation that he would naturally dominate. With the new, combined entity, Nasser and the Soviets were now on Iraq's western border. Two weeks later, Iraq and its sister Western-leaning Hashemite monarchy, Jordan, responded by declaring their own confederated Arab Union. Foreign and defense policies were to be unified and domestic administration would continue as before. With Iraq naturally dominating the partnership, Nuri Pasha was the Union's prime minister and Faisal II its head of state.

Nuri Pasha's Arab Union felt reactive and flaccid. Its unconvincing nature reminded Iraqis of Nuri's humiliating pro-British stance when two years earlier Nasser, proclaiming a new postcolonial world of Arab greatness despite his Soviet clienthood, had seized Suez. Now, in early 1958, in every Iraqi barracks and large military unit, there were the tentacles of an Iraqi Free Officers movement, inspired by Nasser's original organization of the same name. The leader of the Iraqi Free Officers was a forty-three-year-old brigadier called Abdul Karim Qasim, born poor in Baghdad and educated up through the ranks in the Iraqi monarchy's atmosphere of urban Sunni social mobility.

On July 14, 1958, King Faisal II was due to fly to Ankara for a meeting of the Baghdad Pact. Nasser had threateningly massed troops on the eastern border of his new Syrian satellite. The Jordanians were also concerned about a spillover of anti-Western violence in Lebanon. Nuri Pasha, now prime minister for the fourteenth time since 1930, had decided to send a force west to support Iraq's Arab Union partner and fellow Hashemite monarchy.

Of the units that Nuri ordered to Jordan, one was a brigade commanded by Qasim and another was a battalion commanded by his chief associate, Abdul Salam Arif. On July 13 Arif chose a route through the capital for his westward-bound troops. This was unusual. More unusual, for troops entering Baghdad, was the fact that they were carrying live ammunition. With "unceasing attacks on Iraq by Nasser's radio, which remained unjammed, and the activities of his agents in Iraq,"[47] Nuri Pasha and the king had received numerous warnings of an impending coup attempt. The Egyptians, working with their local Baath and Communist allies, had already tried at least two plots that year. Now, in the heat of mid-July, Arif's army column emptied a prison full of Communists at Baqubah, an hour outside the capital. Whether the Iraqi Free Officers were at this point directly working with Nasser and the Soviets, or merely inspired by them and united with them in their attacks on the Western-backed monarchy, the strong connections were clear.

On the evening of July 13, as Arif marched through Baghdad and Qasim lurked outside it with his brigade, Iraq's last king was staying at the Palace of Welcome, a modest royal house in Baghdad. In the early evening, King Faisal arranged a magician for some children of the palace. He himself watched Doris Day in *The Pajama Game*, a romantic comedy about union workers in Iowa. Then Faisal II went to bed.

In the small hours of July 14, Arif seized the central radio station and announced the revolution. According to some accounts, Faisal, on waking to the news, ordered his palace guard not to resist when Arif sent a unit there. A little after six a.m., as Faisal II was being shaved, the shooting began in his palace garden. With the young king that morning were a few servants, two aunts, and the Crown Prince Abdulillah, the uncle who had served as regent during Faisal's fourteen-year minority. Outside the little palace, Faisal and the others, lined up against a wall in one account, were cut down by Arif's men and finished off in repeated sprays of bullets from an automatic weapon. King Faisal was the only one to live for another hour or two, although he never regained consciousness. He was the only grandson of Faisal I. After thirty-seven years, this was the end of their dynasty.

Nuri Pasha, who had fought with the first King Faisal and Lawrence of Arabia against the Turks in the Syrian desert years before a nation of Iraq was imagined, died as he had partly lived, like an Abbasid vizier.*

---

* Nuri Pasha's methods and demise were not his only Abbasid qualities. De Gaury recalls lending Nuri a house, rented in turn from Jafar, for parties involving singing girls and

Well-informed, Nuri had wanted to escape Baghdad the night before. It would have been his fourth time doing so. Instead he waited up all night for his son, who was on the town. Facing the putschists in the early morning, the young man "died bravely, with a taunt on his lips and a glass in his hand."[48]

Nuri Pasha himself, at daybreak, in his pajamas and holding a pair of pistols, forced two fishermen to row him across the Tigris. At a friend's house he put on a woman's veil and long cloak, but as he tried to escape through the city, his disguise was discovered. With his pajamas showing underneath the cloak, he died exchanging bullets on a Baghdad street. After a hasty burial the same day, Nuri's body was dug up on July 15 and repeatedly run over by a city bus until it was said to resemble a local type of flat sausage known as *basturma*. Then the mob strung up the corpse of the fourteen-time prime minister, took it down, cut it to pieces, and burned it. A Reuters report from shortly after the coup, based on an account given by "a retired Turkish Army Captain back in Istanbul" after witnessing several of the revolutionary events in Baghdad, does not mention the *"basturma"* incident. Unlike most other accounts, this one claims that young King Faisal and his cousin the regent were shot in the palace garden while putting up resistance.

In 1941, the British had responded to the Rashid Ali coup by defending Habbaniya and firmly returning their allies to power. Immediately after the 1958 coup, the British and Americans sent troops to Beirut and Amman, but these then stayed in place. Soon the British ambassador in Baghdad was meeting with the junta of General Qasim, who had immediately declared himself prime minister and defense minister. The accommodating line taken by the British and Americans was the unwitting signal for a humble coup, if a singularly gruesome one, to become something far bigger. Jails were emptied of criminals and filled with the powerful, the well-connected, and the rich. In the prisons their "names

---

other entertainment. Nuri knew the exotic musical instruments as well as the band did, and in the early hours became rather animated at these affairs. He would call for the band to play the "then most popular song, 'Cocaine.'" Then Nuri would ask them to play it again, and again. De Gaury, *Three Kings*, p. 49.

read like a guest list for a party given by one of their number." But unlike at a dinner party from the past, they were now locked "twelve or so in a room and in their pyjamas."[49]

In foreign affairs, the major result of the 1958 coup was Iraq's entry into the Soviet orbit. General Qasim immediately dissolved the hasty confederation with Jordan. In an interview in Lebanon a year after the revolution, Qasim explained the debt the Soviets owed him. "When giving us aid, Moscow is paying us only part of what she owes us for having destroyed the Baghdad Pact."[50]

James Morris, the Welsh travel writer and journalist who later became Jan Morris, filed a report from Baghdad for the *Manchester Guardian* eleven days after the coup. It was too soon, Morris wrote, to know whether the country's new leaders "want Iraq to maintain her condition of prosperous independence."[51] But it was clear that real change was coming. "It is a new world in Baghdad to-day," Morris wrote. "The dear old London buses still lurch down Rashid Street and the British still drink their gin happily enough in its bars; but behind the familiar façade of the city, that mercurial mixture of the sleazy and the brilliant, all is changed."

The work of revolution continued long after the initial slaughters. General Qasim's many hasty trials were like Stalin's. "Across the wide Tigris in the darkness the dreadful orchestration of evil can be plainly heard," wrote an English journalist attending the Baghdad show trials. "The brutish laughter of the courtroom," he continued, "picked up on thousands of radio and television sets, is magnified by a whole city full of sadists."[52] Years later, many of Iraq's former elite who had not fled or been murdered were still in prison.

———————

Thirty-seven years previously, a couple of weeks after the enthroning of her friend King Faisal I, Gertrude Bell wrote home to her parents about the annual Shia festival of grief then taking place in Najaf, Kerbala, and the other shrine cities of Iraq.

"It may have escaped your notice," wrote Bell to her parents in Yorkshire, "that we are in the middle of Muharram."

As she explained, Muharram is a period (ten days long, during the month of the same name) when "the Shiahs mourn for Hussain, the prophet's grandson who was invited over from Mecca by the Iraqis to be Khalif." It had been 1,241 years earlier, on the parched plain of Kerbala sixty miles south, facing the well-organized Umayyad army, that Hussein, son of Ali, grandson of the Prophet Mohammed, had watched "his followers die of thirst and wounds," before himself being slaughtered.

"One small son escaped," wrote Bell, "and from him Faisal is descended."

As Bell penned this letter to England, Faisal, son of Hussein, the last Sharif of Mecca, had recently arrived in Iraq, just like his father's namesake twelve centuries before. For Bell, as she considered the fragile project before them, "the story of his ancestor was always in my mind."

"The parallel was so complete," she wrote, "the invitation from Iraq, the journey from Mecca, the arrival with nothing but his formal following."[53] Bell could also have mentioned, had she known what was to happen there in Baghdad a few decades later, other parallels with the massacre from Umayyad days: the army, its roots in European ways adopted by a new Arab world, Sunni in identity, secular in point of view.

Bell congratulated herself, in that letter home during the heady optimistic days of mid-1921, that despite the parallels things had turned out differently this time.

Epilogue

The Free Officers group that undertook Iraq's 1958 coup d'état embodied, principally, two factions opposed to the liberal idea of constitutional parliamentary government under a nonpolitical crowned head of state. Both called themselves Arab Socialists. The first, led by Qasim, had an Iraqi nationalist focus, while the second was pan-Arab in aspiration, looking to Nasser and hoping to join his United Arab Republic. The two blocs fell out almost immediately after the July 14 coup.

Compared to what followed, Qasim's five-year rule is remembered as something of a golden period among Iraqi anti-monarchists and socialists. In October 1958 the new government instituted agrarian reforms that did much to diminish the wealth and political power of the landowning class. In 1959 he appointed the first female cabinet minister in the Arab world, outlawed polygamy, and tore up the current treaty with the British. In May of that year, the last British forces left Habbaniya. In 1961, Qasim created the Iraqi National Oil Company. Iraq took control over those IPC oil blocks that were not already producing, representing over 99 percent of the acreage marked for exploration and production.

Qasim was not personally corrupt, and his idealistically patriotic foreign policy—standing up to Nasser, threatening Iran over its Arab-dominated province of Khuzestan on the southern border with Iraq (home to ancient Elam), and voicing loud claims to Kuwait before the British sent troops there to shore up the local ruler—gave him a quixotic, somewhat pure and saintly persona. His mother's family were Kurdish Shias, setting him apart from the Sunni Arab officer class that dominated his coup.

In October 1959, Qasim survived a Baath Party assassination attempt in which a Tikriti former schoolteacher called Saddam Hussein was one of the gunmen. But in February 1963, in the "Ramadan Revolution," the Baath succeeded in toppling and killing Qasim. Nine months later, pro-Nasser officers within the ruling junta launched a successful coup against their Baathi colleagues. Finally, in 1968, in the "17 July Revolution," the Iraqi Baath seized power back from the Nasserites.

In 1968, Saddam Hussein became vice president of Iraq. After eleven years he became president, pushing aside his cousin and Baathi predecessor, Ahmed Hasan al-Bakr, after several years in effective control of the party and country.

Throughout the post-1958 period, there had been trouble between Baghdad and the Kurds of the former Mosul vilayet. From the beginning they had hoped for autonomy within a federal Iraq, had sometimes been promised it, and had never received it. The first Iraqi-Kurdish War came in 1961, three years into Qasim's rule, and lasted nine years. The Second Iraqi-Kurdish War, from 1974 to 1975, saw Saddam's government take control of the Kurdish provinces and begin a policy of settling Arabs in oil-rich areas such as Kirkuk. In 1977 Kurdish guerrilla actions prompted a two-year campaign by Saddam that saw hundreds of Kurdish villages destroyed and as many as two hundred thousand Iraqi Kurds forcibly resettled. Saddam's 1980–1988 war against Iran gave the Iraqi Kurds an opportunity to return to the offensive in their region. Saddam's "Anfal" campaign in response, from February to September 1988, used chemical weapons and airpower in addition to massive ground forces and led to hundreds of thousands of Kurdish casualties in conditions described by Human Rights Watch as genocide.

Saddam's 1980 invasion of Iran and the subsequent eight-year Iran-Iraq War had seen him using chemical weapons for the first time. In June 1981, a year into the war, an Israeli air strike destroyed Saddam's French-supplied nuclear facility, known as Osirak, just south of Baghdad. Supported by the United States in fighting the Khomeini regime in Tehran, Saddam concluded the Iran-Iraq War in 1988 without achieving either of his goals—making himself a new Nasser-like hegemon among the Arabs, or toppling the Khomeinist government that was inciting Iraq's

Shias against the Iraqi Baath's Sunni Arab regime. The war ended with essentially no territorial adjustments and half a million combatants killed on the two sides. Hoping to attract Arab support against the Persians, Saddam's regime called the conflict the *Qadissiyah*, after the battle in 636 AD in which the Arabs had defeated the Sasanians in the time of the Caliph Omar.

In August 1990, Saddam's forces invaded Kuwait, accusing it of illegally extracting Iraqi oil. He had made a similar allegation against Iran ten years previously. Kuwait had been part of the Ottomans' Basra vilayet, but so had other parts of the Gulf region, including much of Saudi Arabia, on which Saddam now had his eyes. His army was the fifth largest in the world, battle-hardened after the war with Iran, and experienced in the expansive use of its chemical weapons of mass destruction delivered by SCUD ballistic missiles and other means. By January 1991, for the planned liberation of Kuwait, the United States assembled a coalition of over thirty countries massing more than 750,000 military personnel in Saudi Arabia. After a thirty-four-day aerial campaign, and a four-day ground invasion of Kuwait, the Coalition declared a ceasefire. In the eventual peace terms, Saddam agreed to eliminate or surrender Iraq's nuclear, biological, and chemical weapons.

On March 1, 1991, the day after the Coalition declared its ceasefire in Kuwait, a Shia uprising began in Basra against Saddam's Sunni Arab–dominated government. Over the coming weeks revolts spread to all but four of Iraq's eighteen provinces. Fearing a Khomeinist takeover, the George H. W. Bush administration allowed the Baath government to regain control relatively quickly in the south, earning for the United States the lasting distrust of the Shia population. Eventually the US-led coalition declared a no-fly zone over the north and south of the country. In the north this allowed the dominant Kurdish factions to declare an autonomous zone outside of Baghdad's control.

United Nations Security Council Resolution 687, in April 1991, demanded that Saddam's Iraq give up all ballistic weapons programs; give up all nuclear, chemical, and biological weapons; and submit to a UN inspections regime for enforcement. The resolution's conclusion stated that the Security Council was authorized to "take such further steps as may be required for the implementation of the present resolution and to secure peace and security in the area."

Under this proviso, in 1996 the United States launched a cruise missile attack on targets in southern Iraq following Iraqi aggression in the Kurdistan region. On October 31, 1998, United States President Bill Clinton signed into law the Iraq Liberation Act, stating that the United States' policy was "to support efforts to remove the regime headed by Saddam Hussein from power in Iraq and to promote the emergence of a democratic government to replace that regime."[1]

Claiming that Iraq had failed to abide by Resolution 687 in either eliminating its weapons of mass destruction or allowing the UN-sponsored inspections, the Clinton White House in December 1998 embarked on a four-day bombing campaign, involving 600 air sorties and 325 land-based cruise missiles, against targets considered to be part of a suspected ongoing Iraqi WMD program.

In 1999, the United Nations passed Security Council Resolution 1284, establishing a UN WMD inspections body for Iraq (UNMOVIC). The resolution, referring to eleven previous resolutions directed at Iraq over the previous nine years, stated that "in particular . . . Iraq shall allow UNMOVIC teams immediate, unconditional and unrestricted access to any and all areas, facilities, equipment, records and . . . all officials and other persons under the authority of the Iraqi Government."

In November 2000, George W. Bush was elected president of the United States on a party platform that stated, in its section on Middle East policy, "We support the full implementation of the Iraq Liberation Act, which should be regarded as a starting point in a comprehensive plan for the removal of Saddam Hussein and the restoration of international inspections in collaboration with his successor." The statement concluded that "peace and stability in the Persian Gulf is impossible as long as Saddam Hussein rules Iraq."[2]

Ten months later the United States suffered its worst-ever foreign attack on home soil, on September 11, 2001. Many drew links to Saddam, and the domestic US atmosphere became notably more hawkish.

In November 2002, the Security Council unanimously passed Resolution 1441, "recalling" the many previous resolutions and "deploring" the fact that "Iraq has not provided an accurate, full, final, and complete disclosure, as required . . . of all aspects of its programmes to develop weapons of mass destruction and ballistic missiles . . . as well as all other nuclear programmes." With Russian and Chinese support, the new resolution also "deplored" Iraq's failure to comply with various previous resolutions regarding terrorism, "repression of its civilian population," and Kuwaiti restitutions.

Resolution 1441 concluded that Iraq was "in material breach of its obligations" and gave Iraq "a final opportunity to comply," namely thirty days to produce an "accurate, full, and complete declaration of all aspects of its programmes to develop chemical, biological, and nuclear weapons, ballistic missiles, and other delivery systems."

Iraq agreed to the new resolution on November 13, 2002, five days after it was passed. Two weeks later UN and International Energy Agency inspectors returned to the country for the first time in four years. Their initial work on the ground, and findings from reviewing the twelve-thousand-page report that Iraq now produced on its banned programs, yielded reports of numerous breaches. All of these were of secondary importance at worst. The inspectors were finding no stockpiles of banned weapons nor any production of those weapons, but they did find, among other infractions, ballistic weapons with ranges greater than allowed and a failure to account for certain stockpiles of nerve agents and anthrax that were not found.

With Iraq clearly still in breach of its obligations under the numerous Security Council resolutions and the country now missing this "final opportunity" to avoid the "serious consequences" that Resolution 1441 threatened, the debate turned to the issue of a "second resolution." The question was whether, before any war to force compliance, further Security Council action was required. The United States and its allies argued that the extant resolutions provided all the authorization necessary. Others, led in the West by France, argued that a further, dedicated resolution would be necessary.

The argument was posturing at this point. Those who claimed that a further, war-authorizing resolution was necessary were opposed to military action in Iraq and would have voted against the resolution. Those on the other side, arguing against a further resolution, were in favor of military action and would have voted for it. The various parties were using the UN legal arguments for stances to which they had already committed.

In November, US President George W. Bush had said, in a speech to NATO in Belgium, "Should Iraqi President Saddam Hussein choose not to disarm, the United States will lead a coalition of the willing to disarm him." A month before that, in October 2002, the United States Congress had voted, by majorities of over two to one in the House of Representatives and over three to one in the Senate, to give President Bush authority to go to war in Iraq.

On February 5, 2003, US secretary of state Colin Powell delivered a speech to the United Nations detailing the intelligence findings that, in his view, proved that Saddam Hussein continued to maintain and develop stocks of the banned material. "Here," said Powell in one example from his presentation, "you see 15 munitions bunkers in yellow and red outlines. The four that are in red squares represent active chemical munitions bunkers."*

On February 14, Hans Blix, chief of the United Nations inspection program for Iraq, delivered his last preinvasion report to the Security Council. "How much, if any, is left of Iraq's weapons of mass destruction and related proscribed items and programmes?" he asked.

"So far," Blix reported, "UNMOVIC has not found any such weapons, only a small number of empty chemical munitions, which should have been declared and destroyed. Another matter—and one of great significance—is that many proscribed weapons and items are not accounted for."[3]

---

* Of the various post-invasion reports about the decision-making leading up to the war, the most credible, or at least the most nonpartisan, was the US Senate's "Report of the Select Committee on Intelligence on the U.S. Intelligence Community's Prewar Intelligence Assessments on Iraq." The report was endorsed unanimously by its authors, including the eight Democratic Party members of the Senate's Intelligence Committee. With regard to Powell's United Nations presentation, the Senate report concluded that "much of the information provided or cleared by the Central Intelligence Agency for inclusion in Secretary Powell's speech was overstated, misleading, or incorrect." The Senate report additionally cited broader intelligence failings, concluding that "most of the major key judgments" from the US intelligence community "either overstated, or were not supported by, the underlying intelligence reporting." In particular, according to the bipartisan review, failures in "analytic trade craft" led to a "mischaracterization" of the underlying intelligence. S. Rep. 108-301 (2004). https://www.govinfo.gov/content/pkg/CRPT-108srpt301/pdf/CRPT-108srpt301.pdf.

Blix concluded by noting that, while in terms of physical inspections his team had met with essentially full access within Iraq, overall the "immediate, active and unconditional cooperation" required in 2002's Resolution 1441 had not been forthcoming. The upshot of Blix's report was that there was significant material for both sides of the disagreement about the looming invasion. There were breaches of Resolution 1441, but were they material? In terms of the proscribed weapons, they were not. In terms of the complete and immediate Iraqi cooperation that the United Nations demanded after a dozen previous Security Council resolutions, they were.

By February 18, the United States had over a hundred thousand troops in Kuwait. American forces had entered Iraqi Kurdistan some weeks previously.[4] American and British diplomats, meanwhile, were preparing the "second resolution." It soon became clear that the Security Council would not adopt any such thing, and one was never introduced.

On March 20, 2003, the ground forces of President Bush's "Coalition of the Willing," comprising 160,000 troops from the United States and the United Kingdom, in a proportion of roughly three to one, plus much smaller numbers from Australia and Poland, invaded Iraq.*

The record of the Iraqi Army by that point was remarkable: in 1932, massacring the Assyrian Christians as its first important act; in 1936, murdering its own founder, Jafar Pasha, while perpetrating the first coup in the Arab world; in 1941, staging a pro-Nazi putsch that was the second coup in the Arab world; defeated in this by a tiny group of trainee airmen and convalescing teachers forced to bolt bomb racks onto training airplanes; in 1948, suffering humiliation by an Israeli army then only a few years old; in 1958, killing their young king and his aged relatives in a garden; in 1980, invading Iran; in that and following years, using mustard gas, sarin, and other chemical weapons against Iran; in the 1980s, serially gassing large numbers of their own citizens in Kurdistan; in 1990, invading Kuwait; and in 1991, massacring tens of thousands of Shia countrymen in the post-Kuwait uprisings.

---

* Japan, Italy, Spain, South Korea, Denmark, and thirty-two other countries joined the coalition in providing troops on the ground in Iraq after the initial invasion.

Under Saddam Hussein, the Iraqi military, led as it had been since its founding in the 1920s by representatives of the nationalist element within the Sunni Arab secular middle class, had invaded two of its neighbors, repeatedly used WMD against its own people, and launched near-genocides against the Kurds in the north and the Shia Marsh Arabs in the south. In 1991 the army of Iraq had launched missile attacks against five regional countries: Saudi Arabia, Israel, Bahrain, the UAE, and Kuwait. Regardless of the role, large or small, of faulty intelligence in the lead-up to the 2003 invasion, the one element without which there never would have been an invasion of Iraq in 2003 was a certain DNA in the Iraqi Army that, present in its founders, predated even its birth.

In March 2003, when the invasion began, the Iraqi Army, including Saddam's Republican Guard and Special Republican Guard, numbered about 185,000 men, not counting conscripts. Outgunned, out-led, lacking airpower and working armor, with the exception of brief resistance in a small number of relatively minor engagements, they collapsed.

By April 9 the coalition had taken Baghdad. Within a week the rest of the country was conquered. On May 1, President Bush announced on the USS *Abraham Lincoln*, in front of a sign reading MISSION ACCOMPLISHED: "Major combat operations in Iraq have ended. In the battle of Iraq, the United States and our allies have prevailed."

The major justification for the invasion had been the issue of weapons of mass destruction. A secondary argument had been alleged links between Saddam Hussein and Al Qaeda, the Sunni Islamist terrorist group that had, two years earlier, launched the 9/11 attacks on the United States. In the aftermath of the invasion, the truth behind both of these claims was revealed to be a matter of historical issues far deeper than any of the news headlines of the day.

In April 2003, immediately following the invasion, the United States government formed an "Iraq Survey Group" to continue the work of UNMOVIC, the United Nations inspections body that had been led by Hans Blix. (UNMOVIC was removed from Iraq two days before the ground invasion.)

The Iraq Survey Group concluded, in its report a year and a half after the invasion: "While a small number of old, abandoned chemical munitions have been discovered, ISG judges that Iraq unilaterally destroyed its undeclared chemical weapons stockpile in 1991. There are no credible indications that Baghdad resumed production of chemical munitions thereafter."

Having dismantled and destroyed his unconventional weapons program more or less entirely soon after the First Gulf War in 1991, and the rest later in the 1990s, why had Saddam Hussein not complied with the rest of the United Nations requirements? He no longer had the weapons and was no longer developing more in any material way. He could also have complied with the obligations that dealt with verification, but he did not. Had he done so, Saddam Hussein could have avoided the 2002 Resolution 1441 that provided the justification, such as it was from a UN point of view, for the war.

Saddam Hussein was no spiritual mystic or ideological zealot, prone to inspiration by forces beyond the ordinary and the pragmatic. He had an ideology—the collectivist pan-Arab nationalism of the Baath Party—but this ideology was of a mundane, malignant, essentially practical nature.

The reasoning behind Saddam's calculations, as the war clouds gathered in the period 2000 to 2003, was as ancient as any with which a Mesopotamian ruler has had to reckon: Iran. For Saddam the larger, Persian, Shia neighbor was the most immediate threat, foreign or domestic, to his Sunni-minority regime in Baghdad. His unconventional weapons had saved him from the ayatollahs once, in the 1980–1988 Iran-Iraq War. These weapons would do so again if necessary—even if he did not have them. In Saddam's relations with Washington and the UN, WMD attracted trouble. In his relations with Tehran, their presumed existence was a regime-saving deterrent. Saddam's calculus, to which he held until late in 2002, when it was already too late, was that the latter was more important to his survival. The variable that Saddam miscalculated was the political will in the Bush White House, its determination to follow through on the Clinton era's official policy of regime change, which that latter administration had pursued only halfheartedly.

As for the alleged connection between Saddam Hussein and Al Qaeda, numerous post-invasion reports disproved the notion of significant links.

In the world of Middle Eastern terrorist groups and criminal regimes, minor contacts between various players up to a certain level were inevitable. But between Saddam Hussein and Al Qaeda, the links would never be material in scale or implication. This was because, as anyone who understood the region's history would know, they could not be so.

A Pentagon-funded 2007 report by the Institute for Defense Analyses, entitled "Saddam and Terrorism: Emerging Insights from Captured Iraqi Documents," summarized this well. Both Saddam Hussein and Al Qaeda had a common foe in the United States. (They were also both Sunni.) But as the two parties were inherently at odds with each other, "the similarities ended there: bin Laden wanted to restore the Islamic caliphate while Saddam dreamed more narrowly of being the secular ruler of a united Arab nation."[5]

The nostalgic Sunni revivalism of Al Qaeda, the modern secular national socialism of the Baath: these two outlooks were fundamental enemies. Shia Iran was an even bigger foe for each. And then there were the foreigners from the world to the west. There was nothing new about any of it.

Acknowledgments

I owe utmost thanks to my agent, Andrew Wylie. I have been extraordinarily fortunate in my editor, George Gibson, and my publisher, Morgan Entrekin, and would like to thank our copyeditor, Alicia Burns. My late editor Joan Bingham was a true friend to this project and to me personally. Emma Parry and Toby Mundy were also early supporters of the book, and I am grateful for their contributions.

As a journalist in the Middle East, I had the privilege of working with the most talented people in that field. Lewis Lapham of *Harper's* and Gwen Robinson at the *Financial Times* gave me early breaks, while Toby Harshaw, then at the *New York Times*, and David Goodheart, then with *Prospect*, stand out as brilliant people with whom I greatly enjoyed working repeatedly.

My wife, Claudia, has been immensely supportive. Matias Rojas, Michaela and Pablo Born, Mita Corsini, Maria Tholstrup, Nick Emmanuel, Edouard and Mathilde Guerrand, Tom and Polly Coke, Annabelle Gundlach, Miles and Kilks Montgomerie, Alex and Amy Beard, Taran and Natalie Davies, and Jane Willoughby have all been splendid hosts in beautiful places where I did significant work on this project.

The London Library, the New York Society Library, and the British Institute of Persian Studies in Tehran provided excellent support in research as well as fine locations for writing. Zaab Sethna has taught me much about the last century of history in the region. Nur Yalman, a dear friend and former professor of mine, provided early inspiration, and then three decades of priceless insight and intellectual generosity, and finally looked at parts of the manuscript.

There are countless individuals in Iraq, Iran, and Syria to whom I owe debts that can never be repaid. Thank you.

Selected Bibliography

Prologue

Bottéro, Jean. *Mesopotamia: Writing, Reasoning, and the Gods.* Chicago: University of Chicago Press, 1992.

Crawford, Harriet. *Sumer and the Sumerians.* Cambridge: Cambridge University Press, 1992.

Dalley, Stephanie. *Myths from Mesopotamia: Creation, the Flood, Gilgamesh and Others.* Oxford: Oxford University Press, 2000.

Damrosch, David. *The Buried Book: The Loss and Rediscovery of the Great Epic of Gilgamesh.* New York: Henry Holt, 2006.

Daniel, Glyn. *The First Civilizations: The Archaeology of Their Origins.* London: Phoenix Press, 2003.

Delaporte, L. *Mesopotamia: The Babylonian and Assyrian Civilization.* Translated by V. Gordon Childe. London: Kegan Paul, 1925.

Glassner, Jean-Jacques. *The Invention of Cuneiform: Writing in Sumer.* Translated and edited by Zainab Bahrani and Marc van de Mieroop. Baltimore: Johns Hopkins University Press, 2003.

Jacobsen, Thorkild. *The Treasures of Darkness: A History of Mesopotamian Religion.* New Haven, CT: Yale University Press, 1976.

Kramer, Samuel Noah. *The Sumerians: Their History, Culture, and Character.* Chicago: University of Chicago Press, 1971.

Leick, Gwendolyn. *Mesopotamia: The Invention of the City.* London: Penguin, 2002.

Leick, Gwendolyn. *Who's Who in the Ancient Near East.* New York: Routledge, 2002.

Luckenbill, D. D. *Ancient Records of Assyria and Babylonia.* 2 vols. Chicago: University of Chicago Press, 1926.

Oppenheim, A. Leo. *Ancient Mesopotamia: Portrait of a Dead Civilization.* Chicago: University of Chicago Press, 1977.

Postgate, Nicholas. *Early Mesopotamia: Society and Economy at the Dawn of History.* New York: Routledge, 2004.

Reader, John. *Cities.* New York: Grove Press, 2004.

Roux, Georges. *Ancient Iraq*. 3rd ed. London: Penguin, 1992.

Van de Mieroop, Marc. *A History of the Ancient Near East*. London: Blackwell, 2004.

Chapter 1

Bottéro, Jean. *Mesopotamia: Writing, Reasoning, and the Gods*.

Crawford, Harriet. *Sumer and the Sumerians*.

Dalley, Stephanie. *Myths from Mesopotamia*.

Damrosch, David. *The Buried Book*.

Daniel, Glyn. *First Civilizations: The Archaeology of Their Origins*.

Delaporte, L. *Mesopotamia: The Babylonian and Assyrian Civilization*.

Foster, Benjamin R. *The Epic of Gilgamesh*. Norton Critical Editions. New York: W. W. Norton, 2001.

Gardner, John, and John Maier. *Gilgamesh: Translated from the Sin-Leqi-Unninni Version*. New York: Vintage Books, 1985.

Heidel, Alexander. *The Gilgamesh Epic and Old Testament Parallels*. Chicago: University of Chicago Press, 1963.

Jacobsen, Thorkild. *The Treasures of Darkness: A History of Mesopotamian Religion*.

Kramer, Samuel Noah. *The Sumerians*.

Leick, Gwendolyn. *Mesopotamia: The Invention of the City*.

Leick, Gwendolyn. *Who's Who in the Ancient Near East*.

Lloyd, Seton. *Foundations in the Dust: The Story of Mesopotamian Exploration*. London: Thames & Hudson, 1980.

Luckenbill, D. D. *Ancient Records of Assyria and Babylonia*.

Meador, Betty De Shong, and Judy Grahn. *Inanna, Lady of Largest Heart: Poems of the Sumerian High Priestess Enheduanna*. Austin: University of Texas Press, 2001.

Postgate, Nicholas. *Early Mesopotamia*.

Reader, John. *Cities*.

Roth, Martha T. *Law Collections from Mesopotamia and Asia Minor*. 2nd ed. Atlanta, GA: Society of Biblical Literature, 1997.

Roux, Georges. *Ancient Iraq*.

Sandars, N. K., trans. *The Epic of Gilgamesh*. London: Penguin, 1972.

Van de Mieroop, Marc. *History of the Ancient Near East*.

Chapter 2

Baden, Joel S. *The Composition of the Pentateuch: Renewing the Documentary Hypothesis*. Anchor Yale Bible Reference Library. New Haven, CT: Yale University Press, 2012.

Bottéro, Jean. *Mesopotamia: Writing, Reasoning, and the Gods*.

Crawford, Harriet. *Sumer and the Sumerians*.

Daniel, Glyn. *First Civilizations: The Archaeology of Their Origins*.

Friedman, Richard Elliott. *Who Wrote the Bible?* New York: Summit Books, 1987.

Heidel, Alexander. *Gilgamesh Epic and Old Testament Parallels*.

Heschel, Abraham J. *The Prophets*. New York: Perennial Classics, 2001.

Jacobsen, Thorkild. *The Treasures of Darkness: A History of Mesopotamian Religion*.

Johnson, Paul. *A History of the Jews*. New York: Harper Perennial, 1987.

Klinghoffer, David. *The Discovery of God: Abraham and the Birth of Monotheism*. New York: Doubleday, 2004.

Kramer, Samuel Noah. *The Sumerians*.

Leick, Gwendolyn. *Mesopotamia: The Invention of the City*.

Leick, Gwendolyn. *Who's Who in the Ancient Near East*.

Luckenbill, D. D. *Ancient Records of Assyria and Babylonia*.

Milgrom, Jacob. "Bible Versus Babel: Why Did God Tell Abraham to Leave Mesopotamia, the Most Advanced Civilization of Its Time, for the Backwater Region of Canaan?" *Bible Review* 11:2 (April 1995). http//baslibrary.org/bible-review/11/2/5.

Postgate, Nicholas. *Early Mesopotamia*.

Reader, John. *Cities*.

Rosenberg, David. *Abraham: The First Historical Biography*. New York: Basic Books, 2007.

Roux, Georges. *Ancient Iraq*.

Shanks, Hershel, ed. *Abraham and Family: New Insights into the Patriarchal Narratives*. Washington, DC: Biblical Archaeology Society, 2000.

Van de Mieroop, Marc. *History of the Ancient Near East*.

Woolley, Sir Leonard. *The Sumerians*. New York: W. W. Norton, 1965.

Woolley, Sir Leonard. *Ur of the Chaldees: A Record of Seven Years of Excavation*. London: Penguin, 1952.

Chapter 3

Chandler, Tertius. *Four Thousand Years of Historical Growth: An Historical Census*. Lewiston, NY: Edwin Mellen, 1987.

Cook, J. M. *The Persian Empire*. New York: Schocken, 1983.

Delaporte, L. *Mesopotamia: The Babylonian and Assyrian Civilization*.

Foltz, Richard C. *Spirituality in the Land of the Noble: How Iran Shaped the World's Religions*. London: Oneworld, 2004.

Frye, Richard N. *The Heritage of Persia: The Pre-Islamic History of One of the World's Great Civilizations*. Cleveland, OH: World Publishing, 1963.

Gershevitch, Ilya, ed. *Cambridge History of Iran*. Vol. 2, *The Median and Achaemenian Periods*. Cambridge: Cambridge University Press, 1985.

Herodotus. *The Histories*. Norton Critical Edition. Translated by Walter Blanco. Edited by Walter Blanco and Jennifer Tolbert Roberts. New York: W. W. Norton, 1992.

Herodotus. *The Histories*. Penguin Classics. Translated by Aubrey de Selincourt. London: Penguin, 2003.

Holland, Tom. *Persian Fire: The First World Empire and the Battle for the West*. New York: Anchor Books, 2007.

Johnson, Paul. *History of the Jews*.

Leick, Gwendolyn. *Mesopotamia: The Invention of the City*.

Leick, Gwendolyn. *Who's Who in the Ancient Near East*.

Luckenbill, D. D. *Ancient Records of Assyria and Babylonia*.

Oates, Joan. *Babylon*. Ancient Peoples and Places. London: Thames & Hudson, 2003.

Oppenheim, A. Leo. *Ancient Mesopotamia*.

Reade, Julian. *Assyrian Sculpture*. 2nd ed. London: British Museum Press, 1998; reprint 2004.

Roux, Georges. *Ancient Iraq*.

Saggs, H. W. F. *The Might That Was Assyria*. Great Civilizations Series. London: Sidgwick & Jackson, 1984.

Spector, Jack J. *Delacroix: The Death of Sardanapalus*. Art in Context. London: Allen Lane, 1974.

Sykes, Sir Percy. *A History of Persia*. 3rd ed. Vol. 1. London: Macmillan, 1930. Reprint 1963.

Chapter 4

Aeschylus. *The Persians and Other Plays*. Penguin Classics. Translated by Alan H. Sommerstein. London: Penguin, 2010.

Anderson, J. K. *Xenophon*. London: Bristol Classical Press, 2001.

Boyce, Mary. *Zoroastrians: Their Religious Beliefs and Practices*. New York: Routledge, 2006.

Burckhardt, Jacob. *The Greeks and Greek Civilization*. Edited by Oswyn Murray. Translated by Sheila Stern. New York: St. Martin's Griffin, 1998.

Cook, J. M. *Persian Empire*.

Delaporte, L. *Mesopotamia: The Babylonian and Assyrian Civilization*.

Foltz, Richard C. *Spirituality in the Land of the Noble: How Iran Shaped the World's Religions*. London: Oneworld, 2004.

Freeman, Charles. *The Greek Achievement: The Foundation of the Western World*. New York: Viking, 1999.

Frye, Richard N. *Heritage of Persia*.

Gershevitch, Ilya, ed. *Cambridge History of Iran*. Vol. 2, *The Median and Achaemenian Periods*.

Hastings, James, ed. *The Encyclopedia of Religion and Ethics*. New York: Scribner, 1908. Reprint, Whitefish, MT: Kessinger, 2003.

Herodotus. *The Histories*. Norton Critical Edition.

Herodotus. *The Histories*. Penguin Classics.

Hobhouse, Penelope. *Gardens of Persia*. Carlsbad, CA: Kales Press, 2004.

Holland, Tom. *Persian Fire: The First World Empire and the Battle for the West*. New York: Anchor Books, 2007.

Johnson, Paul. *History of the Jews*.

Jones, Lindsay, ed. *Encyclopedia of Religion*. 2nd ed. New York: Macmillan Reference USA, 2004.

Kitto, H. D. F. *The Greeks*. 2nd ed. London: Penguin, 1976.

Kriwaczek, Paul. *In Search of Zarathustra: The First Prophet and the Ideas That Changed the World*. London: Weidenfeld & Nicolson, 2002.

Kuhrt, Amélie. *The Persian Empire: A Corpus of Sources from the Achaemenid Period*. New York: Routledge, 2010.

Livius.org. http://www.livius.org/aa- ac/achaemenians/DSf.html.

Marozzi, Justin. *The Way of Herodotus: Travels with the Man Who Invented History.* Boston: Da Capo, 2008.

Matheson, Sylvia A. *Persia: An Archaeological Guide.* London: Faber, 1972.

Nadon, Christopher. *Xenophon's Prince: Republic and Empire in the Cyropaedia.* Berkeley: University of California Press, 2001.

Pope, Arthur Upham. *Introducing Persian Architecture.* Tehran: Asia Institute Books, 1976.

Reade, Julian. *Assyrian Sculpture.*

Roux, Georges. *Ancient Iraq.*

Spector, Jack J. *Delacroix: The Death of Sardanapalus.*

Sykes, Sir Percy. *History of Persia.* Vol. 1.

Waterfield, Robin. *Xenophon's Retreat: Greece, Persia, and the End of the Golden Age.* London: Faber & Faber, 2006.

Wilber, Donald N. *Persepolis: The Archaeology of Parsa, Seat of the Persian Kings.* New York: Thomas Y. Crowell, 1969.

Xenophon. *Cyropaedia.* Loeb Classical Library. Translated by Walter Miller. Cambridge, MA: Harvard University Press, 1914. Second reprint, 2000.

Zaehner, R. C. *The Dawn and Twilight of Zoroastrianism.* New York: G. P. Putnam's Sons, 1961.

Chapter 5

Appian. *The Roman History.* Translated by Horace White. Vol. 1, *The Foreign Wars.* New York: George Bell and Sons, 1899.

Arrian. *The Campaigns of Alexander.* Penguin Classics. Translated by Aubrey de Selincourt. Annotated by J. R. Hamilton. London: Penguin, 1971.

Barker, Philip. *Alexander the Great's Campaigns: A Guide to Ancient Political and Military Wargaming.* Cambridge: Patrick Stephens, 1981.

Bevan, Edwyn Robert. *The House of Seleucus.* 2 vols. London: Edward Arnold, 1902.

Boyce, Mary. *Zoroastrians.*

Cummings, Lewis V. *Alexander the Great.* New York: Grove Press, 2004. First published 1940 by Houghton Mifflin.

Diodorus Siculus. *The Library of History.* Vol. 8, Books 16.66–17. Translated by C. Bradford Welles. Loeb Classical Library. Cambridge, MA: Harvard University Press, 1963.

Eiler, W. "Iran and Mesopotamia." In *The Cambridge History of Iran,* edited by Ehsan Yarshater. Vol. 3, *The Seleucid, Parthian and Sasanian Periods.* Cambridge: Cambridge University Press, 1983.

Errington, R. Malcolm. *A History of the Hellenistic World: 323–30 BC.* Blackwell History of the Ancient World. Oxford: Blackwell, 2008.

Frye, Richard N. *Heritage of Persia.*

Grainger, John D. *Seleukos Nikator: Constructing a Hellenistic Kingdom.* London: Routledge, 1990.

Hammond, N. G. L. *Philip of Macedon.* London: Duckworth, 1994.

McGroarty, Kieran. "Did Alexander the Great Read Xenophon?" *Hermathena,* 181 (2006): 105–124. http://www.jstor.org/discover/23041624

Plutarch. *The Age of Alexander*. Penguin Classics. Translated and annotated by Ian Scott-Kilvert. London: Penguin, 1973. Reprint 1976.

Renault, Mary. *The Nature of Alexander*. New York: Pantheon, 1976.

Romm, James, ed. *Alexander the Great: Selections from Arrian, Diodorus, Plutarch, and Quintus Curtius*. Translated by Pamela Mensch and James Room. Indianapolis: Hackett, 2005.

Tarn, W. W. *Hellenistic Civilisation*. 3rd ed. Cleveland, OH: World Publishing, 1967.

Worthington, Ian. *Alexander the Great: Man and God*. London: Pearson, 2004.

Zaehner, R. C. *Dawn and Twilight of Zoroastrianism*.

Chapter 6

Appian. *Roman History*.

Arrian. *Campaigns of Alexander*.

Bevan, Edwyn Robert. *House of Seleucus*.

Boyce, Mary. *Zoroastrians*.

Cummings, Lewis V. *Alexander the Great*.

Eiler, W. "Iran and Mesopotamia."

Errington, R. Malcolm. *History of the Hellenistic World: 323–30 BC*.

Frye, Richard N. *Heritage of Persia*.

Grainger, John D. *Seleukos Nikator*.

Plutarch. *Age of Alexander*.

Renault, Mary. *Nature of Alexander*.

Romm, James, ed. *Alexander the Great*.

Tarn, W. W. *Hellenistic Civilisation*.

Yarshater, Ehsan, ed. *The Cambridge History of Iran*. Vol. 3 (I), *The Seleucid, Parthian and Sasanian Periods*. Cambridge, University of Cambridge Press, 1983.

Chapter 7

Ammianus Marcellinus. *The Later Roman Empire (A.D. 354–378)*. Penguin Classics. Translated by Walter Hamilton. London: Penguin, 2004.

Ball, Warwick. *Rome in the East: The Transformation of an Empire*. London: Routledge, 1999.

Bevan, Edwyn Robert. *House of Seleucus*.

Boyce, Mary. *Zoroastrians*.

Brown, Peter. *The World of Late Antiquity: AD 150–750*. New York: W. W. Norton, 1989. First published 1971 by Thames & Hudson.

Campbell, Brian. "War and Diplomacy: Rome and Parthia, 31 BC–AD 235." In *War and Society in the Roman World*, edited by John Rich. London: Routledge, 1993.

Canepa, Matthew P. *The Two Eyes of the Earth: Art and Ritual of Kingship between Rome and Sasanian Iran*. Berkeley: University of California Press, 2010.

Cassius Dio. *Roman History*. Vol. 3. Loeb Classical Library. Translated by Earnest Cary. Cambridge, MA: Harvard University Press, 1914.

Christensen-Ernst, Jorgen. *Antioch on the Orontes: A History and a Guide*. Lanham, MD: Hamilton Books, 2012.

Colledge, Malcolm A. R. *The* Parthians. Westport, CT: Praeger, 1967.

Daryaee, Touraj. *Sasanian Iran (224–651 CE): Portrait of a Late Antique Empire.* Costa Mesa, CA: Mazda Publishing, 2008.

Daryaee, Touraj. *Sasanian Persia: The Rise and Fall of an Empire.* London: I. B. Tauris, 2009.

Debevoise, Neilson Carel. *A Political History of Parthia.* Chicago: University of Chicago Press, 1938.

Dignas, Beate, and Engelbert Winter. *Rome and Persia in Late Antiquity: Neighbours and Rivals.* Cambridge: Cambridge University Press, 2007.

Errington, R. Malcolm. *A History of the Hellenistic World: 323–30 BC.*

Fakhry, Majid. *Averroes (Ibn Rushd): His Life, Works and Influence.* Great Islamic Thinkers. London: Oneworld, 2001.

Ferguson, R. James. "Rome and Parthia: Power Politics and Diplomacy across Cultural Frontiers." Research Paper No. 12, Centre for East-West Cultural and Economic Studies, Faculty of Humanities and Social Sciences, Bond University, Australia, December 2005.

Frankopan, Peter. *The Silk Roads: A New History of the World.* New York: Knopf, 2016.

Frye, Richard N. *The Golden Age of Persia.* New York: Harper & Row, 1976.

Frye, Richard N. *Heritage of Persia.*

Gibbon, Edward. *The History of the Decline and Fall of the Roman Empire.* Vols. 2 and 3. New York: Everyman's Library, 1993.

Hill, John E., trans. *The Western Regions according to the* Hou Hanshou. "Chapter on the Western Regions." http://depts.washington.edu/silkroad/texts/hhshu/hou_han_shu.html.

Hirth, Friedrich. *China and the Roman Orient: Researches into Their Ancient and Medieval Relations as Represented in Old Early Chinese Records.* Leipzig, 1885.

Maenchen-Helfen, Otto J. *The World of the Huns: Studies in Their History and Culture.* Berkeley: University of California Press, 1973.

Plutarch. *The Lives of the Noble Grecians and Romans.* Translated by John Dryden. New York: Modern Library, 1975.

Pope, Arthur Upham. *Introducing Persian Architecture.*

Procopius, History of the Wars. Vol. 1, Books 1 and 2. "The Persian War." Loeb Classical Library. Translated by H. B. Dewing. Cambridge, MA: Harvard University Press, 1914.

Rawlinson, George. *The Sixth Great Oriental Monarchy; or the Geography, History, & Antiquities of Parthia.* London: Longmans, Green, 1873.

Renan, Ernest. *The Apostles.* New York, 1866.

Rosenberg, Matt. "Largest Cities Throughout History." ThoughtCo., November 4, 2019. http://geography.about.com/library/weekly/aa011201a.htm.

Sheldon, Rose Mary. *Rome's Wars in Parthia: Blood in the Sand.* London: Vallentine Mitchell, 2010.

Stark, Freya. *Rome on the Euphrates.* London: John Murray, 1966.

Sykes, Sir Percy. *History of Persia.*

Tacitus. *Annals and Histories.* Translated by Alfred John Church and William Jackson Brodribb. New York: Everyman's Library, 2009.

Thorley, J. "The Silk Trade between China and the Roman Empire at Its Height,'Circa' A.D. 90–130." *Greece & Rome* 18, no. 1 (April 1971): 71–80.

Wells, H. G. *The Outline of History: The Whole History of Man.* New York: Garden City, 1956.

Wilcox, Peter, and Angus McBride. *Rome's Enemies (3): Parthians and Sassanid Persians.* Men-at-Arms Series. Oxford: Osprey Publishing, 2000.

Yarshater, Ehsan, ed. *Cambridge History of Iran.*

Zaehner, R. C. *Dawn and Twilight of Zoroastrianism.*

Chapter 8

Akram, A. I. *Khalid bin Al-Waleed: Sword of Allah.* Birmingham, UK: Maktabah Publishers, 2007.

Ball, Warwick. *Rome in the East.*

Brown, Peter. *World of Late Antiquity.*

Burns, Ross. *Damascus: A History.* New York: Routledge, 2007.

Campbell, Brian. "War and Diplomacy: Rome and Parthia, 31 BC–AD 235."

Chadwick, Henry. *The Early Church: The Story of Emergent Christianity from the Apostolic Age to the Dividing of the Ways Between the Greek East and the Latin West.* Penguin History of the Church. London: Penguin, 1993.

Colledge, Malcolm A. R. *The Parthians.*

Dawoud, N. J., trans. *The Koran.* Penguin Classics. London: Penguin, 2003.

Dignas, Beate, and Engelbert Winter. *Rome and Persia in Late Antiquity.*

Ferguson, R. James. "Rome and Parthia: Power Politics and Diplomacy across Cultural Frontiers."

Frye, Richard N. *Golden Age of Persia.*

Frye, Richard N. *Heritage of Persia.*

Gibbon, Edward. *The History of the Decline and Fall of the Roman Empire.* 6 vols. New York: Everyman's Library, 1993.

Goldziher, Ignaz. *Introduction to Islamic Theology and Law.* Translated by Andras and Ruth Hamori. Princeton, NJ: Princeton University Press, 1981.

Grunebaum, G. E. von. *Islam: Essays in the Nature and Growth of a Cultural Tradition.* Menasha, WI: George Banta, 1955.

Hitti, Philip K. *The Arabs: A Short History.* Washington, DC: Regnery Publishing, 1996. First published 1949 by Princeton University Press.

Holt, P. M., Ann K. S. Lamb, and Bernard Lewis, eds. *The Cambridge History of Islam.* Vol. 1, *The Central Islamic Lands from Pre-Islamic Times to the First World War.* Cambridge: Cambridge University Press, 1970.

Holt, P. M., Ann K. S. Lamb, and Bernard Lewis, eds. *The Cambridge History of Islam.* Vol. 2, *The Further Islamic Lands.* Cambridge: Cambridge University Press, 1970.

Hourani, Albert. *A History of the Arab Peoples.* London: Faber and Faber, 2002.

Ibn Ishaq. *Sirat Rasul Allah (Life of the Messenger of God).* Translated by A. Guillaume (as *The Life of Muhammad*). Oxford: Oxford University Press, 1955.

Karsh, Efraim. *Islamic Imperialism: A History.* New Haven, CT: Yale University Press, 2007.

Kennedy, Hugh. *The Great Arab Conquests: How the Spread of Islam Changed the World We Live In.* London: Phoenix, 2008.

Lawrence, Bruce. *The Qur'an: A Biography.* Books That Changed the World. New York: Atlantic Monthly Press, 2006.

Le Strange, Guy. *The Lands of the Eastern Caliphate: Mesopotamia, Persia, and Central Asia, from the Moslem Conquest to the Time of Timur.* Cambridge: Cambridge University Press, 1905.

Madelung, Wilferd. *The Succession to Muhammad: A Study of the Early Caliphate.* Cambridge: Cambridge University Press, 1997.

Muslim, I. *Sahih Muslim.* Translated by A. H. Siddiqui. Delhi: Kitab Bhavan, 2000.

Nicolson, Reynald A. *A Literary History of the Arabs.* London: T. Fisher Unwin, 1907.

Qutb, Sayyid. *Milestones.* Self-published, 2005.

Rahman, Fazlur. *Islam.* 2nd ed. Chicago: University of Chicago Press, 1979.

Rawlinson, George. *The Sixth Great Oriental Monarchy.*

Sheldon, Rose Mary. *Rome's Wars in Parthia.*

Sykes, Sir Percy. *History of Persia.*

Tabari, al-. *The History of al-Tabari.* Edited by Ehsan Yarshater. 40 vols. Albany: State University of New York Press, 1989–2007.

Tabari, al-. *The History of al-Tabari.* Vol. 7, *The Foundation of the Community.* Translated by M. V. McDonald. Albany: State University of New York Press, 1987.

Tabari, al-. *The History of al-*Tabari. Vol. 8, *The Victory of Islam.* Translated by Michael Fishbein. Albany: State University of New York, 1997.

Toynbee, Arnold J. *Mankind and Mother Earth: A Narrative History of the World.* Oxford: Oxford University Press, 1976.

Waqidi, Al-. *Kitab Al-Maghazi.* Oxford: Oxford University Press, 1966.

Wells, H. G. *Outline of History.*

Chapter 9

Abbas, Hassan. *The Prophet's Heir: The Life of Ali ibn Abi Talib.* New Haven, CT: Yale University Press, 2021.

Bodley, R. V. C. *The Messenger: The Life of Mohammed.* Westport, CT: Praeger, 1970.

Bukhari, Mohammed al-. *Sahih al-Bukhari.* Book 5. Riyadh: Darussalam Publishers, 1987.

Bukhari, Mohammed al-. *Sahih al-Bukhari.* In www.sunnah.com.

Crone, Patricia. *God's Rule: Government and Islam.* New York: Columbia University Press, 2004.

Frye, Richard N. *Golden Age of Persia.*

Frye, Richard N. *Heritage of Persia.*

Gibbon, Edward. *The History of the Decline and Fall of the Roman Empire.* Vols. 5 and 6. New York: Everyman's Library, 1993.

Glubb, John Bagot. *A Short History of the Arab Peoples.* New York: Dorset Press, 1969.

Goldziher, Ignaz. *Introduction to Islamic Theology and Law.*

Grunebaum, G. E. von. *Classical Islam: A History, 600 A.D. to 1258 A.D.* London: Routledge, 1970.

Hazleton, Lesley. *After the Prophet: The Epic Story of the Shia-Sunni Split.* New York: Anchor Books, 2009.

Ibn Ishaq. *Life of Muhammad.*

Kennedy, Hugh. *Great Arab Conquests.*

Lewis, Bernard. *The Arabs in History.* 6th ed. Oxford: Oxford University Press, 2002.

Madelung, Wilferd. *Succession to Muhammad.*

Rahman, Fazlur. *Islam.*

Rogerson, Barnaby. *The Heirs of Muhammad: Islam's First Century and the Origins of the Sunni-Shia Split.* New York: Overlook Press, 2007.

Tabari, al-. *The History of al-Tabari.* 40 vols.

Tabari, al-. *The History of al-Tabari.* Vol. 6, *Muhammad at Mecca.* Translated by W. Montgomery Watt and M. V. McDonald. Albany: State University of New York Press, 1989.

Tabari, al-. *The History of al-Tabari.* Vol. 15, *The Crisis of the Early Caliphate.* Translated by R. Stephen Humphreys. Albany: State University of New York Press, 1987.

Tabari, al-. *The History of al-Tabari.* Vol. 16, *The Community Divided.* Translated by Adrian Brocket. Albany: State University of New York, 1996.

Tabari, al-. *The History of al-Tabari.* Vol. 17, *The First Civil War.* Translated by G. R. Hawting. Albany: State University of New York Press, 1996.

Tabari, al-. *The History of al-Tabari.* Vol. 18, *Between Civil Wars: The Caliphate of Muawiyah.* Translated by Michael G. Morony. Albany: State University of New York Press, 1987.

Tabari, al-. *The History of al-Tabari.* Vol. 19, *The Caliphate of Yazid B. Mu'awiyah.* Translated by I. K. A. Howard. Albany: State University of New York Press, 1991.

Watt, W. Montgomery. *Muhammad: Prophet and Statesman.* Oxford: Oxford University Press, 1961.

Yeor, Bat. *The Dhimmi: Jews and Christians Under Islam.* Cranbury, NJ: Associated University Presses, 1985.

Chapter 10

Bennison, Amira K. *The Great Caliphs: The Golden Age of the Abbasid Empire.* New Haven, CT: Yale University Press, 2009.

Browne, Edward Granville. *A Literary History of Persia.* Vol. 1. London: T. Fisher Unwin, 1902.

Burns, Ross. *Damascus: A History.*

Burns, Ross. *Monuments of Syria: An Historical Guide.* New York: New York University Press, 1999.

Burton, Sir Richard, trans. *Arabian Nights: A Selection.* London: Penguin Books, 1997.

Crone, Patricia. *God's Rule: Government and Islam.*

Dozy, Reinhart. *Spanish Islam: A History of the Moslems in Spain.* Translated by Francis Griffin Stokes. London: Chatto & Windus, 1913.

Fernandez-Morera, Dario. *The Myth of the Andalusian Paradise: Muslims, Christians, and Jews under Islamic Rule in Medieval Spain.* Wilmington, DE: ISI Books, 2016.

Frye, Richard N. *The Cambridge History of Iran.* Vol. 4, *The Period from the Arab Invasion to the Saljuqs.* Cambridge: Cambridge University Press, 1975.

Frye, Richard N. *Golden Age of Persia.*

Glubb, John Bagot. *Short History of the Arab Peoples.*

Goldziher, Ignaz. *Introduction to Islamic Theology and Law.*

Grunebaum, G. E. von. *Islam: Essays.*

Grunebaum, G. E. von, ed. *Studies in Islamic Cultural History.* Menasha, WI: George Banta, 1954.

Gutas, Dimitri. *Greek Thought, Arabic Culture: The Graeco-Arabic Translation Movement in Baghdad and Early Abbasid Society*. London: Routledge, 2005.

Hawting, G. R. *The First Dynasty of Islam: The Umayyad Caliphate AD 661–750*. 2nd ed. London: Routledge, 2000.

Hitti, Philip K. *The Arabs: A Short History*.

Holt, P. M., Ann K. S. Lamb, and Bernard Lewis, eds. *The Cambridge History of Islam*. Vol. 1.

Kennedy, Hugh. *The Armies of the Caliphs: Military and Society in the Early Islamic State*. London: Routledge, 2001.

Kennedy, Hugh. *The Court of the Caliphs: The Rise and Fall of Islam's Greatest Dynasty*. London: Weidenfeld & Nicolson, 2004.

Kennedy, Hugh. *The Early Abbasid Caliphate: A Political History*. London: Croom Helm, 1981.

Khadduri, Majid. *Islamic Jurisprudence: Shafii's Risala*. Baltimore: Johns Hopkins University Press, 1961.

Le Strange, Guy. *Lands of the Eastern Caliphate*.

Lewis, Bernard. *The Crisis of Islam: Holy War and Unholy Terror*. London: Modern Library, 2003.

Maqqari, Ahmed ibn Muhammad al-. *The History of the Mohammedan Dynasties in Spain*. Translated by Pascual de Gayangos. London: RoutledgeCurzon, 2002.

Masudi. *From The Meadows of Gold*. Translated by P. Lunde and C. Stone. London: Penguin, 2007.

Misri, Ahmad ibn Naqib al-. *Reliance of the Traveler*. Translated by Nuh Ha Mim Keller. Beltsville, MD: Amana Publications, 1994.

Nicolson, Reynald A. *A Literary History of the Arabs*.

Rahman, Fazlur. *Islam*.

Schacht, Joseph. *An Introduction to Islamic Law*. Oxford: Clarendon Press, 1964.

Schacht, Joseph. "Law and Justice." In *The Cambridge History of Islam*. Vol. 2, *Islamic Society and Civilization*. Cambridge: Cambridge University Press, 1970.

Shaban, M. A. *The Abbasid Revolution*. Cambridge: Cambridge University Press, 1970.

Sharon, Moshe. *Black Banners from the East*. Vol. 1, *The Establishment of the Abbasid State: Incubation of a Revolt*. Jerusalem: Hebrew University, 1990.

Sharon, Moshe. *Black Banners from the East*. Vol. 2, *Revolt: The Social and Military Aspects of the Abbasid Revolution*. Jerusalem: Hebrew University, 1990.

Sykes, Sir Percy. *History of Persia*.

Tabari, al-. *The History of al-Tabari*. 40 vols.

Tabari, al-. *The History of al-Tabari*. Vol. 25, *The End of Expansion*. Translated by Khalid Yahya Blankinship. Albany: State University of New York Press, 1989.

Tabari, al-. *The History of al-Tabari*. Vol. 26, *The Waning of the Umayyad Caliphate*. Translated by Carole Hillenbrand. Albany: State University of New York Press, 1989.

Tabari, al-. *The History of al-Tabari*. Vol. 27, *The Abbasid Revolution*. Translated by John Alden Williams. Albany: State University of New York Press, 1985.

Tabari, al-. *The History of al-Tabari*. Vol. 28, *Abbasid Authority Affirmed: The Early Years of Al-Mansour*. Translated by Jane Dammen McAuliffe. Albany: State University of New York Press, 1995.

Watt, W. Montgomery. *Islamic Philosophy and Theology*. Edinburgh: Edinburgh University Press, 1962.

Wells, H. G. *Outline of History*.

Chapter 11

Adamson, Peter, and Richard C. Taylor, eds. *The Cambridge Companion to Arabic Philosophy*. Cambridge: Cambridge University Press, 2005.

Averroes. *The Incoherence of the Incoherence*.

Bennison, Amira K. *The Great Caliphs*.

Berkey, Jonathan P. *The Formation of Islam: Religion and Society in the Near East, 600–1800*. Cambridge: Cambridge University Press, 2003.

Bosworth, C. E. *The Arabs, Byzantium, and Iran*. London: Routledge, 1996.

Boyce, Mary. *Zoroastrians*.

Boyle, J. A., ed. *The Cambridge History of Iran*. Vol. 5, *The Saljuq and Mongol Periods*. Cambridge: Cambridge University Press, 1968.

Browne, Edward Granville. *Literary History of Persia*.

Bulliet, Richard W. *Islam: The View from the Edge*. New York: Columbia University Press, 1995.

Caswell, Fuad M. *The Slave Girls of Baghdad: The Qiyan in the Early Abbasid Era*. London: I. B. Tauris, 2011.

Cooperson, Michael. *Classical Arabic Biography: The Heirs of the Prophets in the Age of al-Ma'mun*. Cambridge: Cambridge University Press, 2000.

Crone, Patricia. *God's Rule: Government and Islam*.

Frye, Richard N. *Cambridge History of Iran*. Vol. 4.

Frye, Richard N. *Golden Age of Persia*.

Frye, Richard N. *Heritage of Persia*.

Glubb, John Bagot. *Short History of the Arab Peoples*.

Godefroy, Gilles. *The Adventure of Numbers*. Translated by Leslie Kay. Providence, RI: American Mathematical Society, 2004.

Goldziher, Ignaz. *Introduction to Islamic Theology and Law*.

Grunebaum, G. E. von. *Classical Islam*.

Gutas, Dimitri. *Greek Thought, Arabic Culture*.

Hitti, Philip K. *The Arabs: A Short History*.

Holt, P. M., Ann K. S. Lamb, and Bernard Lewis, eds. *The Cambridge History of Islam*. Vol. 1.

Hoodbhoy, Pervez. *Islam and Science: Religious Orthodoxy and the Battle for Rationality*. London: Zed Books, 1991.

Hourani, George F. *Reason and Tradition in Islamic Ethics*. Cambridge: Cambridge University Press, 1985.

Hurvitz, Nimrod. *The Formation of Hanbalism: Piety into Power*. New York: Routledge, 2002.

Kennedy, Hugh. *Court of the Caliphs*.

Khadduri, Majid. *Islamic Jurisprudence*.

Khalili, Jim al-. *The House of Wisdom: How Arabic Science Saved Ancient Knowledge and Gave Us the Renaissance*. London: Penguin, 2011.

Le Strange, Guy. *Baghdad during the Abbasid Caliphate: From Contemporary Arabic and Persian Sources.* 2nd ed. Oxford: Clarendon Press, 1922.

Lewis, Bernard. *The Middle East: A Brief History of the Last 2,000 Years.* New York: Scribner, 1996.

Lewis, Bernard. *The Muslim Discovery of Europe.* London: Weidenfeld & Nicolson, 2001.

Lewis, David Levering. *God's Crucible: Islam and the Making of Europe, 570–1215.* New York: W. W. Norton, 2008.

Lyons, Jonathan. *The House of Wisdom: How the Arabs Transformed Western Civilization.* London: Bloomsbury, 2009.

Martin, Richard C., Mark R. Woodward, and Dwi S. Atmaja. *Defenders of Reason in Islam: Mu'tazilism from Medieval School to Modern Symbol.* London: Oneworld, 1997.

Masudi. *From The Meadows of Gold.*

Misri, Ahmad ibn Naqib al-. *Reliance of the Traveler.*

Muir, William. *The Caliphate: Its Rise, Decline, and Fall, from Original Sources.* London: The Religious Tract Society, 1891.

Peters, F. E. *Aristotle and the Arabs: The Aristotelian Tradition in Islam.* New York: New York University Press, 1968.

Rahman, Fazlur. *Islam.*

Reilly, Robert R. *The Closing of the Muslim Mind: How Intellectual Suicide Created the Modern Islamist Crisis.* Wilmington, DE: Intercollegiate Studies Institute, 2010.

Rosenthal, Franz. *The Classical Heritage in Islam.* Arabic Thought and Culture. London: Routledge, 1975.

Schacht, Joseph. *Introduction to Islamic Law.*

Tabari, al-. *The History of al-Tabari.* 40 vols.

Tabari, al-. *The History of al-Tabari.* Vol. 30, *The Abbasid Caliphate in Equilibrium: The Caliphates of Musa al-Hadi and Haroun al-Rashid A.D. 785–809.* Translated by C. E. Bosworth. Albany: State University of New York Press, 1989.

Tabari, al-. *The History of al-Tabari.* Vol. 31, *The War Between the Brothers: The Caliphate of al-Amin A.D. 809–813.* Translated by Michael Fishbein. Albany: State University of New York Press, 1992.

Tabari, al-. *The History of al-Tabari.* Vol. 32, *The Reunification of the Abbasid Caliphate: The Caliphate of Al-Mamun.* Translated by C. E. Bosworth. Albany: State University of New York Press, 1991.

Watt, W. Montgomery. *Islamic Philosophy and Theology.*

Yeor, Bat. *The Dhimmi: Jews and Christians Under Islam.*

Chapter 12

Bennison, Amira K. *The Great Caliphs.*

Frye, Richard N. *Golden Age of Persia.*

Holt, P. M., Ann K. S. Lamb, and Bernard Lewis, eds. *The Cambridge History of Islam.* Vol. 1.

Javad Anvari, Mohammad. "al-Ash 'Ari." Translated by Matthew Melvin-Koushki. In *Encyclopaedia Islamica*, edited by Farhad Daftary. First published online by Brill: 2015.

Kennedy, Hugh. *Court of the Caliphs.*

Le Strange, Guy. *Baghdad during the Abbasid Caliphate: From Contemporary Arabic and Persian Sources.* 2nd ed. Oxford: Clarendon Press, 1922.

Nicolson, Reynald A. *A Literary History of the Arabs.*

Posamentier, Alfred S., and Ingmar Lehmann. *The (Fabulous) Fibonacci Numbers.* Amherst, NY: Prometheus Books, 2007.

Tabari, al-. *The History of al-Tabari.* Vol. 30., *The Abbasid Caliphate in Equilibrium: The Caliphates of Musa al-Hadi and Haroun al-Rashid A.D. 785–809.*

Tabari, al-. *The History of al-Tabari.* 40 vols.

Chapter 13

Adamson, Peter, and Richard C. Taylor, eds. *The Cambridge Companion to Arabic Philosophy.*

Averroes. *The Incoherence of the Incoherence.*

Caswell, Fuad M. *The Slave Girls of Baghdad.*

Goldziher, Ignaz. *Introduction to Islamic Theology and Law.*

Javad Anvari, Mohammad. "al-Ash 'Ari." Translated by Matthew Melvin-Koushki. In *Encyclopaedia Islamica*, edited by Farhad Daftary. First published online by Brill: 2015.

Kennedy, Hugh. *Court of the Caliphs.*

Khadduri, Majid. *Islamic Jurisprudence.*

Misri, Ahmad ibn Naqib al-. *Reliance of the Traveler.*

Rahman, Fazlur. *Islam.*

Tabari, al-. *The History of al-Tabari.* 40 vols.

Watt, W. Montgomery. *Islamic Philosophy and Theology.*

Chapter 14

Adamson, Peter, and Richard C. Taylor, eds. *The Cambridge Companion to Arabic Philosophy.*

Averroes. *The Incoherence of the Incoherence.*

Boyle, J. A., ed. *Cambridge History of Iran.* Vol. 5.

Byron, Robert. *Road to Oxiana.* London: Penguin, 1992.

Coke, Richard. *Baghdad: The City of Peace.* London: Thornton Butterworth, 1927.

Fakhry, Majid. *Averroes.*

Frankopan, Peter. *The First Crusade: The Call from the East.* Cambridge, MA: Belknap Press, 2012.

Freely, John. *Storm on Horseback: The Seljuk Warriors of Turkey.* London: I. B. Tauris, 2008.

Frye, Richard N. *Golden Age of Persia.*

Frye, Richard N. *Heritage of Persia.*

Gibbon, Edward. *Decline and Fall of the Roman Empire.* Vol. 6.

Glubb, John Bagot. *Soldiers of Fortune: The Story of the Mamlukes.* New York: Dorset Press, 1973.

Goldziher, Ignaz. *Introduction to Islamic Theology and Law.*

Jackson, Peter, and Lawrence Lockhart, eds. *The Cambridge History of Iran*. Vol. 6, *The Timurid and Safavid Periods*. Cambridge: Cambridge University Press, 1986.

Jenkins, Philip. *The Lost History of Christianity: The Thousand-Year Golden Age of the Church in the Middle East, Africa, and Asia—and How It Died*. New York: Harper-One, 2008.

Kennedy, Hugh. *Court of the Caliphs*.

Le Strange, Guy. *Mesopotamia and Persia under the Mongols, in the Fourteenth Century A.D*. London: Royal Asiatic Society, 1903.

Lewis, Bernard. *The Arabs in History*.

Maalouf, Amin. *The Crusades Through Arab Eyes*. New York: Schocken [Pantheon/Random House], 1984.

Mackey, Sandra. *The Iranians: Persia, Islam and the Soul of a Nation*. New York: Plume, 1996.

Marozzi, Justin. *Tamerlane: Sword of Islam, Conqueror of the World*. Boston: Da Capo, 2006.

Miles, Samuel Barrett. *The Countries and Tribes of the Persian Gulf*. 2 vols. London: Harrison and Sons, 1919.

Misri, Ahmad ibn Naqib al-. *Reliance of the Traveler*.

Morgan, David. *Medieval Persia 1040–1797*. London: Routledge, 2016.

Mottahedeh, Roy. *The Mantle of the Prophet: Religion and Politics in Iran*. London: Oneworld, 2005.

Nakash, Yitzhak. *The Shi'is of Iraq*. Princeton, NJ: University Press, 1994.

Nicolle, David. *The Mongol Warlords: Genghis Khan, Kublai Khan, Hulegu, Tamerlane*. New York: Firebird Books, 1990.

Norwich, John Julius. *A Short History of Byzantium*. New York: Knopf, 1997.

Peacock, A. C. S. *The Great Seljuk Empire*. Edinburgh: Edinburgh University Press, 2015.

Peters, Edward, *The First Crusade: The Chronicle of Fulcher of Chartres and Other Source Materials*. 2nd ed. Philadelphia: University of Pennsylvania Press, 1998.

Pope, Arthur Upham. *Introducing Persian Architecture*.

Rahman, Fazlur. *Islam*.

Riley-Smith, Jonathan. *The Crusades: A History*. London: Bloomsbury, 2005.

Saunders, J. J. *The History of the Mongol Conquests*. New York: Barnes & Noble, 1971.

Sebag Montefiore, Simon. *Jerusalem: The Biography*. New York: Knopf, 2011.

Stevens, Roger. *The Land of the Great Sophy*. London: Methuen & Co., 1965.

Sykes, Sir Percy. *History of Persia*.

Tabari, al-. *The History of al-Tabari*. 40 vols.

Tabari, al-. *The History of al-Tabari*. Vol. 31. *The War Between the Brothers: The Caliphate of Muhammad al-Amin A.D. 809–813*. Translated by Michael Fishbein. Albany: State University of New York Press, 1992.

Tabari, al-. *The History of al-Tabari*. Vol. 32. *The Reunification of the Abbasid Caliphate: The Caliphate of al-Mamun A.D. 813–833*. Translated by C. E. Bosworth. Albany: State University of New York Press, 1987.

Tabari, al-. *The History of al-Tabari*. Vol. 33, *Storm and Stress Along the Northern Frontier of the Abbasid Caliphate: The Caliphate of al-Mutasim A.D. 833–842*. Translated by C. E. Bosworth. Albany: State University of New York Press, 1991.

Toynbee, Arnold J. *Mankind and Mother Earth*.

Tyerman, Christopher. *God's War: A New History of the Crusades*. Cambridge, MA: Belknap Press, 2007.

Watt, W. Montgomery. *Islamic Philosophy and Theology*.

Wells, H. G. *Outline of History*.

Chapter 15

Agoston, Gabor, and Bruce Masters, eds. *Encyclopedia of the Ottoman Empire*. New York: Facts on File, 2008.

Blow, David. *Shah Abbas: The Ruthless King Who Became an Iranian Legend*. London: I. B. Tauris, 2009.

Busbecq, Ogier de. *Turkish Letters*. Translated by Edward Seymour Forster. London: Eland, 2005. First published 1927 by Clarendon Press.

Byron, Robert. *Road to Oxiana*.

Coke, Richard. *Baghdad: The City of Peace*.

Faroqhi, Suraiya N. *The Cambridge History of Turkey: The Later Ottoman Empire, 1603–1839*. Cambridge: Cambridge University Press, 2006.

Finkel, Caroline. *Osman's Dream: The History of the Ottoman Empire*. New York: Basic Books, 2005.

Gibb, H.A.R., and Harold Bowen. *Islamic Society and the West: A Study of the Impact of Western Civilization on Moslem Culture in the Near East*. Oxford: Oxford University Press, 1967.

Glubb, John Bagot. *Soldiers of Fortune: The Story of the Mamlukes*.

Goodwin, Jason. *Lords of the Horizons: A History of the Ottoman Empire*. New York: Henry Holt, 1999.

Graf, Tobias. "Best of Enemies: Europeans in the Ottoman Elite." *History Today*, January 2, 2018.

Graf, Tobias. *The Sultan's Renegades: Christian-European Converts to Islam and the Making of the Ottoman Elite, 1575–1610*. Oxford: Oxford University Press, 2017.

Hathaway, Jane. *The Arab Lands Under Ottoman Rule, 1516–1800*. 2nd ed. London: Routledge, 2019.

Holt, P. M. *Egypt and the Fertile Crescent: A Political History, 1516–1922*. Ithaca, NY: Cornell University Press, 1975.

Holt, P. M., Ann K. S. Lamb, and Bernard Lewis, eds. *Cambridge History of Islam*. Vol. 1.

Inalcik, Halil. *The Ottoman Empire: The Classical Age, 1300–1600*. London: Weidenfeld & Nicolson, 1973.

Jackson, Peter, and Lawrence Lockhart, eds. *The Cambridge History of Iran*. Vol. 6.

Kinross, Lord. *The Ottoman Centuries: The Rise and Fall of the Turkish Empire*. New York: William Morris, 1977.

Lewis, Bernard. *The Arabs in History*.

Longrigg, Stephen Hemsley. *Four Centuries of Modern Iraq*. Oxford: Oxford University Press, 1925.

Malcolm, Noel. *Useful Enemies: Islam and the Ottoman Empire in Western Political Thought, 1450–1750*. Oxford: Oxford University Press, 2019.

Misri, Ahmad ibn Naqib al-. *Reliance of the Traveler*.

Morgan, David. *Medieval Persia 1040–1797*. London: Routledge, 2016.

Mottahedeh, Roy. *Mantle of the Prophet: Religion and Politics in Iran.*

Murphey, Rhoads. *Ottoman Warfare, 1500–1700.* London: Routledge, 1998.

Nakash, Yitzhak. *Shi'is of Iraq.*

Newman, Andrew J. *Safavid Iran: Rebirth of a Persian Empire.* London: I. B. Tauris, 2006.

Savory, Roger. *Iran under the Safavids.* Cambridge: Cambridge University Press, 1980.

Stevens, Roger. *Land of the Great Sophy.*

Stubbs, William. *Lectures on European History.* London: Longman's, Green and Co., 1904.

Sykes, Sir Percy. *History of Persia.*

Tavernier, Jean-Baptiste. *The Six Voyages of John Baptista Tavernier, Noble Man of France now living, through Turky into Persia, and the East-Indies, finished in the year 1670.* London, 1678.

Chapter 16

Adkins, Lesley. *Empires of the Plain: Henry Rawlinson and the Lost Languages of Babylon.* New York: Thomas Dunne Books, 2003.

Anderson, J. K. *Xenophon.*

Brackman, Arnold C. *The Luck of Nineveh: Archaeology's Great Adventure.* New York: McGraw-Hill, 1978.

Buckingham, James Silk. *Travels in Mesopotamia.* 2 vols. Cambridge, Cambridge University Press, 2012. First published in 1928.

Cregan-Reid, Vybarr. *Discovering Gilgamesh: Geology, Narrative and the Historical Sublime in Victorian Culture.* Manchester, UK: Manchester University Press, 2013.

Finkel, Caroline. *Osman's Dream.*

Goodwin, Jason. *Lords of the Horizons.*

Kubie, Nora Benjamin. *Road to Nineveh: The Adventures and Excavations of Sir Austen Henry Layard.* New York: Doubleday, 1964.

Larsen, Mogens Trolle. *The Conquest of Assyria: Excavations in an Antique Land.* London: Routledge, 1996.

Layard, Sir Austen Henry. *Autobiography and Letters from His Childhood until His Appointment as H.M. Ambassador at Madrid.* London, 1903.

Layard, Sir Austen Henry. *Discoveries in the Ruins of Nineveh and Babylon: With Travels in Armenia, Kurdistan and the Desert.* London: John Murray, 1853.

Layard, Sir Austen Henry. *Early Adventures in Persia, Susiana, and Babylonia: Including a Residence among the Bakhtiyari and Other Wild Tribes Before the Discovery of Nineveh.* 2 vols. London: John Murray, 1887.

Layard, Sir Austen Henry. *The Monuments of Nineveh.* 2 vols. London: John Murray, 1849–1853.

Layard, Sir Austen Henry. *Nineveh and Its Remains: A Narrative of an Expedition to Assyria during the Years 1845, 1846, and 1847.* Abridged by the author from his larger work. London: John Murray, 1882. Reprint, 2001.

Layard, Sir Austen Henry. *A Popular Account of Discoveries at Nineveh.* London: John Murray, 1851.

Lloyd, Seton. *Foundations in the Dust.*

Longrigg, Stephen Hemsley. *Four Centuries of Modern Iraq.*

Lucian. *Charon*. Translated and edited by H. E. Gould. London: Macmillan, 1932.

Mitford, Edward Ledwich. *A Land March from England to Ceylon Forty Years Ago*. London: W. H. Allen, 1884. Reprint, Elibron Classics, 2005.

Rawlinson, George. *A Memoir of Major-General Sir Henry Creswicke Rawlinson*. London: Longmans, Green, 1898.

Shakespeare, William. *Twelfth Night*. In *William Shakespeare: Four Comedies*. Penguin Classics. Edited by G. R. Hibbard and Stanley Wells. London: Penguin, 1995.

Sykes, Sir Mark. *The Caliph's Last Heritage*. London: Macmillan, 1915.

Tudela, Benjamin of. *The Itinerary of Benjamin of Tudela*. Translated by Marcus Nathan Adler. London, 1907. Reprint, New York: Phillip Feldheim.

Waterfield, Gordon. *Layard of Nineveh*. London: John Murray, 1963.

Waterfield, Robin. *Xenophon's Retreat*.

Xenophon. *The Persian Expedition*. Penguin Classics. Translated by Rex Warner. London: Penguin, 1972.

Chapter 17

Adelson, Roger. *Mark Sykes: Portrait of an Amateur*. London: Jonathan Cape, 1975.

Allawi, Ali. *Faisal I of Iraq*. New Haven, CT: Yale University Press, 2014.

Askari, Jafar Pasha al-. *A Soldier's Story: From Ottoman Rule to Independent Iraq: The Memoirs of Jafar Pasha Al-Askari*. London: Arabian Publishing, 2003.

Bashkin, Orit. *New Babylonians: A History of Jews in Modern Iraq*. Redwood City, CA: Stanford University Press, 2012.

Batatu, Hanna. *The Old Social Classes and the Revolutionary Movements of Iraq*. New York: St. Martin's Press, 1979.

Bell, Gertrude. *The Letters of Gertrude Bell, Selected and Edited by Lady Bell, D.B.E*. 2 vols. New York: Boni and Liveright, 1927.

Bell, Gertrude. *Selected Letters of Gertrude Bell: Selected by Lady Richmond from Lady Bell's Standard Edition*. London: Penguin, 1953.

Benjamin, Israel Joseph. *Eight Years in Asia and Africa, from 1846 to 1855*. Hanover, 1859.

Burgoyne, Elizabeth. *Gertrude Bell from her Personal Papers 1914–1926*. London: Benn, 1961.

Busch, Briton Cooper. *Britain, India, and the Arabs, 1914–1921*. Berkeley: University of California Press, 1971.

Busch, Briton Cooper. *Mudros to Lausanne: Britain's Frontier in West Asia, 1918–1923*. Albany: State University of New York Press, 1976.

Catherwood, Christopher. *The Battles of World War I*. London: Allison & Busby, 2014.

Catherwood, Christopher. *Churchill's Folly: How Winston Churchill Created Modern Iraq*. New York: Carroll and Graf, 2004.

Civil Commissioner of Iraq, Arnold Talbot Wilson, and Gertrude Bell. *Review of the Civil Administration of Mesopotamia*. London: H.M. Stationery Office, 1920.

De Gaury, Gerald. *Three Kings in Baghdad: The Tragedy of Iraq's Monarchy*. London: Hutchinson, 1961.

Dockter, Warren. "Flying in a Hurricane: Winston Churchill and T. E. Lawrence Shape the Middle East." *Finest Hour: The Journal of Winston Churchill and His Times* 170 (Fall 2015, p. 28 and ff.).

Dodge, Toby. *Inventing Iraq: The Failure of Nation-Building and a History Denied.* New York: Columbia University Press, 2003.

Edmonds, C. J. *Two Years in Kurdistan: Experiences of a Political Officer, 1918–1920.* London: Sidgwick & Jackson, 1921.

Findley, Carter Vaughan. *Bureaucratic Reform in the Ottoman Empire: The Sublime Porte, 1789–1922.* Princeton: Princeton University Press, 1980.

Finkel, Caroline. *Osman's Dream.*

Foster, H. A. *The Making of Modern Iraq.* Norman: University of Oklahoma Press, 1935.

Freeman, David. "Midwife to an 'Ungrateful Volcano': Churchill and the Making of Iraq." *Finest Hour: The Journal of Winston Churchill and His Times* 132 (Autumn 2006).

Gilbert, Martin. *Winston S. Churchill.* Vol. 4, *The Stricken World, 1916–1922.* Boston: Houghton Mifflin, 1975.

Graves, Philip. *The Life of Sir Percy Cox.* London: White Eagle Books, 1941.

Haldane, Lieutenant General Sir Aylmer. *The Insurrection in Mesopotamia 1920.* London: Naval & Military Press, 1922.

Huxley, Julian. *From An Antique Land: Ancient and Modern in the Middle East.* New York: Crown, 1955.

Ireland, Philip Willard. *Iraq: A Study in Political Development.* London: Jonathan Cape, 1937.

Jackson, Iain. "The Architecture of the British Mandate in Iraq: Nation-Building and State Creation." *Journal of Architecture* 21, no. 3 (2016): 375–417.

Kedourie, Elie. *England and the Middle East: The Destruction of the Ottoman Empire, 1914–1921.* Boulder, CO: Westview Press, 1987.

Kedourie, Elie. *In the Anglo-Arab Labyrinth: The McMahon-Husayn Corrsepondence and Its Interpretations, 1914–1939.* Cambridge: University of Cambridge Press, 1976.

Kent, Marian. *Oil and Empire: British Policy and Mesopotamian Oil, 1900–1920.* New York: Barnes & Noble, 1976.

Kilidar, Abbas, ed. *The Integration of Modern Iraq.* New York: St. Martin's Press, 1979.

Landau, Jacob M. *The Politics of Pan-Islam.* Oxford: Oxford University Press, 1990.

Lawrence, T. E. "A Report on Mesopotamia." *Times* (London), August 22, 1920.

Lawrence, T. E. *The Seven Pillars of Wisdom.* London: Jonathan Cape, 1952.

Lloyd, Seton. *Foundations in the Dust.*

Longrigg, Stephen Hemsley. *Four Centuries of Modern Iraq.*

Longrigg, Stephen Hemsley. *Iraq, 1900 to 1950: A Political, Social, and Economic History.* Oxford: Oxford University Press, 1953.

Lukitz, Liora. *A Quest in the Middle East: Gertrude Bell and the Making of Modern Iraq.* London: I. B. Tauris, 2006.

MacMillan, Margaret. *Paris 1919: Six Months That Changed the World.* New York: Random House, 2002.

Marr, Phebe. *The Modern History of Iraq.* London: Longman Group, 1985.

McDowall, David. *A Modern History of the Kurds.* London: I. B. Tauris, 1996.

Mejcher, Helmut. *Imperial Quest for Oil: Iraq 1910–1928.* Ithaca, NY: Ithaca Press, 1976.

Morris, James. *The Hashemite Kings.* New York: Pantheon, 1959.

Morris, Jan. *Farewell the Trumpets: An Imperial Retreat.* New York: Harcourt Brace Jovanovich, 1978.

Nakash, Yitzhak. *Shi'is of Iraq.*

Nezir-Akmese, Handan. *The Birth of Modern Turkey: The Ottoman Military and the March to WWI.* London: I. B. Tauris, 2005.

Omissi, David E. *Air Power and Colonial Control: The Royal Air Force, 1919–1939.* Manchester, UK: Manchester University Press, 1990.

Paris, Timothy J. *Britain, the Hashemites, and Arab Rule, 1920–1925.* London: Routledge, 2005.

Provence, Michael. *The Last Ottoman Generation and the Making of the Modern Middle East.* Cambridge: Cambridge University Press, 2017.

Rogan, Eugene. *The Fall of the Ottomans: The Great War in the Middle East.* New York: Basic Books, 2015.

Rutledge, Ian. *Enemy on the Euphrates: The British Occupation of Iraq and the Great Arab Revolt, 1914–1921.* London: Saqi Books, 2014.

Shwadran, Benjamin. *The Middle East, Oil and the Great Powers.* New York: Frederick A. Praeger, 1955.

Sluglett, Peter. *Britain in Iraq: Contriving King and Country.* New York: Columbia University Press, 1976.

Soane, Major Ely Banister. *To Mesopotamia and Kurdistan in Disguise, with Historical Notices of the Kurdish Tribes and the Chaldeans of Kurdistan.* London: John Murray, 1926.

Sykes, Sir Mark. *The Caliph's Last Heritage.*

Tripp, Charles. *A History of Iraq.* Cambridge: Cambridge University Press, 2002.

Wilson, Arnold T. *Loyalties: Mesopotamia, 1914–1917: From the Outbreak of the War to the Death of General Maude.* Oxford: Oxford University Press, 1930.

Wilson, Arnold T. *Loyalties: Mesopotamia, 1917–1920: A Clash of Loyalties.* Oxford: Oxford University Press, 1931.

Winstone, H. V. F. *Gertrude Bell.* London: Barzan, 2004.

Witts, Frederick. *The Mespot Letters of a Cotswold Soldier.* Edited by Jasper Hadman. Stroud, UK: Amberley, 2009.

Young, Major Sir Hubert. *The Independent Arab.* London: John Murray, 1933.

Chapter 18

Barrett, Roby. "Intervention in Iraq 1958–1959." Middle East Institute, April 1, 2008. https://www.mei.edu/publications/intervention-iraq-1958-1959.

Bashkin, Orit. *New Babylonians: A History of Jews in Modern Iraq.*

Batatu, Hanna. *The Old Social Classes and the Revolutionary Movements of Iraq.*

Bell, Gertrude. *Letters of Gertrude Bell, Selected and Edited by Lady Bell.*

De Gaury, Gerald. *Three Kings in Baghdad.*

Deighton, Len. *Blood, Tears and Folly: An Objective Look at World War II.* London: Jonathan Cape, 1993.

Dodge, Toby. *Inventing Iraq: The Failure of Nation-Building.*

Dudgeon, Air Vice Marshall A. G. *Hidden Victory: The Battle of Habbaniya, May 1941.* Stroud, UK: Tempus, 2000.

Haberman, S. J. "The Iraq Development Board: Administration and Program." *Middle East Journal* 9, no. 2 (1955): 179–186. http://www.jstor.org/stable/4322695. Accessed May 1, 2023.

Kedourie, Elie. *England and the Middle East: The Destruction of the Ottoman Empire.*

Longrigg, Stephen Hemsley. *Iraq 1900 to 1950.*

Marr, Phebe. *Modern History of Iraq.*

Nakash, Yitzhak. *Shi'is of Iraq.*

Playfair, I. S. O. *The Mediterranean and Middle East.* 4 vols. Uckfield, UK: Naval & Military Press, 2004.

Roberts, Andrew. *The Storm of War: A New History of the Second World War.* London: Allen Lane, 2009.

Rommel, Erwin. *The Rommel Papers.* Translated by Paul Findlay. Edited by B. H. Liddell Hart. London: Collins, 1953.

Tripp, Charles. *History of Iraq.*

Woods, Kevin M., and James Lacey. "The Business of Terror." *Iraqi Perspectives Project: Saddam and Terrorism: Emerging Insights from Captured Iraqi Documents.* Vol. 1 (Redacted). Institute for Defense Analyses, 2007.

Illustration Credits

Notes

Prologue

1 Georges Roux, *Ancient Iraq*, 3rd ed. (London: Penguin: 1992), p. 66.
2 John Reader, *Cities* (New York: Grove Press, 2004), p. 39.
3 Sir Leonard Woolley, *Ur of the Chaldees: A Record of Seven Years of Excavation* (London: Penguin, 1952), pp. 20–26.
4 Gwendolyn Leick, *Mesopotamia: The Invention of the City* (London: Penguin, 2002), p. 46.
5 Nicholas Postgate, *Early Mesopotamia: Society and Economy at the Dawn of History* (New York: Routledge, 2004), p. 206.
6 Leick, *Mesopotamia*, p. 48.
7 Ibid.
8 Postgate, *Early Mesopotamia*, p. 64.
9 Jean Bottéro, *Mesopotamia: Writing, Reasoning, and the Gods* (Chicago: University of Chicago Press, 1992), p. 78.
10 Bottéro, *Mesopotamia: Writing*, pp. 84–86.

Chapter 1

1 N. K. Sandars, trans., *The Epic of Gilgamesh* (London: Penguin, 1972), p. 61.
2 Ibid., p. 12.
3 Ibid., p. 2.
4 Roux, *Ancient Iraq*, 3rd ed., p. 115.
5 Ibid., p. 120.
6 Ibid., p. 121.
7 Ibid., p. 123.
8 Ibid., p. 123.
9 Ibid., p. 135.

10 Ibid., p. 140.

11 Charles Burney, *The Ancient Near East* (Oxford: Phaidon Press, 1977), p. 59.

12 Leick, *Mesopotamia*, p. 33

13 Burney, *Ancient Near East*, p. 50.

14 *The Epic of Gilgamesh*, trans. Benjamin R. Foster (New York: W. W. Norton, 2001), Tablet VII, p. 58.

15 Alexander Heidel, *The Gilgamesh Epic and Old Testament Parallels* (Chicago: University of Chicago Press, 1963), p. 9.

16 Sandars, *Gilgamesh*, p. 45; T. R. Bryce, "Ahhiyawans and Mycenaeans. An Anatolian Viewpoint," *Oxford Journal of Archaeology* 8 (1989): 297–310, http://www.aakkl.helsinki.fi/melammu/database/gen_html/a0000770.php.

17 *The Epic of Gilgamesh*, Tablet XI, pp. 84–95.

Chapter 2

1 Gen. 12:1 (KJV).

2 Reader, *Cities*, p. 25.

3 Paul Johnson, *A History of the Jews* (New York: Harper Perennial, 2008), pp. 13–14.

4 Gen. 14:14 (ESV).

5 Gen. 12:1 (KJV).

6 "mother of harlots": Rev. 17:5; "fornication": Rev. 19:2.

7 Heidel, *Gilgamesh Epic*: flood sent to chastise sinful man, p. 225; pitch, p. 235; seed, p. 237; mountain, p. 250; harbinger bird, p. 251.

8 Jacob Milgrom, "Bible Versus Babel: Why Did God Tell Abraham to Leave Mesopotamia, the Most Advanced Civilization of Its Time, for the Backwater Region of Canaan?" *Bible Review* 11, no. 2 (April 1995): 1.

9 For a full list, see Martha T. Roth, *Law Collections from Mesopotamia and Asia Minor*, 2nd ed. (Atlanta, GA: Society of Biblical Literature, 1997).

10 Roux, *Ancient Iraq*, p. 162.

11 Ibid., p. 182.

12 Gen. 11:4 (KJV).

13 David Rosenberg, *Abraham: The First Historical Biography* (New York: Basic Books, 2007), p. 57.

14 Gen. 12:1–2.

15 For more background on the textual origins of the Pentateuch, see Joel S. Baden, *The Composition of the Pentateuch: Renewing the Documentary Hypothesis* (New Haven, CT: Yale University Press, 2012); and Richard Friedman, *Who Wrote the Bible?* (New York: Simon & Schuster, 1987).

16 For more information on Babylon and its prestige at the time the Torah was produced there, see Milgrom, "Bible Versus Babel."

17 Roux, *Ancient Iraq*, p. 395.

18 Thorkild Jacobsen, *The Treasures of Darkness: A History of Mesopotamian Religion* (New Haven, CT: Yale University Press, 1976), p. 87.

19 This idea is posited in Rosenberg, *Abraham*, p. 79. He also argues that the absence of "significant" concern for the afterlife, an absence conspicuous in the Abraham

story, is a feature of the Sumerian religious outlook. The dreary afterworld seen in *Gilgamesh* would support this.

20 Samuel Noah Kramer, *The Sumerians: Their History, Culture, and Character* (Chicago: University of Chicago Press, 1971), p. 97.

Chapter 3

1   Tertius Chandler, *Four Thousand Years of Urban Growth: An Historical Census* (Lewiston, NY: Edwin Mellen, 1987), p. 460.

2   Marc van de Mieroop, *A History of the Ancient Near East* (London: Blackwell, 2004), p. 252.

3   Roux, *Ancient Iraq*, p. 376.

4   Ibid., pp. 278–280.

5   Ibid., p. 289.

6   Ibid., pp. 286–294.

7   D. D. Luckenbill, *Ancient Records of Assyria and Babylonia* (Chicago: University of Chicago Press, 1926), vol. 1, p. 147.

8   Luckenbill, *Ancient Records of Assyria and Babylonia*, p. 180.

9   Roux, *Ancient Iraq*, p. 294.

10 L. Delaporte, *Mesopotamia: The Babylonian and Assyrian Civilization*, trans. V. Gordon Childe (London: Kegan Paul, 1925), p. viii.

11 Roux, *Ancient Iraq*, p. 285.

12 Ibid., p. 322.

13 Ibid., p. 323.

14 2 Kings 17:6.

15 2 Kings 19:35–36.

16 2 Kings 24:14–15.

17 Isa. 13:9.

18 Dan. 5:1–28.

19 Roux, *Ancient Iraq*, pp. 140, 335.

20 Sir Percy Sykes, *A History of Persia*, 3rd ed. (London: Macmillan, 1930, 1963 reprint), vol. 1, p. 93.

21 Ezek. 32:24.

22 Richard C. Foltz, *Spirituality in the Land of the Noble: How Iran Shaped the World's Religions* (London: Oneworld, 2004), p. 5.

Chapter 4

1   Herodotus, *The Histories*, Norton Critical Edition, Book 1, trans. Walter Blanco, ed. Walter Blanco and Jennifer Tolbert Roberts (New York: W. W. Norton, 1992), p. 107.

2   Xenophon, *Cyropaedia*, Loeb Classical Library, Book 8, trans. Walter Miller (Cambridge, MA: Harvard University Press, 1914), p. 355.

3   Paul Kriwaczek, *In Search of Zarathustra: The First Prophet and the Ideas That Changed the World* (New York: Knopf, 2002), p. 178.

4   Sykes, *History of Persia*, vol. 1, p. 152.

5 Amélie Kuhrt, *The Persian Empire: A Corpus of Sources from the Achaemenid Period* (New York: Routledge, 2010), p. 72.

6 Adapted from www.britishmuseum.org/collection/object/W_1880-0617-1941

7 Roux, *Ancient Iraq*, p. 490.

8 Nebuchadnezzar's sack of Jerusalem, 587 BC: Roux, *Ancient Iraq*, pp. 379–380; destruction of the temple and exile to Babylon are punishment: Isa. 44:9–20; exile is a trial: Ezek. 14:3ff, 21:31ff; see also *Encyclopedia of Religion*, 2nd ed., ed. Lindsay Jones (New York: Macmillan Reference USA, 2004), s.v. "Exile."

9 Ezra 6:5.

10 Ezra 1:4.

11 Isa. 44:28.

12 Isa. 44:25–28 and 45:1–4.

13 Foltz, *Spirituality*, p. 47.

14 Kriwaczek, *Zarathustra*, p. 205.

15 Mary Boyce, *Zoroastrians: Their Religious Beliefs and Practices* (New York: Routledge, 2006), p. 18.

16 Ibid.

17 J. K. Anderson, *Xenophon* (London: Bristol Classical Press, 2001), pp. 1–8.

18 Quoted in Kriwaczek, *Zarathustra*, p. 182.

19 Herodotus, *Histories*, Penguin Classics (London: Penguin, 2003), p. 68.

20 Ibid., p. 69.

21 Roux, *Ancient Iraq*, p. 276; Richard N. Frye, *The Heritage of Persia: The Pre-Islamic History of One of the World's Great Civilizations* (Cleveland, OH: World, 1963), pp. 99–100, 121, 141.

22 Justin Marozzi, *The Way of Herodotus: Travels with the Man Who Invented History* (Boston: Da Capo, 2008), p. 70

23 Ibid., pp. 7–9.

24 Johnson, *History of the Jews*, p. 85.

25 Sykes, *History of Persia*, vol. 1, p. 158.

26 Livius.org, http://www.livius.org/aa-ac/achaemenians/DSf.html.

27 Freya Stark, *Rome on the Euphrates* (London: John Murray, 1966), p. 241.

28 Jacob Burckhardt, *The Greeks and Greek Civilization*, ed. Oswyn Murray, trans. Sheila Stern (New York: St. Martin's Griffin), 1998, p. 216.

29 Charles Freeman, *The Greek Achievement: The Foundation of the Western World* (New York: Viking, 1999), p. 95.

30 Sykes, *History of Persia*, vol. 1, p. 195.

31 *Guinness Book of World Records*, https://www.guinnessworldrecords.com/world-records/largest-empire-by-percentage-of-world-population.

32 Freeman, *Greek Achievement*, p. 175.

33 Sykes, *History of Persia*, vol. 1, p. 196.

34 Herodotus writes of Xerxes' invasion force, "The army was indeed far greater than any other of which we know." *The Histories*, trans. Aubrey de Selincourt (London: Penguin, 2003), Book 7, p. 425. Two hundred thousand men is a mid-range estimate of current historians.

35 Freeman, *Greek Achievement*, p. 184.

36 Ibid., p. 171.

37 Ibid., p. 184

38 Burckhardt, *The Greeks*, p. 216.

39 Kriwaczek, *Zarathustra*, p. 167; Sandra Mackey, *The Iranians: Persia, Islam and the Soul of a Nation* (New York: Plume, 1996), p. 17.

40 Foltz, *Spirituality*, p. 49.

41 For more on "Yahweh-ism," see Johnson, *History of the Jews*.

42 Resurrection: Dan. 12:1; end times: Dan. 12:4, 12:13.

43 Penelope Hobhouse, *Gardens of Persia* (Carlsbad, CA: Kales Press, 2004), p. 8.

44 Kriwaczek, pp. 194–195.

45 Donald N. Wilber, *Persepolis: The Archaeology of Parsa, Seat of the Persian Kings* (New York: Thomas Y. Crowell, 1969), p. 57.

46 Sylvia A. Matheson, *Persia: An Archaeological Guide* (London: Faber, 1972), p. 228.

Chapter 5

1 Plutarch, *The Age of Alexander*, trans. Ian Scott-Kilvert, Penguin Classics (London: Penguin, 1986), p. 255.

2 Philip Barker, *Alexander the Great's Campaigns: A Guide to Ancient Political and Military Wargaming* (Cambridge: Patrick Stephens, 1981), p. 96. Barker is an excellent source for military details in the various events of Alexander's career.

3 W. W. Tarn, *Hellenistic Civilisation* (New York: New American Library, 1974), p. 149.

4 Arrian, *The Campaigns of Alexander*, trans. Aubrey de Selincourt, Penguin Classics (London: Penguin, 1971), pp. 349–350.

5 Arrian, *Campaigns*, p. 173.

6 Plutarch, *Age of Alexander*, p. 254.

7 Ibid., pp. 253–254.

8 Ibid., pp. 257–258.

9 Arrian, *Campaigns*, p. 282.

10 Plutarch, *Age of Alexander*, p. 258.

11 Plutarch, *Age of Alexander*, p. 261.

12 Ibid.

13 Lewis V. Cummings, *Alexander the Great* (New York: Grove Press, 2004; first published Boston: Houghton Mifflin, 1940), p. 108.

14 Ian Worthington, *Alexander the Great: Man and God* (London: Pearson, 2004), p. 55; reproducing table from N. G. L. Hammond, *Alexander the Great: King, Commander and Statesman* (London: Bloomsbury Academic, 1989).

15 J. R. Hamilton footnote to Arrian, *Campaigns*, p. 105.

16 Barker, *Alexander the Great's Campaigns*, p. 81.

17 Arrian, *Campaigns*, pp. 112–113.

18 Another version says they came to him.

19 Plutarch, *Age of Alexander*, p. 276.

20 Mary Renault, *The Nature of Alexander* (New York: Pantheon, 1976), p. 106.

21 Cummings, *Alexander the Great*, p. 199.

22 Worthington, *Man and God*, p. 86.

23 Plutarch, *Age of Alexander*, p. 291.

24 Worthington, *Man and God*, p. 101.
25 Herodotus, *Histories*, p. 87.
26 Arrian, *Campaigns*, p. 179.
27 Plutarch, *Age of Alexander*, p. 295.
28 Ibid., p. 300.
29 Worthington, *Man and God*, pp. 113–114.
30 Plutarch, *Age of Alexander*, pp. 301–302.
31 Arrian, *Campaigns*, p. 213.
32 Ibid., p. 397.
33 Plutarch, *Age of Alexander*, p. 303.
34 Ibid., pp. 324–325.
35 Ibid., p. 326.
36 As with almost everything else about Alexander, the various accounts of his life differ about the number of officers whom Alexander forcibly married to Asian women at Susa. Arrian, a sober chronicler who relied on two contemporaneous memoirs, says "about eighty."
37 Plutarch, *Age of Alexander*, p. 366.
38 Arrian, *Campaigns*, p. 375.
39 Edwyn Robert Bevan, *The House of Seleucus*, 2 vols. (London: Edward Arnold, 1902), vol. 1, p. 246.

Chapter 6

1 Edwyn Robert Bevan, *The House of Seleucus*, 2 vols. (London: Edward Arnold, 1902), vol. 1, p. 28.
2 *Funeral Games* is the name of a novel about the period after Alexander's death, by Mary Renault. It is the third in her highly recommended Alexander trilogy.
3 Bevan, *House of Seleucus*, vol. 1, p. 28.
4 Ibid., p. 252.
5 John D. Grainger, *Seleukos Nikator: Constructing a Hellenistic Kingdom* (London: Routledge, 1990), p. 54.
6 Bevan, *House of Seleucus*, vol. 1, p. 26.
7 Ibid., p. 72.
8 Ibid.
9 Ibid.
10 Ibid.
11 Ibid., p. 136. Bevan says Ptolemy Keraunos was killed in 280. Some sources say it happened in 279.
12 Ibid., vol. 2, p. 23.
13 Stark, *Rome on the Euphrates*, p. 29.
14 Tarn, *Hellenistic Civilisation*, pp. 48–49.
15 Ibid., pp. 128, 133.
16 Ibid., pp. 137–138.
17 Ibid., p. 135.
18 Ibid., p. 139.
19 Ibid.

20 Tarn, *Hellenistic Civilisation*, p. 295.
21 Ibid., p. 296.
22 Ibid., p. 1.

Chapter 7

1 Justinus, quoted in Peter Wilcox and Angus McBride, *Rome's Enemies (3): Parthians and Sassanid Persians* (Oxford: Osprey Publishing, 2000), p. 6.
2 Herodotus, *Histories*, pp. 260–261 (blood, scalps, and skulls); p. 264 (hemp seed smoke); and pp. 277–278 (Amazons).
3 Plutarch, *The Lives of the Noble Grecians and Romans*, trans. John Dryden (New York: Modern Library, 1975), p. 674.
4 Stark, *Rome on the Euphrates*, p. 173.
5 Sykes, *History of Persia*, vol. 1, p. 366.
6 Wilcox, *Rome's Enemies*, p. 15.
7 Matt Rosenberg, "Largest Cities Throughout History," ThoughtCo., November 4, 2019, http://geography.about.com/library/weekly/aa011201a.htm.
8 Sykes, *History of Persia*, vol. 1, p. 367, citing Philostratus.
9 Ibid.
10 Tacitus, *Annals and Histories* (New York: Everyman's Library, 2009), p. 50.
11 Malcolm Colledge, *The Parthians* (Westport, CT: Praeger, 1967), pp. 46–47.
12 John E. Hill, trans., *The Western Regions according to the Hou Hanshou*, Section 10, http://depts.washington.edu/silkroad/texts/hhshu/hou_han_shu.html.
13 J. A. Thorley, "The Silk Trade Between China and the Roman Empire at Its Height, circa A.D. 90–130," *Greece and Rome* 18, no. 1 (April 1971): 71–80.
14 Hill, *Hou Hanshou*, Section 12.
15 Thorley, "Silk Trade," p. 71, citing Cassius Dio XLIII 24.
16 Peter Frankopan, *The Silk Roads: A New History of the World* (New York: Knopf, 2016), p. 19.
17 Thorley, "Silk Trade," p. 71.
18 *Hou Hanshou*, ch. 88, translated in Friedrich Hirth, *China and the Roman Orient: Researches into Their Ancient and Medieval Relations as Represented in Early Chinese Records I.* (Leipzig, 1885), p. 42.
19 Tacitus, *Annals and Histories*, p. 50.
20 Plutarch, *Noble Grecians and Romans*, p. 666.
21 Ibid., p. 673.
22 Ibid.
23 George Rawlinson, *The Sixth Great Oriental Monarchy; or the Geography, History, & Antiquities of Parthia* (London, Longmans, Green, 1873), p. iii.
24 Warwick Ball, *Rome in the East: The Transformation of an Empire* (London: Routledge, 1999), p. 13, quoted in R. James Ferguson, "Rome and Parthia: Power Politics and Diplomacy across Cultural Frontiers," Research Paper No. 12, Centre for East-West Cultural and Economic Studies, Faculty of Humanities and Social Sciences, Bond University, Australia, December 2005.
25 For more about Armenia as the recurring "casus belli," see Sykes, *History of Persia*, vol. 1.

26 Plutarch, *Noble Grecians and Romans*, p. 661.

27 Roman casualties at Carrhae: Rose Mary Sheldon, *Rome's Wars in Parthia: Blood in the Sand* (London: Vallentine Mitchell, 2010), p. 38, ref. Pliny *Historiae Naturae* 6.47; the Romans first irreversible loss: Arnold J. Toynbee, *Mankind and Mother Earth: A Narrative History of the World* (Oxford: Oxford University Press, 1976), p. 266.

28 Sheldon, *Rome's Wars in Parthia*, p. 39.

29 Stark, *Rome on the Euphrates*, quoting T. Rice Holmes, *The Architect of the Roman Empire* (Oxford: Oxford University Press, 1928).

30 Sheldon, *Rome's Wars in Parthia*, pp. 66-73. The losses are approximately as follows: two legions (with eagles) on the way into Parthia from the west, twenty-four thousand men during the retreat to Armenia, and a further eight thousand in the march from Armenia to the coast of Syria.

31 Ibid., p. 74.

32 Edward Gibbon, *The History of the Decline and Fall of the Roman Empire*, 6 vols. (New York: Everyman's Library, 1993), vol. 1, p. 3.

33 Ibid.

34 Cassius Dio, *The History of Dion Cassius, in Two Volumes, Done from the Greek by Mr. Manning* (London, 1704), vol. 2, pp. 121-122.

35 Frankopan, *Silk Roads*, p. 22.

36 Sheldon, *Rome's Wars in Parthia*, pp. 125-143.

37 Cassius Dio, *History of Dion Cassius*, vol. 2, p. 53.

38 From *The Chronicle of John Malalas*, pp. 284-285, quoted in Jorgen Christensen-Ernst, *Antioch on the Orontes: A History and a Guide* (Lanham, MD: Hamilton Books, 2012), p. 30.

39 Ernest Renan, *The Apostles* (New York, 1866), p. 199.

40 Sheldon, *Rome's Wars in Parthia*, pp. 159-176.

41 Plutarch, *Noble Grecians and Romans*, p. 666.

42 Quoted in Stark, *Rome on the Euphrates*, p. 119.

43 Rawlinson, *The Sixth Great Oriental Monarchy*, p. 327.

44 Tacitus, *Annals and Histories*, p. 203.

45 Plutarch, *Noble Grecians and Romans*, p. 662.

46 Sykes, *History of Persia*, vol. 1, p. 391.

47 W. Eilers, "Iran and Mesopotamia," in *Cambridge History of Iran*, ed. Ehsan Yarshater (Cambridge: Cambridge University Press, 1983), vol. 3, p. 485.

48 Sykes, *History of Persia*, vol. 1, p. 397.

49 Respectable histories of the early Sasanian period differ in the dates and even sequence of major events; we rely here mostly on *The Cambridge History of Iran*.

50 Eilers, "Iran and Mesopotamia."

51 Otto J. Maenchen-Helfen, *The World of the Huns: Studies in Their History and Culture* (Berkeley: University of California Press, 1973), p. 58.

52 Procopius, *History of the Wars*, vol. 1, trans. H. B. Dewing (Cambridge, MA: Harvard University Press, 1914), p. 11.

53 Ibid., p. 49.

54 Ibid., p. 155.

55 Ibid., p. 349.

56 Ibid., pp. 382–383.

57 H. G. Wells, *The Outline of History: The Whole History of Man* (New York: Garden City, 1956), vol. 1, pp. 417, 422.

58 Gibbon, *Decline and Fall*, vol. 4, p. 337.

59 Subsequent use of Chosroes's name: Frye, *Heritage*, p. 215.

60 Majid Fakhry, *Averroes (Ibn Rushd): His Life, Works and Influence* (London: Oneworld, 2001), pp. ix and x.

Chapter 8

1 Mohammed al-Bukhari, *Sahih al-Bukhari*. Book 5 (Riyadh: Darussalam Publishers, 1987), 8:387. Also, I. Muslim, *Sahih Muslim*, trans. A. H. Siddiqui (Delhi: Kitab Bhavan, 2000), 1:33.

2 Events, color, and quotations from Khalid's life are taken from his biography by A. I. Akram, *Khalid bin al-Waleed: Sword of Allah* (Birmingham, UK: Maktabah Publishers, 2007); Omar and Hafsa at Medina: Akram, p. 443ff.

3 Al Misri, *Reliance of the Traveler*, trans. Nuh Ha Mim Keller (Beltsville, MD: Amana Publications, 1994), p. viii.

4 G. E. von Grunebaum, *Islam: Essays in the Nature and Growth of a Cultural Tradition* (Menasha, WI: George Banta, 1955), p. 1.

5 Koran, 37:43–49, 52:17–24, 55:51–76, 56:12–37, 76:12–21, 78:32–35.

6 On the nature of jihad: Koran 2:191–193, 2:216, 3:151, 4:104, 8:12, 8:59–60, 8:65, 9:5, 9:14, 9:20, 9:29, 9:41–42, 9:123, 17:16, 25:52, 47:3–4, 66:9, etc.; Bukhari 8:387, 52:65, 52:256, etc.; Muslim 1:30, 1:33, 19:4294, 20:4645, etc.; Ibn Ishaq, *The Life of Muhammad*, trans. A. Guillaume (Oxford: Oxford University Press, 2006), 484, etc.; on jihad not conceived as personal or spiritual struggle: Koran 4:95, 9:20, 9:38–39, 9:41, 9:88, 9:111, 25:52, 48:17, 61:10–12, 66:9, etc.

7 Koran 9:29; Muslim 9:4294; Bukhari 53:386; Ibn Ishaq 956, 962; see also various texts in the main schools of Sunni Islam.

8 Hugh Kennedy, *The Great Arab Conquests: How the Spread of Islam Changed the World We Live In* (London: Phoenix, 2008), p. 62.

9 Akram, *Sword of Allah*, p. 443ff.

10 Ibid., p. 443.

11 Ibid., p. 1.

12 Efraim Karsh, *Islamic Imperialism: A History* (New Haven, CT: Yale University Press, 2007), p. 5.

13 Philip Hitti, *The Arabs: A Short History* (Washington, DC: Regnery Publishing, 1996), pp. 50–65.

14 Bukhari, hadith no. 6982. www.sunnah.com.

15 Ignaz Goldziher, *Introduction to Islamic Theology and Law*, trans. Andras and Ruth Hamori (Princeton, NJ: Princeton University Press, 1981), p. 6.

16 Quoted in Akram, *Sword of Allah*, p. 10.

17 Koran, Surah 93.

18 Koran 74:11–29.

19 Ibn Ishaq, *Life of Muhammad*, p. 464; Tabari, vol. 2, pp. 479–83, 550–55, 581–94; Toynbee, *Mankind and Mother Earth*, p. 368.
20 Koran 33:26.
21 Goldziher, *Islamic Theology and Law*, p. 8.
22 Koran 2:278.
23 Ibn Ishaq, *Life of Muhammad*, p. 289.
24 Goldziher, *Islamic Theology and Law*, pp. 11–12.
25 For an excellent summary of the nature of the changes at Medina versus the earlier Mecca period, see Goldziher, p. 810.
26 Koran 2:215.
27 Koran 4:43 and 5:6.
28 Koran 5:90.
29 Koran 29:46.
30 Koran 5:51.
31 Koran 66:9.
32 Koran 9:5.
33 Von Grunebaum, *Cultural Tradition*, p. 12.
34 Koran 2:106, 16:101.
35 Koran 9:5.
36 Koran 29:46.
37 Koran 2:256.
38 Koran 48:29.
39 Koran 33:50.
40 Koran 66.
41 Koran 33:37, 33:4–5, 33:40.
42 Koran 33:30–33.
43 Koran 33:53.
44 Bukhari, hadith no. 4788. www.sunnah.com.
45 See Tabari, *The History of al-Tabari*, Vol. 8, *The Victory of Islam*, trans. Michael Fishbein, (Albany: State University of New York Press, 1997).
46 Koran 9:5.
47 Goldziher, *Islamic Theology and Law*, p. 23.
48 Akram, *Sword of Allah*, p. 129.
49 Ibid., p. 144.
50 Ibid., p. 163.
51 Ibn Ishaq, *Life of Muhammad*, pp. 659–660.
52 Koran 9:29.
53 Toynbee, *Mankind and Mother Earth*, p. 370.
54 Kennedy, *Conquests*, p. 106.
55 Wells, *Outline of History*, vol. 1, p. 452, quoting Sir Mark Sykes, *The Caliph's Last Heritage* (London: Macmillan, 1915).
56 Koran 9:111.
57 Tabari, vol. 2, p. 544, quoted in Akram, *Sword of Allah*, p. 206.
58 Kennedy, *Conquests*, p. 75.
59 Ross Burns, *Damascus: A History* (New York: Routledge, 2007), p. 96.
60 Kennedy, *Conquests*, p. 82.

Chapter 9

1 Ibn Ishaq, *Life of Muhammad*, p. 112.
2 Quoted at http://ismaili.net/histoire/history03/history336.html.
3 John Bagot Glubb, *A Short History of the Arab Peoples* (New York: Dorset Press, 1969), p. 42.
4 Tabari, vol. 8, p. 3, and elsewhere.
5 Tabari, vol. 8, pp. 59–60.
6 Koran 24:11.
7 Bukhari, hadith no. 4141. www.sunnah.com
8 The exact date of the battle is uncertain. "Arabic sources are typically contradictory about the dates, suggesting anything from 535 to 638, with most historians settling for 636." Kennedy, *Conquests*, p. 109.
9 Glubb, *A Short History of the Arab Peoples*, p. 63.
10 G. E. von Grunebaum, *Classical Islam: A History, 600 A.D. to 1258 A.D.* (London: Routledge, 1970), p. 57.
11 Karsh, *Islamic Imperialism*, p. 26.
12 Glubb, *A Short History of the Arab Peoples*, p. 55.
13 Ibid.
14 Lesley Hazleton, *After the Prophet: The Epic Story of the Shia-Sunni Split* (New York: Anchor Books, 2009), p. 86.
15 Wilferd Madelung, *The Succession to Muhammad: A Study of the Early Caliphate* (Cambridge: Cambridge University Press, 1997), p. 84.
16 Tabari, *The History of al-Tabari*, vol. 15, *The Crisis of the Early Caliphate*, trans. R. Stephen Humphreys (Albany: State University of New York Press, 1987), p. 120.
17 Madelung, *Succession to Muhammad*: "fart," p. 97; "garden," p. 84.
18 Hazleton, *After the Prophet*, p. 88.
19 Barnaby Rogerson, *The Heirs of Muhammad: Islam's First Century and the Origins of the Sunni-Shia Split* (New York: Overlook Press, 2007), p. 275.
20 Ibid., pp. 274–275
21 Hazleton, *After the Prophet*, p. 88.
22 Ibid., p. 89.
23 Glubb, *A Short History of the Arab Peoples*, p. 66.
24 Tabari, *The History of al-Tabari*, vol. 16, *The Community Divided*, trans. Adrian Brocket (Albany: State University of New York, 1996), p. 38.
25 Ibid., p. 90.
26 Ibid., p. 91.
27 Ibid., p. 88.
28 Ibid., p. 118.
29 Hazleton, *After the Prophet*, p. 128 ff.
30 Tabari, *History of al-Tabari*, vol. 16, p. 30.
31 Tabari, *The History of al-Tabari*, vol. 17, *The First Civil War*, trans. G. R. Hawting (Albany: State University of New York Press, 1996), p. 70.
32 Glubb, *A Short History of the Arab Peoples*, p. 68.
33 Madelung, *Succession to Muhammad*, p. 326.

34 Tabari, *The History of al-Tabari*, vol. 19, *The Caliphate of Yazid B. Mu'awiyah*, trans. I. K. A. Howard (Albany: State University of New York Press, 1991), pp. 120–161.

35 I. K. A. Howard, footnote 407 to Tabari, vol. 19, p. 121.

36 Tabari, *History of al-Tabari*, vol. 19, p. 121.

37 Ibid., p. 123.

38 Ibid., p. 152.

39 Ibid., p. 160.

40 Ibid., p. 160.

41 Ibid., p. 161.

42 "The Largest Contemporary Muslim Pilgrimage Isn't the Hajj to Mecca, It's the Shiite Pilgrimage to Karbala in Iraq," *The Conversation*, September 9, 2020, https://theconversation.com/the-largest-contemporary-muslim-pilgrimage-isnt-the-hajj-to-mecca-its-the-shiite-pilgrimage-to-karbala-in-iraq-144542.

Chapter 10

1 Hitti, *The Arabs*, pp. 98–99.

2 Joseph Schacht, "Law and Justice," in *The Cambridge History of Islam*, vol. 2, *Islamic Society and Civilization* (Cambridge: Cambridge University Press, 1970), pp. 553–560.

3 Ibid., p. 551.

4 Ibid., p. 553.

5 Majid Khadduri, *Islamic Jurisprudence: Shafii's Risala* (Baltimore: Johns Hopkins University Press, 1961), p. 5.

6 Schacht, "Law and Justice," p. 554.

7 Ibid., p. 555.

8 Fazlur Rahman, *Islam*, 2nd ed. (Chicago: University of Chicago Press, 1979), p. 59.

9 Schacht, Joseph, *An Introduction to Islamic Law* (Oxford: Clarendon Press, 1964), p. 74.

10 Kennedy, *Great Arab Conquests*, p. 132.

11 Wells, *Outline of History*, p. 484.

12 Goldziher, *Islamic Theology and Law*, p. 27.

13 M. A. Shaban, *The Abbasid Revolution* (Cambridge: Cambridge University Press, 1970), pp. 86–92.

14 Edward Granville Browne, *A Literary History of Persia* (London: T. Fisher Unwin, 1902), vol. 1, p. 234, citing Dozy.

15 Tabari, *The History of al-Tabari*, vol. 26, *The Waning of the Umayyad Caliphate*, trans. Carole Hillenbrand (Albany: State University of New York Press, 1989), pp. 24–25.

16 Tabari, *History of al-Tabari*, vol. 15, pp. 47–51.

17 P. M. Holt, Ann K. S. Lamb, and Bernard Lewis, eds., *The Cambridge History of Islam*, vol. 1, *The Central Islamic Lands* (Cambridge: Cambridge University Press, 1970), p. 102.

18 Shaban, *Abbasid Revolution*, p. 158.

19 Browne, *Literary History of Persia*, p. 246.

20 Shaban, *Abbasid Revolution*, p. 151.

21 Glubb, *A Short History of the Arab Peoples*, p. 55.

22 Dimitri Gutas, *Greek Thought, Arabic Culture: The Graeco-Arabic Translation Movement in Baghdad and Early Abbasid Society* (London: Routledge, 2005), p. 14.

23 Sykes, *History of Persia*, vol. 1, p. 557.

24 Tabari, *The History of al-Tabari*, vol. 27, *The Abbasid Revolution*, trans. John Alden Williams (Albany: State University of New York Press, 1985), p. 148.

25 Ibid., pp. 162–164.

26 Ibid., pp. 168–170.

27 Ibid., p. 212.

28 Browne, *Literary History of Persia*, p. 245.

29 For more information about Muslim Spain, rhapsodizing, and norms, see esp. Dario Fernandez-Morera, *The Myth of the Andalusian Paradise: Muslims, Christians, and Jews under Islamic Rule in Medieval Spain* (Wilmington, DE: ISI Books, 2016).

30 Reinhart Dozy, *Spanish Islam: A History of the Moslems in Spain*, trans. Francis Griffin Stokes (London: Chatto & Windus, 1913), p. 207.

31 Masudi, *From The Meadows of Gold*, trans. P. Lunde and C. Stone (London: Penguin, 2007), p. 40.

32 Gutas, *Greek Thought, Arabic Culture*, p. 13 and ff.

33 Kennedy, *The Court of the Caliphs: The Rise and Fall of Islam's Greatest Dynasty* (London: Weidenfeld & Nicolson, 2004), p. 20.

34 Browne, *Literary History of Persia*, p. 243, quoting Gerlof van Vloten, *Recherches sur la Domination arabe, Chiitisme et les Croyances Messianiques sous le Khalifat des Omayades (1894)*, pp. 65–68.

35 Sykes, *History of Persia*, vol. 1, p. 561.

36 Browne, *Literary History of Persia*, p. 243.

37 Tabari, *The History of al-Tabari*, vol. 28, *Abbasid Authority Affirmed: The Early Years of Al-Mansour*, trans. Jane Dammen McAuliffe (Albany: State University of New York Press, 1995), p. 39.

38 Gutas, *Greek Thought, Arabic Culture*, p. 63, quoting Masudi.

39 Browne, *Literary History of Persia*, p. 251, quoting Muir, *The Caliphate: Its Rise, Decline, and Fall*, pp. 430–432.

40 Sir Richard Burton, trans., *Arabian Nights: A Selection* (London: Penguin, 1997), p. 211.

Chapter 11

1 Richard Coke, *Baghdad: The City of Peace* (London: Thornton Butterworth, 1935), p. 48.

2 Gutas, *Greek Thought, Arabic Culture*, p. 98.

3 Kennedy, *Court of the Caliphs*, p. 95.

4 Tabari, *History of al-Tabari*, vol. 31, pp. 134–181.

5 Kennedy, *Court of the Caliphs*, p. 106.

6 Ibid., p. 105

7 Robert R. Reilly, *The Closing of the Muslim Mind: How Intellectual Suicide Created the Modern Islamist Crisis* (Wilmington, DE: Intercollegiate Studies Institute, 2010), pp. 198–199ff.

8 Gutas, *Greek Thought, Arabic Culture*, p. 103.

9 Browne, *Literary History of Persia*, p. 261, citing Al Waqidi.

10 Gutas, *Greek Thought, Arabic Culture*, pp. 39–45.

11 Ibid., pp. 118, 133.

12 Amira K. Bennison, *The Great Caliphs: The Golden Age of the Abbasid Empire* (New Haven, CT: Yale University Press, 2009), p. 181.

13 Gutas, *Greek Thought, Arabic Culture*, p. 14.

14 Ibid., pp. 14–16.

15 Browne, *Literary History of Persia*, p. 304.

16 Bernard Lewis, *The Muslim Discovery of Europe* (London: Weidenfeld & Nicolson, 2001), p. 74.

17 Gutas, *Greek Thought, Arabic Culture*, p. 18.

18 Ibid., pp. 84–85.

19 Ibid., p. 95.

20 Coke, *City of Peace*, pp. 87–88.

21 Browne, *Literary History of Persia*, p. 281.

22 Reilly, *Closing of the Muslim Mind*, p. 47.

23 Bennison, *Great Caliphs*, p. 35.

24 Roger Scruton, foreword to Reilly, *Closing of the Muslim Mind*, p. xi.

25 The story comes from Ibn Khallikan, the thirteenth-century author of a biographical dictionary of great men of the Islamic world. This version is from William McGuckin de Slane's 2,700-page 1842–1871 translation, in which de Slane converts farsakhs, an Abbasid measure of distance, into miles.

26 Bennison, *Great Caliphs*.

27 Coke, *City of Peace*, p. 91.

28 Ibid.

29 Bennison, *Great Caliphs*, p. 190.

30 Reilly, *Closing of the Muslim Mind*, p. 41.

31 Boyce, *Zoroastrians*, p. 158.

32 Coke, *City of Peace*, p. 91.

33 Masudi, quoted in Kennedy, *Court of the Caliphs*, p. 24.

34 Kennedy, *Court of the Caliphs*, p. 240.

35 Browne, *Literary History of Persia*, p. 290.

36 Schacht, "Law and Justice," p. 555.

37 Browne, *Literary History of Persia*, p. 283: "The Shiite doctrine current in Persia at the current day is in many respects Mutazilite."

38 *"Cette antique Babylonie, ou la race semitique et la race perse se recontraient et se melangaient."* Browne, *Literary History of Persia*, p. 282, quoting Dozy's *Het Islamisme* in V. Chauvin's 1879 French translation.

Chapter 12

1 Tabari, *History of al-Tabari*, vol. 30, p. 321.

2 Coke, *City of Peace*, p. 15.

3 Jer. 50:29.

4 Nah. 3:3.

5 Kennedy, *Court of the Caliphs*, p. 1.

6 British Museum website, photograph of an Offa dinar from the kingdom of Mercia, http://www.britishmuseum.org/explore/highlights/highlight_objects /cm/g/gold_imitation_dinar_of_offa.aspx.

7 Kennedy, *Court of the Caliphs*, p. 194.

8 Ibid., p. 167.

9 Ibid., p. 172 and ff.

10 Kennedy, *Court of the Caliphs*, p. 253.

11 Caswell, *Slave Girls of Baghdad*, p. 25.

12 Quoted in Reynald A. Nicolson, *A Literary History of the Arabs* (London: T. Fisher Unwin, 1907), p. 300.

13 Quoted in Caswell, *Slave Girls of Baghdad*, p. 29.

14 Franz Rosenthal, *The Classical Heritage in Islam*, Arabic Thought and Culture (London: Routledge, 1975), p. 10.

15 Kennedy, *Court of the Caliphs*, p. 258.

16 Quoted in Alfred S. Posamentier and Ingmar Lehmann, *The (Fabulous) Fibonacci Numbers* (Amherst, NY: Prometheus Books, 2007), p. 23.

17 Lewis, *Muslim Discovery of Europe*, p. 74.

18 Gutas, *Greek Thought, Arabic Culture*, p. 34.

19 Rosenthal, *Classical Heritage in Islam*, p. 10.

20 Hitti, *The Arabs*, p. 147.

21 Bennison, *Great Caliphs*, p. 214

22 Kennedy, *Caliphs*, p. 131.

23 Ibid., p. 296.

Chapter 13

1 Reilly, *Closing of the Muslim Mind*, p. 47.

2 Browne, *Literary History of Persia*, p. 6.

3 Quoted in Caswell, *Slave Girls of Baghdad*, p. 28.

4 Gutas, *Greek Thought, Arabic Culture*, p. 76.

5 Pervez Hoodbhoy, *Islam and Science: Religious Orthodoxy and the Battle for Rationality* (London: Zed Books, 1991), p. 120.

6 Khadduri, *Islamic Jurisprudence*, p. 17.

7 Schacht, *Islamic Law*, pp. 47–48.

8 Al Misri, *Reliance of the Traveler*, trans. Keller. From the translator's Introduction, p. VII.

9 Ibid., p. 292.

10 Schacht, "Law and Justice," pp. 563–565.

11 Article, "al-Ashari" by Anvari, M. and Koushki, M.M., *Encyclopedia Islamica*, eds. Madelung, W. and Daftary, F.

Chapter 14

1 Christopher Marlowe, *Tamburlaine* (2 I.iii), quoted in David Nicolle, *The Mongol Warlords: Genghis Khan, Kublai Khan, Hulegu, Tamerlane* (New York: Firebird Books, 1990), p. 146.

2 Kennedy, *Caliphs*, p. 213.

3 Ibid., p. 214.

4 Tabari, *History of al-Tabari*, vol. 33, p. 27.

5 Ibid., pp. 25 (Samarra bought from a Christian monastery), and 26, footnote (eight monasteries in the area).

6 John Julius Norwich, *A Short History of Byzantium* (New York: Knopf, 1997), p. 242 (from John Scylitzes, collected in Georgius Cedrenus).

7 Toynbee, *Mankind and Mother Earth*, p. 451.

8 Coke, *City of Peace*, p. 112.

9 Samuel Barrett Miles, *The Countries and Tribes of the Persian Gulf*, 2 vols. (London: Harrison and Sons, 1919), vol. 1, p. 128.

10 Gibbon, *Decline and Fall*, vol. 6, pp. 13–15.

11 Sykes, *History of Persia*, vol. 2, p. 30.

12 Ibid., p. 30; paraphrasing Gibbon, *Decline and Fall*, vol. 6, p. 14.

13 Wells, *Outline of History*, p. 500.

14 Miles, *Tribes of the Persian Gulf*, vol. 1, p. 128.

15 Sykes, *History of Persia*, vol. 2, p. 34.

16 Norwich, *Short History of Byzantium*, p. 236.

17 Gibbon, *Decline and Fall*, vol. 6, p. 20.

18 Norwich, *Short History of Byzantium*, p. 242.

19 Sykes, *History of Persia*, vol. 2, p. 33.

20 For a concise political account of the Seljuks, see Sykes, *History of Persia*, vol. 2, pp. 30–36.

21 Solomon ben Joseph Ha-Kohen, *The Turkoman Defeat at Cairo*, ed. and trans. Julius H. Greenstone (Chicago: Chicago University Press, 1906), p. 163, quoted in A. C. S. Peacock, *The Great Seljuk Empire* (Edinburgh: Edinburgh University Press, 2015), p. 64.

22 Gibbon, *Decline and Fall*, vol. 6, p. 38.

23 Quoted in Christopher Tyerman, *God's War: A New History of the Crusades* (Cambridge, MA: Belknap Press, 2007), p. 49.

24 Byzantine call for help is the lead proximate cause of Urban's calling the First Crusade: Riley-Smith p. 1, Freely p. 1 ("Seljuk conquest of a large part of the Byzantine Empire . . . led to the First Crusade") and elsewhere.

25 Gibbon, *Decline and Fall*, vol. 6, p. 85.

26 Ibid., p. 86.

27 Fulcher of Chartres, from Edward Peters, *The First Crusade: The Chronicle of Fulcher of Chartres and Other Source Materials* (Philadelphia: University of Pennsylvania Press, 1998), p. 84.

28 Ralph of Caen, quoted in Maalouf, *The Crusades Through Arab Eyes* (New York: Schocken, 1984), p. 39.

29 Tyerman, *God's War*, pp. 157–158.

30 B. Spuler, "The Disintegration of the Caliphate in the East," in *Cambridge History of Islam*, vol. 1, p. 156.

31 *Cambridge History of Islam*, vol. 1, p. 156.

32 Sykes, *History of Persia*, vol. 2, p. 34.

33 Coke, *City of Peace*, p. 115.

34 Toynbee, *Mankind and Mother Earth*, p. 430 (Al Ghazali's "retreat"); W. Montgomery Watt, *Islamic Philosophy and Theology* (Edinburgh: Edinburgh University Press, 1962), p. 121 (inner "states").

35 Toynbee, *Mankind and Mother Earth*, p. 450 ("tour de force"), p. 431 ("hold on human hearts").

36 Averroes, *The Incoherence of the Incoherence*, trans. Simon van den Bergh (Oxford: Oxford University Press, 1954), p. 317.

37 Fakhry, *Averroes*, p. 25.

38 Ibid., p. 132.

39 Wells, *Outline of History*, p. 502.

40 Fakhry, *Averroes*, p. 96.

41 Wells, *Outline of History*, p. 500.

42 Robert Byron, *The Road to Oxiana* (London: Penguin, 1992), p. 197.

43 Mackey, *The Iranians*, p. 72.

44 Watt, *Islamic Philosophy*, pp. 54–56; Peter Adamson and Richard C. Taylor, *The Cambridge Companion to Arabic Philosophy* (Cambridge: Cambridge University Press, 2005), pp. 107–108.

45 Coke, *City of Peace*, p. 144.

46 Nicolle, *Mongol Warlords*, p. 109.

47 Ibid.

48 Coke, *City of Peace*, p. 148.

49 Ibid., p. 152.

50 Nicolle, *Mongol Warlords*, p. 109.

51 Quoted in Coke, *City of Peace*, p. 151.

52 Small provincial town: *Cambridge History of Islam*, vol. 1, p. 165.

53 *Cambridge History of Islam*, vol. 1, p. 165.

54 Ahmad ibn Naqib al-Misri, *Reliance of the Traveler*, trans. Nuh Ha Mim Keller (Beltsville, MD: Amana Publications, 1994), pp. 2–3.

55 Ibid., p. 9.

56 Ibid., pp. 8–14.

57 Byron, *Road to Oxiana*, pp. 50–51.

58 Arthur Upham Pope, *Introducing Persian Architecture* (Tehran: Asia Institute Books, 1976), p. 66.

59 Coke, *City of Peace*, p. 165.

60 Frankopan, *Silk Roads*, p. 421.

61 Nicolle, *Mongol Warlords*, p. 161.

62 P. M. Holt et al., *Cambridge History of Islam*, vol. 1, p. 170.

63 Coke, *City of Peace*, p. 176.

64 Ibid., p. 177.

65 Byron, *Road to Oxiana*, p. 90.

66 Coke, *City of Peace*, p. 183.

Chapter 15

1 The material from Ogier de Busbecq's *Letters* is taken from Ogier de Busbecq, *Turkish Letters* (London: Eland, 2005).

2 William Stubbs, *Lectures on European History* (London: Longmans, Green, and Co., 1904), p. 122.

3 Ralph Fitch, quoted in Stephen Hemsley Longrigg, *Four Centuries of Modern Iraq* (Oxford: Oxford University Press, 1925), p. 10.

4 Longrigg, *Four Centuries of Modern Iraq*, p. 10.

5 Ibid., p. 1.

6 Gabor Agoston and Bruce Masters, eds., *Encyclopedia of the Ottoman Empire* (New York: Facts on File, 2008), s.v. "Baghdad and the Ottoman Empire."

7 Longrigg, *Four Centuries of Modern Iraq*, p. 3.

8 Ibid., p. 11.

9 Ibid., p. 8.

10 Mackey, *The Iranians*, p. 26.

11 Sykes, *History of Persia*, vol. 2, p. 164, quoting "Angiolello" in *Travels of Venetians in Persia*," p. 111.

12 Sykes, *History of Persia*, vol. 2, p. 160.

13 David Blow, *Shah Abbas: The Ruthless King Who Became an Iranian Legend* (London: I. B. Tauris, 2009), p. 4.

14 Mackey, *The Iranians*, p. 85.

15 *Cambridge History of Islam*, vol. 1, pp. 398–399.

16 Ibid., p. 400.

17 Busbecq, *Turkish Letters*, p. 44.

18 Jacopo Soranzo, *Relazione e Diario*, p. 237, quoted in Caroline Finkel, *Osman's Dream: The History of the Ottoman Empire* (New York: Basic Books, 2005), p. 166.

19 Tobias Graf, "Best of Enemies: Europeans in the Ottoman Elite," *History Today*, January 2, 2018; see also Graf, *The Sultan's Renegades: Christian-European Converts to Islam and the Making of the Ottoman Elite, 1575–1610* (Oxford: Oxford University Press), 2017; for Campanella and Cigalla, see Noel Malcolm, *Useful Enemies: Islam and the Ottoman Empire in Western Political Thought, 1450–1750* (Oxford: Oxford University Press, 2019).

Chapter 16

1 Sir Austen Henry Layard, *Nineveh and Its Remains: A Narrative of an Expedition to Assyria during the Years 1845, 1846, and 1847* (London: John Murray, 1882; reprint, 2001), p. 2.

2 Ibid.

3 Ibid.

4 Edward Ledwich Mitford, *A Land March from England to Ceylon Forty Years Ago* (London: W. H. Allen, 1884), vol. 1, p. 280.

5 Sir Austen Henry Layard, *Autobiography and Letters from His Childhood until His Appointment as H.M. Ambassador at Madrid* (London, 1903), vol. 1, p. 11.

6 Ibid., p. 14.

7 Ibid., p. 21.

8 Ibid., p. 26.

9 Ibid., p. 38.

10 Gen. Chapter 10, verse 11.

11 Xenophon, *The Persian Expedition*, trans. Rex Warner (London: Penguin, 1972), pp. 162–163.

12 Ibid., p. 163.

13 Layard, *Autobiography*, vol. 1, p. 306.

14 Arnold C. Brackman, *The Luck of Nineveh: Archaeology's Great Adventure* (New York: McGraw-Hill, 1978), p. 11.

15 Lucian, *Charon*, trans. and ed. H. E. Gould (London: Macmillan, 1932), p. 23.

16 Benjamin of Tudela, *The Itinerary of Benjamin of Tudela*, trans. Marcus Nathan Adler (London, 1907; reprint, New York: Philipp Feldheim), pp. 24–25.

17 Shirley, quoted in Sir Austen Henry Layard, *Discoveries in the Ruins of Nineveh and Babylon* (London: John Murray, 1852), p. 660.

18 Mogens Trolle Larsen, *The Conquest of Assyria: Excavations in an Antique Land* (London: Routledge, 1996), pp. 7–9.

19 Nora Benjamin Kubie, *Road to Nineveh: The Adventures and Excavations of Sir Austen Henry Layard* (New York: Doubleday, 1964), p. 60.

20 Ibid., p. 59.

21 Layard, *Autobiography*, vol. 1, p. 327.

22 Kubie, *Road to Nineveh*, p. 65.

23 Ibid., p. 118.

24 Larsen, *Conquest of Assyria*, p. 16.

25 Ibid., p. 16.

26 Brackman, *Luck of Nineveh*, p. 98.

27 Ibid., p. 100.

28 Brackman, *Luck of Nineveh*, pp. 105–113; Kubie, *Road to Nineveh*, pp. 131–146; Layard, *Autobiography*, vol. 2, p. 108.

29 Seton Lloyd, *Foundations in the Dust: The Story of Mesopotamian Exploration* (London: Thames & Hudson, 1980), pp. 96–97.

30 Layard, *Autobiography*, vol. 2, p. 107.

31 Layard, *Nineveh and Its Remains*, p. 10.

32 Jason Goodwin, *Lords of the Horizons: A History of the Ottoman Empire* (New York: Henry Holt, 1999), p. 304.

33 Finkel, *Osman's Dream*, p. 450.

34 Ibid., p. 427.

35 Layard, *Nineveh and Its Remains*, p. 11.

36 Ibid.

37 Ibid., p. 12.

38 Ibid., p. 13.

39 Ibid.

40 Ibid., p. 15.

41 Ibid., p. 16.

42 Ibid., p. 19.

43 Ibid., p. 20.

44 Ibid., p. 25.

45 Sir Austen Henry Layard, *A Popular Account of Discoveries at Nineveh* (London: John Murray, 1851), pp. 24–25.

46 Nah.: 3:1, 3:3, 3:7.

47 Layard, *Nineveh and Its Remains*, p. 29.

48 Ibid., p. 30.

49 Brackman, *Luck of Nineveh*, p. 21.

50 Layard, *Nineveh and Its Remains*, p. 31.

51 Ibid., p. 32.

52 Ibid., p. 33.

53 Larsen, *Conquest of Assyria*, p. 97.

54 Brian Fagan, introduction to Layard, *Nineveh and Its Remains*, p. 18.

Chapter 17

1 Gertrude Bell, *Selected Letters of Gertrude Bell: Selected by Lady Richmond from Lady Bell's Standard Edition* (London: Penguin, 1953), p. 304.

2 Quoted in Gerald de Gaury, *Three Kings in Baghdad: The Tragedy of Iraq's Monarchy* (London: Hutchinson, 1961), p. 40.

3 De Gaury, *Three Kings in Baghdad*, p. 29.

4 Christopher Catherwood, *Churchill's Folly: How Winston Churchill Created Modern Iraq* (New York: Carroll and Graf, 2004), pp. 91 (Churchill note to Lloyd George) and 94 (Churchill note to Cabinet).

5 Ali Allawi, *Faisal I of Iraq* (New Haven, CT: Yale University Press, 2014), pp. 11 (seven years among the "desert tribes") and 14 (reasons for Hussein's sojourn in Mecca). The debt this chapter owes to Dr. Allawi's tour de force is enormous. Unless otherwise noted, most citable material in the chapter comes from this source.

6 De Gaury, *Three Kings in Baghdad*, p. 31.

7 Goodwin, *Lords of the Horizons*, p. 313.

8 Ibid.

9 Ibid., p. 311.

10 Longrigg, *Four Centuries of Modern Iraq*, p. 313.

11 Finkel, *Osman's Dream*, pp. 491–492.

12 Quoted in Finkel, *Osman's Dream*, p. 492.

13 Finkel, *Osman's Dream*, p. 492.

14 De Gaury, *Three Kings in Baghdad*, p. 32.

15 Allawi, *Faisal I*, p. 14.

16 De Gaury, *Three Kings in Baghdad*, p. 32.

17 Allawi, *Faisal I*, p. 43.

18 Quoted in Allawi, pp. 47–48.

19 Quoted in Allawi, p. 53.

20 Allawi, p. 53.

21 Letter from Sir Henry McMahon, H.M. High Commissioner at Cairo, to Sharif Hussein of Mecca, October 24, 1915.

22 Quoted in Allawi, *Faisal I*, p. 100.

23 Jan Morris, *Farewell the Trumpets: An Imperial Retreat* (New York: Harcourt Brace Jovanovich, 1978), p. 171.

24 Christopher Catherwood, *The Battles of World War I* (London: Allison & Busby, 2014), p. 95.

25 "imperial school": Charles Tripp, *A History of Iraq* (Cambridge: Cambridge University Press, 2002), p. 36; "outright colony": Allawi, *Faisal I*, p. 196.

26 Quoted in Allawi, *Faisal I*, p. 309.

27 Longrigg, *Iraq 1900 to 1950*, p. 113.

28 De Gaury, *Three Kings in Baghdad*, p. 16.

29 Longrigg, *Iraq 1900 to 1950*, p. 113.

30 Benjamin Shwadran, *The Middle East, Oil and the Great Powers* (New York: Frederick A. Praeger, 1955), p. 200.

31 Quoted in Allawi, *Faisal I*, p. 203.

32 Quoted in Allawi, p. 204.

33 Quoted in Allawi, p. 200.

34 Allawi, *Faisal I*, p. 198.

35 Text of the Covenant of the League of Nations (see Article 22): https://avalon.law.yale.edu/20th_century/leagcov.asp#art22.

36 Shwadran, *Middle East, Oil and the Great Powers*, p. 235.

37 Tripp, *History of Iraq*, p. 41.

38 Churchill, Chartwell Papers 16/48, quoted in Catherwood, *Churchill's Folly*, p. 88.

39 Quoted in David Freeman, "Midwife to an 'Ungrateful Volcano': Churchill and the Making of Iraq," *Finest Hour: The Journal of Winston Churchill and His Times* 132 (Autumn 2006).

40 Text of the Treaty of Sèvres, https://wwi.lib.byu.edu/index.php/Section_I,_Articles_1_-_260: frontiers of Turkey, Article 27; "autonomy" for Turkish Kurdistan but not Kurds of Mosul vilayet, Article 62.

41 Martin Gilbert, *Winston S. Churchill*, vol. 4, *The Stricken World, 1916–1922* (Boston: Houghton Mifflin, 1975), p. 488.

42 Churchill, Chartwell Papers 16/48, quoted in Catherwood, *Churchill's Folly*, pp. 87–88.

43 Bell, *Selected Letters*, p. 265.

44 Ibid., p. 217.

45 Longrigg, *Iraq 1900 to 1950*, p. 113.

46 Bell, *Selected Letters*, p. 243.

47 Allawi, *Faisal I*, p. 366.

48 Bell, *Letters*, vol. 2, p. 604.

49 De Gaury, *Three Kings in Baghdad*, p. 25.

50 Quoted in Allawi, *Faisal I*, p. 371.

51 Allawi, *Faisal I*, p. 372.

52 Gertrude Bell, *The Letters of Gertrude Bell, Selected and Edited by Lady Bell, D.B.E.*, 2 vols. (New York: Boni and Liveright, 1927), vol. 2, pp. 613–614.

53 Quoted in Allawi, *Faisal I*, p. 373.

54 Bell, *Letters*, vol. 2, p. 612.

55 Longrigg, *Iraq 1900 to 1950*, p. 10.

56 Ibid.

57 Jer. 29:5–6.

58 Tripp, *History of Iraq*, p. 11.

59 Israel Joseph Benjamin, *Eight Years in Asia and Africa, from 1846 to 1855* (Hanover, 1863), p. 112.

60 Jer. 29:7.

61 De Gaury, *Three Kings in Baghdad*, p. 23.

62 Allawi, *Faisal I*, p. 375.

63 Quoted in Allawi, *Faisal I*, p. 375,

64 Allawi, *Faisal I*, p. 375.

65 De Gaury, *Three Kings in Baghdad*, p. 55.

66 Ibid., p. 17.

67 Text of the Treaty of Lausanne, transl. from the French: https://wwi.lib.byu.edu/index.php/Treaty_of_Lausanne.

68 Quoted in numerous secondary sources. Primary source obscure.

69 Tripp, *History of Iraq*, p. 29.

70 Allawi, *Faisal I*, p. 451.

71 Tripp, *History of Iraq*, p. 31.

72 Gilbert, *Winston S. Churchill*, p. 817.

73 Toby Dodge, *Inventing Iraq: The Failure of Nation-Building and a History Denied* (New York: Columbia University Press, 2003), p. 24.

74 Quoted in Dodge, *Inventing Iraq*, p. 24.

75 Catherwood, *Churchill's Folly*, p. 197.

76 Tripp, *History of Iraq*, p. 53.

77 Allawi, *Faisal I*, p. 406.

78 Shwadran, *Middle East, Oil and the Great Powers*, p. 236.

79 Tripp, *History of Iraq*, p. 47.

80 Elizabeth Burgoyne, *Gertrude Bell from Her Personal Papers 1914–1926* (London: Benn, 1961), p. 318.

81 Longrigg, *Iraq 1900 to 1950*, p. 139.

82 Ibid., p. 147.

83 Ibid., p. 163.

84 Ibid., p. 166.

85 Ibid.

86 Treaty Between the United Kingdom and Irak, Regarding the Duration of the Treaty Between the United Kingdom and Iraq of October 10, 1922, Signed at Bagdad January 13, 1926, Article 3. UK Foreign, Commonwealth, and Development Office, UK Treaties Online: https://treaties.fcdo.gov.uk/data/Library2/pdf/1926-TS0010.pdf#:~:text=Treaty%20between%20the%20United%20Kingdom%20and%20Irak%20regarding,1926.%20%5BRatifications%20exchanged%20at%20London%2C%20March%2030%2C%201926.%5D.

87 De Gaury, *Three Kings in Baghdad*, p. 39.

88 Allawi, *Faisal I*, pp. 431–432.

89 Ibid., p. 466.

90 Quoted in Allawi, *Faisal I*, p. 467.

91 Allawi, *Faisal I*, p. 432 (bridge partners); De Gaury, *Three Kings in Baghdad*, p. 86 (Prince Usama).

92 Allawi, *Faisal I*, p. 468, quoting the "unpublished papers of Sir Henry Dobbs."

93 Burgoyne, *Gertrude Bell from Her Personal Papers*, p. 359.

94 De Gaury, *Three Kings in Baghdad*, p. 53.

95 Burgoyne, *Gertrude Bell from Her Personal Papers*, p. 356.

96 Schwadran, *Middle East, Oil and the Great Powers*, p. 233, fn 45.

97 Allawi, *Faisal I*, p. 399.

98 Jafar Pasha al-Askari, *A Soldier's Story: From Ottoman Rule to Independent Iraq: The Memoirs of Jafar Pasha Al-Askari* (London: Arabian Publishing, 2003), p. 112.

99 De Gaury, *Three Kings in Baghdad*, p. 48.

100 Allawi, *Faisal I*, p. 477.

101 De Gaury, *Three Kings in Baghdad*, p. 49.

102 Allawi, *Faisal I*, p. 477.

103 Ibid.

104 Quoted in Allawi, *Faisal I*, p. 482.

105 "Note on the Internal Situation in Iraq" by the high commissioner, June 27, 1927, quoted in Allawi, *Faisal I*, p. 477.

106 Dobbs unpublished papers, letter of December 29, 1928, quoted in Allawi, *Faisal I*, p. 509.

107 Allawi, *Faisal I*, p. 518.

108 Ibid.

109 Ibid.

110 Ibid.

111 Ibid., p. 532.

112 Ibid., pp. 532–533.

113 Ibid., p. 533.

Chapter 18

1 Lloyd, *Foundations in the Dust*, p. 182.

2 Baghdad 1932: Longrigg, *Iraq 1900 to 1950: A Political, Social, and Economic History* (New York: Oxford University Press, 1953), pp. 168–170.

3 Ibid., p. 174.

4 Shwadran, *Middle East, Oil and the Great Powers*, p. 194.

5 Ibid., p. 203.

6 Tripp, *History of Iraq*, p. 71, citing Peter Sluglett, *Britain in Iraq: Contriving King and Country* (New York: Columbia University Press 1976), p. 198.

7 Longrigg, *Iraq 1900 to 1950*, p. 221.

8 De Gaury, *Three Kings in Baghdad*, p. 83.

9 Longrigg, *Iraq 1900 to 1950*, p. 223.

10 Allawi, *Faisal I*, p. 560.

11 De Gaury, *Three Kings in Baghdad*, p. 87.

12 Ibid., p. 52.

13 Ibid., p. 111.

14 Air Vice Marshall A. G. Dudgeon, *Hidden Victory: The Battle of Habbaniya, May 1941* (Stroud, UK: Tempus, 2000), p. 19.

15 Ibid.

16 Ibid., p. 21.

17 Milton Shulman, *Defeat in the West*, p. 115, quoted in Andrew Roberts, *The Storm of War: A New History of the Second World War* (London: Allen Lane, 2009), p. 284.

18 Roberts, *Storm of War*, p. 129.

19 Ibid., pp. 411, 551.

20 Longrigg, *Iraq 1900 to 1950*, p. 292.

21 Dudgeon, *Hidden Victory*, p. 50.

22 Ibid., p. 5.

23 Ibid.

24 Quoted in Dudgeon, *Hidden Victory*, p. 130.

25 Dudgeon, *Hidden Victory*, p. 21.

26 Longrigg, *Iraq 1900 to 1950*, p. 380.

27 De Gaury, *Three Kings in Baghdad*, p. 141.

28 Ibid., pp. 153–154.

29 Ibid., p. 162.

30 Ibid., p. 170.

31 Longrigg, *Iraq 1900 to 1950*, p. 380.

32 Ibid., p. 390.

33 Ibid., p. 391.

34 Ibid., p. 380.

35 Ibid., p. 378.

36 Ibid., p. 365.

37 S. J. Haberman, "The Iraq Development Board: Administration and Program." *Middle East Journal* 9, no. 2 (1955): pp. 179–186, http://www.jstor.org/stable/4322695, accessed May 1, 2023.

38 De Gaury, *Three Kings in Baghdad*, p. 171.

39 Ibid., p. 170.

40 Ibid.

41 Ibid., p. 176.

42 Z. E. Zeine, *Anglo-Turkish Relations and the Emergence of Arab Nationalism*, quoted in De Gaury, *Three Kings in Baghdad*, p. 55.

43 Longrigg, *Iraq 1900 to 1950*, p. 395.

44 Ibid.

45 De Gaury, *Three Kings in Baghdad*, p. 178.

46 Ibid., p. 186.

47 Ibid., p. 189.

48 Ibid., p. 195.

49 Ibid., p. 200.

50 *Daily Telegraph*, August 4, 1959, quoted in De Gaury, *Three Kings in Baghdad*, p. 203.

51 James Morris, "Uncertain Character of New Iraqi Government," *Guardian*, July 25, 1958, https://uploads.guim.co.uk/2017/07/25/iraq1958.jpeg.

52 *Daily Telegraph*, May 19, 1959, quoted in De Gaury, *Three Kings in Baghdad*, p. 206.

53 Bell, *Letters*, vol. 2, p. 244, Sept. 11, 1921.

Epilogue

1 Iraq Liberation Act of 1998, https://www.govinfo.gov/content/pkg/PLAW-105publ338/html/PLAW-105publ338.htm.

2 GOP platform, 2000 US Presidential election, http://www.cnn.com/ELECTION/2000/conventions/republican/features/platform.00/.

3 Hans Blix's final UNSC briefing, February 2022, https://www.theguardian.com/world/2003/feb/14/iraq.unitednations1.

4 "U.S. Has 100,000 Troops in Kuwait," *Iraq Banner*, February 18, 2003, https://edition.cnn.com/2003/WORLD/meast/02/18/sprj.irq.deployment/index.html.

5 Kevin M. Woods and James Lacey, "The Business of Terror," Iraqi Perspectives Project: Saddam and Terrorism: Emerging Insights from Captured Iraqi Documents Volume 1 (Redacted), Institute for Defense Analyses, 2007, p. 41.

Index